HANDBOOK OF
Professional
Ethics FOR
Psychologists

Issues, Questions, and Controversies

William O'Donohue
University of Nevada, Reno

Editors ## Kyle Ferguson
University of Nevada, Reno

SAGE Publications
International Educational and Professional Publisher
Thousand Oaks ▪ London ▪ New Delhi

1191993

For information:

Sage Publications, Inc.
2455 Teller Road
Thousand Oaks, California 91320
E-mail: order@sagepub.com

Sage Publications Ltd.
6 Bonhill Street
London EC2A 4PU
United Kingdom

Sage Publications India Pvt. Ltd.
B-42 Panchsheel Enclave
Post Box 4109
New Delhi 110 017 India

Printed in the United States of America

Library of Congress Cataloging-in-Publication Data

Handbook of professional ethics for psychologists / editors, William T. O'Donohue, Kyle E. Ferguson.
    p. cm.
Includes bibliographical references and index.
ISBN 0-7619-1188-X-ISBN 0-7619-1189-8 (pbk.)
  1. Psychologists-Professional ethics. I. O'Donohue, William T.
II. Ferguson, Kyle E.
BF76.4 .H36 2003
174´.915—dc211

                              2002013230

02   03   04   05   10   9   8   7   6   5   4   3   2   1

Acquiring Editor:	Jim Brace-Thompson
Editorial Assistant:	Karen Ehrmann
Production Editor:	Claudia A. Hoffman
Copy Editor:	Carla Freeman
Indexer:	Molly Hall

Contents

Preface

This book is designed to fill a gap in the literature on professional ethics for psychologists. First, it seeks to be more comprehensive than existing books and therefore covers topics typically neglected, such as moral reasoning and the ethics of professional licensing. Second, this book, at times, is more radical and controversial than much of the literature in this area. Too many authors take ethical pronouncements associated with some organizations as dogmatic authoritarian edicts not to be questioned, but simply to be understood and observed. We, on the other hand, encourage a questioning, critical attitude that attempts to root out both error and ethical slovenliness (think Socrates as a model). This book in part is an attempt to push harder on the ethical impulse in psychologists to expose quality as well as mendacity. Ethics need not be as comfortable as it is for most psychologists. Moral leadership often disturbs.

There are many individuals we wish to thank. All the chapter authors deserve thanks—particularly the ones who submitted their chapters on time. We owe a large debt of gratitude to Jim Brace-Thompson for his patience and excellent stewardship. We would also like to thank Sara Ashby for her administrative assistance. Finally, we wish to thank our families Jane Fisher, Katie and Anna and Robin Ferguson for their patience and support.

William T. O'Donohue
Kyle E. Ferguson
Reno, NV

CHAPTER 1

Introduction

Ethics: The Good, the Bad, and the Ugly

WILLIAM T. O'DONOHUE
*Nicholas Cummings Professor of
Organized Behavioral Healthcare Delivery
University of Nevada, Reno*

KYLE E. FERGUSON
University of Nevada, Reno

Ethical codes, or any ethical claim for that matter, should not in our view be taken without critical thought. They should not be taken implicitly to say, "You should not think . . ." Rather, psychologists as critical thinkers should respond rationally and fairly to any proffered ethical code and its enforcement in an attempt to find any errors and correct them. All too often, we have seen psychologists treating the ethics code and its implementation in an authoritarian manner, as if it were beyond error and criticism. This probably is derived from the traditional connection between ethics and authoritarian religions. One does not generally debate the Ten Commandments ("I think it ought to be winnowed down to nine"). We want to remind psychologists that the current code and its implementation are human efforts, and as such are bound to contain error. This chapter may appear to be "gadflyish" (as ethical discourse often is—Christ, Gandhi, and King did not preserve the status quo). However, we hope that the reader can see that this critical posture is taken in an effort to increase the likelihood that these codes are sound and reasonable.

One of the most basic questions one can ask about any moralizing is an existential one: To what extent is this moralizing genuine, or to what extent is it a farce to allow mediocrity and comfortableness? Even more radically, to what extent is moralizing itself problematic? A quote from Nietzsche raises an interesting issue: "Isn't a moral philosopher the opposite of a puritan? Namely, insofar as he is a thinker who considers morality questionable, as calling for question marks, in short as a problem? Should moralizing not be—immoral?" (Nietzsche, 1887/1998, p. 12).

This is a radical question. On the surface, moralizing seems to be among the best activities in which humans can engage—after all, isn't it an attempt to find out and do what is right, good, and just? In what ways can moralizing be immoral? We submit that there are two: (a) when it involves wrong claims (either by commission or omission) and (b) when it is an attempt to hide "lies, hypocrisy, and comfortableness."

When the ethics code prescribes behaviors that ought not to be prescribed or proscribes behaviors that ought not to be prohibited (i.e., when it moralizes incorrectly), it can do vast amounts of harm to individuals. The kinds of harm are obvious. Less obvious is how to respond to the question "How does moralizing itself meet the moral maxim of 'At least do no harm'"?

A decent case can be made regarding the second manner of problematic moralizing. For example, it would seem that a core focus of the ethics code should be the quality of services psychologists give their consumers. Tests given should have the best psychometric properties for that construct. Therapies should be delivered that have the best evidence of effectiveness for the patient's particular problem. Is this the case in contemporary practice? To what extent does the ethics code hide the "lies, hypocrisy, and comfortableness" associated with the general practice of psychology?

We all know that psychologists administer and make judgments on tests that have little or no psychometric data at all or violate standardization in the contexts in which they are using them (e.g., O'Donohue & Bradley, 1999). We know

that many therapies are given with no evidence of their effectiveness, even for problems for which there are empirically supported treatments (Chambliss, 2000). In fact, both of these are fairly common practices, perhaps even more the rule than the exception. Why does so little of the ethics code focus on this issue of quality? Why is there so little enforcement regarding this? Why isn't any psychologist delivering, for example, sand tray therapy, brought up on ethical charges? To the extent that this is true, can it be validly said that the ethics code is a disingenuous attempt to allow such problematic but popular practices to go on while shifting too much attention to more minor issues (e.g., bartering)? To what extent is the ethics code a scam on the unsuspecting public?

It may be that the ethics code is a reflection of an era that likes its moralizing to be cheap. Easy morality can come in many forms. To what extent does psychologists' concern with "cultural sensitivity" reflect a quick and cheap response to terribly complex and important social problems? A diligent use of the hyphen does not really do all that much to resolve these problems. How are those who engage in such facades pushed to more genuine (and perhaps difficult) moral positions?

Psychologists uniquely face several interesting issues that we will discuss in this chapter. First, some of our theories and models assume determinism. What room does this leave for legitimate psychological discourse? Second, we have indigenous theories of moral development. This raises the question of how these interact with our ethical code. Finally, psychologists look at motivation, self-control, and other issues that have an impact on the practice of morality. For example, Kauffman (1992) states, "Morality always consists in not yielding to impulses; moral codes are systems of injunctions against submission to various impulses, and positive moral commandments always enjoin a victor over animal instincts" (p. 214). This raises the question of the extent to which psychologists can shed light on the moral battles between our urges and our rules, both to understand moral infractions and to help individuals decrease them.

EVIDENCE, ARGUMENT, AND THE ETHICS CODE

Apparently, the American Psychological Association (APA) believes that it has discovered how psychologists *qua* psychologists should behave. How can we defend these ethical judgments? By what method were these ethical claims produced? To what degree are these claims warranted by evidence and argument?

Because of the authoritative and regulative role of the code, it may be useful to very briefly argue for the possibility of error in the code. Three considerations are relevant here. First, the code itself has undergone seven previous revisions (APA, 1958, 1963, 1968, 1977b, 1979, 1981a, 1990). Thus, the possibility of flaws is uncontroversial even to the APA itself. However, admittedly, there might be some ambiguity in this matter. The APA can of course argue that its code has always perfectly tracked the ethics but the revisions were necessary because the underlying ethics have changed. However, no such argument has been advanced, and because morality commonly has been viewed as being fixed, the first interpretation seems more plausible. (It is interesting to note the issues of ethical responsibilities of the APA toward individuals who have been judged as engaging in unethical behavior by a previous code, such as barter arrangements and client sexual

contact, but whose behavior would no longer be judged unethical by a revised code.)

Second, the ethics code is not based on an allegedly infallible procedure, but rather a human product (and a committee at that). Thus, unlike certain systems of theological ethics, which posit ethical standards as emanating from an infallible god, there is no reason internal to the code to believe that it is epistemologically incorrigible.

Third, other professional organizations have devised their own ethics codes, and these are different from the APA code in many respects. This inconsistency raises the question of which of them is "right." For example, the ethics code of the Association for the Advancement of Behavior Therapy (AABT, 1977) contains the following: "B. Has the choice of treatment methods been adequately considered? 1. Does the published literature show the procedure to be the best one available for that problem?" (p. v). In contrast, the APA ethics code (APA, 1992b, p. 1600) states, "Psychologists rely on scientifically and professionally derived knowledge when making scientific or professional judgments or when engaging in scholarly or professional endeavors." Although the general "drift" of the codes is similar, the APA ethics code seems to be looser because it renders a decision as ethical as long as the decision was based on scientific and professional knowledge. In fact, in a previous standard, "Maintaining Expertise" (APA, 1992b, p. 1600), the code states that the professional should "maintain a reasonable level of awareness of current scientific and professional information." The AABT code is much more rigorous in that it requires specific knowledge—that is, rather thorough knowledge of the scientific-outcome literature regarding the most effective treatment— and does not appear to countenance the relevance of "professional knowledge." However, given these inconsistencies, both cannot be correct, which therefore raises the possibility that the APA ethics code is not correct.

The question becomes this: Are the assertions of the APA ethics code correct? This, unfortunately, is a very difficult question to address because the code itself simply makes assertions without any appeals to evidence or arguments. If we take the hallmark of rationality to be the explicit consideration of all relevant evidence, arguments, and counterarguments in arriving at a conclusion, then the code does not appear to be a document as presented, but simply a series of bald, undefended, unargued, authoritarian fiats. If we as psychologists want to be rational and to form our beliefs on the basis of argument and evidence, then the ethics code appears to present us with serious problems.

As a case in point, the ethics code now states, "Psychologists do not engage in sexual intimacies with a former therapy patient or client for a least two years after cessation or termination of professional services" (APA, 1992b, p. 1605; APA, 2002). The question is whether this ethical standard is correct. In evaluating this claim, one is immediately confronted with the (unanswered) question considered in the previous section; that is, what ethical premises and theories underlie this claim? Therefore, one is in the unfortunate position of guessing what is the relevant ethical premise on which to construct a possible argument. If one adopts a utilitarian ethical standard, then one needs to examine data concerning the effects of sexual intimacies on former patients. However, the ethics code does not cite data, nor is there any companion document that provides the evidence and argument. Questions such as this arise: What evidence or arguments resulted in this change from previous ethics codes? What evidence is there that the passage of 2 years is relevant to the effects of sexual intimacies on former clients? How good is the evidence? How good

is the total body of evidence in supporting the notion that after 2 years, the net amount of happiness relative to the net amount of pain renders this sexual contact as ethically permissible?

In summary, because the ethics code does not argue or cite evidence but rather simply asserts, it provides no acceptable warrant for its assertions. Epistemologically, its acceptance relies on an authoritarian appeal (because the APA says so) rather than on an epistemology that recognizes the importance of defending one's claims by arguments and the importance of evidence and critiques of counterarguments and opposing positions. It is suggested that at a minimum, the APA prepare a companion document to provide evidence and arguments in defense of these now bald assertions.

THE ETHICS CODE AND ETHICAL THEORY

In this section, we will examine the relationship between the APA ethics code and ethical theory. When the code states that some act is unethical, what general ethical standards are being relied on to make this claim? The broader ethical theory that is implicit in the APA code is important because it has direct implications for three critical issues: (a) for precisely understanding what an ethical standard may mean; (b) for evaluating the ethics code; that is, if the implicit ethical theory is problematic, then it may be the case that the ethics code is flawed; and (c) for identifying relevant issues for determining whether an ethical standard has been violated. For example, if the broader ethical theory holds that an act is bad only when a person *intends* bad consequences, then ascertaining the individual's intentions can become critical in ethical investigations. On the other hand, if the broader ethical theory evaluates the moral worth of an action only by a consideration of the act's consequences relative to other possible acts, then only actual consequences and the possible effects of alternative acts need to be assessed. Conversely, if an individual is to have a fair opportunity to defend his or her actions, then the ethical premises of the ethical code must be clear. Without this, the grounds for indicating that an ethical violation has occurred (as opposed to, say, a violation of organizational procedure) are unclear. Moreover, a legitimate ground is not clearly open that may be used to base the defense "My actions were not unethical in some fuller sense implied by the code or principle." Thus, it appears important to both potential defendants and to potential complainants that they fully understand the content and exact nature of the ethical principles, and to do this, we claim, involves an explication of the ethical premises and assumptions involved in the ethics code.

It is difficult to answer questions concerning the underlying ethical theory that is relied on by the APA ethical code because the code itself is silent on this issue. There is no explicit mention in the code regarding what general standard or standards were relied on to produce the specific ethical pronouncements contained in the code. Moreover, the language it uses to express ethical standards is somewhat unusual and puzzling. It uses the indicative mode ("Psychologists do not engage in sexual intimacies with current patients or clients," APA, 1992b, p. 1605) rather than one using the language in which ethical statements are usually made: *ought, must,* or *should.* However, it is clear that the code does not intend these statements to be simple indicative claims. For example, it would be absurd to argue that the ethical standard quoted above is not true because some psychologists do in fact engage in sexual intimacies. This kind of statement involving "facts of the matter" is not relevant to

this or other normative claims. Rather, this claim and other ethical claims deal with what *should* be the case. However, it is unclear why the APA has chosen this indirect form of ethical language rather than the more straightforward "Psychologists *should not* engage in sexual intimacies with current patients or clients."

Although the code does not explicate the general ethical theory on which it is based, it appears clear that certain candidates can be ruled out. For example, this is not a theologically based ethical code. No appeals appear to be made concerning issues such as "Whatever God wills is what ought to be done." This is not surprising given the secular nature of psychology. Moreover, the code does not appear to rely on ethical relativism. The code views itself as applying to all psychologists (or at least all those practicing in North America). It makes no appeal that this code is not relevant to different groups of individuals. This is interesting because internally the code suggests that there are situations in which differences in "age, gender, race, ethnicity, national origin, religion, sexual orientation, disability, language or socioeconomic status" necessitate that psychologists make certain adjustments or special treatments (APA, 1992b, p. 1601). However, it appears to view professional ethics absolutistically and therefore as equally applicable to all psychologists, regardless of their differences.

Important to an issue that we discuss below, on the compatibility of science and morality, the ethics code is not based on ethical nihilism. Ethical nihilism suggests that nothing is morally right or morally wrong. This is obviously not relevant in that an ethical nihilist cannot consistently produce an ethics code. Relevant to the next issue we discuss, justifying an ethics code, the code is not based on ethical skepticism. This is the view that it is impossible to know what is ethically right or ethically wrong. The code also is not based on ethical egoism (each person ought to act to maximize his own good or well-being).

Two influential ethical theories that may function as the general ethical grounds of the code are *utilitarianism* and *deontological* ethics. Eyde and Quaintance (1988) have interpreted the previous version of the code as subsuming Kantian deontological ethics. Kant (1943) suggested that the highest good was a good will. Kant rejected the notion that an act was good because of its consequences: "The good will is not good because of what it effects or accomplishes or because of its adequacy to achieve some proposed end" (p. 49). Thus, Kant believed that when a person acts with a good will, the person acts out of respect for moral laws. The moral law is embodied in Kant's *categorical imperative*, which may be stated in two forms that Kant took to be equivalent: (a) Act only according to that maxim that should become a universal law, and (b) act so that you treat humanity, whether in your own person or in that of another, always as an end and never as a means only. From the categorical imperative, Kant thought that specific duties can be derived. In this view, the ethics code would be an attempt to derive from the absolute moral law the duties a psychologist holds by virtue of being a psychologist. One criticism of Kant's deontological theory is that it is difficult to derive specific duties from his categorical imperative, and thus many different and even conflicting duties are derived. However, it would be useful if the APA ethics committee would indicate the extent to which the ethics code is based on an account of a psychologist's duties. It would be useful to ascertain whether these duties have been accurately enumerated and would also be important because it would indicate the irrelevance of an act's consequences in a deontological ethical theory in ascertaining the ethical appropriateness of certain behaviors.

A utilitarian theory, in direct contrast to a deontological theory, judges the ethical worth of an act by the act's consequences. Utilitarian theories differ according to what kind of consequences are of importance (e.g., happiness vs. pleasure). Utilitarian theories also differ in the extent to which they believe that the consequences of each individual act need to be considered separately (i.e., act utilitarianism), as opposed to the belief that acts fall into some broad classes and therefore rules can be constructed regarding which classes of acts generally have better consequences (i.e., rule utilitarianism). Given the fact that the ethics code consists of general rules, it seems reasonable to believe that if the code is based on a utilitarian theory, it is based on rule utilitarian theory. Otherwise, it would simply need to indicate that each act be considered in a casuistic manner.

But if the code is based on utilitarian ethics, it is not clear what kinds of consequences the ethics code considers in judging the moral worth of actions. For example, John Stuart Mill (1863) criticized Bentham's (1838) version of utilitarian ethics on the grounds that Bentham failed to distinguish between the qualities of pleasure. Mill thought it better to be Socrates unsatisfied than a pig satisfied. Thus, to have a clearly workable utilitarian ethic, it is not only important to specify what kinds of consequences are morally relevant but also to specify a weighing of these consequences. (A weighing of consequences to clients vs. consequences to others might also be necessary, e.g., family members, society, and even the therapist.)

Finally, there are indigenous psychological theories of morality, and the relationship between these and the APA ethics code is also unclear. Kohlberg (1981) has arguably the most influential psychological account of moral development. Kohlberg has claimed to have found culturally universal stages of moral development. Six developmental stages fall within three moral levels (preconventional, conventional, and postconventional or autonomous). Two issues are of concern here. First, Kohlberg's theory is at least partly deterministic. That is, the extent to which one advances along these stages is determined at least in part by the quality of one's environment (e.g., schooling, parenting, models). Thus, could a legitimate defense against a moral failing be that one has been a victim of one's poor environment and therefore has not developed morally as one should? If "ought implies can," then the argument is that I am not morally culpable because I could not have done otherwise. The second and more serious issue is that in Kohlberg's conception, the highest stage of moral development is characterized by individual principles that are not concrete, but abstract, general, and universal. The second level of moral development, on the other hand, is oriented to obeying authority or concrete rules. The question becomes this: Does the APA's concrete ethics code influence one to behave in a manner that psychological theory itself indicates is a lower stage of moral reasoning?

In summary, it is not clear in which account of morality the ethics code is grounded. This is problematic for several reasons but particularly because it vitiates the process of fair ethical inquiries. It is recommended that the ethical grounds of the code be explicated and defended both to better understand the code and its application and to expose it to the light of criticism so that improvements can be made.

THE ETHICS CODE AND PSYCHOLOGICAL ACCOUNTS OF HUMAN BEHAVIOR

What is the relationship between the factual claims of science, "is" statements, and the normative claims of ethics, "ought" statements? There are several basic schools of thought on this important issue. One is that of *ethical naturalism,* which asserts that ethical claims can be derived from factual claims. Skinner (1971) provides an example of this when he attempts to define "what is morally good" with the empirical matter of "what is reinforcing."

This attempt has been criticized on many grounds, but one that strikes at the heart of ethical naturalism is G.E. Moore's (1960) naturalistic fallacy. This fallacy states that one cannot define ethical terms such as "good" or "what ought to be done" in terms that are purely factual, descriptive, and nonevaluative. Moore has argued that this is fallacious because it would make many open and debatable questions closed and trivial. As Moore states, "Whatever definition be offered, it may always be asked, with significance, of the complex so defined, whether it is itself good" (p. 19).

For example, if we follow Skinner's suggestion and define *good* as that which is reinforcing, when we ask "Is X good?" we also need to ask "Is X reinforcing?" However, if we ask the seemingly open and debatable question "Is that which is reinforcing good?" our question becomes (using the definition) the closed and trivial question "Is that which is reinforcing reinforcing?" Although the first question seems worth debating, the second question does not. Thus, Moore presents some reasons to believe that moral terms cannot be defined in terms of nonevaluative natural properties.

The second school of thought on the relationship between science and morality is that the two are incompatible. For example, Carl Hempel (1965) also argued that science cannot establish objective standards of right and wrong. According to Hempel, at best, science can provide us with instrumental judgments of value. That is, science can only tell us which means are instrumental for bringing about certain ends. Hempel illustrates the relevance of science for normative ethics by involving Laplace's demon—a perfect scientific intelligence that knows all the laws of nature, knows everything that is going on in the universe at any given moment, and at any particular moment can calculate with infinite speed and precision from the state of the universe its state at any other past or future moment:

> Let us assume, then, that faced with a moral decision, we are able to call upon the Laplacean demon as a consultant. What help might we get from him? Suppose that we have to choose one of several alternative courses of action open to us and that we want to know which of these we ought to follow. The demon would then be able to tell us, for any contemplated choice, what its consequences would be for the future course of the universe, down to the most minute detail, however remote in space and time. But, having done this for each of the alternative courses of action under consideration, the demon would have completed his task; he would have given us all the information that an ideal science might provide under the circumstances. And yet he would not have resolved our moral problem, for this requires a decision as to which of the several alternative sets of consequences mapped out by the demon as attainable to us is best; which of them we ought to bring about. And the burden of the decision would still fall upon our shoulders; it's we who would have to commit ourselves to an unconditional (absolute) judgment of value by singling out one of the sets of consequences as superior to the alternatives. (pp. 88-89)

Kant (1943) has claimed that "ought implies can." That is, to meaningfully claim that someone *ought* to do X is to imply that he *could* do X. Thus, it is contradictory to assert that someone ought to so something that the person cannot do: It is wrong to claim that Jane ought to have jumped 18 feet in the air without any aid when Jane simply cannot do this.

Science has been considered by some as a search for universal laws. All general scientific laws state impossibilities. Newton's second law, for example, states that it is impossible for any two objects to behave differently than to be attracted to each other in direct proportion to their masses and in inverse proportion to the square of the distance between them. Thus, a deterministic universal scientific law states that it is impossible for the entity to behave in any other way.

Thus, if human behavior can be subsumed under deterministic scientific laws (as many would as the goal of scientific psychology), then this same behavior falls outside the purview of morality. The prominent psychologist B.F. Skinner (1971) clearly realized the incompatibility of a scientific determinism and morality:

> In what we may call the prescientific view (and the word is not necessarily pejorative) a person's behavior is at least to some extent his own achievement. He is free to deliberate, decide, and act possible in original ways, and he is to be given credit for his successes and blamed for his failures. In the scientific view (and the word is not necessarily honorific) a person's behavior is determined by a genetic endowment traceable to evolutionary history of the species and by the environmental circumstances to which as an individual he has been exposed. Neither view can be proved, but it is in the nature of the scientific inquiry that the evidence should shift in favor of the second. (p. 101)

It is also important to realize that this incompatibility is held not only by radical behaviorists but also by other psychological determinists (perhaps the early Freud and most physiological psychologists).

An interesting aspect of this incompatibility is illustrated in the dispositions of ethical violations. At times, violators of the ethics code are required to enter into psychotherapy. But, then, how are we to understand this: Is psychotherapy an application of scientific principles for the treatment of moral failings?

Therefore, the question arises: To what extent is the ethics code consistent with the science of human behavior or its regulative principles? If morality implies human agency—the freedom to make choices—and if a science of human behavior (or at least some influential version of it) presumes determinism—the impossibility to behave otherwise—then to what extent does it make sense to have an ethics code for psychologists?

ISSUES IN ENFORCEMENT: DETECTION, ADJUDICATION, AND DISPOSITION

Even if one grants that the current APA code or some future revision of it are generally sound as a document, the question of how well it is being implemented remains. We recommend that the reader take a careful look at the Ethics Committee of the American Psychological Association's Rules and Procedures (APA, 1992a) to see what seems sound and what seems problematic. The broad function of this code presumably is to proscribe ethically problematic behaviors and to prescribe positive behaviors. When infractions or failures occur, at what rate are these detected (true positives)? That is, how sensitive is the enforcement mechanism that supports the code? On the other hand, how often are individuals accused and punished falsely (false positives)? Currently, the answers to these questions are unknown, and although they are difficult to answer, there appears to be little or no effort on the part of the APA to attempt to discover information relevant to these important questions.

Related to the issue of detection, if adjudication and disposition are not handled well, the code becomes either an impotent charade or a damaging weapon hurting the innocent (or a bit of both). These issues become enormous when one is either making an accusation or defending oneself.

Detection

What barriers are there to accurate detection? Currently, detection relies heavily on parties initiating official complaints on their own. But there are at least two major potential problems with this. First, this is a heavy burden to be placed on individuals (e.g., patients, students, colleagues) who for their own vested interests or other legitimate factors (e.g., unassertiveness, lack of knowledge of what actually counts as a violation) may fail to make legitimate complaints. On the other hand, their interconnectedness may produce interests to use the ethics code as a weapon to harm the alleged violator. Psychologists deal with issues that have huge stakes, and to what extent do those who are disappointed with decisions attempt to seek retribution by filing false complaints? To what extent are certain kinds of patients (e.g., individuals with borderline personality disorder or antisocial personality disorder) disposed to make false complaints? Should there be research on types of individuals who either fail to make legitimate complaints or who are inclined to make false complaints? This is a difficult issue, and there has been little recognition of it in the literature and consequently little work on how to improve this situation. Second, should the APA have more of an active role in policing by conducting proactive audits, for example? Should the current relatively passive approach be supplemented by a more active detection process? Certainly, in the criminal justice system, active policing is viewed as necessary to properly detect violations. Why isn't this model applied in professional ethics?

Adjudication

How are complaints, once brought, fairly adjudicated? What is proper due process? What are the rights of the accuser and accused? Who has the burden of proof? What evidential standard must be met (e.g., preponderance of the evidence)? Or is the accused "innocent until proven guilty" or "guilty until proven innocent"? Who decides the outcome (e.g., jury of one's peers)? Are special skills or qualifications needed for this? Should there be representation of all stakeholders (e.g., patients)? Do the accused have the right to "face their accusers"? Should there be some sort of indictment process before a full investigation/hearing is conducted? Is legal representation permissible? Who bears the responsibility and expense of gathering evidence? What procedures are followed in the adjudication process? (Is hearsay permissible, or cross-examination, and what are the rules of evidence?) What, if at all, is the appeals process like?

These are all enormously complex questions. But they need to be answered well so that both the accused and the accuser are treated justly. There are important tradeoffs in doing this. Again, unfortunately, there is little discussion currently, and practically no efforts have been made at improving the quality of the adjudication of complaints by the APA and state boards.

Disposition

What are fair "sentences" for violations? What are the aims that resolutions are attempting to achieve? Above, we have discussed conceptual conflicts in prescribing therapy for ethical violations. The intent seems sound—to help induce reform, perhaps even moral reform. But the question remains as to how best to do this. What is needed is an overall theory of such reform, a subtheory of how this is to be applied in individual cases, and empirical demonstration of particular methods to achieve this and the extent to which these are actually achieved.

Dispositions can go beyond the intent to reform and function to seek either retribution or punishment. Is this a legitimate part of giving consequences for violations of the code? If so, what are just punishments? Just

punishments must "fit their crimes." Are the punishments meted out by the APA or state boards too lenient, thus producing a farce? Or on the other hand, are punishments too harsh, thus creating a reasonably feared quasi-inquisitional process? Can punishments be reduced for "good behavior"?

A disposition can also be used to set an example so that others learn from this and are less likely to make a similar mistake. Should dispositions be made as public as soon as possible to maximize this aim? Or should dispositions be confidential to reduce potential harm to the accuser or accused? Should this be decided on a case-by-case basis? If so, by what criteria?

Moreover, dispositions can be constructed to make restitution. What is proper restitution for each violation? How is this to be decided? Finally, given these multiple functions of dispositions (restitution, public examples, reform, retribution), how are they to be properly balanced in cases?

A final issue is this: How are any of these dispositions properly monitored to ensure quality compliance and that the intent of the disposition is being achieved? For example, suppose a therapist is given the consequence of having his or her therapy supervised to prevent the recurrence of a certain violation. How does the controlling body ensure that this supervision is achieving this aim?

CONCLUSIONS

We conclude that the full functions of the APA ethics code are unclear; that the ethical theory or premise on which the code is based is not explicit and is poorly understood; that because no evidence or arguments for the claims within the code are provided, it is epistemologically undefended; and that it is inconsistent with influential scientific accounts of human behavior.

This is a most unfortunate state of affairs for the public as well as psychologists. These problems raise such profound questions about the status of the code that in its current form, it should not be regarded as an acceptable document on which psychologists can guide their actions or evaluate the actions of others. Admittedly, these problems are not easily resolved, and some of them directly involve difficult and fundamental philosophical issues. However, we suggest that this is not an artifact of our arguments, but rather an inevitable consequence of being involved in the types of complex activities that comprise the profession of psychology.

Thus, these issues need to be addressed by adequately consulting the relevant literature. Although it is beyond the scope of this chapter to present and argue for concrete proposals, one possibility deserves mention. The prominent philosopher of science Sir Karl Popper (1992) has recently provided an interesting and somewhat radical proposal for professional ethics based on his epistemological fallibilism. Popper suggests the following ethics code:

2. It is impossible to avoid all mistakes, or even all those mistakes that are, in themselves, avoidable. All scientists are continually making mistakes. The old idea that one can avoid mistakes and is therefore duty bound to avoid them, must be revised: it is itself mistaken. . . .

5. We must therefore revise our attitude to mistakes. It is here that our practical ethical reform must begin. For the attitude of the old professional ethics leads

us to cover up our mistakes, to keep them secret and to forget them as soon as possible. . . .

6. The new basic principle is that in order to learn to avoid making mistakes, we must learn from our mistakes. To cover up mistakes is, therefore, the greatest intellectual sin. . . .

9. Since we must learn from our mistakes, we must also learn to accept, indeed accept gratefully, when others draw our attention to our mistakes. When in turn we draw other people's attention to their mistakes, we should always remember that we have made similar mistakes ourselves. And we should remember that the greatest scientists have made mistakes. I certainly do not want to say that our mistakes are, usually, forgivable; we must never let our attention slacken. But it is humanly impossible to avoid making mistakes time and again. (pp. 201-202)

Thus, Popper calls for a radical new orientation to ethical mistakes based on his notion of the inevitability of errors in human knowledge and conduct. This might provide an interesting epistemological grounding for the construction of the code as well as providing useful guidelines for the broader aims of the code. However, additional work is required regarding identifying acceptable ethical standards to define a "mistake" as well as understanding what is legitimately subject to ethical evaluation (human agency) and what is outside the purview of moral discourse (determine behavior).

REFERENCES

American Educational Research Association, American Psychological Association, and National Council on Measurement in Education. (1985). *Standards for educational and psychological tests*. Washington, DC: American Psychological Association.

American Psychological Association. (1953). *Ethical standards of psychologists*. Washington, DC: Author.

American Psychological Association. (1958). Standards of ethical behavior for psychologists. *American Psychologist, 13,* 268-271.

American Psychological Association. (1963). Ethical standards of psychologists. *American Psychologist, 18,* 56-60.

American Psychological Association. (1968). Ethical standards of psychologists. *American Psychologist, 23,* 357-361.

American Psychological Association. (1977a). *Ethical guidelines for the delivery of human services.* Washington, DC: American Psychological Association.

American Psychological Association. (1977b, March). Ethical standards of psychologists. *APA Monitor,* pp. 22-23.

American Psychological Association. (1979). *Ethical standards of psychologists.* Washington, DC: Author.

American Psychological Association. (1981a). Ethical principles of psychologists. *American Psychologist, 36,* 633-638.

American Psychological Association. (1981b). Specialty guidelines for the delivery of services by clinical (counseling, industrial/organizational, and school) psychologists. *American Psychologist, 36,* 639-981.

American Psychological Association. (1982). *Ethical principles in the conduct of research with human participants.* Washington, DC: Author.

American Psychological Association. (1983). Casebook for providers of psychological services. *American Psychologist, 38,* 708-713.

American Psychological Association. (1985). Standards of ethical behavior for psychologists. *American Psychologist, 13,* 268-271.

American Psychological Association. (1987). General guidelines for providers of psychological services. *American Psychologist, 42,* 712-723.

American Psychological Association. (1990). Ethical principles of psychologists (amended June 2, 1989). *American Psychologist, 45,* 390-395.

American Psychological Association. (1992a, October). APA council adopts new ethics code. *APA Monitor,* pp. 5-7.

American Psychological Association. (1992b). Ethical principles of psychologists and code conduct. *American Psychologist, 47*(12), 1597-1612.

American Psychological Association. (2002). Ethical principles of psychologists and code of conduct 2002. Retrieved December 12, 2002, from www.apa.org/ethics/code2002.html#10_08

Association for Advancement of Behavior Therapy. (1977). Ethical issues for human services. *Behavior Therapy, 8,* v-vi.

Bentham, J. (1838). *The works of Jeremy Bentham.* London: Hutchinson.

Chambliss, C. H. (2000). *Psychotherapy and managed care: Reconciling research and reality.* Boston: Allyn & Bacon.

Eyde, L., & Quaintance, M. (1988). Ethical issues and cases in the practice of personnel psychology. *Professional Psychology: Research and Practice, 19,* 148-154.

Freedman, B. (1978). A meta-ethics for professional morality. *Ethics, 89,* 1-19.

Hall, J., & Hare-Mustin, R. (1983). Sanctions and the diversity of ethical complaints against psychologists. *American Psychologist, 38,* 714-729.

Hempel, C. G. (1965). Science and human values. In C. G. Hempel (Ed.), *Aspects of scientific explanation.* New York: Free Press.

Kant, I. (1943). *Kant's groundwork of the metaphysic of morals.* London: Hutchinson.

Kauffman, S. A. (1992). *Origins of order: Self-organization and selection in evolution.* New York: Oxford University.

Kohlberg, L. (1981). *Essays in moral development.* New York: Harper & Row.

Mill, J. S. (1863). *Utilitarianism.* London: Hutchinson.

Moore, G. E. (1960*). Principia ethica.* New York: Cambridge University Press.

Morris, W. (Eds.). (1970). *The American heritage dictionary of the English language* (pp. 1044-1045). New York: Houghton Mifflin.

Nielsen, K. (1967). Problems of ethics. In P. Edwards (Ed.), *The encyclopedia of philosophy*. New York: Macmillan.

Nietzsche, F. W. (1998). *On the genealogy of morals* (D. Smith, Trans.). Oxford, England: Oxford University Press. (Original work published 1887)

O'Donohue, W., & Bradley, A. R. (1999). Conceptual and empirical issues in child custody evaluations. *Clinical Psychology: Science & Practice, 6,* 310-322.

O'Donohue, W., Fisher, J. E., & Krasner, L. (1987). Ethics and the elderly. In L. Cartensen & B. Edelstein (Eds.), *Handbook of clinical gerontology*. New York: Pergamon.

Popper, K. (1965). *The logic of scientific discovery* (2nd ed.). New York: Harper & Row.

Popper, K. (1992). *In search of a better world*. London: Routledge & Kegan Paul.

Skinner, B. F. (1971). *Beyond freedom and dignity*. New York: Alfred A. Knopf.

Part I

FOUNDATIONS

CHAPTER 2

Philosophical Foundations of Professional Ethics

ANDREW LLOYD AND JOHN HANSEN
University of Nevada, Reno

This chapter is designed to provide a brief introduction to the field of ethics. Although this text is devoted to covering ethical topics specific to the field of psychology, a more general understanding of traditional ethical questions, principles, and theories may facilitate an understanding of ethics as it is applied to the professional domain of psychology. The study of ethics can be broken down into four primary domains: metaethics, normative ethics, virtue ethics, and applied ethics. This chapter deals with the first three domains, while subsequent chapters deal with applied ethics.

Metaethics, as the name suggests, is an investigation into the underlying assumptions of our ethical systems and beliefs (Fieser, 2000). What beliefs do we rely on (intentionally or unintentionally) when we reason ethically about a situation? Does ethical thinking differ from other sorts of thinking? It is here that questions of moral relativism, absolutism, and skepticism are explored. Are humans naturally egoistic or altruistic? Finally, metaethics explores the meanings of indispensable ethical terms such as *the good, evil, happiness, duty, right,* and so on. Reaching answers to these fundamental questions goes a long way toward helping a person think more clearly about the more practical ethical issues.

The domain of *normative ethics* is probably more familiar to the reader. It is here that the classical ethical theories are found. The utilitarianism (consequentialist ethics) of John Stuart Mill, the deontological (absolutist ethics) approach of Immanuel Kant, and natural law ethics (also referred to as divine command theory) are likely the most familiar approaches and will be dealt with in this chapter.

Finally, the domain of *virtue ethics* will be explored. The study and discussion of virtues and their development was a cornerstone of ethical theory for the ancient Greeks (White, 2000, p. 7). It is often believed that there is something inherently good about being courageous, wise, temperate, and so on. The study of virtue ethics explores the reasons for such beliefs. Following the classical Greek and Roman period, interest in such issues slowly subsided. Recently, however, there has been a resurgence of interest in the topics of virtue, character, and personality. Although the question, "What constitutes the good life?" is dealt with at all levels of ethical thinking, it is here that this question evokes the most insightful and thought-provoking perspectives. In the following sections of this chapter, we will deal with the following:

- The general role of ethics in life
- The ethical environment
- Metaethics
- Normative ethics
- Virtue ethics

These topics will be covered in such a way as to facilitate a more robust understanding of the topics covered in the latter chapters. Although these issues are sometimes philosophically complicated, every effort has been made to enhance both their clarity and relevance to psychologists.

THE GENERAL ROLE OF ETHICS IN LIFE

Why study ethics? Some think that ethics is just highbrow moralizing that has no practical implications. Doesn't it amount to imposing our own personal values on others? Don't we already know that coloring the world in terms of right and wrong can lead to personal distress (see, e.g., Beck, Rush, Shaw, & Emery, 1979; Ellis & Blau, 1998)? Unfortunately for some people, the answers to these questions is "Yes." These individuals may view the study of ethics as little more than an opportunity for moral bullies to force their outdated views and predilections on others. Indeed, some people may even think that they live their lives in complete isolation from

ideas such as "right," "wrong," "good," and "virtuous." Although these criticisms may highlight some of the limitations of ethical thinking, the conclusions often drawn from them are extreme (if not absurd):

- Whatever anyone wants to do is "OK" by me because I cannot judge them.
- To judge another's behavior or beliefs is just wrong.
- Ethics is merely a tool of religious people to oppress others.

Although reasoning about what one ought and ought not do can be complicated and lack universal agreement, it is neither impossible nor without value.

There seem to be two overlapping criticisms of ethics. First, that it is too divorced from the practical day-to-day affairs of life to be relevant or worthwhile. Second, that it represents a way of thinking (e.g., in terms of right and wrong) that is best left in antiquity. We will address these criticisms in order. Aristotle *(Ethics)* provided a rationale for studying ethics that still holds today:

> Our present inquiry does not aim, as our others do, at study; for the purpose of our examination is not to know what virtue is, but to become good, since otherwise the inquiry would be of no benefit to us. (Aristotle, 2000, pp. 764-823)

The sentiment being expressed here is important. We do not study ethics to be more interesting cocktail party guests or, more problematically, to be able to point out everyone else's ethical failures and shortcomings (which would amount to moralizing). We study ethics so that our lives might be enriched. We study ethics so that we can live happily and in harmony with others.

The second complaint regarding ethics represents yet another fundamental misconception regarding ethical thinking. This misconception is that ethics, morality, good, evil, and so on are no longer relevant concepts in our modern scientific world. Let us see what a world without ethics might be like.

You wake up in the morning and go to the bathroom only to find that your husband has failed to clean up as promised. To make things worse, you have no clean clothes to wear because he did not do the laundry as promised. You are quite agitated. Why? You go to the bedroom and confront him about his broken promises and he responds, "So what? I have no *duty* to keep promises. What kind of world are you living in?" He chuckles and returns to sleep as if nothing were wrong. You put some dirty clothes on and head off to work.

When you arrive at work, you are informed that you, along with all the other women at the office, have been replaced with the CEO's male golfing buddies. Clearly agitated, you seek answers for this obvious injustice. After all, you are a stellar employee, and there is no just cause for your firing. When asked why he has fired all, and only, the female employees, the CEO rolls his eyes and responds, "Well, obviously, these new guys are my friends, and I prefer working with them over working with women." You are dumbfounded. Why? When you inform the CEO that you will be seeking legal recourse to this obviously unjust act, the CEO replies, *"Justice?* What kind of world are you living in?" You leave work and drive to a local café where you and your friends often meet for lunch.

When you arrive at the café, you order the usual. The waiter instructs you that you must sit in a special section designated for female customers. Speechless, you do as instructed— only to find that the new female menu prices are twice as much as the old prices. When you inquire about the price changes, the waiter slaps you upside the head with a service tray and warns, "Look you stupid woman, you are lucky that we serve your

kind here. I'd just be quiet and pay the price we ask if I were you." As he says this, he moves his apron aside to reveal a pistol. You are speechless. Why? When your food finally arrives, a man from the front of the café rushes over to take your food and pocketbook. You shriek out, "Help me! That man just assaulted me and stole my property!" A woman huddling at a table next to you looks at you sternly and warns, "Shut up. You'll ruin it for us. You have no *right* to property. What kind of world do you think this is?"

The story could go on, but it doesn't have to. The picture is clear enough. The world described above is decidedly not the kind of world most of us would choose to live in. It is an ugly world in which injustice is on an equal par with justice and rights and duties have no place. Duty, justice, and rights are the kinds of things we take for granted in our society. These are ethical notions. A sense of duty, for example, is not born with humans. It must be cultivated. It wasn't always this way. As Thomas Hobbes (1668/1994) is famous for saying, "In the state of nature people live in a war of all against all, . . . in which their lives are solitary, poor, nasty, brutish and short" (xxi).

The "state of nature" to which Hobbes refers is best understood as a time when people lived together without guidance, laws, rules, and morals. As society developed, so too did the ethical environment, including ideas of rights, duties, justice, parity, and so on.

We are not too far removed from societies that did not value such things. Just over 50 years ago, Germany, under the control of Hitler's national socialist movement, was making a bold push to dominate the world. Genocide, racism, homophobia, radical scientific experimentation on human guinea pigs, and other atrocities may have become the norm had Hitler succeeded. Indeed, relatively minor changes in strategy and tactics could have changed the course of the war. Had

Germany decided to focus on one front at a time rather than waging a war on multiple fronts, the outcome of World War II might have been radically different. It is an unfortunate fact that the society we live in, even taking into account its faults, is a fragile one that must always compete with forces that draw us back toward Hobbes's state of nature.

THE ETHICAL ENVIRONMENT

Humans have evolved to respond to the natural environment. We naturally avoid objects and behaviors that cause pain and gravitate toward those that bring pleasure. For the most part, this natural environment is obvious. A snarling dog and the aroma of a pleasing meal motivate us to behave in certain predictable ways. The natural environment shapes the very course of our lives in important ways. People living in the tropical South Sea islands need not worry about bitter winters, have little (if any) access to red meat, tend to eat more fish and fruit, and must deal with dangerous venomous insects more than those who live in more temperate climes. These are differences that make a difference. The physical environment that we live in shapes the kinds of lives we live. This is not the only environment we live in. We also live in an *ethical environment*.

Unlike the natural environment, the ethical environment can be difficult to discern. Nonetheless, the ethical environment shapes our lives in the most profound ways. The ethical environment legitimizes certain practices and makes others taboo. Prior to the abolishment of slavery in the South, many southerners saw nothing wrong with owning other human beings. This was legitimate practice, and it shaped the lives of both slave and slave owner. Not too long ago, it was considered legitimate practice for a man to

have sex with his wife even if she did not want to. In some places in the world today, it is legitimate practice to kill those who speak against you, castrate the female clitoris and labia, and force women to cover every inch of their bodies with clothing while in public. These practices are supported not by the natural environment (otherwise they would be common practice in all similar climes), but by the ethical/normative environment. Whereas the natural environment dictates what is possible, the ethical environment selects out of the many possibilities those that ought and ought not be done.

The norms, mores, and practices unique to each society are heavily infused with ethical assumptions. Though these assumptions are often unspoken and difficult to unambiguously define, they are nonetheless vital to the identity of a society and its people. These practices and values do not disappear when ignored, nor do they tend to improve on their own when dissatisfaction with them grows. A great part of the value of studying ethics is the extent to which it facilitates an understanding of our own circumstances and enhances our ability to work for positive change. Noticing the ethical environment can be like asking a fish to notice the water it swims in and breaths. This difficulty may be part of what leads people to claim that they do not think in terms of right and wrong even when they clearly do.

Large societies are not the only contexts capable of supporting ethical dimensions. More discrete contexts, such as the office place, can support and perpetuate ethical environments as well. Valuing the practice of promoting from within the ranks and hiring a diverse workforce are examples of such contexts. It is still acceptable in many American workplaces for men to be paid more than women for the same work. This is part of the ethical environment, or that which is valued. Noticing these values is the first step toward any attempt to improve on them or replace them with other values.

Ethical environments change over time as well. Americans do not value the same behaviors and attitudes that we did 200 years ago. The same is true of almost any other society in the world. Samurai values and practices no longer play a significant role in Japanese culture, and few countries in the world recognize monarchies as legitimate political arrangements.

Although ethical principles and moral sentiments change over time, it would be premature to conclude that ethics is relative. The debate over whether or not our ethical beliefs are absolute or relative is independent of the fact that such beliefs do change over time and from place to place. In the next section, we turn to an examination of this and many other questions encountered in metaethics.

METAETHICAL ISSUES: HOW TO THINK ABOUT ETHICS

In this section, we outline seven basic metaethical issues. Some of these issues involve serious debate (e.g., relativism/absolutism), whereas others are more principle oriented (e.g., ought implies can). We begin by addressing a critical ethical distinction.

1. The Is/Ought Distinction

A distinction is often made between what "is" and what "ought" to be. The 18th-century British philosopher David Hume is famous for having stressed that you cannot derive an ought from an is. In other words, simply because a particular behavior or practice is common (e.g., slavery in early 19th-century America), it cannot be concluded that things ought to be that way. If it were legitimate to reason this way, then ethics would be reduced to a descriptive scientific

practice and social change would be without normative support. Slavery, for example, would still be an institution in America because it was once a matter-of-fact practice. Fortunately, this is not the case. Ethics deals with what ought to be, not with what is.

Criticisms of this distinction have been advanced by those who argue that ethical language is not fundamentally different from factual language. Therefore, the terms *is* and *ought* are functionally identical. That is, they accomplish the same semantic purpose. One rather famous, and extreme, example of such a theory is *emotivism*. Emotivism is a theory of ethics advocated by A.J. Ayer, a 20th-century logical positivist. According to Ayer, "ought" claims and assertions serve the following purposes:

> [They] merely (1) express our feelings and (2) function as commands to other people. For example, when I say, "It is good for Jones to donate to charity," I am (1) expressing my favorable emotions about Jones, and (2) commanding you to endorse Jones's conduct. (Fieser, 2000, pp. 124-125)

In other words, ethical assertions do not appeal to a normative metaphysical principle, as some earlier philosophers claimed (e.g., Plato). Many contemporary clinicians advocate similar emotivist theories (e.g., Hayes, Strosahl, & Wilson, 1999).

Another motivation for criticism of the is/ought distinction can be found in the misuse of ethical standards in the history of humankind. Many examples could be cited here. Slavery, genocide, sexism, racism, and so on are examples of practices that have been supported by corrupt ethical environments. These practices were often supported by a select group (often self-selecting) of people who "knew" how things ought to be done. There is no denying that great injustices have come to pass under the banner of terms such as ought. Notice, however, that when it is claimed, for example, that "Slavery is bad," an ethical claim has been made. Most criticisms of the harm that has come from corrupt ethical principles actually amount to ethical criticisms based on unique ethical principles in their own right. To think that there is something wrong with X is, at least implicitly, to think that an ethical standard has been violated.

2. Ought Terms

In this section, we discuss a few terms that are often used in lieu of ought but that still carry a sense of moral obligation. Although it might seem unnecessary to provide a discussion of "ought terms," we do so because it is far too easy to think that a claim does not involve an ethical dictate when in fact it does. Everyday terms that do not seem to be ethically laden, such as *appropriate, healthy, legitimate,* and so on, are normative and evaluative terms and as such fall within the domain of ethics. They are ethical terms. We use them to praise and blame our own as well as others' behavior. Praise and blame are exclusively ethical notions.

To better explicate this point, imagine the woman from the earlier example responding to the waiter's threats by saying either "Your actions are inappropriate" or "Your actions are wrong." Although some may claim that these two statements are different, it appears that they are not. We can see this by asking, "Inappropriate (or wrong) according to what, or whose, standard?" The answer to this question on both counts will be the same. The woman might appeal to her own personal standards of human conduct to justify her claims. Likewise, she might be a born-again Christian who appeals to religious scripture to justify her claims. In either case, her justification for the terms *inappropriate* and *wrong* will appeal to some ethical standard. Consequently, the

person who says "I'm not saying that what you have done is wrong, it is just that you have behaved inappropriately" seems to have created a difference where none exists.

Should is a common term that is used instead of ought. Should is a synonym of ought. *Must* is another term that is sometimes used in lieu of ought. Although the term can have a strictly descriptive connotation, as in the statement "All humans must eventually die," it can also be used in an obligatory sense, such as "You must wash your hands before eating." In the former sense of the term, no sense of obligation is felt. It is simply a statement of fact. A clear sense of obligation is implied in the latter use of the term. A person could easily, for example, eat a meal without washing his or her hands. A similar analysis could be provided for phrases such as "You *have to* _____" and "You *need to* _____." They could either point to a descriptive necessity or a moral obligation. A good test of such terms and phrases would be to ask yourself, "Is it possible to not do _____?" If it is possible, then the statement carries with it a sense of moral obligation. When asking this question, it is important that you do not think of the consequences of failing to perform the action. The question seeks only to determine whether or not it is possible regardless of any potential consequences.

3. Ought Implies Can

When we claim that someone ought to do something, we necessarily assume that they can do it, in other words, that it is possible for them. Because terms such as ought carry with them a moral obligation, and because performance with regard to a moral obligation can be followed by praise or blame, the person who is under the mandate of an ought must at least be capable of carrying out the obligation. Otherwise, we would be able to blame people, for example, for not curing cancer during their lunch break. This would be absurd. If a person is physically incapable of performing an act (e.g., unaided flight), then it cannot be said that they ought to perform that act. This reasoning assures that people cannot be blamed for actions that are beyond their control. As such, being able to perform an action is a necessary prerequisite for the moral obligation to do so.

The ability to perform an action, however, does not itself dictate any moral obligation to perform that act. Simply because you can give blood every two weeks does not oblige you to do so, no matter how much good might result from it. This is an interesting wrinkle in moral theory. Clearly, we could all be better people (e.g., be more honest, give to charity, spend every waking hour working toward the good of humanity), and it would be splendid if we all did so. But we are not obligated to do so. Such acts are sometimes referred to as *super-ogatory acts*. These are acts that go beyond the call of duty and obligation. Donating a kidney to a stranger who needs it is an example. Such acts of kindness and goodness are often inspiring, but never obligatory. Indeed, if they were obligatory, then they would cease to be inspiring because we would just be doing what we ought to do. A world such as this would be an uninspiring world. It may be because of this that no moral theory requires such a level of performance.

4. Rights and Duties

For it to be meaningfully said that people have rights, people must also have duties. Duties support and ensure rights. Let us think about a clear example of a right. Americans have a right to free speech. How do we know we have this right? We could simply appeal to the Bill of Rights, couldn't we? Sure. But this would be an empty right, a right in words only. The best way to exercise your rights is to act on them. This is the true test of any right. One way to do

this is to go to a public meeting and voice your opinion about a civic matter. Let's say you do this. Now let's imagine that your opinion is not shared by many. Maybe you want to reinstate racial segregation. Why don't those who disagree simply throw stones at you or try to silence you by killing you?

The answer is simple. They cannot do so because they have a duty (backed by civil law) to refrain from harming you without just cause. Their anger at your opinion does not constitute just cause. Therefore, they must (in the obligatory sense) allow you to speak your piece (assuming that you are following all the particular rules of discourse for the meeting). Your right to free speech is created out of the duty of others to allow you the freedom to do so. A similar analysis can be provided for all other rights. They all depend on duties (both yours and others'). An interesting ethical question that can always be asked when thinking about rights is this: "What duties guarantee this right, and who is bound by such duties?"

People possess rights because they possess some status that is deemed to be *right conferring*. There are civil rights, human rights, and employee rights, to name just a few categories. There are at least two senses of the term *right* that are relevant: a weak sense and a strong sense. According to the weak sense of a right, when someone is said to have a right, what we are really saying is that it is not wrong for the person to act a certain way. This being said, it does not follow that individuals must act in accordance with their rights. Just because one has a right to refuse to help a person in need, it does not follow that it would be wrong to fail to act in accordance with that right. In short, according to the weak sense of a right, we are each free to act in ways that might be deemed impolite or even mean. According to the strong sense of right, when someone is said to have a right, what we are really saying is that exercising the right is good.

5. Rules, Laws, and Values

We have all probably said something like this in the past: "It's not that I think X is wrong ethically, but my hands are tied by the law (or a rule), and I have to do as it states." Maybe a competent employee failed to fill out a form in the right way, and even though this happens with employees all the time, you are forced as his supervisor to suspend him on the basis of the company procedures book. In such instances, we often make a distinction between ethics (values) and rules (laws). We want to make it clear that we are not making a moral judgment in such cases. The rules are the rules. Unfortunately, it is not always this clear-cut. Two issues can muddle such situations: (a) Sometimes we hide behind rules and laws, and (b) rules and laws are often based on ethical assumptions and principles.

As for the first issue, in some instances people hide behind the law to shelter themselves from any accusation of being moralistic or of passing judgment. Most people don't want to be viewed as overly judgmental or as believing that they are operating from a morally superior position. Because of this, people sometimes attempt to hide their ethical views behind laws. This practice can be relatively innocuous, or it can be dangerous. An innocuous example might be that of a supervisor at a restaurant firing a well-liked employee for failing to call in sick when she did not show up for work. Maybe the supervisor really did want to fire the employee because she thought that her behavior was inappropriate. And at the same time, she wanted to maintain a friendship with her into the future. Being judgmental might threaten that relationship, so she hides behind the restaurant policy on absenteeism when explaining her decision. A dangerous example is provided by Nazi concentration camp workers, some of whom are known to have claimed "I don't have anything against

Jews, I was just following orders." It is often all too easy to hide behind laws to avoid taking ethical responsibility for our actions.

As for the second issue, think about any law. Why is it a law? In all likelihood, the law is based on some moral principle or belief. This is clear with regard to capital crimes and the laws that prohibit them. The link between laws and rules and ethics is not always so clear. Take the speed limit, for example. There is no obvious connection here to an ethical principle unless we consider what speed limit laws are designed to prevent. Speed limits are not designed to limit speed per se, they are designed to limit the possibility of accidents, fatalities, and similar unfortunate things occurring on the roadways. If people could drive their cars at any speed without fatalities resulting, then speed limits might not exist.

Now the connection may be more clear. We value health and personal happiness. Accidents can hamper, or altogether destroy, our pursuit of such ends. Therefore, we prohibit activities that can unnecessarily hamper such ends. Similar reasoning can be applied to other laws and institutional rules. Exploring the ethical basis for a law or rule can be a way to understand the ethical environment within which the law operates. Even if we are simply following the rules, it does not follow that our behavior has nothing to do with ethics.

6. Relativism and Absolutism

Probably the most debated ethical question concerns the extent to which our ethical values are absolute or relative. Either murder (rape, incest, etc.) is objectively wrong for everybody, all around the world, or murder is wrong only in cases in which certain cultural practices and beliefs prevail.

The issue is dichotomized this way for logical reasons. Any principle that fails to be absolute is by definition relative. Mathematical statements such as "2 + 2 = 4" are often used as exemplars of absolute statements. This mathematical expression is true under all possible conditions. Most topics, however, do not involve the analytic rigor of mathematics and fall short of being absolute. Many thinkers believe that ethical claims and principles fail to be absolute in this mathematical sense. We turn now to the relativist position.

To say that an ethical principle is *relative* is to say that there are circumstances under which the principle could be violated without incurring reproach. The belief that, for example, "Killing is wrong" is an example of an ethical principle that many people view as relative. Some people may believe that killing is wrong except in cases of self-defense, capital punishment, war, euthanasia, and abortion. This is an example of a principle with exceptions, or a relative principle. If a rule or principle has exceptions, then it is relative. If a rule or principle is without exception, then it is absolute.

Sometimes ethical discussions can become sidetracked by loose use of terminology. The example above is a good one. Notice that the concept under consideration is "killing," not "murder," which would likely be conceptualized differently. One obvious difference is that although all acts of murder involve killing another person, not all instances in which a person is killed amount to murder. Murder is a legal term, whereas killing is generally considered a descriptive term.

Relativist reasoning suggests that ethical principles are always context (time and place) specific and as such are never absolute. A statement that most of us are familiar with is "Western practices and values are just that, Western values and practices." The function of this statement is typically to draw attention to the inherently biased sources of our ethical beliefs. As Simon Blackburn (2001) claims,

[Relativists] suppose that if our standards of conduct are "just ours," then that strips them of any real authority. We might equally well do things differently, and if we come to do so there is neither real gain nor real loss. What is just or right in the eyes of one people may not be so in the eyes of another, and neither side can claim real truth, unique truth, for its particular rules. (p. 21)

The relativist position can be broken down into two similar but conceptually distinct theses: (a) general ethical relativism and (b) ethical subjectivism. Each of these approaches will be explored.

The ethical relativist's primary point is that there are no universal ethical truths or standards. The values of a society are unique to that society and have no special claim to truth. To strengthen this argument, a great deal of emphasis is placed on the diversity of practices and opinions in the world. Some Hindu practitioners condemn the killing and eating of animals, whereas many people in America see nothing wrong with eating a hamburger. Who is to say who's right? Although the belief that "Everyone is on an ethical par" comes across as a very tolerant and agreeable position, there are some difficulties associated with such an extreme view.

According to the relativist position, slavery was a just and moral practice prior to the abolitionist movement. After all, who could prove it unjust? Once slaves were freed and our society condemned slavery, then the practice of slavery became immoral. This reversal-of-fortune effect of ethical relativism can be unnerving to some. Taken to its extreme, we must accept the fact that in "the big picture," our current values and practices are not objectively any better than those we adopted when we subjugated human beings to slavery and treated women as second-class citizens. To say otherwise is to say that our position here and now is objectively better and that we can prove it. This claim would contradict the relativist's primary claim that there are no objectively superior or "true" ethical standards.

According to the relativist, the prevailing ethical environment of a people or culture cannot be questioned or criticized unless we do so from our own ethical positions. But who is to say that we are right or just in our ways? Clearly, those who adopt other views would claim that we are wrong in our practices. Who is following the objectively true ethical principles? The relativist recognizes the eventual absurdity of such disagreements (e.g., "I am right"—"No, I am right") and maintains the belief that no comparisons can be made. All moral positions are equally valid to the relativist.

The moral subjectivist takes the relativist's position one step further. The subjectivist's primary point is that ethical beliefs are the result of an individual's upbringing and have no claim to objectivity or universality. Each person, according to the subjectivist, constitutes his or her own moral standard. Not all people in a particular culture share the same values, so relativism does not accurately capture the nature of ethics. If Shelly believes that it is right to lock her children in the closet when they have misbehaved, then it is her right to do so. This is the way Shelly was raised, and as such, no one can say it is wrong without appeal to what they think is right. Thus, the subjectivist relies on similar reasoning that the relativist does but takes this reasoning to its logical conclusion.

Positive aspects of ethical relativism: Ethical relativism highlights our ethical biases and recognizes multiple legitimate ethical systems. It also highlights the inherent difficulties in comparing ethical systems.

Criticisms of ethical relativism: Ethical relativism often rests on an apparent contradiction, for example, "To judge another person or culture based on your own ethical standards is wrong because there are no universal objective ethical standards by which you can legitimately do so."

Another line of reasoning suggests that true ethical principles such as the dictate that we ought not murder are true, regardless of where and when we live. Such principles are absolute, and as such, this position is referred to as *ethical absolutism*. Although absolutism appears to be the venerable default ethical position against which relativism reacts, the reverse of this order is a more accurate description of the history of ethics. Absolutism is a reaction to relativism. We can see this as far back as Plato. Socrates is often depicted arguing against ancient Greece's relativists, the sophists.

The moral absolutist's position is more subtle than is generally assumed. In short, the absolutist claims that true ethical standards hold for all people, regardless of their personal preferences or cultural upbringing. The standards can consist of particular beliefs. Rape, for example, is simply wrong. That is, there are no conditions under which the act of rape can be justified and right. The absolutist often appeals to our basic human reactions to injustices we see around the world to support his position. Don't we all have a negative reaction to children forced into slave labor? How about the image of children being forced into prostitution? What is the source of this reaction if not the belief that children ought not be forced into slave labor or prostitution under any circumstances?

Because the absolutist recognizes the problems highlighted by both the relativist and subjectivist, a more subtle claim is often made. It is not the particular ethical beliefs that are relevant. Rather, it is the clear need for some sort of universal standard that should be focused on. As the philosopher says in Tom Stoppard's play *Jumpers*, "Certainly a tribe which believes it confers honour on its elders by eating them is going to be viewed askance by another which prefers to buy them a little bungalow somewhere." But he also goes on to point out that in each tribe, some notion of honour or some notion of what it is fitting to do is at work (Blackburn, 2001, p. 21).

The argument being made is that some sense of obligation is common across all peoples; only the details are different. In the United States and Europe, for example, people drive on the right, and in Britain and Australia on the left, but in each country there has to be one rule or chaos reigns and traffic grinds to a halt (Blackburn, 2001, p. 22).

> **Positive aspects of absolutism:** Absolutism accounts for the fact that people judge and evaluate actions and events according to standards. In its sophisticated forms (such as the one presented), it deals with the basic human need for rules, orderly social interaction, and the importance of equity.
>
> **Criticisms of absolutism:** Absolutism can be accompanied by intolerance, and in this combination can be found the makings of tyranny, suffering, and everything that might be wrong with ethics.

Thus, the absolutist claims that ethics is a reflection of a basic human need to behave according to standards in certain areas of conduct. Moreover, the absolutist is apt to point out that the relativist has focused on the details (e.g., "Which side of the road is it objectively right to drive on?") rather than on the more fundamental principles. In doing so, argues the absolutist, the relativist has missed the point.

Although the absolutist admits that moral standards change over time, he or she stresses that this has no bearing on whether or not the standards are absolute. Maybe, for example, societies simply make mistakes with their moral standards. Moreover, if we adopt a relativist position, then not only are we forbidden from judging the practices of other societies but we are also without cause for judging and improving our own practices because "If right and wrong are relative to culture, this must be true for our own culture just as much as for other cultures" (Fieser, 2000, p. 15).

The debate between a relativist ethics and an absolutist-based ethics is made even more difficult because it is common for individuals on each side of the debate to simply miss the other person's point. A humorous anecdote retold by Simon Blackburn (2001) captures this difficulty well:

> This is illustrated by a nice anecdote of a friend of mine. He was present at a high-powered ethics institute which had put on a forum in which representatives of the great religions held a panel debate. First the Buddhist talked of the ways to calm, the mastery of desire, the path of enlightenment, and the panelists all said, "Wow, terrific, if that works for you that's great." Then the Hindu talked of the cycles of suffering and birth and rebirth, the teachings of Krishna and the way to release, and they all said, "Wow, terrific, if that works for you that's great." And so on, until the Catholic priest talked of the message of Jesus Christ, the promise of salvation, and the way to life eternal, and they all said, "Wow, terrific, if that works for you that's great." And he thumped the table and shouted, "No! It's not a question of if it works for me! It's the true word of the living God, and if you don't believe it you're all damned to hell!"
>
> And they all said, "Wow, terrific, if that works for you that's great." (p. 26)

7. Altruism and Egoism

The fundamental question being explored here is "Why be moral?" Do we do what is right because it is right, or do we do what is right because it is somehow pleasing for us to do so? Are our actions motivated by a sense of what is right or by a basic drive for self-interest? The altruist claims that it is possible for people to act against their own basic self-interests in doing what is right. A person may, for example, risk her life to snatch a child from the path of an oncoming car. Altruists claim that this act conflicts with any conceivable gain that the woman might enjoy. Acts of self-sacrifice are common examples for the altruist.

> **Positive aspects of altruism:** Self-sacrifice for the good of another, or the greater good, has always been valued in societies. The altruist position acknowledges the possibility, even though it is rare, of such self-sacrificing actions.

> **Criticisms of altruism:** Every seemingly self-sacrificing action admits of many alternative egoistic interpretations. No example of self-sacrifice has yet to overcome this obstacle.

The egoist claims that seemingly altruistic acts can be viewed as veiled acts of egoism. According to the egoist, people's behavior can be motivated by only two ends: pleasure and the removal of pain. A distinction is typically made between two variants of egoism: (a) psychological egoism and (b) ethical egoism. *Psychological egoism* is the thesis that humans act merely out of self-interest in all cases. As such, psychological egoism is a descriptive theory of human behavior, not a normative theory. Even if it is true that people always act out of self-interest, it does not necessarily follow that people ought to behave this way. *Ethical egoism* is a much bolder thesis. According to the ethical egoist, people ought to act out of self-interest in all cases. In fact, the ethical egoist claims that such a standard of conduct might actually be beneficial to humankind (Rachels, 2000).

A common complaint haunting the egoist is that the position is just too selfish and ugly

to really give any credit to. One way to explore this criticism is to ask whether self-interest and selfishness are identical. One conceptualization distinguishes the two as follows: "Selfish behavior is behavior that ignores the interests of others, in circumstances in which their interests ought not to be ignored" (White, 2000, p. 13). Self-interest, on the other hand, is to be viewed as a result of the basic drive for survival and the pursuit of pleasure.

> **Positive aspects of egoism:** The egoist relies on substantial empirical support that points to the fact that like it or not, people are complicated stimulus-response organisms that don't go about sacrificing positive stimulation very often (if ever).

> **Criticisms of egoism:** A major criticism of egoism is that most egoists are merely psychological egoists and do not really consider whether self-interest is a good ethical position.

NORMATIVE ETHICS

In this section, we will outline three of the major ethical theories in contemporary philosophy. We begin by discussing *utilitarianism* (also known as consequentialist ethics), then the *deontological* (e.g., duty-based) ethical theory, and finally *natural law theory* (also known as divine command theory). Each of these theories explicates a unique method that people can follow to determine how they ought to act in a given situation. We begin with what is likely the most well-understood ethical theory, utilitarianism.

Utilitarianism

Utilitarianism is often referred to as "consequentialist ethics" due to its focus on the outcomes of behavior when assessing their status as just or unjust, right or wrong, or ethical or unethical. According to this theory, one should act in such a way as to increase the total amount of happiness for society in general. There are two forms of utilitarianism: (a) act utilitarianism and (b) rule utilitarianism. The former is most often associated with Jeremy Bentham, who claimed that the pleasure and pain of each act must be calculated according to a utilitarian calculus, whereas the latter is associated with J.S. Mill, who asserted that we ought to follow a general rule with respect to actions.

Because of its implausibility, act utilitarianism is rarely treated as a serious attempt to describe how we ought to act. To explicate this implausibility, we have included a brief description of Bentham's utilitarian calculus. Seven factors are weighed with respect to each potential act.

1. Intensity of the pleasures and pains

2. Duration of the pleasures and pains

3. Certainty of the pleasures and pains

4. Remoteness of the pleasures and pains

5. Fecundity of the pleasures and pains

6. Purity of the pleasures and pains

7. Extent of the pleasures and pains

Answers to each of these questions must be quantified according to a rule that is similar to that used when constructing decision trees; then, the answer will be evident. Clearly, however, basing each of our decisions on such a complicated calculation is not realistic. We would spend all of our time calculating instead of behaving.

Mill identifies the ideal perfection of utilitarian morality with the following phrase, "To do as you would be done by, and love your neighbor as yourself" (Mill, 1948/2000, p. 39). Mill argues that the general happiness is that which ought to be worked toward because "Each person's happiness is a good to that person, and the general happiness, therefore, a good to the aggregate of persons." (Mill, 1948/2000, p. 40).

Deontology

The famous German philosopher Immanuel Kant popularized deontological ethics. Thinking about deontological ethics in relation to utilitarian ethics helps foster understanding, because Kant's writing is both dense and philosophically complicated. In contrast to utilitarian ethics, deontological ethics focuses on duty and does not accept consequences coming into play when determining the ethical status of a behavior. Unlike utilitarian ethics, which focuses on the future consequences and pleasure(s) associated with a particular course of action, deontological ethics looks backward at the intent of an action. Deontological ethics focuses on two important concepts: (a) duty and (b) the good will.

Deontological ethics can be encapsulated by what is known as the *categorical imperative:* "Act only on that maxim through which you can at the same time will that it should become a universal law" (Kant, 1948/2000, p. 46). This means that we should only behave in ways that we can truly imagine everybody acting all around the world. In a sense, Kant developed an absolutist ethic by requiring that each person ask the absolutist question "What if everybody acted this way? Would that be a world I want to live in?" If the answer is "Yes," then it is permissible. If the answer is "No," then it is not permissible. After such reasoning, we develop maxims (rules) that guide our behavior. For example, a person might wonder if it would be permissible to lie to a friend in order to avoid embarrassment. Following Kant's advice, the person should ask, "Would it be okay if everyone lied to others in order to avoid embarrassment?" The answer would likely be "No," and as such, the maxim cannot be universalized. Many of our behaviors reflect one or more ethical maxims, but not all. For example, the following maxims seem to make little sense even though they could be universalized: "When alone in the dark, whistle" or "Tie your left shoestring first."

Interestingly enough, deontological ethics does not actually specify what particular behaviors ought to be done. Rather, it provides us with a method by which we can think about our behavior in an ethical manner. Kant seems to be making these three points:

1. It is permissible to act on a maxim if and only if one can will it to be a universal law.

2. It is wrong to act on a maxim if and only if one cannot will it to be a universal law.

3. It is a duty to act on a maxim if and only if one cannot will its opposite to be a universal law.

Another expression of the categorical imperative is found in Kant's means/ends analysis, "Act in such a way that you always treat humanity, whether in your own person or in the person of any other, never simply as a means but always at the same time as an end" (Kant, 1948/2000, p. 50). It is generally agreed that this claim is equivalent to the previous expression of the categorical imperative. It should be emphasized that Kant does not claim that we should not use people as means, simply that we should never use them as mere means. "To use someone as a *mere means* is to involve them in a scheme of action *to which they could not in principle consent*" (O'Neill, 2000, p. 50).

With regard to the notion of a "good will," Kant seems to suggest the opposite of what the utilitarian might say regarding happiness and pleasure. Kant seems to

require hardship and even unhappiness for the clear expression of action from the motive of duty:

> When, on the contrary, disappointments and hopeless misery have quite taken away the taste for life; and when a wretched man, strong in soul and more angered at his fate than faint-hearted or cast down, longs for death and still preserves his life without loving it—not from inclination or fear but from duty; then indeed his maxim has a moral content. (Kant, 1948/2000, p. 45)

The deontologist wants to see that an individual has performed a good act out of a sense of duty to a maxim rather than from inclination. Moral worth (acting from duty) is worthy of esteem, whereas simply doing good (acting from inclination) is worthy of encouragement.

Natural Law Ethics

The final ethical theory we will consider is natural law ethics. This is a religious approach to ethics that stresses that God had a plan when the world was created and that insight into this plan will provide answers to our ethical questions. Although there are many religions, the natural law approach is a Catholic theory. Sources for natural law ethics are not limited to the Bible. The writings of church philosophers such as Saint Thomas Aquinas and Saint Augustine often prove to be sources of the natural law perspective. The basic assumptions of this approach are as follows:

1. Religion is necessary for morality because otherwise there would be no right or wrong.

2. Religion provides us with guidance as to what is right and what is wrong.

3. Religion is a necessary source of motivation for people to do right.

Natural law ethics are most often encountered in conjunction with sexual ethics. An example would be the church's prohibition of certain sexual acts that are not designed to result in conception: masturbation, birth control, and homosexual sex. According to the church, sex is an act that has procreation as its function. This is the state of nature as God created it, and the aforementioned acts cannot produce the natural consequence.

A problem commonly cited regarding natural law ethics is that it rests on the assumption that morality is arbitrary and based on the whim of God. Here is a brief outline of this argument:

1. God's commands can create right and wrong.

2. There is no other source for rights and wrongs.

3. God is all-powerful.

4. God could change (reverse) rights and wrongs.

5. Therefore, murder, rape, torture could become right (good) if God simply commanded it so.

Even religiously minded people are often troubled by the notion that according to natural law ethics, God could simply mandate that, for example, "We ought to murder," and because of this, murder would be praiseworthy. Most people are unwilling to accept the fact that morality is so radically contingent, even if the contingency is associated with God's wishes.

VIRTUE ETHICS

Aristotle defines *virtue* as the excellence of a thing. A thing's excellence is, in turn, defined as its disposition to perform its proper function. The proper function of a knife is to cut things, so an excellent knife is one that cuts well. Similarly, the proper function of a therapist is to improve the condition of his or her client's life, so an excellent therapist is one who does so with efficiency and regularity. These observations seem commonsensical. This is a distinguishing feature of Aristotle's approach to philosophy in general. It is also the feature that may have been partly responsible for Plato overlooking Aristotle when it came time to nominate a successor to the Academy (Albert, Denise, & Peterfreund, 1953).

The topic of moral virtue is of particular interest in Aristotle's ethics because an understanding of this topic is likely to result in happiness. We acquire intellectual virtue through teaching, but we acquire moral virtue through habit. Aristotle claims that moral virtue is not a matter of nature (as opposed to nurture). That is, we are not born with the predisposition to act morally; we learn to do so. What we are born with is a predisposition to adapt accordingly. Through practice, we develop habits. One does not become a painter by thinking about painting nor a pianist by thinking about playing the piano. The same is true of the moral virtues: One becomes courageous by engaging in courageous behaviors.

The goal of such practice is to develop habits that are conducive to happiness. Once these habits are sufficiently developed, a person is more likely to associate virtuous behavior with happiness. When a person is honest in his or her relationships, then this person is likely to be treated well and respected. Respect and good treatment are generally pleasing and tend to result in happiness. The virtuous person, according to Aristotle, is the person who is made happy by being virtuous. The person who derives happiness from virtuous activities is better off than the person who is honest only because she has been told to be honest.

Aristotle asserted that the characters of men who seem to fulfill their proper function (e.g., virtuous people) tend to be characterized by moderation. The courageous person is neither fearful nor foolhardy. If we think of courage as a continuum of potential behavior, then the fearful person is lacking in courage (Aristotle refers to this as "defect"), whereas the foolhardy person is foolishly courageous (Aristotle refers to this as "excess"). Each of these extremes is undesirable in that behaving in these ways is not conducive to happiness.

For Aristotle, the good life is the life of happiness. Hence, ethics is the examination of happiness. Aristotle emphasized the attainment of virtue and happiness through moderation in all things. Aristotle further noticed that people tend to identify happiness with something that they lack: The poor think it is money, the sick think it is health, and the ugly think it is beauty.

Whatever happiness might be, however, Aristotle was convinced that it must be something that is sought for its own sake. Money, health, and beauty are indeed worthy things, but these are sought for the sake of happiness. That is, money is only a good insofar as it is a means to the procurement of material goods and services. If money failed to be a means for attaining such things, then money would quickly cease to be sought. Happiness, on the other hand, must be something else, or more basic, than these obviously desirable things. Aristotle defines happiness as an activity of the soul in accordance with virtue.

Consider the following maxim: "Always act in the right way, at the right time, in the right place, and for the right reasons." This maxim captures the meaning of Aristotle's famous doctrine of the mean or, as it is sometimes referred to, the "Golden Mean." The Golden Mean applies also to the passions and emotions. Anger is an appropriate response in the right way, at the right time, in the right place, and for the right reasons. One who is always angry is flawed in the same way as one who never gets angry, on Aristotle's account. Aristotle's definition of moral virtue is as follows:

> Virtue, then, is a state of character concerned with choice, lying in a mean, i.e., the mean relative to us, this being determined by a rational principle, and by that principle by which the man of practical wisdom would determine it. (Albert et al., 1953, p. 51)

Not all behaviors admit of a virtuous mean. Aristotle mentions adultery, thievery, and murder as activities that though one may engage in them moderately, will never generate a virtue.

Aristotle identified many particular virtues. The virtue of courage has already been mentioned. Bertrand Russell (1945), the famous 20th-century logician, captures Aristotle's doctrine of the mean in the following passage:

> Every virtue is a mean between two extremes, each of which is a vice . . . Courage is a mean between cowardice and rashness; liberality, between prodigality and meanness; proper pride, between vanity and humility; ready wit, between buffoonery and boorishness; modesty, between bashfulness and shamelessness. (pp. 173-174)

The person who most completely exemplifies the virtuous life is the magnanimous person. *Magnanimous* is a Greek term that literally means "great-souled" or "proud." In addition to being virtuous, the magnanimous person requires friends.

CONCLUSION

Ethics infuses our daily lives. As psychologists, we face unique challenges in carrying out our professional duties as therapists, teachers, and researchers. Subsequent chapters focus on these topics. As you read through them, you will notice many of the themes, distinctions, and theories that have been discussed in this chapter. The relationship between ethical theory and applied ethics is a straightforward one. Applied ethics, when done well, does not amount to a simple list of rules that has been arrived at during a committee meeting. The reasoning that goes into applied ethics is based on ethical principles and assumptions that go beyond the circumscribed settings to which they are applied. Applied ethics is an extension of ethical theory.

REFERENCES

Albert, E. M., Denise, T. H., & Peterfreund, S. P. (1953). *Great traditions in ethics: An introduction*. New York: American Book Company.

Aristotle. (2000). Nicomachean ethics. In S. M. Cohen, P. Curd, & C. D. C. Reeve (Eds.), *Ancient Greek philosophy from Thales to Aristotle* (pp. 764-823). Indianapolis, IN: Hackett.

Beck, A. T., Rush, A. J., Shaw, B. F., & Emery, G. (1979). *Cognitive therapy for depression*. New York: Guilford.

Blackburn, S. (2001). *Being good: A short introduction to ethics*. Oxford, UK: Oxford University Press.

Ellis, A., & Blau, S. (1998). *The Albert Ellis reader: A guide to well-being using rational emotive behavior therapy*. Secaucus, NJ: Citadel.

Fieser, J. (2000). *Metaethics, normative ethics, and applied ethics*. Stamford, CT: Wadsworth.

Hayes, S. C., Strosahl, K. D., & Wilson, K. G. (1999). *Acceptance and commitment therapy*. New York: Guilford.

Hobbes, T. (1994). *Leviathan*. Cambridge, UK: Hackett. (Original work published 1668)

Kant, I. (2000). The categorical imperative. In J. E. White (Ed.), *Contemporary moral problems* (pp. 43-49). Belmont, CA: Wadsworth. (Original work published 1948)

Mill, J. S. (2000). *Utilitarianism*. In J. E. White (Ed.), Contemporary moral problems (pp. 36-43). Belmont, CA: Wadsworth. (Original work published 1948)

O'Neill, O. (2000). A simplified account of Kant's ethics. In J. E. White (Ed.), *Contemporary moral problems* (pp. 49-55). Belmont, CA: Wadsworth.

Rachels, J. (2000). Egoism and moral skepticism. In J. E. White (Ed.), *Contemporary moral problems* (pp. 9-17). Belmont, CA: Wadsworth.

Russell, B. (1945). *A history of western philosophy*. New York: Touchstone.

White, J. E. (Ed.). (2000). *Contemporary moral problems*. Belmont, CA: Wadsworth.

CHAPTER 3

Thinking Well About Ethics
Beyond the Code

MICHAEL LAVIN
Private Practice

Philosophical ethics is an all-out assault on the question "How should I live?" Contending schools of philosophy have given competing answers to the question. Consequentialists say we ought to live so as to make the consequences as good as possible. Kantians say we ought to live so that we always treat other persons as ends in themselves, never merely as means. Virtue theorists say that we should live virtuously. Casuists say we ought to decide how to live one case at a time. Skeptics say the question has no answer, or if it has, that none of us knows the answer or perhaps even has any reasonable beliefs about the answer, save the skeptic's answer, of course. The intellectually finicky say the question is misstated. Certain religious people say we ought to live in conformance with God's commands, which they claim to know. There is no definite end to the number of answers that the "How should I live?" question pulls for.

To make it more confusing still, answers to the "How should I live?" question have no ready epistemology for answering them. As in mathematics, there is confusion about how knowledge in philosophical ethics is achieved, even when there is agreement about particular cases (e.g., 2 + 2 = 4; psychologists billing clients for unperformed services is wrong). Uncontroversial knowledge claims paradigmatically involve placing myself in a position for my beliefs to be caused in the right kind of way. Further causation is (normally) thought of as a physical transaction. I know that the cat is on the mat if and only if my belief that the cat is on the mat is caused by the cat on the mat. If my belief is not caused by the cat on the mat, then I don't know that the cat is on the mat. Or so a plausible story goes. But it is far from obvious that knowledge in mathematics or philosophical ethics could come about by beliefs having the right causes. For example, many examples of mathematical knowledge involve infinitely large sets or carry claims about their "necessity." But the world of causes experienced by human beings has no infinitely large sets or necessities. I have no sensuous experience of infinitely large sets or necessities, even though I know that there are infinitely large sets. If I "see" them at all, if I indeed have any knowledge of them, it is in my mind's eye. Likewise, no personal experience has caused me to believe that torturing clients is wrong, even though I believe I know that torturing clients is wrong and also think that any person who only believes that torturing them is wrong is either guilty of understatement or a moral imbecile. Philosophical ethics is puzzling.

Fortunately, psychologists have no professional need to answer the "How should I live?" question for all contexts, or even with complete philosophical rigor. Instead, psychologists answer an apparently easier question, with an apparently easier epistemology. They wonder how they should conduct themselves as psychologists. How should psychologists live their professional lives? In their day-to-day work, psychologists can turn to their code of professional ethics (American Psychological Association [APA], 1992) for guidance. If they are members of the APA, they have promised to comply with the APA code as a condition of membership (APA, 1992, Introduction), and this is so even if psychologists wonder if they should have promised. Even if they are not members, if they are licensed, they are likely to have a duty to comply with the APA code imposed on them by state boards of psychology. If they are conducting research in a university, they also have duties, often alleged to be ethical, to comply with various federal ethics requirements and to submit their research protocols for review by an Institutional Review Board or Human Subjects Committee. But in meeting these duties to comply with the code or submit their research for review, psychologists may well wonder why the provisions of ethics code and regulations are what they are and

why somebody would think it wrong to disregard or disobey them. This chapter tries to offer guidance on this question by arguing that psychologists can do a better job of answering ethical questions by viewing them as continuous with their role as scientists. What psychologists need to do when they engage in serious moral thinking is continuous with what they do as scientists, but the similarities between scientific thinking and moral thinking get blurred by too narrow a focus on a code-driven, ethics-driven approach to moral thinking.

THE APA ETHICS CODE

Thinking about the APA ethics code should undermine any easy faith in it. It is incomplete and vague. It has been repeatedly revised and expanded. And its interpretation is a matter of controversy. Its moral underpinnings and the relation of its principles and ethical standards and substandards are unexplained. It is a document that came into being through a political process.

The APA promulgated its first ethics code in 1953 (APA, 1953) and has tinkered with it eight times since then. For the first 60 years of the APA's existence, there was no code, though by 1938, there was a Committee on Scientific and Professional Ethics that handled complaints informally, and by 1947, that committee had urged the development of a formal code (Pope & Vetter, 1992). One reason offered in support of a formal code was that an unwritten code was "tenuous, elusive, and unsatisfactory" ("A Little Recent History," 1952, p. 427, as cited in Pope & Vetter, 1992). The years since 1953 have yielded the present form of the APA code.

The APA's regnant ethical principles are in its 1992 Ethical Principles of Psychologists and Code of Conduct. It has the following structure: Introduction, Preamble, General

Principles, and Ethical Standards. The Introduction stresses that its general principles are aspirational goals that are not enforceable against members. Rather, its General Principles are alleged to be the highest ideals of psychology and are to be used to guide interpretation of the code's ethical standards. The APA does grant itself authority to enforce the code's ethical standards. Members who run afoul of them may be sanctioned (viz., expulsion from the APA). In addition to the aspirational General Principles and the aspirational Preamble, interpretation of the ethical standards is furthered by a variety of supplemental materials that are not enforceable under the APA's ethics code, such as a psychologist's own values. This acknowledgment of the need for interpretation, much of which hinges on idiosyncratic supplemental sources, guarantees that the code is not what mathematicians would call an effective method. It is not an algorithm that generates one and only one assuredly correct answer to a problem in a finite number of steps, as a logician's truth table does (Hunter, p. 14, 1973).

The General Principles asserted by the APA are six in number: Principle A: Competence; Principle B: Integrity; Principle C: Professional and Scientific Responsibility; Principle D: Respect for People's Rights and Dignity; Principle E: Concern for Others' Welfare; and Principle F: Social Responsibility. These principles are all set forth in one-paragraph glosses of a mean length of approximately 110 words.

The enforceable ethical standards, as of 1998, cover eight areas of concern to psychologists. Each standard includes various substandards. So, under General Standards are 27 substandards covering a variety of problems, including the applicability of the ethics code, the relationship of law and ethics, and sexual harassment. The remaining seven standards are "Evaluation Assessment," or "Interventions," with 10 substandards; "Advertising and Other Public Statements," with 6 substandards; "Therapy," with 9 substandards; "Privacy and Confidentiality," with 11 substandards; "Teaching, Training Supervision, Research, and Publishing," with a whopping 26 substandards; "Forensic Activities," with 6 substandards; and "Resolving Ethical Issues," with 7 substandards.

Given the complexity of the code, it is perhaps not surprising that the APA has not thought it possible to rely on letting aspiring clinical psychologists learn their duties from modeling and practice alone. Instead, APA-accredited clinical programs are obligated to include ethics training in their curricula. Increasingly, states have begun to require an ethics course as a condition for a clinical psychologist's licensure. Moreover, like all professional societies, the APA has an interest in having there be, both in fact and in public perception, devotion to high ethical standards by APA programs and members.

Though most psychologists will have acquired sound hunches about what is moral, ethical, and legal, this is partly a result of the formal training they receive. As already indicated, APA-accredited clinical programs must include elementary training in ethical and legal issues relating to practice and research (APA Committee on Accreditation, 1996). Undoubtedly, numerous formal (courses) and informal (modeling) sources in a psychologist's training, as well as social forces, go into creating the average psychologist's intuitions about what kinds of activity are moral, ethical, and legal. In fact, if properly understood, a psychologist's scientific training is a superb foundation for moral and ethical thinking. In fact, if psychologists recognized the similarities between their scientific thinking and moral ethical thinking, there could well be a deeper understanding about what their moral responsibilities are and what psychology's code of ethics ought to say.

MORAL THINKING AS QUASI-SCIENTIFIC

Characteristics of Scientific Thinking

It is almost part of the zeitgeist to believe that moral thinking is soft in a way that scientific thinking is not. Scientific thinking is data driven and bristles with devices for making tight connections between scientific evidence and scientific conclusions. In a good, albeit simplified, account of scientific thinking, Quine and Ullian (1978) explain that scientific thinking involves the construction of conservative, modest, simple, general, refutable theories.

A theory is *conservative* if it minimizes the need to change previously held beliefs. Perhaps it is true that schizophrenia is caused by witchcraft, but such a belief would require massive revision of orthodox scientific beliefs about the way the world works. The witchcraft hypothesis is unconservative in a way that the dopamine hypothesis, false though they both may be, is not.

Scientific thinking is *modest*. Modest hypotheses do not depend heavily on the unusual. The hypothesis that a stenographer mistyped a word owing to carelessness is more modest than one blaming his typos on brain disease. As Quine would say, even if brain disease is rife, carelessness is rifer.

Simplicity is a third characteristic of scientific thinking. What makes a theory or hypothesis simple is hard to define. Researchers recognize it when they see it. Linear relation between variables is simpler than a periodic function. The Copernican theory of the planet moving around the sun in elliptical orbits is simpler than the Ptolemaic system that has them doing epicircles. An ecological theory that derives behavioral principles from Darwin is simpler than a theory that derives them from Darwin, computer science, and the will of the creator.

Scientific thinking attains *generality* when its theories and hypotheses enjoy a wide range of application; the greater the range, the greater the generality. Whatever one thinks of the truth of psychoanalytic theory, it has greater generality than Gibson's theory of vision.

Refutability is perhaps the sine qua non of a scientific hypothesis. The theory should make predictions and retrodictions that if mistaken, refute it. However, it's important to be somewhat lenient about what counts as a refutation. Refutation may seldom be as simple as a theory getting a prediction wrong. First, sometimes theories are revised rather than refuted. Even Freud, often the whipping boy of philosophers (Popper, 1959) seeking an example of a theory that allows no refutations, often revised his theories in response to what he saw as their clinical failures. For example, Freud moved from an early topographic system of Cs, Pcs, and Ucs that did not include the Id, Ego, and Superego as constructs to a structural system that did. However, a bad predictive record is indeed taken to be one of the better marks of a theory that needs burying. There is a reason why people are more trusting of the predictions of physicists than of Watsonian behaviorists. A refusal to accept an avalanche of counterexamples is the mark of the true believer, not the scientist.

As will be seen, once these normative characterizations of rational hypotheses-making in scientific thinking are kept in mind, moral thinking looks more like a variant of scientific thinking than a species of its own.

Characteristics of Moral Thinking

Moral thinking has at least three salient characteristics (Rachels, 1998). It is *universal*. It is *impartial*. It is *reason driven*.

Universality means that morality's claims are not local. It would be odd to claim that cheating a client is morally permissible if he has the misfortune to live in Cleveland in February rather than Cleveland in April. Also, it would be odd for me to claim that it is permissible for me to have sexual relations with former clients simply because I am who I am, but would be wrong if you and I swapped places.

Impartiality requires that likes be treated alike. It is morally unsustainable to argue that Sam and Suzy are alike in all relevant respects but that Sam has a particular right that Suzy does not have. If their moral claims differ, impartiality requires that there be at least one relevant difference between them.

Finally, when we make moral claims, we have an obligation to defend the claims with *reason*. If I say I like rhubarb, I don't need to have a reason for liking it, but if I claim Maslow was a good man or Napoleon a bad one, I do need to have reasons. Expressions of taste do not require a justification. Moral judgments do.

The Role of Moral Principles

These three characteristic features of moral thinking do not answer substantive moral problems. To do that, one also needs to apply substantive moral principles to the facts. Deciding what moral principles should regulate the behavior of psychologists is a controversial matter. There is disagreement. For example, even if somebody believes that persons should act on the basis of virtuous dispositions—courage, prudence, conscientiousness, and the like—rather than from principles, there is still a governing moral principle, namely, act from virtue.

Several principles have attained prominence, especially in writings on medical ethics. Beauchamp and Childress (1994), writing in the tradition of the highly influential *Belmont Report* (National Commission for the Protection of Human Subjects of Biomedical and Behavioral Research, 1979), have been influential in articulating, defending, and applying four principles that have gained wide allegiance: a principle of autonomy, a principle of beneficence, a principle of nonmaleficence, and a principle of justice. Though the formulation and ultimate justification of these principles is certainly controversial, their relevance to ethical decision making is easy to make clear. Few, if any, psychologists would assert that whether an act limits a person's autonomy or self-determination is morally irrelevant. Few, if any, psychologists would claim that a client's well-being is irrelevant in deciding what to do. Few, if any, psychologists would claim that whether a client is harmed is irrelevant to their deciding what to do. And, finally, few, if any, psychologists would think that issues of justice are irrelevant to ethical decision making.

Many psychologists might have other principles, as well as moral or religious ideals, that help them to reach morally sound decisions, but these four principles identify features that the overwhelming majority of psychologists would be willing to acknowledge as relevant to their moral thinking. The four principles may well represent a minimum consensus on principles that should guide psychologists in their moral decision making and the APA in formulating its ethical principles and standards of conduct. An ethics code that conflicted with these moral principles would stand in need of justification or, more likely, revision. For example, regulating any sexual conduct between *competent* clients and therapists, as the APA standards do (Standard 4.05, "Sexual Therapy With Former Sexual Partners"; Standard 4.07, "Sexual Intimacies With Former Therapy Patients"), arguably violates the principle of autonomy. Nevertheless, one plausible justification for this infringing on client and therapist autonomy is that the infringement is minor and regulation arose only because of egregious violations by therapists of the principle of nonmaleficence at the expense of clients.

Psychologists with a sound understanding of moral principles are well positioned to appraise the APA Ethical Principles and Code of Conduct (1992). They are also better prepared than psychologists schooled only in the code to know how to think about the many issues not covered by the code.

THE FOUR PRINCIPLES AND SCIENTIFIC THEORIZING

With knowledge of moral principles in hand, psychologists can recognize moral theory as having a structure isomorphic to scientific theories. To see the isomorphism, psychologists can trace this moral theory of four principles in terms of its being conservative, modest, simple, general, and refutable.

To begin with, the principles of autonomy, beneficence, nonmaleficence, and justice are conservative. They were selected to agree with widely held moral beliefs. Tests of the conservatism of moral principles are best thought of as analogous to tests of grammaticality by a native speaker of a language. Chomsky (1957) has made it clear that a linguist need not conduct a survey of speakers to determine the grammaticality of all sentences:

> We assume for discussion that certain sequences of phonemes are definitely sentences, and that certain other sequences are definitely nonsentences. In many intermediate cases we shall be prepared to let the grammar [we are seeking to elucidate] itself decide, when the grammar is set up in the simplest way so that it includes the clear sentences and excludes the clear nonsentences. (pp. 13-14)

So, ordinary judgment suffices to tell us that "The president invited me to dinner" is a grammatical sentence and "Me dinner invited president the" is not. Likewise, these principles seem consistent with ordinary, uncontroversial moral beliefs. Ordinary moral beliefs about the wrongfulness of billing clients for unperformed services or of having sex with a client who has passed out in one's office or, to take a happier instance, the duty to make competent treatment recommendations to clients are consistent with or derivable from the four principles. A sense of morality will prove indispensable for moral theorizing, as has been indicated in this sketch of why the four principles are conservative. However, just as the use of "intuitions" in linguistics does not count against its being a science, so the use of moral intuitions should not count against morality being rationally grounded.

The four principles are also modest. They do not imply simpler deontological or consequentialist moral theories. Beauchamp and Childress, the authors of *Principles of Biomedical Ethics* (1994), accept different moral theories. Beauchamp is a consequentialist (consequentialists hold that we ought to act to make the consequences as good as possible; Parfit, 1984). Childress is a deontologist (deontologists hold that there are right- and wrong-making features of an act other than its consequences; Donagan, 1977). Nevertheless, they believe that their theories support the use of the four principles in moral thinking. Likewise, this conjunction of moral principles is more modest than, to take one example, a divine-command theory that depends on revelations from God to determine right and wrong.

Furthermore, these principles are simple. They make no grave demands on a psychologist's trying to remember what principles to consider when engaged in moral thinking. They are even easier to keep in memory than the Decalogue.

The four principles are also general. It is not claimed that the principles apply only on Thursdays in Belgium. In fact, the requirements imposed on moral thinking, that it be universal and impartial, guarantee a high degree of generality.

The contestable feature of moral, as opposed to scientific, theories is in their refutability. Refutability is not easy to specify. If freshmen in a physics lab attempt to replicate a classic experiment and all the students get disparate results, physics is not tottering. Likewise, if a classroom of students claimed to have falsified the law of effect, it would be so much the worse for them, not the law. However, there is perhaps a sense that no data serve a disconfirming role in moral theory. But the notion that refutation has no role in moral theories is too extreme. The issue, just as it is in science, is not whether everybody is convinced that a position is mistaken, but whether everybody should be convinced. The arguments establishing the impossibility of a perpetual-motion machine are not refuted by the invincible beliefs of an addled inventor. Refutations of cruder versions of egoism ("I ought always to do what is best for me") are not mistaken just because there continue to be devotees of Ayn Rand.

How ethical theories and principles are refuted may appear different from how hypotheses are refuted in the behavioral sciences. For one thing, the "data" of ethics are rooted in human emotional responsiveness. Judge Posner (1995) has put it well:

> We reason from our bedrock beliefs, not to them. Infanticide and slavery are not forbidden in our society because the arguments against these practices are stronger than the arguments in favor of them, but because the practices revolt us. We would not listen to anyone who cared to make arguments in favor of them. . . .

Our primary motives for not killing children are indeed biological and sentimental—and provide a solider basis for a civilized morality than philosophical reflection, which notoriously has difficulty drawing moral distinctions among computers, talking apes, and retarded human beings. (p. 191)

Or, in the same vein, Posner (1995) continued:

> Our deepest values . . . live below thought and provide warrants for action even when we cannot give those values a compelling or perhaps any rational justification. (p. 192)

Posner (1992) also stressed the role of emotion as moral data:

> Disgust and other strong emotions in fact supply the sturdiest foundations for moral feelings. You cannot convince a person by argument that infanticide is a bad thing. If he demands an argument—seriously, and not just when playing philosophy—this merely shows that he inhabits a different moral universe from you, and there is no arguing between universes. The revulsion that modern Americans feel against infanticide is deeper than any reason they could give for the revulsion. An even clearer case is sexual intercourse between men and animals. Most people in our society find this a disgusting practice, yet it is hard to give reasons why. We do not scruple to eat lambs or make their skins into clothing; why do we worry about inserting the human penis into one of their orifices? Does it hurt or degrade them? Does it brutalize a man to copulate with an animal? Such questions are irrelevant, because the disgust we feel is not the product of utilitarian calculations. (pp. 230-231)

Posner's identification of the importance of emotions to morality as well as his noticing the rootedness of moral judgment in emotions are crucial to thinking about the refutability of moral hypotheses. It is all too easy, when thinking about morality, to believe that if no intellectual reason against a practice comes to mind, then it is irrational or mistaken to condemn it. Human emotions give the moral theorist data to heed.

Posner is not to be taken as saying that our moral emotions are infallible indicators of moral truth. Human emotions can mislead in moral theorizing just as human perceptions can mislead in scientific theorizing. Some of our emotions undoubtedly are misleading, but we come to see them as misleading as inquiry proceeds. And seeing them as misleading will (presumably) lead to a realignment of our emotional world. A wide knowledge is a protector against moral parochialism and its associated bigotting of feelings. It helps, for example, to know that Indonesians see nothing wrong with eating dogs, even though most Americans are disgusted at the idea and undoubtedly support laws against it. What is crucial for moral inquiry, though, is that moral emotions be taken seriously. They do test and constrain moral theorizing.

Like sensory observations in the sciences, emotions become the data from which inquiry begins and against which inquiry is checked. In this, their role resembles the role of observations in physical science. To the senses, the world does appear to be a flat, stationary object, whereas the sun and stars appear mobile. It takes training to see that these beliefs and supporting observations are mistaken, need revision, or need to be understood against a theoretical background that explains them. No pretense is made that either our moral emotions or our commonsense observations from which science derives are independent of a background of ordinary belief or, to put it only a bit too grandly, theory. Instead, the observations and feelings from which both science and moral theorizing begin are rooted in social practices and psychological facts about human beings. It is known that beliefs can be mistaken and feelings inapt. But to discover which beliefs are mistaken and which feelings inapt, it is necessary to start with them.

The situation is similar to Chomsky's previously cited statement on method in linguistics. We have commonsense views about what sentences are grammatical. As linguists discover rules of grammar, they may revise their commonsense beliefs about whether a sentence is grammatical. All serious inquiry starts with the acceptance of "can't help" beliefs and emotions that arise from human experience. As inquiry proceeds, some of the "can't helps" disappear as more is learned, and sometimes new "can't helps" succeed them. A "can't help" is always relative to a particular agent in particular contexts. And the method is not limited to linguistics.

Goodman (1951, 1978), Quine (1960), and Kuhn (1970) are only a few of many philosophers of science to notice the interplay of observation (the stuff of data) and theorizing. Science begins with observation-supported beliefs that are taken to be true. As science continues, it may lead to revision of previously held beliefs, if the payoffs are big enough. Improved predictive validity, for example, may justify the overthrow of seemingly obvious beliefs. When surprising results occur, we may even be led to deny that we saw what we thought we were seeing. Because scientific theories are tested as wholes, scientists also have latitude in deciding what to reject. Experiments may lead to the rejection of a theory, to its revision, to its reinterpretation, or even to a rejection of the data on which it was based. For example, Gould (1996) reinterpreted Burt's use of factor analysis, while also accepting Dorfman's (1978) contention that Burt's data themselves were fraudulent and should be rejected. On the basis of Gould's analysis, he rejected Burt's hereditarian theory of intelligence rather than revising it or offering new data.

However, as Posner recognizes, if strong pro and con feelings are the fundamental data of moral theorizing, not all strong feelings are equal. Posner's *Sex and Reason* (1992) was his own attempt to bring readers and himself up-to-date on the facts of sex. He recounted his own astonishment at learning that Plato's *Symposium* was a defense of homosexual love. As he learned more, his feelings changed. Feelings of disgust, to take one example, have a relationship to beliefs. Trustworthy feelings are those that arise from true beliefs. Revulsion at the idea of an SS officer stomping a baby to death has no dependence on false beliefs. However, disgust at same-sex sex, Jewishness, or race do, at least in many cases, depend on false or zany beliefs.

From the standpoint of evolutionary psychology, it is plausible that strong positive feelings aroused by bravery or kindness are rooted in generally accurate, evolutionarily advantageous beliefs about heroes and caregivers. Likewise, strong negative feelings aroused by patricide and cowardice are rooted in generally accurate, evolutionarily advantageous beliefs about murderers and cowards.

The importance of distinguishing feelings that have moral weight from those that do not has a long tradition in moral philosophy. Richard Brandt (1979) is one recent champion of the idea that morally important feelings can remain intact when confronted with true and only true beliefs. Brandt's idea is that a person tests moral feelings by subjecting them to rational cognitive psychotherapy. This therapy involves putting cognitive pressure on one's feelings and wishes. If somebody is disgusted by homosexuality, he might well wish that homosexuals be punished. Rational cognitive psychotherapy would test the rationality of a desire by seeing if it would be present "in some persons if their total motivational machinery were fully

suffused by available information" (Brandt, 1979). He argues that many irrational desires depend on four sources of mistakes. First, a person can have false beliefs (e.g., homosexuals are inordinately wicked or pedophiles). Second, a person could have prevailing prejudices transmitted to him (e.g., women belong in the home). Third, a person may generalize from untypical examples (e.g., this Jew cheated me, so all Jews are cheats). Fourth, a person may exaggerate feelings that arose from early deprivation (e.g., I was poor as a child, so I must save more no matter how wealthy I am now). Even though the practical possibility of such psychotherapy is fanciful, the theoretical role of it is clear. Strong feelings are best relied on in moral thinking when they grow from and are nourished by true beliefs, cosmopolitan influences, judicious inferences, and apt feelings. It is worth adding that the relevant information includes information about how one's desires will make other people feel. It is, for example, horrible to be homosexual in a society in which many people hold false and hateful beliefs about homosexuals and consequently wish them oppressed. It is plausible that many prejudiced desires would not survive a vivid and repeated confrontation with accurate information, including information about the genesis of the desire. Brandt's view is that only beliefs and feelings that could survive rational cognitive psychotherapy are rational and that only those beliefs and feelings are entitled to moral consideration.

The refutability of moral theories is indeed possible once moral feelings are counted as data. Refutation occurs when a proposed moral theory collides with the moral data provided by justifiable moral beliefs, the kind of beliefs whose underpinnings would survive Brandt's brand of psychotherapy. But as in scientific theorizing, refutation is not always a straightforward matter. Moral feelings and the related moral beliefs and preferences that they sustain are, to return to a previous point, similar to commonsense beliefs and supporting observations about the physical world. Just as observations and commonsense beliefs can be surrendered if the payoffs of a theory are good enough, so can initially strong moral feelings and beliefs be rejected if they conflict with a powerful enough moral theory. For example, if the theory systematizes a large number of strong moral beliefs while only requiring the surrender of a few strongly held moral beliefs, then it may be wiser to reject the authority of the initial feelings and beliefs than to insist on their truth. So, a deeply held repugnance toward homosexual acts might give way to a theory that makes sense of our other moral beliefs, that is, a theory that is conservative, modest, simple, and general. We decide that the theory has survived a refutation challenge arising from our initial beliefs and feelings. This picture of the creative adjustment of both moral principles and strong moral feelings and beliefs has been described by Rawls (1971), who refers to his version of this process of reciprocal adjusting of principles, feelings, and beliefs as an effort to achieve a "reflective equilibrium." To repeat, for psychologists who accept the picture of scientific theorizing found in thinkers such as Goodman (1951, 1977) or Kuhn (1970), as well as behavioral science methodologists Cook and Campbell (1979), this account of refutability is familiar. Cook and Campbell (1979, pp. 20-25) are strikingly useful in their reminder to behavioral scientists that not just discordant facts, but plausible alternative theories are crucial in deciding whether a theory has been refuted. So, when there are no good alternative moral theories, refutation of the few that are in contention may well prove difficult.

Fortunately, most psychologists do not need to have formulated a complete moral theory to engage in accurate thinking about their professional obligations. They have access to their own strong moral feelings. Their life experiences are likely to have taught them which of their feelings are judged idiosyncratic by their colleagues. They have training enough to take responsibility for ascertaining which of their beliefs are supported by plenty of evidence and which are supported by little evidence or even run contrary to what is presently known. They should have enough scientific discipline to be cautious in making inferences.

Moreover, it appears that *any* viable morality is going to have to include principles similar to the principles of autonomy, beneficence, nonmaleficence, and justice, because few psychologists are likely to disavow these principles as relevant to reaching decisions about professional obligations. Further still, the importance of these principles is likely to be thought overriding of a professional society's ethical code. In particular, a code that flouted these principles or prescribed behavior contrary to them is morally refuted, because the situation in moral philosophy is that these principles have survived examination to date. In short, there is a justificatory structure here. A code of professional ethics must be at least consistent with the four principles of autonomy, beneficence, nonmaleficence, and justice. It is far from obvious that the APA code of ethics is derivable from or even consistent with the four principles. However, that is a determination that the readers of this chapter are invited to consider on their own.

CONCLUSION

This chapter has sought to point to a different way for psychologists to think about their moral and ethical (where *ethical* means code-derived) duties. On this view, *the moral stands above any ethics code.* It is from moral concepts that defensible codes are derived. Although the APA code has the advantage of letting psychologists and their clients publicly know what minimal standards of behavior can be expected from a psychologist, codes often give scant evidence that their principles and standards were rationally derived from a defensible moral theory. Furthermore, codes are necessarily silent on what their morally indefensible, if any, provisions are. Readers interested in more comment on the advantages and disadvantages of the codes can consult Lavin and Sales (1998).

Rather than focusing exclusively on the APA code, this chapter has considered how moral inquiry is continuous with a wide range of rational inquiry, both in and out of psychology. At a minimum, it sought to show that morally thinking has a strong analogue in scientific thinking. Still, psychologists may want suggestions about how to think through morally and ethically difficult problems. One method, derived from Jameton (1984), is to do the following: First, identify the problem. Second, gather whatever facts seem necessary. Third, identify a set of feasible alternatives. Fourth, gather more information, if necessary, about the alternatives and their probable consequences. Fifth, apply a moral theory (the one you think best) to evaluate the alternatives (e.g., if you are one type of utilitarian, you rank alternatives by expected utility; if you are a Kantian, you rank alternatives in terms of those that either violate no rights or duties or, if violations are impossible to avoid, in terms of the least-serious violations). Sixth, pick the best alternative. Seventh, assess for code compliance. Eighth, if code compliant, implement alternative. If non–code compliant, is disobedience to the code justified? If it is justified, implement it. If not justified, return to Step 3. Finally, after the alternative is implemented, evaluate it. Again, this metric for ethical decision making has clear similarities to conducting research. And just as obviously, it is not an effective method for getting the "right" answer any more than so-called scientific method is. Instead, it is a heuristic that may be of help. Thinking through a problem, be it scientific or moral, requires creativity and the ability to notice connections that others have ignored, failed to notice, or may be missing. It is a dialectical process. And one can be wrong. There is that risk in all serious inquiry.

REFERENCES

American Psychological Association. (1953). *Ethical standards of psychologists.* Washington, DC: Author.

American Psychological Association. (1992). Ethical principles of psychologists and code of conduct. *American Psychologist, 47,* 1597-1611.

American Psychological Association Committee on Accreditation. (1996). *Guidelines and principles for accreditation of progams in professional psychology.* Washington, DC: Author.

Beauchamp, T. L., & Childress, J. F. (1994). *Principles of biomedical ethics* (4th ed.). New York: Oxford University Press.

Brandt, R. B. (1979). *A theory of the good and the right.* Oxford: Clarendon.

Chomsky, N. (1957). *Syntactic structures.* The Hague, Netherlands: Mouton.

Cook, T. D., & Campbell, D. T. (1979). *Quasi-experimentation: Design & analysis for field settings.* Boston: Houghton Mifflin.

Donagan, A. (1977). *The theory of morality.* Chicago: University of Chicago Press.

Dorfman, D. D. (1978). The Cyril Burt question: New findings. *Science, 201,* 1177-1186.

Goodman, N. (1978). *Ways of worldmaking.* Indianapolis, IN: Hackett.

Goodman, N. (1951). *The structure of appearance.* Cambridge, MA: Harvard University Press.

Gould, S. J. (1996). *The mismeasure of man* (Revised and expanded edition, new introduction). New York: Norton.

Hunter, G. (1971). *Metalogic: An introduction to the metatheory of standard first order logic.* Berkeley: University of California Press.

Jameton, A. (1984). *Nursing practice: The ethical issues.* Englewood Cliffs, NJ: Prentice Hall.

Kuhn, T. S. (1970). *The structure of scientific revolutions* (2nd ed., enlarged). Chicago: University of Chicago Press.

Lavin, M., & Sales, B. D. (1998). Moral and ethical considerations in geropsychology. In M. Hersen & V. B. Van Hagselt (Eds.), *Handbook of clinical geropsychology* (pp. 71-86). New York: Plenum.

A little recent history. (1952). *American Psychologist, 7,* 426-428.

National Commission for the Protection of Human Subjects of Biomedical and Behavioral Research. (1979). *Belmont report* (DHEW Publication OS 79-0012). Washington, DC: U.S. Government Printing Office.

Parfit, D. (1984). *Reasons and persons.* New York: Oxford University Press.

Pope, K. S., & Vetter, V. A. (1992). Ethical dilemmas encountered by members of the American Psychological Association: A national survey. *American Psychologist, 47,* 397-411.

Popper, K. (1959). *The logic of scientific discovery.* New York: Basic Books.

Posner, R. A. (1992). *Sex and reason.* Cambridge, MA: Harvard University Press.

Posner, R. A. (1995). *Overcoming law.* Cambridge, MA: Harvard University Press.

Quine, W. V. O. (1960). *Word and object.* Cambridge: MIT Press.

Quine, W. V., & Ullian, J. S. (1978). *The web of belief* (2nd ed.). New York: Random House.

Rachels, J. (1998). *Elements of moral philosophy* (3rd ed.). New York: McGraw Hill.

Rawls, J. (1971). *A theory of justice.* Cambridge, MA: Belknap.

CHAPTER 4

Moral Reasoning and Development

KARL H. HENNIG
St. Francis Xavier University, Canada

LAWRENCE J. WALKER
University of British Columbia, Canada

The moral concerns that face societies, professional groups, and individuals are many and varied. Most decisions involve little deliberation, but conflicting interests, responsibilities, and moral principles can occasion uncertainty. Working with vulnerable populations (children, developmentally disabled) and within certain contexts and clinical modalities (sexual, family, and multicultural) can increase the need for moral clarity. The term *moral reasoning* as it is used here describes the process of adjudicating between prescriptive moral claims ("What should I do?"). In contrast to explanatory reasons (financial gain, pragmatics, lack of competence, etc.), moral reasons are overriding in giving precedence to doing what is "right." We may offer our gratitude and appreciation to charity-contributing businesses but withhold moral praise to the extent that donations were made for reasons of furthering business interests.

The study of *moral development* seeks to locate within the normal course or trajectory of human development grounds for determining the adequacy of our moral reasons and responses. The reasoning and sensitivity of 8-year-olds is considerably different from that of 16-year-olds, which is different again from 65-year-olds. We frequently regard the reasoning of older individuals as more "mature," both in form and complexity. Questions of how we arrive at our moral considerations in the course of human development are thus relevant to questions about what considerations we ought to have.

Domains of scientific inquiry, however, have to be first identified before they can be measured, and moral psychology received its assumptive start by investigating the philosophical ideals of justice reasoning. The theory of Lawrence Kohlberg (1971, 1981), which has dominated the field these past several decades, proposed developmental stages in justice reasoning. Later stages were regarded as superior to earlier stages.

Criticisms that the theory was too narrow, rationalistic, dispassionate, partisan, and so forth encouraged Kohlberg to expand the moral domain to include moral emotions, such as empathy (Kohlberg, Levine, & Hewer, 1983). Martin Hoffman's (1991, 2000) theory of empathy development will be illustrative here of this broadening emphasis within moral psychology. Because the twin principles of *justice* (equality, respect, and dignity of persons) and *beneficence* (empathy, care) have so dominated many professional codes of ethics and the field of moral psychology, Lawrence Kohlberg and Martin Hoffman will form this chapter's central focus. But whereas the basic terms of philosophy used to be divided into two camps (Muirhead, 1938), thus positioning Kohlberg and Hoffman as potential rivals, a more recent point of division would locate both together against communitarian or personal theories (Taylor, 1989; Williams, 1981).

The "personal" emphasis, I will argue, has been most visibly represented in the field of moral psychology by the work of Carol Gilligan (1982). What identifies the moral within personal accounts has less to do with identifying a narrow set of distinctly "moral" principles than with negotiating concrete decisions within the particular histories and relational affiliations of those individuals involved. Moral or principled reasoning is regarded as more of a postdecisional justification than as a central component of a predecisional process. A personal approach would stress clinical training for interpersonal and transcultural empathy over philosophical training in the application of abstract ethical principles. The *practical* decision-making model on which this chapter concludes incorporates features from all these accounts. At a *theoretical* level, however, this is no easy alliance.

KOHLBERG'S COGNITIVE DEVELOPMENTAL THEORY

All cultures make domain distinctions between moral and social transgressions (Turiel, 1998). Stopping at a red light is an arbitrary norm that derives its force from *social* convention. In contrast, *moral* standards are considered to be serious, unalterable, not contingent on authorities or arbitrary social agreement, and universal or "natural." Anthropologists and cross-cultural psychologists, however, note the lack of consensus regarding what is considered "natural" (Shweder, 1991). A lack of shared ideals is problematic among culturally and religiously pluralistic societies such as our own, particularly with weaponry capable of mass destruction.

Instead of societies determining what was right, Kohlberg (1981) believed that it was for the *individual* to determine issues of morality and criticize conventional culture when necessary. One thinks here of the hippies and the various protest movements of the 1960s. Arising "in part as a response to the Holocaust" (1981, p. 470), Kohlberg sought an evaluative base within the study of psychological development from which to examine the validity claims of social norms. Kohlberg (1971) slid from the facts of human development—our developing capacity to reason morally within a "later-is-better stage" sequence—to an account of what the highest moral principles *should* be. That societies practice racial segregation (or keeping the law) is one thing; that they prescriptively *ought* to do so is another. The first involves matters of fact, the second, matters of value. More hopeful than finding cross-culturally shared moral standards would be to clarify a set of underlying principles capable of rationally guiding and compelling the cooperation of individuals who are otherwise committed to a plurality of ideals and self-identifying projects.

Kohlberg makes, as do most codes of ethics, a strong distinction between rules (or standards) and principles. Moral education, in so far as it had sought to instill moral rules and virtues, had become discredited in Kohlberg's estimation by the work of Hartshorne and May (1928-1930), who found a low correlation between the "Boy Scout" approach (be honest, loyal, brave) and specific moral behaviors. Similarly, "best practice" professional models of ethics based on clearly articulated principles and values are generally viewed in the field as preferable to "worst (or minimal) practice" models that emphasize rules and proscriptions/prescriptions (Stark, 1998). An ethical code should inspire moral identity and not just detail infractions. "General Principles are not themselves enforceable rules, they should be considered by psychologists in arriving at an ethical course of action and may be considered by ethics bodies as interpreting the Ethical Standards" (American Psychological Association [APA], 1992, Introduction). What gives moral standards their enforceable clout, however, is their greater behavioral specificity.

Kohlberg's Stages of Moral Development

To investigate moral reasoning within Kohlberg's model, research participants are asked to discuss a number of hypothetical dilemmas encountered in moral philosophy. In one moral dilemma, the protagonist, Heinz, considers stealing an unaffordable drug for his terminally ill wife. Heinz has explored every option. Should Heinz obey the law or steal the drug to save his wife's life? The research participant's *prescriptive* responses are assigned a stage score ranging from 1 to 6. Kohlberg's (1981, 1984) stage sequence proceeds as follows:

Stage 1 (The punishment and obedience orientation: Do as you're told). Young children are impressed by the physical features and power of others. Large and powerful others define what is right, and failing to comply results in punishment. For example, Heinz should not steal the drug that would save his wife's life because "He will be caught, locked up, or put in jail" (Colby & Kohlberg, 1987, p. 57).

Stage 2 (The instrumental-exchange orientation: Let's make a deal). Children come to reject being bossed around by other people who are recognized as pursuing desires and interests distinct from their own. Doing good resolves into "doing what is in my self-interest," not necessarily what others demand of me. Although this appears to be self-focused, there is here the notion that cooperation can be achieved by striking deals and exchanging favors.

Stage 3 (The "good boy/girl" orientation: Be nice and you'll have friends). In seeing that relationships can be more enduring and of intrinsic enjoyment, Stage 3 individuals seek to maintain the affection and approval of those close to them by being a "good person." Stage 3 expressions presuppose reciprocal perspective taking. Each trying to imagine what it is like for the other promotes a mutuality of support and a coordination of interests. When societies grow in size and complexity beyond the face-to-face community, efforts to coordinate action can quickly encounter a disturbing plurality of norms.

Stage 4 (The social-order-maintaining orientation: We are all obligated to and protected by the law). The recognition of interdependence at Stage 3 is broadened to a Stage 4 societal perspective, in which the promotion of peace and harmony within a complex society requires balancing rights and claims to personal freedom with a corresponding respect owed to others' rights and freedoms. As one 18-year-old put it, the function of law is "to set up a standard of behavior for people, for society living together so that they can live peacefully and in harmony with each other" (Adelson, Green, & O'Neil, 1969, p. 328).

Note that developmental movement from one stage to the next involves a logical increment in reciprocal perspective-taking and social coordination. Of most interest is the *postconventional* thought that emerges at Stages 5 and 6, reflecting a level of perspective taking capable of critically evaluating as well as justifying social "systems" themselves.

Postconventional or Principled Reasoning

Major principles within moral philosophy and professional codes of ethics appear in postconventional Stages 5 and 6; however, in Kohlberg's developmental scheme, the Stage 6 principle of justice trumps all Stage 5 competitors.

Stage 5 (The morality of due process). This stage includes a number of moral principles commonly found in philosophy and professional codes. Ideal societies are founded on (a) a free and willing participation in a common agreement (or contract) to live together in a law-structured society;

(b) respect for individual rights ("Obey the law only to the extent that it . . . protect[s] fundamental individual or human rights"; Colby & Kohlberg, 1987, p. 63); and (c) a cost-benefit analysis of consequences to society for one's actions ("In deciding whether or not to obey the law one should evaluate the proposed action in terms of its consequences for all of the people involved and . . . for social norms"; Colby & Kohlberg, 1987, p. 64). Stage 5 conceptions of individual "rights," however, are understood as products of "nature" rather than human rationality.

At a Stage 5 level of perspective taking, the possibility of alternative social and professional codes is conceivable, and the fairness in the procedures for interpreting and modifying regulations is emphasized. We could have a well-ordered and law-abiding society (like the ancient Egyptians) wherein the vast majority of its members toil for the comfort of the few. Similarly, newer associations of psychologists could adopt one of several already-developed codes of ethics. Principles can also be used to justify an association's existence.

The relationship between society and a profession (e.g., accrediting agencies, codes of ethics), for example, assumes or is explicitly framed by the profession as a rationally organized form of mutual consent undertaken for the betterment of both parties.

Every discipline that has relatively autonomous control over its entry requirements, training, development of knowledge, standards, methods, and practices does so only within the context of a contract with the society in which it functions. This *social contract* is based on attitudes of mutual respect and trust, with society granting support for the autonomy of a discipline in exchange for a commitment by the discipline to do everything it can to assure that its members act ethically in conducting the affairs of the discipline within society.

(Canadian Psychological Association [CPA], 2000, Preamble; italics provided)

Stage 5 reflects a political approach to questions of morality (Rest, 1994). But what makes the principles *right* that societies and professional associations invite their members to enjoin?

Stage 6 (The morality of universal ethical principles). Historically, a variety of principles for ordering a utopian society have been proposed (see Stage 5 above). Consider a simple analogy. The only safe principles for determining how to divide a pie among several people would be fair principles, because you do not know which slice will be yours and who will suffer or benefit from your method. In the "real world," pie slices are not all equal in size. The distribution of assets and abilities vary as do differences in nationality, religion, sex, race, and the various values and commitments (or identity projects) that distinguish groups of people. Thinking about the problem from behind a hypothetical "veil of ignorance" (Rawls, 1971), not knowing which pie slice will be the cutter's, increases the likelihood that all slices will be cut evenly in size. Behind the impartial veil of ignorance, no personally identifying features can bias the procedures for distributing pie slices and social resources. Analogously, from the impartial Stage 6 perspective, which moral principles appear as those most likely to ensure fairness? Kohlberg, following Rawls, proposes principles of justice: equality of human rights and respect for the dignity of all individuals. (In what follows, Rawls's veil of ignorance will be used to illustrate Stage 6, though it is recognized that Kohlberg considered other philosophical accounts as representative of Stage 6 as well, i.e., Habermas, 1990.)

A considerable body of research has confirmed that individuals do progress through Kohlberg's stages in the proposed invariant order. Across several longitudinal studies ranging in duration from 2 to 20 years, the data show few instances of regression (Stage transitions 1 to 2 to 1) or stage skipping in modal score (Stage transition 1 to 3; for a review, see Walker, 1988; Walker, Gustafson, & Hennig, 2001). As more morally advanced levels of reasoning are understood and applied, lower levels of reasoning are simultaneously rejected. Research has also shown that in studies of *recognition,* participants prefer higher-stage reasoning while rejecting lower-stage reasoning (Carroll & Rest, 1981; Davison, Robbins, & Swanson, 1978; Rest, 1973). When tested for *comprehension,* participants understand lower-stage reasoning and distort higher-stage reasoning (Walker, 1988). Recognition of the superiority of higher stages precedes their comprehension and verbal expression (Rest, 1994).

Empirical evidence, however, has not supported Kohlberg's Stage 6 commitment to the superiority of impartial procedures capable of compelling rational persons to accept principles of justice. The problem was not that people failed to go through the stages in sequential order, but that relatively few people move beyond conventional Stage 4. Stage 6 has now been dropped from the scoring manual (Colby & Kohlberg, 1987), no small loss given that it was from the specter of Stage 6 that the entire stage sequence derived its theoretical thrust as a stage model of *justice* reasoning (Puka, 1991). With the loss of Kohlberg's pinnacle stage, the abovementioned mixed bag of Stage 5 philosophical competitors once again jockey with one another for the philosophical top spot.

Those with varying degrees of sympathy to Kohlberg's vision have proposed several reformulations, most of which have left the issue of ultimate principles in the hands of philosophers. Although in no way attempting to be exhaustive, one category of responses would be to avoid taking Kohlberg's (Stage 6) theorizing too seriously. Perhaps least sympathetic to Kohlberg would be to see within a thematic analysis of the stages only "five loosely related ethical systems which replace each other cognitively, the way particular beliefs or ideologies do" (Puka, 1991, p. 389). Somewhat more sympathetic, the remaining Stages 1 though 5 can be morally valued for their "developmental continuity of logical, role [perspective]-taking, and moral operations that become successively more differentiated, integrated, and equilibrated" (Puka, 1991, p. 389).

Kohlberg Summary

Kohlberg sought to discover which of the many philosophical theories emerged as correct within the trajectory of human development. In Kohlberg's ordering, a Stage 6, right-based theory proposing universal principles of justice overrode its major philosophical contenders: Stage 5 principles of social contract, safeguarding individual rights, and utilitarian cost-benefit analysis. The compelling character of Kohlberg's account is evidenced by its dominance within the field of moral psychology as well as the extent to which it has drawn criticism. The general thrust of recent reinterpretations of the theory is to markedly temper the later-is-better construal by narrowing the value of later stages while promoting earlier stages. Justice reasoning itself is seen as just one component of a larger picture of moral functioning.

What right-based accounts of morality seek to capture is our intuition that certain actions or principles are morally right, *in and of themselves*. What is right in this sense is an "irreducible moral notion" (Freeman, 1990). The contingency inherent in financial interest, or any other motivation including prosocial motivations, cannot guarantee an action being objectively right. Ethical funds that

mix business with ethics may be fashionable or good for the bottom line one year, but not another. On the other hand, Hoffman's model of empathy development exemplifies the critique that right-based models lack a sufficiently compelling account of moral motivation. The Kohlbergian moral agent is characterized as rather pathetically acting on "duty alone," consulting,

> The stage structure of their development to locate the relevant general rule or principle that will decide the issue by transcending its content and its social-personal context. . . . When the additional judgment of self-responsibility is made, people will act in accordance with their stage. . . . In this view actors have a certain *detachment* from moral conflict. (Haan, 1986, p. 1272; italics added)

In contrast to a strictly "moral motive" or "duty motive," Hoffman's account highlights the motivating capacity of emotion, in particular the prosocial emotion of empathy.

HOFFMAN'S SOCIALIZATION THEORY OF EMPATHY DEVELOPMENT

Whereas Kohlberg stands in the tradition of thinkers emphasizing impartial reasoning (Kant, Rawls), members of Hoffman's family tree (Hume, Freud, Durkheim) share the fundamental belief that reasons never determine ends; they only guide the means to prior ends provided by our emotions. Hoffman (1991, 2000) believes his theory accounts for moral motivation by reference to the primacy of affect, specifically the benevolent and biologically rooted disposition of empathy.

What moral dilemmas share is concern over victims who are the potential beneficiaries of the actions of others. In Kohlberg's "Heinz dilemma," for example, a terminally ill woman needs a lifesaving drug she can't afford. Should Heinz steal the drug that would save his wife's life? We could ask how Heinz would morally justify an act of theft. We could also ask what would motivate Heinz to risk a prison sentence? For Hoffman, empathy is the motivational base (Eisenberg & Fabes, 1998; Ickes, 1997), but as a developmental model, stress is placed on the emergent capacity to take the perspective of another's general life condition. Cognitive perspective-taking directs empathic feeling and gives empathy its accuracy.

Hoffman's Levels of Empathy Development

Hoffman proposes a sequence of levels in empathy development that moves as follows:

[From a relatively] unclear or confused self/other differentiation [to an] awareness of self and others as separate physical entities; awareness of self and others as having independent internal states; [to an] awareness of self and others as having their own personal histories, identities, and lives beyond the immediate situation. (Hoffman, 2000, p. 64)

A fuller account of Hoffman's proposed sequence is as follows:

1. Newborn Reactive Cry. Within the first year of life, a child witnessing another in distress may respond reflexively in distress. Infants can respond to the cue of distress in others as if they themselves were distressed. At this level, the infant's mimicking cry is regarded as a precursor to empathic distress in that the distress of the other is perceived as connected to the self. Self and other are yet in large part fused and undifferentiated.

2. Egocentric Empathic Distress. Toward the end of the first year of life, children begin

to become aware of the physical distinctiveness of others and with it, the early beginnings of a separation of the distress of others from one's own distress. Toward the end of the first year, reactive crying is accompanied by more passive responses. Hoffman cites the example of a 10-month-old girl who on witnessing another child's distress responded with efforts to comfort herself rather than the victim.

3. Quasi-Egocentric Empathic Distress. Within months thereafter, children's reactive distress becomes less frequent, and efforts are made to comfort the other person. Toddlers recognize that others are distinct from self but remain sufficiently egocentric in responding to others in ways *they* find comforting. As with self-understanding, gains in emotional understanding lead to greater situational appropriateness in empathic responding (Ricard & Kamberk-Kilicci, 1995; Roberts & Strayer, 1996).

4. Veridical Empathic Distress. Around the middle of the first year, major developments occur in a child's sense of self, indicated by a toddler's first self-recognition in a mirror. An objective self, visible to self and others, emerges as distinct from the kinesthetically experienced subjective self. Awareness emerges in the second year of life that others have inner states (beliefs and desires) and that at times, these may differ from one's own inner states. After 2-year-old David fails to comfort a child with *his* teddy bear, David goes to retrieve the child's own teddy bear. Hoffman proposes a series of further substages extending into adulthood that reflect further key milestones in self-development.

5. Empathic Distress Beyond the Situation. With advances in perspective taking and a richer understanding of a person's psychological continuity through time (Hennig & Walker, 2002a), the plight of an entire group or class of people can be envisioned. Empathy can be experienced for those with whom one has no direct face-to-face contact, differentiating situational cues from broader considerations. Faint glimpses of such a capacity may be already evident quite early. For example, information about another's prior experiences (e.g., their having been bitten by a gerbil) to infer current emotional reactions (e.g., to a currently present gerbil) is not used by kindergartners but is used by fifth-grade children. This ability gains in sophistication over time (Gnepp, 1983; Wiggers & van Lieshout, 1985).

The general outline of Hoffman's account of empathy development has found general empirical support (Eisenberg & Fabes, 1998). Assumptions concerning the motivational priority of emotions over cognition, however, are more problematic (Cicchetti & Pogge-Hesse, 1981). Insofar as morality is a practical matter—in prescribing right action and prosocial behavior—it is, finally, about motivated *action*. Indices of moral reasoning as well as several measures of empathy have been correlated with hundreds of measures of behavior (Eisenberg & Fabes, 1998; Rest, 1994). Although the link between moral reasoning and action is only moderate (Blasi, 1980; Rest, 1994), predictions based on measures of empathy vary as a function of the measure employed. The better measures of empathy fair about as well as measures of moral reasoning (Eisenberg & Fabes, 1998).

Hoffman Summary

In summary, Hoffman's primary critique is that the vision of the rationally motivated individual lacks credibility. Kohlberg stood in the tradition that believed "The ground of [right-based] obligation must be looked for, not in the nature of man [sic] nor in the circumstances in the world in which he [sic] is

placed, but solely a priori in the concepts of pure reason" (Kant, 1785/1964, p. 57). Although humans possess a range of temperamental tendencies, perhaps even some malevolent tendencies (Glover, 2000), Hoffman's research emphasizes the importance of socializing those tendencies to emotionally "feel with" others as these motivate prosocial responding. Similar to Kohlberg, although requiring less from the notion, Hoffman proposes a later-is-better stage sequence of empathy development. Later stages of development, particularly self-other differentiation and perspective taking, extend the quality and range of empathic responding.

What precisely makes empathic responding morally "right," to use Kant's and Kohlberg's terminology, cannot be stated without further qualification. Why should anyone—the insecurely attached, Machiavellian, or psychopathic individual incapable of empathy—be obliged to foster greater empathic concern? Where empathy is lacking, efforts to foster such qualities may require lengthy and costly therapeutic intervention and/or medications. For these reasons, the principle of benevolence frequently takes a backseat to, and looks for justification from, principles of justice.

> While sympathy could be strengthened to the force of habit, and trained . . . toward impartial response, it would still generate morally correct actions only by accident. For while sympathy can give an interest in an action that is (as it happens) right, it cannot give an interest in its *being right*. (Herman, 1993, p. 5; italics added)

Consistent with this and unique to the Canadian Code of Ethics for Psychologists (CPA, 2000), for example, is the inclusion of a decision-making model that prioritizes Principle I (Respect for the Dignity of Persons) over Principle II (Responsible

Caring). As with Kohlberg, justice trumps benevolence. What Hoffman's account does highlight is the importance of a multifaceted model of morality that includes both cognition and emotion, withholding a decision as to which takes precedence (Cicchetti & Pogge-Hesse, 1981).

"PERSONAL" THEORIES AND GILLIGAN'S ETHIC OF CARE

The twin considerations of *benevolence* and *justice* have occasioned no small amount of investigation and discussion (Blum, 1980; Taylor, 1989; Williams, 1981). The largest challenge to Kohlberg's theory, including efforts to "elevate" empathic concern to a principle of benevolence (Hoffman), has come from Carol Gilligan. Her internationally acclaimed work *In a Different Voice* (1982) found fault with Kohlberg for overvaluing (a) themes of justice, (b) abstract principles, (c) right-based ethics, (d) Western classical liberalism, (e) the priority of individual rights, and (f) the detached impartiality of the "veil of ignorance." Gilligan's move was to link what she refers to as an "ethic of care" with gender differences in self-construal. Owing to the proposed requirement in men's developmental trajectory that they detach from the mother to identify with the father, men understand, reason by, and apply *impartial* principles of justice. Men construe themselves independently, whereas women, for whom attachment and gender identification are not in conflict, construe themselves as interdependent. Issues of adjudicating competing rights or claims are central for men, whereas issues of maintaining self in relationships are central for women. The independent male is characterized as standing apart from the concerns of individuals in concrete situations to adjudicate impartially from behind the veil of

ignorance what is the "right" thing to do. Women are said to be more responsive or attuned to the concrete concerns and welfare of those involved.

Part of the problem in empirically evaluating Gilligan's claims stems from a lack of consensus regarding measures by which to assess a care "orientation" (cf. Skoe, 1996; Wark & Krebs, 1996). Gilligan and her colleagues themselves have abandoned conducting quantitative research in favor of a "'relational' method for reading and interpreting interview narratives of individuals' lived experiences of conflict and choice" (Brown, Debold, Tappan, & Gilligan, 1994, p. 25). The general opinion of those whom Gilligan initially set out to critique is that "After 10 years, there is pitifully little empirical evidence for Gilligan's theory. The Gilligan phenomenon underscores the view that popularity has little to do with evidence" (Rest, 1994, p. 2). The comment may, however, not give sufficient credit to the larger *communitarian* or *personal* movements that have recently arisen within philosophy and psychology. (For details of research regarding gender differences, see Walker, 1991; for a review confirming gender differences in self-construal, see Cross & Madson, 1997; Hennig & Walker, 2002b.)

Gilligan rejects universal principles. Divergent moral orientations are said to be rooted in fundamentally incommensurate gender identity projects. Personal accounts of morality reflect a more thorough affirmation of a differences approach. Not only do men and women have fundamentally different values, commitments, and self-construals, but by extension, the differences that divide individuals and cultures outweigh and hold suspect any appeal to notions of a common humanity, common rationality, or common morality. The only thing in common is what can be socially constructed through curiosity, conversation, and the mutual exploration of one another's self-understanding and experience. This applies to the therapeutic encounter (Anderson & Goolishian, 1992; Gilligan, 1991) as it does to the political (Taylor, 1989). These are local dialogues creating local meanings.

From the personal perspective, moral ideals and the various life or cultural projects deemed praiseworthy are intimately linked to an individual's (or group's) identity. In the process of abstracting moral principles, what gets left out are the deeper or tacit "frameworks" that inform one's self-understanding and sense of self-worth (Hennig, in press; Taylor, 1989). By construing others and by extension ourselves, in this blindly minimal way we risk losing our identities. Answers to the question "Who am I?" (or "Who are we?") reflect *particular* conceptions of what it means to be human. These are particular human ontologies. Abstract principles within ethical codes are frequently characterized as "aspirational goals" (APA, 1992, Introduction), but what is to inspire such aspiration and "a personal commitment to a lifelong effort to act ethically" (APA, 1992, Preamble)? Questions of moral aspiration cannot be separated from questions of "Who do I (we) want to become?" The moral personality on which much of Western ethics has been premised is said to thus have become "thin as a needle" (Murdoch, 1970), "ghostlike" (MacIntyre, 1984), and "skeletal" (Walker & Hennig, 1997).

By overvaluing abstract moral principles, the Enlightenment tradition that Gilligan opposes may have undervalued the complexity of practical moral decision-making. For example, in Toulmin's (1981) experience working with the National Commission for the Protection of Human Subjects, he observed that commissioners could reach consensus on specific cases, but not on what abstract principles might justify their decisions. Beauchamp and Childress (1994)

similarly report that in developing a framework to guide decisions relevant to medical ethics, consensus through dialogue on individual cases preceded the application of moral principles that were found difficult to apply. Haidt (2001) argues that moral reasoning functions not as a predecisional guide to action, but as a post hoc justification that only creates the "illusion" of objective reasoning.

From a critical historical perspective, moral reasoning cannot be dissociated from its use to justify the exercise of power wielded as a form of argumentation, as a lawyer or politician would do against an opposition. The development of a professional code of ethics is frequently a first move in establishing a group's hegemony, by which they thus "attain exclusive social and legal recognition" (Dunbar, 1998, p. 3). Professional governing bodies must protect and be seen as protecting the public to which it is responsible, for purposes of collective power, lobbying for tax exemptions, securing the freedom of its research pursuits by justifying its social relevance, and so forth. Psychologists must establish "socially convincing means of distinguishing themselves (the 'real psychologists') from pretenders to the title" (Dunbar, 1998, p. 3). Associating moral reasoning with the exercise of power, however, does not necessarily taint the well, but it does invite a critical awareness (Glover, 2000).

Within clinical practice, the diversity of today's client population has drawn attention to the area of educating for cultural competence. However, lest increasing one's cultural knowledge risks enforcing cultural stereotypes, training has placed even greater therapeutic and ethical importance on empathic listening skills, openness to diversity, clarification of impediments to clinical receptivity, and so forth. What is emphasized is the complexity of the communicative task of clarifying *particular* frameworks embedding the sense of who clients perceived themselves to be and who they seek to become (Draguns, 1995).

At first blush, this may appear similar to the ethical relativism that Kohlberg sought to head off. But as Taylor (1989) points out, what can make moral decisions difficult is not so much the absence of higher principles capable of overriding lesser principles, but the recognition that something is vitally at issue. Hard deliberation suggests precisely the importance of the moral domain, not its irrelevance and incapacity (cf. Sartre, 1946/1977). This may, however, be little consolation within practical settings in which moral decisions need to be made decisively and justifiably. What does one do when the number of premature infants delivered exceeds available incubators? Does the decision give precedence to those infants at greatest risk, or is it first come, first served? Problems multiply, but personal accounts do sketch out a broader, more complex picture of the moral domain (Rehg, 1994).

THE FOUR-COMPONENT MODEL

In the four-component model, moral judgment is just one component within a broader framework. Rather than dividing up the moral domain into cognition, affect, and behavior, the question might rather be "What must we suppose happens psychologically in order for moral behavior to take place?" (Rest, 1994, p. 23). At least four components covering as many kinds of moral failure should be considered in a comprehensive model of moral functioning: moral sensitivity, moral judgment, moral motivation, and moral character.

Component 1 (Moral sensitivity). The first component involves the basic recognition that a moral issue is at stake and that one's choice of action has implications for the interests and

welfare of others. That a moral norm or principle is in danger of violation is an indicator. Ensuing courses of action are identified along with an analysis of attendant short-term and possible long-term risks and benefits. Hoffman's work clarifies the potential for individual differences both in capacity to experience empathic affect and associated perspective-taking processes that extend the range and sensitivity of one's empathic concern. Reformulating Kohlberg's model in the ways identified above similarly places emphasis on a developmentally increasing capacity for moral perspective-taking. The presence of individual differences in moral reasoning competency involves a sensitivity component that culminates in moral judgment. From the personal perspective, this component also highlights the importance of surfacing the "thicker" identity questions raised by Gilligan and expressed in cross-cultural empathy training. Morality includes one's basic relational stance relative to the client. The relevance of moral sensitivity within the contexts of nursing (Duckett & Ryden, 1994), sports (Bredemeier & Shields, 1994), and dental practice (Bebeau, 1994) have been demonstrated. If no moral issues are detected in a situation, then moral reflection never gets under way.

Component 2 (Moral Judgment). Limitations in this second component arise in overly simplistic ways of justifying one's actions. The process of moral judgment includes much of what has been said above concerning the place of moral reasoning and principled reasoning in particular, within predecisional and postdecisional component processes. In cases in which weightier issues are involved, individuals with limited moral perspective-taking competencies may not have adequate means for determining a sound judgment.

Component 3 (Moral Motivation). Although Piaget stated that "morality is the logic of action" (1965, p. 398), moral reasoning may not compel moral motivation in the way that logic compels the answer 4 to the problem "What is 2 + 2?" The necessity of what we ought to do may not deductively follow in quite this way. Hoffman's work thus highlights the importance of motivation and the role of empathy. Second, doing what is right may lack moral worth if not accompanied by actual felt concern for the other person. Acting begrudgingly out of "duty alone" hardly warrants our moral praise. Evidence further suggests what clinicians have long known (Shapiro, 1986), that the experience of moral "oughts" as overly ego-alien is a better predictor of psychopathology than moral excellence in character (Deci & Ryan, 2002; Higgins, 1987).

Component 4 (Moral Character). The sustained exercise of previous components passes into the habitual texture of one's moral character, strengthening the degree of ego strength that one has to follow through on one's best reasoning and decisions. Moral character is fostered in the context of relationships and in clinical practice by experience gained in ethical consultation with more experienced practitioners. If one wants to become a great archer, the best thing may be to watch what great archers do (Aristotle, c. 325 B.C.E./1984). Component 4 stresses the wisdom gained in the concrete practice of moral decision making within respective areas of professional competence. Professional codes of ethics hope to inspire "a personal commitment to a lifelong effort to act ethically" (APA, 1992, Preamble). That the moral domain should exclude one's self-identifying projects and actions as morally special lacks credibility. "Too much moral energy is expended on self-improvement and the refinement of character, on respectful interactions with loved ones, friends, and strangers, and on supererogation for

such a claim to be acceptable without considerable defense" (Flanagan, 1991, p. 223). The moral exemplars of Colby and Damon's (1992) case study analysis detailed the lives of American individuals whose commitment had taken them to various impoverished regions of the world to provide aid. The authors highlight four developmental processes that characterized these individuals: (a) an openness to progressive social influence and the capacity for personal change; (b) evident certainty about moral values and principles in conjunction with truth seeking and openness; (c) optimism, humility, compassion for others, and religious commitment; and (d) a strong moral identity, fusing personal and moral domains of their lives. Although their level of moral reasoning exceeded that of the average citizen, little evidence was found for any "dilemma-busting" cognition. In a study in which participants were asked to nominate moral exemplars, the expected categories (humanitarians, social activists, politicians, and religious leaders) were among the ranks; however, most commonly elected were family and friends (Walker, Pitts, Hennig, & Matsuba, 1995). In situations in which moral decision-making is not clear-cut, particularly when ethical principles conflict and situations are complex, the inclusion of a comprehensive decision-making model can assist in the effortful process of moral deliberation and temporal monitoring. Decision-making models have been incorporated into some ethical codes (e.g., CPA, 2000).

DISCUSSION

Kohlbergian moral subjects have been portrayed as *cold-cognizing individuals* acting rather pathetically for the sake of "duty alone" rather than out of empathic concern for the welfare of others. Moral deliberation over what one is obliged to do in the face of others' distress is regarded as one thought too many (Williams, 1981). Sharing the critique, Hoffman proposes a socialization account of prosocial norms. Starting with the assumption that emotions are primary, prosocial norms acquire their motivational force by association with our biologically given capacity to empathize with others. The development of empathy expands one's range of concern within a later-is-better stage scheme, tempering the problem of empathic bias. Empathic bias may (a) respond only to the immediacy of the in-your-face distress of others and (b) may lack impartiality with regard to offering care to genetically, culturally, geographically, and racially foreign others. Although Kohlberg believes in the automotivating character of moral cognition, Hoffman is less convinced. What both share, however, is a concern with principles of justice.

Kohlberg's increasing interest in supporting and interpreting his empirical work by appeal to certain philosophers (Habermas, 1990; Rawls, 1971) was laudable in its effort toward developing a coherent right-based theory but simultaneously left him open to charges of philosophical abstraction and partisanship. In the absence of an empirical Stage 6, Kohlberg's stages could no longer be interpreted specifically as stages of justice reasoning. Later reformulations of Kohlberg's account dispense with many of his philosophical commitments, generally emphasizing the increasing capacity for moral perspective-taking and social coordination that accompanies stage progression (Puka, 1991; Rest, Narváez, Bebeau, & Thoma, 1999). Within a stage model more restricted in range and philosophical commitment, the evidence suggests,

People who develop in moral judgment are those who love to learn, who seek new challenges, who enjoy intellectually stimulating environments, who are reflective, who make plans and set goals, who take risks, who see themselves in the larger contexts of history and institutions and broad cultural trends. (Rest, 1994, p. 15)

Revisions to Kohlberg's stage theory have now come to include the once rival Hoffman as part of an integrated model (Gibbs, 1991).

A more recent division within the field of moral philosophy and psychology would place all accounts involving impartial principles against personal or communitarian accounts. Gilligan's ethic of care has more in common with efforts to train for cross-cultural empathy than it does with the study of ethical principles accompanying professional codes of conduct. A personal model of moral functioning would highlight the importance of individual case discussions, moral self-identity, and the ongoing role of consulting with more experienced moral decision makers. Rather than disproving Gilligan's theory, perhaps much of the current (Aristotelian) shift in the field of moral psychology reflects these same "personal" movements. Current research has moved away from an exclusive focus on justice reasoning in favor of studying: persons within real-life contexts (Walker, de Vries, & Trevethan, 1987), moral personality and identity (Blasi, 1984), lay conceptions of moral maturity (Walker & Pitts, 1998), moral exemplarity and commitment (Colby & Damon, 1992; Walker & Hennig, 2002), and "bottom-up" moral consensus-seeking (Rest et al., 1999; Toulmin, 1981). Finally, a four-component model (Rest, 1994) was used to incorporate some of the many facets of moral development that inform a comprehensive model of moral decision-making.

REFERENCES

Adelson, J., Green, B., & O'Neil, R. (1969). Growth of the idea of law in adolescence. *Developmental Psychology, 1,* 327-332.

American Psychological Association. (1992). *Ethical standards of psychologists.* Washington, DC: Author.

Anderson, H., & Goolishian, H. (1992). The client as the expert: A not-knowing approach to therapy. In S. McNamee & K. Gergen (Eds.), *Therapy as social construction.* Newbury Park: Sage.

Aristotle. (1984). The Nichomachean ethics. In Jonathan Barnes (Ed.), *The complete works of Aristotle.* Princeton, NJ: Princeton University Press. (Original work published c. 325 B.C.E.)

Beauchamp, T. L., & Childress, J. F. (1994). *Principles of biomedical ethics* (4th ed.). New York: Oxford University Press.

Bebeau, M. J. (1994). Applied ethics and moral reasoning in sport. In J. Rest & D. Narváez (Eds.), *Moral development in the professions* (pp. 121-146). Hillsdale, NJ: Lawrence Erlbaum.

Blasi, A. (1980). Bridging moral cognition and moral action: A critical review of the literature. *Psychological Bulletin, 88,* 1-45.

Blasi, A. (1984). Moral identity: Its role in moral functioning. In W. M. Kurtines & J. L. Gewirtz (Eds.), *Morality, moral behavior, and moral development* (pp. 128-139). New York: Wiley.

Blum, L. (1980). *Friendship, altruism, and morality.* London: Routledge & Kegan Paul.

Bredemeier, B. J. L., & Shields, D. L. L. (1994). Applied ethics and moral reasoning in sport. In J. Rest & D. Narváez (Eds.), *Moral development in the professions* (pp. 213-224). Hillsdale, NJ: Lawrence Erlbaum.

Brown, L. M., Debold, E., Tappan, M., & Gilligan, C. (1991). In W. M. Kurtines & J. L. Gewirtz (Eds.), *Handbook of moral behavior and development* (Vol. 2, pp. 25-62). Hillsdale, NJ: Lawrence Erlbaum.

Canadian Psychological Association. (2000). *Canadian code of ethics for psychologists: Revised.* Ottawa, Canada: Author.

Carroll, J. L., & Rest, J. R. (1981). Development in moral judgment as indicated by rejection of lower-stage statements. *Journal of Research in Personality, 15,* 538-544.

Cicchetti, D., & Pogge-Hesse, P. (1981). The relation between cognition and emotion in infant development: Past, present, and future perspectives. In M. Lamb & L. Sherrod (Eds.), *Infant social cognition* (pp. 205-272). Hillsdale, NJ: Lawrence Erlbaum.

Colby, A., & Damon, W. (1992). *Some do care: Contemporary lives of moral commitment.* New York: Free Press.

Colby, A., & Kohlberg, L. (1987). *The measurement of moral judgment* (Vol. 2). New York: Cambridge University Press.

Cross, S. E., & Madson, L. (1997). Models of the self: Self-construals and gender. *Psychological Bulletin, 133,* 5-37.

Davison, M. L., Robbins, S., & Swanson, D. B. (1978). Stage structure in objective moral judgments. *Developmental Psychology, 14,* 137-146.

Deci, E. L., & Ryan, R. M. (2002).The paradox of achievement: The harder you push, the worse it gets. In A. Joshua (Ed.), *Improving academic achievement: Impact of psychological factors on education* (pp. 61-87). San Diego, CA: Academic Press.

Draguns, J. (1995). Human universal and culturally distinctive: Charting the course of cultural counseling. In P. B. Pederson, J. G. Draguns, W. J. Loner, & J. E. Trimble (Eds.), *Counseling across cultures* (pp. 1-19). Thousand Oaks, CA: Sage.

Duckett, L. J., & Ryden, M. B. (1994). Education for ethical nursing practice. In J. Rest & D. Narváez (Eds.), *Moral development in the professions* (pp. 85-100). Hillsdale, NJ: Lawrence Erlbaum.

Dunbar, J. (1998). A critical history of CPA's various codes of ethics for psychologists (1939-1986). *Canadian Psychology, 39,* 177-186.

Eisenberg, N., & Fabes, R. A. (1998). Prosocial development. In N. Eisenberg (Ed.), *Handbook of child psychology: Vol. 3. Social, emotional, and personality development* (5th ed., pp. 701-778). New York: Wiley.

Flanagan, O. (1991). *Varieties of moral personality: Ethics and psychological realism.* Cambridge, MA: Harvard University Press.

Freeman, S. (1990). Reason and agreement in social contract views. *Philosophy and Public Affairs, 19,* 122-157.

Gibbs, J. C. (1991). Sociomoral developmental delay and cognitive distortion: Implications for the treatment of antisocial youth. In W. M. Kurtines & J. L. Gewirtz (Eds.), *Handbook of moral behavior and development* (Vol. 3, pp. 95-108). Hillsdale, NJ: Lawrence Erlbaum.

Gilligan, C. (1982). *In a different voice: Psychological theory and women's development.* Cambridge, MA: Harvard University Press.

Gilligan, C. (1991). Women's psychological development: Implications for psychotherapy. *Women & Therapy, 11,* 5-31.

Glover, J. (2000). *Humanity: A moral history of the twentieth century.* New Haven, CT: Yale University Press.

Gnepp, J. (1983). Children's social sensitivity: Inferring emotions from conflicting cues. *Developmental Psychology, 19,* 805-814.

Haan, N. (1986). Systematic variability in the quality of moral action, as defined by two formulations. *Journal of Personality and Social Psychology, 50,* 1271-1284.

Habermas, J. (1990). Justice and solidarity. In T. Wren (Ed.), *The moral domain: Essays in the ongoing discussion between philosophy and the social sciences. Studies in contemporary German social thought* (pp. 224-251). Cambridge: MIT Press.

Haidt, J. (2001). The emotional dog and its rational tail: A social intuitionist approach to moral judgment. *Psychological Review, 108,* 814-834.

Hartshorne, H., & May, M. A. (1928-1930). *Studies in the nature of character* (3 vols.). New York: Macmillan.

Hennig, K. H. (in press). *Care gone awry.* In T. A. Thorkildsen, J. Manning, & H. J. Walberg (Eds.), *Nurturing morality.* Washington, DC: Child Welfare League of America Press.

Hennig, K. H., & Walker, L. J. (2002a). *Continuities of selfhood: Conceptualization and clinical implications.* Manuscript submitted for publication.

Hennig, K. H., & Walker, L. J. (2002b). *The two faces of unmitigated communion.* Manuscript submitted for publication.

Herman, B. (1993). *The practice of moral judgment.* Cambridge, MA: Harvard University Press.

Higgins, T. E. (1987). Self-discrepancy: A theory relating self and affect. *Psychological Review, 94,* 319-340.

Hoffman, M. L. (1991). Empathy, social cognition, and moral action. In W. M. Kurtines & J. L. Gewirtz (Eds.), *Handbook of moral behavior and development* (Vol. 1, pp. 275-301). Hillsdale, NJ: Lawrence Erlbaum.

Hoffman, M. L. (2000). *Empathy and moral development: Implications for caring and justice.* New York: Cambridge University Press.

Ickes, W. (1997). *Empathic accuracy.* New York: Guilford.

Kant, I. (1964). *Groundwork of the metaphysic of morals* (H. J. Patton, Trans.). New York: Harper & Row. (Original work published 1785)

Kohlberg, L. (1971). From is to ought: How to commit the naturalistic fallacy and get away with it in the study of moral development. In T. Mischel (Ed.), *Cognitive development and epistemology* (pp. 151-235). New York: Academic Press.

Kohlberg, L. (1981). *Essays on moral development: Vol. 1. The philosophy of moral development.* San Francisco: Harper & Row.

Kohlberg, L. (1984). *Essays on moral development: Vol. 2. The psychology of moral development.* San Francisco: Harper & Row.

Kohlberg, L., Levine, C., & Hewer, A. (1983). *Moral stages: A current formulation and a response to critics.* New York: Karger.

MacIntyre, A. (1984). *After virtue.* Notre Dame, IN: University of Notre Dame Press.

Muirhead, J. H. (1938). *A hundred years of British philosophy.* New York: Allen & Unwin.

Murdoch, I. (1970). *The sovereignty of good.* London: Routledge.

Piaget, J. (1965). *The moral judgment of the child* (M. Gabain, Trans.). New York: Free Press.

Puka, M. L. (1991). Toward the redevelopment of Kohlberg's theory: Presenting essential structure, removing controversial content. In W. M. Kurtines & J. L. Gewirtz (Eds.), *Handbook of moral behavior and development* (Vol. 1, pp. 373-394). Hillsdale, NJ: Lawrence Erlbaum.

Rawls, J. (1971). *A theory of justice.* Cambridge, MA: Harvard University Press.

Rehg, W. (1994). *Insight and solidarity: The discourse ethics of Jürgen Habermas.* Berkeley: University of California Press.

Rest, J. (1973). The hierarchical nature of moral judgment: A study of patterns of comprehension and preference of moral stages. *Journal of Personality, 41,* 86-109.

Rest, J. R. (1994). Background: Theory and research. In J. R. Rest & D. Narvaez (Eds.), *Moral development in the professions.* Hillsdale, NJ: Lawrence Erlbaum.

Rest, J. R., Narváez, D., Bebeau, M. J., & Thoma, S. J. (1999). *Postconventional moral thinking: A neo-Kohlbergian approach.* Mahwah, NJ: Lawrence Erlbaum.

Ricard, M., & Kamberk-Kilicci, M. (1995). Children's empathic responses to emotional complexity. *International Journal of Behavioral Development, 18,* 211-225.

Roberts, W., & Strayer, J. (1996). Empathy, emotional expressiveness, and pro-social behavior. *Child Development, 67,* 449-496.

Sartre, J. P. (1977). *Existentialism and humanism* (P. Mairet, Trans.). Brooklyn: Haskell House. (Original work published 1946)

Shapiro, D. (1986). *Neurotic styles.* New York: Basic Books.

Shweder, R. A. (1991). *Thinking through cultures.* Cambridge, MA: Harvard University Press.

Skoe, E. E. (1996). The ethic of care: Stability over time, gender differences, and correlates in mid- to late adulthood. *Psychology and Aging, 11,* 280-292.

Stark, C. (1998). Ethics in research context: Misinterpretations and misplaced misgiving. *Canadian Psychology, 39,* 202-211.

Taylor, C. (1989). *Sources of the self: The making of modern identity.* Cambridge, MA: Harvard University Press.

Toulmin, S. (1981). The tyranny of principles. *Hastings Center Report, 11,* 31-39.

Turiel, E. (1998). The development of morality. In N. Eisenberg (Ed.), *Handbook of child psychology: Vol. 3. Social, emotional, and personality development* (5th ed., pp. 863-932). New York: Wiley.

Walker, L. J. (1988). The development of moral reasoning. *Annals of Child Development, 5,* 33-78.

Walker, L. J. (1991). Sex differences in moral reasoning. In W. M. Kurtines and J. L. Gewirtz (Eds.), *Handbook of moral behavior and development* (Vol. 2, pp. 333-364). Hillsdale, NJ: Lawrence Erlbaum.

Walker, L. J., de Vries, B., & Trevethan, S. D. (1987). Moral stages and moral orientations in real-life and hypothetical dilemmas. *Child Development, 58,* 842-858.

Walker, L. J., Gustafson, P., & Hennig, K. H. (2001). The consolidation/transition model in moral reasoning development. *Developmental Psychology, 37,* 187-197.

Walker, L. J., & Hennig, K. H. (1997). Moral development in the broader context of personality. In S. Hala (Ed.), *The development of social cognition* (pp. 297-327). East Sussex, England: Psychology Press.

Walker, L. J., & Hennig, K. H. (2002). *Differing conceptions of moral exemplarity: Just, brave, and caring.* Manuscript submitted for publication.

Walker, L. J., & Pitts, R. C. (1998). Naturalistic conceptions of moral maturity. *Developmental Psychology, 34,* 403-419.

Walker, L. J., Pitts, R. C., Hennig, K. H., & Matsuba, M. K. (1995). Reasoning about morality and real-life moral problems. In M. Killen & D. Hart (Eds.), *Morality in everyday life: Developmental perspectives* (pp. 371-407). Cambridge: Cambridge University Press.

Wark, G., & Krebs, D. (1996). Gender and dilemma differences in real-life moral judgment. *Developmental Psychology, 32,* 220-230.

Wiggers, M., & van Lieshout, C. F. M. (1985). Development of recognition emotions: Children's reliance on situational and facial subjectivity cues. *Developmental Psychology, 21,* 338-349.

Williams, B. (1981). *Moral luck.* New York: Cambridge University Press.

Part II

PSYCHOLOGY AND PROFESSIONAL ETHICS

CHAPTER 5

Ethical Principles of the Psychology Profession and Professional Competencies

Ype H. Poortinga
Tilburg University, Netherlands, &
Catholic University of Leuven, Belgium

Karel A. Soudijn
Tilburg University, Netherlands

I know that what we do has some effect, we only do not have the instruments to measure it; our methods are not sensitive enough to record the changes.

Statement by a psychologist who shall remain anonymous

The ethical codes of psychological associations in various countries testify to the high moral standards of psychologists in their work. This is reflected in the preamble of the American Psychological Association (APA) code of ethics (APA, 1992), which states, "The development of a dynamic set of ethical standards for psychologist's work-related conduct requires a personal commitment to a lifelong effort to act ethically" (p. 1599).

Similarly, the metacode of ethics of the European Federation of Psychologists Associations (EFPA, formerly EFPPA), meant to serve as general guidelines for more specific national codes, has as its first ethical principle "Respect for a Person's Rights and Dignity." This is formulated as follows:

Psychologists accord appropriate respect to and promote the development of the fundamental rights, dignity and worth of all people. They respect the rights of individuals to privacy, confidentiality, self-determination and autonomy, consistent with the psychologist's other obligations and with the law (EFPA, 1997a, Article 2.1, p. 1).

The interests of their clients and respect for human dignity place high demands on the competence of psychologists. Article 2.2. of the EFPA (1997a) metacode reads:

Psychologists strive to ensure and maintain high standards of competence in their work. They recognize the boundaries of their particular competencies and the limitations of their expertise. They provide only those services and use only those techniques for which they are qualified by education, training or experience. (p. 1)

The education and training that the metacode refers to is scientific and professional training in psychology (Lunt et al., 2001). In this chapter, we will draw attention particularly to science.

The APA (1992) code begins its preamble as follows: "Psychologists work to develop a valid and reliable body of scientific knowledge based on research" (p. 1599). The same sentiment is expressed in the EFPA metacode and in numerous national codes, such as the code of the Columbian Federation of Psychology (Federación Colombiana de Psicología, 2000), which states in Article 1.2:

The science of psychology seeks to develop a body of knowledge that is valid and reliable, based in research. . . . The goal of the psychologist is to increase scientific knowledge and to apply it adequately with the aim to improve the conditions of the individual and the society with a view to realize a better quality of life for all. (p. 9)

This formulation refers explicitly to the science of psychology as the basis for professional intervention. The underlying assumption is that there exists a body of "psychological knowledge" that lends itself to application and that psychologists let themselves be guided by this knowledge. The ramifications of this assumption are the main topic of discussion in this chapter.

First, we will argue that psychologists tend to justify their profession as being based in the science of psychology when it is convenient but have difficulty in accepting the constraints and limitations associated with this. Thereafter, we briefly present a few instances in which professional practices appear to be at variance with scientific evidence. In the final section, we discuss possible directions in which psychology could seek to proceed while maintaining high ethical standards.

DOES SCIENTIFIC KNOWLEDGE SERVE AS THE BASIS FOR PROFESSIONAL INTERVENTIONS?

The competence of psychologists is derived first and foremost from their knowledge of scientific psychology. This is clear from examples already given, and it is a point mentioned also in numerous other codes. According to the Austrian Psychological Society, "The psychologist strives at all times to use the methods that are of the highest standard according to the latest scientific developments" (General Principle 3, Austrian Psychological Society, 1990, p. 16).[1] In Scandinavia, it is required that "psychologists work according to scientific principles and substantiated experience and maintain their professional competence at all times" (Principle IIA, Anonymous, 1989, pp. 21/1-21/13).

One finds few attempts to define the "valid and reliable body of scientific knowledge" or "latest scientific developments" or even the broader notion of "scientific principles." It is understandable that the authors of codes have not tried to provide details (a code of professional ethics is not an advanced textbook), but at the same time one cannot deny that much in our literature is controversial, if not demonstrably flawed. One of the few articles we have found that seems to address this issue comes from the code of the Colegio Oficial de Psicólogos in Spain: "Without prejudice towards the actual diversity of theories, schools and methods, psychologists should use neither means nor methods which have not been sufficiently inspected, within the bounds of the scientific knowledge in force" (Article 18, Colegio Oficial de Psicológos, 1990, p. 12).

This code acknowledges diversity and appears to respect it. However, when have methods been sufficiently inspected; what is the knowledge that is "in force"; and what are the consequences when theories and methods have not stood up to closer scrutiny but are still being used by large numbers of practitioners?

In our view, the profession of psychology tends to ignore too often such questions and their consequences. A, in our opinion, poignant set of events happened at the 1997 meeting of the General Assembly of the EFPA. During this meeting, a motion was passed in which the Assembly distanced itself from any formal recognition of work that "ignored the connection between the science of psychology and the practice of psychotherapy." The position of the European psychologists seems clear: The practice of psychotherapy should be rooted in science.

However, less than an hour earlier, the same General Assembly approved a report of the EFPA task force on traffic psychology. On the first page of this report, it is seen as a "sober attitude" of practitioners "not [to] give up work that allows them to make a living just because the scientific character of certain work cannot be clearly proved"

(EFPA, 1997b, p. 1). This viewpoint is elucidated with an appeal to plausibility:

> Thus, unambiguous [proof] for the efficiency of psychological work in the applied sector is something that cannot be gained easily and in a short time, many effects are difficult to be analyzed in a way that everybody agrees with the results. . . . Thus, acceptance of certain types of psychological [evidence] is connected to traditions and they have often developed, because certain measures seemed useful to politicians and policy makers from a plausibility perspective. (EFPA, 1997b, p. 1)[2]

A close relationship between science and practice can also be questioned on other grounds. According to Schönpflug (1993), applied psychology as practiced in clinics and organizations does not originate from basic research. Applied psychology has its own history, characterized by largely autonomous developments. The reason that psychologists like to refer to the science of behavior as the basis for their interventions is that science continues to carry an aura of objectivity and independence. Schönpflug (1993, 1994) has expressed the suspicion that a major function of academic psychology for practitioners lies in the scientific respectability it lends to the profession.

In summary, codes of ethics tend to portray psychology as a science-based profession. The illustrations we have given challenge the common belief expressed in these codes that professional activities of psychologists tend to be based in scientific knowledge.

A DISCREPANCY BETWEEN SCIENTIFIC EVIDENCE AND PROFESSIONAL PRACTICE

Let us take the challenge entailed in the codes a step further. They imply that psychologists have the responsibility to abandon reliance on obsolete theories and the use of methods that have not stood up to critical examination. Presumably, by far most psychologists will agree with this principle. However, when it comes to any concrete issue, opinions differ, and psychologists using particular methods will dismiss negative scientific evidence as irrelevant, misconstrued, or beside the point.

Projective techniques have a long history in psychology. The most outstanding example of this type of diagnostic device is the Rorschach. There is a theoretical premise to the effect that the rather unstructured inkblots provide opportunities for personal reactions of respondents who project their inner mental states and processes in their answers. The technique was initially welcomed not only as a tool to gain insight into the deeper realms of the human mind but also as a basis for predictions of future behavior in vocational guidance and personnel selection (e.g., Wittenborn, 1949/1970). However, the theory was questioned repeatedly, as well as the scoring and standardization (e.g., Sargent, 1953/1970). The most crucial failure was psychometric. When the reliability and validity of all kinds of claims put forward by enthusiastic users were examined, the test showed up dismally poor. In a review of early validation studies, Cronbach (1956) concluded that the test had failed as a predictor of practical criteria and that there was nothing to encourage reliance on Rorschach interpretations. Since then, sophisticated efforts have been made to turn the tables, particularly by Exner (e.g., 1993). But the Dutch Committee on Tests (Evers, Van Vliet-Mulder, & Groot, 2000) has rated the Rorschach as *insufficient* (the lowest rating) in all five evaluation categories (theoretical rationale, quality of materials and manual, availability of norms, reliability, and validity). In various countries, the

Rorschach continues to be a popular instrument. A survey in the United States of America (Watkins, Campbell, Nieberding, & Hallmark, 1995), found that more than 40% of all clinical psychologists used this test frequently and more than 80% at least occasionally. The controversy in the United States was brought to the public domain when Lilienfeld, Wood, and Garb (2001) challenged the use of projective techniques in a popular magazine, *Scientific American*. These authors write,

> We find it troubling that psychologists commonly administer projective instruments in situations for which their value has not been well established by multiple studies; too many people can suffer if erroneous diagnostic judgments influence therapy plans, custody rulings or criminal court decisions. (p. 79)

Of course, we are aware that some psychologists consider psychometrically based criticism as rather irrelevant because they apply assessment instruments not as assessment standards, but as communication aids for soliciting relevant information from clients. However, more than anything else, this obscures issues of validity. It is rarely made clear how information is obtained and how valid inferences are derived from such usage. About a decade ago, during the heyday of the "Anatomically Detailed Dolls" (AD dolls), no less an augurous body than the Council of Representatives of the APA issued a statement mentioning that "There are currently no uniform standards for conducting interviews with the dolls" (Fox, 1991, p. 722). Koocher et al. (1995) underscored this in an extensive review article: "AD dolls are not a psychological test with predictive (or postdictive) validity per se" (p. 218).

Still, the statement of the Council of Representatives argues,

Doll-centered assessment of children when used as part of a psychological evaluation and interpreted by experienced and competent examiners, may be the best available practical solution for a pressing and frequent clinical problem (i.e., investigation of the possible presence of sexual abuse of the young child). (Fox, 1991, p. 722)

A few years earlier, the Council of the Netherlands Institute of Psychologists (NIP) issued a press statement in which a diagnostic function was acknowledged. Although limitations of AD dolls were mentioned, the expertise of the well-trained psychologist was emphasized (NIP, 1989). This somewhat ambivalently phrased statement was a reaction to a cause célèbre in the Netherlands. In a school with developmentally problematic young children, many pupils had been diagnosed by an educational psychologist as victims of sexual abuse. With the expansion of the numbers of alleged victims, irate parents and their legal counsel soon exposed the vacuousness of the evidence, in which AD dolls played an important role.

Positions such as those of the NIP and the APA emphasize the humanitarian aspect of the psychologist's work. It is felt that psychologists cannot ignore important diagnostic questions of their clients (such as possible sexual abuse in early childhood). However, this aspect has to be weighed against the risk of an incorrect interpretation with negative consequences for clients and their social environment.

In fact, simple psychometric principles argue quite convincingly against giving practitioners the proverbial benefit of the doubt. Ever since Taylor and Russell (1939) published their tables on the success of selection decisions, psychologists have known that two factors are important in such decisions, namely, the validity of the selection procedure and the proportions of cases that belong to various categories. Methods of a

low validity can hardly contribute to the quality of a judgment when the criterion that is assessed has a low frequency of occurrence in the population. Diagnosing sexual abuse of children before primary school age is a case in point.

There are numerous estimates of the rate of occurrence of sexual abuse. For example, in a report of the British Psychological Society (BPS, 1995), 6% was mentioned for all girls. In the Netherlands, the most extensive study to date arrived on the basis of retrospective reports at a value of 1.14% before age 7 (Draijer, 1990). In order not to err on the low side, we shall assume a population with a risk of 7%. We shall further assume that the criterion validity (i.e., the correlation between a diagnosis and the "true" state of affairs) is $r = .20$.

In the left-hand pair columns in Table 5.1, the expected distribution is presented if 100 cases come up for diagnosis and if the rate of diagnosed cases is the same as the population rate (cf. Arbous, 1952, for the computations). One victim of the seven is correctly identified, six cases escape identification, and six others are wrongly identified as victims. Please note that the large majority of judgments is correct; of the 93 children with a negative criterion value, 87 are correctly identified. Nevertheless, with six false positives and six false negatives against a single true positive, the added benefit of diagnosis is poor.

Suppose the diagnostician is most concerned about false negatives (unidentified victims) and makes the diagnostic index even more inclusive, let us say to 16% of the children. In the middle columns of Table 5.1, it is shown that one more true positive diagnosis can be expected, but at the cost of 14 false-positive diagnoses.

The standard argument against an approach as presented here is that experienced diagnosticians will combine evidence from

Table 5.1   Expected Distributions of Correctly Identified Cases (+ +)

Criterion		−	+	−	+	−	+
Diagnostic	+	6	1	14	2	5.5	1.5
Index	−	87	6	79	5	87.5	5.5

NOTE: False positives (positive on index, negative on criterion; + −); false negatives (negative on index and positive on criterion: − +); and correct negatives (− −).

several sources. We shall again specify conditions favorable for identification, assuming four different indices with criterion validity of $r = .20, .20, .15,$ and $.15$, respectively, and intercorrelations between each two indices of $r = .10$. The multiple correlation then has a value of $r = .31$. In the right-hand pair of columns in Table 5.1, we can see that this results in an expectation of two more correct decisions compared with the initial expectations. However, with 11 false negatives and false positives to be expected, the outcome is still poor.

In summary, when the a priori probability of a diagnostic category is low and only methods of very limited validity are available, the added value of diagnostic expertise can be only negligible. It is irrelevant whether the methods are standardized tests or a communication aid and whether interpretations are derived in a nomothetic or idiographic (interpretive, hermeneutic) manner.

YOMANDA AND OTHER INSIGHTS

In the Netherlands, there is a national celebrity with the name of Yomanda. She is a kind of faith healer, drawing large crowds and performing miraculous cures. Although we never saw the report, apparently an evaluation study was conducted among people attending the sessions. They were asked whether in their experience and perception, Yomanda's interventions were effective; 80% endorsed this.[3]

In one of the most extensive studies on the effectiveness of psychotherapy (Seligman, 1995), a large panel of consumers in the United States were asked whether they had sought help of a mental health professional in recent years and whether or not this had been beneficial. Major improvements were reported by approximately half of the 1.6% of the original sample who had received help from a psychologist, and more than 90% of the clients reported at least some improvement (a base rate of improvement without professional help is not known).

At face value, Yomanda does not seem less effective than do professional psychologists. Nevertheless, we remain unconvinced by the "evidence" in favor of Yomanda. There are two main reasons for our disbelief. First, we consider the a priori probability that there is any substance to her claims of being in contact with supernatural forces to be extremely low. Stated in plain terms: We do not at all believe in her "theory," which we consider merely a form of superstition. Second, the results of the evaluation study did not in any way change this prior belief, because it is not at all pertinent to our doubts. We could be convinced of Yomanda's special gifts only if she could demonstrate these under controlled conditions with outcome measures that were independent of the opinions of her followers.

There are uncomfortable parallels in design between the study on Yomanda and the consumer survey that open the latter study to similar criticisms. The results confirm the convictions of those who believe in the effectiveness of psychotherapy to begin with, but they do little to convince the skeptics. Serious methodological weaknesses in the consumer study have been pointed out (e.g., Brock, Green, & Reich, 1998; "Outcome Assessment," 1996) but were played down by Seligman (e.g., 1996). Perhaps the beliefs of the believers should not be challenged too much (cf. Dawes, 1994). For the purpose of the present chapter, we are not interested in a precise evaluation of the pros and cons of any particular design or set of findings. We merely wish to draw attention to a problem: If we look at the psychological literature with the same skepsis as we do with Yomanda, the body of accumulated knowledge is open to major questions.

Psychology has a long tradition of helping to understand human judgment processes, including those of psychologists. For example, Michotte (1954) reported experiments on the perception of causality. His respondents looked through a narrow slit in a wooden partition. Behind the slit, a sheet of paper was moving. On the sheet, two lines were drawn that, to the observer, first moved in parallel. After a while, one line would start to move closer to the other, touch it, and then the second line would start to move. To the observer, the first line "pushed" the second one in the same way as one billiard ball impacts another ball. The perception of causality remained forceful even after the sheet of paper with the lines drawn on it had been shown to respondents.

Now imagine a clinical psychologist who engages in a series of therapy sessions with a client. Usually at the start of such interventions, the client is in evident need of help and more often than not shows signs of improvement over time. These improvements are what the therapist aimed at and worked hard for. It is extremely difficult for the therapist not to perceive a relationship between these interventions and the improvement of the client, even when taking into account serious arguments as mentioned here. Moreover, there is a collusion of perceptions of therapist and client. Most clients are feeling badly at the start of an intervention, and this by itself makes it likely that they feel better after some time (known as *regression toward the mean*). And clients often are not much inclined to admit that therapy was a waste of time and money (referred to as the *hello-goodbye effect*).

None of the above arguments are absolute. In final analysis, it is difficult to rule out in a particular instance that the therapist is correct in ascribing positive changes in a client to the intervention, even if the rate of improvement in clients undergoing therapy is hardly higher than spontaneous improvement in a nontreated group. The question is what the consequences should be for the psychologist when scientific findings and arguments are pitted against personal experience.

CLOSING THE GAP BETWEEN ASPIRATIONS AND ACHIEVEMENTS?

In the previous sections, we have illustrated how evidence supporting current professional practices can fall short of the high standards formulated in professional codes of ethics. Our examples have been selective and mainly limited to a single field of practice. Nevertheless, the discrepancies between professed ideals and reality seem so large that they cannot be ignored or covered up, for example, by referring to the ideals as being (merely) aspirational.

We see three directions that can be followed to transcend the dilemma. The first is to define professional practice in psychology independent of traditional scientific criteria, giving up pretensions about a scientific basis that are difficult to maintain. A second way is to redefine standards for the quality of interventions. And a third way is to take the perspective of critical outside agencies on the criteria for success of the profession.

Standards Embedded in Practice

In a previous section, we mentioned an instance in which two national associations, APA (see Fox, 1991) and NIP (1989), emphasized the responsibility of practitioners but largely refrained from criticizing an inherently questionable methodology. This can be interpreted as a shift from scientific standards to practice-based expert judgment of professionals. We also perceive other indications that psychologists may be abandoning the pretension of being part of a science-based profession. In the 1990s, alternative conceptions of science-practice relationship were advocated by postmodernist authors who emphasized skilled reflection and expert practice. These authors do not see complementary roles for practice (generating new knowledge) and science (testing new knowledge). Rather, they call for an "epistemology of practicing knowledge" (Hoshmand & Polkinghorne, 1992, p. 60) that is embedded in the expertise of practitioners. Here, science and practice are no longer seen as both having a more or less independent function; the insight of the practitioner becomes the main criterion for validity.

In many respects, less reliance on the presumed body of scientific knowledge is a welcome development. In the examples we discussed in previous sections, we demonstrated weaknesses, but admittedly we did not offer solutions. However, we also fail to see how the emperor will be dressed in more solid clothes if the presumed body of scientific knowledge is replaced by the presumed expertise of the practitioner. In any case, professional codes will have to be reformulated if psychologists wish to go in this direction.

Toward a More Modest Psychology

Psychologists typically tend to search for convergent rather than for discriminant evidence (Campbell & Fiske, 1959), a tendency also known as *confirmation bias* (Friedrich, 1993). Nevertheless, the percentage of variance in target behaviors that is explained with experiments or psychometric tests and questionnaires generally is small. A statistically significant (nonzero) portion of variance may be accounted for, but a high level of significance often still coincides with a large proportion of unaccounted variance (Cohen, 1988, 1994). Authors such as Hoshmand and Polkinghorne (1992) or Gergen (1994) can rightly argue that quantitative approaches have had limited success and that it is time to consider alternative strategies. However, we contend that the qualitative approaches that are advocated as alternatives have largely failed to demonstrate better results, at least in ways convincing to skeptical outsiders (Poortinga, 1997).

In the natural sciences, the principle of unexplainable variance has gained wide acceptance. For example, mathematical equations describing the movements of a train wheel along the track are known precisely, but the complexity of changes over time and distance make it impossible to calculate the exact position of the wheel past 10 to 20 meters. Similarly, the weather becomes exceedingly difficult to predict after a period of 5 to 6 days. The models of nonlinear dynamics that describe the behavior of the weather or train wheels are known as *chaos models* or *catastrophe models*. They have captured the imagination of psychologists mainly for the analogon of unexplainability (Masterpasqua & Perna, 1997). However, chaos models have not resulted in abandoning quantitative methodologies in the natural science. In fact, they are mainly of interest insofar as they allow a differentiation between chaos (unpredictable) and linear (predictable) change. Meteorologists have learned from chaos theory that weather predictions for a period of 4 days makes sense, but not for a period of 8 days.

In a similar sense, there is an aspect of uncertainty and unpredictability to behavior, but it is not total chaos; in virtually any situation in which a person can act, the range of actual outcomes is smaller than the range of imaginable outcomes. This points to a conceptualization in which there is emphasis on constraints that limit the range of alternative actions actually available to a person in a given situation. Such constraints should become manifest in regularities that are open to analysis by experimental and psychometric methods. If we know what the constraints are, we can predict events that will occur (and perhaps more important, events that will not occur). For example, learning curves and curves of forgetting have been found to follow such precise trajectories that we even speak about "psychological laws" (such as "the law of effect," Thorndike, 1905). Inasmuch as there is freedom from constraints, future events are not predictable beyond their a priori levels of probability; only in retrospect can we observe which alternative actually was realized in a certain instance. Elsewhere, we have described such an orientation in somewhat more detail (Poortinga, 1997; Poortinga & Lunt, 1997; Poortinga & Soudijn, in press).

The practitioner in psychology is often faced with an open problem in which the range of possible solutions is initially undefined. Usually, a search is started for patterns of information that converge on a single best solution. Insofar as there is any merit in our analogy with chaos, such a unitary unambiguous solution is simply not available. On the other hand, even if information is insufficient to point to a single solution, the range of possible solutions is likely to be constrained. That is to say, unpromising courses of action can be identified that the psychologist should avoid. For example, sexual abuse of children can sometimes be identified with high likelihood, and sometimes it can be ruled out with a fair likelihood. However, there is a gray area in which the psychologist neither can rule out this possibility nor find substantial supporting evidence. Rather than resorting to dubious sources of evidence, one has to accept this uncertainty, however unsatisfactory this may be from a helping perspective.

Practitioners already tend to follow an approach that has some similarity with what we are proposing. They will adopt a certain solution tentatively and shift to another one if the first does not seem to work. However, we advocate a further step, namely, to acknowledge a range of alternatives simultaneously. A simple example is a selection situation in which the psychologist may be unable to differentiate between two or three good candidates for a job. If there were five or six candidates to begin with, uncertainty is reduced, but some uncertainty remains; the potential employer would like to be given a single name of "the" most promising candidate. In a clinical setting, the range of alternatives that cannot be ruled out is more diffuse, and some of these alternatives may even be quite incompatible with each other.

In summary, psychology should start to take seriously the uncertainty and the unpredictability that are inherent in behavior. Limited reduction of uncertainty should be the target. We may have to formulate more modest, but presumably more feasible, goals for interventions. Under these conditions, the profession of psychology can remain science informed, if not actually science based.

However, codes of ethics would have to be more explicit as to the limited reach of contemporary psychology.

Public Accountability

Questions of costs and benefits of professional services, particularly in the domain of health, have drawn much attention from outsiders representing public interests. This has been the case in the United States (e.g., Newman & Tejeda, 1996) and elsewhere. We would like to mention a draft regulation on the liability of suppliers of service providers, circularized about 10 years ago by the European Commission (EC, 1991). The starting principle was the protection of customers against poor services of professionals. The EC considered that because of their lack of knowledge and low financial means, customers are at a disadvantage when they have to prove negligence or poor quality of services. Therefore, a reversal of the burden of evidence was suggested. For example, if an adolescent in treatment with a psychologist for anorexia nervosa attempted to commit suicide and her parents lodged a judicial complaint for bad practice, the onus would not be on the complainants to bring evidence of malpractice, but on the psychologist to show that the client had been treated competently. At the time, there was widespread resistance against these plans, and they were shelved for the time being. Let us speculate for a moment about the implications for psychologists if such plans were adopted at some time in the future.

In the absence of any jurisprudence, it is not clear what evidence a court would require, but we can make a few educated guesses. Undoubtedly, a recognized diploma and professional qualifications would be seen as important evidence of competence; absence of proof of professional competence would expose a service provider as incompetent, if not as a charlatan (which almost certainly would happen to Yomanda[4]). In addition, strong claims about the effectiveness of interventions would be associated with responsibility for failure. With an overall success rate of more than 90%, the unsuccessful treatment of a client might require specific explanation, whereas a low overall success rate would testify to the inherent difficulties of intervention. Another aspect of such a court case would be a consultation by the judges of expert witnesses, and here scientific evidence comes in. The user of the Rorschach or AD dolls might have to face one of the authors of the article on projective techniques published in the *Scientific American* or a psychometrician who would produce computations similar to those in Table 5.1. Judges might be convinced by interpretative argument and rely on the professed expertise of the professional; however, it would be a risky strategy to count on this. In fact, existing judicial evidence on controversial issues, such as recovered memories of early traumatic events (BPS, 1995; Lipton, 1999) seems to show that courts tend to be suspicious of subjective evidence that cannot be otherwise supported. Evidence that the professional had worked in-line with best current practices would probably impress a court, even though such practices are defined by the profession itself. On the other hand, adherents of a particular school or method that has been challenged extensively by colleagues on the basis of questionable effectiveness or negative scientific evidence could hardly argue convincingly that they followed best practices.

Let us speculate a bit about the consequences for the profession. Easier access to the courts for clients would probably greatly increase litigation and might bring it to a level in Europe even exceeding that of the United States. No psychologist could be looking forward to that. But there would also be benefits. The most important would be that unqualified providers of psychological services would face hard times and that the recognition of professional expertise would increase. From the perspective of the present chapter, an advantage would be that psychologists would have to more carefully consider the scope of their interventions. We think that this would lead to a somewhat more modest profession and a strengthening of the relationships between science and practice. Our codes of ethics would probably need minimal adjustment if this scenario were realized.

CONCLUSION

In national codes of ethics, psychology is presented as a science-based profession. This does not mean that professional action can be largely accounted for in terms of an accumulated fund of scientific evidence. However, it should mean that there are no major incompatibilities between the (rather limited) reach of contemporary science of behavior and professional practice. We have briefly presented a few discrepancies and indicated ways in which psychologists can deal with them. The burden of evidence can be shifted more away from science and toward the individual expertise of the professional psychologist, but then, we think, the professed status of psychology in our codes of ethics as a science-based profession cannot be sustained. Psychologists can also seek a sharper definition of the current reach of their science and admit to the limitations this imposes on science-informed practice. This is a difficult path to take, not in the least because of the collusion of interests between the psychologist and the client, who both for their own reasons are likely to overestimate positive effects of interventions. However, if we take the high moral values reflected in our codes seriously, psychology also has to take its limitations seriously; it can be only a modest profession, as mentioned above. In the long run, we anticipate that such an orientation serves not only the best interests of the public but also of the profession as it enhances public accountability of our interventions.

NOTES

1. Citations in this section from European codes were mainly taken from English translations published in *News From EFPPA* (see Vol. 3, No. 1; Vol. 4, No. 1; and Vol. 4, No. 2, in 1989 and 1990). In various countries, there may be more recent versions, but we are not aware of English translations.

2. These quotations are from *The Activity Report of the EFPPA Task Force Traffic Psychology 1996/1997; Ralf Risser, Convenor*. The motion concerning psychotherapy was an elaboration on a proposal submitted to the General Assembly by the Colegio Oficial de Psicólogos from Spain.

3. This information was provided to us some years ago by an indignant student who had heard about the study on the radio and felt that the author should be sanctioned for unprofessional conduct.

4 According to news reports of January 2002, the inspection of health in the Netherlands is investigating whether Yomanda's healing practices have demonstrable negative effects.

REFERENCES

American Psychological Association. (1992). Ethical principles of psychologists and code of conduct. *American Psychologist, 47,* 1597-1611.

Anonymous. (1989). Ethical principles for Scandinavian psychologists adopted by the Nordic countries. *News From EFPPA, 3*(1), 21/1-21/13.

Arbous, A. G. (1952). *Tables for aptitude testers.* Johannesburg, South Africa: National Institute for Personnel Research.

Austrian Psychological Society. (1990). Professional code of the Austrian Psychological Society. *News From EFPPA, 4*(2), 15-23.

British Psychological Society. (1995). *Recovered memories* (Report). Leicester, UK: Author.

Brock, T. C., Green, M. C., & Reich, D. A. (1998). New evidence of flaws in the *Consumer Reports* study of psychotherapy. *American Psychologist, 53,* 62-63.

Campbell, D. T., & Fiske, D. W. (1959). Convergent and discriminant validation by the multitrait-multimethod matrix. *Psychological Bulletin, 56,* 81-105.

Cohen, J. (1988). *Statistical power analysis for the behavioral sciences.* Hillsdale, NJ: Lawrence Erlbaum.

Cohen, J. (1994). The earth is round (p <. 05). *American Psychologist, 49,* 997-1003.

Colegio Oficial de Psicológos. (1990). Ethical standards of the psychologist, first edition, 1987. *News From EFPPA, 4*(1), 9-15.

Cronbach, L. J. (1956). Assessment of individual differences. *Annual Review of Psychology, 7,* 173-196.

Dawes, R. M. (1994). *House of cards: Psychology and psychotherapy built on myth.* New York: Free Press.

Draijer, N. (1990). *Sexuele traumatisering in de jeugd* [Sexual traumatization at young age]. Amsterdam: PhD Free University Amsterdam.

European Commission. (1991). *Proposal for a council directive on the liability of the suppliers of services* [KOM(90) 482 final-SYN (91/C 12/11)]. Brussels, Belgium: Author.

European Federation of Psychologists Associations. (1997a). *Meta code of ethics* (Report). Brussels, Belgium: Author.

European Federation of Psychologists Associations. (1997b). *Activity report of the EFPPA task force traffic psychology, 1996/1997; Ralf Risser, convenor.* Brussels, Belgium: Author.

Evers, A., Van Vliet-Mulder, J. C., & Groot, C. J. (2000). *Documentatie van tests en test research in Nederland* [Documentation of tests and test research in the Netherlands]. Amsterdam: Nederlands Instituut van Psychologen.

Exner, J. E. (1993). *The Rorschach: A comprehensive system: Vol. 1. Basic foundations* (3rd ed.). New York: Wiley.

Federación Colombiana de Psicología. (2000). *Código ético del psicólogo* [Ethical code of the psychologist]. Bogota, Colombia: Author.

Fox, R. E. (1991). Proceedings of American Psychological Association, incorporated, for the year 1990: Minutes of the meeting of the council of representatives. *American Psychologist, 46,* 689-726.

Friedrich, J. (1993). Primary error detection and minimization (PEDMIN) strategies in social cognition: A reinterpretation of the confirmation bias phenomenon. *Psychological Review, 100,* 298-319.

Gergen, K. J. (1994). Exploring the postmodern: Perils or potentials? *American Psychologist, 49,* 412-416.

Hoshmand, L. T., & Polkinghorne, D. E. (1992). Redefining the science-practice relationship and professional training. *American Psychologist, 47,* 55-66.

Koocher, G. P., Goodman, G. S., White, C. S., Friedrich, W. N., Sivan, A. B., & Reynolds, C. R. (1995). Psychological science and the use of anatomically detailed dolls in child sexual-abuse assessments. *Psychological Bulletin, 118,* 199-222.

Lilienfeld, S. O., Wood, J. M., & Garb, H. N. (2001). What's wrong with this picture? *Scientific American, 284*(5), 73-79.

Lipton, A. (1999). Recovered memories in the courts. In S. Taub (Ed.), *Recovered memories of child sexual abuse: Psychological, social, and legal perspectives on a contemporary health controversy* (pp. 165-210). Springfield, IL: Charles C Thomas.

Lunt, I., Bartram, B., Döpping, J., Georgas, J., Jern, S., Job, R., Lecuyer, R., Newstead, S., Nieminen, P., Odland, T., Peiro, J. M., Poortinga, Y. H., Roe, R., Wilpert, B., & Hermann, E. (2001). *A framework for education and training for psychologists in Europe* (Report submitted to the Leonardo da Vinci program of the European Union). Brussels, Belgium: EFPA.

Masterpasqua, F., & Perna, P. A. (Eds.). (1997). *The psychological meaning of chaos.* Washington, DC: American Psychological Association.

Michotte, A. (1954). *La perception de la causalité* [The perception of causality]. Leuven, Belgium: Publications Universitaires de Louvain.

Netherlands Institute of Psychologists. (1989). Verklaring van het Hoofdbestuur inzake Bolderkar-affaire [Declaration of the executive concerning the "Bolderkar"-affair]. *De Psycholoog, 24,* 43.

Newman, F. L., & Tejeda, M. J. (1996). The need for research that is designed to support decisions in the delivery of mental health services. *American Psychologist, 51,* 1040-1049.

Outcome assessment of psychotherapy. (1996, October). *American Psychologist* [Special issue].

Poortinga, Y. H. (1994). Defining the competence of psychologists: A European perspective. *News From EFFPA, 8*(4), 4-10.

Poortinga, Y. H. (1997). Brown, Heisenberg and Lorenz, predecessors of 21st century psychology? In R. Fuller, P. N. Walsh, & P. McGinley (Eds.), *A century of psychology: Progress, paradigms and prospects for the new millennium* (pp. 1-15). London: Routledge.

Poortinga, Y. H., & Lunt, I. (1997). Defining the competence of psychologists with a view to public accountability. *European Psychologist, 2,* 293-300.

Poortinga, Y. H., & Soudijn, K. (in press). Behaviour-culture relationships and ontogenetic development. In H. Keller, Y. H. Poortinga, & A. Schoelmerich (Eds.), *Between biology and culture: Perspectives on ontogenetic development.* Cambridge, UK: Cambridge University Press.

Sargent, H. (1970). Review of the Rorschach. In O. K. Buros (Ed.), *Personality tests and reviews* (pp. 626-631). Highland Park, NJ: Gryphon. (Original work published 1953)

Schönpflug, W. (1993). Applied psychology: Newcomer with a long tradition. *Applied Psychology: An International Review, 42,* 5-30.

Schönpflug, W. (1994). Professional training in psychological departments: A critical analysis. *News From EFPPA, 8*(4), 15-17.

Seligman, M. E. P. (1995). The effectiveness of psychotherapy: The *Consumer Reports* study. *American Psychologist, 50,* 965-974.

Seligman, M. E. P. (1996). A creditable beginning. *American Psychologist, 51,* 1086-1088.

Taylor, H. C., & Russell, J. T. (1939). The relationships of validity coefficients to the practical effectiveness of tests in selection: Discussion and tables. *Journal of Applied Psychology, 23,* 565-578.

Thorndike, E. L. (1905). *The elements of psychology.* New York: Seiler.

Watkins, C. E., Campbell, V. L., Nieberding, R., & Hallmark, R. (1995). Contemporary practice of psychological assessment by clinical psychologists. *Professional Psychology: Research and Practice, 26,* 54-60.

Wittenborn, J. R. (1970). Review of the Rorschach. In O. K. Buros (Ed.), *Personality tests and reviews* (pp. 394-395). Highland Park, NJ: Gryphon. (Original work published 1949)

CHAPTER 6

The Mismeasure of Psychologists

A Review of the Psychometrics of Licensing Requirements

WILLIAM T. O'DONOHUE
Nicholas Cummings Professor of
Organized Behavioral Healthcare Delivery
University of Nevada, Reno

JEFFREY A. BUCHANAN
University of Nevada, Reno

The U.S. Department of Health, Education, and Welfare (1977) defines *licensing* as follows:

A process for which an agency of government grants permission to an individual to engage in a given occupation upon finding that the applicant has attained the minimal degree of competence required to ensure that the public health, safety and welfare will be reasonably well protected. (p. 4)

All 50 states require individuals to become licensed before practicing psychology, although specific requirements vary from state to state (Association of State and Provincial Licensing Boards, 1997a). Practicing psychology, and often even calling oneself a psychologist without meeting all of the state's requirements for licensing, is prohibited and punishable by law.

Licensing differs slightly from the related, but less restrictive, process of certification. Certification involves granting recognition to an individual who has met certain qualifications set by a governmental credentialing agency (Shimberg, 1981). Certification, then, protects the title of "psychologist" for only those who meet certain requirements, but differs from licensing in that it does not prevent uncertified individuals from practicing (Lecomte, 1986).

AUTHORS' NOTE: The authors would like to thank David Antonuccio, Dean Hinitz, Scott Lilienfeld, and Lee Sechrest for their helpful comments on an earlier version of this paper.

PURPOSES OF LICENSING

The general purpose of licensing is to protect the public's health, safety, and welfare from incompetent or unqualified practitioners (Shimberg, 1981). Furthermore, Hogan (1983) adds that licensing laws are not intended to guarantee a high degree of competency, only the degree of competency necessary to protect the public from harm. Due to the technical nature of most professions, it is thought that the public is unable to make informed choices concerning the quality of services provided by professionals. Therefore, it is argued, some form of regulation must be in place to protect consumers (Young, 1987). However, historically, the public rarely demands for a profession to be licensed as a result of being victimized by fraudulent practitioners (Friedman, 1962). Instead, it has been members of the profession who have most frequently persuaded the government to enact licensure laws (Friedman, 1962).

Licensure, of course, may have functions other than protecting the public. For instance, licensure may become a kind of "rite of passage" for new psychologists. In other words, older generations of psychologists may feel that because they had to complete the licensure process, newer generations should also. Other functions of licensure may be to promote consumer confidence in our profession or to establish the credibility of our profession compared with other professions. Although these certainly are among the functions of licensure, they seem to be considerations that support the *maintenance* of the current licensing system, but were not the original reasons for *creating* licensure and are not sufficient to support the continuation of the exact procedures currently involved in licensure. Therefore, this paper will primarily focus on the issue of whether or not the current licensing system is serving the function of protecting the public, because this was presumably the most important

impetus for creating a system of licensure in the first place.

REQUIREMENTS FOR LICENSING AND THEIR PROBLEMS

In general, three major requirements must be met for one to become licensed as a psychologist: (a) appropriate education, (b) supervised clinical experience, and (c) successful completion of state and/or national examinations. Each set of requirements will be explained and then critiqued.

Educational Requirements

To be licensed as a psychologist, one must meet certain minimal educational requirements. This seems reasonable, as graduating from an accredited school with a degree in psychology assures some level of knowledge of the field. However, these educational requirements vary from state to state. One thing that is agreed on in every state is that one must have a doctoral degree of some sort (Ph.D., Psy.D., or Ed.D.). However, this is where the consistency ends.

Although all states require a doctoral degree of some kind, only 23 states explicitly state that they require a doctorate *in psychology* (Association of State and Provincial Psychology Boards [ASPPB], 1997a). The other 27 states simply state that a doctoral degree is required. Moreover, only 13 states explicitly require that the program one graduates from be accredited in some form, although all states (except California) require the institution to be regionally accredited (ASPPB, 1997a). Some states specifically require that the program be American Psychological Association (APA) approved (e.g., Hawaii, Kansas), whereas others state that the doctoral program be "ASPPB/National Register designated" (e.g., Maryland, Utah). It seems peculiar that in more than half the states, one could be licensed as a psychologist and not possess a degree in psychology from an accredited program. Allowing persons with little to no formal educational background to practice psychology would not seem to be consistent with the overriding goal of protecting the public. Below, we will argue for a strengthening of this educational requirement.

Nineteen states allow persons with master's degrees to practice in some form (e.g., as a "psychological associate," "psychological examiner," "psychological technician," or "certified psychological associate"; ASPPB, 1997a). With the exception of West Virginia and Vermont, all these states require those with master's degrees to work under the supervision of a doctoral level provider (ASPPB, 1997a).

Licensing Examinations

In psychology, each state requires an applicant to pass a national licensing exam, and most states also require one to pass a state exam. This section will describe these tests and the many problems associated with measuring the construct of *minimal competence* in a valid manner.

Examination for Professional Practice in Psychology (EPPP): Reliability or Validity?

The EPPP is the national licensing examination that potential licensees in all 50 states must pass (ASPPB, 1997a). The EPPP is a 200-question, multiple-choice test that covers a wide variety of subject areas, including biological bases of behavior, assessment and diagnosis, ethical issues, and research methods/statistics, among others (ASPPB, 1997b).

Establishing the reliability and validity of the EPPP is essential for justifying its use as a measure of minimal competence and as a tool for making major decisions, such as whether individuals can practice the profes-

sion for which they have spent many years and dollars preparing. Reliability and validity are concerned with the accuracy of inferences one can make from a test. Classical test theory assumes that an individual's score on the test can be represented as follows:

$$X_{obs} = T + e$$

Where X_{obs} is the score that the test taker actually received on a test, T reflects the test taker's true score on the construct, and e is the amount of error. Thus, studies of reliability and validity are concerned with the size of the error term. The following sections will describe reliability and several types of validity, and when available, psychometric data concerning these properties will be presented. All psychometric data regarding the EPPP were taken from the most recent edition of the ASPPB *Research Digest: The Examination for Professional Practice in Psychology* (1991).

Reliability. The EPPP's internal consistency has been fairly well established. For instance, the last 16 forms of the EPPP have demonstrated split-half reliabilities in the range of .89 to .93. Likewise, Kuder-Richardson 20 reliabilities range from .89 to .93.

Although these reliability coefficients appear to be quite high, these correlations may not actually reflect high internal consistency. A test's internal consistency is determined by the average inter-item correlation of test items and the length of the test (Cortina, 1993). Thus, the average inter-item correlation for the 200 items on the EPPP could be as low as .05 and the test could still achieve a Kuder-Richardson 20 coefficient of .90 (Sechrest, personal communication, March 20, 1998). High KR-20 coefficients can be due to the length of the test, not the interrelatedness of the test items (Cortina, 1993). However, the constraints on coherence of the EPPP may reflect the heterogeneity in the field itself. Given inconsistencies in graduate curricula, the lack of coherence in the ways in which students are taught, and the controversies concerning what actually is knowledge in the field, it is admittedly difficult to construct a test with high internal consistency.

The *Research Digest* fails to mention any other indices of reliability. For instance, information concerning test-retest reliability would be informative regarding the consistency with which the test measures competence over time, assuming the absence of factors that could legitimately affect the construct. It would be hoped that a person deemed "knowledgeable" or "competent" by this test would pass the test again at a later date. Thus, overall, the EPPP has demonstrated at best only weak internal consistency, and it has not been demonstrated that it is a consistent measure across time. This is an important concern if crash test preparation courses produce transient score increases.

Content Validity. For a licensing exam to demonstrate content validity, it would have to be shown that scores could be interpreted in terms of degree of competence in some content domain or domains (Kane, 1985). For a licensing exam in psychology, the content domain would include knowledge and skills deemed necessary for safe and effective delivery of psychological treatment and other services (Kane, 1985).

One possible way to determine the appropriate content of a licensing exam is to conduct a task analysis (Shimberg, 1981). Several analyses designed to delineate the primary domains of psychological practice and the specific responsibilities germane to each of these domains have been conducted (ASPPB, 1991). However, none of these have actually been task analyzed. Rather, psychologists' opinions regarding the relevance and importance of these tasks have been gathered. The results of these various investigations

are summarized in the *Research Digest*. In conducting these analyses, questions on the EPPP were evaluated in terms of their relevance to these roles and responsibilities, thereby possibly improving the content validity of the test.

The most recent of these studies, called a *practice analysis*, determined the content areas covered in the current version of the EPPP examining "what licensed psychologists do and what they need to know to practice psychology in the United States and Canada" (ASPPB, 1997b). To accomplish this goal, surveys were sent to approximately 7,500 licensed psychologists in the United States and Canada. Results of the survey identified eight content domains that were then used to determine the content areas to be covered in the exam. These domains include (with percentage of exam items devoted to each domain in parentheses): assessment and diagnosis (14%); biological basis of behavior (11%); cognitive-affective bases of behavior (13%); ethical/legal/professional issues (15%); growth and life span development (13%); research methods (6%); social and multicultural basis of behavior (12%); and treatment/intervention (16%) (ASPPB, 1997b).

In addition, four major roles in which professional psychologists engaged were identified, as well as specific tasks associated with each role (ASPPB, 1997b). These four roles are (a) direct service that entails activities such as assessment, treatment planning and delivery, and coordinating services with other professionals; (b) outreach and consultation that involves activities such as disseminating knowledge to the public and consultation; (c) academic preparation and professional development that involve teaching and supervising students; and (d) research and evaluation that entails collecting and analyzing research data and preparing proposals and grants.

However, it is important to note that the weighting of the importance of various content domains is not necessarily achieved by varying the number of items in each content domain. The actual weights that each content domain will have will depend on the relative variances of the items in each domain. "Correct/Incorrect" test items have their maximum variance at a difficulty level of .5. If, for example, questions on research methods are more difficult than items in other areas, then they will contribute less variance to the total score than indicated by their number, that is, perhaps even less than 6%. Second, it is not clear that the opinions of 7,500 psychologists actually reflect what psychologists do and need to know, because it is not certain that these opinions identify critical knowledge. Finally, the number of test items in each content domain should be determined by the requirements for adequate testing in that domain. It may take more items to adequately test, for example, growth and life span development than to test multicultural bases of behavior.

One problem with a generic test of general abilities is that not all psychologists are trained to do the same tasks. For instance, if the goal of the exam is to distinguish those who would engage in competent versus incompetent practice, then the content of the EPPP would seem less relevant to an industrial/organizational psychologist (Howell, 1986). If testing is to be used, a series of licensing exams may be more appropriate. Several could be developed and validated for different subspecialties of psychology as opposed to having one all-encompassing test to cover to entire field. In this way, the content of the test would be more relevant to the tasks a particular applicant is likely to be engaged in once licensed. Bernstein and Lecomte (1981) laid out a plan for addressing these issues (as well as others). However, it appears little has been done to carry out this plan.

Efforts to establish the content validity of the EPPP have been commendable. Attempts have been made to determine what psychologists actually do and must know to practice psychology. However, as mentioned previously, to justify its use as part of the licensing procedure, the content domain of the EPPP must test critical abilities deemed necessary for safe and effective delivery of psychological services (Kane, 1985). It is unclear whether the EPPP actually assesses possession of abilities critical for the purpose of protecting consumers. The knowledge tested in this exam may be knowledge we would desire that all psychologists have, but the question "Is there the potential that the public may be harmed if a psychologist does not possess this knowledge?" may still not be addressed by this content.

A major difficulty concerning content validity (and construct validity as well) of the EPPP is the definition of the construct minimal competence. There does not seem to be a consensus regarding the definition of this construct. The problem is that the content of the test must reflect the entire content domain of the construct. In other words, if minimal competence cannot be well-defined, how can the test be said to reflect this construct, and how does one go about establishing construct validity?

This problem may be illustrated with an example. In most states, one can miss 60 of the 200 questions on the EPPP and still pass the exam. The issue is that one can miss *any* 60 of these items and pass the test. This means that, for instance, a person could miss all the questions in the Assessment and Diagnosis content domain and still pass the test. In fact, one could pass the exam when incorrectly answering *all* Assessment and Diagnosis as well as *all* Treatment/Intervention questions. It seems peculiar that one could demonstrate complete ignorance (and perhaps, more strongly, being completely misinformed) regarding two critical content domains and still be deemed minimally competent.

It is not clear why the EPPP relies on such a compensatory model, that is, one in which good performance on one type of domain can compensate for poor performance on some other type of domain. One could instead use a successive-hurdles model in which examinees need to demonstrate minimal competence on what are decided to be key domains. However, one consequence of a successive-hurdles model is almost certainly to be a higher overall failure rate.

Another problem concerning content validity is that the EPPP does not reflect or emphasize issues related to some of the most common ethical violations, such as dual relationships/sexual misconduct, issues regarding insurance and fees, and confidentiality (APA, 1996). Because it is in these areas that malpractice most frequently results, one could argue that they should comprise a large part of the test.

Furthermore, it can be argued that the field of psychology actually has identified some skills that may be considered critical abilities, namely empirically supported treatments (Chambless et al., 1995, 1998). These are arguably essential skills because they have been shown to be effective in reasonably designed experimental investigations and related to positive client outcomes. Because knowledge of these treatments is generally associated with improved patient outcome, they should be highly represented on the licensing exam. This is not the case, however, and calls into question the content validity of the EPPP.

Construct Validity. In the case of the EPPP, the construct that is presumably being measured is competence or minimal competence. Research investigating the construct validity of the EPPP is summarized in the ASPPB's *Research Digest* (1991). Eight studies all found evidence that subjects with more education (i.e., Ph.D.) and better education (i.e., degree from APA-approved institution) scored higher on the EPPP (although it is unclear whether scores were *significantly* higher). Further evidence suggests that scores on the EPPP are related to graduate school GPA and ratings of professional competence by faculty advisors and internship sponsors, as would be predicted. Thus, there is some evidence demonstrating the EPPP's convergent validity.

Although these data are of value, there are still some important unanswered questions regarding the construct validity of the EPPP. For instance, although EPPP scores are related to advisor ratings of competence, a more relevant question seems to be "To what extent are those candidates rated as incompetent by supervisors failing the EPPP, and to what extent are those candidates rated as competent by supervisors passing the EPPP?" Unfortunately, there are no data presented to answer this question. However, there are some indirect negative data. We suggest that any graduate of an APA-accredited program who fails the exam actually provides negative evidence for the construct validity of the EPPP, because these individuals have been judged to be competent by a series of independent raters (i.e., psychology faculty, internship supervisors, and supervisors of postdoctoral experience).

Another deficiency in the existing construct validity studies is that there is no evidence for the discriminant validity of the EPPP. It would seem to be important to know not only whether the EPPP is related to other presumed measures of competence but also whether or not the EPPP is simply measuring some other construct, such as general intelligence, test-taking ability, or short-term memory of "cram course" material. Discriminant validity cannot simply be assumed, but must be established empirically.

The multitrait-multimethod approach to establishing construct validity (Campbell & Fiske, 1959) would be a step in the right direction for empirically determining both convergent and discriminant validity. We are particularly concerned as to whether the EPPP is measuring familiarity with commercial cram course material because it is part of the lore that one needs to study this material to pass the exam. It is important that the test makes this discrimination because the cram course material has a greater likelihood of not being retained and not generalizing to actual behavior.

In general, there is some support for the construct validity of the EPPP, but this evidence is relatively unimportant if the construct being measured is minimal competence in the service of protecting the public. It would be hoped that poor candidates (as indicated by some other measure such as supervisor ratings) would fail the exam, but there is no evidence to support this. Evidence supporting the proposition that all competent candidates pass the exam is also lacking. Overall, it appears as if the factors that influence performance on the EPPP are numerous, complex, and largely unknown.

Criterion-Related Validity. Criterion validity is traditionally divided into two types: concurrent and predictive. Each of these types of validity as it relates to the EPPP will be discussed.

Concurrent Validity. In the context of licensing exams, it would be hoped that scores on the EPPP would predict other measures of current competence (e.g., current supervisor's ratings of competence). As mentioned in the "Construct Validity" section above, there is some evidence that EPPP scores correlate with graduate school GPA and ratings of professional competence by faculty advisors and internship sponsors

(ASPPB, 1991). However, there was no mention that failing scores on the EPPP were able to predict a rating of "incompetence" by supervisors. Overall, there currently is no evidence that EPPP scores can predict other current measures of competence. Moreover, it is interesting to note that the EPPP assumes that competence in clinical psychology is entirely a matter of deficits in knowledge rather than incompetence stemming from other psychological domains such as self-control, judgment, and attitudes.

Predictive Validity. The issue of predictive validity seems to be particularly relevant regarding licensing exams (Bernstein & Lecomte, 1981). Again, it would be hoped that scores on the EPPP would predict future measures of competence or, more important, indices of incompetence such as number of ethical violations, consumer and employer satisfaction ratings, or number of malpractice suits. Ideally, those who are found to be poor clinicians in the future (i.e., incompetent) should fail the exam. This is perhaps the most critical and important function of licensing exams and of the entire licensing process in general. Unfortunately, there is no evidence that indicates the EPPP has predictive validity. To be clear, this means that high or passing scores have not been shown to correlate with any future index of competence, and "low" or "failing" scores have not been shown to correlate with any future index of incompetence. Moreover, there is no published information concerning the false-positive and false-negative rates of this test. These are important indices that must be known to properly evaluate a test, and when these are unknown, it is difficult to argue that the test is adequate.

Of particular importance would be to establish the positive and negative predictive power of the EPPP as indexed against some dichotomous measure of competence.

Positive predictive power would address the following critical question: Given a passing test result, what is the probability that the examinee will prove to be competent in his or her practice? Negative predictive power would address another key question: Given a negative test result, what is the probability that the examinee will prove to be incompetent in his or her practice? However, positive and negative predictive power are influenced by the base rate of the criterion variable, that is, incompetence. Thus, it is essential to know the prevalence of what one is attempting to assess. For example, if the base rate of genuinely incompetent practice (what the test is attempting to screen out) is low, then the positive predictive power will also tend to be low. In practical terms, this means that the test will have a very low hit rate even though it may be high in content validity. If the test has not been shown to be able to successfully identify incompetent practitioners, why use it? Faith? Hope?

As has been pointed out before (Kane, 1986), establishing criterion validity is difficult because those who do not pass the exam are not allowed to practice, and therefore, the relevant data needed to evaluate predictive validity cannot be gathered. Allowing those who do not pass the exam to practice would no doubt be unacceptable to many, but there are compelling reasons why this nonetheless should be done. First, currently, there are no data suggesting that the EPPP is able to predict who will practice in an incompetent/unqualified manner, so we cannot assume that if those that fail the exam are allowed to practice, there actually will be such problems. The claim that candidates who fail will eventually do harm begs the question, because this is the very issue that is not known. In this argument, the validity of the EPPP as a screen for incompetence is assumed rather than demonstrated. Second, if those who fail the exam are allowed to practice, data could be collected on all applicants.

Perhaps relevant criteria that discriminate between competent and incompetent clinicians could then be empirically identified.

Rosen (1986), author of the second edition of the *Research Digest,* argued that the predictive validity model is inappropriate for evaluating licensing exams for at least two reasons. First, predictors (e.g., amount of experience required, amount of education required, the EPPP) and criterion measures vary widely from jurisdiction to jurisdiction due to varying objectives and elements of the licensing process. Therefore, a single index of predictive validity cannot be established, but instead would have to be done on a jurisdiction by jurisdiction basis. It must be recognized, however, that this argument would challenge the possibility of a single-content valid test—thus repudiating the current EPPP. Another problem is that the objectives of licensing are presumably the same regardless of jurisdiction, ensuring a level of competence in order to protect the public. Second, even if one countenances varying definitions of competence, the EPPP can still be evaluated with respect to each of these.

Another reason Rosen claims that the predictive-validity model is inappropriate for licensing exams is because this model is inconsistent with the primary assumptions of the licensure process. He claims that the initial assumption is one of incompetence (Rosen, 1986). Why graduates of APA-approved programs in clinical psychology and graduates of APA-approved internships should be assumed to be incompetent is unclear. It is our clear impression that academic faculty and internship supervisors are taking great pains to ensure that their students are in fact competent in the necessary skills relevant to clinical psychology. In addition, the APA conducts evaluations to assure that training programs (whether it be Ph.D., Psy.D., counseling, or school psychology programs) are providing adequate training.

Another criticism against the predictive-validity model is that it would be very difficult to establish because reliable and valid criterion measures of competence would be required for comparison with EPPP scores (Shimberg, 1981). The criterion problem is always difficult in test construction and validation. If psychologists cannot agree on what constitutes competence and incompetence, then this is an argument against any attempt to construct a test of these constructs, not an argument to have a test but simply ignore the question of the test's predictive validity. However, to our knowledge, the attempt to evaluate the predictive validity of the EPPP has not even been made, so it cannot be argued that the task is impossible.

To summarize, although predictive validity seems to be very important from the standpoint of protecting the public from incompetent clinicians, because candidates take the test once and on the basis of passing it are allowed to practice for many years, there is no evidence in support of the EPPP's predictive validity. Furthermore, some would believe that this is not even an appropriate way to evaluate the EPPP, which is discouraging. The current practice of requiring psychologists to pass this test once in their lives increases the difficulty of the predictive task, because the test is essentially asked to predict lifetime competence. The American Board of Radiology as well as a number of other medical boards require reexamination after certain time periods (e.g., 5-10 years). This decreases the predictive burden of the test.

Incremental Validity. To establish incremental validity in the case of the EPPP, there would need to be evidence showing that the EPPP improves decisions concerning competence of potential clinicians when compared with decisions made using only the criterion of graduation from an APA-approved clinical psychology program and internship program. This is a particularly important issue when the total cost of the testing procedure (particularly on those that fail) is taken into account. Again, there is no evidence supporting the EPPP's incremental validity and some reason to believe that it may not have positive incremental validity. To the extent that graduates from APA-approved graduate programs and internships fail this exam and that graduation from these programs is thought to ensure minimal competence by experts in the field (i.e., psychology faculty), there is some evidence that the EPPP has negative incremental validity.

Other Problems

Beyond having generally unknown psychometric properties, the EPPP has other problems. For instance, there is evidence that the EPPP may be a racially biased test. Werner (1981, as cited in ASPPB, 1991) found the pass rates for whites ($N = 284$), blacks ($N = 20$), and other minorities ($N = 25$) to be 57%, 25%, and 16%, respectively. It is also stated, admittedly vaguely, that these data are consistent with previous research (ASPPB, 1991). In addition, the *Research Digest* claims that the results reported by Werner provided less convincing evidence for racial bias than did previous research (ASPPB, 1991). Although the number of minority subjects in the Werner study was small, the large differences in pass rates provides evidence that the EPPP is perhaps racially biased.

Another problem with the EPPP is that the criterion "passing" cutoff is somewhat arbitrary. Generally, the passing score is 140 (70%), but it is sometimes 1, ½, or ¼ standard deviations below the mean, or may be the mean for all candidates. Assuming a normal distribution, this means that between 16% and 50% of candidates could fail in some states. The point is that there is no independent argument or evidence that the 70% criterion is a valid cutoff score (i.e., separates the competent from the incompetent). The test providers need to answer the question of why we should hold the assumption that X% of test takers do not have minimal competency, particularly when X may be as high as 50%. McGaghie (1980) has previously argued that whether someone passes this test should depend on his or her absolute skill level, not the makeup of the group that happened to take the test at the same time. Moreover, the APA *Standards for Educational and Psychological Testing* (1985) recommends that the standard error of measurement at the cut score should be given, but it is not.

State Licensing Examinations

In addition to the EPPP, 41 states require applicants to take state licensing exams (ASPPB, 1997a). Twenty-six states require oral proficiency examinations, 19 require ethics/law/jurisprudence exams, and another 7 require an exam of unspecified form (ASPPB, 1997a). A Psych-Info search was conducted to locate studies examining the psychometric properties of state licensing exams. To the author's knowledge, there is no published literature regarding the reliability or validity of any of these exams.

As a result, a questionnaire requesting psychometric information was sent to the licensing boards of all 50 states. This questionnaire included questions concerning reliability (test-retest, internal consistency); validity (content, convergent, discriminant, predictive, concurrent, incremental); cultural fairness; whether and how situational factors were taken into account when scoring the exam; how the cutoff score was determined; pass/fail rates for the last 5 to 10 years; presence of a technical manual; factor structure; and in what ways those who pass the exam are different than those who fail.

Although questionnaires were sent to all 50 states, only 41 states actually require state exams in addition to the EPPP. Therefore, these data are relevant only to these 41 states. Responses were obtained from 12 of these 41 states (5 states that do not require state exams also replied). Respondents were board chairs, executive officers, or board members in most cases. Few data were actually reported. Some states admitted the complete absence of psychometric data, some refused to respond to our questions (usually no reason was given, although one state indicated it refused because it was involved in litigation), while the majority did not even respond. (Incidentally, follow-up letters were sent to all nonresponding states a month after the questionnaires were sent, which resulted in two additional responses). The fact that many states did not even reply is disturbing because according to the *Standards of Education and Psychological Testing,* anyone is entitled to this psychometric information (APA, 1985), assuming that there is any available. In any case, it is evident that no state was able to produce (or was willing to share) any sort of data to support any type of psychometric property, with the exception of some explanations of content (i.e., general statements that content was based on state law or APA ethics).

In light of this, the discussion of psychometric properties of the EPPP also applies to these state exams, particularly the oral proficiency exams. State oral examinations, however, carry with them problems in addition to those mentioned with regard to the EPPP. In particular, inter-rater reliability would need to be evaluated because scoring is more subjective when compared with the objective scoring of the EPPP. Moreover, consistency of scoring could be affected by variables such as the differing theoretical orientations of the panel or the lack of blindness of raters with respect to the applicant's history. Again, no psychometric data addressing these issues are available.

Other potential difficulties can arise with an oral exam. For instance, because graders can see the examinees and know their names, biased scoring is a potential problem. Characteristics such as the examinees' gender, race, age, reputation, or prestige of their credentials could affect how they are graded. The APA ethics code dictates cultural fairness, and these tests have not been shown to meet these requirements. Finally, it is not clear how test-taking circumstances are taken into account when scoring these exams. For instance, if an applicant had recently lost a spouse or were feeling ill, it is not clear how these factors would be taken into account when interpreting test performance.

In conclusion, state licensing exams, to our knowledge, have no psychometric data to support their use as reliable and valid measures of competence, even for the restricted constructs some attempt to measure (e.g., "knowledge of state laws"). Therefore, all criticisms leveled at the EPPP apply to these exams. Considering the time and money spent on the part of applicants and board members, their continued use is difficult to justify.

There appear to be many possibilities for improving this situation, including conducting the necessary psychometric examinations of the current EPPP, revising the EPPP and then conducting the necessary psychometric evaluations, or creating and evaluating wholly new licensing tests. However, we believe that there is another legitimate possibility that has received too little consideration in the literature: eliminating testing requirements, at least until empirical data suggest that these possess acceptable incremental validity over educational requirements. This point will be discussed further below.

Potential Ethical Violations of Licensing Exams

It could be argued that the use of these exams is in violation of a number of APA ethical principles. Principle 2.02a states,

> Psychologists who develop, administer, score, interpret, or use psychological assessment techniques, interviews, tests, or instruments do so in a manner and for purposes that are appropriate *in light of the research on or evidence of the usefulness and proper application of the techniques.* (APA, 1992; italics added)

As has been mentioned, there is no research evidence suggesting that these tests actually serve the function of identifying competent and incompetent psychologists.

Because of the lack of important psychometric data, it could also be argued that state and national exams violate Principle 2.04b: "Psychologists recognize limits to the certainty with which diagnoses, judgments, or predictions can be made about individuals" (APA, 1992). We suggest that if the uncertainty and possible error inherent in current licensing examinations were actually recognized, then psychologists would not use these tests. Furthermore, Principle 2.04c states,

> Psychologists attempt to identify situations in which particular interventions or assessment techniques or norms may not be applicable or may require adjustment in administration or interpretation because of factors such as individual's gender, age, race, ethnicity, national origin, religion, sexual orientation, disability, language or socioeconomic status. (APA, 1992)

There is no evidence that this requirement is met either in the national or state exam, despite at least preliminary evidence that the national test may have a lower passing rate for minorities. For example, the test is given only in English, and no alteration in scoring is made for those whose first language is not English or for those who plan to practice using another language. Finally, Principle 2.05 states that "[Psychologists] indicate any significant reservations they have about the accuracy or limitations of their interpretations" (APA, 1992). Given missing validity data, it seems that ethical psychologists administering state tests or requiring the EPPP should have a lot to disclose in the informed consent process.

Potential Violations of the Standards of Psychological Testing

Beyond APA ethical code violations, licensing exams (both the EPPP and state) potentially violate numerous *Standards of Educational and Psychological Testing* (SEPT; APA, 1985). The following paragraphs will describe several of the more important of these violations as a function of various content domains. Many of these violations concern standards that SEPT regards as "primary," that is, that should be met by the test before the test's use.

The first area in which licensing tests are lacking is the publication of a manual. Standard 5.1 states, "A technical manual should be made available to prospective test users at the time the test is published or released for operational use" (APA, 1985, p. 35). The *Research Digest* (ASPPB, 1991) could be considered a manual because it describes pertinent research performed with the EPPP. However, no state licensing board was able to provide us with a manual for state licensing exams. Standard 5.2 states,

> Test manuals should describe thoroughly the rationale for the test, state the recommended uses of the test, and *provide a summary of the support for such uses.* Where particular misuses of a test can be reasonably anticipated, the test manual should provide specific cautions against such misuses. (APA, 1985, p. 36)

Because these tests are used to determine competence, there should be evidence that the scores can be interpreted in this way (APA, 1985, p. 36), but there is no such evidence.

In addition, concerning reliability, Standard 2.1, quoted as follows, is violated by both national and state exams:

> For each total score, subscore, or combination of scores that is reported, estimates of relevant reliabilities and standard errors of measurement should be provided in adequate detail to enable the test user to judge whether scores are sufficiently accurate for the intended use of the test. (APA, 1985, p. 20)

For instance, the EPPP reports only internal consistency measures with no data regarding test-retest stability (also in possible violation of Standard 2.6), and state exams have failed to produce any relevant data, particularly in the critical area of inter-rater reliability for oral exams (also a possible violation of Standard 2.8). Finally, Standard 2.12, concerning dichotomous decisions based on tests (in this case pass/fail), requires that "the percentage of test takers who are classified the same way on two separate occasions or on alternate forms of the test" be reported (APA, 1985, p. 23). Neither the EPPP nor the state tests report this kind of data.

The standards do not grant an exception for professional licensure examinations. They state, "Issues of validity that are discussed in other sections of the *Standards are also relevant to testing for licensure and certification*" (APA, 1985, p. 63, emphasis added). Despite this, validity standards are breached. Again, the first (and presumably the most important) standard in this section appears to be violated. Standard 1.1 states, "Evidence of validity should be presented for the major types of inferences for which the use of a test is recommended. A rationale should be provided to support the particular mix of evidence presented for the intended uses" (APA, 1985, p. 13). Evidence supporting criterion-related (particularly predictive), and incremental validity concerning educational requirements arguably would be necessary to support the inferences these tests are used to make (i.e., whether someone will be an incompetent psychologist and be a threat to public safety). Also, this lack of evidence supporting the accuracy of interpretations that are based on scores seemingly violates Standard 1.2. This standard states,

> If validity for some common interpretation has not been investigated, that fact should be made clear, and potential users should be cautioned about making such interpretations. Statements about validity should refer to the validity of particular interpretations or of particular types of decisions. (APA, 1985, p. 13)

To be clear, we propose that the "potential users" to be informed include state boards, who use the EPPP to make decisions concerning licensure. Presumably, they should understand the limitations of the test they are using to make decisions regarding a person's ability to practice psychology and earn a living. Test takers should also be informed of the limitations of the EPPP for making decisions. Although test takers have little say in the matter, if more individuals were aware of the limitations of the EPPP, a widespread demand for change (such as is provided in this paper) could be generated. Finally, the public should be informed that the test designed to protect their welfare is inadequate for meeting this goal.

Similarly, Standard 6.3 stipulates that the user is responsible for providing evidence of validity if a test is used for a purpose for which it has not been validated. Standards 1.8, 1.9, and 1.10 all make reference to issues associated with discriminant validity or the necessity of differentiating the construct purportedly measured by a test from other constructs (APA, 1985). As has been mentioned, no evidence is presently available concerning discriminant validity of either the EPPP or state licensing exams.

Historically, things seem to be even worse. Licensing exams were distributed for use before there were sufficient data to support their content validity. In fact, the ASPPB (1991) admits this when they state, "In 1978—13 years after Form 1 of the EPPP had been administered—AASPB commissioned PES (Professional Examination Services) to conduct the *first* systematic study of the appropriateness of the content and structure of the examination" (p. 15; italics added). This appears to be in violation of Standard 3.1, which states that "Test developers should compile the evidence bearing on a test, decide which information is needed *prior to test publication or distribution* and which evidence can be compiled later" (APA, 1985, p. 25; italics added).

The *Standards* also outline several specific guidelines for licensing and certification exams. In the comments following Standard 11.1, it is explained that "Skills that may be important to success but are not directly related to the purposes of licensure (i.e., protecting the public) should not be included in a licensing exam" (APA, 1985, p. 64). Again, it has not been established whether any of the knowledge assessed in licensing exams is actually predictive of whether a practitioner will harm the public. Because there is no evidence supporting the notion that test scores can be interpreted as a measure of the construct of "competence" (or potential incompetence), Standard 11.2 may also be violated. Thus, this raises the question of whether the EPPP is even content valid when the question concerns competence.

Next, some possible infractions regarding general principles of testing need to mentioned. First, here a quote from Chapter 6 of the *Standards*:

Although it is not appropriate to tell a test user that particular levels of practice validity and reliability need to be met, *it is appropriate to ask the user to ascertain that procedures result in adequately valid predictions or reliable classifications for the purposes of the testing.* Cost-benefit compromises become as necessary in test use as they do in test development. However, as with standards with test development, *when test standards are not met in test use, reasons should be available.* Here again, the criteria of impact on the test takers applies. *The greater the potential impact, the greater the need to satisfy relevant standards.* (APA, 1985, p. 41; italics added)

The key point here is that because there is no evidence that valid predictions can be made, one of the costs of licensing tests is that the impact on potential licensees can be enormous. Someone can be denied a license and the ability to earn a living in their chosen profession simply because they do not pass a test that has not shown to be valid for making the decisions it is being used to make. The ASPPB claims that the EPPP was never intended as the sole measure of the competence of entry-level practitioners and that it has never been used for this purpose (ASPPB, 1991, p. 9). This may be true in principle, but it is also true that if one does not pass this exam, this is a sufficient condition for denying someone a license.

Given what appear to be numerous ethical/testing violations associated with testing requirements for licensure, we again return to the possibility that testing requirements be eliminated at this point in time and this moratorium continue until any tests meet the minimal requirements for ethical use. Furthermore, this solution does not preclude the notion that psychometric evaluations could be conducted with these tests and that after they are found to be psychometrically adequate, they (or more likely revisions of these) could be reinstated as requirements.

Experience Requirements

Most states require that applicants for licensure in psychology have a certain amount of postdoctoral supervised clinical experience before they can be licensed. These requirements vary greatly from state to state. All the following information was obtained from the *Handbook of Licensing and Certification Requirements for Psychologists in North America* (ASPPB, 1997a). Four states (Indiana, Mississippi, North Dakota, and Vermont) simply require a doctoral degree in psychology. The other 46 states require varying degrees of experience and supervision beyond an internship. For instance, 7 states require 1 year of postdoctoral experience of anywhere between 1,500 to 1,900 hours. These states do not specify that this training must be supervised. Another group of about 16 states requires this 1-year postdoctoral experience to be supervised by a licensed psychologist. Another 9 states require 2 years of postdoctoral training (anywhere between 2,000 to 4,000 hours), most specifying that this must be supervised training. Finally, 12 states simply require a certain number of postdoctoral hours be completed (between 1,500 and 3,000), with most stipulating that at least some of this be supervised experience. In certain jurisdictions, this postdoctoral experience requirement must be satisfied within a specified time frame to be eligible for licensure (for example, 1,800 hours within a 2-year period).

States allowing master's level providers to work in some capacity often require constant supervision by a doctoral level licensed psychologist. Only the states of West Virginia, Oregon, and Vermont allow for the possibility of master's level providers to practice independently.

The issue of incremental validity discussed in the context of licensing examinations can also be applied to the issue of experience

Table 6.1 Responses to Questions Concerning Each State's Postdoctoral Experience Requirements ($N = 18$)

Content of Question	Reported No Data/ Didn't Know	Data/Information Provided
Evidence concerning the superiority of candidates who have met these requirements versus those who have not	18	0
How requirements were chosen (i.e., what evidence was considered in deciding on the content of the requirements?)	12	6*

NOTE: *But none provided evidence.

requirements. For instance, we wanted to know if there was any evidence that these requirements (i.e., over and above predoctoral clinical internships) actually improves the ability to predict competence (or incompetence) when compared with simply requiring a degree from an APA-approved institution. If these additional requirements were actually found to add to the ability to predict competence, then they could in principle be justified as necessary additional requirements (although even in this case, the cost-benefit ratio would need to be considered). This question was posed to the licensing boards of all 50 states as part of the previously mentioned questionnaire. Table 6.1 includes the results of the survey. Of the 18 replies we received, only 6 states were able to provide an explanation of how experience requirements were defined (most states claimed they were based on board discussion or APA guidelines). No state, however, was able to provide any evidence that these additional requirements improved the ability to predict competence or incompetence.

This lack of evidence for incremental validity makes it all the more surprising that

experience requirements are significant (taking 1 to 2 years of someone's life) and have gradually been increased over time (Stewart & Stewart, 1998). Overall, it seems that if licensing boards are making it increasingly more difficult and costly in terms of time and money to obtain a license, there should be some empirical evidence in terms of less harm to the public to justify this practice.

There are several reasons why extra experience requirements may not be predictive of competency. First, there may be a kind of ceiling effect, in that those candidates taking the EPPP that have completed predoctoral internships have already met minimal standards of competency, making additional experience unnecessary for achieving this goal. Second, some individuals may not obtain the proper type of postdoctoral experiences needed to increase competency, thereby making this extra experience useless for the purposes of licensure. The APA evaluates and approves predoctoral internship training, but there is no direct monitoring of the quality of the postdoctoral clinical experience.

Likewise, there seems to be the assumption that fulfilling all three types of licensing requirements is necessary to ensure competence and that achieving only one or two is simply insufficient. As has been mentioned, the incremental validity of each of these standards above and beyond passing the dual hurdles of having a degree from an APA-approved institution and passing an APA-approved internship has not been established. Moreover, incremental validity needs to be considered in all permutations of the three requirements: education, testing, and postdoctoral clinical experience. It is also possible that these are redundant in that some subset of these is sufficient to make the discrimination between competent and incompetent clinicians. Considering the time and expense needed to complete such an extensive array of requirements, the assumed benefits (i.e., protecting the public from incompetent clinicians) should be more firmly established.

Given this, there again seem to be several possible options for improving the situation. Our proposed solution seems to be at least one of several legitimate possibilities, mainly because doctoral students have already accumulated a great deal of clinical experience under the supervision of clinical faculty and internship supervisors prior to receiving a doctorate. These two groups of evaluators have access to large samples of criterion-relevant behavior and are usually independent, so errors will tend to cancel out. Also, additional postdoctoral experience requirements delay the student's entry into the field (and thereby the student's ability to earn a competitive wage), something that would not occur with our proposed solution.

COSTS OF LICENSING REQUIREMENTS

The costs of licensing exams include, first, costs to consumers in that when supply is reduced, then competition is reduced, and thereby prices are made higher. This particularly affects lower-income consumers who become increasingly disadvantaged as prices rise (Young, 1987). Second, licensing requirements also pose a financial, time, and emotional burden to those wishing to enter the profession of psychology. As has been mentioned, increases in experience requirements have resulted in untold amounts of lost income because applicants must wait to enter the field and must work for lower wages when completing supervised training after obtaining a degree. Furthermore, licensing tests themselves impose a large financial burden. For instance, it costs anywhere from $250 to $500 each time the applicant takes the EPPP (ASPPB, 1997). Oral exam fees can cost up to $200. There are also study materials offered that include items from previous exams ($75) and study courses offered that provide information about how to study and take the EPPP, which can cost between $500 and $1000. Apart from the financial burden of the licensing process is the amount of time candidates must spend studying for exams. There is also a good deal of stress experienced during these exams, particularly when individuals fail. Third, licensing board members spend a great deal of time and money developing, administering, and evaluating these tests and other requirements that have no demonstrated value.

RECOMMENDATIONS FOR CHANGE

Information has been presented in opposition of current licensing requirements, particularly testing and postdoctoral experience requirements. Given the lack of information that the costs of these requirements are offset by the benefits of protecting the public from incompetent psychologists, it appears as if changes in the current licensing system need to be made. As we have suggested throughout this chapter, there are several different possibilities, each with arguable advantages. It is our contention that among these possibilities is to eliminate testing and postdoctoral experience requirements until their incremental validity over educational requirements can be established. We are concerned that this possibility has not been given serious attention in the literature, and one purpose of this chapter is to argue why this possibility ought to be considered. These controversies concerning licensure and the EPPP are not new (Bernstein & Lecomte, 1981; Gross, 1978; Hogan, 1979; Wiens & Menne, 1981; Young, 1987). For instance, Bernstein and Lecomte (1981) discussed the importance of but lack of data concerning predictive validity and the absence of any consensus regarding minimal competence. However, it is also apparent that little (if anything) has been done in the past two decades to effectively respond to these criticisms. In fact, experience requirements have increased over time.

Therefore, we recommend that to practice psychology, one should have a doctorate in psychology (i.e., clinical, counseling, school, applied) from an APA-accredited institution. Some argue that the current licensure system primarily functions to reassure the public, not necessarily protect it (Rosen, 1986). However, we feel that meeting these educational requirements can serve the function of reassuring the public just as well as the current licensure system. The APA conducts comprehensive evaluations of psychology graduate programs with the explicit purpose of ensuring that graduates of these programs are competent. This includes evaluations of course curriculum, research produced by students, and many other aspects of training provided by the program. Furthermore, we believe that the best judges of the competence of an entry-level clinician are not licensing boards, but instead, psychology faculty and internship supervisors who have had extensive criterion-related observations of the individual over many years. For instance, some oral examinations attempt to verbally describe potential clinical situations and evaluate how a candidate performs. However, a clinical supervisor, as well as other clinical faculty, has likely observed the candidate in a far greater number of clinically relevant situations. Therefore, a large number of independent samples of clinically relevant behavior are obtained during graduate training. There is no reason to believe that licensing board members are more qualified judges of clinical competence, particularly in these analogue settings.

Moreover, a truly incompetent student would likely be identified by clinical faculty or internship faculty and would either obtain more supervised training or would not be allowed to graduate. In addition, graduate students take dozens of exams throughout their educational careers. It is difficult to believe that one more exam (i.e., for licensing) is needed to assure an adequate base of knowledge.

One potential criticism of our proposed solution is that we are being inconsistent. We insist the EPPP be abandoned because it does not meet the SEPT, but countenance the legitimacy of numerous course tests and therapy evaluations though these also do not meet SEPT essential psychometric criteria. We believe this criticism is not valid for two reasons: First, SEPT criteria do not apply to tests used to measure knowledge gained from a course. This may be a problem with the purview of the SEPT, but it is an institutional regulatory fact that these sorts of course exams are excluded from being bound by SEPT criteria. On the other hand, SEPT states explicitly that its criteria do apply to licensing examinations. Second, this point also ignores the psychometric point that multiple sources of independent information can cancel out error contained in any one source. Instead of relying on any one test to comprehensively measure minimal competence, the academic experience uses multiple written tests (e.g., across courses) and multiple behavior samples (e.g., across clients) across multiple domains (e.g., research, teaching therapy), across time (multiple years of graduate school), and very importantly, across evaluators. This produces a more representative sample of criterion-relevant behavior than any single test. Moreover, independence is also achieved in that the raters of the predoctoral internship experience are usually entirely independent for the academic faculty initially rating the candidate. Thus, any gross biases of the academic faculty ought to be caught by the internship faculty, if they are doing their jobs. Thus, our argument is that although no one academic evaluation meets SEPT criteria (and ethically they do not need to), the diversity and relevance of evaluation samples by multiple independent evaluators is superior to any single paper-and-pencil test.

Finally, putting the EPPP, postdoctoral experience, and state tests into the mix actually puts academic and internship faculty in a strange position: The faculty are not to finish training until minimal competence is achieved, but rather ought to stop at some ill-defined point at which postdoctoral supervised experience and studying for state and national exams allows the student to finally cross the minimal-competence threshold. It has been our experience that no faculty actually does this. Rather, they at least train to minimal competence. Thus, until incremental validity is shown by any such test, currently, academic/internship evaluations are the best we have to go on.

It may be argued by some that graduate programs actually may not prevent students who are considered incompetent from graduating, for a variety of reasons (e.g., fear of lawsuit, to reflect well on the program). Even if this is true in some cases, one question remains: "Does the EPPP help to identify and protect the public from these potentially incompetent candidates?" In other words, "Do they fail the exam?" If the EPPP is doing its proposed job, the answer should be "Yes." There are no data, however, indicating that this is the case.

REFERENCES

American Psychological Association. (1985). *Standards for educational and psychological testing.* Washington, DC: Author.

American Psychological Association. (1992). *Ethical principles of psychologists and code of conduct.* Washington, DC: Author.

American Psychological Association, Ethics Committee. (1996). Report of the ethics committee, 1995. *American Psychologist, 51,* 1279-1286.

Association of State and Provincial Psychology Boards. (1997a, January). *Handbook of licensing and certification requirements for psychologists in North America.* Montgomery, AL: Author.

Association of State and Provincial Psychology Boards. (1997b, May). *Information for candidates: Examination for professional practice in psychology.* Montgomery, AL: Author.

Association of State and Provincial Psychology Boards. (1991, August). *Research digest: The examination for professional practice in psychology.* Montgomery, AL: Author.

Bernstein, B. L., & Lecomte, C. (1981). Licensure in psychology: Alternative directions. *Professional Psychology, 12,* 200-208.

Campbell, D. T., & Fiske, D. W. (1959). Convergent and discriminant validation by the multitrait-multimethod matrix. *Psychological Bulletin, 56,* 81-105.

Chambless, D. L., Babich, K., Crits-Christoph, P., Frank, E., Gilson, M., Montgomery, R., Rich, R., Steinberg, J., & Weinberger, J. (1995). Training in and dissemination of empirically validated psychological treatments: Report and recommendations. *The Clinical Psychologist, 48,* 3-23.

Chambless, D. L., Baker, M. J., Baucom, D. H., Beutler, L. E., Calhoun, K. S., Crits-Christoph, P., Daiuto, A., DeRubeis, R., Detweiler, J., Haaga, D. A. F., Johnson, S. B., McCurry, S., Mueser, K. T., Pope, K. S., Sanderson, W. C., Shoham, V., Stickle, T., Williams, & Woody, S. (1998). Update on empirically validated therapies II. *The Clinical Psychologist, 51,* 3-16.

Cortina, J. M. (1993). What is coefficient alpha? An examination of theory and applications. *Journal of Applied Psychology, 78,* 98-104.

Friedman, M. (1962). *Capitalism and freedom.* Chicago: University of Chicago Press.

Gross, S. J. (1978). The myth of professional licensing. *American Psychologist, 33,* 1009-1016.

Hogan, D. B. (1979). *The regulation of psychotherapists: Vol. I. A study in the philosophy and practice of professional regulation.* Cambridge, MA: Ballinger.

Hogan, D. B. (1983). The effectiveness of licensing: History, evidence, and recommendations. *Law and Human Behavior, 7,* 117-138.

Howell, W. C. (1986). Industrial/organizational psychology issues on credentialing: Licensure and state board relations. *Professional Practice of Psychology, 7,* 37-48.

Kane, M. T. (1985). Validating licensure examinations. *Professional Practice of Psychology, 6,* 206-218.

Kane, M. T. (1986). The future of testing for licensure and certification examinations. In B. S. Plake & J. C. Witt (Eds.), *Buros-Nebraska symposium on measurement and testing: Vol. 2. The future of testing.* Hillsdale, NJ: Lawrence Erlbaum.

Lecomte, C. (1986). Licensing. In G. S. Tryon (Ed.), *The professional practice of psychology.* Norwood, NJ: Ablex.

McGaghie, W. C. (1980). The evaluation of competence: Validity issues in the health professions. *Evaluation & the Health Professions, 3,* 289-320.

Rosen, G. A. (1986). A perspective on predictive validity and licensure examinations. *Professional Practice of Psychology, 7,* 116-123.

Shimberg, B. (1981). Testing for licensure and certification. *American Psychologist, 36,* 1138-1146.

Stewart, A. E., & Stewart, E. A. (1998). Trends in postdoctoral education: Requirements for licensure and training opportunities. *Professional psychology: Research and Practice, 29,* 273-283.

U.S. Department of Health, Education, and Welfare. Public Health Services. (1977, July). *Credentially health manpower* (DHFW Publication No. 77-50057). Washington, DC: Author.

Wiens, A. N., & Menne, J. W. (1981). On disposing of "straw people": Or an attempt to clarify statutory recognition and educational requirements for psychologists. *American Psychologist, 36,* 390-395.

Young, S. D. (1987). *The rule of experts.* Washington, DC: Cato Institute.

CHAPTER 7

Institutional Review Boards
Balancing Conflicting Values in Research

GREGORY J. HAYES
University of Nevada

Institutional Review Boards (IRBs), those bodies of people charged with protecting human subjects in research settings, go by many names (Human Subjects Review Committee, for example) and can be ubiquitously found in both academic and nonacademic settings. Within our society, a strongly held view has emerged in the decades since World War II, especially since the highly questionable practices of the Tuskegee syphilis experiments came to light, that proposed research must be carefully evaluated by knowledgeable persons not otherwise involved. Proposal review by such persons helps to assure that this research is done in an ethical and responsible manner, especially as regards risk to subjects (risks to animals are also scrutinized by similar committees, but this chapter concentrates on human subjects research). By whatever name they are known, most researchers have experienced the work of an IRB. And at least 1 in 5 psychologists engaged in research involving human subjects are able to detail one or more seemingly unnecessarily frustrating experiences with their review boards (Hayes, Hayes, & Grundt, 2002). To assist in making the research proposal review process run more smoothly, researchers would do well to gain a greater understanding of and insight into why and how IRBs came to be, the purpose and scope of IRB work, the key characteristics, policies, and procedures of such bodies, the types of problems arising from the IRB-researcher interaction, and some of the strategies for improving IRB function and the relationship between IRBs and researchers.

THE ORIGINS OF IRBS

In a general sense, we know that behavioral science researchers have not always adequately considered the risks assumed by human beings participating in research. A few famous examples are often cited: In the

Milgram obedience study, subjects used what they thought were shocks of increasing voltage on a second "subject" (actually part of the research team), who had also indicated possible underlying heart problems (Milgram, 1964); and in the Zimbardo jail study, actual injury to subjects occurred (Zimbardo, 1981). But the origins of our national effort to protect human subjects comes primarily from problems in biomedical research and from the changing set of societal values regarding those who participate in research.

Careful consideration of risks to human subjects is a fairly new phenomenon. In the decades (and even centuries) prior to World War II, the prevailing view was that researchers had the interests of humanity at the core of their work. They were, it was felt, working for the good of others and had to do what they had to do to gain essential new knowledge. Few philosophers and ethicists, let alone researchers, gave much thought to the risks individuals faced while participating in research. Society and the scientific community simply trusted in the good intentions of those engaged in research. The revelations about World War II research, in Germany primarily but also in the United States, shook this faith forever.

There is no doubt that the atrocities of German medical research took center stage as the postwar Nuremberg trials detailed. The resulting Nuremberg Code described a number of key elements necessary for ethical research involving human beings. For example, it required that "The experiment should be such as to yield fruitful results for the good of society, unprocurable by other methods or means of study" and that "The experiment should be so conducted as to avoid all unnecessary physical and mental suffering and injury." In addition, "The degree of risk to be taken should never exceed that determined by the humanitarian importance of the problem to be solved." The first of the 10 principles of the Nuremberg Code was (and is) the most important: "The voluntary consent of the human subject is absolutely essential" ("Permissible Medical Experiments," n.d., p. 181).

The notion of voluntary consent was the biggest change in public and professional perception, a new value not previously acknowledged. Prior to this time, the need for choice among human subjects was generally not recognized as an important principle in research. Human subjects were viewed in an often utilitarian context that allowed for subtle and not-so-subtle arguments that the end justified the means. The researcher made this determination, and the subjects involved—often drawn from the poor, prison populations, or the chronically, mentally, or terminally ill—were simply expected to bend over and take their medicine for the good of humankind. The Nuremberg Code marked the first time the issue of voluntary consent was brought to the fore.

Interestingly, as dramatic and gripping as the Nuremberg trials were on the public's consciousness, the code had little immediate impact on research practices. But the ball had begun to roll. Coupled with this new input was the less publicly discussed realization that American World War II research had also ignored issues of voluntary consent, for example, by using nonconsenting orphaned children, retarded and mentally ill persons, and nonconsenting and deceived enlisted men in a variety of war-related experiments. Such experiments were undertaken under the assumption that everyone must contribute to the war effort (Vanderpool, 1996). Voluntary consent was not at issue.

Slowly, the wheels turned. Beecher (1966), a noted Harvard professor, shocked the research community with a careful analysis of 100 consecutive human studies published in 1964 in a top-tier medical journal, which revealed 12 of these studies as having been performed unethically. This landmark article underlined just how common unethical behavior (whether intentional or not) appeared to be. A careful look revealed that much of this unethical behavior revolved around the lack of consent and serious risks to the subject's well-being.

In the same year as Beecher's revelations, the U.S. Public Health Service began a policy of peer review of research proposals using federal dollars (Curran, 1970). Soon thereafter, an exposé of the decades-old and soon-to-be-infamous Tuskegee syphilis experiment (in which hundreds of poor black men were denied the benefits of the newly available penicillin so that the full, natural course of syphilis could be studied) underlined the need for such review (Tuskegee Syphilis Ad Hoc Advisory Panel, 1973). By 1974, this initial effort had evolved in a codified set of guidelines and procedures (known in common parlance as "45 CFR 46" and subsequently modified several times) that guide IRB action to this day (Code of Federal Regulations, 1991).

An important additional shift in values also occurred in the several decades it took for the wisdom of Nuremberg to take hold. The Nuremberg Code spoke of voluntary consent. As the years passed, it appeared to those who continued to ponder the principles laid down at Nuremberg that voluntariness was only one element of the consent equation. The second element was the new idea that consent must also be *informed*.

Many people are taken aback when they realize just how new the concept of informed consent really is. One of the earliest acknowledgments of its importance came in the form of an appeals court decision known as *Canterbury v. Spence* (1972). This case dealt with a problem occurring between a physician and a patient in a clinical setting. The court set the stage for what physicians, psychologists, and other health professionals have struggled with ever since, in both the clinical arena and research, by stating that there is a "duty to disclose all options and risks that a reasonable person would need to make an informed choice" (*Canterbury v. Spence,* 1972, p. 72). Although we continue to debate just how much information a "reasonable person" would require to give his or her informed consent, the shift in values from World War II to the present is striking. Simply stated, the prior view strongly came down on the side of the quest for new scientific knowledge. With the exposure of abuses stemming from this quest for knowledge—a quest that sometimes seemed to proceed at almost any cost—came the notion of voluntary consent. The pendulum this shift set in motion continued to swing, producing in the 1970s the more mature notion of informed consent. Since that time, IRBs and others have continued to refine what is meant by informed consent as well as how the other principles of the Nuremberg Code and several subsequent international codes regarding research ethics should be applied. This new prioritization of values has produced a heavy emphasis on the protection of the human subject in research. To many researchers the pendulum has, in fact, swung too far. The call is now to find middle ground that simultaneously honors both the values of new scientific knowledge and the protection of human beings involved in research. The IRB is center stage in seeking this more balanced approach.

THE PURPOSE AND SCOPE OF IRB FUNCTION

Nearly all human research in the United States and many other countries passes through the human subject review process. The general notion of the purpose of an

IRB is to protect the human subject from unnecessary risks and other burdens occurring in the pursuit of knowledge. This, in fact, is not precisely right. Although the need for IRBs arose with the exposure of research excesses that sometimes harmed or even led to the death of research subjects, the purpose of IRBs goes beyond the protection of these individuals. A very important body in the evolution of research ethics, The National Commission for the Protection of Human Subjects of Biomedical and Behavioral Research (1978), wrote soon after 45 CFR 46 came into effect,

> The ethical conduct of research involving human subjects requires a balancing of society's interests in protecting the rights of subjects and in developing knowledge that can benefit the subjects or society as a whole. . . . Investigators should not have sole responsibility for determining whether research involving human subjects fulfills ethical standards. Others who are independent of the research must share this responsibility, because investigators are always in positions of potential conflict by virtue of their concern with the pursuit of knowledge as well as the welfare of the human subjects in their research. (p. 1)

The commission's statement underlines the requirement that IRBs seek out an appropriate balance between the sometimes conflicting values of new scientific knowledge and the protection of human research subjects. In addition, the commission expands on the purpose and scope of IRB practice by stating,

> The rights of subjects should be protected by local review committees operating pursuant to Federal regulations and located in institutions where research involving human subjects in conducted. Compared to the possible alternatives of a regional or national review process, local committees have the advantage of greater familiarity with the actual conditions surrounding the conduct of research. Such committees can work closely with investigators to assure that the rights and welfare of human subjects are protected and, at the same time, that the application of policies is fair to the investigators. They can contribute to the education of the research community and the public regarding the ethical conduct of research. The committees can become resource centers for information concerning the ethical standards and Federal requirements and can communicate with Federal officials and other local committees about matters of common concern. (National Commission for the Protection of Human Subjects of Biomedical and Behavioral Research, 1978, p. 2)

Many IRBs have, at least in the eyes of researchers, sometimes overly emphasized the protection of human subjects rather than keeping the ideal of a balance between knowledge and protection at the forefront of their thinking. In addition, too few IRBs have done a sufficient job of educating researchers and the general public about the ethically appropriate research. Too often, research has shown that the human subjects review process is viewed by researchers as a black box, a mysterious, if well-intentioned, gauntlet to be run (Hayes et al., 2002).

IRB CHARACTERISTICS, POLICIES, AND PROCEDURES

One of the ways we can better understand IRBs and help them evolve into entities that are willing and able to assist researchers in finding the appropriate balance between conflicting values is to dissect these boards as to their key characteristics, including relevant policies and procedures. The first such attempt to do so in the United States surveyed IRBs at 172 Category I institutions, Category I being a designation of the American Association of University Professors that captures all the leading research universities (Hayes, Hayes, & Dykstra, 1995). This attempt to better understand IRBs looked at social/behavioral committees, biomedical committees, and some that handled all types of human subjects research. It is worthwhile to summarize a number of key results from this study and briefly discuss them here.

Composition of the Board. As with most committees at universities and other institutions, there is a certain amount of randomness as to who becomes a member of the group. General notices regarding committee openings were the most common means of finding interested persons. Appointments were generally made outside the IRB by a vice president for research or equivalent person. The groups tended to mirror the composition of the universities in general: 66% of IRBs members at surveyed institutions were male, and 90% were white/non-Hispanic. Some boards were more than 90% male. Policies regarding composition usually included mandates from the federal code (for example, 97% required a community representative, and 81% required gender diversity). However, only 56% of board specifically required active researchers on the board, while 76% required a nonresearcher member—both also federal mandates (Hayes et al., 1995).

Training and Tenure. Once individuals were found who were interested in serving, few boards (28%) had specific guidelines regarding the maximum length of time a person could serve. Fifteen percent of board members had served 6 years or more. As for training, few institutions offered more than a smattering of education: 25% provided less than one hour of training (usually nothing more than an overview of federal codes); 84% provided less than 4 hours of education (Hayes et al., 1995).

Researcher Anonymity and the Review Process. With rare exception (2%), members of the IRB knew the researchers submitting the proposals. In addition, most boards vote by hand or voice vote—secret ballots are rarely used (3%). Most boards appear to interpret their mandates as very broad: Fifty-one percent indicated they would evaluate the adequacy of a proposal's research design above and beyond any human subjects concerns (Hayes et al., 1995).

Complaints and Evaluations. The majority of the time (54%), complaints regarding the IRB review process were handled by the IRB itself, and only on appeal were individuals outside the IRB used. The remainder of IRBs directed complaints immediately to an outside administrator or separate review committee. Twenty-four percent said they did not have formal appeals process experience (although it should be noted that some experienced IRBs indicated that there had never been a demand for such a process). Of importance, only 44% of boards said they were ever evaluated, and about 10% of this group indicated that evaluations done were, in fact, self-evaluations (Hayes et al., 1995).

There are several issues of concern related to the above information. The fact that boards tend to be very white and male is understandable, because this reflects demographics among faculty. However, an IRB in a given area is supposed to reflect the community's values as well as adhering to the requirements in the federal code. To accomplish this, more IRBs should have explicit policies regarding the demographics of their memberships and how a better balance can be obtained. In addition, simply choosing people who are interested in serving on the IRB is probably not the most effective way to assure that the right people reach the board. Besides demographic considerations, members of these important committees should be able to work effectively as a group. To do so, they must avoid personality types that tend toward the authoritarian, those who are not able to tolerate ambiguity, those who harbor excessive prejudices, and those who are dogmatic in their dealings with others. This is one institutional committee in which taking the time to do psychological profiles on potential members would yield dividends. Certainly, there are plenty of useful instruments to address the above concerns and others as well (Robinson, 1973).

Another genuine concern is the number of IRBs that are not systematically evaluated by some impartial outside group or person. Especially with a large percentage of committees allowing membership of unlimited duration, it is crucial to assure that the group has not drifted from its tasks, as research indicates can indeed happen (Kazdin, 1977). The general lack of training merely adds to these concerns—especially training regarding how small-group decision-making processes work.

Yet another concern—created by little screening of potential committee members, little training in small-group dynamics, often unlimited membership duration, nonsecret voting on research proposals, and often no outside evaluation—is the interesting phenomenon of "groupthink." Dominant or authoritarian members can over time help fashion a group that operates as if it were a single individual. Under the influence of this member or members—especially someone with a hidden agenda or underlying prejudice—the group's decisions can move disastrously off course (Janis, 1983).

THE INTERACTION OF IRB AND RESEARCHER

The evidence says that the interaction of IRB and researcher usually goes smoothly, but not always. As noted earlier, at least 1 in 5

psychologists have had what they would describe as unnecessarily negative experiences with their IRBs. One useful starting point in considering the give-and-take between researcher and IRB is to review the criteria for IRB approval of research as set down in the 1991 revision of the federal code:

(a) In order to approve research covered by this policy [45 CFR 46] the IRB shall determine that all of the following requirements are satisfied:

(1) Risks to subjects are minimized: (i) by using procedures which are consistent with sound research design and which do not unnecessarily expose subjects to risk, and (ii) whenever appropriate, by using procedures already being performed on the subjects for diagnostic and treatment purposes.

(2) Risks to subjects are reasonable in relation to anticipated benefits, if any, to subjects, and the importance of the knowledge that may reasonably be expected to result. In evaluating risks and benefits, the IRB should consider only those risks and benefits that may result from the research (as distinguished from risks and benefits of therapies subjects would receive even if not participating in the research). The IRB should not consider possible long-range effects of applying knowledge gained in the research (for example, the possible effects of the research on public policy) as among those research risks that fall within the purview of its responsibility.

(3) Selection of subjects is equitable. In making this assessment the IRB should take into account the purposes of the research and the setting in which the research will be conducted and should be particularly cognizant of the special problems of research involving vulnerable populations, such as children, prisoners, pregnant women, mentally disabled persons, or economically or educationally disadvantaged persons.

(4) Informed consent will be sought from each prospective subject or the subject's legally authorized representative, in accordance with, and to the extent required in 45 CFR 46.116 [the requirements for

informed consent are substantially detailed in this later section].

(5) Informed consent will be appropriately documented in accordance with 45 CFR 46.117 [the requirements for documentation of informed consent are substantially detailed in this later section].

(6) When appropriate, the research plan makes adequate provision for monitoring the data collected to ensure the safety of subjects.

(7) When appropriate, there are adequate provisions to protect the privacy of subjects and to maintain the confidentiality of data.

(b) When some or all of the subjects are likely to be vulnerable to coercion or undue influence, such as children, prisoners, pregnant women, mentally disabled persons, or economically or educationally disadvantaged persons, additional safeguards have been included in the study to protect the rights and welfare of these subjects. (Code of Federal Regulations, 1991)

The above criteria seem surprisingly straightforward. And indeed they generally are. One survey showed that more than 92% of proposals submitted from psychologists were approved without problem—a process that includes reasonable and understandable revisions (Hayes et al., 2002). But obviously the devil is in the details. The requirements for informed consent, for example, continue on for several more pages, and the call for added scrutiny when vulnerable populations are involved probably helps explain why 7.8% of proposals submitted by psychology faculty were considered to be "problem proposals" by these researchers (Hayes et al., 2002). Problem proposals were, in the researchers' view, those for which unnecessary or inexplicable changes were required, for which the IRB in one way or another seemed to overstep its charge or to bury the researcher in nonproductive busywork (Hayes et al., 2002). When such changes overly compromised the scientific integrity of the proposed work, researchers were disinclined to resubmit their proposals. When the impact on the scientific quality of the work was minimal, most researchers resubmitted and tended to be successful in their efforts, but felt that the only real change in doing so was to add time and effort to their workload while doing little to increase the protection of human subjects. Those with such experiences under their belts had become, to some degree, distrustful of their human subjects' review boards and felt that significant changes to IRB structure and function were in order (Hayes et al., 2002).

These problem proposals were most likely to involve informed consent issues (56%), risk to subjects (43%), vulnerable populations (31%), confidentiality (24%), and methodological concerns (17%) (Hayes et al., 2002). Structured interviews with more than 80 survey respondents revealed a great deal of frustration. This frustration with required changes, which in the researchers' view did little to add protection to the subjects of research, revealed a litany of concerns: a lack of appropriate knowledge among board members, inconsistent standards, an emphasis on legalities and protecting the university, a police mentality that often assumed researchers intended to do wrong, bureaucratic delays and busywork, and poor communication (Hayes et al., 2002).

Federal scrutiny of the IRB process has increased of late as well. Testimony before the Subcommittee on Human Resources of the House Committee of Government Reform and Oversight details a list of concerns directed at what was referred to as a "system in jeopardy" (Subcommittee on Human Resources, 1999). In addition, the shutdown of federally funded research at several top-tier research universities in 1999 has merely served to underline governmental concern that IRBs are not yet functioning as they should.

The Office of the Inspector General's (OIG) report before the Subcommittee on Human Resources (1999) noted that in her (the Inspector General's) view, "IRBs review too much, too quickly, with too little expertise" (p. 18). Most university IRBs show substantial increases in workload. Some receive as many as 2,000 proposals annually. Both large and small IRBs are suffering under the load, which in the OIG's opinion threatens the adequacy of the review of proposals. The OIG report also noted that "In some IRBs, unless the assigned reviewer raises a question or concern about the research, the board engages in little or no discussion" (p. 19). Some committees have sought to increase the amount of time they meet—a difficult proposition given the volunteer nature of the endeavor—but most have struggled to "squeeze more reviews into a fixed block of time" (p. 19). Furthermore, the OIG report indicated that "Science is becoming increasingly complex and many IRBs find that they lack sufficient scientific expertise on their boards or staff to adequately assess protocols" (p. 19). This is a more prevalent problem on biomedical IRBs, but psychologists also point to their frustrations with social/behavioral boards that critique methodology when, in fact, no one on the board is familiar with it (Hayes et al., 2002).

An additional concern in the OIG report is that IRB members and researchers alike receive little or no training regarding the complicated ethical concerns and other scientific questions that can arise during proposal review. Consistent with previous findings, the OIG's report noted that "For new IRB members, their orientation to their role is seldom much more than a stack of materials to read and on-the-job training" (Subcommittee on Human Resources, 1999, p. 23). Furthermore, the OIG report argues a controversial and much debated point that IRBs need to do more than review what *should* be

happening and should actually monitor what *is* happening in the research setting (p. 25). Experts testifying at this same hearing took exception to this comment on monitoring. While allowing for possible review in the field in the extreme case, Robert Levine, longtime chair of Yale's biomedical IRB and editor of the leading journal on human subjects research, stated clearly that "IRBs are not policing bodies, watchdogs, or auditing agents" (p. 99).

Dr. Levine also took exception to the tone of the OIG report, which viewed the IRB network as a "system in jeopardy." In fact, he noted, despite its shortcomings, the IRB system does work. He observed, for example, that the OIG report "acknowledges that the study yielded no evidence of harm or abuse" to research subjects (Subcommittee on Human Resources, 1999, p. 100).

RESOLVING THE ISSUES: POSSIBLE SOLUTIONS

The IRB system is with us, and although it may be reformed, it will not go away. Nor should it. Those that have involved themselves in the ethics of human subjects research are generally pleased with the more than quarter-century history of the IRB. As Jonathan Moreno, Director of the Center for Biomedical Ethics at the University of Virginia, pointed out at the hearings previously described, "The current system has worked reasonably well, though some important improvements should be made" (Subcommittee on Human Resources, 1999, p. 117). The data certainly support the view that human subject protection has greatly increased. How, then, to improve the system?

"The single most important factor that contributes to the successful functioning of the IRB is its credibility within the institution that it serves and within the community that its institution serves" (Levine, 1986, p. 341). IRB members must be clear that they represent the institution and the researchers within that institution. They are not an arm of the federal government. They are not a deputy sheriff of a regulatory agency, as Huff (1979) described. They should not, in the view of most IRB experts, do as the OIG report suggests by moving aggressively into on-site monitoring of how research is actually performed. To do so would merely diminish the trust between researcher and IRB, and the ability of the IRB to function successfully would decrease.

The notion of trust is the most important element in establishing the credibility of the IRB. Trust promotes a cordial, cooperative, collegial, productive relationship. This is not to advocate some sort of "good ol' boys" network or a philosophy of "You scratch my back, I'll scratch yours," which some people feel is the inevitable result of friendly relationships between researchers and those who monitor them. Using a slippery-slope analogy, they feel that friendly leads to "too friendly" and objectivity is ultimately lost. It need not be so.

Too many researchers describe their relationships with their IRBs as adversarial—and trust among adversaries is difficult, if not possible. Even the skeptical individuals in the OIG are clear that IRBs need to "work closely and collaboratively with researchers" (Subcommittee on Human Resources, 1999, p. 14). An adversarial relationship is self-defeating, promoting attempts among researchers to circumvent the board's seemingly unfair practices. The credibility of an IRB and the protection of human subjects is not served by researchers clandestinely working without approval or playing the game of describing what the board wants to hear and then executing the project as they had originally intended. An IRB needs to be viewed as a helpful body that can help researchers improve their research proposals so that the benefits are maximized while the risks to subjects are minimized. It can be done. More innovative IRBs, lead by dynamic and proactive chairs, have shown that finding more collegial ways to work with and educate researchers about the important issues in human subjects research can eliminate most problems before they arise and serve to quickly mitigate problems when they do occur (Hayes et al., 2002).

Most researchers *want* to do what is appropriate and right for their research subjects. IRB members should believe in the integrity of researchers at their institutions. When potential problems are found in research proposals, such errors almost always occur out of a lack of understanding or sensitivity to the issues at hand. Researchers mean well, and those who serve on IRBs should believe so until proven otherwise. Better education, collaboration, and a trusting relationship are the keys to solving such problems. There are resources available to help IRB members become better informed about complex research ethics issues and to then take this increased understanding out to the various departments who bring research before the board. As Dr. Levine noted in his testimony before the Subcommittee on Human Resources (1999),

> Another activity that is absolutely key is education and training for both investigators and IRB members, something the [Inspector General's] report emphasizes, and something that the IRBs themselves welcome. Many institutions have made impressive efforts at providing outreach to patient groups, developing mechanisms for educating patients about research protocols, and developing formalized orientation programs for new IRB members. PRIM&R [a national IRB organization, Public Responsibility in Research and Medicine] is also conducting these activities on a national level. . . . PRIM&R will also sponsor an

"IRB Training Institute" which will take a curriculum for new IRB members and administrators "on the road," if you will, making this kind of training—which will be lead by nationally recognized experts— accessible to institutions all around the country. (pp. 102-103)

Although there is hope on the horizon, it should also be pointed out that, despite Dr. Levine's enthusiastic description, such training for IRB members and researchers is still the exception, not the norm. Resources are lacking at many institutions. But new federal pressures along with national efforts by PRIM&R and others will ideally stimulate institutional administrations to see the benefit of preventing problems before they occur or nipping potential problems in the bud by (a) increasing understanding of the ethical issues in human subjects research among both IRB members and researchers and (b) increasing the dialogue between these two groups. It will be money well spent: In situations in which the working relationship between IRB and researcher improved and it became cooperative and collegial, human subjects problems correspondingly diminished (Hayes et al., 2002).

Better understanding of the issues will also help address a second major stumbling block. Too often, researchers report problems, at least at some institutions, with what they view as the inconsistent application of standards. The comment is heard: "An almost identical proposal sailed right through last time, now this time there are all sorts of problems cropping up." When projects involve several universities, this type of inconsistency can be dramatically outlined. "The proposal was alright at three other respected institutions, why isn't it okay at mine?" Whatever the explanation, perceived inconsistency negatively reflects on the reputation of the IRB and decreases researcher willingness to cooperate. The pathway through the IRB process becomes confused and suspect—a crapshoot, at best, to be circumvented if possible. This circumstance in no way helps the protection of human subjects. If anything, it works against such protection as researchers move into the "game mode" to deal with this inexplicable barrier. Most essential to solving this sort of problem is better communication. The very best strategy, once IRBs are sufficiently well educated on matters of research ethics, is to *proactively* take the important messages of the board—who they are, what they do, what the important issues are—to each department or other unit bringing proposals before the board. Engaging active researchers and enlightening them about the hows and whys of getting the job done can go a long way toward moving the relationship between researcher and IRB in a positive direction.

The IRB process need not be an inexplicable black box producing inconsistent results. There is no reason why the process cannot be open and cooperative. Particularly helpful in this regard are model proposals and informed consent documents to guide the researcher. These should be discussed with each department so that written documents are put to work in thoughtful and appropriate ways and not just reduced to boilerplate language to be mindlessly copied. Once researchers are clear on the issues and the practical how-to ways to get the work done correctly, they can avoid most errors from the outset. Given a good working relationship, additional errors or problems can often be quickly addressed.

Though some institutional administrators may feel differently, IRBs do not exist to protect the institution from legal entanglements. IRBs are charged with addressing the *ethical* issues involved in human subjects research. They must consider the important ethical principles underlying research: respect for persons, subject autonomy, justice, and the interplay between beneficence ("to be of benefit") and nonmaleficence ("to do no harm"). They must, in the context of this ethical analysis, hold these principles to the fore and try to strike a balance, as we have previously acknowledged, between the competing values of new scientific knowledge and the protection of research subjects. This balancing act has nothing directly to do with legalities. History has underlined the fact that what is ethical and what is legal may not necessarily be the same (the legality of slavery is one striking example in our history, as is the exclusion of women from voting). IRBs must take a stand on what is ethically appropriate given the careful analysis of what is morally acceptable behavior within the context of a research project. Legalities, though of practical importance, should not rule the day.

In addition, to promote a better working relationship between themselves and researchers, IRBs should do all they can to minimize the red tape and mindless bureaucratic paperwork that can dominate this interaction. If federal rules seem to be at issue, IRB chairs and administrators should take a stand for simplifying paperwork whenever appropriate so that more researchers are happy with the process and more IRB time can be spent on the sometimes truly difficult ethical issues arising out of certain research proposals. Seemingly endless delays and unnecessary paperwork merely lower IRB credibility and increase the desire among researchers to find a way around the roadblock. This should not be an us-versus-them relationship. If both groups can learn to understand the issues and to work together to address them, the dual values of knowledge and subject protection can both be honored.

If your institutional IRB is not yet addressing its relationship with researchers in such a positive way, consider advocating for change. Consider being part of the IRB; discussing more innovative strategies to improve the IRB-researcher relationship with the appropriate administrators; encouraging your institution to make educational materials available to IRB members and researchers to help them unravel the practical problems that can arise when writing a proposal or informed consent document; consider encouraging your institution to bring in expert training help through organizations such PRIM&R (prmr@aol.com). Working together, we can assure that the IRB process will serve all of us well.

REFERENCES

Beecher, H. K. (1966). Ethics and clinical research. *New England Journal of Medicine, 274,* 1354-1360.

Canterbury v. Spence, 464 F. Rep.2nd 72 (CA, DC) (U.S. Ct. App. 1972).

Code of Federal Regulations. (1991). *Title 45, Public Welfare; Part 46, Protection of Human Subjects.* Washington, DC: Government Printing Office.

Curran, W. J. (1970). Government regulation of the use of human subjects in medical research: The approaches of two federal agencies. In P. A. Freund (Ed.), *Experimentation with human subjects* (pp. 402-454). New York: Braziller.

Hayes, G. J., Hayes, S. C., & Dykstra, T. (1995). A survey of university institutional review boards: Characteristics, policies and procedures. *IRB: A Review of Human Subjects Research, 17*(3), 1-6.

Hayes, G. J., Hayes, S. C., & Grundt, A. (2002). *The trouble with IRBs: Researcher perspectives on problems with the human subjects review process.* Manuscript submitted for publication.

Huff, T. A. (1979). The IRB as deputy sheriff: Proposed FDA regulation of the institutional review board. *Clinical Research, 27,* 103-108.

Janis, I. L. (1983). *Groupthink: Psychological studies of policy decisions and fiascoes.* Boston: Houghton Mifflin.

Kazdin, A. E. (1977). Artifact, bias, and complexity of assessment: The ABCs of reliability. *Journal of Applied Behavioral Analysis, 10,* 141-150.

Levine, R. J. (1986). *Ethics and regulation of clinical research* (2nd ed.). Baltimore, MD: Urban & Schwarzenberg.

Milgram, S. (1964). Issues in the study of obedience: A reply to Baumrind. *American Psychologist, 19,* 848-852.

National Commission for the Protection of Human Subjects of Biomedical and Behavioral Research. (1978). *Institutional review boards: Report and recommendations.* Washington, DC: U.S. Government Printing Office.

Permissible medical experiments. (n.d.). In *Trials of war criminals before the Nuremberg military tribunals under control council law no. 16: Nuremberg, October 1946-April 1949* (Vol. 2, pp. 181-182). Washington, DC: U.S. Government Printing Office.

Robinson, J., & Saver, P. (1973). *Measures of social psychological attitudes.* Ann Arbor, MI: Institute for Social Research.

Subcommittee on Human Resources. (1999). *Hearing before the Subcommittee on Human Resources of the Committee on Government Reform and Oversight, House of Representatives, 105th Congress, June, 11, 1998.* Washington, DC: U.S. Government Printing Office.

Tuskegee Syphilis Ad Hoc Advisory Panel. (1973). *Final report of the Tuskegee syphilis ad hoc advisory panel, Department of Health, Education, and Welfare.* Washington, DC: U.S. Government Printing Office.

Vanderpool, H. Y. (1996). Introduction and overview: Ethics, historical case studies, and the research enterprise. In H. Y. Vanderpool (Ed.), *The ethics of research involving human subjects: Facing the 21st century.* Frederick, MD: University Publishing.

Zimbardo, P. G. (1981). The ethics of introducing paranoia in an experimental setting. *IRB: A Review of Human Subjects Research, 3*(10), 10-11.

Part III

SPECIAL TOPICS

CHAPTER 8

Ethics and the Allocation of Healthcare

Nicholas A. Cummings

The industrialization of healthcare since 1985 has solved a number of problems, mostly economic, but it has left in its wake vexing issues that are of paramount importance to practitioners whose practices have been decimated. Incomes of psychotherapists and other behavioral health specialists have diminished considerably since the halcyon days of the cottage industry, and practitioner reaction has reached the boiling point (Holstein, 1995; Shore, 1995). Mental health professionals would prefer to couch these issues in ethical terms aimed at embarrassing managed care, while invoking lofty ethical motives of patient welfare, thus often disguising self-interest. This is reminiscent of the struggle to obtain statutory licensure decades ago. The issue was always presented to state legislative bodies as one of protecting the public from the untrained, whereas in private, the issue was unabashedly one of protecting practice and reducing competition from the unlicensed.

This chapter will endeavor to separate issues that are clearly not matters of ethics from those that are; it will further delineate the differences among ethics, professional morality, and common sense, all of which have been homogenized into our current legalistic system, which is both brittle and outmoded. Our current system is overly detailed, yet it leaves enormous gaps in our thinking and practice and is woefully inadequate in meeting the challenges posed by the allocation of healthcare in this era of managed care. First, it will be important to engage the reader in a historical perspective, tracing the progression of a voluntary ethos, to one of professional sanction, and finally to its present statutory enforcement.

HISTORICAL PERSPECTIVE

The Beginnings of Ethics

The first recorded conceptualization of professional ethical principles in Western civilization is embodied in the Hippocratic Oath, named after the celebrated Greek physician who was born around 460 B.C. The school of medicine prevalent at the time also bears his name, and the chief therapeutic agents were diet, medicinal waters, fresh air, and gymnastics. Hippocrates did not have at his disposal a formal professional society to enforce appropriate physician conduct, so he relied on the concept of *ethos,* a Greek word that can be equated with character. It was decidedly a moral question, with *character* loosely defined as the ability to do the right thing even when no one is looking. Hippocrates saw ethos as the best that a profession can be, whereas our modern legalistic code of ethics (American Psychological Association [APA], 2002) defines the lowest common denominator in terms of its sanctions. Everything above that line is permissible, though not necessarily desirable, whereas conduct seen as falling below the least common denominator is punishable.

The Hippocratic Oath was taken by students as they entered training with their mentors. It was surprisingly simple as compared to our overly complex code of today. The first admonition was "Do no harm," and from this followed the prohibitions against all forms of exploitation, whether sexual, financial, or otherwise. The physician was thereby exhorted to constantly improve treatment and in return had the right to collect a fee. A little-noted feature of the Hippocratic conceptualization was that the patient also had a set of obligations, which included compliance with treatment, respecting one's own health, and payment of the bill.

The Unraveling of the Oath of Hippocrates

The remarkable aspect of this moral imperative to do no harm, with its unceasing striving for the profession to be the best it can be, is that it lasted almost 2,000 years as a voluntary exhortation. It had to be augmented during the Middle Ages by the reaffirmation to profess, from which our word

profession derives. In other words, by the Middle Ages, there were demonstrable practitioners who wished to affirm a voluntary but highly aspirational code of conduct through which the public could be reassured. Used much differently today, the original professions were religion, teaching, law, and medicine. A profession was defined as a body of knowledge and practice in which its practitioners professed to the public a self–imposed commitment to a moral code of conduct, all leading to making the profession the best it could be. It cannot be overly emphasized that the conceptualization was moralistic and voluntary, enforced only by self-denial and peer consensus—much different than the legalistic sanctions of today. The conceptualization survived relatively unchanged until about the middle of the 20th century. What changed everything was the emergence of third-party reimbursement for health services, a modern invention that preceded managed care and removed from the patient the obligation to pay the bill.

As long as the patient was responsible for the bill, the amount of care was balanced with need. Practitioners were obligated not to overtreat or overcharge, and patients could be expected to balk at unnecessary services or exorbitant fees. Once the insurance company, the health plan, or the government paid the bill, more became better. As desirable as the bringing of healthcare to those who otherwise could not afford it may be, it did nonetheless erode the ethos on which practice was based and ushered in the inflationary spiral characteristic of modern healthcare delivery. The patient did not mind that an increasing number of procedures were performed, believing that more is better, while the size of the fee became irrelevant as long as the third party paid the bill. It behooved hospitals to have longer stays, and it benefited the chemical dependency industry to hospitalize all addicts. In psychotherapy, practitioners saw the patient for as long as the latter was willing to come in, which often coincided with how long the insurer would continue to pay. It could all be rationalized that even in the absence of any pain, anxiety, or depression, the ethereal goal of "self-actu-alization" made longer-term therapy desir-able, if not laudatory. After all, the patient enjoyed being the weekly focus of such an attentive and prestigious practitioner, while the therapist was rewarded for doing "good," with a handsome reimbursement that did not affect the patient's income. The patient and the provider unconsciously col-luded to defraud the payor; the Hippocratic Oath was badly eroded, if not altogether rendered obsolete.

Once the mutual set of obligations that comprised the foundation for moral practice was removed, other unprecedented forces emerged to hasten its demise. These will be discussed below, but it may be useful to recall that the first APA code of ethics had a greater resemblance to that of Hippocrates than its own current version.

The First APA Code of Ethics

The years immediately following World War II saw growing numbers of psycholo-gists, and somewhat later, social workers, going into independent solo practice. This movement was vehemently opposed by orga-nized psychiatry, which pointed to a lack of licensure, precedent, and standards. In advance of statutory recognition (licensure) that was to come much later, these pioneer-ing privately practicing psychologists saw the need for an ethical code to bolster their cred-ibility and pressured the APA to create one. Painfully aware of the lack of historical precedents to the private practice of profes-sional psychology, the APA proceeded cau-tiously and produced by the early 1950s a

rather remarkable document, which had two aspects in common with Hippocratic concep-tualizations.

First, this early code of ethics was more a guide for doing the right thing through a moral consensus employing commonsense conduct than it was a compendium of what to do and what not to do. It proceeded through a series of vignettes and hypothetical situa-tions to describe commonsense conclusions to practice dilemmas, precisely the teaching method employed by the mentors of the Hippocratic School almost 2,500 years earlier.

The second feature was that on seeing pos-sible unethical behavior on the part of a col-league, a psychologist was required to meet informally, perhaps over dinner, with the offending colleague. More often than not, this would include one or two other colleagues who were close to and respected by the poten-tial offender. This was not intended to over-whelm or to pressure the potentially unethical psychologist, but to have an open, common-sense discussion about doing the right thing. Every psychologist was obligated to confer with the colleague, with the intention of resolving the issue without invoking formal ethics procedures. It was highly successful inasmuch as more than 90% of perceived vio-lations were settled without recourse to formal ethics charges, either by virtue of the psychol-ogists altering their practice behavior or through the realization of the inquiring col-leagues that, indeed, the colleague's practices were sound and beneficial to the patient. The following is an example from the late 1950s.

The Therapist Who Came to Dinner

It came to the attention of a psycholo-gist that a colleague specializing in child psychology had dinner with the entire family of a 10-year-old patient in the family home. He arranged a meeting with him and another friendly colleague, in which it was learned that this was not only true, but was a routine procedure. On receiving a referral of a child, the psychologist would invite himself to dinner, using the setting and family interaction as a gold mine of insight into the family dynamics. He had been trained in this method of family evaluation by none other than Erik H. Erikson, who had an impressive theoretical framework as well as many years of successfully employing the technique. The psychologist was well trained by Erikson, was highly skilled and effective, and his inquiring colleagues came to the commonsense conclusion that this was in the best interest of the patient and no therapeutic boundaries had been violated to the detriment of the patient. Not only was there no harm, the technique over the years had been highly beneficial to a large number of families and their children.

One cannot help but wonder whether this same conclusion would be reached under the current highly legalistic ethical code (APA, 2002) and whether perhaps not only Erik Erikson but also a number of other legendary psychotherapists would be found culpable in today's climate. Before the advent of third-party reimbursement, this kind of local consensus worked well. And if a formal ethics committee had to be convened, it was on the local level; everyone knew all those involved as well as the practice patterns in the community. Few cases were remanded to the national ethics committee, scandals were rare, and a sense of

professional cohesiveness, collegiality, and integrity, all based on common sense about doing the right thing, seemed to prevail. The system was never perfect, but compared with today's lack of common sense and inflexibility, which threaten to stifle innovation and creativity, to say nothing of the proliferation of arrogant, punitive licensing boards, it was like a breath of fresh air.

THE FURTHER DECLINE OF MORALITY AND ETHOS

Swiftly, in the latter part of the 20th century, healthcare practice became much more detailed and codified, eliminating ethos as the guiding principle of practitioner conduct. This was justified in part with the recognition that American society was multicultural and diverse, and morality was viewed as relative with no definitive rights and wrongs. Certain consequences emerged from such a view, but along with the demise of ethos came the disappearance of commonsense judgment.

Enter the Plaintiff's Lawyer

It may be said that an industrialized society is out of balance when it supports more lawyers than it has engineers. With the decline of the moral view, our society became more litigious, with plaintiffs' lawyers winning cases not on their merits, but on obscure or minute technicalities. The response was increasingly detailed statutory and regulatory codes, with an undue reliance on the letter of the law so as to avoid litigation on the basis of such technicalities. Bureaucracies, whether those of the professional guilds or of the state licensing boards, became more and more inflexible. Commonsense decisions were not safe for the bureaucrats and were avoided. As codes of conduct became more brittle and more detailed, anyone accused of unethical conduct could find a lawyer who easily forged a loophole. In frustration, ethics committees lost their collegiality and became punitive. Similarly, licensing boards matched frustration with arrogance and even began to wield their power not in the interest of the profession being its best, but in the limiting of competition by failing applicants for licensure through capricious oral examinations contrived for that purpose. We had lost our way, but the response seemed to be to create more of what got us into trouble in the first place.

As our society continued to become more litigious, it had a profound effect on the benevolent relationship between the insurer and the patient. The following is not an atypical example. One health maintenance organization (HMO) had a maximum medical/surgical hospitalization of 110 days per year. One woman who had successive surgeries for multiple cancers was continuously hospitalized for more than 3 years. This was accomplished by discharging and readmitting her on paper every 111th day. A journalist learned of this, published a laudatory story, and within 30 days, a lawyer filed a class action suit charging that the HMO was discriminatory in violating its own rules. Although the case was thrown out of court eventually, the HMO became meticulous thereafter in applying its benefits to the letter of the contract.

Meehl (1997) takes issue with the use of credentials as a substitute for knowledge. He decries the anecdotal base on which practice rests resulting in the profession, through its ethics structure and licensing boards, rendering judgments concerning treatment and other clinical procedures that are not scientifically determined. Yet practitioners have not been congenial to evidence-based treatment protocols (DeLeon & Williams, 1997), fearing that outcome studies will not support traditional and customary approaches.

Overcodification and Its Shortcomings

Psychology's ethical code (APA, 2002) emphasizes the significance of integrity, respect, informed consent, and confidentiality, and it decries harassment, exploitation, discrimination, and harm. These lofty motives are often lost when well-intentioned guidelines are taken too far and become transformed into artificial boundaries that serve as destructive prohibitions that undermine clinical effectiveness. This is eloquently affirmed by Lazarus (1994), who believes that many of our proscribed boundaries are outmoded concepts from psychoanalysis. Yet Freud gave gifts to some patients, loaned books to others, offered a meal to the Rat Man, and even provided financial support in a few cases. Nonetheless, Gutheil and Gabbard (1993) insist that "These are no longer acceptable practice regardless of their place in the history of our field" (p. 189).

Lazarus (1994) particularly takes issue with clinicians who espouse what he regards as dehumanizing boundaries. He gives as an example the telephoning of a patient who had, with considerable anxiety, undergone a biopsy for cancer. The patient was very grateful for the therapist's concern, but his spouse, herself a clinical psychologist, complained to colleagues that Lazarus had overstepped therapeutic boundaries. To her, this was a clinical assault, not a simple act of human decency.

Lazarus and other gifted therapists (e.g., Ellis, M. Erickson, E. Erikson, Haley, Perls, Watzlawick) regard the ignoring of

Cognitive Tennis, Anyone?

A patient, a middle-aged corporate CEO, was so competitive that he regarded any interpretation or observation that he had not seen himself to be a personal defeat. Often, he would avoid engagement by looking out the therapist's office window at the tennis court adjoining the building and would challenge the therapist to a game of tennis. For weeks, the patient's pervasive competitiveness stalled therapy; progress would mean the therapist had won. Eventually, the therapist accepted the tennis challenge and was quickly defeated. Thereafter, the patient could accept help, and there was rapid progress. He prefaced every insight or comment by the therapist with a jocular, "Well, I can still beat you at tennis." In time, even this small defensiveness disappeared as the patient rapidly gave up his overcompetitiveness. The breakthrough had been the tennis game.

traditional boundaries to be a very rare event and one that is undertaken only after a great deal of deliberation. Some of the considerations employed by skilled, innovative and flexible therapists are discussed in a later section.

Codification Does Not Necessarily Make It Right

The opposite of stifling overcodification is the attempt to render a wrong into a right by codifying it. An excellent example is the APA's debate of several years as to how long it should be after termination before a therapist could engage in a dual relationship

(romantic, financial, etc.) with a patient: 1, 3, 5, or 10 years (Pope, Shoverm, & Levenson, 1980). Eventually, the consensus was 5 years. This is a decidedly therapist-centric conclusion that ignores the fact that the patient's transference vulnerability may extend far beyond 5 years, even to a lifetime. The intense regard the patient has for the therapist is subject to therapist exploitation, and it is better to err on the side of caution.

The X-File

Seven years after termination of treatment, a psychologist found himself serving on the same civic committee with a former patient. He had helped her through a severe depression attendant to a difficult divorce, and she had remained unattached. They became friendly at first and then plunged into a torrid 6-week affair, essentially at her instigation. The therapist, a short, fat, balding, middle-aged man, immediately saw this as his attractiveness rather than her misplaced transference. Suddenly, there was a return of the depression that had initially driven her to seek therapy. She now began to compare him to her husband, who had cheated on her, and her father, whose infidelity had made her mother's life a continual nightmare. The psychologist was, of course, married. During their pillow talk he had confided he had found her attractive during her therapy. She now doubted his objectivity, obsessed as to whether the divorce was warranted, and abruptly terminated the affair. Feeling depressed, betrayed, and panicked, she sought treatment with another male psychologist, who quickly discerned that he would be inheriting profound distrust. He referred her to an older female social worker, in whom, being neither male nor a psychologist, the patient was able to regain therapeutic trust. Fortunately for the first therapist, she decided to resolve her turmoil through therapy rather than to prolong it through an ethics charge or malpractice suit. However, she poignantly referred to the paradox of the 5-year "rule" by calling it the APA code of "ethical stupidity." In conversations with colleagues, her first therapist still believes his conduct fulfilled the letter of the law and that he did no wrong.

Flexibility With Caveats

It is often difficult to maintain therapeutic innovation and spontaneous skill in the face of frightening warnings of unwarranted law suits (Keith-Spiegel & Koocher, 1985). However, by following a few simple caveats, a skillful therapist can safeguard practice and reputation. This author had practiced, before recently retiring, for half a century in San Francisco, with a difficult addicted or Axis II specialization, without even a threat of an ethics complaint or malpractice suit. These caveats are based on the exhortation to "Do no harm."

Prior to disregarding any boundary and before embarking on something highly innovative, ask the question "Is this for the benefit of the patient or the therapist?" Even if exploitation does not seem present, if the answer is not resoundingly unequivocal, refrain from it. Here, the concept of ethos with its three elements is useful: self-denial, commitment to the patient, and clinical integrity. In the current let-it-all-hang-out

culture, self-denial may seem monastic at worst and quaint at best. Yet as Hippocrates pointed out, without self-denial, commitment to the patient is tenuous and clinical integrity is readily compromised, both in self-interest. Interestingly, most patients know on an intuitive level when something extraordinary is for their benefit or when it is for therapist aggrandizement. The following types of patients are those who are unlikely to make this distinction, so that the technique may backfire:

1. Severely disturbed patients with a distorted sense of reality or anyone with a thought disorder

2. Personality disorders, especially manipulative persons

3. Borderline personality disorders who have difficulty maintaining boundaries of any kind

4. Narcissistic patients who will seek to dethrone the therapist if they do not get their way

5. Hysterics, dissociative disorders, and other patients given to an eroticized transference

6. Litigious persons, patients ordered into therapy by the courts, or others who really are not seeking treatment

7. Paranoid personalities

Cummings and Sayama (1995) offer the following Patient Bill of Rights as a guiding principle in all therapy: "The patient is entitled to relief from pain, anxiety and depression in the shortest time possible and with the least intrusive intervention" (p. 1).

It follows from this that all therapists have an obligation to so hone their skills that they can fulfill this Patient Bill of Rights. In these authors' view, this requires a strong theoretical grounding, followed by skill, innovation, and creativity in an aura of compassion and human decency. It may also require the undertaking of spontaneity within the context of prudent, well-designed therapeutic risk.

When Therapy Is Harmful: Disclosing Side Effects

In view of the large body of research that has demonstrated the potential harmful side effects of psychotherapy under various conditions, it is curious that the APA code of ethics has never seriously considered this as part of patient informed consent prior to beginning treatment. Cummings, Budman, and Thomas (in press) have listed dozens of studies that have documented deterioration in patients, even for those who participate in carefully controlled research protocols. Indeed, studies that use controls generally find that deterioration is lower in the control groups than in the treated groups. This has led Lambert and Bergin (1994), in their review of negative effects of psychotherapy, to conclude that the "occurrence of therapy or therapist-induced worsening was widespread, occurring across a variety of treatment modalities" (p. 176). Perhaps the most thorough and objective review is that of Mohr (1995), who finds ample evidence in 46 studies for negative outcomes in outpatient psychotherapy.

Side effects from psychotherapy can include overdependence; deterioration resulting from therapy with patients whose thought disorder was undetected; escalation of acting out in personality disorders in which a well-intentioned therapist failed to insist on boundaries and/or "tough love"; therapist inexperience, incompetence, or misdiagnosis; and the failure to detect suicidal risk or hidden drug/alcohol abuse. These side effects can be found with conscientious therapists. They also occur with insensitive, exploitative,

and greedy therapists. The fact remains that no matter the cause, there is no treatment (behavioral, medical, or surgical) that is without its side effects. One of the most outmoded aspects of the APA code of ethics is the failure to provide for informed consent in psychotherapy.

ETHICS AND THE RATIONING OF HEALTH CARE

The rationing of healthcare is ubiquitous in all modern industrialized nations because there are simply not enough resources to meet the demand. Rationing has existed ever since the advent of third-party payment and is prevalent in nations that have adopted a single payor (government) system. The term *universal healthcare* is essentially an oxymoron inasmuch as rationing is accomplished by definitions of medical necessity that preclude many conditions, with long waiting lists for services in those conditions that do not qualify.

The Silent Rationing of Behavioral Healthcare

In the United States, rationing of behavioral healthcare also includes more or less exclusionary definitions of medical necessity as well as the old standbys such as benefit design, first-dollar amounts (i.e., the amount each year the patient would spend out of pocket before insurance coverage began), caps on total payments, session limits, circumscribed inpatient care, limited access, exclusion of preexisting conditions and Axis II conditions, and so forth. These methods of rationing have been with us for decades and are the product of third-party reimbursement in a reality of insufficient resources. Of interest is the fact that rationing is not only ubiquitous but it is also always *silent,* a term used by health economists to describe the fact that the rationing is hidden through a variety of euphemisms, ranging from allocation to benefit design. Only two notable exceptions to silent rationing exist in the United States.

The first exception is the allocation of organs for transplant. No one denies that there are far more medically desperate potential recipients than there are organs available, and a system for severe rationing is unavoidable. Even here, society attempts to soften the rationing by substituting such terms as *organ allocation,* but the reality of organ transplant rationing is widely recognized. The second notable exception to silent rationing is the courageous decision of the State of Oregon to limit treatment in accordance with financial realities. Even here, state officials would prefer the term *prioritizing* to that of *rationing.* Simply, in its Medicaid system, the state of Oregon rank-ordered all medical conditions on a predetermined system of priority. It added up the costs of each and then drew a line just below the condition where the money ran out. All conditions falling below that line are not covered. Thus, anencephaly, the absence of a brain at birth, is not covered, and most mental health treatment received a low but not as stringent priority. But for the most severe mental/emotional conditions, behavioral care is almost nonexistent in the Oregon Medicaid system.

Ethics and Time-Efficient/ Effective Psychotherapy

In a series of recent articles highly touted by disaffected practitioners, Miller (1996a, 1996b, 1996c) asserts that short-term therapy constitutes "invisible" (ostensibly his term for silent) rationing, with the values and ethics of short-term therapists formulated to justify such rationing. In his stridency, he accuses short-term therapists as being unethical. Such polemics could easily be overlooked

were it not for their widespread resonance among today's struggling solo practitioners. He further insists that the psychotherapist should disclose to the patient what is known about the rationing practices of the managed care company. Miller (1996a) claims that not disclosing this information would adversely affect the therapeutic relationship, though he provides no evidence for this. In his highly selective review of the brief therapy literature, he concludes, curiously, that no evidence exists for the efficacy of short-term therapies. He cavalierly reinterprets studies, arriving at conclusions different from those of the original experimenters, and rejects controlled studies that do not meet his preconception, while accepting uncontrolled studies (e.g., see *Consumer Reports Study* in Seligman, 1995) that agree with him. He glaringly omits large-scale controlled studies (e.g., see Fort Bragg Study in Bickman, 1996; Hawaii Medicaid Project in Cummings, Dorken, Pallak, & Henke, 1993) that demonstrate that long-term therapy significantly increases healthcare costs.

In a response, Cummings, Budman, and Thomas (1998) found Miller's managed care disclosure requirement to be more political than practical. It is information of importance to struggling practitioners, not patients, and it is designed to enlist the patient's indignation toward embarrassing the managed care company to grant more sessions. Austad (1996), in a thorough and thoughtful treatise, reviews the evidence for time-effective therapies and concludes that in light of this evidence, long-term psychotherapy may itself be unethical. She makes an eloquent plea for a social ethic in this era of managed care.

Managed Behavioral Care as Rationing: The Future

There is no question that managed behavioral care is the newest form of rationing, but

The Case of the Dual Duel

A patient had been in therapy with a psychologist for 3 years when his employer changed healthcare coverage to a managed care company. His therapist received authorization for 15 sessions for transitioning the patient to a new therapist in the managed care network, a rather generous allotment in this situation. The 15 sessions were expended, and the therapist engaged the patient in a protracted series of complaints against the managed care company. He warned the patient that he would likely lose the progress he had made in the past 3 years. He urged the patient to protest directly to the managed care company, and the patient obtained an appointment with the case manager. The latter noted that the patient accused the company of interest only in cost containment and used other terminology not known to patients unless they have been coached. The case manager asked the patient to try solution-focused therapy on an unlimited basis, and if he was not satisfied, he would be given authorization to return to the original psychotherapist. The patient agreed, and found not only that he was satisfied, but his conflicts were resolved in 17 sessions. Writing to his previous therapist, he complained that he had wasted 3 years in therapy and further complained that the therapist had attempted to use him in his anger at the managed care company. He copied the case manager, who refrained from coaching the patient that the latter behavior is termed *dual relationships*.

it is a more humane form of rationing than that which has gone on before. It provides the organized setting in which evidence-based protocols, population and diseased-based therapies, and psychoeducational models can be developed, which eventually because of their efficiency (cost-effectiveness) and effectiveness will end rationing in behavioral care (Cummings & Cummings, 1997). The integration of behavioral care with primary care holds even greater promise for the needed parity between physical and mental health because finally, the body and mind will not be treated as separate entities in our health system (Cummings, Cummings, & Johnson, 1997). One must agree with Austad (1996) that ethics and social concern demand that practitioners forge toward the future rather than engage in futile, atavistic polemics.

ETHICS, MORALS, AND INDUSTRIALIZED HEALTHCARE DELIVERY

In an early discussion of clinical, ethical, and practical guidelines for participation in managed care, Haas and Cummings (1991, p. 45) identified three considerations: (a) the dilemmas presented by managed healthcare systems are not unique, but are present (albeit in less stark form) in other financing arrangements; (b) there are particular questions psychologists should ask before associating themselves with particular plans, especially about types of limitations and possible effects on the patient-provider relationship; and (c) if the therapist has appropriate training, there are very few types of patients who could not be provided with at least some benefits in a managed care environment.

The present discussion will focus on the clinical and moral responsibility of practitioners, not only in participating in managed care but also in preparation for the rapidly evolving provider-owned networks (integrated delivery systems, or IDSs) that are emerging as attractive alternatives to the managed care companies (Cummings, 1995). These practitioner-equity groups are in a position to contract directly with purchasers (e.g., large employers, insurers, purchasing alliances, and other payors), cutting out the so-called middleman. The discussion will look at the practitioner side of the equation inasmuch as ethics is a professional matter, and the moral responsibilities of the managed care companies will be addressed only as they relate to practice. Rather than letting the dilemmas posed by managed care off the hook, the intent is to aid the practitioner who wishes to participate in managed care or as a participant-owner of an IDS. The discussion will address training, competency, overdiagnosis, and confidentiality and will conclude with a look at who should and who should not participate in managed behavioral healthcare. Throughout, the emphasis will be on the moral questions pertaining to each issue.

Training

There is a growing arsenal of effective/efficient psychotherapy (Bennett, 1994; Bloom, 1991) that is unknown to most practitioners and, even more surprising, to those who educate and train graduate students. Beginning with Balint (1957), a number of authors have pointed out that brief therapy is not merely a truncated version of long-term therapy. Having its own parameters, additional training is required to master short-term approaches (Bennett, 1994; Bloom, 1992; Budman & Gurman, 1983, 1988; Cummings, 1977), and Friedman and Fanger (1991) have concluded that a number of attitudinal changes must precede or accompany this retraining.

Levenson and Davidowitz (1995) conducted a national survey and found that

although 65% of the respondents were working in managed care, less than 30% had any training in brief therapy, less than 50% had ever read a book on brief therapy, and a staggering 94% responded that they had been inadequately trained and needed to learn more about brief therapy. Is this state of affairs improving with our future practitioners now in training? In his survey of 233 interns in psychology, Kent (1995) found that only 39% had received even one seminar on brief therapy in graduate school, and only 37% were receiving any internship supervision in brief psychotherapy. Yet by an overwhelming 95%, these interns believed it was a valuable treatment, an equal 95% saw it as the most appropriate treatment in the real world, and 87% had already made up their minds to work in managed care after the completion of their internships. In the face of this career decision, the additional finding that only 15% had been formally taught anything about managed care is alarming. Hoyt (1995) found that most therapists entering the job market today get their short-term therapy training on the job, often in uneven and haphazard fashion. He calls for comprehensive training and experience in short-term therapy models. The finding that our level of training has improved only slightly in the past decade suggests that our profession may be teetering on the brink of moral irresponsibility (Cummings, 1998).

Several years ago, the APA appointed a task force on education to address these and other vexing issues. Although the task force completed its work, its report has never been approved, officially released, or widely disseminated. Its impact to date, therefore, has been negligible. An unofficial version of the report has been published by the chair of the task force (Troy & Shuemann, 1996) and is readily available. However, without the APA's endorsement, its incisive recommendations are not likely to be implemented.

Case managers for some time to come will find themselves plagued by network providers who lack adequate training. The following case is typical.

Of Course I Can Be Brief

A psychologist who had been in practice for over 10 years found her practice dwindling, so she joined a managed care network. On the application, she stated that she was skilled in brief therapy, but actually she was not. She did not regard this as a lie, believing that anyone who is a highly trained long-term therapist can easily do brief therapy. In the course of her affiliation with the managed care company, she received over 2 dozen referrals under the company's policy of six sessions per episode. The therapist essentially did with each patient what she had been doing for 10 years: she used all six sessions taking an extensive history and administering a battery of psychological tests in preparation for the long-term therapy that would never take place. After the sixth session, each patient was released without the definition of the problem, goal setting, or even the beginning of treatment. Most patients, though bewildered, did not complain. Three, however, complained bitterly to the payor, who investigated the therapist and terminated her affiliation. She became the community's most outspoken critic of managed care.

Stop That Gag Rule!

A solo practitioner who had consistently been active in the local psychological association was bitter when lack of referrals forced him to join a managed care network. His already hostile attitude toward short-term therapy was now augmented by his anger at the very managed care company with which he was affiliated, blaming it for his declining practice. On the first session with each of the patients referred to him, he cautioned the patient to not expect much because as the therapist, he was being forced to conduct substandard treatment. This was often reiterated in each session. For example, at a certain point, the therapist would declare that he should pursue something or other with the patient, but that would lead to the need for more treatment, which would be disallowed under the terms of the substandard care. The therapist in the preceding example, although inadequately trained, was caring and sincere, so most of her patients did not complain. In this instance, the therapist's anger mitigated any caring, rendering him insensitive. His patients unanimously complained and refused to work with him. In an effort to find a solution, the case manager offered him training in brief therapy, which he used as a platform to berate anything less than long-term therapy. After all efforts at conciliation were exhausted, the therapist was terminated, after which he wrote a volatile letter to the APA complaining that the company was acting unethically toward patients and that he was a victim of their gag rule.

In the author's survey of case managers, it is estimated that 60% to 70% of all therapists who initially join their networks fall into one of two illustrative situations, the preceding and the one to follow.

Competence

The therapist's moral responsibility to the patient as embodied in the Patient Bill of Rights (Cummings & Sayama, 1995, p. 1) cuts across the debate of long-term versus short-term psychotherapy. In honing one's skills, it should be noted that efficient/effective psychotherapy does not mean *quick*. It defies session limits, for some conditions require more therapy than others, but this is on the basis of patient need, not therapist bias or lack of training. A well-constructed treatment plan avoids therapeutic "drift" and eliminates unnecessarily protracted treatment.

In invoking the concept of the least-restrictive alternative within the psychotherapy domain, the patient is encouraged to retain the major responsibility for what decisions are made in the therapeutic encounter. Cummings (1988) states,

> In making the therapeutic contract with the patient, we want to make clear that we are there to serve as a catalyst, but the patient is the one who will do the growing. This contract is stated: "I shall never abandon you as long as you need me, and I shall never ask you to do something until you are ready. In return for this I ask you to join me in a partnership to make me obsolete as soon as possible." (pp. 312-313)

It follows, therefore, that when the patient is ready, the therapist will encourage, gently prod, or generally empower the patient to take the next step. The vehicle throughout is the homework assignments, clinically tailored to the patient's needs and subsequent growth. There is a treatment plan, shared with the patient, that defines the problem, goals, and procedures. The treatment is solution focused, and although there may be interruptions, there is no termination. The patient is free at any time to return with other issues, thus constituting what has been termed "brief, intermittent psychotherapy throughout the life cycle" (Cummings & Sayama, 1995). Interestingly, every healthcare profession functions within this model except for long-term psychotherapy.

Psychotherapy without a treatment plan and focused goals is like trying to fly an aircraft without a flight plan or compass. A persistent complaint of case managers is that most therapists do not have the slightest notion of what constitutes a treatment plan. Many reasonable facsimiles are offered, often with ethereal non-goals such as "self-actualization" and increase in "self-esteem" or the institution of "self-empowerment." The consequences of therapeutic "drift" are demonstrated in the following example.

The Therapy That Went to Pot

A 40-year-old real estate broker had seen four different therapists within a period of 6 years, with a total of more than 200 sessions. When his office signed up with a managed care company, he decided to try one more time. He had no specific complaints other than a lack of zest, which had been previously misdiagnosed as depression, Epstein-Barr Syndrome, or a low-grade virus. There was nothing wrong with his life, but there was nothing good either. All complaints were vague, nonspecific, and "Your guess is as good as mine." In constructing a treatment plan, the new therapist suspected marijuana nonmotivational syndrome, and when he inquired as to drug use, the patient readily admitted extensive daily use of cannabis. After an initial resistance, the patient decided to refrain from drug abuse, essentially to prove that the psychologist was in error. Within a few weeks, his zest and enthusiasm returned, and he decided to give up marijuana forever. The therapist, in a patient-approved exchange of information, asked the previous therapist how he could have missed a classic substance abuse syndrome. The reply was that several times, he had suspected that that might be the case, but to probe into the subject would be a violation of the "unconditional positive regard for the patient."

Confidentiality: A Legitimate Concern With a Dark Side

There is probably no other issue that has generated more passionate discussion than the topic of confidentiality. The issue is not new; it dates back several decades, when psychotherapists first became eligible for third-party reimbursement. It escalated considerably in later decades, when peer review became a requirement, and then exploded with the increased demands of managed care. On one side, practitioners deeply resent anyone looking over their shoulders but feel compelled to cloak this self-interest in lofty concern for the patient's right to privacy. On the other hand, those who pay the bills have the right to determine whether a certain procedure has indeed been performed within acceptable professional standards. They also have the right to determine whether the services delivered are within the scope contracted with the patient. The patient has conceded this reasonable determination in accepting the health plan contract. The managed care company is not interested in the intimate details of a patient's therapy. Why, then, are case managers increasingly demanding to be given the treatment notes?

Case managers have grown increasing skeptical, if not cynical, as to whether the therapist is actually performing the services in the manner prescribed. Unfortunately, more than any other, the issue of confidentiality is used as a "red herring" by practitioners to conceal incompetence or breach of contract with the managed care companies. The unnecessarily intrusive procedures by managed care are intended to catch the therapist at his or her own game. The limits and necessities of information conveyance will eventually have to be resolved by a task-oriented, mutually conscientious joint effort between the professions and the managed care companies.

Of Course You're Guilty

Repeatedly, there came to the attention of the case manager gross inconsistencies between what a therapist claimed she had done and the therapeutic outcome. Her treatment plans were requested, which she steadfastly refused to turn over on the basis of patient confidentiality. A tug-of-war ensued, during which time the psychologist wrote two inflammatory letters to the state psychological association, which aggressively took up her cause. Eventually, the therapist admitted she had no treatment plans for any of the referrals she had accepted. She apologized, but the state association never did, stating that to do so might excuse "unethical behavior" on the part of the managed care company that had not yet come to light.

In contrast to this example, one of the network's most effective and reliable providers, who stubbornly refused to convey information beyond the bare essentials, was excused by the case manager from all case management.

Managed care would be delighted if all providers were not only well trained and competent but also reliable and truthful, thus never having to be case managed. Case management is expensive, but in the current practitioner climate, vital to those who pay the bills.

Overdiagnosis: Deliberate and Inadvertent

With indemnity insurance, and in times past, psychotherapists consistently underdiagnosed for the protection of the patient. A diagnosis of schizophrenia, for example, could result in the cancellation of a driver's license or the denial of an application for a job or life insurance. In managed care, the opposite is true: With therapists forced to demonstrate concepts of "medical necessity" or "life-threatening," the exaggeration of findings has become widespread. This practice raises serious issues of unethical, immoral conduct that can not be swept aside by a mere "I lied for the sake of my patient." With veracity destroyed, no wonder managed care demands the actual treatment records.

But other factors have contributed to the prevalence of overdiagnosis. The first is that the profession itself has responded to the practitioner glut by creating larger and larger pools of potential patients. For example, depression has been redefined so that even the common "blues" should qualify for intensive psychotherapy. And when 50% to 60% of the boys in a grammar school are diagnosed as suffering from attention deficit disorder (ADD), one must question whether, indeed, there is a definable syndrome at all.

A second source of overdiagnosis stems from the overspecialization of many therapists in controversial, marginal, or yet to be accepted syndromes. They become blind activists on behalf of their patients, labeling skepticism from payors or colleagues as injustice.

Accumulated national data by managed care companies (American Biodyne, 1992) on tens of thousands of therapists and hundreds of thousands of patients indicate that common areas of overdiagnosis are multiple personality disorder; ADD; post-traumatic stress disorder (PTSD) for the most common of life's stresses; survivors of incest often based on a hypnosis-induced "memory"; depression redefined to include slight common mood alterations, and all manner of somaticized responses. These provider profiles reveal that psychotherapists in general do not engage in this kind of overdiagnosis. Rather, there seems to be a segment of practitioners who possess an uncanny ability to find in almost every patient that one psychological condition they most like to treat.

Perhaps Each Patient Should Be in His or Her Own Group Therapy

A practitioner in a small rural community on the border between a midwestern and southern state was treating 4 out of every 5 referrals for multiple personality disorder (MPD). He justified this as a consequence of the patients' living in an unsophisticated "backwoods" environment where dissociation was a way of life. Because psychotherapists were difficult to find in that part of the nation, the managed care company was unusually indulgent. Two years later, when this psychologist moved to a large and far more sophisticated metropolitan area and 4 out of 5 referrals were still being treated for MPD, the managed care company realized this was the propensity of the psychologist, not a characteristic of the population.

Who Should and Should Not Work in Managed Care?

Even though participation in managed care is voluntary, the only alternative to participation may be loss of practice. This does not in any way mitigate the imperative that if one signs onto a network, it cannot be done under a cloak of deceit. But it also does not mean giving up one's right to strive to change managed care, either through the professional societies, the legislative process, or in direct negotiations with the managed care companies. However, false reporting, inciting patients, and practicing beyond one's training and skills are forms of morally irresponsible conduct once participation is established. Cummings (1998) has delineated a set of five considerations that must be addressed by each practitioner before making the decision to work or not work with managed care.

1. How Will It Affect My Conscience?

Despite its diversity, managed care can generally be defined as the partial subordination of clinical considerations to business principles in the interest of rendering healthcare delivery economically viable. This is a tough-minded, no-nonsense definition that also acknowledges the reality that no system of healthcare delivery existent in the world today, be it market oriented or socialistic, is without some inherent form of healthcare rationing.

Practitioners who have strong philosophical disagreements with market-oriented solutions to health reform will not be happy in this system. This does not mean that those who work in managed care have to accept the inordinately high compensation some CEOs receive while providers are relegated to "employee" status, or any other conditions that are clearly business abuses. But those who are opposed philosophically can only transfer their unhappiness on their patients.

2. Is It Compatible With My Core Professional Beliefs?

Some psychotherapists steadfastly believe that only long-term therapy is effective and are inured to any evidence to the contrary. To compromise one's cherished beliefs in the hope of working with managed care will create a tug-of-war that can only result in unenthusiastic outcomes for the patient and demoralized unhappiness for the practitioner.

3. Do I Have the Requisite Training and Competence?

It is every practitioner's responsibility to practice within one's competence and training, and this also applies to a decision to work with managed care. This does not mean that a practitioner must demonstrate master competency in brief therapy before enrolling in a network, but it does mean obtaining serious requisite training. Anyone not willing to do this should not work in managed care, because it would be deleterious to one's patients.

4. Do I Have the Stamina?

Brief psychotherapy, with its rapid turnover and high volume of patients, is hard work. As Haley (1976) has pointed out, therapists accustomed to seeing eight patients, four times a week find themselves readily overwhelmed. In addition, a therapist must learn to carry a large caseload of patients who need to be seen only occasionally. Many therapists thrive on this kind of schedule, whereas others are dismayed and even exhausted.

5. Do I Have the Appropriate Personality?

As was discussed in a previous section, success in short-term therapy is in large part a function of the patient as a partner to one's own treatment. This is part of the minimization of the transference and the enhancement of self-reliance, thus rendering the therapy time- effective. When successful, patients conclude treatment with the conviction that they have solved their own problems, with the therapist as a valued catalyst. Long-term patients are likely to express much gratitude, often accompanied by gifts. The short-term therapist is aware of the patient's satisfaction mainly through the referral of friends. Managed care practice is not for psychotherapists who need narcissistic supplies as accorded by grateful, adoring patients.

SUMMARY AND CONCLUSIONS

Although many of the limitations and reporting requirements existed prior to the industrialization of healthcare, an ethical code that represents professional consensus achieved essentially before the healthcare revolution often does not directly address the dilemmas confronting practitioners in the current era. In achieving a new consensus that will lead to

updating this ethical code, the profession must address issues of moral responsibility that are broader than codification of minimum acceptable conduct. In essence, practitioners must ask what is the very best that the profession can be in the new healthcare environment. Abuses by a business-driven system do not justify deceit by the practitioner, no matter how well couched it is in lofty concern for the patient. Moral responsibility must consider issues of adequate training and supervision, as well as the applicability of the therapist's core beliefs that may render him or her ineligible for participation. Ultimately, moral responsibility is the concern for the patient, not protection of the profession. Many, if not most, practitioners who currently participate in managed care are not qualified either by training or attitude to do so. As long as this condition exists, practitioners must come to terms with the fact that those who pay the bills will be intrusive in their requirement of accountability. The best way to serve the patient is to be well trained and competent, and maintain both clinical and moral integrity.

REFERENCES

American Biodyne. (1992). *Profiles of frequency of diagnosis by practitioner and geographical location: Studies in over-diagnosis.* South San Francisco: American Biodyne. Unpublished in-house document.

American Psychological Association. (2002). Ethical principles of psychologists and code of conduct. American Psychological Association Monograph.

Austad, C. S. (1996). *Is long-term therapy unethical?* San Francisco: Jossey-Bass.

Balint, M. (1957). *The doctor, his patient and the illness.* New York: New York International Universities Press.

Bennett, M. J. (1994). Can competing psychotherapists be managed? *Managed Care Quarterly, 2*(2), 29-35.

Bickman, L. (1996). A continuum of care: More is not always better. *American Psychologist, 51,* 689-701.

Bloom, B. L. (1991). *Planned short-term psychotherapy: A clinical handbook.* Boston: Allyn & Bacon.

Budman, S. H., & Gurman, A. S. (1983). Short-term group psychotherapy. In H. Kaplan & B. Sadock (Eds.), *Comprehensive group psychotherapy* (pp. 138-144). Baltimore, MD: Williams Wilkins.

Budman, S. H., & Gurman, A. S. (1988). *Theory and practice of brief therapy.* New York: Guilford.

Cummings, N. A. (1977). Prolonged (ideal) versus short-term (realistic) psychotherapy. *Professional Psychology: Research and Practice, 8,* 491-505.

Cummings, N. A. (1988). Emergence of the mental health complex: Adaptive and maladaptive responses. *Professional Psychology: Research and Practice, 19*(3), 308-315.

Cummings, N. A. (1995). Behavioral health after managed care: The next golden opportunity for professional psychology. *Register Report, 20*(3), 1, 30-32.

Cummings, N. A. (1998). Moral issues in managed mental healthcare. In R. F. Small & L. R. Barnhill (Eds.), *Practicing in the new mental health marketplace: Ethical, legal and moral considerations* (pp. 76-84). Washington, DC: APA Books.

Cummings, N. A., Budman, S. H., & Thomas, J. L. (1998). Efficient psychotherapy as a viable response to scarce resources and rationing of treatment. *Professional Psychology: Research and Practice, 29*(5), 460-469.

Cummings, N. A., & Cummings, J. L. (1997). The behavioral health practitioner of the future: The efficacy of psychoeducational programs in integrated primary care. In N. A. Cummings, J. L. Cummings, & J. N. Johnson (Eds.), *Behavioral health in primary care: A guide for clinical integration* (pp. 325-346). Madison, CT: Psychosocial Press.

Cummings, N. A., Cummings, J. L., & Johnson, J. N. (Eds.). (1997). *Behavioral health in primary care: A guide for clinical integration.* Madison, CT: Psychosocial Press.

Cummings, N. A., Dorken, H., Pallak, M. S., & Henke, C. J. (1993). Medicaid, managed behavioral health, and implications for public policy. *The HCFA-Hawaii Medicaid report and other readings: Vol. 2. Healthcare and utilization cost series.* South San Francisco: Foundation for Behavioral Health.

Cummings, N., & Sayama, M. (1995). *Focused psychotherapy: A casebook of brief intermittent psychotherapy throughout the life cycle.* New York: Brunner/Mazel.

DeLeon, P. H., & Williams, J. G. (1997). Evaluation research and public policy formation: Are psychologists collectively willing to accept unpopular findings? *American Psychologist, 52,* 551-552.

Friedman, S., & Fanger, M. T. (1991). *Expanding therapeutic possibilities: Getting results in brief psychotherapy.* Lexington, MA: Lexington.

Gutheil, T. G., & Gabbard, G. O. (1993). The concept of boundaries in clinical practice: Theoretical and risk-management dimensions. *American Journal of Psychiatry, 150,* 188-196.

Haas, L. J., & Cummings, N. A. (1991). Managed outpatient mental health plans: Clinical, ethical and practical guidelines for participation. *Professional Psychology: Research and Practice, 22,* 45-51.

Haley, J. (1976). *Problem solving therapy.* San Francisco: Jossey-Bass.

Holstein, R. M. (1995). Taking on managed care and winning: One practitioner's story. *Independent Practitioner, 15*(2), 77-79.

Hoyt, M. F. (1995). *Brief therapy and managed care: Readings for contemporary practice.* San Francisco: Jossey-Bass.

Keith-Spiegel, P., & Koocher, G. P. (1985). *Ethics in psychology.* New York: Random House.

Kent, A. J. (1995, August). *Survey of interns' knowledge of brief therapy and managed care* (Presentation 5164). Paper presented at the American Psychological Association Annual Convention, New York.

Lambert M. J., & Bergin, A. E. (1994). The effectiveness of psychotherapy. In A. E. Bergin & S. L. Garfield (Eds.), *Handbook of psychotherapy and behavior change: An empirical analysis* (4th ed., pp. 143-189). New York: Wiley.

Lazarus, A. A. (1994). How certain boundaries and ethics diminish therapeutic effectiveness. *Ethics & Behavior, 4*(3), 255-261.

Levenson, H., & Davidowitz, D. (1995, August). *National survey of mental health professionals on brief therapy* (Presentation 4172). Paper presented at the American Psychological Association Annual Convention, New York.

Meehl, P. E. (1997). Credentialed persons, credentialed knowledge. *American Psychologist, 4*(2), 91-98.

Miller, I. P. (1996a). Ethical and liability issues concerning invisible rationing. *Professional Psychology: Research and Practice, 27*(6), 583-587.

Miller, I. P. (1996b). Some "short-term therapy values" are a formula for invisible rationing. *Professional Psychology: Research and Practice, 27*(6), 577-582.

Miller, I. P. (1996c). Time-limited brief therapy has gone too far: The result is invisible rationing. *Professional Psychology: Research and Practice, 27*(6), 567-576.

Mohr, D. C. (1995). Negative outcomes in psychotherapy: A critical review. *Clinical Psychology: Science and Practice, 2*, 1-27.

Pope, K. S., Shoverm, L. R., & Levenson, H. (1980). Sexual behavior between clinical supervisors and trainees: Implications for professional standards. *Professional Psychology: Research and Practice, 11*, 157-162.

Seligman, M. E. P. (1995). The effectiveness of psychotherapy: The *Consumer Reports* Study. *American Psychologist, 50*, 965-974.

Shore, K. (1995). Managed care as a totalitarian regime. *Independent Practitioner, 15*(2), 73-77.

Troy, W. G., & Shuemann, S. A. (1996). Program redesign for graduate training in professional psychology: The road to accountability in a changing professional world. In N. A. Cummings, M. S. Pallak, & J. L. Cummings (Eds.), *Surviving the demise of solo practice: Mental health practitioners prospering in the era of managed care* (pp. 55-79). Madison, CT: Psychosocial Press.

CHAPTER 9

Fees and Financial Arrangements

ROBERT MIRANDA JR.
Brown University

BRIAN P. MARX
Temple University

Despite the unavoidable significance of fees and financial matters for psychologists who provide services to others, these topics are often neglected by the curricula of many training programs. Likewise, many professional psychologists often neglect to discuss issues related to fees and financial arrangements with other colleagues. A potential consequence of such a state of affairs is that despite their undeniable importance, psychologists may remain unfamiliar with the ethical issues concerning fees and financial arrangements for services provided. Also, psychologists may choose to ignore the financial aspects of their professional duties as a result of their limited knowledge of and subsequent discomfort caused by such issues. The topic of fees and financial arrangements related to the provision of services may also cause uneasiness for practicing psychologists who see the topic as inherently incompatible with their role as compassionate helpers.

Yet psychologists are not solely compassionate helpers but are also paid professionals who often work within a creditor-debtor professional relationship and encounter ethical dilemmas involving fees and financial transactions. As a result, it is important that psychologists recognize and thoroughly understand the ethical issues related to fees and financial arrangements, because any breach of ethical behavior may result in undesirable consequences for both clients and service providers. Likewise, psychologists who offer services for financial compensation should be aware that disputes regarding financial arrangements are a common focus of legal complaints filed by clients against service providers (Knapp & VandeCreek, 1993).

Psychologists face numerous possible consequences for unethical practices involving fees and financial matters, whether deliberate or unintentional. Such practices may result in emotional and financial harm done to individuals seeking services. Unethical financial practices may also do irrevocable damage to any preexisting client-therapist relationship. Furthermore, professionals who engage in unethical financial practices not only risk harm to others but also risk compromising their own future financial stability by tarnishing their professional reputations. Ultimately, unethical practices related to fees and financial arrangements can taint the client's view of psychotherapy as well as those providing services.

In an effort to prevent such consequences and reduce speculation with regard to ethical dilemmas, the American Psychological Association (APA, 1992) has furnished a set of ethical principles and standards that include rules for governing ethical professional behavior regarding fees and other financial arrangements. Practicing psychologists have a responsibility to familiarize themselves with the ethical standards concerning their professional behavior involving financial matters, recognize potential ethical dilemmas involving fees and financial arrangements, and respond in accordance with the ethical standards in situations in which fees and financial arrangements are relevant issues.

The purpose of this chapter is to present and discuss the current ethical standards set by the APA as they relate to fees and financial arrangements. Specifically, this chapter will be devoted to addressing specific financial issues and ethical dilemmas inherent in the provision of services by professional psychologists. Issues, both those explicitly addressed and those merely implied by the current APA ethical standards relating to financial intricacies of service provision, will be discussed. Although an exhaustive discussion of the ethical dilemmas potentially encountered by psychologists regarding fees and finances is not feasible here because the possibilities are essentially limitless, many important ethical issues will be discussed.

With respect to each issue, directive guidance will be provided in accordance with the APA ethical standards.

DETERMINING FEES FOR SERVICES

The significance of fee payment for individuals who receive services from psychologists has received much speculative attention. For instance, it has been previously hypothesized that psychotherapy may be less successful when the client does not make a relatively sufficient financial sacrifice for those psychological services (e.g., Freud, 1913/1958; Halpert, 1972; Koren & Joyce, 1953; Kubie, 1950; Menninger & Holzman, 1973; Nash & Cavenar, 1976). As such, it has been suggested that the service provider set a fee for services by taking into consideration the financial status of each client and tailoring the fee to be a "reasonable sacrifice" for the individual based on that established financial status (Herron & Sitkowski, 1986). Despite the assumed relationship between therapeutic success and fee payment, empirical evidence has not consistently supported such assertions (e.g., Pope, Geller, & Wilkinson, 1975; Yoken & Berman, 1984, 1987). In a review of the literature, Herron and Sitkowski (1986) concluded that despite theorized links between payment of fees and successful intervention, little empirical evidence exists to support or refute the validity of these claims.

Regardless of the debate over the significance of fee payment for individuals who receive services, psychologists usually require reimbursement for the services they provide in order to maintain their livelihood. The APA ethical standards (APA, 1992) do not explicitly dictate how much a psychologist should charge for services. The ethical standards do, however, state that an agreement specifying the fee and billing arrangements should be established as early as possible in the professional relationship.

In addition, psychologists should always genuinely represent their fee policy and not exploit recipients of services with respect to payment. Examples of fee exploitation include waiting to increase the fee for services until after a rapport with a client has been developed, or not genuinely representing fee policies to individuals who may be naive and/or cognitively or judgmentally impaired (Keith-Spiegel & Koocher, 1985). Psychologists should always carefully assess clients' vulnerability to exploitation and treat fairly those who may be especially suggestible or otherwise susceptible to financial mistreatment.

When determining fees and financial arrangements, psychologists should base their rates on regional costs of living and economic conditions, as well as on their level of competence (e.g., degree completed), special skills or training, operating expenses, competition from other psychotherapists, and other relevant variables (Woody, 1989). In addition, the APA ethical standards state that when establishing a fee policy, psychologists should always ensure that their financial arrangements are consistent with any existing state laws.

PRO BONO SERVICES

The APA ethical principles (APA, 1992) encourage psychologists to donate a portion of their professional time for little or no personal advantage. However, neither the ethical principles nor standards explicitly state how a psychologist should ethically provide services free of charge, or pro bono. As a result, previous authors have speculated on how this obligation could be ethically fulfilled. For example, Knapp and VandeCreek

(1993) suggest that therapists can ethically fulfill their social responsibility obligation by providing pro bono services to nonprofit organizations in need, such as domestic violence shelters, rape crisis programs, shelters for the homeless, or organizations that assist individuals who may be traumatized (e.g., American Red Cross).

Psychologists may also fulfill their social responsibility obligations by providing pro bono services through their supervisory roles. As supervisors or consultants for other clinicians, psychologists may offer their expertise for little or no fee. For example, an established licensed clinician may supervise less experienced, unlicensed practitioners free of charge while they obtain the clinical hours necessary for licensing. Likewise, a psychologist with expertise in a particular clinical area may provide pro bono consultation to a colleague who lacks similar specialized training.

Another avenue through which psychologists may provide pro bono services is to offer a first session free of charge. However, caution should be exercised here, as there are ethical considerations when offering free first sessions. First, any client who is given a free first session should be made well aware of such an arrangement, as well as of the fee for any subsequent sessions at the outset of the professional relationship. Second, the use of a free first session merely as a strategy to lure clients into seeking services or as an advertising or marketing strategy violates the spirit of the ethical principle of social responsibility, which states that such a service is not for the purpose of self-gain. If used unethically, a free first session could be emotionally and financially harmful to some clients and may jeopardize any therapeutic relationship that develops during the course of the first session. Such a scenario might involve a client disclosing intimate details about his or her life during the initial free session and establishing an emotional connection with the service provider. On learning that subsequent services may not be offered free of charge, the client may feel betrayed and decline further services or even a referral to a clinician he or she can better afford. Therefore, although offering a free first session is generally not an illegal practice, service providers should engage in such behavior carefully and with the client's best interest in mind.

BARTERING

The APA ethical standards (APA, 1992) explicitly state that psychologists should "ordinarily refrain from accepting goods, services, or other non-monetary remuneration from patients or clients in return for psychological services because such arrangements create inherent potential for conflicts, exploitation, and distortion of the professional relationship" (p. 1602). Bartering for services potentially eradicates the common value of the exchanged goods, which are ordinarily maintained in monetary transactions. Although the value of currency is preestablished, other forms of compensation may not possess a predetermined, agreed-on financial value. Consequently, using such nonmonetary goods for compensatory purposes can often lead to disagreement regarding the equivalence of the goods in relation to the services provided.

Despite these concerns, clinicians may deem it appropriate to barter at certain times, such as when clients are unable to compensate monetarily for services provided. In these circumstances, the APA ethical standards state that "Psychologists may participate in bartering only if 1) it is not clinically contraindicated, and 2) the relationship is not exploitative" (p. 1602). In cases in which bartering will be employed as the method of payment, the therapist and client should agree on the market value of the goods to be exchanged prior to the provision of services (Haas & Malouf, 1989).

INCREASING FEES

As the cost of living and expenses associated with service provision increase, psychologists may find it necessary to increase charges for their services to keep abreast with these changes. Although such fee increases will not likely affect new clients, they may affect individuals already in treatment. In cases in which a fee increase is necessary, psychologists should address the issue with sensitivity, courtesy, and respect. In addition, psychologists should provide established clients with adequate advance notice of any anticipated fee increases. An ethical approach sometimes used by practitioners is to maintain established clients at their previously determined fee rate, while increasing the fee charged to any new clients. This practice allows the clinician to uphold previously agreed-on financial arrangements with established clients, while still responding to inflation or other costs associated with maintaining a professional practice.

ADVANCE PAYMENTS FOR SERVICES

Though an unusual practice, some clinicians may require clients to pay fees in advance of receiving services as a type of retainer. Such a practice is more prevalent among relationships in which the practitioner is asked to hold time available on short notice. For example, this practice may be used in certain types of corporate counseling or cases in which litigation is involved. This practice is not unethical according to the standards set by the APA so long as the contingencies are mutually agreed on at the outset of the professional relationship.

CHARGING FOR
MISSED SESSIONS

Whether clients should be charged for missed sessions has remained a contentious issue among psychological service providers. Arguments in support of this practice have stated that if clients do not reimburse therapists for missed sessions, they are unlikely to take the therapeutic process seriously and therefore not fully benefit from services. In addition, charging clients for sessions they miss may enhance their perceptions of self-responsibility and decrease resistance to services provided. Finally, the ability to charge for missed sessions prevents a psychologist who has reserved a time slot for a client from losing any profits. When viewed in the light of these arguments, charging for missed sessions may be seen as an ethically valid and clinically beneficial practice.

On the other hand, some psychologists have argued against the practice of charging clients for missed sessions. It has been suggested that charging for a missed session is an unethical practice because the service provider receives reimbursement for services he or she did not provide. This argument reflects the philosophy that a client purchases a service provided by the psychologist, rather than a time slot (Fay, 1995). Furthermore, charging for a missed session has been deemed unethical by some because it may result in distress for clients with limited financial means. As such, this practice may hinder the client-service provider relationship.

Although no conclusion to this debate has been reached, it is important that psychologists consider client-specific factors when deciding whether to charge for missed sessions. Fay (1995) has suggested that psychologists consider such factors as the frequency with which a client misses sessions, the degree of notice given by the client (e.g., advance notification of the missed session vs. no notification), the extent of a

client's financial resources, and the degree of functional impairment exhibited by the client.

The APA ethical standards (1992) do not explicitly provide ethical policies regarding the collection of fees for missed sessions. As with all financial matters, practitioners should inform clients of their policies regarding missed sessions as early as is feasible in the professional relationship.

BILL COLLECTING

When clients withhold payment for services provided, it is generally not considered unethical for the psychologist to refuse further services (APA, 1992). However, refusal to provide future services should occur only after the psychologist has made certain that the client has been sufficiently assessed for any future psychological vulnerability or risk. For clients judged to be at risk for experiencing significant distress and engaging in behavior that may be harmful to themselves or others as a result of termination, the psychologist is ethically obligated to take measures or precautions to ensure the client's psychological and physical integrity. Measures may include facilitating appropriate referrals, reducing the fee, extending the length of time between sessions, or providing pro bono services (Knapp & VandeCreek, 1993).

In cases where a client has accrued an outstanding balance and is unwilling or neglecting to pay for provided services, psychologists may use a collection agency to obtain payment. However, before using such an agency, there are ethical considerations of which the therapist should be aware. According to the APA (1992) ethical standards,

> If the patient, client, or other recipient of services does not pay for services as agreed, and if the psychologist wishes to use collection agencies or legal measures to

collect fees, the psychologist first informs the person that such measures will be taken and provides that person an opportunity to make prompt payment. (p. 1603)

Furthermore, "Psychologists may not withhold records under their control that are requested and imminently needed for a patient's or client's treatment solely because payment has not received, except as otherwise provided by law" (p. 1607). Although regulations will vary between states, it is possible for psychologists to be held liable for any "improper, abusive, invasive or otherwise noxious collection activities initiated in her or his name" (Keith-Spiegel & Koocher, 1985, p. 170). Though it is ethical to take legal measures to obtain outstanding payments, any subsequent emotional damage to the client directly linked to collection procedures may result in malpractice claims against the psychologist. Therefore, "Psychologists may decide that occasionally writing off unpaid bills is better than facing malpractice suits or ethical charges—even if the charges are unfounded and frivolous" (Knapp & VandeCreek, 1993, p. 30).

THIRD-PARTY RELATIONSHIPS

Increasingly, practitioners must obtain compensation for services they provide from third-party payors, such as Health Maintenance Organizations (HMOs), Preferred Provider Organizations (PPOs), and insurance companies. Within a third-party payment arrangement, an insurance company, government agency, or employer reimburses the clinician, fully or partially, for services provided to an individual client. Although reimbursement policies often decrease the client's cost for services, such practices may involve further administrative responsibilities and clinical implications for therapy (Chodoff, 1978; Dorken, 1980; Dorken & Webb, 1980; Dujovne, 1980; Julius & Handal, 1980).

In cases where the third-party payor only partially reimburses a psychologist for services rendered, the client is required to make a copayment to cover any residual fee. For example, a third party may cover 80% of the cost of services provided, leaving the client to pay the remaining 20%. Yet despite the substantially lower costs, it is possible that clients may still be unable to cover the copayments. Although some practitioners may be tempted to resolve a client's inability to make the copayment by augmenting the fee charged to the insurance company, thereby lessening the client's portion of the bill, this practice is deemed unethical and often illegal. According to the APA ethical standards, psychologists are not allowed to misrepresent their fees, nor are they to make statements pertaining to fees that are false, deceptive, misleading, or fraudulent. As discussed earlier (see "Pro Bono Services"), practitioners may elect to reduce or waive a client's portion of the fee. Such a practice is ethical and can reduce financial hardship for the client.

Another important issue involved in third-party reimbursement is the client's stated diagnosis. Prior to reimbursement, many third-party payors require the psychologist to provide a definitive diagnosis for a client. The ethical standards (APA, 1992) state,

In their reports to payors for services or sources of research funding, psychologists must accurately state the nature of the research or service provided, the fees or charges, and where applicable, the identity of the provider, the findings, and the diagnosis. (p. 1603)

Explicit in the aforementioned ethical guideline is the principle that assigning an invalid diagnosis for the sole purpose of obtaining reimbursement is an "unethical practice."

In dealing with third-party reimbursement, psychologists may encounter incongruity between the maximum amount paid by a third party and the scope of treatment necessary. Although research indicates that 85% of clients will terminate treatment within 25 sessions, a significant minority of individuals will require extended services (Welch, 1990). Because managed care systems often predetermine the number of sessions it will fund, psychologists may reach a policy's reimbursement limit before termination of services is clinically indicated. When this loss of reimbursement occurs, psychologists must consider options for continuing therapy with their clients. In such instances, a clinician may elect to provide pro bono services, as discussed earlier in this chapter, or make an appropriate affordable referral.

A potentially unethical practice occurs when a service provider takes on a new client, sees the client until his or her third-party coverage expires and he or she can no longer afford treatment, and then terminates services. Such a practice is called "creaming and dumping," in which "creaming" involves using up a client's third-party coverage and subsequently "dumping" the client from the therapist's caseload or, possibly, referring the client to a more affordable service provider (Keith-Spiegel & Koocher, 1985; Knapp & VandeCreek, 1993). This practice can be considered unethical and may be a disservice to clients because it does not generally consider their best interests, nor does it allow other agencies (e.g., community mental health centers), who might continue to see the client pro bono when third-party reimbursement ceases, to receive initial third-party reimbursement. Furthermore, such a practice may be counterproductive to clients' therapeutic progress because termination of services may not be clinically indicated when reimbursement expires. Moreover, such a practice depletes a client of much-needed resources that he or she may have elected to not use had he or she known the circumstances under which services were being provided. Although it is impossible for clinicians to consistently make accurate predictions about the length of treatment and the client's prognosis, psychologists are always ethically obligated to make clinically rather than financially motivated judgments with regard to their clients.

Increasingly, psychologists have been concerned about their professional and legal liability for potential harm done to clients who could no longer afford services and as a result were terminated from their care (e.g., see termination of third-party reimbursement, Knapp & VandeCreek, 1993). Clinicians should be aware that before terminating services, they are always ethically obligated to assess for psychological vulnerability in their clients and take measures to ensure the client's psychological and physical safety. Service providers should be cognizant that they may be held legally accountable for any harm done to clients, because there is legal precedent for the court system to hold health care providers liable for a client's harm when termination is based on third-party reimbursement expiration (e.g., *Wickline v. State of California*, 1986).

By and large, third-party reimbursement can lessen the financial burden of psychotherapy for clients. However, when working within managed care systems, psychologists should be aware of the breadth of their legal and ethical responsibilities to both clients and their reimbursing corporations. When third-party favor arrangements are used, psychologists and their clients should be aware of potential reimbursement limitations and anticipate the likely course of action should payment cease.

INTERPROFESSIONAL FINANCIAL ARRANGEMENTS (FEE SPLITTING)

An interprofessional financial arrangement of particular relevance is an arrangement commonly referred to as *fee splitting*. In the context of health care, fee splitting, sometimes referred to as a *kickback,* involves a portion of the compensation received for services provided being paid out as the result of a prearranged agreement or coercion (Keith-Spiegel & Koocher, 1985). In clinical practice, fee splitting may involve one practitioner receiving compensation for referring a client to another practitioner without actually providing a service. Such practices are considered unethical. According to the APA (1992) ethical standards, "When a psychologist pays, receives payment from, or divides fees with another professional other than in an employer-employee relationship, the payment to each is based on services provided (clinical, consultative, administrative, or other) and is not based on the referral itself" (p. 1603). A primary concern regarding such practices is that the client's best interest may be sacrificed. For example, individuals may be referred for unnecessary services that will subsequently lead to increased health care costs.

Another context in which fee splitting may be relevant is in group practice. As the cost of private practice increases, many practitioner-entrepreneurs are joining with other professionals in practice in an effort to conserve revenues. Often inherent in these arrangements is the sharing of costs and resources with fellow professionals. For example, practitioners in a collaborative practice may apportion such expenses as rent, utility costs, secretarial wages, and technological investments. These expenses may result in a portion of the client's fee being directly allocated to the group practice, with the clinician not directly receiving the total amount billed to clients. Generally, this practice is considered ethical. However, when using this method, partners should (a) predetermine the amount due from each party and (b) ensure that the amount paid is independent from and not contingent on client fees, but rather on actual facility use (Keith-Spiegel & Koocher, 1985).

Within group practices, it is also ethically important that practitioners provide clients with referrals that are in their best interest. Therefore, it is necessary that practitioners have the professional liberty to refer clients to nonpartner therapists (practitioners outside the group practice) if such a referral is clinically indicated. As discussed earlier, in either case, the receiving service provider should not financially reward the referring professional solely on the basis of the referral. In addition, when referring a client, he or she should be accurately informed of the basis on which a referral to a specific provider is made.

FURTHER CONSIDERATIONS

Although the APA has provided a code of ethical standards and governing principles designed to guide the professional behavior of practicing psychologists with respect to financial matters, the ethical standards themselves may be problematic. As they stand, the current ethical standards related to fees and financial arrangements are limited in their specificity. It is likely that this evident ambiguity was purposely built in so that the ethical standards could be applied easily to a wide range of questionable circumstances. Although this ambiguity may indeed mean that practitioners might be able to apply the ethical standards to a wide range of situations, it also means that the ethical standards may be subject to varied interpretation by psychologists who may be left on their own to determine how the guidelines should be applied. As a result, psychologists' ethical behavior as it pertains to financial matters may involve a significant degree of subjectivity, possibly resulting in a lack of consistency in ethical behavior among professionals.

One other possible problem related to the ambiguity of the ethical standards for fees and financial arrangements is that professional psychologists who behave unethically with regard to fees and financial arrangements may be able to bend the standards, or find loopholes, such that their dubious professional behaviors would fall within the confines of ethicality. The obvious danger here is that those service providers who practice unethically may be able to justify their behavior, despite any risk to those who seek services.

Despite the fact that the ethical standards for fees and financial arrangements are so broadly written that they may apply to a wide variety of situations, the current ethical standards neglect to address one very important issue. The APA ethical standards for fees and financial arrangements neither explicitly state the types of psychological services that warrant payment, nor do they provide guidelines regarding the price tag for specific psychological services. This situation is problematic because it suggests that service providers can legitimately expect compensation simply for their professional time, without accounting for any type of treatment plan or for what may or may not have been accomplished during time spent with a client. It also suggests that specialty training is unnecessary to obtain a desired amount of compensation for the provision of services. The absence of guidelines given by the APA regarding the price tag for specific services lastly suggests that when determining a client's fee, practitioners need not concern themselves with whether an assessment or treatment procedure has been empirically validated. Indeed, as the ethical standards currently stand, a service provider who does not use empirically validated assessment and treatment procedures in his or her practice is ethically entitled to request and receive the same compensation as another practitioner who does use empirically validated assessment and treatment procedures. Despite this,

the ethicality of receiving compensation for providing unproved treatments for psychological disorders remains questionable to some psychologists. The APA should properly address these issues by adopting a set of ethics policies regarding fees for specific types of services provided, fees and specialty training, and the compensation practitioners may receive for using either empirically validated or unproved treatment and assessment approaches.

CONCLUSIONS

Psychologists provide services to clients in the context of a therapeutic relationship, while seeking compensation. With respect to matters of compensation and other financial arrangements, the APA has provided a collection of ethical standards to be used as enforceable guidelines for the professional conduct of psychologists. The ethical standards relevant to fees and financial matters in the provision of services discussed in this chapter provide the necessary foundation on which psychologists should base their professional behavior and are necessary to ensure the integrity of the client-therapist relationship.

There are advantages to being familiar with and adhering to the APA ethical standards regarding the governance of fees and other financial matters related to clinical practice. By following these ethical standards, psychologists will likely avoid any professional and legal sanctions for their professional behavior. This is especially the case because most of the ethical standards discussed in this chapter are written so broadly that they will apply to psychologists working in varied roles and contexts. Furthermore, professionals who adhere to these ethical standards will maintain their professional integrity.

Yet psychologists may find that even if they are completely familiar with the ethical standards for fees and financial arrangements and act accordingly, they may not be able to avoid ethical dilemmas or professional and legal entanglements. This is a result of the fact that many of the current ethical standards are written so broadly that they do not specifically address many ethical issues encountered by psychologists who provide services for compensation. As a result, practitioners are often required to demonstrate a substantial degree of interpretative competence when considering ethical issues regarding finances. This strong reliance on subjectivity can lead to inconsistency in interpretation and application of the guidelines. Thus, in ethically ambiguous situations, practitioners may find it advantageous to consult with other professionals before acting. In doing so, uniformity in ethical decisions concerning finances will likely increase and potential unethical practices avoided.

In the process of making decisions regarding their professional behavior in relation to fees and other financial matters, psychologists must consider not only the ethics code but also applicable laws and state psychology board regulations as well. If the ethics code establishes a higher standard of conduct than is required by law, psychologists must meet the higher ethical standard. If the ethics code standards appear to conflict with the requirements of law, then psychologists make known their commitment to the ethics code and take steps to resolve the conflict in a responsible manner. If neither law nor the ethics code resolves an issue, psychologists should consider other professional materials and the dictates of their own conscience and/or, when practical, consult with others within the field.

The purpose of this chapter was to familiarize psychologists with the issues related to fees and financial arrangements for the provision of services and the ethical considerations relevant to such issues. Discussion was devoted to issues, both mentioned and neglected in the current ethical standards, that may be encountered by professional psychologists who provide services to others for compensation. With respect to each issue, direct guidance, based on the ethical standards contained in the current version of the ethical principles of psychologists and code of conduct provided by the APA, was given to the reader.

It is hoped that the preceding discussion of the ethical issues related to fees and financial arrangements provides less experienced psychological service providers, who may have limited knowledge with respect to fees and financial matters, with a more thorough understanding of these important issues. Finally, the directive guidance offered here may assist professional psychologists who encounter future ethical dilemmas related to fees and financial arrangements. As the debates continue on issues of ethics relevant to fees and finances for services rendered (e.g., the importance of the fee in psychotherapeutic interventions or the clinical benefit or detriment of charging for missed sessions), guidelines regarding ethical practice will likely change and perhaps become more specific. As the ethical standards and state laws change, psychologists are obligated to be aware of those changes and incorporate them into their clinical practices.

REFERENCES

American Psychological Association. (1992). Ethical principles of psychologists and code of conduct. *American Psychologist, 47*, 1597-1611.

Chodoff, P. (1978). Psychiatry and the fiscal third party. *American Journal of Psychiatry, 135*, 1141-1147.

Dorken, H. (1980). National health insurance: Implications for mental health practitioners. *Professional Psychology: Research and Practice, 11,* 664-671.

Dorken, H., & Webb, J. T. (1980). 1976 third-party reimbursement experience: An interstate comparison by insurance carrier. *American Psychologist, 35,* 355-363.

Dujovne, B. E. (1980). Third-party recognition of psychological services. *Professional Psychology: Research and Practice, 11,* 574-581.

Fay, A. (1995). Ethical implications of charging for missed session. *Psychological Reports, 77,* 1251-1259.

Freud, S. (1958). On beginning the treatment: Further recommendations on the technique of psycho-analysis I. In J. Strachey (Ed.), *The standard edition of the complete works of Sigmund Freud* (Vol. 12, pp. 123-144). London: Hogarth. (Original work published 1913)

Haas, L., & Malouf, J. (1989). *Keeping up the good work: A practitioner's guide to mental health ethics.* Sarasota, FL: Professional Resource Exchange.

Halpert, E. (1972). The effect of insurance on psychoanalytic treatment. *Journal of the American Psychoanalytic Association, 20,* 122-133.

Herron, W. G., & Sitkowski, S. (1986). Effect of fees on psychotherapy: What is the evidence? *Professional Psychology: Research and Practice, 17,* 347-351.

Julius, S. M., & Handal, P. J. (1980). Third-party payment and national health insurance: An update on psychology's efforts towards inclusion. *Professional Psychology: Research and Practice, 11,* 955-964.

Keith-Spiegel, P., & Koocher, G. P. (1985). *Ethics in psychology: Professional standards and cases.* Hillsdale, NJ: Lawrence Erlbaum.

Knapp, S., & VandeCreek, L. (1993). Legal and ethical issues in billing patients and collecting fees. *Psychotherapy: Theory, Research, Practice, Training, 30,* 25-31.

Koren, L., & Joyce, J. (1953). The treatment implications of payment of fees in a clinic settings. *American Journal of Orthopsychiatry, 23,* 350-357.

Kubie, L. S. (1950). *Practical and theoretical aspects of psychoanalysis.* New York: International Universities Press.

Menninger, K. A., & Holzman, P. S. (1973). *Theory of psychoanalytic technique* (2nd ed.). New York: Basic Books.

Nash, J. L., & Cavenar, J. O. (1976). Free psychotherapy: An inquiry into resistance. *American Journal of Psychiatry, 133,* 1066-1069.

Pope, K. S., Geller, J. D., & Wilkinson, P. S. (1975). Fee assessment and outpatient psychotherapy. *Journal of Consulting and Clinical Psychology, 43,* 835-841.

Welch, B. (1990, May 16). *Testimony on DOD medical programs including the CHAMPUS reform initiative* (Before the Senate Committee on Armed Services, Subcommittee on Manpower and Personnel). Unpublished manuscript.

Wickline v. State of California, 228 Cal. Rptr. 661 (Cal. Ct. App. 1986); review granted 231 Cal. Rptr. 560 (Cal. 1986); review dismissed, 239 Cal. Rptr. 805 (Cal. 1987).

Woody, R. H. (1989). *Business success in mental health practice: Modern marketing, management, and legal strategies.* San Francisco: Jossey-Bass/Pfeiffer.

Yoken, C., & Berman, J. S. (1984). Does paying a fee alter the effectiveness of treatment? *Journal of Consulting and Clinical Psychology, 52,* 254-260.

Yoken, C., & Berman, J. S. (1987). Third-party payment and the outcome of psychotherapy. *Journal of Consulting and Clinical Psychology, 55,* 571-576.

CHAPTER 10

The Termination and Referral of Clients

NATALIE M. RICE AND VICTORIA M. FOLLETTE
University of Nevada, Reno

The processes of termination and referral are common occurrences in therapy, yet many authors have commented on the lack of attention given to these processes in the literature as well as in training programs for psychologists, psychiatrists, counselors, and social workers (Fox, Nelson, & Bolman, 1969; Goodyear, 1981; Kramer, 1986; McRoy, Freeman, & Logan, 1986; Nelson & Politano, 1993; Ward, 1984; Weddington & Cavenar, 1979; Wetchler & Ofte-Atha, 1993; Wolitzky, 1995). The authors emphasize the importance of attending to these processes because they assert that an effective termination/referral can maximize and help maintain treatment gains, whereas a poorly handled termination/referral can undo or weaken strong therapy gains. They describe the termination process as a growth opportunity for both the client and therapist. This chapter will address issues regarding effective termination and referral practices as well as

critically examine the relevant principles in the American Psychological Association (APA) ethics code published in 1992 (all citations will refer to this source).

THE TERMINATION OF THERAPY

Termination refers to the process of ending therapy between a therapist and a client. A 1993 review of the cognitive-behavioral literature revealed an absence of writing concerning the conceptual aspects of termination and found only one article focusing on the mechanics of termination (Nelson & Politano, 1993). Writers from the areas of social work and counseling psychology have also reported a lack of practical and theoretical literature on the subject (Goodyear, 1981; McRoy et al., 1986; Wetchler & Ofte-Atha, 1993). The majority of the literature on the termination process comes from the psychodynamic perspective and tends to focus primarily on the theoretical meaning of termination as opposed to a focus on practical application (Kramer, 1986).

In the psychodynamic literature, termination is discussed in terms of previous and current losses, transference, and countertransference issues. *Transference* can be described as a set of issues based on experiences from the client's history and reflected in the client's feelings and behaviors toward the therapist, and *countertransference* is described as the therapist's reactions to the particular client and the client's transference (Greenberg & Cheselka, 1995). Termination tasks for the client include experiencing and resolving their reactions to the loss and separation from the current therapist, gaining insight into their thoughts and feelings regarding their past losses, and preparing to deal more effectively with future good-byes (Dewald, 1982; Maholick & Turner, 1979; McRoy et al., 1986).

From a behavioral perspective, transference has been defined as "the shared behavioral functions for a client of current and historical contexts due to either their formal similarity or to verbal relations that tie the current event to past events" (Hayes, Follette, & Follette, 1995, p. 161). Nelson and Politano (1993) address cognitive-behavioral theory and termination and assert that termination is a focal point that is evident at each phase of treatment: goal setting, intervention, generalization, and maintenance of changes in target behaviors. The "time-limited" or "short-term" nature of cognitive-behavioral therapy is said to facilitate setting and achieving realistic goals for therapy in a way that discourages unnecessary dependence and beliefs of a miracle cure. As Nelson and Politano summarize it, "Structurally and conceptually, the beginning goal of therapy is to achieve the end of therapy as it was defined at the beginning" (p. 254). Termination for some is therefore a stage of the psychotherapy process with its own tasks to be completed;

for others, it is a process that is present from the beginning of therapy and assists in providing the structure for the general tasks of therapy; still others do not address termination at all. Regardless of the view one holds of an ideal termination, all therapeutic relationships between therapists and clients end at some point, and termination is consequently an important topic for all clinicians.

An Effective Termination

Depending on theoretical orientation, an effective termination could be defined in a number of ways, ranging from the resolution of transference and countertransference issues to the acquisition, generalization, and maintenance of target behavior/skills. There is no consensus on what constitutes an effective termination and thus no consensus on how one goes about achieving such an outcome. Writers and clinicians report differing views on who should decide when termination is appropriate, the criteria for termination readiness, and how the mechanics of termination are approached.

The American Psychological Association Ethics Code

The APA ethics code, though "intended to provide both the general principles and decision rules to cover most situations encountered by psychologists" (Preamble, p. 1599), does not offer comprehensive guidance in the area of ethical behavior with respect to termination and referral practices. According to the ethics code, psychologists apply scientific, research-based knowledge to human behavior in a pragmatic manner that improves "the condition of both the individual and society" (p. 1599). The ethics code's primary stated goal is to provide for the "welfare and protection of the individuals and groups with whom psychologists work" (Preamble,

p. 1599). As O'Donohue and Mangold (1996) point out, however, it is not clear what the underlying ethical theory or theories are that guided the creation of the ethics code. They offer two possible theories, deontological ethics and utilitarianism, which use as criteria for ethical behavior the good will of the psychologist and the consequences of a psychologist's behavior, respectively.

With respect to the practical application of the ethics code to the behavior of psychologists, the absence of an identified underlying ethical theory becomes a problem when a question of ethical behavior arises that is not specifically covered in the ethics code. Even if one is looking only at the practices of termination and referral, countless complicated issues and situations confront practicing psychologists every day. Because it is impossible for any ethics code to predict and address all these potential issues, it therefore seems necessary to have an ethics code based on a theory that can be turned to in these cases to guide decisions concerning ethical behavior. If the underlying theory for the current ethics code were better explicated, the current ethics code might be sufficient for practical purposes; but without a clear guiding base theory, more detailed guidelines are needed in the field.

Who Decides When to Terminate?

Mutual agreement to terminate, regardless of who initiates the process, is often described as the ideal approach to termination (Weddington & Cavenar, 1979). It has been pointed out, however, that a mutually agreed-on termination does not implicitly translate into an effective or ineffective experience for the client and therapist (Levenson, 1976). Kramer (1986) reports that most of the therapists interviewed in his study did not use an explicit approach to talking about termination with their clients; rather, they used

vague, indirect interactions around termination and allowed the clients to bring up the subject. Cognitive-behavioral therapists generally advocate an active, collaborative relationship between therapist and client in which the two collaborate on goal setting, treatment, and termination. They report that the therapist usually makes the suggestion for termination, with the expectation that the client will agree (Nelson & Politano, 1993).

Some authors suggest that the therapist unilaterally set either a tentative or definite termination date from the beginning of therapy or when there is an impasse in the therapy. These authors have described this practice as functioning as a catalyst in accelerating the therapeutic process (Dewald, 1965; Weddington & Cavenar, 1979). It has been suggested that therapists inform the clients of their expectations regarding termination, regardless of how they will approach it. Kramer (1986) states that even if a therapist is not going to set a termination date or initiate termination, the therapist should discuss the process with the client at the beginning of therapy and inform him or her that he or she will be expected to initiate termination.

Standard 4.01a of the APA ethics code states that "Psychologists discuss with clients or patients as early as is feasible in the therapeutic relationship appropriate issues, such as the nature and anticipated course of therapy, fees, and confidentiality" (p. 1605). One could interpret the "anticipated course of therapy" to include a discussion of termination and who will be expected to initiate ending therapy as well as when therapy will end. In Standard 4.09b, the ethics code clearly places certain responsibilities on the therapist. It states that "Psychologists terminate a professional relationship when it becomes reasonably clear that the patient or client no longer needs the service, is not benefiting, or is being harmed by the service" (p. 1606). This standard sets the expectation that the psychologist will determine the client's progress or lack of progress and initiate termination based on it. The criteria for the determination of progress is not specified by the ethics code and is another issue that varies widely in the literature.

When Does One Terminate?

In general, termination in a successful treatment can be said to begin when the therapist, client, or both recognize that the major goals of therapy have been reached and the achievement of other goals is approaching (Dewald, 1982). In his review of the literature, Kramer (1986) found criteria cited for termination, such as the emergence of themes of loss or separation, resolution of transference, improvements in ego functioning (with the ego developed enough to be able to tolerate unhappiness and maintain resiliency), and symptom relief. From a cognitive-behavioral perspective, Nelson and Politano (1993) assert that termination is appropriate when the behavior targets occur enough to be reinforced by naturally occurring consequences in their environment.

Views on the issue of power differential or relationship structure with respect to termination represent the continuum from emphasizing the therapeutic significance of an egalitarian relationship to emphasizing the importance of retaining the therapist-client hierarchical structure. Some view the emergence of egalitarian client behavior toward the therapist as an indication of therapy progress toward termination (Levenson, 1976; Weigert, 1952), whereas others suggest that the therapist facilitate such behaviors (Wechler & Ofte-Atha, 1993), and still others warn against therapist or client drifting toward such behaviors that are viewed as a threat to therapeutic progress (Dewald, 1982; Kubie, 1968). Although authors differ on these issues of equality and candor, many

warn therapists of the possibly harmful effects of entering into a friendship/collegial relationship with a client posttermination (Dewald, 1982; Kubie, 1968; Robbins, 1975). Their caution with respect to multiple relationships and sexual relationships with former clients is also reflected in the APA ethics code (Standards 1.17, 4.05, 4.06, and 4.07). This topic, however, is beyond the scope of this chapter.

The APA ethics code leaves the decisions of when the client no longer needs therapy, is no longer benefiting from therapy, and/or is being harmed by continued therapy up to the therapist, but offers little assistance in determining which of the numerous available criteria to use. In the Preamble, the ethics code makes reference to "scientific knowledge based on research" as well as the promotion of the welfare of clients. If one assumes an underlying theory of utilitarianism, then one might assert that the criteria to be used should have been empirically demonstrated to result in the desired consequences, with the desired consequences being defined by those that are in the best interests of the client. Although this assumption would ideally provide guidance in choosing criteria, the question still remains as how to choose between multiple conflicting research findings. Presently, there is not a wealth of research to turn to for guidance, and thus this question presently exists only in abstract form. In addition to an explanation of the theory underlying the ethics code, additional guidelines regarding criteria use are currently needed.

In addition to theoretical orientation differences in opinion on the critical dimension to be examined (i.e., spontaneity and equality in the therapeutic relationship, generalization and maintenance of therapy targets, resolution of transference issues, etc.), ethical dilemmas can arise on other levels. Recently, the present authors encountered a situation in which a couple was being seen in therapy and the therapists became aware of domestic violence between the couple. The couple attended sessions sporadically (at times disappearing for weeks at a time without contact information) and continued to engage in physical violence regardless of their stated commitment to nonviolence. They reported that they wished to continue therapy, but their noncompliance with treatment put them in a dangerous position. The continued violence indicated that the couple was not benefiting from therapy and was possibly being harmed by continued treatment, because treatment continuation could be construed as tacit acceptance of the status quo.

The APA ethics code states that the therapist should terminate therapy if the clients are not benefiting from and/or are being harmed by continued service, but it is unclear what one should do if the therapist considers a situation too risky to continue treatment yet considers terminating treatment risky as well (as in this example). The issue was further complicated in this instance because one of the partners required a Spanish-speaking therapist and there were very few Spanish-speaking services available in town. Standard 4.09a states that "Psychologists do not abandon patients or clients" (p. 1606), yet Standard 4.09b instructs therapists to terminate ineffective therapy. One of the partners in this couple reacted to the termination rationale with anger and expressed feelings of abandonment. The supervision team weighed the options of continuing and discontinuing therapy and determined that although terminating therapy carried some risk, continuing therapy carried a greater risk. They decided that terminating therapy was in the best interests of the clients, and each person was encouraged to pursue individual treatment.

How Does One Terminate?

Standard 4.09c of the APA ethics code states,

Prior to termination for whatever reason, except where precluded by the patient's or client's conduct, the psychologist discusses the patient's or client's views and needs, provides appropriate pretermination counseling, suggests alternative service providers as appropriate, and takes other reasonable steps to facilitate transfer of responsibility to another provider if the patient or client needs one immediately. (p. 1606)

To be in compliance with the ethics code, one should therefore ideally have a discussion with the client about termination and the client's views and needs. It is unclear, however, what constitutes "pretermination counseling" according to the ethics code. One therapist might interpret pretermination counseling as a 5-minute explanation of the reason for the therapist's initiation of termination and a single question regarding the client's understanding of that explanation, whereas another therapist might interpret pretermination counseling as discussing the client and therapist's thoughts and feelings about termination over the course of the 6 sessions before the termination date.

If the underlying theory of the ethics code is assumed to be utilitarianism, then one might assert that the characteristics of ethical pretermination counseling are associated with therapeutic benefits (or at least are not iatrogenic). Based on the ethics code's reference to scientific knowledge gained through research, one could claim that this association of pretermination counseling characteristics and therapeutic benefits are to be determined by empirical research. If, however, the underlying theory of the ethics code is assumed to be deontological in nature, a therapist need only have good intentions in approaching pretermination counseling to be behaving in an ethically defensible manner. Assuming a utilitarianism theory, the terms *effective* and *ethical* could be interchangeable in that what is found to be the most effective approach to termination could also be considered the most ethical approach as well. Currently, there is a lack of empirical evidence on the topic, but there is a range of suggestions based on clinical experience offered in the literature on how to most effectively terminate a therapeutic relationship.

Nelson and Politano (1993) describe a cognitive-behavioral approach in which the therapist and therapy are systematically withdrawn, giving the client more responsibility and control over his or her problems. They state that the therapist-client relationship has an impact on skill generalization and maintenance and that the expectation communicated to the client that he or she can deal effectively with problems (self-efficacy) is a main factor mediating therapeutic outcome and maintenance. Predicting and preparing the client for relapses and scheduling follow-up sessions or having an open-door policy for booster sessions are included in the process. They offer six suggestions for fading the therapeutic relationship, enhancing generalization, and reducing relapse. They suggest (a) setting the final sessions 2 or 3 weeks apart or using booster sessions, (b) giving homework to self-monitor progress between sessions, (c) scheduling one follow-up session after 4 weeks or intermittently for a few months to check on maintenance, (d) having check-in reports through the mail or telephone at regular intervals (such as once every 2 weeks for 12 weeks after termination), (e) having more than one person involved in the treatment with changing settings (to facilitate generalization), and (f) using self-control methods so that the client is the primary change agent.

Termination in the structural/strategic theory has been described as a "mutually agreed upon ending between the family and the therapist that presumes that the presenting problem of the family has been solved" (Wetchler & Ofte-Atha, 1993, p. 35). They note that in this framework, the therapist is higher in the hierarchy than the clients, which can lead to disempowerment of families in that families may believe that the therapist is the one who has the power to solve their problems. Techniques to empower families at termination are offered, including "praising the family for resolving the problem better than therapist could" (p. 38) and "using the family as a consultant to the therapist" (p. 39). The emphasis on having "systemic flexibility" reflected in an egalitarian relationship between clients and the therapist is critical. Other suggestions include having families engage in activities during the normal therapy appointment time (when tapering therapy sessions) and predicting relapses.

Although spacing sessions farther apart as termination is approaching is a commonly suggested practice, some authors disagree with this practice. Kubie (1968), for example, asserts that when sessions are spaced farther apart, the longer intervals "give freer rein to the patient's fantasies, with less opportunity to bring them into the open in the analysis, or to subject them to corrective experiences" (p. 340). As with other practices, it appears that views on this technique vary with conceptualization of the therapy and termination tasks.

McRoy et al. (1986), from the social work field, offer "basic practice principles" for termination, including not waiting until the last session to introduce termination and being aware of and using relevant theoretical material as a guide in planning a termination. Also included in the principles are recommendations to consider the influence of past experiences of separation/loss for the therapists as well as the clients, and to teach the clients about predictable reactions to loss, help them identify their reactions, and normalize the reactions.

Kramer (1986) presented guidelines for termination based on a 1982 survey of termination practices, theoretical models, and clinical experience. He advocated an overt discussion of termination with the client (from the beginning of therapy and continuing throughout) even if the therapist is going to let the client decide when it will happen; respecting a client's decision to terminate and providing feedback and a clinical opinion if the therapist disagrees with the client's decision; being aware of and dealing with countertransference; being sensitive to termination cues from the client (such as client reducing the frequency of sessions, not having much to talk about, and requiring less input from the therapist); reviewing treatment progress; and having an open-door policy in which clients are told they can return for follow-up or further treatment if necessary (the majority of his subjects reported that they had this). Kramer also suggests using a cost-benefits analysis to help determine whether termination is appropriate (looking at time, energy, and money spent compared to the therapeutic gains).

A review of the client's progress is commonly recommended in the literature. Bostic, Shadid, and Blotcky (1996) offer eight areas of progress that can be discussed with the client when reviewing client progress at termination, including changes in the capacity to love and be loved; symptoms/problems; resolution of precipitating stressors; coping ability; awareness, appreciation, and acceptance of self and others; daily functioning; quality of life; and ability to observe self and analyze situations. They suggest reframing termination as coming away with a new perspective and skills that will help them continue their therapeutic work even after therapy. If clients require help transitioning out of therapy, they suggest that brief letters (that do not address specific therapy issues) can be written in response to letters from clients.

Although there is a range of suggestions on how to terminate therapeutic relationships,

there are some general commonalities across viewpoints, such as an emphasis on the importance of attending to client and therapist reactions to termination, working to maximize the transfer of treatment gains outside of the therapy context, increasing client self-reliance and confidence, and acknowledging the loss of the relationship and the gains the client has made in therapy (Bostic et al., 1996; Dewald, 1982; Kramer, 1986; Hayes et al., 1995; Maholick & Turner, 1979; Nelson & Politano, 1993; Ward, 1984). These client-oriented suggested practices could be presented as the pretermination counseling and discussion of the client's views and needs advocated by the APA ethics code. If the underlying theory of the ethics code were identified, these practices could then be evaluated in terms of that theory.

Barriers to an Effective Termination

The above suggestions from the literature reflect the authors' ideas regarding an ideal termination. As therapists know all too well, however, countless factors can interfere with ideal therapy practices. Commonly discussed factors that can interfere with an effective termination include "forced" terminations; "premature" terminations; client variables, including transference issues; therapist variables, including countertransference issues; and a lack of adequate supervision/training with respect to termination.

Forced Termination: Therapist Initiated

The extent to which an interrupted termination disrupts treatment can depend on the nature of the therapeutic relationship, the length and intensity of treatment to the point of the interruption, the nature of treatment at the time of the interruption, how the termination is presented, how much time is left to deal with termination, and whether the termination is therapist (forced) or patient (premature) initiated (Smith, 1983). In the case of forced termination, the therapist initiates termination because of extratherapeutic parameters such as therapist relocation (training rotation, job change, or move out of the area), therapist retirement, therapist illness, or therapist death (Bostic et al., 1996). Writers have stressed the importance of preparing students to handle forced terminations, given the institutionalization of these practices in training programs through policies such psychiatric rotations each semester (Bostic et al., 1996; Dewald, 1965; Keith, 1966; Smith, 1983; Weddington & Cavenar, 1979).

Often cited in discussions of forced terminations is the Veterans Administration Mental Hygiene Clinic study in which Pumpian-Mindlin (1958) found that clients experienced the most difficulty when the termination was presented to them as an order declared by some higher authority. The study also revealed that the less content the residents were about an upcoming rotation, the more problems their clients had when transferred. Authors generally suggest that therapists avoid portraying themselves as passive victims and blaming the system for the termination (Bostic et al., 1996; O'Reilly, 1987).

Bostic et al. (1996) offer nine general guidelines to follow when carrying out a forced termination, to be combined with consideration for the details of the individual case. They discuss providing termination notice based on the client's best interests; deciding how much to divulge about the therapist's situation leading to the termination (i.e., relocation details, etc.); dealing with client issues that surface after the announcement; countertransference issues; transfer to another therapist; concluding remarks and empowering clients; dealing

with client gifts; balancing the therapist as a transitional object while allowing the formation of a new relationship; and what to say in the last session.

Although they can present challenges to the therapist and client, there is some evidence that forced terminations can result in positive therapeutic outcomes. As evidenced by the Pumpian-Mindlin (1958) study, the manner in which the therapist and client reactions are dealt with in therapy are important factors to consider. Dewald (1965) documented positive outcomes in situations in which the forced termination served as a catalyst that accelerated the emergence of negative transference reactions and previous reactions to loss and separation.

Standard 4.08a in the APA ethics code states, "Psychologists make reasonable efforts to plan for facilitating care in the event that psychological services are interrupted by factors such as the psychologist's illness, death, unavailability, or relocation or by the client's relocation or financial limitations." According to Standard 4.08b,

> When entering into employment or contractual relationships, psychologists provide for orderly and appropriate resolution of responsibility for patient or client care in the event that the employment or contractual relationship ends with paramount consideration given to the welfare of the patient or client. (p. 1606)

The ethics code is unclear regarding what constitutes "reasonable efforts" or "appropriate resolution," but it is clear that therapists have a responsibility to consider the welfare of their clients and take action in an attempt to ensure their welfare.

Standard 4.09a states that "Psychologists do not abandon patients or clients" (p. 1606). As Pope and Vasquez (1998) point out, however, insurance companies and managed care policies can pose a challenge with respect to this standard. As Pope and Vasquez assert, insurance and managed care companies can refuse continuing services with a client when the therapist believes that terminating therapy could be harmful to the client (possibly resulting in the client's suicide). This situation, regardless of company policy, they explain, could constitute abandonment of the client. In its current form, the ethics code is written to supercede the law (Standard 1.02, p. 1598); the therapist's personal values, culture, and experience (p. 1599); and organizational demands (Standard 8.03). In the event of a conflict between the demands of the law and the ethics code, the ethics code instructs therapists to "make known their commitment to the ethics code and take steps to resolve the conflict in a responsible manner" (p. 1600). In the event of a conflict between ethics and organizational demands, the ethics code advises therapists to "clarify the nature of the conflict, make known their commitment to the ethics code, and to the extent feasible, seek to resolve the conflict in a way that permits the fullest adherence to the ethics code" (p. 1611).

Even as the APA ethics code is written to supercede other demands, it also simultaneously detracts from its original assertions with phrases such as "to the extent feasible" and "the fullest adherence." This wording implies that the therapist may balance the demands of the ethics code with other demands and still behave in an ethical manner. If this is the case, nothing is resolved, and the therapist is left alone to decide how to balance the conflicting demands. We recommend that the ethics code explain in more detail how one is to weigh conflicting demands between the ethics code and the law and/or organizations, because having clear standards for this practice is becoming increasingly important.

Premature Termination: Client Initiated

Premature termination can be defined as the case in which "The client believes or purports to believe that the process [therapy] is complete, despite the counselor's judgment and concern that it is not" (Ward, 1984, p. 24). Circumstances for these terminations include events external to therapy (such as clients moving out of the area or physical illness); clients unexpectedly dropping out of therapy without explanation; financial considerations; therapist-client mismatch; clients unsatisfied with therapy; and clients reporting that they have finished their work in therapy (Smith, 1983).

In the case of premature termination, the therapist is faced with not only the task of deciding whether the client's decision reflects a mature, thoughtful decision or whether it reflects resistance or avoidance; the therapist must also be aware of his or her own actions and reactions in an effort to examine what he or she may have done to influence the premature termination or whether he or she has a wish to prolong therapy for personal reinforcement or to avoid negative feelings (Robbins, 1975). As with forced terminations, it has been pointed out that premature terminations can result in positive therapeutic outcomes if there is enough notice to effectively handle the termination and the time pressure functions to intensify the work done in the remaining time left (Smith, 1983).

University counseling center studies have examined reasons for client premature termination. One study found that clients were more likely to terminate after one session when problem recognition by the therapist was absent, and this finding was more pronounced for experienced counselors compared with trainees (Epperson, Bushway, & Warman, 1983). In another university counseling center study, administrative factors (length of intake, time between intake to assignment, and days from intake to first session) were found to be the major factors related to premature termination (Rodolfa, Rapaport, & Lee, 1983). There have been conflicting findings for the relationship between gender of intake therapist and premature termination (Rodolfa et al., 1983).

As previously discussed, the APA ethics code instructs therapists "prior to termination for whatever reason" to discuss the client's views and needs, to provide pretermination counseling, to suggest alternative service providers if appropriate, and to facilitate client transfer if appropriate. Client conduct that precludes such practice is not specified by the Standard 4.09c. Not coming into a session is one behavior that would obviously preclude such practices, but there are other less extreme behaviors, often referred to as "client reactions," that may be unpleasant to work with. Presently, a therapist could ethically claim that the client's conduct precluded the practices listed above even though it may have been possible to work with the client toward a more effective termination.

Client Reactions

Client responses to termination may mirror earlier responses to past losses (Dewald, 1965). Common client responses to termination cited in the literature include feeling unworthy, feelings of guilt, denial, acting out, self-defeating behaviors, searching for substitute transference objects, symptom increase or reemergence of old symptoms, devaluation of therapy, attempts to prematurely terminate, feelings of anger, feelings of resentment, feelings of abandonment, feelings of anxiety or depression, feelings of pain, attempts to delay termination, and an inability to generalize learned behaviors (Bostic et al., 1996; Dewald, 1965, 1982;

Fox et al., 1969; Keith, 1966; Ward, 1984; Wetchler & Ofte-Atha, 1993; Weigert, 1952).

In the case of a forced termination, Bostic et al. (1996) assert that the more forced termination resembles a client's past losses, the more the client needs to know about the therapist's situation in order to gain some control over their transference feelings and fantasies. The more reality provided to clients, they claim, the greater the distinction will occur between the past relationships and the current therapist-client relationship. This distinction is said to help them cope with the current loss in an effective way.

Bostic et al. (1996) also suggest allowing clients to make some decisions regarding continuing therapy to give them some mastery over the situation. They note that late or nonpayment of fees may signal anger, a wish to maintain a connection to the therapist, an attempt to punish the authority ordering the termination, or a wish for special treatment to prove the client is viewed as special to the therapist. Gifts from the client, they observe, may signal a need to be remembered.

Therapist Reactions

Termination has been described as a learning opportunity for both clients and therapists (Weddington & Cavenar, 1979). When termination is discussed in the literature, the importance of attending to therapist reactions is often emphasized. Authors strongly advise therapists and supervisors to explore, be aware of, and assess the therapist's feelings and thoughts about termination. Feelings of sadness, denial, anger, relief, resentment, anxiety, rejection, fear, and evaluation anxiety are described as common therapist reactions that if not dealt with properly could prevent the therapist from facilitating an effective termination (Dewald, 1965; Goodyear, 1981; Keith, 1966; Maholick & Turner, 1979; McRoy et al., 1986; Scher, 1970).

For the counselor, termination can be a loss of gratification, for example, when termination is the end of a significant relationship; when it evokes the counselor's anxieties about the client's ability to function without the therapist; when it arouses guilt in the therapist about not being as effective as he or she would have liked to have been; when the therapist's professional sense of self is threatened by an angry/abrupt departure of a client; when it is the end of a learning experience for the therapist; when it ends the therapist's experience of living vicariously through a client; when it becomes a symbolic recapitulation of other good-byes for the therapist; and when it evokes therapist conflicts about his or her own individuation (Goodyear, 1981). If clients detect countertransference, Bostic et al. (1996) maintain that the appropriate response is to validate that experience.

Feelings of therapist guilt at deserting clients or not obtaining desired outcomes are commonly reported, particularly in the case of forced terminations. Authors have associated therapist guilt with denial reactions and the following nontherapeutic therapist behaviors: acting in inappropriate ways (such as offering the client a ride in his or her car or meeting socially), minimizing and avoiding recognizing the client's reactions, increasing the client's medication, automatically arranging for a transfer to another therapist, denying the significance of the relationship to themselves or the client, delaying telling the client about the termination, and focusing on practical details at the expense of attention to client/therapist reactions (Beatrice, 1983; Bostic et al., 1996; Dewald, 1965; Keith, 1966; O'Reilly, 1987; Smith, 1983; Weddington & Cavenar, 1979). Dewald (1965) observes that with the presence of therapist guilt, the problems of client responses of aggression to termination and therapist counteraggression are compounded. Increased countertransference and an

increased potential for destructive countertransference, Weddington and Cavenar (1979) claim, are the major factors that separate mutually agreed-on termination from termination initiated by the therapist.

In the case of therapist-initiated termination not due to external pressures, Smith (1983) warns therapists and supervisors to be aware of the involvement of possible therapist countertransference variables guiding the decision. He states that when a therapist abruptly ends an ongoing treatment, it is often the case that the therapist has found the client to be too overwhelming and reacts with anxiety, frustration, and/or guilt until he or she becomes convinced that the therapist-client match is inappropriate. He cites behaviors such as forgetting a client's appointment, not being able to remember the client's name, complaining that a client is boring, and blaming the client for difficulties in therapy as possible signs that this is an issue to be explored. Kramer (1986) emphasizes the importance of differentiating between the goals of the clients and the goals of the therapist for the client.

In summary, based on the available literature and the APA ethics code, the following practices are recommended for therapists regarding termination:

1. Take responsibility at the beginning of a therapy contract for educating the client on how the termination process will unfold and what criteria you will be using to evaluate their progress.

2. Plan for discussing the client's experience of the process, needs, and concerns, and set time aside as termination approaches for this discussion.

3. Choose criteria for evaluating termination readiness in a thoughtful manner that takes into consideration current scientific knowledge on the issue and the client's best interests.

4. Be aware of your own reactions and how they might affect the client. Take responsibility for getting consultation or support if needed.

THE REFERRAL AND TRANSFER OF CLIENTS

Authors have commented on the frequency of client transfer from one therapist to another in mental health care settings ranging from training clinics to private practices (Keith, 1966; O'Reilly, 1987; Scher, 1970; Tryon, 1983; Wapner, Klein, Friedlander, & Andrasik, 1986). In a national survey of full-time private practitioners, almost 85% of respondents reported that they sometimes or often referred clients to other therapists (Tryon, 1983). In a survey of psychology training clinics, one third of the clinics reported transferring more than 10% of their clients (Wapner et al., 1986). Although not commonly addressed in the literature, clients may also initiate a transfer. Perhaps this is due to the categorization of occurrences such as premature termination.

An Effective Transfer of a Client

When to Refer Clients

Transferring clients may occur when therapists leave their clinical settings, change their professional roles, change their professional activities, or decide for whatever reason that it is not beneficial to the client to continue working together (Keith, 1966; Wapner et al., 1986; Wood & Wood, 1990). The most frequently mentioned reasons for referral in Tryon's (1983) national survey were for specialized treatment for the client, for client medication, not enough available hours for the client, and because the client was a friend or family member of another client seen by the therapist.

The APA ethics code implicitly advocates the referral of clients when client's needs are outside the therapist's boundaries of competence (Standard 1.04a); the therapist's personal problems and conflicts may interfere with the therapist's effectiveness and are likely to harm a client (Standard 1.13); there are potentially harmful multiple relationships or the possibility of multiple relationships (Standard 1.17), including conflicting couples and family therapy relationships (Standard 4.03) and sexual relationships (Standards 4.06 and 4.07); and the therapist or client relocates, the client encounters financial limitations, or the therapist becomes ill or dies (Standard 4.08). The issues of boundaries of competence, a therapist's personal problems, multiple relationships, and financial limitations can be complicated. What are the therapist's responsibilities, for example, when a client who is at high risk for self-harm can no longer afford to pay the therapist's regular fee or presents with an issue that the therapist is personally struggling with?

The issue of cultural competence and culturally sensitive therapy is one such example of an issue that is fraught with controversy and ethical dilemmas. Suppose, for example, that a therapist limits his practice to Caucasian, heterosexual clients and refers all other clients to other practitioners, citing APA ethics code Standard 1.04a as his reason. Standard 1.10 states that psychologists do not discriminate based on race/ethnicity or sexual orientation, yet Standard 1.04a prohibits psychologists from practicing outside their boundaries of competence. In the APA *Guidelines for Providers of Psychological Services to Ethnic, Linguistic, and Culturally Diverse Populations* (1993), Guideline 2 asserts that "Psychologists are cognizant of relevant research and practice issues as related to the population being served" (p. 46), and Guideline 2b instructs psychologists to "seek out educational and training experiences to enhance their understanding and thereby address the needs of these populations more appropriately and effectively" (p. 46).

One could technically engage in a circular pattern of reasoning and justify such a limited practice, keeping in line with the above ethical standards. The therapist could reason, for example, that he is not serving populations other than the one he is most familiar with and therefore does not need to seek out any additional education and training. He can then argue that he is not discriminating against ethnic minorities or nonheterosexual clients, but rather, he is refraining from practicing outside the boundaries of his competence. This is a more extreme example, but many other less obviously questionable situations can arise in the everyday practice of therapy. It is impossible for therapists to maintain current knowledge in every area of psychology, yet it is unclear where the boundary exists between the ethical and unethical referral of clients based on the therapist's areas of competence. At what point does a psychologist draw his or her boundary of competence, and at what point is a psychologist expected to seek out educational and training experiences to expand his or her boundaries of competence? This is an issue that remains to be addressed by the ethics code.

Finances are another major area of potential ethical dilemmas. The APA ethics code prohibits paying or accepting a fee for a referral (Standard 1.27) but is not as specific with respect to other financial aspects of referral practice. The ethics code lists financial limitations as a possible reason for the interruption of services. Under Standard 1.25, therapists are advised to discuss with the client "as early as is feasible" potential limitations in service if the therapist anticipates limitations in financing on the part of

the client. Currently, there are no explicit sanctions against referral practices based on the client's financial situation. In some cases, it might be to the therapist's or agency's benefit to maintain more wealthy clients and refer out the less wealthy clients. The ethics code specifies the best interests of the client as the primary consideration in referral practices, but how does one determine the client's best interests, and how does one weigh the other secondary considerations? With the involvement of more agencies and the managerial involvement of more people with a business (as opposed to psychological) orientation, it seems necessary for the next ethics code to expand on their existing standards and take more stances on practices that are deemed harmful enough to be prohibited.

Who Is the New Therapist?

When referring a client, level of professional competency has been suggested in the literature by some authors as the primary criterion to consider (Wood & Wood, 1990), whereas others suggest focusing on the match between the characteristics of the former therapist the client was responding to and the characteristics of the referral therapist (Bostic et al., 1996). Patterson (2001) advocates the creation of competence criteria within the specialty area and use of these criteria when making a referral.

Authors have documented a number of informal criteria used by therapists in choosing a referral. The therapist may, for example, refer a challenging client to a therapist he or she feels competitive with in the hope that the new therapist will struggle or fail with the client; feel obligated to the therapist who accepts a difficult client; attempt to obligate the therapist he or she refers a "good" client to; or refer the client to a therapist whose empathy and skill are admired in an effort to facilitate future progress for the client (Scher,

1970). Wood and Wood (1990) list personal friendships, jealousies, professional and personal competition, social motivations, the wish to offer a favor or receive a favor, personality characteristics similar to the referring therapist, training program/theoretical orientation/ethnic background/age/gender/religious allegiances, and ability of the therapist to reciprocate a favor as factors that can influence the choice of a referral.

Some clients, Scher (1970) states, may benefit from taking a break from therapy at the time of transfer (for example, no therapy for a month). Dewald (1982) advocates not assuming that a client needs to be transferred in the event of a forced termination. He suggests delaying this decision until the therapist can observe how effectively the client can work through his or her reactions to the termination.

Standard 1.20 of the APA ethics code directly addresses the referral of clients. It states that "Psychologists arrange for appropriate consultation and referrals based principally on the best interests of their patients or clients, with appropriate consent, and subject to other relevant considerations, including applicable law and contractual obligations" (p. 1602). The ethics code thus indicates that clients' best interests are the *primary* criterion to be used when deciding whom to refer clients to. How to determine what is in the best interests of the client is left up to the therapist to decide. Wood and Wood (1990) suggested professional competency and Bostic et al. (1996) suggested that matched characteristics are criteria that seem to be reasonable candidates for effective and ethical practice in the best interests of the client. In using the word *primarily,* however, the ethics code also leaves the door open for considerations other than the client's best interests. An ethical referral could therefore include the informal criteria cited by Scher (1970) and Wood and Wood

(1990), such as personal obligations and jealousies, as secondary considerations. Although they do not appear to be based on the client's best interests, they are currently not prohibited by the ethics code.

How to Transfer Clients

In their review of the literature, Wapner et al. (1986) concluded that clinicians seem to be handling the transfer of clients on the basis of intuition, and there appears to be no theoretical or empirical basis for handling the various issues in the transfer process. In their survey of directors of psychology training clinics, Wapner et al. found that there was significant concern about the transfer process, but there was not a consensus on how it is done most effectively. In general, the clinics surveyed appeared to have few specific policies standardizing the transfer process. On the basis of their literature review and analysis of clinical records, Wapner et al. concluded that they could not find clear evidence of a relationship between an effective transfer and any client, therapist, or treatment variable. They found a "marginal" relationship between a successful outcome and clients having previous therapy experiences before arriving at their clinic.

Common suggestions in the literature for client transfer include telling the client about the transfer within a time frame that allows room for discussion and planning; involving the client in the process and decisions to be made; exploring client and therapist reactions to the transfer; having the client meet with the new therapist (preferably while still seeing the departing therapist); engaging in sufficient communication with the new therapist; and presenting the transfer within a positive framework (Bostic et al., 1996; Dewald, 1982; O'Reilly, 1987; Scher, 1970; Wapner et al., 1986). As Wapner et al. (1986) note, authors vary in their suggestions of how much advance notice of the transfer should be given. Some authors assert that telling a client too early can complicate the remaining therapy work (Pumpian-Mindlin, 1958), whereas others suggest that the earlier a therapist tells the client about the upcoming transfer, the more time the client has to work through his or her reactions and be able to accept the new therapist (Dewald, 1982; O'Reilly, 1987).

As with the common suggestion with respect to termination, O'Reilly (1987) cautions therapists not to assign blame for the situation to a higher authority and to be aware of their own feelings of anxiety or resentment about their next placements. He offers a rule of thumb to institutions that once a client is transferred by a trainee, he or she should be assigned to a permanent staff member to avoid setting the client up to be transferred again. Reider (1953, as cited in Keith, 1966) recommended that a partial solution to the problem of multiple transfers could be to actively foster positive client feelings to the service setting as a whole or permanent staff (i.e., receptionists, nurses, etc.) rather than to individual, nonpermanent therapists.

As discussed earlier, Standard 1.25 instructs therapists to tell clients "as early as is feasible" about possible limitations in service anticipated due to limitations in financing, which could be interpreted to include the possibility of a referral and generalize to other referral situations. The other common suggestions of discussing the client's thoughts and feelings about the termination and referral and engaging in sufficient communication with the new therapist also appear to be compatible with the APA ethics code. Standard 4.09c, as previously discussed, directs therapists to have a discussion with the client before termination/referral about the client's views and needs; provide pretermination counseling; and take other "reasonable steps to facilitate the transfer of

responsibility to another provider if the patient or client needs one immediately" (p. 1606). What constitute "reasonable steps" to facilitate a transfer, however, is not clear.

Referral practices can range from handing the client a card with other service providers' names and numbers to having joint transfer sessions with the client and the client's new therapist before the transfer is complete. Matters become even more complicated when one considers how to handle cases in which the current therapist is the only one who can provide a particular type of service and needs to refer a client (such as in the case of therapists serving rural areas, bilingual therapists, or therapists providing specialized treatment). What constitute reasonable steps on the part of the therapist is even less clear in such examples than it is in more straightforward cases.

Potential Barriers to an Effective Transfer of a Client

Client Reactions

The "transfer syndrome" is a term Keith (1966) used to describe "the cluster of symptoms which result from an inadequately understood loss of a therapist occurring in a clinic setting in which periodic transfers of therapy patients are dictated by administrative necessities rather than patient needs" (p. 186). The observed symptoms, he reports, are an attempt by the unconscious ego to deal with the anxiety from the loss of the therapist. The syndrome is said to be commonly manifested in clients in the forms of anger and hostility, which may be directed at the departing therapist, new therapist, institution, and/or mental health community. Expression of the anger/hostility is reported to occur in the form of verbal attacks, missed appointments, tardiness, irritability in session, noncompliance with treatment, and unfavorable comparisons of the new therapist to the past therapist (O'Reilly, 1987). Clients may also exhibit other reactions such as those listed previously (under "Client Reactions to Termination"). According to Keith, the manifestation of the reaction varies with the client's developmental stage.

Scher (1970) described the "therapeutic triangle" that the departing therapist, new therapist, and client comprise. Within the therapeutic triangle, Scher describes the client as not only having to deal with reactions related to the loss of the last therapeutic relationship (such as those discussed under "Termination Reactions") but also having to be in a position of being exposed to a new therapist with less control than the client had over his or her exposure with the previous therapist. Scher points out that with the previous therapist, the client could control how much to reveal at what point. With the new therapist, however, the client does not have as much control given that the previous therapist may have already discussed the case with the new therapist. This, Scher comments, may evoke the client's fear of "disapproval, distortion, and misperception." If the client makes therapeutic progress with the new therapist, Scher explains, he or she may feel disloyal to the previous therapist. If he or she deteriorates, however, the client may feel that he or she has disappointed the person who stepped in to save him or her. Scher concludes, in order to be impartial, that the client cannot change, yet if he or she does not change, the client hurts all three people in the triangle.

The Previous Therapist's Reactions

According to Keith (1966), the transfer syndrome affects both the client and the therapist. For the departing therapist, O'Reilly (1987) reports, the main issue is one of guilt for either deserting the client or failing to cure the client. When the case has been

difficult, therapist relief is a commonly described reaction that is usually mixed with guilt (O'Reilly, 1987). Depression in response to not "curing" the client or in response to losing the relationship has also been observed (Keith, 1966; O'Reilly, 1987). Similar to the case with termination, the therapist may respond to guilt and/or depression by denying the upcoming transfer, denying the significance of the relationship, delaying telling the client about the transfer, focusing on the practical details at the expense of focusing on emotional reactions, making inappropriate attempts to maintain the relationship, and prematurely terminating the client (Bostic et al., 1996; Keith, 1966; O'Reilly, 1987). Fear of evaluation by peers or supervisors, anxiety concerning what the client might expose about him or her, and anxiety about the new placement have also been noted as potentially important complicating factors to be aware of (O'Reilly, 1987; Scher, 1970).

In describing the therapeutic triangle, Scher noted that a smooth client transfer is a "rare phenomenon" and that the three-sided awkwardness is more common. Dewald (1982) warns that if responses to termination with the previous therapist are not acknowledged and addressed with the previous therapist, the client may transfer to the new therapist with inappropriate expectations and unfinished business.

The New Therapist's Reactions

Like the previous therapist, the new therapist can be subjected to scrutiny and comparison by the client and the other therapist (Scher, 1970). In deciding to accept a referral, a range of factors has been implicated in the process, including time and scheduling concerns, personal factors, and obligation (Scher, 1970; Wood & Wood, 1990). As the new therapist is advised to process the loss of the previous therapist with the client, Scher (1970) notes, "For the time being, the new therapist must weather the indignity of being less important to the patient" (p. 282). Therapists are cautioned, however, to be aware of the fine line between exploring feelings and agreeing with criticism of the past therapist (O'Reilly, 1987) and not to give in to the impulse to "lay the previous therapist to rest" and move forward with a treatment plan (Scher, 1970). These authors advise the new therapist to take advantage of the opportunity the transfer offers with respect to providing material to explore previous losses.

Standard 1.20b of the APA ethics code states, "When indicated and professionally appropriate, psychologists cooperate with other professionals in order to serve their patients or clients effectively and appropriately" (p. 1602). The ethics code thus advises both the previous and the new therapists to cooperate with each other in the best interests of the client. The level of the involvement, however, is not outlined.

SUGGESTIONS FOR ORGANIZATIONS

Thus far, termination and referral issues have been presented primarily at the level of the individual therapist. Based on the available literature, the following guidelines are offered for dealing with issues of termination and referral at the organizational level.

1. Incorporate the concepts of termination and transfer into theoretical orientation formulations.

2. Include issues of termination and referral in training curricula reflecting both theoretical knowledge and practical application. McRoy et al. (1986) offer suggestions for teaching about termination.

3. Provide ongoing supervision to students and staff (when possible) with careful attention to therapist and client positive and negative reactions to termination and referral.

4. Provide a forum for students and staff therapists to regularly share termination and referral strategies, challenges, and lessons learned.

5. When creating policies in service settings, make every effort to take into consideration and plan for the multiple terminations and transfers that result when therapists-in-training are required to rotate through settings or specialties. Keith (1966), O'Reilly (1987), and Wapner et al. (1986) offer recommendations for dealing with this issue.

6. To address potential ethical dilemmas, use Pope and Vasquez's (1998) suggested processes of "careful, imaginative awareness" and thinking through a worst-case scenario to help generate possible situations and solutions.

RECOMMENDATIONS TO THE APA

We recommend that the ethical theory or theories that guided the APA ethics code be explicated in a way that facilitates the comprehension and application of the ethics code with respect to the provision of psychological services. If a utilitarian ethic is identified, for example, we concur with O'Donohue and Mangold's (1996) assertion that it would be important to specify what types of consequences would be morally relevant as well as specifications on how to weigh the various consequences. As previously discussed, the interests of the client, therapist, agency, and other involved parties are all relevant to decisions made regarding termination and referral practices. Currently, the ethics code states that the therapist should act primarily in the best interests of the client but does not offer further guidance on the matter.

We also agree with O'Donohue and Mangold's (1996) suggestion that the APA provide a companion piece that provides evidence and arguments for the assertions of the ethics code. Ideally, the ethics code would be updated to reflect the synthesized research findings on termination and referral practices. The standards would then call for behavior that is supported by these findings, and more detailed actions could be specified (such as when termination and referral are appropriate, when they are not appropriate, how they should be carried out, and what practices therapists should not engage in).

As more agencies become involved in the provision of therapy services, it seems that the APA will need to increase their list of practices that are not ethical or permissible in the delivery of services. We recommend that the APA take a stronger stance on practices that compromise the profession as defined by the ethical theory behind the ethics code, and we recommend that they work with other organizations to make their position known. This would clarify their position for all parties involved and serve as a buffer for therapists who currently carry the responsibility to make their commitment to the ethics code known in the event of a conflict of demands and to decide how to balance the conflicting demands.

CONCLUSION

Considering the presence of the termination process in all therapeutic relationships and the frequency with which referrals are made to other therapists, there is a need for more research in this area of psychotherapy. Therapists and therapists-in-training need to be aware of the issues concerning these topics, and they need accessible resources that can offer guidance in dealing with these matters. It has been repeatedly pointed out that ineffective termination and referral practices can undo or weaken therapy gains. Conversely, well-carried-out termination and referral practices have the potential to strengthen and expand on the original therapy work.

Given that academics and researchers cannot agree on criteria and procedures for effective processes of termination and referral at the academic level, these issues are magnified at the practice level. The issues involved in the termination and referral processes are further complicated when one considers the ethical dilemmas faced by therapists in their daily practice. The APA Ethical Principles of Psychologists and Code of Conduct (1992), offers only general guidelines for client termination and transfer, thus leaving complicated ethical dilemmas unaddressed. We call for explication on the part of the APA with respect to the theory underlying the ethics code, more specification with respect to how therapists should balance the multiple interests and demands involved in the provision of services, and more clarity on what practices we, as a profession, want to be in support of or against.

REFERENCES

American Psychological Association. (1992). Ethical principles of psychologists and code of conduct. *American Psychologist, 47,* 1597-1611.

American Psychological Association. Office of Ethnic Minority Affairs. (1993). Guidelines for providers of psychological services to ethnic, linguistic, and culturally diverse populations. *American Psychologist, 48*(1), 45-48.

Beatrice, J. (1983). Premature termination: A therapist leaving. *International Journal of Psychoanalytic Psychotherapy, 9,* 313-336.

Bostic, J. Q., Shadid, L. G., & Blotcky, M. J. (1996). Our time is up: Forced terminations during psychotherapy training. *American Journal of Psychotherapy,*
50(3), 347-359.

Dewald, P. A. (1965). Reactions to the forced termination of therapy. *Psychiatric*
Quarterly, 39, 102-126.

Dewald, P. A. (1982). The clinical importance of the termination phase.
Psychoanalytic Inquiry, 2, 441-462.

Epperson, D. L., Bushway, D. J., & Warman, R. E. (1983). Client self-terminations
after one counseling session: Effects of problem recognition, counselor gender,
and counselor experience. *Journal of Counseling Psychology, 30,* 307-315.

Fox, E., Nelson, M., & Bolman, W. (1969). The termination process: A neglected
dimension in social work. *Social Work, 14*(4), 53-63.

Goodyear, R. K. (1981). Termination as a loss experience for the counselor.
Personal and Guidance Journal, 59, 347-350.

Greenberg, J., & Cheselka, O. (1995). Relational approaches to psychoanalytic psychotherapy. In A. S. Gurman & S. B. Messer (Eds.), *Essential psychotherapies:*
Theory and practice. New York: Guilford.

Hayes, S. C., Follette, W. C., & Follette, V. M. (1995). Behavior therapy: A contextual approach. In A. S. Gurman & S. B. Messer (Eds.), *Essential psy-*
chotherapies: Theory and practice. New York: Guilford.

Keith, C. (1966). Multiple transfers of psychotherapy patients. *Archives of General*
Psychiatry, 14, 185-189.

Kramer, S. A. (1986). The termination process in open-ended psychotherapy:
Guidelines for clinical practice. *Psychotherapy, 23*(4), 526-531.

Kubie, L. S. (1968). Unresolved problems in the resolution of the transference. *The*
Psychoanalytic Quarterly, 11, 211-227.

Levenson, E. A. (1976). Problems in terminating psychoanalysis (a symposium): The
aesthetics of termination. *Contemporary Psychoanalysis, 12*(3), 338-342.

Maholick, L. T., & Turner, D. W. (1979). Termination: That difficult farewell.
American Journal of Psychotherapy, XXXIII(4), 583-591.

McRoy, R. G., Freeman, E. M., & Logan, S. (1986). Strategies for teaching students
about termination. *The Clinical Supervisor, 4*(4), 45-56.

Nelson, W. M., & Politano, P. M. (1993). The goal is to say "good-bye" and have
the treatment effects generalize and maintain: A cognitive-behavioral view of
termination. *Journal of Cognitive Psychotherapy: An International Quarterly,*
7(4), 251-263.

O'Donohue, W., & Mangold, R. (1996). A critical examination of the ethical
principles of psychologists and code of conduct. In W. O'Donohue, &
K. F. Kitchener (Eds.), *The philosophy of psychology* (pp. 371-380). Thousand
Oaks, CA: Sage.

O'Reilly, R. (1987). The transfer syndrome. *Canadian Journal of Psychiatry, 32,*
674-678.

Patterson, T. (2001). Does anybody know a good couple therapist? *The Behavior*
Therapist, 24(4), 85-86.

Pope, K. S., & Vasquez, M. J. T. (1998). *Ethics in psychotherapy and counseling:*
A practical guide (2nd ed.). San Francisco: Jossey-Bass.

Pumpian-Mindlin, E. (1958). Comments on techniques of termination and transfer
in a clinic setting. *American Journal of Psychotherapy, 12,* 455-464.

Robbins, W. S. (1975). Termination: Problems and techniques. *Journal of the*
American Psychoanalytic Association, 23, 166-176.

Rodolfa, E. R., Rapaport, R., & Lee, V. E. (1983). Variables related to premature
termination in a university counseling service. *Journal of Counseling*
Psychology, 30, 50-87.

Scher, M. (1970). The process of changing therapists. *American Journal of Psychotherapy, 24,* 278-286.

Smith, S. (1983). Interrupted treatment and forced terminations. *International Journal of Psychoanalytic Psychotherapy, 9,* 337-352.

Tryon, G. S. (1983). Why full-time private practitioners refer patients to other professionals. *Psychotherapy in Private Practice, 1*(2), 81-83.

Wapner, J. H., Klein, J. G., Friedlander, M. L., & Andrasik, F. J. (1986). Transferring psychotherapy clients: State of the art. *Professional Psychology: Research and Practice, 17*(6), 492-496.

Ward, D. E. (1984). Termination of individual counseling: Concepts and strategies. *Journal of Counseling and Development, 63,* 21-25.

Weddington, W. W., & Cavenar, J. O. (1979). Termination initiated by the therapist: A countertransference storm. *American Journal of Psychiatry, 136*(10), 1302-1305.

Weigert, E. (1952). Contribution to the problem of terminating psychoanalyses. *Psychoanalytic Quarterly, 21,* 465-480.

Wetchler, J. L., & Ofte-Atha, G. R. (1993). Empowering families at termination: A structural/strategic orientation. *Journal of Family Psychotherapy, 4*(1), 33-44.

Wolitzky, D. L. (1995). The theory and practice of traditional psychoanalytic psychology. In A. S. Gurman & S. B. Messer (Eds.), *Essential psychotherapies: Theory and practice.* New York: Guilford.

Wood, E. C., & Wood, C. D. (1990). Referral issues in psychotherapy and psychoanalysis. *American Journal of Psychotherapy, XLIV*(1), 85-94.

CHAPTER 11

Ethical Principles of the Psychology Profession and Involuntary Commitment

DEREK TRUSCOTT AND LORI GOODKEY
University of Alberta

Psychologists sometimes encounter clients who are a threat to their own safety or to the safety of others. In such situations, we may consider whether it would be best to have the client placed in a restrictive environment, typically a psychiatric hospital or unit, to protect them from themselves or to protect others. If a client refuses to consent to such a treatment decision, they can, under certain specific conditions established by law, be detained against their will. Doing so is called *involuntary commitment*. Needless to say, taking away someone's freedom, even if temporarily and with the best intentions, is a serious matter fraught with legal, ethical, and practical difficulties.

Laws are created on the foundation of shared societal values. Internationally recognized as one of the most fundamental values in our society is the right to personal freedom and liberty. So entrenched is this value that it is protected by the Canadian Charter of

Rights and Freedom and the American Constitution. Involuntary commitment is a major violation of the right to liberty. The only other legally sanctioned process that deprives individuals of liberty is criminal justice. In the case of involuntary commitment, however, no crime need have been committed to have the individuals detained against their will.

Professional ethics are meant to reflect the shared values of a profession. One of the most strongly held values of psychologists is respect for the dignity of persons, of which self-determination and personal liberty are central. Thus, obtaining informed consent from our clients for all services provided (or not provided) to them or on their behalf is a requirement of the code of ethics of both the Canadian (CPA) and American Psychological Associations (APA). Involuntary commitment, however, involves going against the wishes of our clients and restricting their personal liberty, albeit with their best interests at heart.

Finally, psychologists placed in a circumstance of deciding whether an individual should be involuntarily committed are faced with difficult practical tasks. We must determine if our client is dangerous, take appropriate steps to reduce that dangerousness, and then, if all else fails, initiate involuntary commitment proceedings.

In this chapter, each of these issues—legal, ethical, and practical—is considered in turn. We make an effort to highlight the importance of determining our clients' competence to decide for themselves what treatment will be initiated and how we should make decisions on their behalf—only if they are not competent to make those decisions.

LEGAL CONSIDERATIONS

Before discussing the legal rationales and criteria for involuntary commitment, an overview of the history of confining persons with mental disabilities is presented to give the reader a sense of the societal values reflected in our laws.

Historical Overview

The customs and laws governing involuntary commitment in North America have their origins in English common law. In 1255, the "Prerogative of the King" was enacted, in which the king served as guardian of the lands of a person who "hath had understanding, but . . . hath lost the use of reason." Any profits were applied to the maintenance of the subject's lands and household (Brakel & Rock, 1971). This custom arose not out of humanitarian motives, however, but out of the king's interest in preventing the lands of deranged noblemen becoming the property of those who might not be supportive of the

crown. Indeed, the principle was not applied to those who were poor; they were either placed in debtors' prison, criminal prison, or cast out of their communities (Bromberg, 1979). Around the 18th century, the *parens patriae* concept arose, in which the state acted in the role of "parent" to detain persons if it is in their "best interests" to do so because they were unable to care for themselves. Mentally disordered persons were often committed to the care of friends or relatives who received an allowance from the state for the cost of care. The management of their estates was usually given over to their heirs or nearest relatives to prevent their depletion (Brakel & Rock, 1971).

In colonial America, mentally disordered persons were usually cast out and would often form bands, wandering the countryside subject to ridicule and cruelty, and even public whippings (Brakel & Rock, 1971). The first asylum whose sole purpose was for the care of mentally disordered persons in America was built in Pennsylvania in 1752, in response to a petition penned by Benjamin Franklin. In the 1800s, Dorothea Dix was a prime motivator for the institutionalization of homeless and mentally disordered persons, and in response to her efforts, some 30 mental hospitals were established (Dakin, 1987). Admission was almost exclusively involuntary, primarily to prevent people from taking advantage of free food and shelter (a most tragic example of a "Catch 22"). Although official public rationale for the existence and functioning of these institutions was to care for and treat the patients admitted to them, in reality they were cold, harsh, and unpleasant places that were very often worse than prisons, and there were no real treatments available (Bromberg, 1979). They were used to confine violent mentally disordered persons, and procedural safeguards were so lacking that admission could be secured on the request of a friend or relative to the staff of the institution (Brakel & Rock,

1971). Persons who were involuntarily committed were considered to be globally incompetent and were afforded no rights to communicate with others, let alone receive legal representation. There was no mechanism for persons committed to request discharge except by obtaining a court order to have a legal determination of whether his or her liberty had been deprived in violation of due process. Few patients knew about such means, and fewer courts accepted them (Miller, 1985).

Given the opportunity for abuse of such a system and society's general attitude to persons who are mentally disordered, it comes as no surprise to learn that the population of persons confined to mental hospitals grew to 560,000 in 1955 (Stromberg & Stone, 1983). With the introduction of powerful tranquilizing drugs that could suppress the upsetting behavioral manifestations that were the impetus for detainment and successful lawsuits that gained more extensive rights for persons being involuntarily committed—most notably *Wyatt v. Stickney* (1971, 1972) and *Donaldson v. O'Connor* (1974)—people actually began to be discharged. By 1975, the confined population dropped to less than 220,000, and by 1981 to about 138,000 (Stromberg & Stone, 1983). Some of the monies that had been spent on maintaining institutions, along with additional state and federal monies, were initially diverted to community mental health centers. A wave of optimism swept over those who were providing treatment, as well as some belated criticism of past practices (Solomon, 1958).

Sadly, this optimism was misguided. Pressure from neighborhood community groups and politicians seizing an opportunity to reduce budget expenditures resulted in inadequate resource allotments to support community mental health centers (Dakin, 1987). In California, for example, 35,000 persons were released from a hospital population of 40,000 (Kirp, 1985). Yet only 11% of the state budget for mental health went to community programs, with 70% allocated for hospitals (Swenson, 1997). And although the total inpatient population has dropped dramatically, it has come about by way of increased numbers of discharges from mental health facilities; the total number of admissions has actually continued to increase (Kiesler & Simpkins, 1991). The reality is that persons with mental disorders have swelled the ranks of the homeless. In Los Angeles, California, a large urban center with a warm climate, an estimated 40,000 persons who suffer from chronic severe mental disorder live on the streets in extreme deprivation (Goldin, 1987). So it appears that we have reached a consensus as a society, as articulated through our laws, that persons with mental disorders should not be denied the same rights as persons without such disorders. What has not yet occurred is a societal consensus to provide care.

Rationales for Involuntary Commitment

As described above, involuntary commitment is originally derived from the parens patriae model of the state's powers; an individual who is incapable of taking care of themselves due to mental disorder is taken care of by the state. The theoretical motivation for such action was benevolent, and the argument ran that because the state was acting not to punish, but to treat, the attendant loss of liberty was justified (Ennis, 1972; Wexler, 1981). Because individuals were being restrained for their own protection and welfare, the courts reasoned, the infringement of their liberty was not the same infringement of liberty as was protected by constitutional provision (*Proschaska v. Brinegar,* 1960). Furthermore, working from the assumption that mental illness was an identifiable entity, like physical illness, courts and legislators identified physicians as the primary decision makers. Professional and legal debates during the 1970s, however, questioned the validity of the concept of mental illness (*Lessard v. Schmidt*, 1972) and the role of the medical profession as agents of social control rather than healers (Szasz, 1963). Eventually, a consensus was reached that the rationale for involuntary commitment was unduly broad, and it evolved into the much narrower *harm-to-self* criterion. This criterion, discussed in the next section, is usually interpreted as requiring a life-threatening situation, with suicide as the quintessential example.

In addition to harm to self, however, involuntary commitment can also be undertaken if an individual is a threat to the safety of others. As a result of the reforms of the 1970s and the subsequent refinement of the harm-to-self criterion, the courts were forced to more clearly articulate justification for commitment when it was not in the interests of the individual. Hence, the establishment of the *harm-to-others* criterion. This criterion arises out of the state's police power, in which an individual is detained to protect the community. Curiously, this criterion has received scant critical attention in and of itself. Its application has come under intense criticism because of the question of the accuracy of mental health professionals' predictions of dangerousness (Ennis & Litwack, 1974), but not its appropriateness. Perhaps this rationale and the lack of criticism it has received is yet another reflection of how we as a society continue to fear those who behave in ways that make us uncomfortable.

Criteria for Involuntary Commitment

Currently, all jurisdictions in the United States and Canada have laws that set out procedures for involuntary commitment. These laws typically contain detailed procedures for ensuring that the rights of the person being committed are not violated any more than is necessary and that hospitalization is truly necessary. However, despite guidelines, professional judgment remains essential to determine the need for commitment. Although there are some differences in the precise criteria across jurisdictions, all require that a person (a) be mentally ill and (b) pose a threat to self or others. The definition of mental illness differs significantly across jurisdictions, with some providing a functional definition, such as "a disorder of thought, perceptions, feelings, or behavior that seriously impairs a person's judgment, capacity to recognize reality, ability to associate with others or ability to meet the ordinary demands of life, in respect of which treatment is advisable," whereas others merely require "a disease or disability of the mind."

The definition of threat to self or others is similarly disparate. Some jurisdictions have broadly defined criterion, such as "for the person's own protection or the protection of others," and others are more specific: "likely to cause serious harm to himself or herself or to another person, or to suffer substantial mental or physical deterioration." Case law in each jurisdiction has typically evolved to refine these definitions, sometimes interpreting them more broadly and other times more specifically. Psychologists involved in these decisions must be aware of the law in their jurisdictions.

ETHICAL CONSIDERATIONS

The ethics of involuntary commitment are complex. As discussed in the preceding section, psychologists are expected to intervene in our clients' lives, but as a society, we are ambivalent about how persons with mental disorders should be treated. This places a responsibility on the psychologist to carefully consider the ethical values intrinsic to each individual situation. When considering the ethics of involuntary commitment, the following questions can help to guide our deliberations:

- What values am I violating?
- What values am I promoting?
- Does bias influence my decision?
- What is my overall evaluation?

What Values Am I Violating?

The codes of ethics of both the APA (1992) and CPA (2000) accept as fundamental the principle of respect for the dignity of persons (APA, Principle D; CPA, Principle 1). This principle is reflected in acknowledging that all persons have a right to have their innate worth as human beings appreciated and that this worth is not dependent on any personal characteristic, condition, or status. Rights to self-determination, personal liberty, autonomy, privacy, and confidentiality arise out of this respect for the dignity of persons, and it is generally recognized that we have a responsibility to protect and promote these rights in our dealings with our clients. This responsibility is realized primarily by ensuring that we obtain informed consent from our clients in all of our dealings with them. Ordinarily, then, a psychologist would not consider undertaking any professional activity with a client without their informed consent. To do so would be in violation of the value of autonomy and self-determination inherent in the principle of respect for their dignity as persons.

Involuntary commitment will also violate our clients' freedom. We need to consider both what freedom is to be violated and what sort our client values. If we hospitalize people against their will, we violate their freedom to make decisions about their own lives, their freedom of movement, and their privacy.

Remembering that typically the means by which we come to be involved in this situation in the first place was because a client trusted us with personal information, another value that will very likely be violated is our client's trust in us and our profession, as well as mental health professionals or persons in authority in general.

What Values Am I Promoting?

Decisions about involuntary commitment usually rest on a utilitarian rubric: Will the *ends* justify the *means?* Will the violation of my client's autonomy, freedom, and perhaps trust be outweighed by the value of protecting him or her from harm or by protecting someone else from being harmed?

The most important value that is promoted when seeking to have someone involuntarily committed who is a risk to themselves is whether doing so is likely to enhance their well-being in the long term. Involuntary commitment is almost always done in consideration of short-term necessity in the hope that long-term gains will accrue. But is this necessarily so? A comparison of patients discharged by a review panel, and thereby against the opinions of their attending physicians, found that such patients did not have more difficulty in the community following discharge nor were they more likely to be admitted more frequently or more quickly than patients released by physicians (Ledwidge et al., 1987).

When considering involuntarily commitment because an individual poses a threat to someone else, there may be circumstances in which we are promoting that individual's well-being and the well-being of the threatened third party. If the harm arises out of a mental disorder, such as paranoia, the individual could feel intense guilt once the paranoid condition abates. But the most common circumstance involves an individual feeling entirely justified in their anger and murderous desires, and in such cases the value we are promoting is saving the life of a third party.

Does Bias Influence My Decision?

Because of our power relative to our clients, we must be careful that we do not impose on clients standards that others in society do not have to meet. Most persons for whom we would never consider making a decision make their own decisions with very little thought to the risks and benefits of their choices or alternate choices. Our expertise is a kind of power: The expert assumes superior knowledge and skills in evaluating a client and proposing intervention. It is all too easy in this circumstance to judge a client incompetent by virtue of his or her role: dependent, needy, bewildered, and so on. We tend to feel more responsible for making decisions for those who have less power than we do, further eroding their power. In extreme situations, such as prisons, persons have so little control over their lives that interventions that are not controversial in most situations can result in a further reduction of autonomy such that they are unjustified, even with consent. It can be helpful to ask ourselves how we would make or consider our decisions if individual characteristics of our clients that have no bearing on our decisions were different. If a mentally disturbed person of high income versus one of low income presented with the same issues, would we still consider involuntary commitment? Or would we more actively pursue other supportive services to reduce dangerousness while promoting a sense of freedom, empowerment, and well-being?

All involuntary commitment laws require that the individual be mentally disordered and a danger to self or others. But why should this be? Why allow some people to make some decisions about themselves and not others? And why only people who are mentally disturbed? Let us consider two scenarios. In the first, an individual is depressed and takes long, aimless walks that find him in very rough parts of the city where he has been severely beaten and robbed on a number of occasions. In the second, an individual who never learned to read because of a learning disorder assaults a bus driver who, when asked which bus to take, rudely advises him to consult the signs on the buses (Schopp, 2001). Both of these individuals have mental disorders, according to the *Diagnostic and Statistical Manual of Mental Disorders* (American Psychiatric Association, 2000), that play causal roles in their dangerousness. But few, if any, would consider them for involuntary commitment. The mere fact that mental disorder contributes to their life-threatening behavior provides no justification for treating them any differently than someone without a mental disorder who behaves in a similar manner.

There is also the issue of whether we should ever involuntarily commit persons who are mentally disordered because they represent a threat to others. Dangerous persons who are not mentally disordered are dealt with through the criminal justice system, which prohibits actions that cause harm to others. The underlying assumption of criminal law is that persons generally choose to conform or not conform to rules governing social behavior. Persons who choose not to conform to these rules are seen as deserving of legal sanctions. We are all capable of unlawful acts, but only those who choose to commit them are held accountable. Detaining someone to prevent some possible criminal act is counter to the value our society places on individual self-determination, liberty, and responsibility. Again, we must ask ourselves to what extent the individual's status as having a mental disorder is biasing our decision.

What Is My Overall Evaluation?

When attempting to balance in an unbiased manner the values promoted and those violated, it is important to consider that within our society, the values of autonomy and self-determination are given higher priority than well-being. As a society, we regularly allow people to make decisions that are of questionable benefit to their well-being, such as smoking and consuming unhealthy foods. Equally important is that we normally allow members of our society to make these decisions regardless of any personal characteristics, conditions, or status. At the individual level, therefore, empowering others to decide for themselves should normally be given precedence over promoting their well-being.

When hospitalization is for the benefit of the individual to prevent self-harm, free and informed consent, including the choice of not being hospitalized, should normally be respected. We should respect their decisions regardless of our appraisal of what would promote their well-being. The only ethically justifiable circumstance in which we would decide for others whether they should be hospitalized (or be subjected to any form of treatment) is when they are not competent to decide for themselves. Note that the fact that someone is mentally disordered should not, in and of itself, have any bearing on our decision. Indeed, the extent to which it does is an indication of the degree to which we are biased in our decision making. The relative weighting of self-determination over well-being is now adjusted by virtue of the individual being unable to make decisions in his or her own best interest. The principle of protecting another's well-being now takes on much greater importance. Considerations of self-determination are now subsumed under considerations of well-being. When individuals are incompetent by virtue of mental disorder to make decisions for themselves,

therefore, we should attempt to replicate as much as possible the decision that they would make under the circumstances if they were competent. We should also attempt to respect and integrate as much as possible their opinions and wishes.

A related consideration is the distinction between an individual's preferences and choices. We might have a preference for one course of action over another but may not always choose the most preferred one. Many competent people have said that they would not wish to have their lives sustained by artificial medical means if they were to suffer severe brain injury. Although this may well be an accurate expression of their preferences at a given point in time, it does not constitute a deliberate choice not to have a particular treatment under the circumstances of actually being brain injured. When considering involuntary commitment of others, therefore, we must attempt to incorporate what they would choose to do under conditions of informed consent, not just what they might prefer to do. If they have previously made choices about hospitalization while competent to do so, it carries a much greater obligation to not hospitalize them against their will than if they have simply expressed a preference. Unfortunately, this does not make our decisions any easier.

The preceding considerations apply most directly to commitment decisions when an individual is at risk to harm themselves. Deciding to involuntarily commit an individual to protect others from harm involves additional considerations, however. The involuntary commitment of mentally disordered persons because they are a danger to others will often involve not making decisions *for* others, but rather making decisions *about* others. Some people who are a threat to the safety of others, mentally disordered or not, will give more weight to the danger they pose to others when weighed against their own loss of personal freedom and liberty if involuntarily committed. In the case of a mother suffering from postpartum depression who has thoughts of harming her child, for example, we may well have good reason to believe, on the basis of her predepressed state of mind, that she would not want to harm her child. But it cannot be assumed for all persons who are mentally disordered and represent a danger to others that they would choose to have themselves committed to hospital in order to protect others. Indeed, most persons who are competent and not mentally disordered choose most of the time to give greater weight to their own interests. Thus the individual's competence to decide whether or not to be hospitalized may well not be a consideration in such circumstances. The central determination is the individual's dangerousness to others, regardless of his or her capacity to make a decision about the need for hospitalization.

PRACTICAL CONSIDERATIONS

Involuntarily commitment is the end result of a process that begins with a determination of dangerousness. If that determination is made in the affirmative, we must attempt to collaboratively prevent the life-threatening event from occurring. If we are unable to do so and in our best clinical judgment, hospitalization is the best option for preventing dangerousness, we must consider involuntary commitment. Then we must assess whether our client is competent to consent to hospitalization and what he or she would decide.

Predicting Dangerousness

Our ability to make accurate predictions of violent behavior is difficult for at least two reasons. First, violent behavior is relatively rare. Given that only approximately 1 out of every 1,000 people will commit a violent act against another, if we were able to predict violence with 99% accuracy (no method for predicting violence even approaches this level), then for every person correctly identified as dangerous, at least 10 other nondangerous persons would be incorrectly identified as dangerous. Second, violent behavior does not result from stable individual traits, as the concept of *dangerousness* implies. Rather, it results from an interaction between characteristics of individuals and characteristics of their environments. Virtually anyone is capable of violent behavior given the right circumstances despite possessing few violent traits, whereas even the most violently predisposed individual is not always behaving violently. Stated differently, individual characteristics are neither necessary nor sufficient causes of violent behavior, whereas situational characteristics can be. Individual characteristics can alter the threshold at which situational characteristics precipitate violence. An individual who possesses many characteristics typical of violence-prone persons would be considered at high risk for violence given relatively fewer situational precipitants.

Assessing Dangerousness to Self

There is no established and generally accepted procedure for assessing suicide risk (Bongar, 2001; Rudd & Joiner, 1998), but the following individual and situational characteristics are adapted from Bednar, Bednar, Lambert, and Waite (1991), Bongar (2001), and Sommers-Flanagan and Sommers-Flanagan (1995).

Individual Characteristics

The more closely an individual resembles a fictional modal suicidal person, the lower the threshold for current risk. The following characteristics typify persons who carry out suicide. To what extent do these describe your client?

- Male
- Late 40s or early 50s
- History of psychoactive substance abuse
- History of unstable social support
- History of suicidal behavior
- Depressed
- Feelings of hopeless, helpless, guilt, worthless, shame, anger, or self-loathing
- Thoughts of suicide or self-destructive thoughts

Situational Characteristics

The more of the following characteristics that are present in an individual's situation, the higher the current risk for harm to self. To what extent do these describe your client's situation?

- Has access to weapons
- Has access to psychoactive substance(s) that they have a history of abusing
- Feels stress related to family/relationship, peer group, finances, or employment
- Lacks persons available for support or to intervene if an attempt is made

Assessing Dangerousness to Others

As with suicide, there is no established and generally accepted procedure for assessing homicide risk, but the following individual and situational characteristics are adapted from Meloy (1987) and Monahan (1981).

Individual Characteristics

The more closely an individual resembles a fictional modal violent person, the lower the threshold for current risk. The following characteristics typify persons who commit violent acts. To what extent do these describe your client?

- Male
- Nonwhite
- Late teens or early 20s
- History of opiate or alcohol abuse
- Low IQ and education
- Unstable residential and employment history
- History of violent behavior

Situational Characteristics

The more of the following characteristics that are present in an individual's situation, the higher the current risk for harm to others. To what extent do these describe your client's situation?

- Knows intended victim
- Has access to intended victim
- Has access to weapons
- Has combat or martial arts training, or possess great strength
- Has access to psychoactive substance(s) and a history of abusing them
- Feels stress related to family/relationship, peer group, finances, or employment

Preventing Harm to Self or Others Collaboratively

Central to responding to risk for harm to self or others is to do everything reasonably possible to influence clients in such a way that violence toward themselves or others will not occur. From an ethical point of view, it is most desirable to avoid breaking confidentiality and avoid resorting to initiating actions outside the consulting room. From a therapeutic point of view, it is vital for psychologists to maintain a good working relationship with a client who is threatening to engage in violence. This is consistent with decades of psychotherapeutic research that finds that a strong therapeutic alliance is the cornerstone of a positive outcome in psychotherapy (Bachelor & Horvath, 1999).

Attending to the degree of risk and the strength of the therapeutic alliance is central to effective treatment *and* the protection of the client and others. The therapeutic alliance should also be strengthened because acting only to prevent a current episode without attending to the therapeutic alliance may enrage and disappoint a client and thereby increase the risk of future harm (Truscott, Evans, & Mansell, 1995), while simultaneously deterring the client from seeking further psychological services for dealing with any future violent impulses. Only if the risk cannot be adequately reduced via the therapeutic alliance should our energies be directed toward seeking involuntary commitment. Psychologists responding to dangerous clients, therefore, should attend to two key dimensions: (a) the degree of risk and (b) the strength of the therapeutic alliance.

Assessing Alliance Strength

A strong therapeutic alliance is present when your client feels a positive affective bond with you and believes that the tasks and goals of therapy are a collaborative effort. Note that the client's perception of the alliance is especially predictive of therapy outcome and should therefore be the focus of an assessment of alliance strength. To what extent do the following describe your client?

- Has positive (nonromantic) feelings toward you
- Perceives you as supportive, concerned, empathic, nonjudgmental, and respectful
- Trusts you
- Feels confident that what is being discussed during therapy will be kept private
- Feels comfortable with the tasks and interventions of the therapy
- Feels confident that therapy will bring about desired changes
- Believes that his or her goals and expectations for seeking help are being addressed
- Believes that his or her goals are consistent with your therapeutic goals

Reducing Dangerousness

If the risk of violence is high and the therapeutic alliance is strong, therapy should be intensified and the therapeutic alliance used to help the client make his or her environment less lethal. Sessions can be scheduled more frequently and weapons removed (Monahan, 1993; Roth & Meisel, 1977; Wulsin, Bursztajn, & Gutheil, 1983).

When a client is at high risk for violence and the therapeutic alliance is weak, the psychologist should attempt to strengthen the alliance. If an alliance has not yet been established, the psychologist should endeavor to behave in an affiliative, autonomy-granting manner and refrain from responding in a hostile or controlling manner (Henry & Strupp, 1994). If the therapeutic alliance has already been established and is strained by the current situation, the psychologist should openly identify and discuss the client's perception of the alliance, listen nonjudgmentally, identify any misperceptions, and make any necessary adjustments to the therapeutic relationship (Safran, Muran, & Samstag, 1994). Simultaneously or in sequence, psychologists should work with clients to alter the aspects of their situations that are promoting and/or maintaining violence.

If the alliance cannot be strengthened, the situational characteristics promoting violence should be eliminated or significantly reduced so that risk is lessened. This will often involve including significant others such as the client's family members or possibly the police, but a warning to potential victims should not be issued at this stage. A warning may result in needless psychic harm if violence is prevented and could even form the basis for a lawsuit against the therapist (Lewis, 1986). The client should be informed of the limits of confidentiality and the steps that will be taken.

Involuntary Commitment

Only if the alliance cannot be strengthened and risk-reducing interventions cannot be implemented collaboratively should involuntary commitment proceedings be considered. If time and circumstances permit, the limits of confidentiality and the steps that will be taken should be discussed openly with the client. If the psychologist has to break confidentiality, it will likely damage the therapeutic alliance and change the relationship between the client and the psychologist from a positive to a negative one, thereby severely curtailing the therapeutic influence. Psychologists must be prepared to breach confidentiality and ignore clients' wishes only to the extent necessary to transfer them to a safe environment. Involuntary commitment does not waive all the usual protections of client rights and privacies. For example, if police officers are called to transport the client to hospital, the officers should be given only that information they need to safely do so.

If, in the best judgment of the psychologist, hospitalization is the means most likely to reduce the client's risk of harm to self or others, the client's reasons for refusing consent should be determined. If it becomes apparent that he or she has misunderstandings or lacks information, you should attempt to correct any misunderstandings or provide the relevant information. If your client still refuses, an assessment of his or her competence to consent to hospitalization should be made.

Assessing Competence

Competence (or incompetence) does not describe a trait or even state of an individual; it describes an individual's ability (or inability) to perform a particular task. Thus, it is decision relative, not global. A person may be competent to make a particular decision under certain circumstances but not competent to make a different decision, or even the same decision under different circumstances. Assessing competence, therefore, should involve a determination of an individual's ability to make a particular decision at a particular time under particular circumstances.

In relation to involuntary commitment, the assessment to be made is whether or not individuals are capable of giving informed consent to being hospitalized in order to protect them from harming themselves or prevent them from harming others. Presenting hypothetical treatment decisions and then probing the client's understanding and reasoning may be helpful, but care must be taken not to be confusing about what decision the client is being asked to make. Does your client understand the following?

- The nature and purpose of hospitalization
- The risk and benefits of hospitalization
- The nature, purpose, risks, and benefits of alternatives to hospitalization

If the client does not understand all three of the above issues due to a mental disorder and in the best judgment of the psychologist would consent if they were competent, then involuntary commitment procedures should be initiated.

Procedures for Involuntary Commitment

Specific procedures differ by jurisdiction, but usually the basic mechanism for commitment begins with a statement from a petitioner. The petitioner may in theory be anyone, but is typically a concerned relative, law enforcement officer, or mental health practitioner. The petition is presented to a judicial official, who will decide if the facts warrant an examination. If the judge finds the examination justified, a custody warrant is issued and paramedics will pick up the allegedly mentally disordered person or serve him or her with an order to report for examination. If the designated evaluators, usually one or two physicians or psychiatrists, agree that the person meets the criteria for commitment, a preliminary hearing is conducted so that a judge can determine whether involuntary hospitalization is legally warranted. Many jurisdictions also have procedures for emergency commitment intended as a temporary measure to deal with prevention of life-threatening conduct. In these instances, law enforcement officials are typically empowered to initiate the process following citizen request or complaints.

Psychologists involved in such proceedings should be very careful to avoid exceeding the limits of their expertise. Because of the great deference given to mental health professionals in these matters, we must take care to avoid giving ultimate issue opinions (i.e., whether to commit or not) and to make clear the uncertainties of our opinions on dangerousness and its recommended treatment.

CONCLUSION

In this chapter, it has been argued that we have a societal obligation to participate in the process of involuntary commitment when we are privy to information about the threat of clients to themselves or others and when we are in a position to be able to influence client behavior. Any information or influence that we have arises out of our clients' trust in us, however, and so we also have an ethical duty to strive above all else to uphold that trust. We do this by acting as a surrogate decision maker on behalf of the client in an attempt to balance the values violated and promoted by the decision. When doing so, we must be particularly sensitive to how the imbalance of power inherent in the situation can bias our decision. We must, therefore, carefully assess risk of life-threatening behavior to self or others and make every effort to reduce that risk within the boundaries of the professional relationship. If we are unable to do so, we should be prepared to carefully assess competence to consent to hospitalization and then initiate involuntary commitment proceedings if the client would consent to that treatment were he or she competent.

REFERENCES

American Psychiatric Association. (2000). *Diagnostic and statistical manual of mental disorders: DSM-IV-TR* (4th ed., Text rev.). Washington, DC: Author.

American Psychological Association. (1992). Ethical principles of psychologists and code of conduct. *American Psychologist, 47,* 1597-1611.

Bachelor, A., & Horvath, A. (1999). The therapeutic relationship. In M. A. Hubble, B. L. Duncan, & S. C. Miller (Eds.), *The heart and soul of change: What works in therapy* (pp. 133-178). Washington, DC: American Psychological Association.

Bednar, R. L., Bednar, S. C., Lambert, M. J., & Waite, D. R. (1991). *Psychotherapy with high-risk clients: Legal and professional standards.* Pacific Grove, CA: Brooks/Cole.

Bongar, B. (2001). *The suicidal patient: Clinical and legal standards of care* (2nd ed.). Washington, DC: American Psychological Association.

Brakel, S. J., & Rock, R. S. (1971). *The mentally disabled and the law.* Chicago: University of Chicago Press.

Bromberg, W. (1979). *The uses of psychiatry and the law*. Westport, CT: Quorum.

Canadian Psychological Association. (2000). *Canadian code of ethics for psychologists* (3rd ed.). Ottawa, ON: Author.

Dakin, L. S. (1987). Homelessness: The role of the legal profession in finding solutions through litigation. *Family Law Quarterly, 21*, 93-126.

Donaldson v. O'Connor, 493 F.2d 507 (5th Cir., 1974).

Ennis, B. J. (1972). *Prisoners of psychiatry: Mental patients, psychiatrists, and the law*. New York: Harcourt, Brace, and Jovanovich.

Ennis, B. J., & Litwack, T. L. (1974). Psychiatry and the presumption of expertise: Flipping coins in the courtroom. *California Law Review, 62*, 693-752.

Goldin, G. (1987). Gimme shelter. *California Lawyer, 7*, 28-34.

Henry, W. P., & Strupp, H. H. (1994). The therapeutic alliance as interpersonal process. In A. O. Horvath, & L. S. Greenberg, (Eds.), *The working alliance: Theory, research, and practice* (pp. 51-84). New York: Wiley.

Kiesler, C. A., & Simpkins, C. (1991). The de facto national system of psychiatric inpatient care: Piecing together the national puzzle. *American Psychologist, 46*, 579-584.

Kirp, D. L. (1985). The road from neglect. *California Law Review, 5*, 70-73.

Ledwidge, B., Glackman, W., Paredes, J., Chen, R., Dhami, S., Hansen, D., & Higenbottam, J. (1987). Controlled follow-up of patients released by a review panel at one and two years after separation. *Canadian Journal of Psychiatry, 32*, 448-453.

Lessard v. Schmidt, 349 F. Supp. 1078, 1094 (E.D. Wis. 1972).

Lewis, M. B. (1986). Duty to warn versus duty to maintain confidentiality: Conflicting demands on mental health professionals. *Suffolk University Law Review, 20*, 579-615.

Meloy, J. R. (1987). The prediction of violence in outpatient psychotherapy. *American Journal of Psychotherapy, 41*, 38-45.

Miller, R. D. (1985). Clinical and legal aspects of civil commitment. In C. P. Ewing (Ed.), *Psychology, psychiatry, and the law: A clinical and forensic handbook* (pp. 149-180). Sarasota, FL: Professional Resource Exchange.

Monahan, J. (1981). *Predicting violent behaviour: An assessment of clinical techniques*. Beverly Hills: Sage.

Monahan, J. (1993). Limiting therapist exposure to *Tarasoff* liability: Guidelines for risk containment. *American Psychologist, 48*, 242-250.

Proschaska v. Brinegar, 251 Iowa 834, 102 N.W.2d 870, 872 (1960).

Roth, L. H., & Meisel, A. (1977). Dangerousness, confidentiality, and the duty to warn. *American Journal of Psychiatry, 134*, 508-511.

Rudd, M. D., & Joiner, T. (1998). The assessment, management, and treatment of suicidality: Toward clinically informed and balanced standards of care. *Clinical Psychology: Science and Practice, 5*, 135-150.

Safran, J. D., Muran, J. C., & Samstag, L. W. (1994). Resolving therapeutic alliance ruptures: A task analytic investigation. In A. Horvath & L. S. Greenberg (Eds.), *The working alliance: Theory, research and practice* (pp. 225-255). New York: Wiley.

Schopp, R. F. (2001). *Competence, condemnation, and commitment*. Washington, DC: American Psychological Association.

Solomon, H. (1958). Presidential address. *American Journal of Psychiatry, 115*, 1-9.

Sommers-Flanagan, J., & Sommers-Flanagan, R. (1995). Intake interviewing with suicidal patients: A systematic approach. *Professional Psychology: Research and Practice, 26*, 41-47.

Stromberg, C. D., Stone, A. A. (1983). A model state law on civil commitment of the mentally ill. *Harvard Journal on Legislation, 20*, 275-396.

Swenson, L. C. (1997). *Psychology and law for the helping professions.* Pacific Grove, CA: Brooks/Cole.

Szasz, T. (1963). *Law, liberty, and psychiatry.* New York: Macmillan.

Truscott, D., Evans, J., & Mansell, S. (1995). Outpatient psychotherapy with dangerous clients: A model for clinical decision making. *Professional Psychology: Research and Practice, 26,* 484-490.

Wexler, D. (1981). *Mental health law: Major issues.* New York: Plenum.

Wulsin, L. R., Bursztajn, H., & Gutheil, T. G. (1983). Unexpected clinical features of the *Tarasoff* decision: The therapeutic alliance and the "duty to warn." *American Journal of Psychiatry, 140,* 601-603.

Wyatt v. Stickney, 325 F. Supp. 781 (M.D. Ala., 1971), enforcing, 344 F. Supp. 373 (M.D. Ala., 1972).

CHAPTER 12

Ethics of Multiple and Overlapping Relationships

JANET SCHANK
Minneapolis, MN

RACHEL SLATER, DEVJANI BANERJEE-STEVENS,
AND THOMAS M. SKOVHOLT
University of Minnesota

T he charge of the psychotherapist is to build relationships with people who have difficulty building relationships with others—a daunting task, indeed. As psychologists work to build trusting and collaborative relationships with clients (a prerequisite if progress is to occur), their own complex emotions often pull them into roles they had not anticipated. Throughout a psychologist's work with a client, the potential exists for developing multiple relationships. Some of these relationships are consistent with the goals of therapy; but many of them could destroy the therapeutic alliance, perhaps leaving deep emotional scars for all parties involved. It would be naive for psychologists to ignore the potential for multiple relationships and dangerous to minimize the negative consequences such relationships might have on clients.

This chapter explores the nature and types of dual relationships that may arise in the practice of psychology. We will discuss the nature of overlapping relationships, identify some of the potential consequences of overlapping relationships, and offer guidelines for ethical practice. To illustrate the complex and ambiguous nature of dual relationships, we give examples of the dilemmas psychologists face as they try to maintain standards of ethical practice.

WHAT ARE MULTIPLE RELATIONSHIPS?

Multiple role relationships, also referred to as *dual* or *overlapping,* occur when psychologists have other relationships with clients in addition to that of therapist-client. Such

AUTHOR'S NOTE: Portions of this chapter were previously published in J. A. Schank and T. M. Skovholt (1997), Dual-Relationship Dilemmas of Rural and Small-Community Psychologists, *Professional Psychology: Research and Practice, 28,* 44-49.

blending of this professional role with other roles can happen concurrently or consecutively with the therapy relationship. Some examples of multiple relationships include (a) functioning in another professional role with a client, for example, when a supervisor is also the therapist of the supervisee, (b) maintaining a personal relationship or close friendship with a client, or (c) going into business with a former client.

Multiple role relationships occur when a therapist crosses or blurs the boundaries that define the therapeutic relationship. Gutheil and Gabbard (1993) defined *boundary crossing* as making a change in the therapist role that could potentially benefit the client. They defined a *boundary violation,* on the other hand, as a serious breach of treatment boundaries that results in exploitation of the client. Gutheil and Gabbard (1993) suggested that not all boundary crossings could be considered boundary violations but agreed that crossing boundaries can lead to a pattern of blurring professional and personal roles. So how do we decide whether and when a boundary crossing is ethical? The evolution of the American Psychological Association's (APA) ethics code throughout the past 50 years illustrates psychology's struggle to answer this question.

THE EVOLUTION OF MULTIPLE RELATIONSHIPS AS AN ETHICAL ISSUE

When APA published its first ethics code in 1953, psychologists were cautioned to avoid relationships that might jeopardize the welfare of their clients. At that time, more explicit guidelines may have seemed unnecessary because the complexities of multiple relationships had not yet surfaced as an ethical issue. During the 1960s and 1970s, therapists began to stretch the standards of their practices and developed "innovative" techniques to help clients break down inhibitions and take risks in therapy (Koocher & Keith-Spiegel, 1998). As the number of reports rose regarding therapists who sexually or financially exploited their clients, it became clear that more attention should be paid to the nature of multiple relationships. Research on different types of boundary crossings emerged, and many studies offered new proscriptions for therapist behavior. Studies of dual relationships, therapist self-disclosure, therapist-client physical contact, and therapist-client sexual contact led to a consensus that multiple relationships can be dangerous (Smith & Fitzpatrick, 1995). Revisions of the APA ethics code reflected this pendulum swing.

Four decades after the first APA ethics code was published and despite the APA's attempt to limit dual relationships between psychologists and clients, different variations of multiple relationships continued. Between 1990 and 1992, nearly half of all complaints to the APA Ethics Committee involved incidents of blurred boundaries (Sonne, 1994). If research indicated the risks inherent in therapist-client boundary crossing, why did psychologists continue with them?

In 1992, the APA Ethics Committee addressed the complex nature of multiple relationships. The 1992 ethics code formally recognized that some nonprofessional contact with clients may be difficult to avoid. The code also rescinded previous prohibitions on bartering in some situations. The 2002 ethics code more explicitly defined multiple relationships as occurring

> When a psychologist is in a professional role with a person and (1) at the same time is in another role with the same person, (2) at the same time is in a relationship with a person closely associated with or related to the person with whom the psychologist has the professional relationship, or (3) promises to enter into another relationship in the future with the person or a person closely associated with or related to the person. (Standard 3.05, APA, 2002, p. 6)

While recognizing that a total prohibition against multiple relationships is unrealistic, psychology continues to clarify issues surrounding such relationships. One area of complexity is that the code places more responsibility on psychologists to judge when "out-of-therapy" contact might result in harm to the client.

WHEN ARE MULTIPLE RELATIONSHIPS UNETHICAL?

The relationships psychologists form with their clients are complex and multidimensional, which may mean that right and wrong answers may not be readily available. The 1992 and 2002 APA ethics codes reflect the complex ambiguity of multiple relationships by avoiding explicit statements regarding the appropriateness of current or posttherapy social, business, or professional relationships with clients. Psychologists are instead cautioned about entering into out-of-therapy relationships with clients,

> If the multiple relationship could reasonably be expected to impair the psychologist's objectivity, competence, or effectiveness in performing his or her functions as a psychologist, or otherwise risks exploitation or harm to the person with whom the professional relationship exists.

> Multiple relationships that would not reasonably be expected to cause impairment or risk exploitation or harm are not unethical. (Standard 3.05, APA, 2002, p. 6)

This concept of *impaired objectivity* is essential in considering whether or not a particular situation conforms to the ethical standard. A central tenant of the profession is the necessity for the psychologist to maintain objectivity and not pursue self-interest at the expense of client (Borys, 1992). Psychologists must place the client's best interest first in return for the special fiduciary status accorded mental health professionals (Pope, 1985). Psychologists are powerful

"by virtue of the client's need for professional services and the structure of the relationship itself" (Pope, 1985, p. 5). Clients may be vulnerable and lack "the objectivity and ability to exercise genuinely free choice" (Pope, 1985, p. 5). This power continues even after the therapy relationship ends.

Serious violations can result from a slow process of boundary erosion. This happens when a therapist's objectivity becomes clouded in small steps that are often unrecognized and that are likely to result in impaired objectivity. For example, Strasburger, Jorgenson, and Sutherland (1992) argued that therapists who blur nonsexual boundaries with clients are more likely to become sexually involved with clients.

Accurate prediction of the risks and benefits of boundary crossings is not a simple exercise in judgment. Koocher and Keith-Spiegel (1998) asserted that "Lax professional boundaries are often a precursor of exploitation, confusion, and loss of objectivity" (p. 172). They go on to suggest that "For psychologists already predisposed to blend roles, rationalization processes are probably well under way, thus subverting the caliber of any risk assessment" (p. 173). How, then, can we ensure that our objectivity is not or will not become impaired?

HOW DO DUAL RELATIONSHIPS AFFECT THE THERAPEUTIC RELATIONSHIP?

Unimpaired objectivity is an important goal, but difficult to ensure. There are a number of internal and external bases for decision making that we can turn to in assessing and resolving ethical concerns. One basis for decision making is an understanding of the theoretical importance of boundaries in the therapeutic relationship.

The importance of the therapeutic alliance must be of central concern for therapists who strive to practice ethically and successfully.

The relationship between clients and therapists is unique. Their alliance is essential to the success of therapy, for without a sound relationship, the best therapy techniques fail miserably (Bachelor & Horvath, 1999).

Tomm (1993) argued that maintaining interpersonal distance from clients may lead to an objectification of the therapeutic relationship and an intensification of the power differential between therapist and client. Others argue that blending boundaries is inevitable and, in fact, fundamental to playing out the therapeutic relationship through the processes of transference and countertransference (Hedges, 1993).

Is the maintenance of therapeutic distance beneficial or possible in all practice settings? This topic has been a subject of debate within the field of ethics in psychology. St. Germaine (1993) asserted that dual relationships may not necessarily be problematic if client welfare remains primary. Situations involving overlapping relationships may even become opportunities for effective role modeling by psychologists in small communities. In some small communities—rural, ethnic, disability, gay/lesbian, military, and others—psychologists may be sought out by clients because of familiarity. Clients may want to know that their therapists have children in the same schools or are involved in similar community activities. These perceived similarities may enhance client motivation and trust (Catalano, 1997).

The traditional model of ethical psychological practice holds professionals responsible for maintaining distance from clients outside the therapy session. Treatment boundaries provide "a therapeutic frame which defines a set of roles for the participants in the therapeutic process" (Smith & Fitzpatrick, 1995, p. 499).

Borys (1994) argued that professional boundaries need not be associated with rigidity or dehumanization. She suggested that therapists can set limits while still being empathic and warm.

Boundaries may also serve "as a metaphor for the internal structure of the patient's emotional life" (Borys, 1994, p. 270) and may be necessary for the progress of clients in therapy. Clients with internal structures that are chaotic and unpredictable need the structure and stability that are provided by clear and consistent boundaries. The therapeutic hope is that they will eventually internalize "the calming and organizing experience of this structure as a model for a more organized inner life" (p. 270).

Dual relationship with clients can "jeopardize professional judgment, clients' welfare, and the process of therapy itself" (Pope & Vasquez, 1991, p. 115). Dual relationships may create conflicts of interest that compromise the professional distance and judgment necessary to best serve clients. Clients may alter their own behavior in therapy if there is a possibility of a relationship outside therapy. Psychologists may lose their ability to confront clients, may lose objectivity, and may struggle with the need to be liked by clients with whom they have a relationship outside therapy (Corey, Corey, & Callanan, 1998). Butler (1990) emphasized:

> A key question to ask is whether or not the dual relationship will in any way inhibit the client's actions and choices in other areas of their [sic] life, and if there are ways in which the client will feel that he or she cannot disagree with the therapist because of outside demands of any sort. (p. 23)

SEXUAL MULTIPLE RELATIONSHIPS

Sexual relationships with therapy clients are among the most serious of all boundary violations. Olarte's (1997) review of research on sexually abusive therapists noted that therapists who engage in sexual misconduct are typically described as being in a "lovesick" state, with clouded judgment. The prohibition of sexual intimacies between patient and health care provider outlined 2,500 years ago in the Hippocratic Oath is the basis of current standards outlawing such relationships. Brodsky (1989) indicated that it was addressed even earlier in the ancient code of Nigerian healing arts. Although laws differ from state to state in length of time that is necessary posttermination before psychologists can engage in sexual relationships with former clients (or whether or not such relationships can ever be considered acceptable), none allow sexual relationships between psychologists and current clients. As Pope and Vasquez (1991) pointed out, "That this prohibition has remained constant over so long a time and throughout so many diverse cultures reflects to some extent the recognition that such intimacies place the patient at risk for exceptional harm" (p. 101). Such harm can include exploitation of the client through abuse of power, role confusion, and undermining therapy by mishandling transference in the client-therapist relationship.

Sexual contact between therapists and current clients is forbidden in all professional codes, but these codes vary in how they deal with posttermination relationships. Before 1992, the APA ethics code gave no guidance on the question of posttermination sexual relationships with clients. In response to complaints about the harmful consequences of irresponsible termination of therapy, the 1992 APA ethics code revision team put this standard into place:

> Psychologists do not engage in sexual intimacies with a former therapy patient or client for at least 2 years after cessation or termination of professional services. (Standard 4.07a, p. 1605)

Within the revision task force, there were strong arguments for prohibiting all sexual contact with ex-clients. The following quote on this issue is from the task force:

> Because sexual intimacies with a former therapy patient or client are so frequently harmful to the patient or client, and because such intimacies undermine public confidence in the psychology profession and thereby deter the public's use of needed services, psychologists do not engage in sexual intimacies with former therapy patients and clients even after a two year interval except in the most unusual circumstances. The psychologist . . . bears the burden of demonstrating that there has been no exploitation. (Standard 4.07b, p. 1605)

In addition, the 1992 APA ethics code defined as unethical a therapist suggesting to a client the possibility of a posttherapy sexual relationship. The 2002 APA ethics code continues the prohibition against sexual contact with a former client for at least two years post termination. It further expands on the psychologist's responsibility to avoid exploitation and specifies relevant factors that may be considered as exploitative (Standard 10.08, p. 15).

Schoener (1986) offered a list of useful factors to consider when thinking of posttherapy relationships: (a) the length and level of therapeutic involvement; (b) the degree of transference, dependency, or power inequity that remains after termination; (c) personality variables and therapy style; (d) whether or not there has been therapeutic deception; (e) whether or not there was an actual termination; (f) who initiated the posttermination contact; (g) whether the pros and cons of such a relationship have been discussed; (h) whether the psychologist sought consultation; and (i) consideration of the legal context, professional setting, and local standards.

These factors illustrate the complexities and ambiguity contained in any discussion of a posttermination sexual relationship—factors that may become more complicated within some cultural or other small-community settings. Psychologists can never be completely sure about their own objectivity. Another factor is that when people enter a romantic relationship, they never know how it will end. If a posttherapy sexual relationship ends badly, the client may claim damage by the psychologist. These kinds of factors, therefore, make such relationships high risk. For example, psychologists may have to prove that they are not responsible if former clients claim exploitation through a complaint. As Vasquez (1991) cautioned, "To rationalize the acceptability of sex after termination, one must demonstrate that transference no longer exists, and we know of no good research that demonstrates that the transference is usually resolved" (p. 51). In addition to "interrupting the posttherapy integration process" (p. 52), clients no longer have the option of returning to therapy with a psychologist with whom they had or are having a sexual posttherapy relationship.

Gabbard (1994a) identified five concerns in initiating posttermination sexual relationships with clients: transference, internalization of the therapist, continuing professional responsibilities, unequal power, and harm to patients and the therapeutic process. He suggested that an honest and complete examination of the issue of a posttermination sexual relationship is clouded by several factors:

- The tendency to blame the victim (even though maintenance of boundaries is always the therapist's responsibility)
- The prospective financial burden of prosecuting violators under a more rigorous standard
- The difficulty of confronting colleagues who are involved in sexual relationships with former clients
- The confusion and guilt often felt by therapists who are attracted to clients but do not act on that attraction

The power differential between client and therapist "can and does continue beyond termination," and "it is the therapist's responsibility to prove that no such power differential exists before pursuing a sexual relationship with a former client" (Shopland & VandeCreek, 1991, pp. 40-41). The debate over this issue is ongoing and sometimes contentious. It is important that the voices of all psychologists be included in the discussions, however difficult or trying those discussions might be.

EVALUATING NONSEXUAL MULTIPLE RELATIONSHIPS

Therapists need to carefully consider their own objectivity, along with the potential risks and benefits to clients, when considering nonsexual multiple relationships. One of the most descriptive examples of the problems inherent in multiple relationships comes from Gabbard (1994b): "The problem lies in knowing when to disregard boundaries and when to honor them. Clinical judgment in this regard is highly variable from one therapist to another. Though many musicians can play the scales, not all can improvise" (p. 283). Herlihy and Corey (1992) suggested that multiple relationships can be problematic for several reasons. Such relationships can be pervasive, difficult to recognize, sometimes unavoidable, the subject of conflicting advice, a risk to consumers and professionals, and may affect a range of other people.

How do nonsexual multiple relationships develop? Bartering, counseling friends or family members of clients, socializing with former clients, and supervising former clients are just a sample of the possibilities (Herlihy & Corey, 1992). Dual, multiple, or overlapping relationships are often easier to define than to recognize. Does the degree of involvement affect the definition? How do the elements of the therapy and out-of-therapy relationship affect each other? What kinds of posttherapy relationships—if any—are acceptable or ethical? It may be difficult to know whether the potential for a dual or multiple relationship may exist. Psychologists cannot always predict who will come for therapy in the future or even who might be related to whom.

The argument sometimes put forth by psychologists, particularly within small communities, is that multiple relationships are unavoidable. The distinction of *sometimes* unavoidable is an important one. Without careful consideration of alternatives, this argument can lead to widespread acceptance of any and all multiple relationships. Psychologists who view multiple relationships as unavoidable risk the unfortunate mind-set that they have little control over situations. This can then lead to feeling no responsibility for maintaining appropriate professional relationships (Pope, 1991). Herlihy and Corey (1992) also pointed out that boundaries between overlapping relationships can be unclear. A real-life example is the distinction between a friendship and a professional therapy relationship. It may be all too easy for the conversation within a therapy session to shift to a more casual and mutual level. It may also be too easy for a psychologist to let information shared within a therapy session affect the dynamics of an out-of-therapy friendship.

As noted earlier, the 1992 and 2002 APA ethics codes make no explicit statements regarding the appropriateness of engaging in nonsexual multiple relationships. Although not specifically prohibited, psychologists are urged to avoid nonsexual posttherapy relationships that could create a risk for harm—a possibility not easily or accurately predictable. Many mental health professionals report friendships with former clients and view those friendships as appropriate under some circumstances (Salisbury & Kinnier, 1996). The degree to which psychologists can differentiate between themselves and their clients in the maintenance of appropriate interpersonal boundaries is an important factor in the ethical success of these relationships. If compounded by significant life stress on the part of a psychologist, it is likely that the risk of less insightful and more harmful decisions will increase (Baer & Murdock, 1995).

There are risks to both clients and therapists in multiple relationships. Clients who feel exploited by overlapping relationships may feel confused, hurt, angry, and betrayed. The therapy process may be jeopardized, and clients may feel that they lose their freedom of choice and action in both their therapy relationships and their outside lives. This betrayal may have long-lasting consequences and may preclude such clients from ever seeking help from other professionals. Alternatively, they may feel trapped and dependent on the relationship, despite feelings of anger and confusion (Herlihy & Corey, 1992).

A nonsexual posttherapy relationship between a psychologist and former client precludes the client from returning to that psychologist for therapy in the future. Because it is difficult to predict the path, length, depth, or importance of the posttherapy relationship, it is not easy to assess whether it is worthwhile for the client to give up the possibility of a future therapeutic relationship. It may also be awkward to shift the dynamics of a therapy relationship to that of a posttherapy relationship with more mutual advice giving and support.

Although psychologists are not legally obligated to take someone back as a client, Pipes (1999) suggested that the nature of the therapy relationship is of utmost consideration. He went on to advise that many clients may remain vulnerable following termination or may continue to have very strong feelings about their psychologists or about therapy. Pipes (1999) also reminded us that former clients may request records or require court testimony from psychologists. It would be difficult in such a situation to argue that a psychologist's objectivity was not impaired by the occurrence of a nonsexual posttherapy relationship. Many therapy relationships could be further strengthened if the possibility for posttherapy contact did not exist, leaving clients with fewer inhibitions about what they might say in therapy or with fewer fantasies about the possibility of an outside-of-therapy relationship.

Psychologists involved in overlapping relationships that turn negative or acrimonious risk loss of professional credibility and professional reputation, possible litigation, complaints to licensing boards, and possible restrictions to or loss of licensure. Even problematic overlapping relationships that are undetected or unreported affect the psychologists involved, may lead them to doubt their competence and sense of self, and may make it easier to commit further violations (Herlihy & Corey, 1992).

A client who is not involved in an overlapping relationship with a particular psychologist may resent that other clients have the opportunity to be involved in more than a professional relationship with the psychologist. Although it may be difficult for those other clients to openly question overlapping relationships between their psychologist and other clients, they may be harmed and may be less likely to refer others to that psychologist (Chapman, 1997; Herlihy & Corey, 1992).

Former clients or individual therapists are not the only ones who might be damaged. The resultant negative publicity can spread to other professionals, to others in the community, and to the larger society (Chapman, 1997; Herlihy & Corey, 1992; Pipes, 1999). Nonpsychologist colleagues may be reluctant to work with such psychologists and may resent having to explain negative fallout from overlapping relationships that psychologists have with clients. Sell, Gottlieb, and Schoenfeld (1986) suggested that the effects of unethical and criminal actions by psychotherapists have had a profound effect on all mental health professionals, both in terms of negative publicity and increased liability insurance premiums.

It is difficult to confront other psychologists who are engaged in damaging overlapping relationships. It is also difficult to ignore what is happening and to condone it through default. Such a situation can create morale problems within an agency and promote an unfortunate image of psychology among other nonpsychologists who may be unfamiliar with the standards of the profession (Herlihy & Corey, 1992).

Thus, ill-considered behavior can be deleterious to the reputation of particular psychologists and to the profession of psychology in general, especially in some small communities in which psychology may already be regarded with suspicion and distrust. If psychologists do not take on the responsibility of regulating their own profession, regulatory agencies may increase their efforts to do so and potential clients may hesitate to seek assistance (Herlihy & Corey, 1992).

LESSONS FROM THE MULTIPLE-RELATIONSHIP DILEMMAS OF SMALL-COMMUNITY PSYCHOLOGISTS

The limitations of strict ethical dictums in all situations are best illuminated by examples from small- and contained-community practice. Small and contained communities include rural areas, communities of color, small colleges, military, disability, sexual orientation, and others. Most of the research on small-community dilemmas has been with rural practice (Schank, 1994, 1998; Schank & Skovholt, 1997). Rural psychologists face ethical decisions about multiple relationships that are unique to their particular circumstances. But if we consider minority populations in urban areas, we can see that many of the ethical dilemmas of rural psychologists generalize to urban psychologists practicing in any circumscribed environment. In our research, we have seen that common ethical dilemmas connect the American military psychologist working on a small base, the lesbian psychologist who primarily serves the gay community, the Native American psychologist working on a reservation, the deaf practitioner who works solely with deaf clients, and the staff psychologist at a small liberal arts college.

The lessons we learn from any of these scenarios may clarify how all psychologists might better cope with sticky multiple relationships. To shed light on the ethical dilemmas unique to these small-community practitioners, Schank and Skovholt (1997) interviewed 16 licensed psychologists practicing in rural towns and small communities. Interview questions were based on six main topics: (a) maintaining professional boundaries, (b) limited resources and limits of competence, (c) community expectations and values differences, (d) interagency issues, (e) peer helpers and other alternatives to traditional treatment methods, and (f) burnout (Schank & Skovholt, 1997).

All the participants in this study indicated that the dilemmas they faced in maintaining professional boundaries presented the most frequent and complicated ethical problems in their practices. From this one interview question, four subtopics emerged: (a) the reality of overlapping social relationships, (b) the reality of overlapping business or professional relationships, (c) the effects of overlapping relationships on members of the psychologist's own family, and (d) working with more than one family member as clients or with others who have friendships with individual clients (Schank & Skovholt, 1997).

All the participants indicated that simultaneous or overlapping relationships were commonplace. Because their communities were so small, the only way these psychologists could avoid interacting with clients outside their offices was to avoid church activities, social gatherings, eating out in local restaurants, school events, and volunteer activities. This was often extremely difficult, so psychologists found themselves facing multiple relationship dilemmas on a regular basis:

> When I moved here, I got a membership to the YMCA to go to exercise classes. After running into a couple of clients in the locker room, I decided that this was just so uncomfortable for me. So I'm not going to continue my membership in the YMCA. It was just really awkward. It's not like there are a huge number of athletic clubs here that you can have a choice of which one you go to. (Schank & Skovholt, 1997, p. 46)

The psychologists indicated that they made decisions about whom they would see as clients on the basis of three criteria: (a) their own comfort level with managing overlapping relationships with the client, (b) the client's input about whether boundaries could be maintained, and (c) the type and severity of the client's presenting problems. Some of the psychologists were forced to consider the complications that could arise from treating a child who was in the same school or activities as their own children. Others reported that their spouses' professional or business relationships with potential clients influenced their decisions about whether they could successfully manage dual roles. Some psychologists were more apt to see a client for situations that involved more problem solving and advice giving but would not enter into overlapping relationships with clients with more serious personality disorders. The majority of the participants chose to talk directly with their clients about the high probability of nonprofessional contact in the hope that clients could anticipate how and if they would acknowledge their therapists in public. This open dialogue about boundaries often occurred throughout clients' therapy:

It is always establishing boundaries. I live on a very busy street in town and was doing some landscaping and working out in the front yard. One of my clients must have seen me and later said, "Oh, is that where you live? I saw you." I said yes, and she said, "Well, I noticed that the house next to you is for sale. Wouldn't that be cool? You know, my parents are thinking of helping me buy a house." I said, "No, that would not be cool because you are my client—you are not a friend. If you moved in next door to me, it would be extremely uncomfortable. I know what you are saying—I listen to you, I care about you—but friends know about one another. You don't come in, and I sit and tell you about my problems and my life. I don't call you when I am hurting or need a friend for support. . . ." She said, "Oh, yeah. I didn't even think about that." And so it's continually having to establish boundaries with a number of clients. (Schank & Skovholt, 1997, p. 47)

Overlapping social relationships with clients was a reality for these small-community practitioners, but overlapping business relationships also posed their own difficulties. For example, shopping in a store in which a client was working was less troubling than doing business with a client or client's family. Other overlapping roles forced some psychologists to choose between competing ethical obligations:

I do consulting at a fair number of group homes. Sometimes I'm in that dilemma where there is someone [working there] that I've seen as a client. In fact, I can think of two instances where I currently was seeing people as clients and subsequently discovered that they had obtained employment at one of the group homes. So I was dealing with them as clients, as well as in a professional relationship in terms of some of the consulting. (Schank & Skovholt, 1997, p. 47)

The effects of overlapping relationships on the psychologists' family were profound.

The 12 psychologists who identified this as a major ethical issue agreed that their relationships with clients sometimes made it difficult to balance professional and family roles. This seemed especially true for the psychologists who were parents. Having to choose between a client's best interest and their children's social interests was not uncommon: "Do they have to accept having clients in their homes as guests of their children, or do they break confidentiality by setting limits on whom their children can have as friends?" (Schank & Skovholt, 1997, p. 47). Two psychologists faced a pronounced ethical dilemma when their teenage children unknowingly began dating clients:

I think the more difficult situation is interaction that my daughter has had. She is now away at college, but when she was here she would end up dating clients—only to find out and just be absolutely horrified and angry. That is probably the most difficult circumstance that we have been in. The confidentiality piece is really difficult because she would confront me with, "Is so and so your client?" She is real glad to be done with that. (Schank & Skovholt, 1997, p. 48)

Because there are limited choices for therapists in rural and small communities, psychologists often felt obligated to work with more than one family member as clients or with friends of current clients. Nine of the psychologists indicated that this was a frequent problem, and it was especially upsetting when they knew there was no other therapist they could feasibly turn to as a referral source. If the psychologist was not aware that two clients knew each other, quick decisions had to be made:

As a matter of fact, one time I had—I did not know this—I had two new clients starting. They didn't know that the other one was coming here, and they were having affairs with each other's mates. Well, I had to make a choice of whom I was going to see. In that particular case, it worked out fine. But just to let you know—there is tremendous overlapping. (Schank & Skovholt, 1997, p. 48)

This case is an example of the unique predicaments small-community practitioners face. Had both of these clients been in serious distress, would the psychologist have been justified in seeing both simultaneously? What are the ethical implications of refusing service to a client who has no alternatives? Could the psychologist build a trusting relationship with both clients, knowing each of their stories? In an urban setting, the psychologist could easily refer one of the clients to a trusted colleague and quickly sidestep this ethical dilemma. A rural psychologist, however, might be forced to make a decision that many would claim violates psychology's ethical code. We suggest that these small-community dilemmas deserve significant consideration and reflection.

SUMMARY AND RECOMMENDATIONS

Although initially conceived for small-community practitioners, the following safeguards can minimize risk for all psychologists:

1. Nonsexual overlapping relationships are not a matter of *if* as much as *when* in the daily lives of many small- and contained-community psychologists (Barnett & Yutrzenka, 1995). Ethical codes or standards are necessary but not sufficient and are tempered by experience and context (Barnett & Yutrzenka, 1995). Although it may seem obvious, knowledge of these codes and of state laws is an essential base for all psychologists, but continuing education and discussion of ethical issues must inform how these codes are implemented.

2. Clear expectations and boundaries, whenever possible, strengthen the therapeutic relationship. This is especially important in situations in which out-of-therapy contact cannot be closely controlled. Obtaining informed consent, sticking to time limits, protecting confidentiality (and explaining its limits), and documenting case progress (including being explicit about any overlapping relationships) diminishes the risk of misunderstandings between client and psychologist.

3. Ongoing consultation and discussion of cases, especially those involving dual roles, provide a context for psychologists to get additional perspectives and decrease the isolation that sometimes accompanies practice, especially in small communities. Each of us has blind spots; trusted colleagues can help us constructively examine them.

4. Self-knowledge and having a life outside work lessens the chances that we as psychologists will use, even unknowingly, our clients for our own gratification.

As identified earlier in this chapter, boundaries in therapeutic relationships provide the safety necessary for clients to explore difficult and painful issues within a therapeutic framework. Prohibitions against dual relationships have served a vital purpose in maintaining the integrity of the therapy process. However, it is also important to consider issues that arise within contained-community contexts that may complicate boundaries. Therapists must make informed, careful decisions when faced with the dilemmas presented by overlapping relationships.

REFERENCES

American Psychological Association. (1992). Ethical principles of psychologists and code of conduct. *American Psychologist, 45,* 1597-1611.

American Psychological Association (2002). Ethical principles of psychologists and code of conduct. Retrieved December 1, 2002, from http://apa.org/ethics.html.

Bachelor, A., & Horvath, A. (1999). The therapeutic relationship. In M. A. Hubble, B. L. Duncan, & S. D. Miller (Eds.), *The heart and soul of change: What works in therapy* (pp. 133-178). Washington, DC: American Psychological Association.

Baer, B. E., & Murdock, N. L. (1995). Nonerotic dual relationships between therapists and clients: The effects of sex, theoretical orientation, and interpersonal boundaries. *Ethics & Behavior, 5,* 131-145.

Barnett, J. E., & Yutrzenka, B. A. (1995). Nonsexual dual relationships in professional practice, with special applications to rural and military communities. *Independent Practitioner, 14,* 243-248.

Borys, D. S. (1992). Nonsexual dual relationships. In L. VandeCreek, S. Knapp, and T. L. Jackson (Eds.), *Innovations in clinical practice* (Vol. 11, pp. 443-454). Sarasota, FL: Professional Resource Press.

Borys, D. S. (1994). Maintaining therapeutic boundaries: The motive is therapeutic effectiveness, not defensive practice. *Ethics & Behavior, 4,* 267-273.

Brodsky, A. M. (1989). Sex between patient and therapist: Psychology's data and response. In G. O. Gabbard (Ed.), *Sexual exploitation in professional relationships* (pp. 15-25). Washington, DC: American Psychiatric Press.

Butler, R. T. (1990, January). Dual relationships and therapy. *Minnesota Psychologist,* p. 23.

Catalano, S. (1997). Challenges of clinical practice in small or rural communities: Case studies in managing dual relationships in and outside of therapy. *Journal of Contemporary Psychotherapy, 27,* 23-35.

Chapman, C. (1997). Dual relationships in substance abuse treatment: Ethical implications. *Alcoholism Treatment Quarterly, 15,* 73-79.

Corey, G., Corey, M. S., & Callanan, P. (1998). *Issues and ethics in the helping professions.* Pacific Grove, CA: Brooks/Cole.

Gabbard, G. O. (1994a). Reconsidering the American Psychological Association's policy on sex with former patients: Is it justifiable? *Professional Psychology: Research and Practice, 25,* 329-335.

Gabbard, G. O. (1994b). Teetering on the precipice: A commentary on Lazarus's "How certain boundaries and ethics diminish therapeutic effectiveness." *Ethics & Behavior, 4,* 283-286.

Gutheil, T. G., & Gabbard, G. O. (1993). The concept of boundaries in clinical practice: Theoretical and risk-management dimensions. *American Journal of Psychiatry, 150,* 188-196.

Hedges, L. E. (1993, July/August). In praise of dual relationships. Part II: Essential dual relatedness in developmental psychotherapy. *The California Therapist,* pp. 42-46.

Herlihy, B., & Corey, G. (1992). *Dual relationships in counseling.* Alexandria, VA: American Association for Counseling and Development.

Koocher, G. P., & Keith-Spiegel, P. (1998). *Ethics in psychology: Professional standards and cases.* New York: Oxford University Press.

Olarte, S. W. (1997). Sexual boundary violations. In *The Hatherleigh guide to ethics in therapy* (pp. 195-209). New York: Hatherleigh.

Pipes, R. B. (1999). Nonsexual relationships between psychotherapists and their former clients: Obligations of psychologists. In D. Bersoff (Ed.), *Ethical conflicts in psychology* (pp. 254-256). Washington, DC: American Psychological Association.

Pope, K. S. (1985). Dual relationships: A violation of ethical, legal, and clinical standards. *California State Psychologist, 20,* 1-3.

Pope, K. S. (1991). Dual relationships in psychotherapy. *Ethics & Behavior, 1,* 21-34.

Pope, K. S., & Vasquez, M. J. T. (1991). *Ethics in psychotherapy and counseling: A practical guide for psychologists.* San Francisco: Jossey-Bass.

Salisbury, W. A., & Kinnier, R. T. (1996). Posttermination friendship between counselors and clients. *Journal of Counseling and Development, 74,* 495-500.

Schank, J. A. (1994). *Ethical dilemmas of rural and small-community psychologists.* Unpublished doctoral dissertation, University of Minnesota, Minneapolis.

Schank, J. A. (1998). Ethical issues in rural counseling practice. *Canadian Journal of Counseling, 32,* 270-283.

Schank, J. A., & Skovholt, T. M. (1997). Dual-relationship dilemmas of rural and small-community psychologists. *Professional Psychology: Research and Practice, 28,* 44-49.

Schoener, G. R. (1986). Sexual involvement of therapists with clients after therapy ends: Some observations. In G. R. Schoener, J. H. Milgrom, J. C. Gonsiorek, E. T. Luepker, & R. M. Conroe (Eds.), *Psychotherapists' sexual involvement with clients* (pp. 265-287). Minneapolis, MN: Walk-In Counseling Center.

Sell, J. M., Gottlieb, M. C., & Schoenfeld, L. (1986). Ethical considerations of social-romantic relationships with present and former clients. *Professional Psychology: Research and Practice, 17,* 504-508.

Shopland, S. N., & VandeCreek, L. (1991). Sex with ex-clients: Theoretical rationales for prohibition. *Ethics & Behavior, 1,* 35-44.

Smith, D., & Fitzpatrick, M. (1995). Patient-therapist boundary issues: An integrative review of theory and research. *Professional Psychology: Research and Practice, 22,* 235-239.

Sonne, J. L. (1994). Multiple relationships: Does the new ethics code answer the right questions? *Professional Psychology: Research and Practice, 25,* 336-343.

St. Germaine, J. (1993). Dual relationships: What's wrong with them? *American Counselor, 2,* 25-30.

Strasburger, L. H., Jorgenson, L., & Sutherland, P. (1992). The prevention of psychotherapist sexual misconduct: Avoiding the slippery slope. *American Journal of Psychotherapy, 46,* 544-555.

Tomm, K. (1993, January/February). The ethics of dual relationships. *The California Therapist,* pp. 7-19.

Vasquez, M. J. (1991). Sexual intimacies with clients after termination: Should a prohibition be explicit? *Ethics & Behavior, 1,* 45-61.

CHAPTER 13

Ideals and Realities in the Development and Practice of Informed Consent

WILLIAM C. FOLLETTE,
DEBORAH DAVIS, AND MARKUS KEMMELMEIER
University of Nevada, Reno

Psychologists in the United States engage in a variety of activities that require participants to provide informed consent. These activities range from delivery of therapy services to assessment to intramural research in institutional settings all the way to federally funded research. At each of these levels, the specific nature of informed consent must meet standards at several levels and comply with multiple ethical, regulatory, and statutory codes.

HISTORICAL CONTEXT OF INFORMED CONSENT IN APPLIED RESEARCH

Federal guidelines and Institutional Review Boards (IRBs) have been established in part because of several infamous blatant violations of human rights, dignity, and participants'

trust. The Nuremberg trials following World War II documented atrocities of many kinds, including "medical experiments" conducted in concentration camps (Caplan, 1992). One outcome of the these trials was the adoption of the Nuremberg Code, a 10-point code of research conduct, the cornerstone of which was the establishment of the principle of *informed consent (Trials of War Criminals Before the Nuremberg Military Tribunals Under Control Council Law,* 1949). In 1964, the World Medical Association adopted the Declaration of Helsinki, which further elaborated the ethical principles for medical research involving human subjects. This document has been amended in 1975, 1983, 1989, 1996, and most recently, in 2000 (World Medical Association Declaration of Helsinki, 2000). In the United States, additional national efforts to define and refine protections for human subjects participating in research have continued (e.g., National Bioethics Advisory Commission, 2001a, 2001b; National Commission for the Protection of Human Subjects of Biomedical and Behavioral Research, 1979).

Sadly, prior to Nazi atrocities of World War II and continuing for decades after the Nuremberg Code, deceptive and harmful human research was conducted in the United States. In the case of the Tuskegee syphilis study, which began in 1932, under the auspices of the U.S. Public Health Service, 399 African Americans who had contracted syphilis and 200 African American controls were followed to study the natural course of the disease, until the experiment came to light in 1972 (see Jones, 1993; Kampmeier, 1974; Wolinsky, 1997). Information about the existence of treatment was withheld from the infected subjects despite the fact that penicillin had been identified as an effective cure for the disease around 1947.

Another well-documented example of biomedical experimentation leading to subject harm without informed consent occurred when the CIA and U.S. Army exposed both uninformed and partially informed subjects to hallucinogenic drugs, resulting in the deaths of at least two persons (Commission on CIA Activities within the United States, 1975; U.S. Senate Select Committee to Study Governmental Operations With Respect to Intelligence Activities, 1976). A final illustration of the blatant violation of informed consent is the long history of experimentation involving human exposure to radiation. A great deal of this research was conducted with insufficient knowledge of the effects of radiation to adequately inform subjects, even had investigators wished to do so.

Deception occurred to different degrees in these experiments, ranging from none to complete (see President's Advisory Committee, 1996). Thus, although there was international outrage at Nazi "experiments," the history of unethical research without informed consent in the U.S. demonstrates how *self*-deceptive researchers can be when justifying their own actions.

The history of the blatantly unethical experiments that can occur when no monitoring is in place is long; it clearly supports the need for standards for conducting experiments ensuring sufficiently informed and wholly voluntary participation. The current nature of such standards, how well they function, and what problems still exist will constitute the topics in the remainder of this chapter.

Although ethical standards for biomedical research began to emerge with the Nuremberg Code (see Box 13.1), formal oversight for biomedical, behavioral, and psychological research was slow to evolve. National Institutes of Health guidelines for the protection of human subjects were first issued in 1966 but were not given regulatory status until 1974. Prior to the adoption of these initial regulations, scientists made a variety of decisions of poor ethical quality, including those leading to the design and implementation of the Tuskegee study.

Box 13.1   **Nuremberg Code**

1. The voluntary consent of the human subject is absolutely essential. This means that the person involved should have legal capacity to give consent; should be so situated as to be able to exercise free power of choice, without the intervention of any element of force, fraud, deceit, duress, over-reaching, or other ulterior form of constraint or coercion;

and should have sufficient knowledge and comprehension of the elements of the subject matter involved as to enable him to make an understanding and enlightened decision. This latter element requires that before the acceptance of an affirmative decision by the experimental subject there should be made known to him the nature, duration, and purpose of the experiment; the method and means by which it is to be conducted; all inconveniences and hazards reasonable to be expected; and the effects upon his health or person which may possibly come from his participation in the experiment.

2. The duty and responsibility for ascertaining the quality of the consent rests upon each individual who initiates, directs or engages in the experiment. It is a personal duty and responsibility which may not be delegated to another with impunity.

3. The experiment should be such as to yield fruitful results for the good of society, unprocurable by other methods or means of study, and not random and unnecessary in nature.

4. The experiment should be so designed and based on the results of animal experimentation and a knowledge of the natural history of the disease or other problem under study that the anticipated results will justify the performance of the experiment.

5. The experiment should be so conducted as to avoid all unnecessary physical and mental suffering and injury.

6. No experiment should be conducted where there is an *a priori* reason to believe that death or disabling injury will occur; except, perhaps, in those experiments where the experimental physicians also serve as subjects.

7. The degree of risk to be taken should never exceed that determined by the humanitarian importance of the problem to be solved by the experiment.

8. Proper preparations should be made and adequate facilities provided to protect the experimental subject against even remote possibilities of injury, disability, or death.

9. The experiment should be conducted only by scientifically qualified persons. The highest degree of skill and care should be required through all stages of the experiment of those who conduct or engage in the experiment.

10. During the course of the experiment the human subject should be at liberty to bring the experiment to an end if he has reached the physical or mental state where continuation of the experiment seems to him to be impossible.

11. During the course of the experiment the scientist in charge must be prepared to terminate the experiment at any stage, if he has probable cause to believe, in the exercise of the good faith, superior skill and careful judgment required of him that a continuation of the experiment is likely to result in injury, disability, or death to the experimental subject.

SOURCE: Reprinted from *Trials of War Criminals Before the Nuremberg Military Tribunals* under Control Council Law No. 10, Vol. 2, pp. 181-182. Washington, DC: U.S. Government Printing Office, 1949.

In 1954, a new ethical problem of informed consent arose. Thoughtful consideration was given to the design and implementation of the field trial of the Salk poliomyelitis vaccine involving more than 2 million children. It was decided that a control group blind to the fact they were receiving a placebo was necessary (Meier, 1989). At the time, and for many years to come, the use of a placebo arm characterized the gold standard design for many types of clinical trials.

A decade later (1963), psychological research joined the ranks of ethically questionable violations of informed consent with the famous research of Stanley Milgram on obedience to authority (Milgram, 1963). Milgram actively deceived his "teacher" participants to convince them they were delivering dangerous electric shocks to a "learner," who was actually a confederate of the experimenter, revealing that the majority of participants would obey the experimenter's instruction to delivery potentially lethal levels of shock to a strongly objecting "learner." This study, a classic in social psychology, has been the focus of a great deal of debate surrounding deception and informed consent (see Kemmelmeier, Davis, & Follette, Chapter 14, this volume).

CURRENT GUIDELINES FOR INFORMED CONSENT

As seen in the Nuremberg code and elsewhere, informed consent is the cornerstone to the ethical treatment of humans participating in a variety of activities, ranging from simple forms of research participation to complex therapies or clinical trials. Standards for the practice of informed consent exist at the level of professional ethical codes and guidelines on up to regulatory control. We will look briefly at two important

social influences, the American Psychological Association Ethical Principles for Psychologists and Code of Conduct (APA, 2002; henceforth "APA code") and the Code of Federal Regulations concerning the use of human subjects and informed consent (U.S. Department of Health and Human Services, 2001).

This chapter does not address superordinate ethical principles that a particular individual may embrace. The reason this chapter addresses the APA code is pragmatic. Though the APA code is not directly binding on individuals, particularly those outside the APA, many states in granting licensure make reference to the code as the operative guide for licensed individuals. In addition, the existence of the code is perceived by some jurisdictions as evidence of standards of practice that may be applied in civil cases, such that those who operate outside the code may be at some risk for liability.

An interesting feature of the APA code of ethics derives from the way the initial version was drafted (APA, 1953). In contrast to a select committee meeting to determine the ethical code on the basis of some unknown doctrine and relying primarily on the collective wisdom of the committee members, the committee decided to develop an empirically based code, the content of which was based on a survey of practicing psychologists in various professional arenas. The survey solicited descriptions of situations representing ethical dilemmas actually encountered by members. The rationale for this approach to developing the code was that it was important to prioritize which issues to develop first so that it would address problems that psychologists actually faced (for a brief history, see Pope & Vetter, 1992).

Ethical codes always evolve. There have been eight versions of the ethical guidelines, with a ninth now in its seventh draft (for a history of the revisions, see APA, 2002). Though more recent iterations of the code have been informed by surveys similar to the initial *critical incidents* analysis, it is now influenced by many other factors, including legal rulings as well as applicable regulatory rules and guidelines.

Whether or not one falls under the purview of the APA guidelines, any behavioral researchers who conduct research at institutions that receive federal monies or who receive federal monies themselves are subject to federal regulations that supply a structure and procedures for evaluation of studies and informed consent procedures by IRBs established to ensure the protection of experimental participants.

Pragmatic Notions of Informed Consent

The spirit of informed consent is given in the first principle of the Nuremberg code, and it has come to encompass three basic elements: competence, comprehension, and freedom to consent or decline. *Competence* is the ability to make informed decisions that are in one's own best interests. *Comprehension* is the capacity to understand the information presented that is relevant to making an informed decision. This entails the potential participant's cognitive capacity to understand the information presented as well as the clarity and completeness of the presentation of information. The *freedom to consent or decline* is an assessment of the real voluntary nature of the decision without undue influence, coercion, fraud, misrepresentation, or duress. For informed consent to be legitimately granted, these conditions must be met. Even in the presence of these conditions, for informed consent to be credible, there is also a community standard; namely, the

community must perceive that a reasonable person with an average degree of self-interest, altruism, and risk aversion would voluntarily consent to participate in the specific study described.

Informed Consent and the APA

The APA addresses informed consent in several different domains (APA, 2002). Section 3.10(a) states, "When psychologists conduct research or provide assessment, therapy, counseling, or consulting services . . . they obtain the informed consent of the individual or individuals using language that is reasonably understandable to that person or persons." The code does not provide a definition of precisely what constitutes informed consent. However, the general principles outlined in the draft are headed Principle A: Beneficence and Non-maleficence; Principle B: Fidelity and Responsibility; Principle C: Integrity; Principle D: Justice; and Principle E: Respect for People's Rights and Dignity. At least principles E, A, and D are direct parallels to the terminology found in the so-called *Belmont Report,* which defines the principles of respect for persons, beneficence, and justice as the cornerstones for the ethical principles and guidelines for the protection of human subjects (National Commission for the Protection of Human Subjects of Biomedical and Behavioral Research, 1979).

APA Guidelines for Consent for Therapy

The APA code (2002) Section 10.01(b) states,

When obtaining informed consent for treatment for which generally recognized techniques and procedures have not been established, psychologists inform their clients/patients of the developing nature of treatment, the potential risks involved, alternative treatments that may be available, and the voluntary nature of their participation.

This abbreviated definition of informed consent (compared with the spirit of Principle 1 of the Nuremberg Code) still places a significant burden on the psychologist.

At a pragmatic level, the process of obtaining informed consent provides the therapist with an opportunity to explain some of the important mechanics of therapy and limits of the therapeutic relationship. A partial list of issues that can and should be addressed in an informed consent form between client and therapist includes (a) a description of the credentials of the therapist and any relevant treatment staff, (b) the definition and limits of confidentiality in the jurisdiction where services are provided, (c) issues of fees and privacy (e.g., how to contact the client without violating his or her privacy at home or work), (d) a description of how goals are established for therapy, (e) how and why assessment is conducted, and (f) the nature, rationale, and data in support of the proposed treatment, along with what alternative treatments might be available.

One might ask why the therapy enterprise requires informed consent. In Part A of the *Belmont Report*, the distinction between research and practice is discussed. In the case of practice, interventions are intended to solely benefit the individual patient, with a reasonable expectation that the intervention will indeed provide benefit. In contrast, research is intended to test hypotheses in order to contribute to "generalized knowledge" in form of theories, principles, or empirical findings (National Commission for the Protection of Human Subjects of Biomedical and Behavioral Research, 1979).

The key distinction for therapy is the expectation of individual benefit for the patient. Over the last several years, there has been an effort to identify interventions for specific problems that have an empirical basis for predicting benefit for a patient. The APA appointed a committee to identify empirically supported treatments, which has issued evaluation criteria and lists of interventions for specific problems. A large literature is emerging on the state of this effort (e.g., Borkovec & Castonguay, 1998; Chambless et al., 1996; Chambless et al., 1998; Chambless & Hollon, 1998; Weisz, Hawley, Pilkonis, Woody, & Follette, 2000). At the same time, there is considerable debate on whether such an effort is appropriate in either principle or practice (cf. Beutler, 1998; Bohart, 2000; Bohart, O'Hara, & Leitner, 1998; Chambless & Ollendick, 2001; Crits-Christoph, 1997; Garfield, 1998; Henry, 1998; Wampold, Mondin, Moody, & Ahn, 1997; Wilson, 1996; see also a special issue of *Behavior Modification,* in press). The importance of the discussion about empirically supported treatments is that those therapies that are not *"generally recognized techniques and procedures"* should require the therapist to engage in an informed consent disclosing the unrecognized nature of the procedures. To the extent that a positive expectancy is an important part of therapy, one can understand why a therapist might be reluctant to qualify his or her intervention as not being generally recognized as beneficial.

*APA Guidelines for
Informed Consent for Research*

Psychologists do research in many settings, ranging from their own offices, to workplaces, to public and research institutions. When soliciting informed consent under the APA code , Standard 8.02 states,

> (a) When obtaining informed consent as required in Standard 3.10, Informed Consent, psychologists inform participants about (1) the purpose of the research, expected duration, and procedures; (2) their right to decline to participate and to withdraw from the research once participation has begun; (3) the foreseeable consequences of declining or withdrawing; (4) reasonably foreseeable factors that may be expected to influence their willingness to participate such as potential risks, discomfort, or adverse effects; (5) any prospective research benefits; (6) limits of confidentiality; (7) incentives for participation; and (8) whom to contact for questions about the research and research participants' rights. They provide opportunity for the prospective participants to ask questions and receive answers. (See also Standards 8.03, Informed Consent for Recording Voices and Images in Research; 8.05, Dispensing with Informed Consent for Research, and 8.07, Deception in Research)

These principles correspond rather closely to other codified regulations but do not specify a procedure for assuring that these goals have been met.

Federal Regulations and Informed Consent

Institutions or individuals receiving federal funds in the United States have to abide by federal regulations that are designed to review research before it is ever presented to a potential participant, to ensure that it passes some (unspecified) risk-benefit analysis conducted by someone other than the researcher and that there is an adequate consent form available for a participant to consider (U.S. Department of Health and Human Services, 2001). These regulations include regulations defining the constitution of the membership of IRBs, descriptions of its functions and operations, rules approving research, and special protections for special populations, including pregnant women, neonates, fetuses, and prisoners. The information required in the informed consent document is detailed in 45 CFR §46.116. The elements of the required informed consent are quite similar to APA principles, though there is predictably much more detail and structure.

Other Cases Requiring Informed Consent

Because they have the potential to greatly affect the lives of individuals, APA ethical principles require informed consent (and grant exceptions to it) around issues relating to assessment. For a detailed discussion of the issues related to assessment, see the chapter in this volume on psychological assessment (Adams & Luscher, Chapter 16).

ETHICAL CONTROVERSIES SURROUNDING INFORMED CONSENT PROCEDURES

When Is the Requirement of Informed Consent Negated?

Informed consent is not required in all circumstances. For example, requirements for informed consent may be negated during emergency situations when no proxy can be located. Although controversial in such circumstances, patients may qualify for clinical trials involving experimental treatments under restricted circumstances (for full explanation, see Davis, 1998; Kraybill & Bauer,

1999) and otherwise for standard treatments. The full list of exclusions under the APA code can be found in Section 8.05, "Dispensing With Informed Consent," and in federal regulations 45 CFR §46.101.

Competency to Consent

Federal regulations and professional codes of ethics address treatment and research with those unable to meet requirements of informed consent, either due to impaired understanding or impaired capacity to exercise choice. However, although some populations, such as younger children, may generally be deemed unable to consent, individuals must often be individually assessed to evaluate capacity to consent—such as those potentially impaired by physical or mental illness or cognitive decline. To facilitate these assessments, instruments have been developed to assess pertinent elements of decision-making capacity. Space does not permit detailed consideration here, but the reader is referred to a recent book by Grisso and Appelbaum (1998), offering comprehensive instructions and illustrations for conducting such assessments.

Those whose competency to consent is limited are subject to possible coercion and/or exploitation. Thus, controversies have developed surrounding appropriate use of such populations in research and appropriate circumstances for treatment without consent.

Safeguards Against Coercion in Therapeutic Settings

Coercion is widely practiced in therapeutic settings, particularly in terms of involuntary hospital admissions (see Truscott & Goodkey, Chapter 11, this volume), and coercive treatments such as restraint, involuntary medication, isolation, and so on (Høyer et al., 2002). Impairment through mental illness represents a serious threat to both cognitive and voluntary elements of the informed consent process. Thus, temptations toward paternalism or coercion are common for therapists dealing with impaired clients, in and outside mental institutions. Leaving aside strictly involuntary procedures, for others, while apparently offering choice, various degrees of persuasion or pressure may in effect coerce compliance (see Høyer et al., 2002).

Partly to track the impact of such practices, various instruments have been developed to assess perceived coercion, for example, the MacArthur Perceived Coercion Scale (Gardner et al., 1993); the Circumstances, Motivation, Readiness, and Suitability Scale (De Leon, Melnic, Kressel, & Jainchill, 1994); and the Coercion/Noncoercion Matrix (Marlowe et al., 1996). At least a subset of patients in Europe and North American report feeling coerced (e.g., Hiday, Swarz, Swanson, & Wagner, 1997; Høyer et al., 2002; Lidz et al., 1995).

Safeguards Against Exploitation In Research

Although regulations permit research involving those unable to reasonably offer voluntary informed consent, ethics surrounding use of such populations have been widely discussed, and a variety of guidelines have been offered to minimize the potential for exploitation (see review in Wendler, 2000). Discussions of these issues are available for the specific populations of various dementias (e.g., Dresser, 2001; Fisher & Craig Yury, Chapter 25, this volume; Marson, 2001; Stelmach, Konnert, & Dobson, 2001), frontal lobe dysfunctions (e.g., Fitten, 1999), mentally challenged (e.g., Arscott, Dagnan, & Kroese, 1998; Reder & Fitzpatrick, 1998; Williams & Williams, Chapter 20, this volume), mentally ill (e.g., Pinals & Appelbaum, 2000), those cognitively impaired due to chronic or acute physical illness (e.g., Dymek, Atchison, Harrell, & Marson, 2001; Montgomery, Lydon, & Lloyd, 1999), and children (e.g., Richards, Chapter 22, this volume; Hermann & Yoder, 1998; Hurley & Underwood, 2002; *Journal of Family Nursing,* February, 2001, special issue; Koocher & Keith-Spiegel, 1990), specifically, populations of victimized children (for example, *Journal of Interpersonal Violence,* July 2000, special issue on this topic).

Concerns regarding capacity for informed consent center largely around (a) the ability of persons in these populations to adequately comprehend the information provided and to integrate it to make reasonable decisions and (b) their ability to exercise voluntary choice. In turn, to the extent that such capacities are limited, ethical concerns center around the potential for exploitation of these populations and development of guidelines that would minimize this potential (see Wendler, 2000).

Decisions to involve vulnerable populations are to be guided by the *necessity requirement,* which suggests that those unable to consent should be enrolled *only* where their participation is scientifically necessary, *unless* exclusion would deprive them of the opportunity to personally benefit from participation (such as potential treatment benefits). Some argue that this principle should limit use of vulnerable populations to research addressing issues specific to the population (termed the *subject's condition requirement*). In some more ethically problematic cases, it is used to refer to necessities to include large numbers that cannot be achieved with normal populations only. Thus, overall, the necessity requirement is not considered sufficient protection, because a number of other issues regarding fairness and exploitation remain possible (for detailed discussion of other issues, see Buchanan & Brock, 1990; Wendler, 2000).

Cease and Desist: What Level of Impairment Should Preclude Participation?

Disagreement exists regarding whether impairment should categorically preclude research participation. The American College of Physicians, for example, supports the view that impaired persons should be precluded from any and all research in which their participation is unnecessary—even when it may offer potential benefit to participants. Others counter that impaired individuals should not suffer discrimination that would deprive them of potentially beneficial (and even lifesaving) procedures that would be otherwise unavailable, as in clinical trials (for detailed discussion of these and related issues, see Wendler, 2000).

Ethical Issues Regarding Consent Through Proxy

Those who are unable to consent for themselves must have a *proxy* consent to research or treatment. Proxies are to make decisions based either on individuals' assumed *preferences,* on what individuals *would decide* in the situation if they were competent, or if such information is unclear or unknowable, on what would be *in the individuals' best interest* (e.g., Buchanan & Brock, 1990). However, although required by regulations and professional standards, consent by proxy raises serious practical and ethical issues of its own (see reviews in Buchanan & Brock, 1990; Wendler, 2000).

Perhaps the most serious issues involve the ability of proxy decision makers to accurately perceive or infer either the wishes of the impaired persons (i.e., what they would decide if able) or what might be in their best interest. For example, children may tend to react in a fundamentally different manner or magnitude than adults to specific treatments, research, or debriefing procedures—and in ways their adult proxies are unable to anticipate (see detailed discussions of these issues with children in Batten, 1996; Hermann & Yoder, 1998; Melton, Koocher, & Saks, 1983). Similar difficulties arise with regard to a competent adult's understanding of the likely preferences and reactions of moderately to profoundly impaired adults (see review in Dresser, 2001). Furthermore, written or verbal advance statements from persons who later decline physically and cognitively cannot be assumed to remain constant in the context of profound changes in mental and physical status (e.g., Dresser, 1995; High, 1992; Wendler, 2000). Finally, research has shown that the judgments of proxies correspond poorly to those of their charges (e.g., Seckler, Meier, Mulvihill, & Cammer, 1991; Suhl, Simons, Reedy, & Garrick, 1994; Sulmasy, Terry, & Weisman, 1998). Thus, the quality of proxy decisions is called into question.

Moreover, although deemed incompetent, some individuals may function at the higher end of this continuum, where they still have preferences and the desire to make their own choices. Thus, although proxy decision makers may be necessary to fully protect them, the proxy's decisions may conflict with the person's preferences and thereby pose a threat to autonomy. With regard to research participation, the proxy may override the desire of his or her charge to participate. However, under circumstances in which a potential or actual subject objects to participation or continued participation, the proxy's authority is superceded by the wishes of his or her charge (National Bioethics Advisory Commission, 1998). Generally, risk is to take precedence over benefit such that proxies should not enroll individuals in even minimal risk protocols in the absence of some evidence that the person wants to enroll.

Similar issues arise in the context of treatment decisions. That is, the proxy may or may not understand or choose what the impaired person would want (for example, aversive treatments, Murphy, 1993) and/or may fail to choose what is in the person's best interest. In some cases, choices may reflect self-interest rather than the best interest of the charge. For example, pharmacological treatments of behavioral problems for mentally retarded people may be convenient for the caretaker, but not in the best interest of the retarded person (e.g., Poling, 1994).

DECEPTION

"Illusions of (Informed) Choice" as the "Ultimate Deception"

The APA ethics code requires that consent be freely given such that the person has an understanding of relevant information under conditions that do not coerce, unduly influence, or otherwise engineer the outcome. These requirements of informed consent provide a special challenge to virtually all research on university students, as well as most others, and to clients undergoing therapeutic procedures. We argue that pervasive *illusions of (informed) choice* permeate both research and therapeutic situations, creating what might be called "the Ultimate Deception" for participants in psychological, as well as medical, procedures of all kinds. Immediately below, we discuss barriers to true choice. In later sections, we discuss difficulties in providing complete and fully understandable information that commonly render truly informed consent an illusion.

Illusions of Choice in the Research Process

The *illusion of choice* permeates the research process even though powerful situational forces do in fact "engineer the outcome." For university students, for example, it begins with the requirement of participation.

Even though alternatives (such as brief papers) are offered, almost no students take the alternatives. If the alternatives were equally attractive, one would expect a 50-50 split in student choices, whereas instead the overwhelming majority choose research—indicating that the choice to participate is, in fact, engineered by the structure of incentives and alternatives.

The illusion continues with sign-up procedures, in which participants may be constrained to particular experiments by their schedules. Then, once participants arrive for the experiment, although the informed consent forms and instructions of the experimenter emphasize that they may decline to participate or may withdraw at any point without penalty, again the situational forces are sufficiently powerful to prevent virtually all from withdrawing, even from clearly stressful research situations. In fact, one study found that less than 20% of participants viewed the informed consent process as a decision point (Brody, Gluck, & Aragon, 1997).

Research procedures are often constructed specifically to promote the illusion of choice. Dissonance researchers, for example, commonly "ask" participants to engage in counterattitudinal behaviors of various sorts, while simultaneously assuring them that although the experimenter would appreciate it if the participant would perform a particular behavior, the choice is completely the participant's own (e.g., Brehm & Cohen, 1962; Festinger & Carlsmith, 1959). Virtually all participants comply with such requests even though they are clearly inconsistent with the choice the participants would make in the absence of the request.

Finally, as discussed in the earlier section on placebo designs and in subsequent sections on understanding of relevant facts, participants often believe that they have been honestly, correctly, and successfully informed of relevant facts when they actually have not—either due to active deception by

commission or omission, or by unintentional errors in fact or communication.

Illusions of Choice for Treatment

Similar coercive influences, typically unrecognized as such, permeate the therapeutic process. Although clients typically voluntarily visit the therapist, once in therapy, treatment choices tend to be more constrained by the influence of the relatively more expert and more situationally powerful therapist. These occur both through feelings that discourage disagreement or noncompliance with therapist suggestions and through the informational influence resulting from perceptions of the therapist's expertise. Thus, the patient may technically and legally have choices while lacking the psychological forces necessary to exert them. For example, failure to comply with treatment is often interpreted as *resistance* rather than as a possible objection to an element of treatment.

Illusions of Successful Communication: Self-Deception Among Professionals

Before leaving the discussion of illusions, it is important to note that we, as professionals, tend to deceive ourselves regarding the effectiveness of our own communications, as patients and participants often fail to understand or appropriately use the information they are given (see discussion below on "Understanding").

Deception by Commission

Researchers often intentionally deceive participants with regard to the overall purpose of research, the purpose of specific procedures, the true roles of other participants (such as experimental confederates), and even whether the experiment is completed (for example, the experimenter actually collects the dependent measure as the subject leaves the building). Ethical criticisms of such deceptive procedures include the observation that true informed consent is not possible when the person is actually intentionally misinformed (for more detailed discussion of these issues, see Kemmelmeier et al., Chapter 14, this volume).

Deception by Omission

Clearly, the most common form of deception, both in therapy and research, is deception through failure to disclose pertinent information. Legally, therapists are required to disclose information relevant to the decision of a *reasonable person* to undergo the procedure *(Canterbury v. Spence,* 1972). Failure to meet such a standard can result in a finding of malpractice in civil court. This standard is similar to those embodied in federal and state regulations and professional codes of ethics. However, arguably, it is commonly violated.

Clearly, researchers commonly fail to disclose all information regarding the purpose of the experiment and of various procedures and measurements—resulting in an incomplete or misleading understanding of the experimental situation (see a more complete discussion of deception by omission in research by Kemmelmeier et al., Chapter 14, this volume). Similar, but perhaps more consequential, failures occur in the context of treatment settings and clinical research, a topic we turn to in the next section.

HOW INFORMED IS CONSENT? PRACTICAL PROBLEMS WITH RISK-BENEFIT COMMUNICATION

APA and federal requirements specify that the person must be informed of features of the research that might affect his or her agreement to participate. Being informed, in turn, requires both that relevant and accurate information is offered and that it is understood. Although in practice, the researcher and regulatory IRBs tend to judge procedures based on a *reasonable-person* standard with regard to what might be understood and what might affect willingness to participate, the issues surrounding these questions are actually more complex. In fact, we argue, researchers often know neither what risks and benefits are *facts* nor which of them are adequately understood by participants or might be considered important by participants if they did understand.

What Are the Facts?

What Information Is Available?

Ideally, one would want to communicate three facets of risk and benefit to potential participants: (a) the *nature* of potential outcomes, (b) the *likelihood* of these outcomes, and (c) their *extremity,* or magnitude. In addition, one is sometimes obligated to communicate the *relative* risk-benefit (RB) profile of two or more procedures. This occurs both in clinical trials, in which the person will be randomly assigned to one of several treatment alternatives, and in clinical practice, in which a person may want to choose between treatment alternatives. Unfortunately, these requirements pose the first barrier to what might be called *evidence-based informed consent* (EBIC).

More often than not, empirical data pertinent to most potentially relevant risks and benefits are not available. The researchers must first have the foresight to imagine what all risks and benefits might be, and second, must have evidence concerning their likelihood and severity. Unfortunately, little research has been conducted to assess the frequency and magnitude of negative reactions to research procedures, with even less addressing objective or subjective benefits of participation (for a discussion of some research addressing consequences of deception, see Kemmelmeier et al., Chapter 14, this volume). Likewise, the likelihood and magnitude of risks and benefits of therapies or their associated specific procedures are rarely known or systematically recorded or assessed. This deficit is arguably smaller in clinical trials, in which therapeutic outcomes and side effects are the central research issues or data from previous trials are available.

As research or clinical paradigms become more established, RB data can become more available. For example, research on false memories has progressed to the point that for some procedures—such as hypnosis or memory implantation, for example—the likelihood of false memories that are resistant to debriefing can be identified (e.g., Ceci, Bruck, & Loftus, 1998). Typically, however, this knowledge is limited to outcomes the experimenters assess in the course of testing their hypotheses. Rarely do researchers include complex post hoc assessments of participant reactions to the procedures, nor do they report idiosyncratic reactions as a matter of course. Commonly, then, the researcher or clinician does not have access to comprehensive, empirically established risks and benefits of the procedures he or she intends to use—and therefore must rely at least in part on intuition and subjective judgment to select information to convey to participants. In federally regulated clinical trials, *data safety monitoring boards* are now required, which are likely to begin to provide these data. How they are used in the informed consent process remains to be seen.

Quantifying Risks and Benefits

A reasoned decision to undergo a therapeutic or research procedure requires not only knowledge of possible outcomes but also some understanding of their likelihood and magnitude. Imagine being asked to consent to surgery, for which a possible outcome is death. In fact, all surgeries carry greater than zero risk of death (in part due to anesthesia alone), but because the actual base rates of death are typically very low, thousands undergo elective surgical procedures every day. Without explicit assurance of very low base rates, however, surgery with the risk of death, especially one that is elective, would be a very poor decision indeed.

Although such quantitative information is more frequently available in medical research, and to some degree in pharmacological clinical research, it is almost never available for most psychological research. The typical informed consent form may acknowledge the possibility of emotional discomfort, stress, or embarrassment but without indication of the likelihood or frequency of responses of varying severity. Similarly, consent for therapeutic procedures may acknowledge the possibility of such negative outcomes as no improvement and various side effects, but rarely do researchers know, much less communicate, the likelihood and magnitude of the various outcomes. Often, this may be because the line of research or therapeutic technique is new and the outcome profile is not yet known. However, more often, the researcher will not possess this information, because researchers do not systematically measure or code consequences that are not associated with the purpose of their investigation. Unlike drug companies, who request and collect reports of unexpected reactions, we have no central organization designed to track reactions to therapeutic or experimental protocols. Finally, RB profiles for specific therapies may be unknown because well-designed controlled outcome research has not been conducted.

The Importance of Tailored RB Profiles

Last, informed decision making is maximized by knowledge of base rates and severity of outcomes for specific subpopulations to which the individual client or participant may belong. Overall base rates and indices of severity may be completely misleading for particular subpopulations. Unfortunately, tailored RB profiles are rarely available. In fact, lack of patient-specific RB evidence, including evidence related to factors valued by patients, is cited by physicians as one of the most important barriers to evidence-based patient communication (EBPC) (Ford, Schofield, & Hope, 2002).

A Priori Disagreement Among Researchers Regarding Actual Risks and Benefits

Researchers and clinicians commonly disagree a priori about such fundamentals as the likelihood and extremity of risks and benefits projected to be associated with particular procedures, as well as the very basic decision of whether a particular outcome should be classified as harmful or beneficial. Kemmelmeier et al. (Chapter 14, this volume), for example, have highlighted the extreme disagreement among researchers regarding both benefits and risks inherent in deceptive research procedures. A currently hotly contested issue in clinical psychology concerns ethical issues surrounding the use of placebo designs, including both issues of benefits (i.e., whether the use of placebos provides scientific validity beyond that of non-placebo designs) and of costs (i.e., of unnecessary risks or of no benefit). (For special issues debating these concerns, see *Archives of General Psychiatry*, 2000; *Schizophrenia Research*, 1999, 189-236; Amdur, Biddle, 2001; Charney et al., 2002).

Unlike risks in medical research, which are often established and quantified, those in psychological research are often both speculative and unquantified. Thus, both researchers and the IRBs that grant permission for the research must rely on subjective RB analysis.

Even when data regarding consequences of specific procedures are available, researchers still may disagree over their applicability in a specific research context. There are now substantial data, for example, linking various therapeutic procedures such as hypnosis, guided imagery, dream interpretation, and others to the creation or distortion of memories (for reviews, see Davis & Follette, 2001; Davis, Loftus, & Follette, 2001). Notwithstanding these data, some refuse to accept the implications of the laboratory data for actual clinical practice, even asserting categorically that "memory is not externally malleable" (e.g., Blume, 2000). Thus, individual researchers' interpretations of data regarding risks and benefits will guide their own decisions regarding what *facts* to include in their informed consent procedures.

What Facts Are Relevant?

Given that presumed outcomes may vary from those strictly based on intuition or isolated anecdotal reports to those firmly established and quantified through controlled research, an issue arises concerning what criteria should dictate the choice of whether to include a particular outcome among those disclosed to clients or research participants. This issue must be evaluated both with respect to what seems scientifically warranted and what will be subjectively relevant to participants or clients.

Scientific Criteria for Inclusion

Davis et al. (2001) discussed these issues with regard to the tendency of various therapeutic components of *recovered-memory therapy,* such as hypnosis, age regression, dream interpretation, and so on, to lead to development of false "recovered" memories of abuse. There, disagreement abounds with respect to the very existence of pertinent phenomena, their overall base rates, base rates specific to subpopulations of already selected clinical samples, base rates for varying degrees of severity in specific outcomes, and so on. Therapists have recently become subject to lawsuits alleging failure to obtain informed consent for procedures that can lead to false memories of abuse. Thereby, a debate was triggered in the clinical community regarding whether sufficient evidence exists to justify both the assumption that certain therapeutic procedures *can* induce false memories and a duty on the part of therapists to warn clients of these outcomes in informed consent procedures (e.g., Cannell, Hudson, & Pope, 2001; Davis et al., 2001). Central to this debate was the issue of the status of evidence supporting the need for such warning. What, then, should be the evidentiary criteria for inclusion?

Is Imagination Sufficient?

Often, researchers or clinicians attempting to construct an RB assessment for informed consent must guess how participants might possibly react to their procedures. Lacking data from comparable procedures or beginning a novel procedure or protocol, they must rely strictly on what they can imagine to be possible reactions. One might ask, however, whether one should warn participants of effects heretofore only imagined or whether it is less misleading to simply state that probable reactions are as yet undetermined.

Is Experimental or Clinical/ Anecdotal Experience Sufficient?

The sufficiency of anecdotal clinical experience has been highlighted in the recovered-memory debate. Recovered-memory practitioners tend to cite anecdotal clinical instances of recovered memories of abuse, whereas critics tend to cite anecdotal clinical instances of false-memory syndrome regarding abuse, in support of their perceptions of benefits versus risks of recovered-memory therapy and its constituent techniques. In turn, each camp tends to disbelieve the very existence of the phenomenon cited by the other and/or its explanatory status for the anecdote in question. Critics of recovered-memory therapy cite anecdotal evidence to justify the necessity of informed consent for the therapy and associated procedures (e.g., Cannell et al., 2001), whereas practitioners reject the evidence to support them (e.g., Blume, 2000).

What, then, should be the status of such anecdotes? Without experimental controls, how can the causal connection between specific procedures and the outcome be established? Can either a true or false recovered memory be firmly attributed to therapy in general or to specific therapeutic techniques? If not, do such anecdotes demand inclusion of the outcome in informed consent procedures? If anecdotal accounts can justify inclusion of an outcome, *how many* anecdotal observations of a phenomenon are necessary to justify inclusion?

Most would agree that a single instance of an outcome would not justify its inclusion in informed consent procedures and particularly that it would not justify a professional standard requiring informed consent. However, no guidelines exist to suggest the point of accumulation at which anecdotal accounts provide a sufficiently established outcome of the procedure to justify inclusion, or mandated inclusion, in informed consent procedures. Nor do any guidelines exist to aid in assessment of the degree to which a particular anecdote (relatively) clearly ties the outcome to the procedure. In other words, all anecdotes are not equally informative.

These issues are, of course, somewhat less difficult with respect to anecdotal reports of reactions to experimental procedures, in which participants react to a more discrete event and sometimes report on immediate reactions during postexperimental debriefing. Reactions (or alleged reactions) to clinical interventions often occur in a more continuous format, or between sessions, and can be more difficult to clearly tie to the clinical procedures.

If Experimental Data Are Required, at What Point Is the Effect Sufficiently Well Established?

Often, disagreement occurs regarding whether or not phenomena may be regarded as sufficiently well established to justify either informed consent requirements or expert testimony in legal settings (as in the previously referenced recovered-memory literature). Although there appear to be no specific empirical guidelines for such decisions, social psychologist Saul Kassin and colleagues took the approach of surveying "experts" in the field of witness memory (i.e., those who had published in that area) to establish the degree of agreement between experts regarding the reliability of various findings that are commonly the subjects of expert testimony (Kassin, Ellsworth, & Smith, 1989).

Are Experimental Analogues Sufficient, or Is Direct Comparability Required?

Again, the recovered-memory controversy provides an interesting illustration of the issue of how freely one might justifiably extrapolate from experimental analogue data to a particular clinical or experimental protocol. Memory researchers have provided a host of demonstrations of the potential for common interviewing and therapeutic techniques to implant false memories (e.g.,

reviews by Davis et al., 2001; Davis & Follette, 2001), which they regard as sufficient evidence to warrant professional standards requiring informed consent warnings for their therapeutic use (e.g., Cannell et al., 2001; Davis et al., 2001). In contrast, advocates of such techniques regard demonstrations of the malleability of autobiographical memory for the relatively benign events examined in the laboratory as uninformative with regard to the more traumatic, sometimes long-term, and impactful events surrounding abuse and other traumata (e.g., Blume, 2000).

What Degree of Quantification of Risks and Benefits Should Be Available?

Again, the recovered-memory debate illustrates the problem of quantification. No reliable base rates have been established either for the possibility that repressed memories may exist to be exhumed or for the rate at which false memories of abuse tend to result from recovered-memory therapy in its entirety or through its constituent parts. Is it scientifically justifiable, then, to include either expected benefits of the therapy or risks of developing false memories in informed consent procedures?

What Degree of Agreement Within the Scientific Community Is Necessary to Justify Professional Standards of Informed Consent for Specific Outcomes?

Professionals sometimes widely agree on risks or benefits associated with particular research or clinical procedures. However, there is often controversy. The previously discussed controversy over the potential for therapeutic procedures to create false memories provides many such examples, as does the debate regarding use of deceptive research procedures (see Kemmelmeier et al., Chapter 14, this volume). What degree of agreement should be required to justify requirements of inclusion in informed consent procedures? Is agreement even necessary, or instead, should the presence of strong debate justify the requirement of inclusion of a statement that although the specific risk or benefit is debated within the scientific/clinical community, it may result from the procedure in question? Should we adopt a standard for inclusion similar to the Frye standard for admission of expert testimony *(Frye v. United States,* 1923) requiring that the outcome in question be "sufficiently established to have gained general acceptance in the particular field in which it belongs?" No guidelines currently address this question. Rather, both legal (e.g., *Canterbury v. Spence,* 1972) and professional guidelines focus on what might subjectively appear to reasonably affect the decision of the person to undergo a procedure (although it should be noted that where professional standards conflict with the legal reasonable-person standard, the courts recognize the legal standard).

Summary

In summary, the reasonable-person standard for inclusion of outcomes in informed consent procedures specifies only that an outcome must be included if it would affect the decision of a reasonable person to participate. This standard leaves unaddressed the questions surrounding the level of evidence for a particular outcome that would reasonably be required to affect the judgment of a reasonable person. Such questions are vital, because the question of what should affect the decision of a reasonable person is intimately tied to the quality of the information.

PROFESSIONAL DECISIONS REGARDING WHAT TO TELL PARTICIPANTS/CLIENTS

Decisions regarding what to tell clients or research participants are subject to the judgments of clinicians in therapeutic relationships and of researchers and their IRBs. It is to be expected that such decisions will fail to fully represent available knowledge and will instead be limited by several informational and motivational concerns of the decision makers.

Experimenter/Clinician Knowledge and Understanding of Available Findings

To the extent that empirical knowledge of risks and benefits does exist, the second limiting factor for EBIC is the knowledge of researchers or clinicians (Ford et al., 2002). Although we might hope that researchers are aware of the latest knowledge in their fields, it is less likely that practicing clinicians can or do keep up-to-date with the latest evidence. Furthermore, some clinicians are not adept at understanding or interpreting research findings, should they encounter them. Those lacking in-depth research training may be unable to interpret complex designs and statistical analyses or to critically evaluate and integrate the findings of an entire literature. Clients of such practitioners, then, are likely subject to illusions of "informed" consent, in that the professionals they trust may *appear* to provide reliable information even as they mislead their clients completely.

Motivated Resistance to Fully Informed Consent

Ford and her colleagues (2002) pointed out that at least within the medical community, there is motivated resistance to the idea of practicing EBPC. That is, "grass roots" practitioners fear the costs in time and equipment to keep themselves current and to provide rapid access to on-line information when required for specific patient decisions. The authors further pointed out that resistance is created by worries over increased time spent on discussion of alternatives, as well as the fear that patients fully informed of their choices will select one different than those therapists or physicians might prefer, thus limiting control over the therapeutic process.

For example, therapists may resist including information in informed consent procedures due to fear that the patient may weight specific risks or benefits inappropriately. In some cases, a very low base-rate risk may be excluded, due to the therapist's fear that the client may decline inappropriately on the basis of an objectively remote risk. Information, especially poor prognoses, may also be withheld to protect the patient from adverse reactions such as depression, withdrawal from beneficial treatments, and so on. More ethically questionable would be cases in which the therapist's own self-interest may motivate omission of important information—for example, when information about financial costs or short-term alternatives is excluded for fear the patient may decline a lengthy therapy or when the therapist does not disclose the experimental nature of suggested therapies he or she prefers.

Thus, for various reasons, professionals engage in *manipulative* (e.g., Switankowsky, 1998) rather than fully informative EBIC, through mechanisms such as exaggerating outcomes to lead the person to a particular choice, overt persuasion, prioritizing treatment information to create a particular decision, and authoritative or coercive demeanor. Generally, behaviors may be regarded as coercive that lead individuals to feel that if they decline the suggested treatment or research procedures, they will either (a) incur the ill will of investigators/therapists or (b) jeopardize their chances of recovery (Shimm & Spece, 1992), which can be reflected in below-average rates of refusal. In this regard, some have questioned whether efforts to increase treatment compliance might compromise informed consent (Perkins & Repper, 1999).

Biases of a "Point of View"

Within the context of therapy, discussions or formal consent processes designed to inform the client of the RB profile of a particular procedure as compared with others will almost certainly be biased by the theoretical orientation or therapeutic preference of the therapist. In fact, comparative discussions of choices may be omitted completely due to the theoretical or practical preferences of the therapist. Unfortunately, even when therapists are willing to provide such comparisons, established RB analyses (similar to those available for many medical treatments) are not available to provide uniform information to all patients.

Particularly when therapists are committed to a specific school of therapy or specific techniques, they may be unaware of, unwilling to believe, or reluctant to disclose risks such as those of no benefit, foregone benefit by failure to use other alternatives, harm through the process advocated, and other iatrogenic disorders (for discussion of these issues with regard to "recovered-memory therapy and techniques," see Davis et al., 2001).

Concerns Over Client/ Participant Comprehension

As discussed more fully below, professionals must be concerned with the issue of comprehension of information provided in the course of informed consent procedures. With this concern in mind, they must take care to convey information in the most sensitive and comprehensible format. Often, however, concerns regarding comprehension can lead the professional to omit information that clients/participants could in fact understand and find important. Health professionals express concern, for example, that some might be "bewildered" or "overloaded" by a full discussion of RB evidence (e.g., Ford et al., 2002).

Timing of Informed Consent Procedures

Most nontherapeutic psychological research unfolds in a single session. Thus, informed consent procedures can reasonably take place once, before the procedures begin. Therapy, on the other hand, unfolds over a longer period of time, sometimes involving years. As well, it may involve multiple components, each with its own risks and benefits. Thus, the question arises of whether a single informed consent discussion or document offered before therapy begins is sufficient (e.g., Davis et al., 2001). In fact, at least within research contexts, there are increasing efforts to encourage or mandate that experimenters review consent and complications with subjects involved in long-term studies.

Most therapeutic relationships, including medical and psychological, should be viewed as an ongoing process of decision making that should ideally be evidence based. As new problems or issues arise, new solutions are required. Arguably, a client rarely remembers information given as part of a long conversation or document given some time ago, before therapy began, in the current context of a decision to agree to a specific procedure, for example, hypnosis. Davis et al. (2001) argued that informed consent to specific procedures should be offered *at the time* the procedure is to begin and should even be repeated as the client engages in multiple instances of the same procedure. The risks of some procedures would be expected to escalate with successive sessions, as, for example, the risk of false memories with repeated imagination-based techniques (e.g., see review in Davis & Follette, 2001), and thus reminders of the escalating risk, in particular, would be desirable as sessions continue, as would renewal of client consent. Because clients are often unable to accurately anticipate their own reactions a priori (see below), affirmations of continuing consent, once a procedure is experienced, can be very important.

Patient/Participant Motivation and Understanding

Perhaps the most serious barrier to EBIC is patient/participant motivation. As noted by Ford et al. (2002), people vary widely in their desire for information and motivation to actively participate in treatment decisions. Many view such decisions as the role of the medical or psychological professional and in fact find treatment decisions and related information aversive. In such cases, the person may fail to attend to information offered in informed consent procedures and simply comply with the advice of the professional. In turn, if the person is motivated and tries to process the information, problems with either the clarity of the communication or the recipient's ability to understand may nevertheless compromise accuracy.

RISK PERCEPTION AND COMMUNICATION

Research in the decision sciences has generally shown that laypeople's and experts' assessment of risk tend to vary greatly (e.g., Fisher, 1991; Margolis, 1996). Risk communication may fail either at the level of the communicator or the recipient. Incomplete or inaccurate information may be provided by the communicator and/or may be attended to, understood, interpreted, or integrated poorly to arrive at a decision, thus thwarting the central goal of informed consent procedures. In this sense, effective communication of information is not only a practical but also an ethical problem (Mann, 1994). In the following sections, we explore the problems and challenges that may occur in the effective communication of risk.

Communicating the Nature and Potential Severity of Possible Outcomes

As noted earlier, professionals must communicate the nature of potential outcomes of therapeutic or research procedures, both good and bad, as well as their potential severity. For obvious reasons, any such communications must reflect consideration of various characteristics of the participants, such as prior knowledge, educational level, and prior beliefs and assumptions about the contemplated procedures, as well as what information participants are likely to value. To deal with this challenge, Fischhoff and his collaborators have proposed a mental model approach according to which communications and warning about risk need to be carefully tailored to the target recipients. The goal is to enable recipients to generate a representation of the procedure that includes both declarative and functional knowledge; that is, participants should understand not only what happens (e.g., the outcome) but also why and how it happens (e.g., Fischhoff, Riley, Kovacs, & Small, 1998).

Even though participants might understand the professional's explanation of nature and magnitude of possible outcomes, it is nonetheless important to keep in mind that an objective risk or benefit has to be translated into projected personal impact (Yates & Stone, 1992). Research has demonstrated that people tend to be rather imperfect in predicting how they will react, particularly to unfamiliar situations (Kahneman & Snell, 1990), because such subjective predictions are often based on naive theories rather than experience (Loewenstein & Schkade, 1999). This is particularly problematic in situations in which participants either underestimate the magnitude of adverse reactions or underestimate benefit and thus decline helpful treatments.

Communicating Likelihood

As noted earlier, a formidable challenge arises from the fact that even researchers are commonly unaware of the actual likelihood of both beneficial and harmful outcomes—and even more commonly unaware of *relative* RB profiles of alternative procedures. Unfortunately, however, even when such information is available, statistical information is difficult to understand and typically not interpreted or used appropriately.

Processing Statistical Information

There is ample evidence to show that most people cannot make sense of statistical information, either because they fail to comprehend its meaning or fail to apply it correctly (cf. Best, 2001; Fong, Krantz, & Nisbett, 1986). Furthermore, even when they understand the essence of the information, they often neglect to include base rates in their decision making (Bar-Hillel, 1980). In many cases, this failure of comprehension appears to be a function of the way in which likelihood information is presented. Whereas percentage or probabilities seem to be least effective (e.g., "The probability of an adverse event is 25%"), participants are more apt to correctly interpret odds ratios (e.g., "1 in 4 experiences an adverse event") (e.g.,

Bieliauskas, Fastenau, Lacy, & Roper, 1997). More generally, Gigerenzer and Hoffrage (1995) demonstrated that in reasoning tasks, people are much more successful when information is presented as frequencies rather than probabilities (see also Fiedler, 1988). In general, risk magnitude is more easily understood when not communicated in the abstract, but in units of everyday experience (e.g., Weinstein, Kolb, & Goldstein, 1996).

Verbal Quantifiers

Because laypeople have a hard time assigning meaning to statistics, the use of verbal descriptors of likelihood, such as *frequently* or *rarely*, often appears preferable. Even though more user-friendly, the meaning of verbal quantifiers is highly variable such that the same individual will interpret a quantifier differently across different contexts (Beyth-Marom, 1982; Moxey & Sanford, 1993; Wänke, 2002; Weber & Hilton, 1990). Moreover, verbal quantifiers often suggest how a particular statement of uncertainty is to be interpreted. This can be illustrated in the use of the quantifiers *few* and *a few*, which are often used to describe identical numerical quantities (Moxey & Sanford, 1993). A statement such as *"Few* participants will experience *X"* emphasizes that it is "only a few" participants who experience *X*, thus emphasizing the smallness of the number. In contrast, saying *"A few* participants will experience *X"* draws attention to the fact that there are indeed some participants for whom *X* will occur, thus emphasizing largeness.

Interactional Dynamics of Risk Communication

As with all communications, RB communication is subject to a difference between what the speaker *intended* to communicate and how the recipient *interprets* what is said (e.g., Sperber & Wilson, 1995). In other words, even

though terms such as *mild discomfort* are apparently based in a shared everyday experience of people of the same culture and elicit similar understanding, their correct interpretation in the communication between researcher and prospective participant cannot be assumed.

Conversational Dynamics

The first challenge may stem from the fact that interlocutors assume their counterparts to be competent and cooperative communicators—hence the expectations that communication partners will be *relevant* and *informative* (e.g., Grice, 1975; Sperber & Wilson, 1995). Thus, a recipient will tend to assume that the speaker considers the information he or she conveys to be important; at least important enough for him or her to communicate it in the first place. This may have some unintended consequences with regard to the communication of events that are usually considered trivial or not important enough to mention. When a researcher in their informed consent procedure mentions such an event (e.g., a momentary dip in self-esteem, an event that supposedly occurs every day), the recipient will tend to assume it must be noteworthy for the experimenter to have mentioned it at all. Moreover, because the recipient makes the reasonable assumption that the cooperative communicator would never convey trivial information, he or she may arrive at the conclusion that the "momentary dip in self-esteem" is not at all trivial in kind—with the result that he or she may overestimate the intensity of the discomfort relative to what the researcher has in mind (cf. Schwarz, 1998; Winkielman, Knäuper, & Schwarz, 1998).

Status and Benevolence

Another dynamic may occur with regard to the communication of severe events.

Because a psychologist may be perceived as a benevolent authority, participants may presume that he or she would not expose them to any risk that is severe or outrageous. This may be the case because people are motivated to see the world as a predictable place in which good people do good things (Lerner, 1980) or because people are motivated to believe that new information is consistent with their prior beliefs (Brehm & Cohen, 1962; Festinger & Carlsmith, 1959). Making such an assumption, however, may have a number of consequences. First, when researchers' warnings entail ill-defined descriptors of risk (e.g., *moderate levels of pain),* participants may actually underestimate the intensity of risk that the researcher seeks to communicate. Second, the same reason may lead participants to minimize information concerning the likelihood of occurrence. In other words, because of the researcher's status, participants may simply not believe his or her risk warnings. A similar dynamic has been hypothesized with regard to the benevolence of a study. In the pharmaceutical sciences, the goal of a clinical trial is often simply to examine the toxicity of a substance rather than its effectiveness in treating a disorder; yet participants in such trials routinely expect the substance to help them get better, being unable to imagine that a physician would give them a medication that was not supposed to help them (Shimm & Spece, 1992).

Illusions of Invulnerability

There is ample evidence that people are unrealistically optimistic about their own susceptibility to risk (Weinstein, 1980, 1989). It has been suggested that this reflects a motivated tendency to deny harm to the self (e.g., Kirscht, Haefner, Kegeles, & Rosenstock, 1966) or to enhance or preserve self-esteem (e.g., Wills, 1981). More recent work strongly

supports the hypothesis that the illusion of invulnerability is based on an egocentric perception of risk: To the extent that people do not have any direct experience with the risk factor, they find it hard to imagine that it can occur in their own lives (cf. Roe-Burning & Straker, 1997; Weinstein, 1989). The result is that people do not engage in self-protective behaviors, even when they should, because perceived risk to the self and engagement in protective behaviors are highly correlated (Weinstein, 1989). In other words, a deflated sense of vulnerability may cause people to fail to make choices that serve their best interest. Hence, researchers are called on to make sure that participants do not only know about risk in the abstract but also consider themselves vulnerable in a way that is consistent with reality.

Unfortunately, research demonstrates that overcoming unrealistic optimism is no trivial task (e.g., Weinstein & Klein, 1995). From an ethical point of view, enhancing a person's sense of vulnerability may pose a dilemma, contrasting the potential for increased anxiety or decreased confidence and self-esteem against the need to accurately convey risk.

Decision Framing

Even though a treatment decision may remain constant, the specific format in which pertinent information is presented can have a profound impact on the attractiveness of the available choices. Such *framing effects* have been documented in virtually all areas of psychology and the social sciences. For example, people are more likely to find risky choices acceptable when the particular format draws attention to benefits compared with focusing on potential harm (e.g., Fischhoff, Slovic, Lichtenstein, Read, & Combs, 1978; Kahneman & Tversky, 1984). From the perspective of a decision to participate in a study, this is problematic, because the presentation of the decision itself may "engineer" the outcome.

A viable strategy to overcome this problem is to use several representations of the same problem (cf. Arkes, 1991). A different strategy tries to enhance participants' sensitivity to the information presented. By providing multiple choices of a similar nature, participants are able to calibrate their judgment and hence are able to more effectively integrate information to reach better decisions (e.g., Lichtenstein & Fischhoff, 1980).

Emotion and Risk Processing

Emotion can hamper informed consent processes in several ways, beginning with aversion to any pertinent discussions. The communication of risk is often assumed to elicit a sense of threat and hence to be emotionally aversive and anxiety inducing. This may lead researchers or clinicians to try to "spare" their participants from potentially threatening details. However, thus far, research has not reliably shown increases in risk information to be linked to increase in threat (Garrud, Wood, & Stainsby, 2001). One study, for example, found that greater amounts of risk information produced anxiety only when knowledge was low. When knowledge was high, anxiety was reduced (Edwards, Lilford, Thornton, & Hewison, 1998).

Cultural Barriers to Risk Communication

Although there are many potential barriers to the comprehension of warnings and risk messages, the issue of cultural background deserves special attention. Individuals from different cultures vary with regard to their views of and expectations about the world (e.g., Shore, 1996;

Oyserman, Coon, & Kemmelmeier, 2002). This has implications for the informed consent process. Because individuals from so-called collectivist societies are more likely to emphasize and respect interpersonal difference in status and social roles, they may have a high threshold for rejecting the request of a researcher, typically an authority figure, to participate in a particular study or procedure. This may be the case either because they do not question the competence and benevolence of the researcher or because they consider the researcher's judgment of what is good for them to be superior. As a result, they may provide consent without having understood the risks (cf. Saldov, Kakai, McLaughlin, & Thomas, 1998).

The opposite might occur in other cases. Historically disenfranchised groups may be highly suspicious of the consent process, especially when the researcher or clinician is from a dominant group (Earl & Penney, 2001). Such individuals may perceive inflated levels of risk and either refuse participation or feel that they have to be "on guard" during the study and alter their behavior according to their suspicions (for the problem of refusals, see Beauvais, 1999).

The Final Decision

We presuppose that people usually care about safety, carefully weighing risks and benefits to protect their own well-being. However, it appears that when risk is low, participants may primarily focus on potential benefits and not consider risk as long as it remains below a certain threshold of intensity. Only when a particular event surpasses the threshold do participants base their decisions on a personal sense of vulnerability (e.g., Kruglanski & Klar, 1985). With regard to psychological studies or procedures that entail only low levels of risk, prospective participants may focus narrowly on benefits of class credit or their interest in the study, without due regard for risks. This focus on benefits might easily be missed on the part of researchers or clinicians, especially when participants expect benefits that researchers are not planning on providing. For example, in many instances, participants may expect to learn something about themselves by participating in psychological studies (e.g., Baumrind, 1985); yet this is not typically the goal of research. Thus, it is important that researchers not only inform about potential risks but also assess and if necessary, correct participants' expectations with regard to benefits.

GETTING THE MESSAGE ACROSS

Successful EBIC requires careful crafting of both written materials and active communication processes. Below, we summarize factors expected to affect risk communication (for guidelines to the design of warnings about risks, see Fischhoff, Bostrom, & Quadrel, 1993; Fischhoff et al., 1998; Morgan, Fischhoff, Bostrom, & Atman, 2002; Switankowsky, 1998).

Language

Participants are known to have trouble comprehending common words and phrases used in informed consent protocols (for examples from medical research, see Lawson & Adamson, 1995; Waggoner & Mayo, 1995). Even though scientific and technical vocabulary allows the greatest degree of accuracy in representing the research and possible risks, it is often inaccessible to prospective participants because scientific and colloquial meanings may differ (e.g. Jardine & Hrudey, 1997). Thus, researchers need to ensure that consent forms are readable and at the level of comprehension of the target population (e.g., Young, Hooker, & Freeberg, 1990).

Among other things, this implies that researchers choose their vocabulary in ways that simply convey the gist of the researcher's warning. To the extent that technical terms and explanations are necessary, researchers need to illustrate their meanings, potentially relying on metaphor, analogy, or visual and graphic illustrations.

Amount of Information

Researchers might be able to provide a rather extensive list of the specific nature, magnitude, and likelihood of various research or treatment outcomes. However, the sheer amount of information and level of detail are likely to overwhelm the average participant. Hence, researchers are often burdened by the difficulty of including necessary information while avoiding overburdening participants with detail (Edwards et al., 1998; Fischhoff et al., 1993).

Issues of Presentation

Regardless of vocabulary and amount of information, comprehension is primarily determined by the way the information is relayed. Complex sentence structures can obfuscate even the meaning of simple concepts, and too-dense presentations can obscure important details. Also, time pressure interferes with participants' comprehension of consent information (Edwards et al., 1998; Silva & Sorrell, 1988). Thus, researchers and clinicians need to allow adequate time and use strategies to encourage participants to actively process the information presented to them (Wogalter, Howe, Sifuentes, & Luginbuhl, 1999). Furthermore, the greatest readability might be achieved by using graphics and simple declarative statements as headings for each paragraph on the consent form (Peterson, Clancy, Champion, & McLarty, 1992).

Evaluating Risk Communication

Often, communicators' (i.e., experts') intuitions about recipients' risk perceptions cannot be trusted (Fischhoff et al., 1993). Nevertheless, it is central that their participants or clients reach a sufficient level of understanding of the procedure before they assent to participating. Hence, researchers need to follow up to ensure effectiveness. To the extent that verbal affirmations of understanding are not likely to be diagnostic, it may be appropriate to ask participants to summarize the information in their own words and attempt to correct remaining misconceptions.

CONCLUSIONS: WHAT DO INFORMED CONSENT PROCEDURES ACTUALLY ACCOMPLISH?

The evidence presented in this chapter has documented formidable challenges to meaningful informed consent procedures. Prominent among them is the issue of whether the decision to undergo a procedure is complete long before informed consent processes begin. Recall, for example, the finding that less than 20% of participants viewed the informed consent process as a decision point (Brody et al., 1997). Instead, the consent form may be viewed as the first aspect of the research or the procedure itself. This implies that participants may not be motivated to thoroughly process all the information provided during the consent procedure and think about all possible implications for the self. As a result, regardless of what information is presented about risk or benefits, participants may primarily rely on the expertise and authority of the researcher (cf. Petty, Cacioppo, & Goldman, 1981).

However, to the extent that clients or research participants attempt to process and integrate the information provided, the meaningfulness of the process may still be compromised by incomplete or inaccurate information, coercive or unclear communications from professionals, and recipient difficulties in processing and integrating information and actively asserting their preferred choices. Thus, a host of challenges remain for practitioners in our discipline who aspire to truly informed and completely voluntary consent.

To date, the processes of eliciting informed consent have been guided by good intentions and intuition. This chapter has reviewed the psychological science related to problems with the empirical database used to inform participants and has described some of the relevant experimental literature on how information is best presented to increase the likelihood of more genuine informed consent. It remains to be seen whether the field turns to a more empirically based informed consent process.

REFERENCES

Amdur, R. J., & Biddle, C. J. (2001). An algorithm for evaluating the ethics of a placebo-controlled trial. *International Journal of Cancer, 96,* 261-269.

American Psychological Association. (1953). *Ethical standards of psychologists.* Washington, DC: Author.

American Psychological Association. (2002). *Ethical principles of psychologists and code of conduct.* Retrieved December 9, 2002 from http://www.apaorg/ ethics/ code2002html

Archives of General Psychiatry. (2000). Vol. 57.

Arkes, H. R. (1991). Costs and benefits of judgment errors: Implications for debiasing. *Psychological Bulletin, 110,* 486-498.

Arscott, K., Dagnan, D., & Kroese, B. S. (1998). Consent to psychological research by people with an intellectual disability. *Journal of Applied Research in Intellectual Disabilities, 11,* 77-83.

Bar-Hillel, M. (1980). The base-rate fallacy in probability judgments. *Acta Psychologica, 44,* 211-233.

Batten, D. A. (1996). Informed consent by children and adolescents to psychiatric treatment. *Australian & New Zealand Journal of Psychiatry, 30,* 623-632.

Baumrind, D. (1985). Research using intentional deception: Ethical issues revisited. *American Psychologist, 40,* 165-174.

Beauvais, F. (1999). Obtaining consent and other ethical issues in the conduct of research in American Indian communities. *Drugs & Society, 14,* 167-184.

Best, J. (2001). *Damned lies and statistics: Untangling numbers from the media, politicians, and activists.* Berkeley: University of California Press.

Beutler, L. E. (1998). Identifying empirically supported treatments: What if we didn't? *Journal of Consulting and Clinical Psychology, 66,* 113-120.

Beyth-Marom, R. (1982). How probable is probable? *Journal of Forecasting, 1,* 257-269.

Bieliauskas, L. A., Fastenau, P. S., Lacy, M. A., & Roper, B. L. (1997). Use of the odds ration to translate neuropsychological test scores into real-world outcomes: From statistical significance to clinical significance. *Journal of Clinical & Experimental Neuropsychology, 19,* 889-896.

Blume, E. S. (2000). The afterward to secret survivors: Sympathy for the devil. *Treating Abuse Today, 9,* 8-33.

Bohart, A. C. (2000). Paradigm clash: Empirically supported treatments versus empirically supported psychotherapy practice. *Psychotherapy Research, 10,* 488-493.

Bohart, A. C., O'Hara, M., & Leitner, L. M. (1998). Empirically violated treatments: Disenfranchisement of humanistic and other psychotherapies. *Psychotherapy Research, 8,* 141-157.

Borkovec, T. D., & Castonguay, L. G. (1998). What is the scientific meaning of empirically supported therapy? *Journal of Consulting and Clinical Psychology, 66,* 136-142.

Brehm, J. W., & Cohen, A. R. (1962). *Explorations in cognitive dissonance.* New York: Wiley.

Brody, J. L., Gluck, J. P., & Aragon, A. S. (1997). Participants' understanding of the process of psychological research: Informed consent. *Ethics & Behavior, 7,* 85-298.

Buchanan, A. E., & Brock, D. W. (1990). *Deciding for others: The ethics of surrogate decision making.* New York: Cambridge University Press.

Cannell, J., Hudson, J. L., & Pope, H. G. (2001). Standards for informed consent in recovered memory therapy. *Journal of the American Academy of Psychiatry and the Law, 29,* 138-147.

Canterbury v. Spence, 464 F2d 772 (DC Cir 1972); cert. denied, 409 US 1064 (1972).

Caplan, A. L. (Ed.). (1992). *When medicine went mad: Bioethics and the holocaust.* Totowa, NJ: Humana.

Ceci, S. J., Bruck, M., & Loftus, E. F. (1998). On the ethics of memory implantation research. *Applied Cognitive Psychology, 12,* 230-240.

Chambless, D. L., Baker, M., Baucom, D. H., Beutler, L. E., Calhoun, K. S., Crits-Christoph, P., Daiuto, A., DeRubeis, R., Detweiler, J., Haaga, D. A. F., Johnson, S. B., McCurry, S., Mueser, K. T., Pope, K. S., Sanderson, W. C., Shoham, V., Stickle, T., Williams, D. A., & Woody, S. A. (1998). Update on empirically validated therapies, II. *The Clinical Psychologist, 51,* 3-16.

Chambless, D. L., & Hollon, S. D. (1998). Defining empirically supported therapies. *Journal of Consulting and Clinical Psychology, 66,* 7-18.

Chambless, D. L., & Ollendick, T. H. (2001). Empirically supported psychological interventions: Controversies and evidence. *Annual Review of Psychology, 52,* 685-716.

Chambless, D. L., Sanderson, W. C., Shoham, V., Bennett Johnson, S., Pope, K. S., Crits-Christoph, P., Baker, M., Johnson, B., Woody, S. R., Sue, S., Beutler, L., Williams, D. A., & McCurry, S. (1996). An update on empirically validated therapies. *The Clinical Psychologist, 49,* 5-18.

Charney, D. S. et al. (2002). National Depressive and Manic-Depressive Association consensus statement on the use of placebo in clinical trials of mood disorders. *Archives of General Psychiatry, 59,* 262-270.

Commission on CIA Activities within the United States. (1975). *Report to the president.* Washington, DC: Government Printing Office.

Crits-Christoph, P. (1997). Limitations of the dodo bird verdict and the role of clinical trials in psychotherapy research: Comment on Wampold et al. (1997). *Psychological Bulletin, 122,* 216-220.

Davis, A. M. (1998). Exception from informed consent for emergency research: Drawing on existing skills and experience. *IRB: A Review of Human Subjects Research, 20*(5), 1-8.

Davis, D., & Follette, W. C. (2001). Foibles of witness memory for traumatic/high profile events. *Journal of Air Law and Commerce, 66,* 1421-1547.

Davis, D., Loftus, E. F., & Follette, W. C. (2001). How, when, and whether to use informed consent for recovered memory therapy. *Journal of the American Academy of Psychiatry and the Law, 29,* 148-159.

De Leon, G., Melnic, G., Kressel, D., & Jainchill, N. (1994). Circumstances, motivations, readiness and suitability (the CRMS Scales): Predicting retention in therapeutic community treatment. *American Journal of Drug and Alcohol Abuse, 20,* 495-515.

Dresser, R. (1995). Dworkin on dementia: Elegant theory, questionable policy. *Hastings Center Report, 25,* 32-38.

Dresser, R. (2001). Advance directives in dementia research: Promoting autonomy and protecting subjects. *IRB: A Review of Human Subjects Research, 23*(1), 1-6.

Dymek, M. P., Atchison, P., Harrell, L., & Marson, D. (2001). Competency to consent to medical treatment in cognitively impaired patients with Parkinson's disease. *Neurology, 56,* 17-24.

Earl, C. E., & Penney, P. J. (2001). The significance of trust in the research consent process with African Americans. *Western Journal of Nursing Research, 23,* 753-762.

Edwards, S. J. L., Lilford, R. J., Thornton, J., & Hewison, J. (1998). Informed consent for clinical trials: In search of the "best" method. *Social Science and Medicine, 47,* 1825-1840.

Festinger, L., & Carlsmith, J. M. (1959). Cognitive consequences of forced compliance. *Journal of Abnormal and Social Psychology, 58,* 202-210.

Fiedler, K. (1988). The dependence of the conjunction fallacy on subtle linguistic factors. *Psychological Research, 50,* 123-129.

Fischhoff, B., Bostrom, A., & Quadrel, M. J. (1993). Risk perception and communication. *Annual Review of Public Health, 14,* 183-203.

Fischhoff, B., Riley, D., Kovacs, D. C., & Small, M. (1998). What information belongs in a warning? *Psychology & Marketing, 15,* 663-686.

Fischhoff, B., Slovic, P., Lichtenstein, S., Read, S., & Combs, B. (1978). How safe is safe enough?: A psychometric study of attitudes towards technological risks and benefits. *Policy Sciences, 8,* 127-152.

Fisher, A. (1991). Risk communication challenges. *Risk Analysis, 11,* 173-179.

Fitten, L. J. (1999). Frontal lobe dysfunction and patient decision making about treatment and participation in research. In B. L. Miller, & J. L. Cummings (Eds.), *The human frontal lobes: Functions and disorders. The science and practice of neuropsychology series* (pp. 277-287). New York: Guilford.

Fong, G. T., Krantz, D. H., & Nisbett, R. E. (1986). The effects of statistical training on thinking about everyday problems. *Cognitive Psychology, 18,* 253-292.

Ford, S., Schofield, T., & Hope, T. (2002). Barriers to evidence-based patient choice (EBPC) consultation. *Patient Education and Counseling, 47,* 179-185.

Frye v. United States, 293 F. 1013 (D.P.C. Cir. 1923).

Gardner, W., Hoge, S. K., Bennet, N., Roth, L. H., Lidz, C. W., Monahan, J., & Mulvey, E. P. (1993). Two scales for measuring patients' perception for coercion during mental hospital admission. *Behavioral Sciences and the Law, 11,* 307-321.

Garfield, S. L. (1998). Some comments on empirically supported treatments. *Journal of Consulting and Clinical Psychology, 66,* 121-125.

Garrud, P., Wood, M., & Stainsby, L. (2001). Impact of risk information in a patient education leaflet. *Patient Education and Counseling, 43,* 301-304.

Gigerenzer, G., & Hoffrage, U. (1995). How to improve Bayesian reasoning without instruction: Frequency format. *Psychological Review, 102,* 684-704.

Grice, P. (1975). Logic and conversation. In P. Cole & J. L. Morgan (Eds.), *Syntax and semantics: 3 Speech acts* (pp. 41-58). New York: Academic Press.

Grisso, T., & Appelbaum, P. S. (1998). *Assessing competence to consent to treatment: A guide for physicians and other health professionals.* New York: Oxford University Press.

Henry, W. P. (1998). Science, politics, and the politics of science: The use and misuse of empirically validated treatment research. *Psychotherapy Research, 8,* 126-140.

Hermann, D., & Yoder, C. (1998). Revisiting the ethics of memory implantation research with children. *Applied Cognitive Psychology, 12,* 245-249.

Hiday, B. A., Swarz, J. S., Swanson, J., & Wagner, H. R. (1997). Patient perception of coercion in mental hospital admission. *Journal of Law and Psychiatry, 20,* 227-241.

High, D. M. (1992). Research with Alzheimer's disease subjects: Informed consent and proxy decision making. *Journal of the American Geriatric Society, 40,* 950-957.

Høyer, G., Kjellin, L., Engberg, M., Kaltiala-Heino, R., Nilstun, T., Sigurjónsdóttir, M., & Syse, A. (2002). Paternalism and autonomy: A presentation of a Nordic study on the use of coercion in the mental health care system. *International Journal of Law and Psychiatry, 25,* 93-108.

Hurley, J. C., & Underwood, M. K. (2002). Children's understanding of their research rights before and after debriefing: Informed assent, confidentiality, and stopping participation. *Child Development, 73,* 132-143.

Jardine, C. G., & Hrudey, S. E. (1997). Mixed messages in risk communication. *Risk Analysis, 17,* 489-498.

Jones, J. (1993). *Bad blood: The Tuskegee syphilis experiment.* New York: Free Press.

Kahneman, D., & Snell, J. (1990). Predicting utility. In R. M. Hogarth (Ed.), *Insights in decision making: A tribute to Hillel J. Einhorn* (pp. 295-310). Chicago: University of Chicago Press.

Kahneman, D., & Tversky, A. (1984). Choices, values, and frames. *American Psychologist, 39,* 341-350.

Kampmeier, R. H. (1974). Final report on the "Tuskegee syphilis study." *Southern Medical Journal, 67,* 1349-1353.

Kassin, S. M., Ellsworth, P. C., & Smith, V. L. (1989). The "general acceptance" of psychological research on eyewitness testimony: A survey of the experts. *American Psychologist, 44,* 1089-1098.

Kirscht, J. P., Haefner, D. P., Kegeles, S. S., & Rosenstock, I. M. (1966). A national study of health beliefs. *Journal of Health and Human Behavior, 7,* 248-254.

Koocher, G., & Keith-Spiegel, P. (1990). *Children, ethics, and the law.* Lincoln: University of Nebraska Press.

Kraybill, E. N., & Bauer, B. S. (1999). Can community consultation substitute for informed consent in emergency medicine research? In N. M. P. King, G. E. Henderson, & J. Stein (Eds.), *Beyond regulations: Ethics in human subjects research* (pp. 191-198). Chapel Hill: University of North Carolina Press.

Kruglanski, A. W., & Klar, Y. (1985). Knowing what to do: On the epistemology of actions. In J. Kuhl & J. Beckmann (Eds.), *Action control: From cognition to behavior* (pp. 41-60). Berlin: Springer.

Lawson, S. L., & Adamson, H. M. (1995). Informed consent readability: Subject understanding of 15 common consent form phrases. *IRB: A Review of Human Subjects Research, 17*(5-6), 16-19.

Lerner, M. J. (1980). *The belief in a just world: A fundamental delusion.* New York: Plenum.

Lichtenstein, S., & Fischhoff, B. (1980). Training for calibration. *Organizational Behavior & Human Decision Processes, 26,* 149-171.

Lidz, C. W., Hoge, S. K., Gardner, W., Bennett, N. S., Monahan, J., Mulvey, E. P., & Roth, L. H. (1995). Perceived coercion in mental hospital admission: Pressures and process. *Archives of General Psychiatry, 52,* 1034-1039.

Loewenstein, G., & Schkade, D. (1999). Wouldn't it be nice? Predicting future feelings. In D. Kahneman, E. Diener, & N. Schwarz (Eds.), *Well-being: The foundations of hedonic psychology* (pp. 85-105). New York: Russell Sage.

Margolis, H. (1996). *Dealing with risk: Why the public and the experts disagree on environmental issues.* Chicago: University of Chicago Press.

Marlowe, D. B., Kirby, C. D., Boniesky, L. M., Glass, D. J., Dodds, L. D., Husband, S. D., Platt, J. J., & Festinger, D. S. (1996). Assessment of coercive and noncoercive pressures to enter drug abuse treatment. *Drug and Alcohol Dependence, 42,* 77-84.

Mann, T. (1994). Informed consent for psychological research: Do subjects comprehend consent forms and understand their legal rights? *Psychological Science, 5,* 140-143.

Marson, D. C. (2001). Loss of competency in Alzheimer's disease: Conceptual and psychometric approaches. *International Journal of Law & Psychiatry, 24,* 267-283.

Meier, P. (1989). The biggest public health experiment ever: The 1954 field trial of the Salk poliomyelitis vaccine. In J. M. Tanur, F. Mosteller, W. H. Kruskal,

E. L. Lehmann, R. F. Link, R. S. Pieters, & G. R. Rising (Eds.), *Statistics: A guide to the unknown* (3rd ed., pp. 3-14). Belmont, CA: Wadsworth.

Melton, G. B., Koocher, G. P., & Saks, M. J. (Eds.). (1983). *Children's competence to consent*. New York: Plenum.

Milgram, S. (1963). Behavioral study of obedience. *Journal of Abnormal and Social Psychology, 67,* 371-378.

Montgomery, C., Lydon, A., & Lloyd, K. (1999). Psychological distress among cancer patients and informed consent. *Journal of Psychosomatic Research, 46,* 241-245.

Morgan, M. G., Fischhoff, B., Bostrom, A., & Atman, C. J. (2001). Risk communication: A mental models approach. New York: Cambridge University Press.

Moxey, L. M., & Sanford, A. J. (1993). *Communication quantities: A psychological perspective*. Hillsdale, NJ: Lawrence Erlbaum.

Murphy, G. (1993). The use of aversive stimuli in treatment: The issue of consent. *Journal of Intellectual Disability Research, 37,* 211-219.

National Bioethics Advisory Commission. (1998, December). *Final report: Research involving persons with mental disorders that may affect decision making capacity*. Bethesda, MD: Author.

National Bioethics Advisory Commission. (2001a, August). *Ethical and policy issues in research involving human subjects* (Vol. II). Commissioned papers and staff analysis. Bethesda, MD: Author.

National Bioethics Advisory Commission. (2001b, August). *Ethical and policy issues in research involving human subjects* (Vol. I). Report and recommendations of the National Bioethics Advisory Commission. Bethesda, MD: Author.

National Commission for the Protection of Human Subjects of Biomedical and Behavioral Research. (1979). *The Belmont Report: Ethical principles and guidelines for the protection of human subjects of research*. Washington, DC: U.S. Government Printing Office.

Oyserman, D., Coon, H. M., & Kemmelmeier, M. (2002). Rethinking individualism and collectivism: Evaluation of theoretical assumptions and meta-analyses. *Psychological Bulletin, 128,* 3-72.

Perkins, R. E., & Repper, J. M. (1999). Compliance or informed choice. *Journal of Mental Health, 8,* 117-129.

Peterson, B. T., Clancy, S. J., Champion, K., & McLarty, J. W. (1992). Improving readability of consent forms: What the computers may not tell you. *IRB: A Review of Human Subjects Research, 14*(6), 6-8.

Petty, R. E., Cacioppo, J. T., & Goldman, R. (1981). Personal involvement as a determinant of argument-based persuasion. *Journal of Personality and Social Psychology, 41,* 847-855.

Pinals, D. A., & Appelbaum, P. S. (2000). The history and current status of competence and informed consent in psychiatric research. *Israel Journal of Psychiatry & Related Sciences, 37,* 82-94.

Poling, A. (1994). Pharmacological treatment of behavioral problems in people with mental retardation: Some ethical considerations. In L. J. Hayes & G. J. Hayes (Eds.), *Ethical issues in developmental disabilities* (pp. 149-177). Reno, NV: Context.

Pope, K. S., & Vetter, V. A. (1992). Ethical dilemmas encountered by members of the American Psychological Association: A national survey. *American Psychologist, 47,* 397-411.

President's Advisory Committee. (1996). *The human radiation experiments: Final report of the President's Advisory Committee*. New York: Oxford University Press.

Reder, P., & Fitzpatrick, G. (1998). What is sufficient understanding? *Clinical and Child Psychology & Psychiatry, 3,* 103-113.

Roe-Burning, S., & Straker, G. (1997). The association between illusions of invulnerability and exposure to trauma. *Journal of Traumatic Stress, 10,* 319-327.

Saldov, M., Kakai, H., McLaughlin, L., & Thomas, A. (1998). Cultural barriers in oncology: Issues in obtaining medical informed consent from Japanese-American elders in Hawaii. *Journal of Cross-Cultural Gerontology, 13,* 265-279.

Schwarz, N. (1998). Communication in standardized research situations: A Gricean perspective. In S. R. Fussell & R. J. Kreuz (Eds.), *Social and cognitive approaches to interpersonal communication* (pp. 39-66). Mahwah, NJ: Lawrence Erlbaum.

Seckler, A. B., Meier, D. E., Mulvihill, M. P., & Cammer, B. E. (1991). Substituted judgment: How accurate are proxy predictions? *Annals of Internal Medicine, 115,* 92-98.

Shimm, D. S., & Spece, R. G. (1992). Deception and the placebo effect in biomedical research. IRB: *A Review of Human Subjects Research, 9*(4), 5-7.

Shore, B. (1996). *Culture and mind: Cognition, culture, and the problem of meaning.* New York: Oxford University Press.

Silva, M. C., & Sorrell, J. M. (1988). Enhancing comprehension of information for informed consent: A review of empirical research. *IRB: A Review of Human Subjects Research, 10*(1), 1-5.

Sperber, D., & Wilson, D. (1995). *Relevance: Communication and cognition* (2nd ed.). Malden, MA: Blackwell.

Stelmach, L., Konnert, C., & Dobson, K. (2001). Obtaining informed consent from continuing care residents: Issues and recommendations. *Canadian Journal on Aging, 20,* 385-406.

Suhl, J., Simons, P., Reedy, T., & Garrick, T. (1994). Myth of substituted judgment: Surrogate decision making regarding life support is unreliable. *Archives of Internal Medicine, 1511,* 90-96.

Sulmasy, D. P., Terry, P. B., & Weisman, C. S. (1998). The accuracy of substituted judgments in patients with terminal diagnoses. *Annals of Internal Medicine, 12,* 621-629.

Switankowsky, I. S. (1998). *A new paradigm for informed consent.* New York: University Press of America.

Trials of War Criminals Before the Nuremberg Military Tribunals Under Control Council Law. (1949). No. 10, Vol. 2, pp. 181-182. Washington, DC: U.S. Government Printing Office.

U.S. Department of Health and Human Services. National Institutes of Health. Office for Protection From Research Risks. (2001). *Protection of human subjects.* 45 Code of Federal Regulations 46.

U.S. Senate Select Committee to Study Governmental Operations With Respect to Intelligence Activities. (1976). *Foreign and military intelligence* [Church committee report]. (Rep. no. 94-755, 94th Cong., 2d Sess., 394). Washington, DC: Government Printing Office.

Wänke, M. (2002). Conversational norms and the interpretations of vague quantifiers. *Applied Cognitive Psychology, 16*(3), 301-307.

Waggoner, W. C., & Mayo, D. M. (1995). Who understands? A survey of 25 words or phrases commonly used in proposed clinical research consent forms. *IRB: A Review of Human Subjects Research, 17*(1), 6-9.

Wampold, B. E., Mondin, G. W., Moody, M., & Ahn, H. (1997). The flat earth as a metaphor for the evidence for uniform efficacy of bona fide psychotherapies: Reply to Crits-Christoph (1997) and Howard et al. (1997). *Psychological Bulletin, 122,* 226-230.

Weber, E. U., & Hilton, D. J. (1990). Contextual effects in the interpretations of probability words: Perceived base rate and severity of events. *Journal of Experimental Psychology: Human Perception & Performance, 16,* 781-789.

Weinstein, N. D. (1980). Unrealistic optimism about future life events. *Journal of Personality and Social Psychology, 39,* 806-820.

Weinstein, N. D. (1989). Perceptions of personal susceptibility to harm. In V. M. Mays, G. W. Albee, & S. F. Schneider (Eds.), *Primary prevention of AIDS* (pp. 142-168). Newbury Park, CA: Sage.

Weinstein, N. D., & Klein, W. M. (1995). Resistance of personal risk perceptions to debiasing interventions. *Health Psychology, 14,* 132-140.

Weinstein, N. D., Kolb, K., & Goldstein, B. D. (1996). Using time intervals between expected events to communicated magnitudes. *Risk Analysis, 16,* 305-308.

Weisz, J. R., Hawley, K. M., Pilkonis, P. A., Woody, S. R., & Follette, W. C. (2000). Stressing the (other) three Rs in the search for empirically supported treatments: Review procedures, research, quality, relevance to practice and the public interest. *Clinical Psychology: Science and Practice, 7,* 243-258.

Wendler, D. (2000). Informed consent, exploitation and whether it is possible to conduct human subjects research without either one. *Bioethics, 14,* 310-339.

Wills, T. A. (1981). Downward comparison principles in social psychology. *Psychological Bulletin, 90,* 245-271.

Wilson, G. T. (1996). Empirically validated treatments: Reality and resistance. *Clinical Psychology: Science and Practice, 3,* 241-244.

Winkielman, P., Knäuper, B., & Schwarz, N. (1998). Looking back at anger: Reference periods change the interpretation of emotion frequency questions. *Journal of Personality and Social Psychology, 75,* 719-728.

Wogalter, M. S., Howe, J. E., Sifuentes, A. H., & Luginbuhl, J. (1999). On the adequacy of legal documents: Factors that influence informed consent. *Ergonomics, 24,* 593-613.

Wolinsky, H. (1997). Steps still being taken to undo damage of "America's Nuremberg." *Annals of Internal Medicine, 127,* I43-44.

World Medical Association Declaration of Helsinki. (2000). *Ethical principles for medical research involving human subjects.* Retrieved June 16, 2002, from http://www.wma.net/e/policy/17c.pdf.

Yates, J. F., & Stone, E. R. (1992). Risk appraisal. In J. F. Yates (Ed.), *Risk-taking behavior* (pp. 49-85). New York: Wiley.

Young, D. R., Hooker, D. T., & Freeberg, F. E. (1990). Informed consent documents: Increasing comprehension by reducing reading level. *IRB: A Review of Human Subjects Research, 12*(3), 1-5.

CHAPTER 14

Seven "Sins" of Misdirection?

Ethical Controversies Surrounding the Use of Deception in Research

MARKUS KEMMELMEIER, DEBORAH DAVIS,
AND WILLIAM C. FOLLETTE
University of Nevada, Reno

Better a lie that heals than a truth that wounds.

— Proverb

Truth has no special time of its own. Its hour is now-always.
— Albert Schweitzer (1875-1965), Out of My Life and Thought

The use of deceptive methods is arguably one of the most controversial issues in psychological research. Since Milgram's (1963) highly controversial studies on obedience to authority, behavioral scientists have questioned the ethical acceptability of deliberately concealing or misinforming participants about the true purpose of a study or about the various activities involved (e.g., Baumrind, 1964, 1985; Hertwig & Ortmann, 2001; Kelman, 1967, 1972; Warwick, 1975). Others have argued that sometimes deception is required in order to produce informative and valid research findings (e.g., Aronson & Carlsmith, 1968; Bröder, 1998; Schuler, 1982). Indeed, despite the ongoing debate and ethical dilemma, a substantial number of psychologists continue to rely on deception methods. Whereas the practice of deception has been most characteristic of social and personality psychologists (Adair, Dushenko, & Lindsay, 1985;

Nicks, Korn, & Mainieri, 1997; Sieber, Iannuzzo, & Rodriguez, 1995), deception research has also become common in other areas, such as cognitive, developmental, and educational psychology (e.g., Ceci, Bruck, & Loftus, 1998; Rosenthal & Jacobson, 1968). Nevertheless, the use of experimental deception raises a number of important ethical complexities that largely stem from conflicting professional goals such as the simultaneous pursuit of scientific integrity, social responsibility, and human welfare.

In this chapter, we will review the nature of deception and the seven "sins" of misdirection alleged to characterize deception research. We will then consider the current reality of regulatory guidelines and actual deceptive practices in psychological research, and offer commentary on the limitations of current practices.

WHAT CONSTITUTES DECEPTION?

Commentators have contrasted informational definitions with relational definitions of *deception* (Lawson, 2001)—that is, definitions focusing on the discrepancy in information, given the participant and reality, versus violations in the trusting relationship between participant and researcher. Because there is ambiguity with regard to what kind of behavior is and is not expected as part of a particular interpersonal relationship, we argue that deception in psychological research is more adequately captured in terms of informational discrepancy and intentionality. Specifically, we define as deception *any act in psychological research by which a psychologist purposefully creates a situation in which a participant's beliefs about the situation are incongruent with the knowledge that the psychologist has of the same situation* (for similar definitions, see

Sigall, 1997; Toy, Wright, & Olson, 2001). This definition incorporates the two forms of deception most commonly addressed by commentators on ethical dilemmas surrounding deception.

On the basis of a distinction first introduced by Thomas of Aquinas, psychologists often distinguish between *deception by commission* and *deception by omission* (Diener & Crandall, 1978), sometimes also referred to as *active* and *passive deception* (Adair et al., 1985; Kimmel & Smith, 2001). We will first review these major forms of deception and then comment on other mechanisms through which participants *are deceived,* but in the absence of any intention to do so by the experimenter.

Deception by Commission

Deception by commission occurs when researchers deliberately mislead participants about the purpose and nature of a study by making false statements about its purpose or the activities involved or by employing the help of confederates who are not identified as such. Because such procedures involve deliberate acts of "lying" and pretense and because they openly conflict with a researcher's responsibility to protect participants' rights and dignity, they are often viewed as posing the most severe ethical problems.

Deception by Omission

Deception by omission refers to a situation in which the researcher withholds information about the true extent or meaning of research procedures yet without actively providing misleading or false information. Some researchers consider "not telling" a lesser form of deception (e.g., Diener & Crandall, 1978), and others exempt it from this category altogether (Adair et al., 1985; Epley & Huff, 1998; Hey, 1998; Ortmann & Hertwig, 1998).

Functional Equivalence of Commission and Omission

People judge ethical violations involving acts of commission more harshly than those involving acts of omission (e.g., Gonzales, Haugen, & Manning, 1994). Yet both deception by omission and deception by commission involve a deliberate decision on the part of the researcher not to disclose the precise nature of a study, either at the time the person is asked to participate or as the procedure unfolds (Gross & Fleming, 1982; Sieber et al., 1995). In other words, the researchers create an informational discrepancy between themselves and the participants.

The degree of this informational discrepancy may vary independently of whether deception by omission or deception by commission is used. Examples of relatively minor informational discrepancy include cases in which participants are asked to complete a personality questionnaire without being told that the researcher uses the items to assess fascist tendencies (omission) or a psychologist telling participants that two experimental tasks are unrelated when they are in fact related (commission). More extreme examples include cases in which trained observers code a couple's interaction from behind a one-way mirror without their knowledge (omission) or a confederate poses as a fellow participant to whom participants confess their personal problems (commission). As the latter examples illustrate, omission and commission may not only lead to similar levels of informational discrepancy but also to similar levels of feeling "fooled," having one's privacy invaded, or other types of harm.

Participant Naïveté

Whereas our definition focuses on intentionality, in most instances, psychologists do not plan to deceive participants when they do not fully disclose relevant information about a study. This omission of information generally occurs because of the complexity of the information, time constraints, or because researchers want to avoid having their research results contaminated by participant awareness or speculation concerning the hypotheses under investigation. For instance, even though relevant for how they view the task, naïve intelligence test takers rarely receive information about the specific conceptions of mental ability assessed by an intelligence test *before* they are asked to work on it. Similarly, participants in some helping studies are not told ahead of time about the researchers' hypotheses, for example, the fact that the researcher expects prosocial behavior to originate in a person's self-interest—a piece of information that may influence the nature of participants' behavior in the study. Obviously, there is nothing unintentional about keeping participants blind with regard to the purpose or goal of one's research; hence, keeping one's participants naive must be qualified as deception by omission (e.g., Baron, 2001). However, it is certainly a very minor case of deception, and it is unavoidable that the researcher knows more about the study than the participant. Nevertheless, it is important that all material facts presented to the participants during the informed consent process can be taken at face value and that none of the withheld facts can reasonably be expected to alter the likelihood of a person participating in the study.

Inadvertent Misleading

Although technically not deception, other types of nonpurposeful misinformation may be equivalent to deception in their consequences. Psychologists might create a serious informational discrepancy by negligence in communication of information that participants might find important had it been accurate or available. The researcher may unintentionally misrepresent potentially relevant information, may simply not possess it, may intend to provide participants with relevant information but explain it poorly, or may simply be mistaken in his or her assumptions about the type of information that prospective participants would want. Furthermore, participants may fail to comprehend information the researcher does provide and therefore choose to join a study on the basis of false expectations (e.g., Shimm & Spece, 1992). In all these cases there is an unintentional informational discrepancy between participants and researchers. Especially in cases in which participants perceive that researchers could or should have provided relevant or understandable information, they may feel they have been deceived (see further discussion of this issue under "Violations of Rights to Self-Determination").

THE FIRST SIN: MORAL TURPITUDE

The controversy surrounding use of deception is essentially one of morals or ethics. Thus, the first alleged sin of misdirection or deception in research is that of *moral turpitude,* or violation of moral standards. Essentially, two distinct schools of moral thought have been applied to evaluating deception (for reviews, see Lawson, 1997; Kimmel & Smith, 2001), varying in the degree to which they consider deception to necessarily violate moral principles.

The Deontological (Duty-Based) Perspective

Based on the work of philosopher Immanuel Kant, the *deontological* or *duty-based*

approach focuses on the inherent rightness of an act, that is, on the moral quality of the behavior itself, not its consequences (Davis, 1991). Based on the proposition that deception is morally wrong, deontology categorically rejects the use of deception in psychological research. Even though this perspective seems to offer a clear-cut answer to the question of the acceptability of deception, ethical judgments vary depending on whether an act is considered in isolation or in context. This may lead to a limited acceptance of otherwise repulsive acts (such as killings) if they occur in situations in which higher moral values are at stake (e.g., defending democracy). Nonetheless, for deontology, maximizing human welfare itself is not a primary consideration, although morality is viewed as important for human welfare.

Consequentialist Perspectives

Consequentialist theories define the rightness of an act relative to another act by focusing on the consequences of the acts. *Utilitarianism,* as the dominant perspective in this school, champions the welfare of individuals as the ultimate value and evaluates acts on the basis of whether they promote this value (Pettit, 1991). Utilitarianism is an ethically demanding position because it obligates decision makers to act in ways that will produce the greatest overall amount of good in the world, even though this may entail acting against their own self-interest. Because this perspective emphasizes that decision makers must evaluate the consequences of their actions, utilitarianism considers science and scientific knowledge as relevant to ethical decision making. There are two basic forms of utilitarianism, one focusing on individual acts (act utilitarianism), the other focusing on rules.

Rule Utilitarianism

Rule utilitarianism emphasizes the beneficial nature of social rules for human welfare, such as the proscription of lying and deception. Even though rules provide a good compass for ethical decision making, sometimes it is not clear which of several rules should be applied in a given situation. Other times, it is difficult to know to what extent certain rules actually promote human welfare, with some accepted rules actually obstructing social welfare. For example, rules against deception may be counterproductive in research on subtle racism. When participants in such studies are suspect or aware of the fact that the research deals with racial prejudice, otherwise occurring racial biases are wiped out (e.g., Sommers & Ellsworth, 2000). This could lead to the erroneous conclusion that subtle racism does not exist and hamper efforts to overcome biases in hiring or legal judgment.

Act Utilitarianism

Act utilitarianism seeks to establish the rightness of specific acts on a case-by-case basis, with decision makers assessing known or expected utilities to all parties that might be affected by an action. Using cost-benefit analysis, the alternative promising the greatest overall benefit to most is chosen, regardless of whether it conforms with social rules or not. Act utilitarianism makes no a priori determination with regard to the moral status of deception, and in some cases, such as the subtle racism example above, even obliges psychologists to use deceptive procedures if they promote the welfare of the largest number of individuals. However, in practice, act utilitarianism is a difficult proposition because decision makers need to evaluate all possible direct and indirect consequences to a potentially vast number of parties, easily exceeding human evaluative capabilities. Also, because maximization of the common good is the only accepted criterion, apparent moral fixtures, such as human

rights, are not recognized unless they result in a benefit.

Psychology's Stance

Most psychologists, through their professional organizations, have implicitly and explicitly adopted a mixture of deontological (duty-based) and consequentialist approaches (Kimmel & Smith, 2001). Specifically, the most recent version of the American Psychological Association Ethical Principles of Psychologists and Code of Conduct (2002; henceforth "APA code") establishes the promotion of human welfare as the supreme goal for psychologists but also specifies moral principles, such as integrity and honesty, from which rules of the profession are derived. The consequentialist stance of the APA code is reflected in the acknowledgment of cases in which these rules (e.g., the prescription to tell the truth) may be overridden on the basis of a cost-benefit analysis in which the benefits flowing from a study outweigh its potential harm. With APA code as context, in the following sections, we review some of the remaining issues commonly raised with regard to the acceptability and usefulness of deception in psychological research.

ETHICAL ISSUES IN DECEPTION RESEARCH

In the sections to follow, we address the remaining six alleged sins of misdirection. Two are methodological, including the issue of whether deception is ever *necessary* and the question of whether deception research can be *valid*. The final four concern the extent to which deception necessarily violates participant rights and causes harm to all participants (including subjects and researchers), to the discipline, and to society.

THE SECOND SIN:
IS DECEPTION UNNECESSARY?

APA code 8.07a specifies that "Psychologists do not conduct a study involving deception *unless* they have determined that the use of deceptive techniques is justified by the study's significant prospective scientific, educational, or applied value, *and* that effective non-deceptive alternative procedures are not feasible" (emphases ours). Thus, critics have questioned the necessity of deceptive methods, arguing that nondeceptive methods are equally or more effective. Most opponents and supporters agree that deceptive research methods should be considered only if they significantly increase the likelihood of valid research findings compared with nondeceptive techniques. Yet the assumption that deceptive techniques are ever superior to nondeceptive techniques is controversial.

Are Nondeceptive Research Methods Equally Effective?

Opponents of deception have generally questioned the superior validity of deceptive methods. Some commentators have argued that deception is never a necessity and proposed alternative methods such as role play or other "as if" techniques that avoid deception's ethical problems (Baumrind, 1985; Freedman, 1969; Geller, 1982; Hertwig & Ortmann, 2001). Indeed, sometimes such methods yield outcomes indistinguishable from those obtained with deception methods (Krupat & Garonzik, 1994).

Most commentators, however, have taken the position that it is naive at best to assume that all questions can be addressed without deception. Psychologists "find themselves in the troublesome position of concealing the truth from their subjects in order to *reveal* the truth about human behavior" (Aronson, Ellsworth, Carlsmith, & Gonzales, 1990, p. 89; emphasis in original).

Thus, deception researchers have generally refuted methodological criticisms of deception research.

Certain Behaviors Can Only Be Studied Using Deception

The most frequent argument for using deceptive methods is that socially sensitive behaviors and those not open to accurate introspection cannot be examined without deception (e.g., Aronson et al., 1990; Baron, 2001; Bröder, 1998). Participants' awareness of the focal behavior leads to evaluation apprehension, self-presentational concerns, or demand effects—all factors that undermine the validity of the research. Hence, it is not surprising that most instances of experimental deception, particularly by commission, are found in research on issues such as expectancy effects, false memory, incidental learning, compliance/conformity, helping, aggression, and prejudice (cf. Gross & Fleming, 1982). Moreover, by definition, the study of unintentional and spontaneous behavior precludes awareness on the part of research participants. A particularly interesting case occurs when participants' self-knowledge is at odds with their spontaneous behavior. Researchers working on aversive racism theory (Gaertner & Dovidio, 1986) and similar theories have shown that most European Americans harbor considerable levels of unacknowledged racial prejudice and under certain circumstances discriminate against minorities—while endorsing a self-image as egalitarian and nonprejudiced. A test of such a theory requires deception, because self-reports are necessarily inaccurate (see also Jones & Sigall, 1971).

Equivalence of Nondeceptive and Deceptive Techniques Cannot Be Assumed

Even though some studies found that deceptive and nondeceptive methods produce similar results, others yield strikingly different findings. There is often a gulf between self-reports or simulated behaviors, on one hand, and the actual behavior by "naive" participants, on the other hand. This is best illustrated by Milgram's classic obedience research, in which the experimenter instructed participant "teachers" to deliver increasingly severe electric shocks to "learners" (actually confederates of the experimenter) until participants either obediently employed levels of shock described as highly dangerous or refused to continue (Milgram, 1963). When people from the same population as those in the experiments received a description of them and were asked how many people they thought would deliver the highest level of electric shocks, the highest estimate was 3%, but the actual number in Milgram's experiment was 65% (Milgram, 1974). The obedience paradigm is a clear example of a situation not amenable to accuracy in either self-report or prospective judgments regarding others' behavior. For other situations, such judgments may be more accurate. Indeed, the functional equivalence of various techniques is an empirical question within each topic area and cannot be assumed a priori.

Self-Reports Do Not Represent an Alternative to Deception Methods

Because most techniques proposed as alternatives to deception include self-report, it has to be assumed that the validity of these methods is compromised by self-presentational concerns, especially when the research focuses on socially sensitive research topics. Other research has documented that self-reports are limited because participants are not aware of their behavior (e.g., nonverbal behavior) or are unable to report on the true causes for their behavior; and in many cases, self-reports seem to reflect merely post hoc rationalizations of one's behavior (e.g., Nisbett & Wilson, 1977). Research on

autobiographical memory reveals systematic distortions, as does research on eyewitness reporting (see reviews in Davis & Follette, 2001; Schacter, 2001; *Review of General Psychology,* Vol. 5(2), special issue on autobiographical memory). Thus, the accuracy of self-reports is often low or uncertain, even though accuracy might be higher for topics or situations that are more familiar to the person than for those that the person has rarely or never encountered.

Naturalistic Observation Does Not Represent an Alternative to Deception Methods

Observational methods may avoid the necessity to actively deceive participants, but at a considerable price. Observational data do not allow any conclusions about causal processes. Thus, whenever researchers are interested in causal questions with regard to sensitive behaviors, the experiment, potentially involving experimental deception, is the method of choice. Furthermore, naturalistic observation studies are often deceptive themselves (at least by omission) and do not offer a priori ethical advantages.

Summary

In summary, although researchers might choose to employ nondeceptive procedures for questions that do not truly require them, most researchers would agree that it is simply not possible to address all questions of interest with nondeceptive methods.

THE THIRD SIN: ARE DECEPTIVE METHODS NECESSARILY INVALID?

An argument commonly attributed to Kelman (1967) focuses on the notion that the repeated use of deception creates distrust toward psychologists and psychological studies in general. Indeed individuals, once deceived, are likely to distrust any other experimenters, to the point that they assume deception even when there is none (Epley & Huff, 1998; MacCoun & Kerr, 1987). This may have a number of unintended consequences. First, suspicion makes it more difficult for researchers to successfully deceive subjects, thereby compromising the ability to create the level of "experimental realism" (Aronson & Carlsmith, 1968) that will elicit natural and spontaneous behavior. Second, the behavior of suspicious participants may differ from those of nonsuspicious participants, thus compromising the validity of the research results (Silverman, Shulman, & Wiesenthal, 1970). Third, participants are likely to share the experience of having been deceived with others. Even though participants are often asked to keep details of the research confidential until it is completed, studies show, for example, that while promising the experimenter to keep procedures and the purpose of an experiment confidential, many students in university subject pools readily share their experiences with other members of the same subject pool (e.g., Horka & Farrow, 1970; Lipton & Garza, 1978). This has the potential of creating a ripple effect with prospective participants (Kelman, 1967). In brief, the argument is that deception will create suspicion, which in turn undermines the effectiveness of deception procedures. Just like an antibiotic in the treatment of bacterial infections, experimental deception is thought to become less effective the more often it is applied (Weiss, 2001).

Success of Deception Cannot Be Reliably Established

In deception research, researchers rely on their intuition or pretesting to assess what participants might believe about a particular study. However, because during the study researchers may not communicate with participants about their perceptions of the study, assumptions about what participants may believe about the study are never verified, leading to unexamined variation in how participants understand an experimental situation (e.g., Agryris, 1968; Kelman, 1967). Furthermore, even though researchers often employ suspicion checks at the end their research, participants may be reluctant to admit that they were suspicious or saw through the deception (e.g., Newberry, 1976; Taylor & Shepperd, 1996). Furthermore, Baumrind (1985) suggested that even when participants seem to be willing to admit suspicion, most suspicion checks do not accurately assess actual levels of suspicion (e.g., Page, 1973). As a result, a basic premise of deception research, namely that researchers are able to reliably misinform participants in intended ways, has not generally been verified, and therefore the validity of deception research is called into question. To the extent that participants see through the deception, the goal of increasing experimental validity will be compromised, thus necessarily decreasing the benefit of deception research in any cost-benefit analysis.

Participants Just Don't Buy It!

Some commentators have argued that much deception research is inherently flawed because the information provided in these studies is not credible to participants (Lawson, 1997). For example, some participants become aware of deception because the experimenter-provided information is at odds with their expectations, self-concepts, or world knowledge (Glinski, Glinski, & Slatin, 1970; Patten, 1977), as, for example, when false-negative feedback regarding abilities may conflict with confident self-perceptions.

Effectiveness of Deceptive Methods Depends on Researcher Skill

The success of any psychological research depends on it being high in experimental or mundane realism and on its ability to elicit the same psychological processes as those occurring in everyday life (Aronson & Carlsmith, 1968). This translates into researchers having to generate situations that are involving and in which participants are likely to behave naturally. Although this applies equally to deceptive and nondeceptive research, the former poses a formidable challenge in that it takes ingenuity and skill, for example, to maintain experimental validity while constructing a highly involving and credible experimental situation. Conversely, the existence of studies in which participants were able to "see through" the deception (Taylor & Shepperd, 1996) or doubted the soundness of information provided by the researcher (Glinski et al., 1970) may be more likely to reflect lack of skill or an inadequate operationalization than a fundamental flaw of deception research.

THE FOURTH SIN: DOES DECEPTION NECESSARILY VIOLATE PARTICIPANT RIGHTS?

In much ethical reasoning, human rights and human dignity are considered central and intuitively compelling concepts. Thus, the fourth alleged sin of deception is that of violation of human rights to dignity, privacy, and self-determination.

Especially to deontological thinkers, human rights serve as axiomatic starting points from which moral guidelines and maxims for ethical behavior are derived. Hence, along with the principles of beneficence and nonmaleficence, fidelity and responsibility, integrity, and justice, respect for rights and human dignity forms one of APA's central principles to guide the conduct of psychologists (APA, 2002). Sometimes, with explicit reference to this professional principle, commentators in the deception

debate have argued that deceptive research, regardless of its validity, disrespects human dignity and violates basic human rights, such as privacy, dignity, and self-determination (e.g., Geller, 1982; Ortmann & Hertwig, 1997; Smith, 1976). Conversely, supporters of deception research have argued either that basic human rights are not necessarily violated or that to the extent they are infringed on, violations are minor and of only a temporary nature.

Dignity

It is safe to assume a general agreement among psychologists that participants should not be treated merely as research material (cf. Kelman, 1972). Rather, they are to be treated as human beings and individuals of value who deserve respect and consideration from those with whom they interact. Consequently, researchers who intentionally mislead their participants are alleged to show disrespect and to compromise participants' dignity by subjecting them to embarrassing or otherwise unpleasant consequences of the deception (e.g., Geller, 1982). Such a concept of human dignity implies that any act of deception is morally repulsive. However, in everyday life, a certain degree of dishonesty, for example, as part of polite behavior, is tolerated without any apparent implications for a person's dignity. Individuals sometimes accept overriding reasons for dishonesty, such as when a person makes obviously untrue statements to protect another's dignity. Similarly, there seem to be no objections to the idea of not communicating true but hurtful information.

Deception is similarly accepted in the entertainment industry, as with magician performers and popular shows such as Allen Funt's *Candid Camera,* a TV show in which innocent people were covertly filmed in potentially compromising situations. Thus, even though there is little doubt that human dignity generally demands honesty, in many cases, this may not be a rigid proposition, as shown by the many popular exceptions to the rule.

Advocates of deception research have further argued that one should not consider deceptive aspects of the research in isolation, but rather that the impact of the research experience *in its entirety* should be considered (Schuler, 1982). The argument is that even though some aspects of the experiment involve deliberate misinformation, on the whole, research procedures safeguard participants' rights. For example, participants may be informed about the possibility of deception beforehand, they are free to withdraw from the experiment at any time, they are fully debriefed about all aspects of the deception, and they are free to have all their own data destroyed (see below). Arguably, in most instances, the deception is mild and without any apparent implications for human dignity. Most research participants, for example, report that they do not mind it (e.g., Gerdes, 1979) and even find deception research, on the average, to be more enjoyable (Christensen, 1988).

Self-Determination

The right of self-determination is arguably one of the most serious issues in deception research. Participants are not given the opportunity to decide whether they are willing to participate in a particular procedure with full knowledge of what they are actually agreeing to (e.g., Baumrind, 1985; Kitchener, 1996). Although prospective participants are never to be deceived about potential harm, a person's decision to participate in a study involving deception is necessarily based on false or incomplete information.

Researchers and institutions have dealt with this informed consent problem in various ways. Especially at universities operating large subject pools, participants are sometimes asked for their general consent to be involved in deception studies without the nature of any individual experiment being revealed to them. In other instances, participants are informed at the beginning of the experimental session that there is a chance that the experimenter may not be fully truthful. These procedures maintain the contractual nature of the relationship between researcher and participants (Kitchener, 1996; Lawson, 1995; Schuler, 1982) and do not appear to influence the experimental outcome (e.g., Finney, 1987). However, both procedures offer only a partial remedy, as participants may agree to the general idea of being misled but reject a particular type of deception that occurs in a specific experiment.

These problems may be exacerbated in cases in which prospective participants are from a particularly vulnerable group or when there is a power differential between participant and researcher (Baumrind, 1985; Kelman, 1972). For example, children or clinical populations may not be able to appreciate a researcher's warning or simply not believe that the researcher, presumably a benevolent authority, would mislead them or have them participate in a study that is not beneficial to them (cf. Herrmann & Yoder, 1998). Moreover, participants are often from lower-power groups, in which prospective participants are given only an *apparent* choice with regard to their participation (Kelman, 1967). Poor people's need for even small amounts of money to be earned in exchange for their participation may override any ethical concern they may have with regard to being deceived. Also, the status of the researcher may bias some participants' judgment of the appropriateness of a particular research procedure such that perceived status leads to greater acceptance of an ethically dubious research procedure (Tanke, 1979).

Participants are often told that they are free to terminate their participation without prejudice if they choose to do so (APA, 2002, 8.02a). However, even though participants might prefer to terminate their participation if they knew that they were being deceived, in a successful deception, experiment participants do *not* know that they are being misled; hence, they may not see any reason to withdraw. In addition, the situational dynamic of experimental participation may discourage participants from leaving, even though they might be suspicious of deception and experience some discomfort as a result. Despite an earlier verbal assurance, participants may be unsure that they will receive the reward promised for their participation (e.g., credit, money) if they decide to leave early, because this would not fit their experience of exchange relationships. Potentially, participants would not want to exit because of overriding considerations such as the desire to be cooperative and helpful to the researcher or for fear leaving would make them look bad in the eyes of the experimenter or other participants (Orne, 1962). In sum, it appears that researchers conducting deception research provide their participants with only an *illusion of choice,* which Follette, Davis, and Kemmelmeier (see Chapter 13, this volume) have termed the "Ultimate Deception" characterizing much of psychological research, particularly informed consent processes (cf. Kelman, 1972; Lawson, 1995). Because situational forces urge students (and sometimes others) to participate, discourage individuals from discontinuing their participation, and dissuade them from withdrawing their data during debriefing, participants' agreement at various phases may be viewed as being *engineered* by situational forces. Such a situation is inconsistent with the requirements of informed consent. Thus, although many persons may actually find the situation acceptable or even enjoyable, those who do not may find it very difficult to withdraw.

A different challenge to a person's self-determination lies in the fact that participants may be confronted involuntarily with certain unpleasant facts about themselves. For example, 65% of all participants in Milgram's (1963) famous obedience experiment were made to learn that they are capable of risking electrocution of an innocent person, one who had repeatedly begged to be released. The very fact that participants learn that they can be deceived rather easily in an experiment may be another issue that participants would otherwise prefer not to know. Interestingly, this argument implies that in their daily lives, participants can pick and choose when and what they would like to know about themselves and their behavior. This conception is exaggerated, if not incorrect. Everyday life is full of novel situations and problems, and people can rarely choose, nor do they know what they will learn from a particular situation.

Privacy

Deception research has the potential of violating a person's privacy, because the researcher may gain access to behaviors that the person would not want to share with others. It is clear, on the other hand, that invasion of privacy is not a necessary characteristic of deception in research, because researchers are often interested in mundane and public behavior. Nevertheless, privacy issues are highly pertinent to deception research.

Problems of privacy may occur with either deception by omission or commission. A typical case of omission may involve covert observation in field settings in which participants may engage in nonpublic behavior or divulge personal information without any knowledge that they are being observed or recorded, either because the researcher is hidden or not identified as such. For example, in a naturalistic study at an airport, Fraley and Shaver (1998) observed the relationship behavior of couples when one person was leaving while the other stayed behind. And, for his research on human gossip, Dunbar (1996) systematically eavesdropped on private conversations in public places. These examples constitute clear invasions of privacy. If a researcher learns or is able to infer participants' identities, he or she is required to fully inform participants about the extent of their observation and obtain permission to use a participant's data. This procedure amounts to obtaining informed consent retroactively, and to the extent that participants do not give permission, APA code specifies that any data pertaining to the person must be destroyed immediately. This procedure helps to protect participants' rights of self-determination and privacy.

Typically, studies invading participant privacy are considered less ethically problematic to the extent that participants remain completely anonymous to the researcher and participants never learn that they have been observed or data about them recorded. Nonetheless, there might be a fine line between the observation of behaviors that people might be willing to share with those close to them and the observation of behaviors that are usually not shared with anyone. For instance, in a widely criticized study by Middlemist, Knowles, and Matter (1976), researchers observed men urinating in a public restroom. Participants remained anonymous because researchers focused exclusively on the space between their genitals and the urinal. Nevertheless, given the presence of the confederate and other details of procedure, this kind of measurement may be viewed as severe invasion of privacy (Koocher, 1977).

Invasions of privacy might also occur with deception by commission in that persons are led to entertain feelings and thoughts that either otherwise occur only in private situations or are erroneously considered outside a researcher's influence. For example, in a case reported by Oliansky (1991), psychology students assumed the role of counselors and tried to help a peer in psychological distress who was really a confederate. This task was emotionally highly engaging to the point that participants related personal problems to benefit their "client." The fact that participants were allowed to develop intense personal feelings for the confederate and that they consequently conveyed personal information they would not have disclosed had they known the true situation constitutes an invasion of privacy. Similarly, in so-called memory-implantation studies, participants may not believe that the experimenter is able to create a highly vivid memory, which they might embrace as a trace of their own personal experience despite assurances to the contrary (e.g., Hermann & Yoder, 1998). Hence, even though participants were debriefed, the participants could feel that their integrity had been violated. Finally, some might argue that to the extent that aspects of the person are revealed without his or her awareness (such as personality or ability scores, moral choices, and so on), privacy has been invaded. This is perhaps the most inclusive view of invasion of privacy in that any experiment that tests anything about a person that they do not explicitly understand as being tested may be considered an invasion of privacy.

A particular controversy has arisen around the invasion of privacy that may result from use of the "bogus pipeline" procedures for measuring attitudes and behavior (Aguinis & Handelsman, 1997; Sigall, 1997). Participants are led to believe that the experimenter has a device that can read the true answer based on participants' physiological responses (Jones & Sigall, 1971). Participants interviewed in such a procedure have been shown to disclose significantly more socially undesirable attitudes and reports on their own behaviors than in anonymous procedures in which they feel they can successfully misreport them (e.g., Tourangeau, Smith, & Rasinski, 1997).

Murray (1982) has argued that rights, such as the right to privacy, show considerable variation with regard to their scope, depending on the specific situation and the consequences of specific research procedures. This notion seems to be substantiated by the fact that participants object to invasions of privacy primarily when personal information is involved (Farr & Seaver, 1975) and do not mind apparent invasions if they do not result in any harm (Tanke, 1979).

THE FIFTH SIN: IS DECEPTION NECESSARILY HARMFUL TO PARTICIPANTS AT ALL LEVELS?

Psychologists are obligated to care for the welfare of the people with whom they work. According to APA code, this includes not only the promotion of good and the avoidance of harm for one's clients and research participants but also responsibility toward "other affected persons" (APA, 2002, Principle A). In this section, we examine the extent to which deception might cause harm to research participants at all levels, including subjects, confederates, and investigators. In the two sections that follow, we will examine the sixth and seventh alleged sins—of harm to the discipline of psychology and to larger society.

Harm to Subject-Participants

Deception as a research strategy is generally considered unacceptable if it causes more than minimal harm in research participants. Several commentators have claimed that

participants find deception offensive. Others have speculated that the experience of being fooled by psychologists necessarily causes harm. That is, deception is assumed to cause embarrassment and shame and to undermine self-esteem and self-confidence as well as interpersonal trust, in psychologists specifically (Baumrind, 1985; Seeman, 1969). Some have argued that the harmful effects of deception on developing self-concepts, trust in authority, and a sense of personal confidence and mastery are particularly strong for children (e.g., Herrmann & Yoder, 1998).

Because psychologists have generally taken a consequentialist stance when discussing the justifiability of deception research, they have advocated the use of empirical evidence in assessing harm (e.g., Aitkenhead & Dordoy, 1985). Note that this approach will not satisfy those with an deontological approach to this matter. In this perspective, deception is wrong regardless of whether it causes measurable harm or not.

Empirical Research

Most empirical research investigation into possible harmful consequences has been designed to assess participant reactions to being deceived.

Studies Showing No or Positive Consequences of Deception. A variety of empirical studies have been conducted to examine the effects of deception on participants. Responding to Baumrind's (1964) criticism of his controversial research on obedience to authority, Milgram (1964) reported that only a small minority (less than 2%) of participants regretted having participated in his highly involving experiments, whereas 84% said they enjoyed their participation (see also Ring, Wallston, & Corey, 1970). In his review of this literature, Christensen (1988) concluded that participants say they enjoy deception studies more than nondeception studies. Smith and Richardson (1983) reported that student participants experienced a greater educational benefit in deception studies (cf. Hilton, 2001), although this finding may be primarily due to debriefings in deception studies being more interesting (Coulter, 1986; Epley & Huff, 1998). Across 15 experiments, Gerdes (1979) found that participants were not annoyed by deception and did not mind its use, and in a 2-year follow up study, none of the participants in an earlier cheating study felt that it was harmful (Smith, 1981). Several studies found that unless it involves invasion of privacy, participants are generally very accepting of the use of deception (e.g., Christensen, 1988; Fisher & Fyrberg, 1994; Sharpe, Adair, & Roese, 1992; Soliday & Stanton, 1995). The reason for this pattern seems to be that participants at least in part base their judgments of the ethical status of a research procedure on the amount of harm that it causes, with innocuous deception being judged as ethically acceptable (e.g., Slone & Hull, 2002; Tanke, 1979).

Epley and Huff (1998) also found support for the idea that the degree of harm is more important than the fact of deception. They examined participant reactions in a false-feedback study, finding that whether participants had been informed about the deception had little effect. Rather, regardless of their knowledge about deception, participants in the negative-feedback condition showed negative reactions toward the experiment. Thus, although they appeared to have no negative reactions to deception per se, they did appear to find negative information offensive, whether deceptive or not.

There also appear to be no negative effects of deception on trust. Even though some of them had been recently deceived on an experimental task, participants in Fillenbaum and Frey's (1970) research acted in a trusting manner on a subsequent task.

Studies Showing Negative Consequences of Deception. Only a few studies have reported negative consequences of deception. Fisher and Fyrberg (1994) found that many participants rejected deception, but this result was based on hypothetical rather then actual participation in a deception study. Oliansky (1991) observed considerable discomfort in participants in a deception study, but it remains unclear to what extent these effects could be generalized beyond the specific study. Overall, the empirical data do not seem to support the idea that deception engenders negative reaction on the part of research participants and certainly do not support the proposition that it necessarily does so.

Limitations. Although to date, there is no reliable evidence showing pervasive negative effects of deception, the research faces a number of serious limitations. Because this research is generally based on self-report, it is unclear to what extent these data fully represent the participant's experience. As found, for example, by Taylor and Shepperd (1996), participants are not always truthful in what they report. Others hypothesized that reports of positive effects of deception show the operation of cognitive dissonance in that participants seek to justify their participation in an otherwise uncomfortable study (Epley & Huff, 1998; but see Berscheid, Baron, Dermer, & Libman, 1973).

Quantitative Data and Protection of Individual Participants

Although the preponderance of data do not suggest that participants are harmed by deceptive research methods, it is an open question as to what extent this absolves researchers from the charge that they do harm to individual participants (e.g., Kitchener, 1996). Even if one has established that a procedure is innocuous for the majority of participants, it is nevertheless possible that a minority of prospective participants could find the procedure unacceptable and experience harm as a result of their research participation. Similarly, the research reviewed above leaves open the possibility that some participants will be harmed.

Whereas this may raise fundamental concerns with regard to researcher responsibility, it is critical to consider that all ethical (and certainly all legal) reasoning is implicitly or explicitly based on a *reasonable-person* standard—that is, the idea that certain behaviors can be viewed as normal by most intelligent individuals. Regardless of whether research involves deception or not, psychologists have to make working assumptions about what can be considered acceptable conduct but, unfortunately, can never guarantee that their assumptions hold for all research participants without exception. Therefore, psychologists are obligated to foresee and avoid possible harm as much as is possible and with reasonable regard to the population they work with.

The Importance of Debriefing

Proponents of deceptive research strategies argue that even though participants may be exposed to moderate levels of discomfort, a thorough debriefing procedure is sufficient to eliminate potential negative effects on most participants (e.g., Holmes, 1976). However, the idea that debriefing removes all relevant ills is disputed by critics (e.g., Kitchener, 1996; Seeman, 1969).

Most of all, the fact that the person was deceived cannot be taken back, regardless of whether participants do not show adverse reactions or even agree with the idea that deception had to be used to investigate the research question. The experience of having been deliberately misled is morally aversive

and may still shake participants' basic trust and change how they approach others. Similarly, information learned about oneself during a deception study cannot be taken back. As mentioned previously, a majority of all participants (65%) in Milgram's (1963) obedience studies learned that they were capable of hurting someone on another person's word. Even though a person might be told that such behavior is relatively "normal," it may forever change the person's self-image or outlook onto the world. Thus, if deception is to be employed at all, researchers need to consider such consequences.

Many psychologists, however, are confident that possible negative effects can be avoided when the experimenter apologizes to participants and successfully conveys the true nature of the research procedures and why a nondeceptive procedure was not viable to obtain valid results. The goals should be to ensure that participants do not leave feeling any more negative than when they first arrived (cf. Slone & Hull, 2002). Generally, research participants have been found to be understanding of deceptive methods, and the absence of negative effects, and even positive reactions, is generally attributed to successful debriefing (e.g., Gerdes, 1979; Smith & Richardson, 1983). However, researchers should carefully monitor the reactions of participants, and in case of unexpected emotional reactions, researchers should be in a position to transfer participants to a counselor. In this context, it is interesting to note that with few exceptions, psychologists' estimates of potential harm are considerably above those of actual or potential research participants (e.g., Sieber, 1983; Sullivan & Deiker, 1973).

As with deceptive research techniques themselves, the use of debriefing can be justified only if it is effective. Thus, psychologists need to take precautions to ensure the effectiveness of their debriefing procedures (Holmes, 1976). Simply informing participants about the facts of the research procedure may neither be enough to convey the extent of misinformation nor to ensure participants' understanding and appreciation of the deceptive procedures. Rather, researchers should actively check on whether participants comprehend the deception, for example, by asking participants to describe the purpose of the study in their own words.

Of particular concern are studies in which participants receive false feedback about their personalities or performance, because beliefs acquired during the experiment may persist even though participants have been debriefed and informed about the spurious nature of the feedback (Ross, Lepper, & Hubbard, 1975). Hence, beyond informing participants about the nature of the deception, Eyde (2000) recommends that researchers help participants revise their false beliefs about themselves. Because participants may discount information presented to them in the debriefing phase as inconsistent with the feedback received earlier, researchers should make participants aware of the operation of this perseverance effect (Ross et al., 1975).

The effectiveness of debriefing is particularly problematic when researchers work with vulnerable populations, such as children or mentally challenged individuals. These groups may not be able to comprehend the purpose and nature of the deception, and they may not be able to rationalize or "brush off" the experience of mild deception as adults can (Herrmann & Yoder, 1998). A similar problem occurs when researchers are certain that even adult participants are unlikely to believe explanations of how false beliefs or other reactions may have been created by deceptive manipulations (for a discussion of the persistence of implanted memories, for example, see Follette et al., Chapter 13, this volume). Hence, psychologists may have to refrain from using certain deceptive techniques on

some groups if the success of a debriefing procedure is uncertain.

Last, a debriefing procedure should not in itself cause negative emotions such as shame, embarrassment, or anger, which may occur in the context of an investigation into socially sensitive behavior. Researchers should do what they can to gently convey the nature of deception and treat participants with respect. Even though debriefing should be as complete as possible with regard to all important characteristics of the design, psychologists may choose to withhold true but hurtful information. On the other hand, if a researcher discovers any information that is important to participants' well-being outside of the research, such as health-related facts, this information should not be omitted. Instead, the researcher needs to ensure an adequate understanding of this information on the part of the participant (for specific guidelines on how to conduct debriefings, see Eyde, 2000; Sieber 1983; Rosenthal & Rosnow, 1991).

Harm to Individual Researchers

Harm to the Main Experimenter

As with harm to individual research participants, there is no general agreement regarding the extent to which deception harms those who employ it in their research. In many areas of psychology, elaborate deception studies yielding interesting results are likely to contribute to a research program and to benefit researchers, aside from generating knowledge, by enhancing their standing in the field. On the other hand, critics have often argued that the use of deception has a morally corrosive effect. Once deception has been used successfully, researchers are more likely to be less critical toward its use and to employ it more lightly in the future, even when it is not needed, thus encouraging a "fun and games" approach to psychology (e.g., Hertwig & Ortmann, 2001;

Ring, 1967). Potentially, this leads researchers onto a slippery slope where they are more willing to use increasingly extreme forms of deception. Unfortunately, no data exist that address this conjecture.

At least anecdotal evidence exists for the idea that deception studies may carry certain unforeseeable risks to the researcher, especially when they occur in a field setting. Latané and Darley (1970) staged a theft from a liquor store of which the storeowner was fully informed. When this study was replicated in the Midwest by other researchers, a customer called the police—who arrived with guns drawn to arrest the researchers (Diener & Crandall, 1978). One of the present authors (MK) conducted a lost-letter study in which a research assistant tucked addressed and stamped envelopes under windshield wipers of parked cars with a note attached creating the impression that someone has found a lost letter and returned it to the wrong owner. Unbeknownst to the researchers, a store employee observed the repeated letter drops by the assistant, inspected the letters and notes, and eventually confronted him, angrily accusing him of deception. Whereas these risks appear to be unique to a certain type of study, they are not a necessary feature of deception studies, as risk of this kind is unlikely to occur in a laboratory setting. Finally, at least one incidence of deception research resulted in a lawsuit against the researcher by an irate participant (Greenberg & Ruback, 1992).

Harm to Research Assistants

A trickier issue of harm to research participants concerns graduate and undergraduate research assistants who collude in deceptions designed by the main experimenter. Like their supervisors, research assistants may also suffer the morally corrosive effects of engaging in deception. However, even more

than their supervisors, they may suffer direct harm in the process of conducting the research. Those of us who have faced the necessity of misleading participants, particularly when the deception is likely to be stressful or uncomfortable to them, know how difficult and stressful deception research can be for those who actually run the sessions.

Oliansky (1991), for example, reported on the stresses he experienced as a confederate playing the role of a distressed student in interaction with another student who was to try to help him. He reported stress due to factors such as negative reactions from those who were deceived, guilt over the deception, embarrassment about engaging in the deception, and embarrassing encounters with previous participants outside the research context. The stressful effects felt by student assistants are arguably the strongest of any participants in research, because they are often stronger than those experienced by participants and are felt with each session, and sometimes beyond. Even so, little attention has been devoted to this potentially harmful consequence of deception.

THE SIXTH SIN: IS DECEPTION RESEARCH HARMFUL TO THE DISCIPLINE?

Some have alleged a sixth sin of misdirection, arguing that deception research has a number of negative consequences for the discipline of psychology (e.g., Kitchener, 1996). In direct contrast, others have pointed to the benefits that deception research methods bring to psychologists (e.g., Jones & Sigall, 1971).

Harm to the Discipline

Effects on Scientific Knowledge

Most of all, deception studies have been a unique source of knowledge about human behavior that has greatly advanced psychological science. For example, even though ethically problematic, Milgram's (1963, 1974) research illustrates the power of situational influences at levels that even professionals had not considered possible. Similarly, false-memory research has reshaped how scientists (and practitioners) think about memory or eyewitness reports (e.g., Davis & Follette, 2001). Classic expectancy manipulations in alcohol research have challenged the disease model of addiction (e.g., Marlatt, Demming, & Reid, 1973). Thus, psychologists from many areas would insist that deceptive research techniques have greatly advanced knowledge about human behavior.

Effects on the
Reputation of the Discipline

Some critics have argued that the reputation of psychology and support for psychology as a science suffers when the public learns of the use of deception (Baumrind, 1985). However, the merits of this argument are at best unclear. As the worldwide popular reception of Milgram's (1963, 1974) experiments demonstrates, the public is generally intrigued by clever studies demonstrating counterintuitive behavioral tendencies. Indeed, popular psychology is an industry because many nonpsychologists are interested in psychological research findings. Arguably, unique insights that were derived from deception research may account for why many college students seem to be fascinated with psychology (cf. Hilton, 2001). Furthermore, scientists from other fields often rely on psychological research to advance knowledge in their own fields (e.g., political science, organizational behavior, medicine, engineering, marketing). Last, policymakers rely on psychological research findings to inform their decisions. In many instances, these "consumers" of psychological science rely on research that involve deception, even though its use is sometimes criticized (e.g., Patten, 1977).

Effects on Future
Participant Populations

A practical consequence of using deception has already been discussed, namely the idea that the use of deception will necessarily exhaust the pool of prospective research participants, either because participant suspicion makes psychological studies ineffective or because people are reluctant to participate in psychological studies in the first place (e.g., Kelman, 1967). Such a tendency would have to hurt all psychological research. Epley and Huff (1998) found some evidence that participants who had been debriefed halfway during the study were more suspicious in the latter part. However, these participants were suspicious of experimental deception but not generally distrustful toward psychologists. A study by Soliday and Stanton (1995) did not find any reliable evidence that deception leads to suspicion or devaluation of scientific and applied psychology; and Smith and Richardson (1983) did not find that deception influenced levels of trust in experimenters. In the only time-series study on this issue, Sharpe et al. (1992) examined levels of trust and suspicion in a university's subject pool and did not find any evidence for a spillover effect across 20 years, suggesting that suspicion is not communicated between cohorts of students.

Effects on Professional Integrity

Another concern centers on the idea that the acceptability of deception research procedures inevitably undermines professional principles of honesty and integrity (APA, 2002). However, the history of the last 40 years seems to tell a different story. Even though the use of deception has not substantially declined during this period (e.g., Nicks et al., 1997), awareness of ethical issues among psychologists and the ethical review of research has increased dramatically, and use of more ethically questionable procedures has declined. In sum, the assumption that a limited use of deceptive techniques leads to moral degradation is not supported. Instead, it was the use of deception that triggered the creation of the APA Ethical Principles of Psychologists and Code of Conduct, as well as the subsequent substantial literature debating a large number of professional ethical issues (including the present handbook).

THE SEVENTH SIN: IS DECEPTION RESEARCH HARMFUL TO SOCIETY?

As noted by Lawson (1997), the debate on the ethical status of deception often narrowly focuses on actual or assumed harm to individual participants in contrast to actual or assumed benefits to society. Yet some argue that society may not only fail to benefit from deception research methods, it may actually be hurt by psychologists' use of deception. Truth telling is essential to human communication and the moral fabric of any society (e.g., Bok, 1999; Kitchener, 1996). Thus, to the extent that psychologists not only undermine interpersonal trust but also model deceptive behavior, one might expect that they facilitate deception becoming a "mass product" (Thielicke, 1958-1959/1979), which has the potential of undermining the well-being and stability of an entire society as people become less and less able to trust each other.

Along these lines, the philosopher Hans Jonas (1970) argued provocatively that the central aim of many scientists using deception methods—quick scientific progress to enhance human welfare—is "an optional goal" (p. 28). He proposed that the speedy improvement of the lives of a minority

through science must be subordinate to the protection of the society, which itself would not be threatened if certain individuals did not receive help immediately, for example, through a lifesaving drug. Rather, Jonas warned of the Pyrrhic victory in improving individual lives while undermining the moral values of an entire society. It is hard to imagine, however, and perhaps unduly grandiose to think that psychological research would account for much of the variance in change in moral values, particularly in the context of political deception, advertising, models by lawyers, and so on.

Does Deception Research Promote Public Welfare?

Proscription of Deception Obstructs Human Welfare. In diametric opposition to Jonas's condemnation, others argue that banning deception would lead to harmful consequences by hampering scientific progress and putting human welfare at risk. In clinical trials in biomedical research, as well as in therapy outcome studies, it is imperative that research participants are not aware of whether they receive an experimental treatment or whether they receive a conventional treatment or a placebo. Only by using deception by omission, and sometimes deception by commission, can researchers accurately assess the effectiveness of a particular therapy. To the extent that this information is not available, practitioners cannot be confident about the effectiveness of various therapeutic approaches. Hence, practitioners are at risk of using ineffective therapies or, worse, using therapies that have negative consequences for the client.

Proscription of Deception Creates Ethical Problems. Whereas the rejection of deception appears to avoid a "sin of commission," this position ignores the possibility of a "sin of omission." Not using deception to study socially sensitive topics or to develop effective therapies and social interventions may lead to lack of scientific or social progress and prolong the suffering of individuals or help maintain social inequality. Thus, although the proscription of deception may avoid one ethical dilemma, it will inevitably create an equally severe moral problem for researchers committed to enhancing human welfare (Rosenthal & Rosnow, 1991). Hence, psychologists have to carefully consider all risks and benefits when making decisions about the use of deception in research.

PLAYING BY THE RULES

Whereas the use of deceptive techniques raises a number of difficult issues, it is common practice in the social and behavioral sciences (but see Hertwig & Ortmann, 2001). According to the guidelines of most professional and regulatory bodies, deception is considered a legal and ethical strategy under specific circumstances.

Professional Standards

Psychologists operating under the APA Ethical Principles and Conduct of Conduct are constrained in the use of deception. According to APA code (2002), the use of deception is limited to the following situations:

1. The study promises significant scientific, educational, or applied benefit, and the research could not be carried out without the deception (Section 8.07a)

2. Participants are not deceived about physical pain or some emotional distress (Section 8.07b)

3. Participants are fully informed about the deception as soon as is feasible (Section 8.07c)

4. Participants are permitted to fully withdraw their data (Section 8.07c)

Note that these guidelines imply that even in the case of deception, the explanation of risks cannot be withheld, with the presumable exception of any risks associated with the act of being deceived.

Regulatory Oversight

In some countries, research involving human participants conducted in institutional settings is subject to review by ethics committees. In the U.S. institutions receiving federal funding, institutional review boards (IRBs) operate under federal guidelines that have been established in part because of the blatant violation of human rights and dignity of uninformed or inadequately informed participants in several infamous studies (see Follette et al., Chapter 13, this volume). The IRB is central in conducting a risk-benefit analysis in which it is determined whether a study sufficiently complies with the principles of respect for persons, beneficence, and justice to maximize protection of the participants (for a detailed explanation of the function of the IRB, see Hayes, Chapter 7, this volume).

With regard to research making use of deception, U.S. federal statute allows for withholding of information from participants under the following conditions: (a) minimal risk to participants, (b) the absence of adverse effects on the rights and welfare of the participant, (c) the fact that the research could not be carried out without deception, and (d) an appropriate debriefing.

Minimal risk is defined to mean that the probability and magnitude of harm or discomfort anticipated in the research are not greater in and of themselves than those ordinarily encountered in daily life or during the performance of routine physical or psychological examinations or tests (see U.S. Department of Health and Human Services, 2001, §46.102i and §46.116d). The definition above provides a rough anchoring point for IRBs in assessing the magnitude of risks. Given that empirical data show that lying is a common feature of interpersonal relationships (e.g., DePaulo, Kashy, Kirkendol, Wyer, & Epstein, 1996; Feldman, Forrest, & Happ, 2002), lying can be considered an everyday risk (without the benefit of debriefing).

Usually U.S. statute requires researchers to obtain a statement of informed consent from participants. Because in a deception experiment, participants cannot be fully or accurately informed about the nature and purpose of the study before they participate, informed consent needs to be obtained following the debriefing procedure (for a detailed discussion of informed consent procedures, see Follette et al., Chapter 13, this volume,). The debriefing must remove any misunderstanding about the real purpose of the study and must contain sufficient information to repair any feelings of mistrust or disrespect that may have resulted from the use of deception (e.g., an apology on the part of the experimenter for having had to deceive). Given that a person's participation is already a material fact, it is following this debriefing procedure that consent must be obtained. Even though the previously mentioned problem of "illusion of choice" cannot be avoided, the researcher must not try to talk participants into acquiescing to the deception, but rather help them understand the entire experiment so that consent can be reasonably given or denied. If any distress is encountered that indicates the presence of more than minimal risk, experimenters must notify the IRB (see U.S. Department of Health and Human Services, 2001).

MEANINGFUL RISK-BENEFIT ASSESSMENT

Risk-benefit assessments (RBAs) are mandated by APA code, as well as by IRBs, and each of the moral perspectives through which deceptive research practices can viewed. Various organizations and commentators differ with respect to the specific risks and benefits they consider appropriate for evaluation and also with respect to the methods and criteria by which such an evaluation is to be performed. One can ask, however, whether truly meaningful RBA is a realistic goal. In the sections below, we will discuss methodological challenges facing any meaningful RBA procedures and offer conclusions regarding probable application of an enlightened RBA.

Practical Challenges

What Costs and Benefits Should Be Examined?

As discussed earlier, contributors to the ethical debate surrounding deception have alleged a variety of harms and benefits potentially resulting from deception research. Neither those who practice deception nor those who criticize it, however, have fairly considered the full range of potential consequences. Critics argue that advocates of deception research focus broadly on benefits ranging from those to society or to the progress of science and the discipline to those specifically to participants—but concentrate selectively on harm to participants without considering harms such as those to society, the researcher, or the discipline (e.g., Lawson, 1997). Arguably, critics also focus narrowly, namely on harm at all levels; however, as far as benefits are concerned, they consider only the benefit to science without taking into consideration the potential benefit to society or to the participants.

We propose that the following types of costs and benefits be considered in a comprehensive and fair RBA: (a) costs and benefits for participants, (b) costs and benefits for scientific progress, (c) costs and benefits for the discipline, (d) costs and benefits for the researchers, and (e) costs and benefits for society.

Only when risks and benefits at all levels are considered can a meaningful determination concerning the acceptability or unacceptability of a deceptive research procedure be made.

What Quantitative Criteria Should Be Applied?

To meaningfully integrate identified consequences into an index of beneficence, all outcomes must first be classified as good or bad, scaled for magnitude and likelihood, and weighted. Not surprisingly, just as commentators disagree on criteria to include, they perhaps disagree even more strongly on quantitative assessments for conceptually agreed-on criteria.

Classification of Consequences as Beneficial Versus Harmful. The first necessary quantitative classification is simply valence (benefit versus neutral or cost/risk). Even this seemingly simple distinction may be subject to disagreement, as clearly illustrated by reactions to Milgram's obedience research. Should one view the outcome for fully obedient subjects in the Milgram paradigm as an acute stressor and long-term threat to their self-concepts? Or might one instead consider it to be a valuable moral lesson and prod to self-insight, with potential to avert future destructive obedience by participants as well as those who have since learned of the research? Many controversial research paradigms have been viewed in similarly contradictory lights.

Scaling of Individual Outcomes. To the extent that there are different types of costs and benefits, decision makers are required to compare them. In an RBA, this implies that different risks and benefits need to be translated onto the same dimension and, either implicitly or explicitly, assigned a scale value. This is naturally challenging, as costs and benefits may occur in different domains and involve different affected parties and are usually considered incommensurable. For example, how can psychological harm to a participant be balanced against the advancement of science (e.g., Smith, 1976)? Or how can the limitations to a person's self-determination, as it occurs in a deception study, be scaled on the same dimensions as the prospective influence that a particular research result may have on the public perception of psychology? Even though such translation to common scales seems farfetched, it is a necessity in any RBA.

Scaling of Magnitude. Although those from different ethical perspectives may agree that a particular outcome is likely to be associated with a procedure *and* agree on the valence of the outcome, they may still disagree strongly on its extremity—as illustrated by a recent exchange among memory researchers studying implantation of false memories (see July 1998 issue of *Applied Cognitive Psychology*). Critics of such research argue that false memories are not always eliminated by debriefing, particularly among children (Herrmann & Yoder, 1998). Furthermore, they argue that *any* false memory is harmful. Researchers in this field, in contrast, argue that a minority of participants maintain false memories long after debriefing and that even for those who do, the very existence of a false memory is not in itself harmful (e.g., Ceci et al., 1998; Goodman, Quas, & Redlich, 1998). Instead, false memories that do not affect the individual's well-being in other ways cannot be viewed as harmful.

Similar debate centers around benefit. Some critics have argued that deception research has no value at all because it is generally invalid (e.g., Baumrind, 1985). An even more startlingly unrealistic proposition of the lack of benefit came from Herrmann and Yoder (1998), who argued that deceptive research on memory implantation was of no benefit because memory implantation had long since been established anecdotally in the writings of Piaget and other distinguished psychologists, such as William James or James Mark Baldwin.

Scaling of Likelihood. Because most consequences of human action do not occur in a deterministic fashion, costs and benefits need to be weighted by their likelihood of occurrence. The objective assessment of risk is not only an important characteristic of our modern evidence-based society but also often a requirement, as in, for example, the legal or the medical arenas. Unfortunately, too often decision makers assess the likelihood of risks and benefits primarily on the basis of a priori intuitions and assumptions rather than through empirical examination. The reason lies in the fact that there may not be any empirical data on the consequences of the use of a certain procedure or that they are not known to the decision maker. Hence, decision makers need to make sure that they are in possession of all available information pertinent to their judgment. Furthermore, ethical decision makers should have an interest in expanding the knowledge base from which to draw information that is pertinent to particular judgments.

Relative Weighting of Outcomes Within and Between Valences. Once the parameters of valence, likelihood, and magnitude have been established for each anticipated outcome, the scored pool of outcomes must somehow be weighted and combined into an overall judgment of the RB ratio for the project in question. Naturally, this poses a challenge, because weighting of risks and benefits necessarily reflects values. In some respects, differences between perspectives are most strongly reflected in the weights they assign to costs, as opposed to benefits. It is worth noting, however, that RBAs are, and should be, weighted to favor the individual. Otherwise, the individual would always come out second, in contrast to projected benefits for so many others at so many levels.

Comparison of Deceptive Versus Nondeceptive Alternative Procedures. Once the RBA is established for the target procedure, similar assessments are mandated for reasonable alternative procedures varying in the degree of deception or other anticipated harms to the participants. The APA code requires that researchers evaluate the relative effectiveness of proposed deceptive procedures as compared with less deceptive or nondeceptive alternatives, with the goal of choosing the least deceptive effective procedure. Disagreement on this assessment is fundamental to the ethical debate regarding deception. Proponents argue that deception is essential for examination of some questions, whereas critics argue for the lack of necessity (benefits of) deception and for the superiority of other methods for all questions.

What Are Appropriate Limits of Tolerance for the Risk-Benefit Balance?

Even if ethical decision makers could reliably assess and quantify the risk and benefits of a particular procedure, the limits of tolerance for the balance of risks to benefits would still be at issue. What is an acceptable balance of harm to benefit? Neither proponents nor critics of deception research have articulated a well-developed rationale for any of several issues regarding the limits of tolerance.

Maximal Tolerance for Risks. One might argue that overall limits of tolerance for deceptive research procedures should be determined solely based on risks (i.e., that benefits are weighted zero). According to such a decision scheme, deception may be unacceptable once a certain level of risk or cost has been reached, regardless of any prospective benefits. If so, two potential limits of tolerance are relevant: (a) those for *maximum degree of harm* and (b) those for the *maximum likelihood of harm* (or maximum proportion of participants harmed). Critics of deception research tend to advocate very low tolerance limits for both, regardless of envisioned benefits (e.g., Seeman, 1969).

In contrast, some view even extreme risks as within the latitude of acceptance. Indeed, our evidence-based, rule-utilitarian society explicitly recognizes the acceptability of such ultimate risk. There exists widespread popular and legal acceptance of clinical trials of procedures for which death is among the risks of participation—either through failure to actually treat a disease (i.e., assignment to the placebo or ineffective standard treatment) or through assignment to the experimental treatment with unknown safety (such as in Phase I toxicity trials). This example seems outrageous with regard to deception research, but consider that risk of death is a possibility in psychological research as well. For example, a person assigned to an ineffective treatment for depression, drug addiction, anger management, and many other disorders may die (and even kill others) as a result. Nevertheless, many ethical commentators view even this risk of death as within the limits of tolerance if justified by anticipated benefits, such as future therapeutic benefits to others.

What combined ratio is appropriate or tolerable? To the extent that neither benefits nor harm are regarded as determinative

alone, RBA may require an assessment of what ratio of the two is to be considered acceptable. Is a tip of the scale away from 50-50 regarded as sufficient for a determination, or must the benefits far outweigh potential harm? This is a particularly pertinent question in situations in which a procedure yields more benefit than harm but the absolute quantity of harm is considerable.

Comprehensive Risk-Benefit Assessment and Reality

To date, there does not appear to be a well-articulated decision scheme for ethical decision making with regard to deception research. Given the complexities elaborated above, it is perhaps not surprising that we hold that meaningful RBA is not currently practiced. To our knowledge, there exists no adequate agreement regarding what to assess, how to assess it, and what to make of it if assessed. Perhaps more important, no empirical methods have been developed to assess many relevant risks and benefits, and disagreement on a priori grounds abounds between critics and proponents.

Current actual practice is to rely on intuitive assessments by the researcher and IRB. Data regarding either anticipated risks or benefits are rarely available and are therefore rarely considered by the researcher or presented to the IRB. Furthermore, the full range of potential risks is rarely considered. Instead, the scientific/practical value of the research is considered and presented in contrast to the harm to participants. Harms to society, the discipline, or the researcher are rarely, if ever, considered—as are benefits to the participants—nor is a balanced consideration of risks and benefits reflected in debates surrounding informed consent. The latter is typically considered in light of how well the participant is informed of what procedures to expect and what risks may be associated with those procedures. No researcher would be slapped by an IRB for failure to fully inform participants of the full range of potential costs at the societal or disciplinary level or of potential benefits, even strictly those to the participant, no matter how great or how small.

The effort and sophistication of methods required for valid and comprehensive RBA are truly daunting. Researchers are unlikely to undertake such a task unless forced by disciplinary codes of ethics, IRBs, and/or state or federal regulatory bodies. Comprehensive RBA, as outlined above, requires a research enterprise dedicated to that goal. Within individual projects, investigators would be obligated to perform pretests of understanding of informed consent procedures and perhaps pretests of reactions to deceptions. Additional assessments during and after the main project would be required to evaluate potential risks and benefits—potentially including those at the researcher, disciplinary, and societal levels. Additional studies specifically designed to assess outcomes of experimental procedures for participants and the effects of the research for the researcher, discipline, or society would be required. Both the costs of the required research enterprise and the lack of available methods to address many of the questions pose serious barriers, which in the absence of any compelling incentives are unlikely to be overcome. Furthermore, even if such empirical efforts were undertaken and were successful, they would not be useful in the absence of standards for how to integrate and weight findings into agreed-on criteria.

CONCLUSIONS

The ethical debate surrounding deception reflects striking differences in moral and professional values, philosophy of science, and methodological positions. As with conflicts of fundamental beliefs and values in politics and other arenas, it is unrealistic to expect widespread consensus to emerge from debate of the deception issue. And just as compromise is the necessary result for those who debate values in politics, neither side of the ethics debate will fully have its way. Thus, we can reasonably expect that researchers will continue to practice deception via commission and omission into the foreseeable future, even as critics continue to advocate stricter guidelines for its use. Deception researchers will modify their procedures in reactions to critics, even as critics will have less to criticize as researchers increasingly address their concerns. In this context, deception researchers can take steps both to increase safeguards to research participants and to address and diffuse critical commentary without sacrifice of the methodological rigor they require.

Although critics of deception have been quick to presume that harms of various sorts are associated with deception, deception researchers have likewise presumed harmlessness. They have tended to presume informed consent procedures adequate, experimental procedures innocuous, and debriefing effective, without adequate evidence, just as critics have presumed the opposite. Many such presumptions can be addressed in pretesting, manipulation checks, debriefing procedures, and postexperimental interviews and assessments—without substantially increased costs in time or resources. Better data on the consequences of deception procedures have no obvious downside. Identification of problems that have previously been presumed absent can promote development of necessary procedural changes that simultaneously promote participant welfare and correct threats to the internal validity of the experiment.

REFERENCES

Adair, J. G., Dushenko, T. W., & Lindsay, R. C. L. (1985). Ethical regulations and their impact on research practice. *American Psychologist, 40,* 59-72.

Agryris, C. (1968). Some unintended consequences of rigorous research. *Psychological Bulletin, 70,* 185-197.

Aguinis, H., & Handelsman, M. M. (1997). Ethical issues in the use of the bogus pipeline. *Journal of Applied Social Psychology, 27,* 557-573.

Aitkenhead, M., & Dordoy, J. (1985). What the subjects have to say. *British Journal of Social Psychology, 24,* 293-305.

American Psychological Association. (2002). *Ethical principles of psychologists and code of conduct.* Retrieved December 9, 2002, from http://www.apaorg/ethics/code2002html

Aronson, E., & Carlsmith, J. M. (1968). Experimentation in social psychology. In G. Lindzey & E. Aronson (Eds.), *The handbook of social psychology* (2nd ed., Vol. 2, 1-79). Reading, MA: Addison-Wesley.

Aronson, E., Ellsworth, P. C., Carlsmith, J. M., & Gonzales, M. H. (1990). *Methods of research in social psychology.* New York: McGraw-Hill.

Baron, J. (2001). Purposes and methods. *Behavioral and Brain Sciences, 24,* 403.

Baumrind, D. (1964). Some thoughts on the ethics of research: After reading Milgram's "Behavioral Study of Obedience." *American Psychologist, 19,* 421-423.

Baumrind, D. (1985). Research using intentional deception: Ethical issues revisited. *American Psychologist, 40,* 165-174.

Berscheid, E., Baron, R. S., Dermer, M., & Libman, M. (1973). Anticipating informed consent: An empirical approach. *American Psychologist, 28,* 913-925.

Bok, S. (1999). *Lying: Moral choice in public and private life.* New York: Vintage Books.

Bröder, A. (1998). Deception can be acceptable. *American Psychologist, 53,* 805-806.

Ceci, S. J., Bruck, M., & Loftus, E. F. (1998). On the ethics of memory implantation research. *Applied Cognitive Psychology, 12,* 230-240.

Christensen, L. (1988). Deception in psychological research: When is its use justified? *Personality and Social Psychology Bulletin, 14,* 664-675.

Coulter, X. (1986). Academic value of research participation by undergraduates. *American Psychologist, 41,* 317.

Davis, D., & Follette, W. C. (2001). Foibles of witness memory for traumatic/high profile events. *Journal of Air Law and Commerce, 66,* 1421-1549.

Davis, N. A. (1991). Contemporary deontology. In P. Singer (Ed.), *A companion to ethics* (pp. 205-218). Cambridge, MA: Blackwell.

DePaulo, B. M., Kashy, D. A., Kirkendol, S. E., Wyer, M. M., & Epstein, J. A. (1996). Lying in everyday life. *Journal of Personality and Social Psychology, 70,* 979-995.

Diener, E., & Crandall, R. (1978). *Ethics in social and behavioral research.* Chicago: University of Chicago Press.

Dunbar, R. (1996). *Grooming, gossip, and the evolution of language.* Cambridge, MA: Harvard University Press.

Epley, N., & Huff, C. (1998). Suspicion, affective response, and educational benefit as a result of deception in psychology research. *Personality and Social Psychology Bulletin, 24,* 759-768.

Eyde, L. D. (2000). Other responsibility to participants. In B. D. Sales & S. Folkman (Eds.), *Ethics in research with human participants* (pp. 61-73). Washington, DC: American Psychological Association.

Farr, J. L., & Seaver, W. B. (1975). Stress and discomfort in psychological research: Subject perceptions of experimental procedures. *American Psychologist, 30,* 770-773.

Feldman, R. S., Forrest, J. A., & Happ, B. R. (2002). Self-presentation and verbal deception: Do self-presenters lie more? *Basic and Applied Social Psychology, 24,* 163-170.

Fillenbaum, S., & Frey, R. (1970). More on the "faithful" behavior of suspicious subjects. *Journal of Personality, 38,* 43-51.

Finney, P. D. (1987). When consent information refers to risk and deception: Implications for social research. *Journal of Personality and Social Behavior, 2,* 37-48.

Fisher, C. B., & Fyrberg, D. (1994). Participant partners: College students weigh the costs and benefits of deceptive research. *American Psychologist, 49,* 417-427.

Fraley, R. C., & Shaver, P. R. (1998). Airport separations: A naturalistic study of adult attachment dynamics in separating couples. *Journal of Personality and Social Psychology, 75,* 1198-1212.

Freedman, J. L. (1969). Role playing: Psychology by consensus. *Journal of Personality and Social Psychology, 13,* 107-114.

Gaertner, S. L., & Dovidio, J. F. (1986). The aversive form of racism. In J. F. Dovidio, & S. L. Gaertner (Eds.), *Prejudice, discrimination, and racism* (pp. 61-89). San Diego, CA: Academic Press.

Geller, D. M. (1982). Alternatives to deception: Why, what, and how? In J. E. Sieber (Ed.), *The ethics of social research: Surveys and experiments* (pp. 40-55). New York: Springer.

Gerdes, E. P. (1979). College students' reactions to social psychological experiments involving deception. *Journal of Social Psychology, 107,* 99-110.

Glinski, R. J., Glinski, B. C., & Slatin, G. T. (1970). Nonnaivety contamination in conformity experiments: Sources, effects, and implications for control. *Journal of Personality and Social Psychology, 16,* 478-485.

Gonzales, M. H., Haugen, J. A., & Manning, D. J. (1994). Victims as "narrative critics": Factors influencing rejoinders and evaluative responses to offenders' accounts. *Personality and Social Psychology Bulletin, 20,* 691-704.

Goodman, G. S., Quas, J. A., & Redlich, A. D. (1998). The ethics of conducting "false memory" research with children: A reply to Herrmann and Yoder. *Applied Cognitive Psychology, 12,* 207-217.

Greenberg, M. S., & Ruback, R. B. (1992). *After the crime: Victim decision making.* New York: Plenum.

Gross, A. E., & Fleming, I. (1982). Twenty years of deception in social psychology. *Personality and Social Psychology Bulletin, 8,* 402-408.

Herrmann, D., & Yoder, C. (1998). The potential effects of the implanted memory paradigm on child subjects. *Applied Cognitive Psychology, 12,* 198-206.

Hertwig, R., & Ortmann, A. (2001). Experimental practices in economics: A methodological challenge for psychologists? *Behavior and Brain Sciences, 24,* 383-451.

Hey, J. D. (1998). Experimental economics and deception: A comment. *Journal of Economic Psychology, 19,* 397-401.

Hilton, D. J. (2001). Is the challenge for psychologists to return to behaviorism? *Behavior and Brain Sciences, 24,* 415.

Holmes, D. S. (1976). Debriefing after psychological experiments: I. Effectiveness of post-deception dehoaxing. *American Psychologist, 31,* 858-875.

Horka, S. T., & Farrow, B. J. (1970). A methodological note on intersubject communication as a contaminating factor in psychological experiments. *Journal of Experimental Child Psychology, 10,* 363-366.

Jonas, H. (1970). Philosophical reflections on experimenting with human subjects. In P. Freund (Ed.), *Experimentation with human subjects* (pp. 1-31). New York: Braziller.

Jones, E. E., & Sigall, H. (1971). The bogus pipeline: A new paradigm for measuring affect and attitude. *Psychological Bulletin, 76,* 349-364.

Kelman, H. C. (1967). Human use of human subjects: The problem of deception in social psychological experiments. *Psychological Bulletin, 67,* 1-11.

Kelman, H. C. (1972). The rights of the subject in social research: An analysis in terms of relative power and legitimacy. *American Psychologist, 27,* 989-1016.

Kimmel, A. J., & Smith, N. C. (2001). Deception in marketing research: Ethical, methodological, and disciplinary implications. *Psychology & Marketing, 18,* 663-689.

Kitchener, K. S. (1996). Professional codes of ethics and ongoing moral problems in psychology. In W. O'Donohue & R. F. Kitchener (Eds.), *The philosophy of psychology* (pp. 361-370). Thousand Oaks, CA: Sage.

Koocher, G. P. (1977). Bathroom behavior and human dignity. *Journal of Personality and Social Psychology, 35,* 120-121.

Krupat, E., & Garonzik, R. (1994). Subjects' expectations and the search for alternatives to deception in social psychology. *British Journal of Social Psychology, 33,* 211-222.

Latané, B., & Darley, J. (1970). The unresponsive bystander: Why doesn't he help? Englewood Cliffs, NJ: Prentice Hall.

Lawson, C. (1995). Research participation as a contract. *Ethics & Behavior, 5,* 205-215.

Lawson, E. (1997). Deception in research: Thirty years of controversy. In M. Bibby (Ed.), *Ethics and education research* (pp. 15-48). Coldstream, Australia: Australian Association for Research in Education.

Lawson, E. (2001). Informational and relational meanings of deception: Implications for deception methods in research. *Ethics & Behavior, 11,* 115-130.

Lipton, J. T., & Garza, R. T. (1978). Further evidence of subject pool contamination. *European Journal of Social Psychology, 8,* 535-539.

MacCoun, R. J., & Kerr, N. L. (1987). Suspicion in the psychological laboratory: Kelman's prophecy revisited. *American Psychologist, 42,* 199.

Marlatt, G. A., Demming, B., & Reid, J. B. (1973). Loss of control drinking in alcoholics: An experimental analogue. *Journal of Abnormal Psychology, 81,* 233-241.

Middlemist, R. D., Knowles, E. S., & Matter, C. F. (1976). Personal space invasions in the lavatory: Suggestive evidence for arousal. *Journal of Personality and Social Psychology, 33,* 541-546.

Milgram, S. (1963). Behavioral study of obedience. *Journal of Abnormal and Social Psychology, 67,* 371-378.

Milgram, S. (1964). Issues in the study of obedience: A reply to Baumrind. *American Psychologist, 19,* 848-852.

Milgram, S. (1974). *Obedience to authority: An experimental view.* New York: Harper & Row.

Murray, T. H. (1982). Ethics, power, and applied social psychology. In L. Bickman (Ed.), *Applied social psychology annual* (Vol. 3, pp. 75-95). Beverly Hills, CA: Sage.

Newberry, B. H. (1976). Admission of suspicion as a function of information sources: Tip-off vs. situational cues. *Memory and Cognition, 4,* 123-127.

Nicks, S. D., Korn, J. H., & Mainieri, T. (1997). The rise and fall of deception in social psychology and personality research. *Ethics & Behavior, 7,* 69-77.

Nisbett, R. E., & Wilson, T. D. (1977). Telling more than we can know: Verbal reports of mental processes. *Psychological Review, 84,* 231-259.

Oliansky, A. (1991). A confederate's perspective in deception. *Ethics & Behavior, 1,* 253-258.

Orne, M. T. (1962). On the social psychology of the psychological experiment: With particular reference to demand characteristics and their implications. *American Psychologist, 17,* 776-783.

Ortmann, A., & Hertwig, R. (1997). Is deception acceptable? *American Psychologist, 52,* 746-747.

Ortmann, A., & Hertwig, R. (1998). The question remains: Is deception acceptable? *American Psychologist, 53,* 806-807.

Page, M. M. (1973). On detecting demand awareness by postexperimental questionnaire. *Journal of Social Psychology, 91,* 305-323.

Patten, S. C. (1977). Milgram's shocking experiment. *Philosophy, 52,* 425-440.

Pettit, N. A. (1991). Consequentialism. In P. Singer (Ed.), *A companion to ethics* (pp. 230-240). Cambridge, MA: Blackwell.

Ring, K. (1967). Experimental social psychology: Some sober questions about some frivolous values. *Journal of Experimental Social Psychology, 3,* 113-123.

Ring, K., Wallston, K., & Corey, M. (1970). Mode of debriefing as a factor affecting subjective reaction to a Milgram-type obedience experiment: An ethical inquiry. *Representative Research in Social Psychology, 1,* 67-88.

Rosenthal, R., & Jacobson, L. (1968). *Pygmalion in the classroom: Teacher expectation and pupils' intellectual development.* New York: Holt, Rinehart & Winston.

Rosenthal, R., & Rosnow, R. L. (1991). *Essentials of behavioral research.* New York: McGraw-Hill Higher Education.

Ross, L., Lepper, M. R., & Hubbard, M. (1975). Perseverance in self-perception: Biased attributional processes in the debriefing paradigm. *Journal of Personality and Social Psychology, 32,* 880-892.

Schacter, D. L. (2001). *The seven sins of memory: How the mind forgets and remembers.* Boston, MA: Houghton Mifflin.

Schuler, H. (1982). *Ethical problems in psychological research.* New York: Academic Press.

Seeman, J. (1969). Deception in psychological research. *American Psychologist, 24,* 1025-1028.

Sharpe, D., Adair, J. G., & Roese, N. J. (1992). Twenty years of deception research: A decline in subjects' trust? *Personality and Social Psychology Bulletin, 18,* 585-590.

Shimm, D. S., & Spece, R. G. (1992). Deception and the placebo effect in biomedical research. *IRB: A Review of Human Subjects Research, 9*(4), 5-7.

Sieber, J. E. (1983). Deception in social research III: The nature and limits of debriefing. *IRB: A Review of Human Subjects Research, 5*(3), 1-4.

Sieber, J. E., Iannuzzo, R., & Rodriguez, B. (1995). Deception methods in psychology: Have they changed in 23 years? *Ethics & Behavior, 5,* 67-85.

Sigall, H. (1997). Ethical considerations in social psychological research: Is the bogus pipeline a special case? *Journal of Applied Social Psychology, 27,* 574-581.

Silverman, I., Shulman, A. D., & Wiesenthal, D. L. (1970). Effects of deceiving and debriefing psychological subjects on performance in later experiments. *Journal of Personality and Social Psychology, 14,* 203-212.

Slone, L. B., & Hull, J. G. (2002). Deception of research subjects. In R. J. Amdur & E. A. Bankert (Eds.), *Institutional Review Board: Management and Function* (pp. 244-249). Sudbury, MA: Jones and Bartlett.

Smith, C. P. (1981). How (un)acceptable is research involving deception? *IRB: A Review of Human Subjects Research, 5*(1), 1-5.

Smith, M. B. (1976). Some perspectives on ethical/political issues in social science research. *Personality and Social Psychology Bulletin, 2,* 449.

Smith, S. S., & Richardson, D. (1983). Amelioration of deception and harm in psychological research: The important role of debriefing. *Journal of Personality and Social Psychology, 44,* 1075-1082.

Soliday, E., & Stanton, A. L. (1995). Deceived versus nondeceived participants' perception of scientific and applied psychology. *Ethics & Behavior, 5,* 87-104.

Sommers, S. R., & Ellsworth, P. C. (2000). Race in the courtroom: Perceptions of guilt and dispositional attributions. *Personality and Social Psychology Bulletin, 26,* 1367-1379.

Sullivan, D. S., & Deiker, T. E. (1973). Subject-experimenter perceptions of ethical issues in human research. *American Psychologist, 28,* 587-591.

Tanke, E. D. (1979). Perceptions of ethicality of psychological research: Effects of experimenter status, experiment outcome, and authoritarianism. *Personality and Social Psychology Bulletin, 5,* 164-168.

Taylor, K. M., & Shepperd, J. A. (1996). Probing suspicion among participants in deception research. *American Psychologist, 51,* 886-887.

Thielicke, H. (1979). In W. H. Lazareth (Ed.), *Theological ethics: Vol. 1. Foundations.* Grand Rapids, MI: Eerdmans. (Original work published 1958-1959)

Tourangeau, R., Smith, T. W., & Rasinski, K. A. (1997). Motivation to report sensitive behavior on surveys: Evidence from a bogus pipeline experiment. *Journal of Applied Social Psychology, 27,* 209-222.

Toy, D., Wright, L., & Olson, J. (2001). A conceptual framework for analyzing deception and debriefing effects in marketing research. *Psychology & Marketing, 18,* 691-719.

U.S. Department of Health and Human Services. National Institutes of Health. Office for Protection From Research Risks. (2001). *Protection of Human Subjects.* 45 Code of Federal Regulations 46.

Warwick, D. P. (1975, February). Social scientists ought to stop lying. *Psychology Today, 8,* 38, 40, 105-106.

Weiss, D. J. (2001). Deception by researchers is necessary and not necessarily evil. *Behavior and Brain Sciences, 24,* 431-432.

CHAPTER 15

Confronting Ethical Issues in the Use of Animals in Biomedical and Behavioral Research

The Search for Principles

JOHN P. GLUCK
University of New Mexico and Georgetown University

JORDAN B. BELL AND MELODY PEARSON-BISH
University of New Mexico

There is strong evidence to support the contention that many scientists assume, or perhaps wish, that the practice of science and research exist in an environment necessarily free from the influence of values and from concerns for ethical principles. This widespread ideology pretends that the reflection on issues of values and ethics should be dealt with by others, while the scientist pursues pure unfettered truth. From this perspective, science is about, as *Dragnet's* detective Joe Friday used to say, "Just the facts ma'am, just the facts." In this view, facts are facts, and scientific theories and research strategies gain dominance or fall from favor on the singular basis of objective data unrelated to the shifting state of

values and assumptions that infect other human activities. Historians of science have shown this ideology to be patently false (e.g., Kuhn, 1973). What constitutes a fact or valid strategy cannot be extricated from the judgments of value. In an interesting example, Paul Forman (1971) convincingly demonstrated that the changes in German social structure between 1918 and 1927 set the stage for the advances in quantum theory. Specifically, he showed that as the social structure opened up to the indeterminacy and freewill arguments of existential thought, work in physics that emphasized related quantum theory concepts prospered. However, scientists in general and perhaps animal researchers in particular have all too often resisted the idea that ethical analysis is a fundamental part of their responsibility. For example, James Wyngaarden, former director of the National Institutes of Health (NIH), declared flatly at a conference at Michigan State University that "Science should not be hampered by ethical judgments" ("Director Addresses," 1989, p. 8).

To make things even more difficult, the history of research in the 20th century has amply demonstrated that the research environment itself can provide serious obstacles to ethical conduct. The extent of human suffering, the fever of scientific investigation and discovery, the requirements of academic promotion and competition, and the joy of personal acclaim and financial advantage may all tempt and perhaps at times seem to sanction inappropriate conduct. This was essentially the claim made over 35 years ago by Henry Beecher in a stunning paper published in the *New England Journal of Medicine*. In that well-known paper, Beecher (1966) outlined 22 examples of human clinical research that were in his view grossly unethical *on their face*. The field of psychology has its own examples of human research to contribute to this body of evidence. For example, we are reminded of the furor created by Stanley Milgram's (1963) work on obedience and cannot ignore some of the experiments conducted by the esteemed developmentalist Wayne Dennis. In these early experiments, Dennis (1935) housed a pair of twins in his back bedroom in extreme sensory and social deprivation so that he might test the various theories about the importance of the environment on the development of reaching behavior.

The crucial point for the present consideration is that the ethical problems of research are amplified enormously when the subjects of the research are beings whose nature and value are unknown or in dispute. When the entity cannot speak to us in our formal or gestural language, its predicament may go unrecognized. This is the reality faced by the researcher who uses animals as subjects of scientific investigation.

The historical evidence that reaches us across the expanse of time and culture attests to the more general conclusion that the ethical foundations that guide human and animal interactions have always been deeply troubled and uncertain (Gluck & Kubacki, 1991). What are we to make of the pictures created by the Ice Age artists in the great caves of northern Spain and southern France, whose sensitive renderings depict many of the animals that were the resources that nurtured human life? At Altamira, the bison stand strong and straight, and at Font de Gaume, reindeer seem to touch affectionately. Perhaps these pictures should be seen as acts of propitiation related to the apology rituals that are an essential part of hunting practices in many more contemporary aboriginal groups. Here, the notion is that the hunter's quarry willingly presents itself to be killed as long as the hunter shows the proper respect to the animal, who is in fact appreciated as a close relative. In other words, the hunter helps to justify the killing by creating the myth of the grateful prey. The Indian emperor Asoka, in the 3rd century B.C., acknowledged the moral status of both human and animals by attempting to create a medical system that was to be available to both humans and animals. Furthermore, his edicts that proscribed certain forms of animal treatment (e.g., blood sport) were publicized on stone pillars throughout the Indian continent. Yi-Fu Tuan's (1984) magnificent historical and psychological analysis of pet keeping shows how the practice is riddled with contradiction, which he summarized as the clash of the needs of domination and affection. In summary, humans have been struggling with the ethical base of the treatment of the animal other for centuries. Need we be surprised that our own relationships are conflicted?

In this context, the task taken up in this chapter is to propose a set of principles to guide the ethical deliberation around the justification of animal experiments. To accomplish this purpose, we will do the following:

1. Examine the important ethical thinking offered in support and in opposition to animal research justification

2. Entertain the question of the nature of animal cognition and its relation to ethical claims

3. Examine the history of regulation and the major components of those schemes

4. Conclude by considering the principles and obligations the researcher should shoulder

THE NATURE OF PRINCIPLES

Principles can be conceptualized in ethics two ways, *robust* or *prima facie*. Robust principles are applicable to a broad range of circumstances, are direct actions in a clear-cut and inflexible way, are unexceptional, and are foundational in that they provide a foundation on which other moral principles are justified by incorporating a theory. On the other hand, prima facie principles are characterized by humility. They are, as the designation implies, relevant to the ethical context in a general sense. However, they can be overridden in certain circumstances and are based on considered judgments instead of being strict derivations from a theory. They should be seen as attempts at capturing the deep intuitions of the best thinking in the common moral life. As a result, conflicts with circumstance and other principles are common and in a way, necessary (Beauchamp & Childress, 2001). For example, the important principle in biomedical ethics, "Do no harm," is a principle of the prima facie type. We can see that a caregiver faced with bad news about a patient must weigh and

balance the impact of the news on the patient's welfare. The potentially damaging effect of knowing the information is balanced against the harm of patient's ignorance. The metaphors of weighing and balancing are important here because they also imply limits to any ethical trade-off. As this example shows, prima facie principles keep the pressure on the decision maker's sensitivity and discernment. In this chapter, we strive toward this latter type of principles.

THE ANIMAL QUESTION AND BIOETHICS

Before we proceed to the body of our discussion, we should point out to the reader the reasons to maintain their attention, even if they are not involved in animal research or may not be concerned with its conflicts. The problem of ethical justification of animal research shares important properties with other crucial questions in the area of bioethics. In one sense, the animal issue poses the following question: What characteristics must an entity possess for it to come under the protection of the moral norms of a society? Presented in this way, we can see that the question is related to other important questions in bioethics, such as abortion, the definition of death, and the creation and use of embryonic stem cells for research purposes (for a more complete discussion, see Veatch, 2000). *Roe v. Wade* (1973) argued that a fetus gains access to the ethical protections of the state when it is potentially capable of living outside the body of the mother. Many disagree and look toward other criteria. Similarly, prior to 1966, a person was considered dead when and only when their heart and lungs lost all function. The Harvard Committee on the Definition of Death, which began to meet in the late 1960s (Harvard Medical School, 1968), argued that a person was dead not when cardiopulmonary function ceased, but when the brain failed to show evidence of any integrated electrical activity. In other words, a person whose heart was still beating due to the provision of artificial life support was nevertheless dead as long as there was no electrical activity in the brain. Some now argue that a person is dead not when the whole brain is dead, but when the parts of the brain that support important human-defining functions such as consciousness and thought no longer operate. The embryonic stem cell issue hinges on the question of what protections we are obliged to provide to a 5-day-old human embryo. Is the fact that this small collection of cells has the potential to develop into a human being sufficient to gain them access to some level of protection? What level? In summary, the questions about the justification of animal research do not stand separate from the matrix of difficult ethical problems in biomedical and behavioral research.

OVERVIEW OF THE PHILOSOPHICAL ISSUES

The Problem of Resistance

Unfortunately, there has been and continues to be a widespread resistance to the application of formal ethical analysis to the questions of animal experimentation. As we have seen, some of that resistance is inherent in an ideology of science that believes that ethics and values are outside the proper responsibility of scientists. Others have wrongly argued that if it is unethical to conduct a given experiment on a human being because of the risks involved, that fact alone justifies the use of animals. In other words, there is a fundamental rejection of the proposition that animal research is a subject worthy or in need of ethical inquiry—and thus a

rejection of the theories used in the analysis. For example, in 1990, the well-respected ethics institute the Hastings Center published a thorough and clearly middle-ground report on the ethics of animal research. Shortly after the issuance of the report, an important biomedical researcher, Professor Robert White, of Case Western Reserve University, contributed a letter to the Hastings Center journal in response to the report:

> I am extremely disappointed in this particular series of articles, which, quite frankly, has no right to be published as part of the Report.
>
> Animal usage is not a moral or ethical issue and elevating the problem of animal rights to such a plane is a disservice to medical research and the farm and dairy industry. (White, 1990, p. 43)

Recently, in what is on balance an interesting book about the proposed benefits produced by animal research for the discipline of psychology, Carroll and Overmier (2001) claim, without serious supportive argument, that the philosophies that question the moral justification of animal research do so "without substantial" foundation. They complain further that the theories are riddled with logical inconsistencies and are based on myth and untruths and imply that they are unworthy of consideration (p. 339). Interestingly, these statements follow an earlier discussion in the book about the historical sources of support for animal research, which draws heavily on biblical injunctions and Cartesian dualism (p. 7). It should also be pointed out that if this standard of total theoretical coherence were uniformly required of all psychological theories, the field would be reduced to a near vacuum. The authors also seem to fail to recognize the fact that their own rather compelling defense of animal research is based on a cost-benefit analysis that is intrinsic to many of the same theories they find seriously wanting. In the same volume, Adrian Morrison (2001), an intelligent and experienced researcher, questions the sources of motivation evident in individuals deeply interested in the animal question and responds with a crude ad hominum attack: "too much free time and money." In a sentence, he attempts to discredit centuries of conflict felt by many people of good faith. He then goes on to compare the animal liberation philosopher Peter Singer to the likes of the Nazi doctor Josef Mengele (p. 351). Still others argue that the character of scientists is such that they are beyond reproach and that everything that happens in the laboratory is the result of clear thinking, superb technique, and a respectful adherence to the law (Novak, 1991). A moment's reflection tells us that no human activity is without defect.

In addition to these factors, it must also be emphasized that resistance to serious ethical analysis on the part of some in the animal research community has been fueled by the radical protection elements. These elements have felt justified in their use of intimidation and acts of violence in their desire to bring a close to animal research. Although these acts may drive some individual investigators away from animal research, which may please them, it disengages the debate from the moral ground on which it belongs. These acts have also had the effect of sealing the laboratory away behind locked doors and security guards, decreasing public knowledge about the nature of animal research, and minimizing the public's input. What is needed is deepened understanding and not pithy one liners or threats. This debate is about the nature of animals, ethical coherency, scientific progress, and the moral identity of the participants of the debate. These issues must remain in focus, regardless of which side of the argument one currently accepts.

Arguments Against the Unrestricted Use of Animals

Most ethicists agree that the serious ethical study on the moral status of animals was reignited in the United States in the 1970s (for an excellent review, see DeGrazia, 1991). A major social theme of the time was a marked resurgence of the concern for the rights of oppressed individuals and populations, women's liberation, as well as a strong opposition to the government's involvement in the Vietnam War. These movements supported a skepticism about traditional conceptions of how some individuals are ordered in society's priorities and systems of justice. Others believed that previous thought on these matters was obsolete. Animals were the beneficiaries of this thinking. For example, in his important book *Animal Liberation* (1975), Peter Singer challenged the reader to evaluate the ethical foundations of the commonly accepted attitudes toward animal life as they had to do with issues such as food consumption and research. The book took the position that the reality of animal suffering taking place on the "factory farm" and in the laboratory was virtually unknown to the average citizen and therefore approved of in ignorance. The basic ethical claim of the book draws on the perspectives of the 18th and 19th-century utilitarians such as Jeremy Bentham and John Stuart Mill. The perspective turns on the idea that any entity capable of feeling pain, distress, and forms of rudimentary pleasure must be included under the umbrella of ethical consideration. Furthermore, equivalent amounts of pain must be considered equally, regardless of the species of the individual having the experience. "Higher" cognitive capabilities beyond the ability to experience pain and distress play a part in ethical judgments about the treatment of an individual insofar as those capabilities add to or detract from the experience of suffering. In other words, a human being facing an impending and untimely death might reflect on the loss of a future, friends, and family, the fact that they may not see their children grow up, and so on. These kinds of considerations are seen as increasing the painful burden of the situation and therefore make the human's situation more ethically problematic, let's say, as compared to a rat facing euthanasia in the laboratory. These same cognitive capabilities at other times may work to decrease the burden of suffering. For example, consider the human experiencing pain as a dentist removes a decayed tooth. Human patients can place the pain in context as they recognize that the pain will be short-lived and result in lowered probability of infection and improved health. A monkey having a decayed canine tooth removed is at a disadvantage resulting in a larger burden of suffering.

Singer further argued that when an entity is capable of feeling pain in response to our interactions with it, the reality of these consequences must be included in calculating needed justifications for the intervention. In short, animals matter ethically because their pain matters just as human pain matters.

> If a being suffers, there can be no moral justification for disregarding that suffering, and for refusing to count it equally with the like suffering of any other being. But the converse is also true. If a being is not capable of suffering, or of enjoyment, there is nothing to take into account. (Singer, 1990, p. 171)

The failure of applying the standard of equal consideration amounts to what Singer called "speciesism," which is akin to sexism and racism. He did not take the position that animals are always off-limits to human use. Rather, he argued that the justification for using animals must reach a very high standard such that the use is seen as maximizing benefits on balance for all those affected and that the benefit is not achievable in any other way.

In analyzing various uses of animals in science, Singer (1990) found this standard to be largely unmet and therefore concluded that the use of animals was unjustified. In fact, Singer leveled some of his most critical comments on research in psychology. In this criticism, Singer asserted that the extreme suffering produced by experiments such as Harry Harlow's work on the effects of early experience (see Harlow, Harlow, & Suomi, 1971) and Seligman's (see Seligman, 1975) work on learned helplessness were particularly egregious. Here, he saw the long line of experiments that repeated the original procedures, with only minor alterations in the variables, as clearly painful to the animals and woefully unjustified by the benefits. One can rightfully question whether Singer's calculations of cost and benefit are accurate, as his conclusion hinges on that accuracy. After all he is a philosopher, not a scientist, and there is enormous room for disagreement about what constitutes a research benefit.

In a related approach, Raymond Frey (2002), an ardent supporter of animal research, argues that as the ability of an entity to experience life increases due to emergence of capabilities such as intelligence, sentience, and self-direction, the value of that life also increases and deserves increasing ethical consideration. Therefore, a human being capable of appreciating the details and subtleties of life possesses a life whose value is greater than that, say, of a mouse who presumably does not possess those abilities. The human therefore deserves a higher level of protection. Frey, however, points out that there are many humans whose quality of life is lower than that of some animals. For example, compare a person in a permanent vegetative state to a healthy chimpanzee, both of whom are physiologically appropriate subjects for a particular research project.

In this particular case, according to Frey, the greater level of protection should go to the chimpanzee because its life is of a higher quality. Frey insists on consistency.

Both Singer and Frey ground their arguments about justification in terms of the consequences of acts that would involve animals in research. Tom Regan, on the other hand, grounds his arguments in the language of rights. Regan (1983) argued that animals have rights not to be harmed by virtue of the fact that they have inherent value and are what he called "subjects of life." By this, he meant that an entity has inherent and not conditional value (i.e., value is not earned) when there is some kind of experience that flows from being that entity. He argued that most animals possess some sense of themselves as entities existing through time. Furthermore, it could be said that they have an interest in their own welfare and rudimentary beliefs about how to carry on a life consistent with that welfare (Gluck & DiPasquale, 2002). For Regan, these rights are absolute, leaving no room for animal use as subjects of even valuable research.

Other philosophers, such as Mary Midgley and Steve Sapontzis, have added to the developing consensus that animals matter morally. Midgley (1984) developed the thesis that although our tendencies toward social bondedness may rightly lead us to prioritize humans, particularly members of our own social network, ahead of animals in many matters of ethical choice, the status of animals cannot be completely dismissed. Sapontzis (1987) further pointed out that attempts to alter the common practices of society that typically ignore the interests of animals are positively grounded in humans' long-accepted, overarching moral goals to become individuals who relieve and reduce suffering and attempt to behave fairly. In this vein, Bernard Rollin (1989) challenged the notion that we have a right to research and pointed out the lengths to which some scientists have gone to deny the reality of animal suffering.

Although all these positions certainly contain limitations and inconsistencies, the weight of the conclusions is that the use of animals for science requires serious reconsideration and alteration, with a burden of proof and standards of evidence.

Arguments in Favor of Animal Use

The views of the philosopher Carl Cohen have been most important to this side of the argument. In 1986, Cohen wrote an important paper titled "The Case for the Use of Animals in Biomedical Research," which was published in the influential *New England Journal of Medicine*. The article was then, and probably still is, the received position among the many biomedical scientists who believe that a theoretical analysis is relevant to the question of animal use. Cohen wants to emphasize the distinction between *obligations* and *rights*. For Cohen, an obligation is a self-generated norm of conduct, whereas rights are brought to bear on an individual in interactions with an outside community. He argued that although we have obligations to animals not to treat them badly or use them unnecessarily in research, any notion of rights, no matter how construed, is ludicrous when applied to animals. Rights, for Cohen, are valid "trump" cards played against external attempts to alter a person's life plans or preferences without their consent. They are trumps in the sense that once they are brought to bear or claimed by an individual, they are absolutely sufficient in negating the ethical foundation of the intended interference. Take, for example, a researcher who has a strong interest in examining the brain of a human patient showing symptoms of a clinically important disorder. It is permissible for the researcher to proceed with that examination only up to the point at which the patient says "Stop." This is the case even if the patient had earlier given his or her informed consent and the predicted benefits of the examination for the patient and society are exceptionally high. For Cohen, rights are relevant only to members of moral communities, places in which these types of reciprocal agreements are negotiated and acknowledged. Therefore, his theory of the basis of the right to ethical protection would appear to be grounded in the possession by community members of a set of cognitive abilities that give rise to the creation and maintenance of true moral communities. These cognitive criteria seem to require at a minimum such things as consciousness, self-awareness, and the ability to raise questions about one's behavioral motives (so-called second-order intentions or reflective consciousness) (Gluck & DiPasquale, 2002). Cohen sees these characteristics as uniquely human. Therefore, he concludes, using animals in research does not violate their rights, because they have none to violate. Instead, we have a moral imperative to do more useful research with animals and obligations to be respectful and humane. This position seems to provide a foundation of secure support for an expansive, nonrestricted animal research enterprise. He also rejects Singer's bleak analysis of the benefits produced by animal research, coming to a very different conclusion.

Since the publication of Cohen's important article, others have raised questions about his analysis. For example, Beauchamp (1997) pointed out that Cohen neglected to acknowledge the long-accepted correlation between obligations and rights: That is, if the common morality contains a consensus that animals should be exposed only to the minimum amount of discomfort consistent with good science and that animal alternatives should be used to reduce animal numbers

and usage, it is clearly appropriate to state that animals have a right to such treatment. Rollin (1989) comes to the same conclusion. Obligations and rights become disconnected only when the sense of obligation arises from a personal feeling, such as a sense of charity, as opposed to a social development of a consensus. Perhaps asking what rights animals have is a better question than whether they have rights at all. In addition, Cohen's analysis would seem to be logically consistent with the use of some human beings in invasive biomedical research. For example, humans who have permanently lost or never had the ability to experience consciousness or themselves as reflective persons (e.g., anencephalic infants and people in a permanent vegetative state) would seem to lose their membership in the rights-owning moral community. This would be consistent with Frey's analysis above. However, Cohen maintains their membership and high level of protection by basically asserting that membership in the human species alone is sufficient to confer rights protection. This begs the question about what is morally relevant about species membership in and of itself, other than it is advantageous to humans. This move further requires, basically, that the Judeo-Christian worldview be accepted as universal. In accepting his arguments without question, members of the research community prematurely raised Cohen's analysis to the level of the indisputable, thereby seriously constricting the discussion by scientists affected by the analysis.

Recently, Baruch Brody (2001) has offered an interesting analysis that grounds the use of animals in research by opposing the equal-consideration notions advanced by utilitarian writers such as Singer and Frey. Recall that impartiality in the consideration of the consequences of an act is a hallmark of utilitarian thinking. Brody begins by first affirming the perspective that it is now well established that animals deserve ethical consideration and that a position favoring the unrestrictive use of animals cannot be supported ethically. He then argues, contrary to Singer and Frey,

> That the same unit of pain counts less, morally, if it is experienced by an animal than it would if it is experienced by a human being, not because of the human's associated experiences, but simply because of the species of the experiencer. (Brody, 2001, p. 141)

He continues to argue that we as humans "have a morally permissible prerogative to pay special attention to our own interests in the fulfillment of some of our central projects" (Brody, 2001, p. 142). He does not argue that human interests always trump animal interests, only that at certain times we are permitted to discount, by some degree, the moral significance of animal pain. Brody goes further by suggesting that the idea of discounting the moral significance of others' interests has a long history in ethics. He asks the reader whether it is morally objectionable to argue that one ought to consider the well-being of one's own children over the well-being of other children. In other words, he rejects the claim of equal and impartial consideration of interests across species. Brody does not specify how we are to determine when discounting is permissible, but would seem to require that any human project that requires animal experimentation be of significant social significance.

The Argument of Benefit

There is no question that since the later part of the 19th century, animal experimentation has been an important part of the arsenal of science (Orlans, 1993). As the previous discussion highlights, it is possible to look at the results of an experiment and come to very different conclusions about whether the experiment produced benefits and whether those benefits were worth the material costs, the labor of the researchers, and the harm to the participants. The typical argument in the animal context pits many of these different conceptions of harm against one another. Those whose objections to animal research are grounded in judgments of insufficient benefit point to the fact that all too frequently, the experimentally produced insights were already well established, the empirical benefits were too meager to justify the harm, or the animal models used mapped poorly on the relevant human disease (see Shapiro, 1998).

Those staunchly in favor of animal research often argue that these considerations set too high a standard for the demonstration of benefit. For example, it has been conclusively shown that although chimpanzees can be infected with the HIV virus, they do not develop AIDS. Does this fact make studying them irrelevant to the worldwide endemic? Some would argue "Yes" to that question, whereas others argue that studying the initial stage of the infection might well provide useful insights into the human disease. Others who agree that the chimpanzee fails the equivalent-model criterion argue that research on them might yield a great deal about retroviruses in general and how they operate in primates (Hahn, Shaw, Cock, & Sharp, 2000). Therefore, arguments from benefit alone will not suffice in an ethical analysis. Rather, the argument from benefit must demonstrate that the benefits are not achievable in an alternative way, are indispensable, and offset the harms to the animals. This latter component requires that prospective researchers lay out for themselves and the review committee an in-depth, good-faith effort at detailing those harms and benefits. Glib explanations that seem to assume justification from the start undermine this necessary step. But just as an example of benefit cannot be used to justify all the experiments that follow the exemplar, neither can the establishment of a failure to produce anything but trivial benefits indict all animal research.

Animal Minds

As the previous discussion suggested, many ethicists have placed a heavy emphasis on the relationship between cognitive characteristics and the level of deserved moral protection. This connection can help inform the degree of pain, discomfort, and suffering that an entity is likely to experience. For example, Peter Carruthers (1992) posed the argument that although many different kinds of animals may seem to behave in ways that look to be versatile, conscious, and sensitive to pain, their experience may be nonconscious. He asked whether the apparent conscious component in animal behavior is like the person who gets in his car in Albuquerque, New Mexico, and drives the 57 miles to Santa Fe. On arrival at the proper highway exit, the driver "comes to" and realizes that he remembers almost nothing about the trip. However, anyone watching the driver from the outside would have noted evidence of supposed consciousness as the person altered speed, changed lanes, made judgments, and avoided danger. If animal behavior is nonconscious in a similar way, then there are no harms to them that we need to ethically consider. Although Carruthers cautioned that this is as yet too controversial and insecure a perspective on which to base standards of animal treatment, he accentuated the importance of knowing about the minds and experiences of animals (Gluck & DiPasquale, 2002). So, what do we know about animal minds?

Donald Griffin (1981, 1984, 1992) wrote a series of books that in effect implored the serious researcher to refocus research activities on the question of animal cognitive capabilities. He argued that one must not ignore the implications of anecdotal accounts of behavior such as cooperative hunting in lions, the activities of honey guides, the symbolic dances of bees, and deception in primates. He called for a thorough examination of these possibilities in both field and laboratory contexts. So began a rebirth of interest in animal consciousness. Where are we now with respect to these issues? We find ourselves in transition, a unique environment in which the remnants of the behaviorist aversion to the study or rejection of the existence of internal states and the sometimes wildly unguided anthropomorphism coexist side by side. Hauser (2000) has claimed that both extremes are off the mark and emphasized that knowledge of the details of the minds of animals cannot be rejected as nonexistent and cannot safely be generalized from what we know about adult human experience. Unique evolutionary pressures and considerations have shaped each animal species' mind.

REGULATORY ISSUES AND ETHICAL PRINCIPLES

Plato long ago pointed out that devices and systems, like law and politics, are ethics "writ large." In other words, codified laws and regulatory schemes (when they are good) reflect the standards of the common morality. In this vein, he humbly suggested that we really don't teach ethics to the people, at most we remind those interested in pursing a moral identity of what norms already exist. Therefore, we review some of the important statutory and regulatory concepts that have been writ large as a way to establish the nature and direction of the ethical evolution in animal research.

An important landmark in animal welfare legislation in the United States appeared in the February 4, 1966, issue of *Life* magazine. A banner headline on the cover declared "Concentration Camps for Dogs!" The story inside was based on an investigation of a private animal dealer who supplied dogs to research facilities. The stark and shocking photographs depicted an open yard full of starving, freezing, and dead dogs. There could be no mistake here. These dogs had suffered terribly during the course of their lives at this facility. The story also advanced the suspicion that some of these dogs were stolen pets. Another picture accompanying the story was striking, but in a different way. The picture was of a large mongrel dog whose chain collar had an ID tag clearly visible. The tag read "HMS M 680." This was a dog that had been returned to the dealer following a stint in a research lab. What lab? It was discovered that "HMS" stood for Harvard Medical School. The question begged to be asked: What was one of the premier research institutions in the United States doing conducting business with a dealer whose standards of animal care could reasonably be referred to as a concentration camp? In one breath, the question seemed to indict both the ethical and research standards of the research profession at large. The story and picture had a profound public impact. Shortly after the story appeared, the U.S. Congress passed the Laboratory Animal Welfare Act, or LAWA (1966). The title was changed in 1970 to the Animal Welfare Act (AWA). This moderate legislation had lain fallow for years prior to the exposé, strongly opposed by the research community. The story neutralized the opposition by raising questions about the integrity of science and scientists and the treatment of animals in research laboratories. Although this was the first national law in the United States, it had been preceded much earlier by international statutes, such as the 1876 Cruelty to Animals Act in England, and local initiatives, such as

the New York Anticruelty Bill of 1866. The 1966 AWA provided for modest changes in the laboratory situation, which centered primarily on the assurance of clean facilities, adequate cages, proper food, and protection to keep pets from being stolen and conscripted into laboratory service. This document made the statement that research animals were not mere laboratory supplies and that dogs and cats that had relationships with humans deserved a degree of increased protection. However, it wasn't until 1985 that major changes in the AWA and the passage of the Health Research Extension Act (1985) led to procedures that were concerned for the first time with both animal care and use in science. The concern of the public for the ways in which animals were treated when they were participating in an experiment was made clear with the creation of the Institutional Animal Care and Use Committee (IACUC). Specifically, these committees were mandated to evaluate the protocols with respect to what are referred to as the "Three Rs" (Russell & Burch, 1959), replacement, reduction, and refinement. The ethic stated that researchers should *replace* the use of animals when useful and effective alternatives are available; *reduce* the number of animals to the minimum necessary to accomplish the research validly; and *refine* experimental procedure so that the animals are exposed to the minimum of pain, distress, and discomfort in accomplishing a valid, useful research project. In addition, researchers using dogs and nonhuman primates were also to make provisions in the housing that showed respect for the animals' "psychological well-being and need for exercise."

Taken together, these provisions expressed a considerable increase in the domains for which the researcher was responsible. He or she was not only to pursue the scientific question at hand but also to concurrently limit the use and harm to which an animal should be exposed. Thus, a series of questions must be asked: What are the species' needs of this animal? What kind of pain or psychological damage might the animal experience in my experiment? What techniques are available to limit or minimize these impacts? Can I do this experiment without animals?

Like the initial passage of the AWA, these latter changes were nurtured by reports of alleged animal mistreatment that became widely known to the public. For example, in 1981, in an incident referred to as the "Silver Springs incident," a researcher named Edward Taub was charged with animal cruelty for what appeared to be slack and negligent treatment of nonhuman primates. Then, in May of 1984, animal activists broke into the laboratory of Thomas A. Gennarelli, of the University of Pennsylvania, who was studying the dynamics of closed head injuries in baboons. The activists stole approximately 30 videotapes that had been taken by the investigators during various experimental procedures. Although the tapes did not picture gratuitous cruelty, they did show surprising examples of sloppy experimental technique, a lack of surgical asepsis, indifference to and inadequate treatment of pain, and expressions of black humor that appeared disrespectful of the animals.

These unfortunate examples as well as the momentum for change that was developing from within some circles of the animal research profession itself led to the establishment of the IACUC. Prior to this point, if an institution had a review committee, its actions were likely limited to nonbinding recommendations. This move mirrored the function of the Human Research Institutional Review Board, which had earlier established the crucial principle of prereview and participant protection. Prereview conducted by a committee made up of scientists, nonscientists, veterinarians, and members of the public instantiates the principle that the decision to proceed with an experiment using live animals is a decision of a community, not just a scientifically committed individual or research team. The IACUC attempts to insure that the values expressed in the project go beyond the individual researcher. In particular, the public member is explicitly expected to represent the societal interests in the humane treatment of animals.

There are a number of important documents relevant to the regulation of animal research (U.S. Department of Agriculture, 1999; Public Health Service [PHS] "Guide," etc.) that are rich with detail and procedure, but the *U.S. Government Principles for the Utilization and Care of Vertebrate Animals Used in Testing, Research, and Training* (Office of Science and Technology Policy, 1985) is particularly noteworthy. Its nine principles describe the ethical foundation in much the same way the *Belmont Report* does for human research. Its influence on other conceptualizations (e.g., *American Psychological Association Guidelines for Ethical Conduct in the Care and Use of Animals;* APA, 1994) is clear. The heart of this document may be summarized as follows (Office of Science and Technology Policy, 1985):

Research on animals is potentially justifiable when it is conducted to advance the good of society in general, human and animal health, and knowledge (Principle II).

Good and worthy ideas are insufficient to justify research; the experimenters must be properly trained and know and follow the applicable laws and guides; and the animals selected must be appropriate and necessary to answer the question (Principles I, III, VIII).

Animal pain must be minimized by the appropriate use of anesthesia, sedatives, analgesia, and timely euthanasia. If a procedure causes pain in humans, it must be assumed that it causes pain in animals (Principles IV, V, VI).

Housing animals in the laboratory is not just a matter of just passive convenience for the researcher. Rather, the housing should contribute to the health and well-being of the animal by incorporating ethological information about the nature of the animal in its design and management (Principle VII).

Any exceptions to these treatment standards should be reviewed and approved by individuals authorized by the responsible institution other than the investigators themselves (Principle IX).

The Exclusion of Rats, Mice, and Birds

As this chapter is being written, a regulatory debate continues to rage in the U.S. Congress about the definition of an *animal.* Under the AWA, the Secretary of the U.S. Department of Agriculture (USDA) is given the responsibility to define which animals are covered by the act. As it currently stands, an animal means any live or dead dog, cat, non-human primate, guinea pig, hamster, rabbit, or any other warm-blooded animal that is being used or is intended for use in research, testing, experimentation, exhibition purposes, or as a pet. However, this definition currently excludes birds, rats of the genus *Rattus,* and mice of the genus *Mus* bred for use in research (USDA, 2001; the regulations, updated annually, also go on to exempt farm animals used for the production of food and fiber and research intended to improve their use as food and fiber, horses not used for research purposes, and other farm animals, such as but not limited to livestock or poultry used or intended for use in improving animal nutrition). In other words, rats, mice, and birds, which make up between 85% and 95% of animals used in

biomedical and behavioral research, are not covered by the AWA. They are, however, covered by the PHS regulations required by institutions taking federal money for research. What is the original meaning of this contradiction? The evidence of this exclusion supports the conclusion that the original exemption was meant by the framers of the AWA to be a temporary step as the law and regulations worked their way into professional practice. Instead, the continued exclusion has been supported by two basic arguments. First, because rats, mice, and birds are already covered under the PHS policy, the vast majority of the animals already receive protection. Here, the number of institutions not receiving federal research money is seen as small and diminishing. Second, extending the umbrella of protection will be a record-keeping and financial nightmare. The extent of this "nightmare" is hard to determine inasmuch as no regulations have been written. Because this phase allows for considerable public input, the concerns of the research community with respect to these issues would be no doubt considered. Whatever the basis of the resistance, it demonstrates a troubling rejection of the need to have our ethical obligations in animal research to be at least coherent. The fact that the APA is on record as opposing the inclusion of rats, mice, and birds under the AWA seems even more absurd given that a survey of the membership showed that more than 70% of nearly 4,000 respondents supported such coverage (Plous, 1996). It is indeed a troubling sign to see that when there is possible conflict between money and ethics, it is the ethical standard that is seen as expendable.

International Perspectives

Focusing on the status of U.S. practices is only part of the picture to which the serious student of these issues must attend. Looking more broadly, 23 countries currently have some form of animal research legislation. The countries included in this group are Australia (some states), Austria, Belgium, Denmark, Finland, France, Germany, Greece, Iceland, Ireland, Italy, Luxembourg, the Netherlands, New Zealand, Norway, Poland, Portugal, Spain, Sweden, Switzerland, Taiwan, the United Kingdom, and the United States (Orlans, 2002). Among members of this group, there is a wide degree of variation concerning the extent of the protection available for research animals. Orlans (2002) has developed a list of eight characteristics on which the various legislative attempts can be graded. She argues that a country with all eight characteristics represents the highest form of protection, while not at the same time excluding the practice (the principality of Liechtenstein is the only country that currently outlaws all forms of animal research or testing). The characteristics are as follows:

1. The provision of basic husbandry requirements and the regular inspection of facilities by an independent review group

2. Requirements that mandate the control of pain and suffering

3. Critical prereview of research proposals

4. Requirements for investigator competence

5. Bans on certain procedures, levels of pain and distress, sources of animals, or use of some species

6. Application of the "Three Rs"

7. The use of ethical criteria in the justification and decisional process

8. Requirements for investigators to rate the level of expected harm to the animals

When the requirements of the United States are compared with European standards, the central difference is related to item #5. In the United States, other than performing surgery with nonanesthetic paralytic agents, any investigative procedure producing any level of pain can conceivably be approved if the argument for benefits is credible. Any level of human benefit may be an adequate justification for any level of experimentally induced animal harm. In other words, there is no point at which animal interests rise to the level of trumping the search for human benefit. On the other hand, in the United Kingdom, the ethic has moved to the position that experimental procedures that produce extreme levels of pain and distress are not permitted, regardless of the predicted benefits. In general, the standards in the European community do not rise to that level of protection, but do require that research in which harms are not balanced by benefits must not proceed (see Brody, 1998).

PRINCIPLES AND CONCLUSIONS

What follows is a limited list of general ethical principles of the prima facie type, which we offer as guidelines. They are meant to supplement and emphasize the core aspects of the more detailed descriptions such as the PHS "Guide" and the *APA Guidelines* and to stimulate reflection. They emerge from the previous considerations of ethical theory, the direction of regulation, and the contributions of animal research to science. The principles assume that the production of human benefit is the primary purpose of the research.

1. *Justification.* Research on animals is potentially justifiable when it is conducted in order to significantly advance the good of society in general, human and or animal health, and knowledge. Justification should be based on the input of the scientific community, the general public, and those concerned with animal welfare.

2. *Standing.* Animals matter morally. Participation as a subject of research typically alters the lives of animals in ways that inherently affect their interests negatively. Consideration of their interests must be

demonstrated in at least the following ways:

a. The appropriateness of the use of an animal must be established first.

b. The beginning presumption ought to be that animal use is considered only after a search for nonanimal alternatives and the conclusion that human participants are scientifically and/or ethically inappropriate. If an animal is to be used, it must be an animal whose attributes are consistent with what is being studied and not just a matter of convenience.

c. Pain, discomfort, and distress must be carefully estimated for each experiment and minimized to the greatest extent possible.

d. There will be circumstances in which the harm to an animal in an experiment will be at such an extreme level that the animal's needs and moral status trump human research goals and therefore its use is precluded.

e. An experimental animal must be housed in a way that reflects its needs. Animals have an evolved and developed nature that connects them to their environments and lives in unique ways, such as what they eat, how they eat, whether and with whom they consort, how they make use of their environment during sleep and wakefulness, and so on. These physical and psychological factors should be accommodated to the greatest extent possible for both the comfort of the animal and the quality of the science.

f. If animals are to be used, only the minimum number necessary to accomplish a valid scientific goal should be used.

3. *Competence.* In addition to the competencies required to carry out the specific scientific goals of research, investigators also need to be knowledgeable about research ethics, the identification and treatment of pain and distress in the animals, ethological and ecological factors relevant to the animals used, and the development and availability of animal alternatives.

4. *Remaining responsibilities.* Animal researchers acknowledge that even when an experiment meets proper standards of justification, animal lives most likely will be harmed. This leaves residual ethical responsibilities to be discharged. In human research, those responsibilities are discharged through procedures such as debriefing, offer of follow-up services, remuneration, feedback about results, and so on. In the case of animals, the discharge of these responsibilities takes the following form:

a. Ensuring continued research competence and skill

b. Supporting reasonable regulatory initiatives that serve to protect the well-being of animals and acknowledge their moral status

c. Helping to ensure the integrity and humaneness of those involved in animal research

d. In some cases, such as those involving the great apes, helping to support animals' postresearch retirement and care

FINAL COMMENT: KEEPING IN TOUCH WITH THE PUBLIC

A few years ago, a well-known psychologist visited our department to discuss his research, which focused on the neurobiological bases of learning. In his research, rabbit subjects were classically conditioned to some criterion and then subjected to various brain lesions. The effects of these lesions on the previously conditioned responses were then evaluated. This researcher had been involved in this work for many years. After his colloquium was concluded and people met to socialize and talk informally, he recounted an encounter that he had as he'd traveled to give the talk. His plane had been delayed, and a small group of passengers sat together in a café to pass the time. Eventually, he was asked about his work. With pride, he began to describe his research and the animal experiments that were an intrinsic part. He described to us his utter shock when some members of the passenger group expressed strong disapproval. He was caught completely off-guard about the existence of public sentiment that questioned the use of animals in research. As I listened, I was shocked that this brilliant scholar could have missed the reality and importance of this controversy.

This story illustrates the result of science education that frequently has asserted that scientists work in a value-free environment and need not be concerned with the ethical beyond being in compliance with the relevant laws. On the contrary, science is not value-free, but operates embedded in the common morality. Therefore, scientists have a responsibility to stay abreast of ethical thought, not just attend to our own limited perspectives. My colleague of many years, Frank Logan, encouraged his students in this regard by always asking the following question at the final Ph.D. defense: "Suppose that you are at a social function and you are introduced as just having received your Ph.D. to a member of the general public. The person is interested and asks about the nature of your work. Describe in less than 5 minutes the nature and significance of this work in language free from scientific jargon." The spirit of the question communicated the fact that we as scientists have a responsibility to the society at large. It also suggested that talking to the public about our work places us in a position to receive feedback from those who support our education and research, both directly and indirectly. Sometimes, we think that we need only to educate the public and they will certainly support us. Although this may frequently be the case, the reality of the contrary must be faced, understood, and integrated. As scientists, we must be receptive to learning from the concerns and insights from representatives of diverse perspectives.

REFERENCES

American Psychological Association. (1994). *Guidelines for ethical conduct in the care and use of animals.* Washington, DC: American Psychological Association.

Beauchamp, T. (1997). Opposing views on animal experimentation: Do animals have rights? *Ethics and Behavior, 7*(2), 113-21.

Beauchamp, T., & Childress, J. (2001). *The principles of biomedical ethics.* New York: Oxford University Press.

Beecher, H. (1966). Ethics and clinical research. *New England Journal of Medicine, 274,* 1354-1360.

Brody, B. (1998). *The ethics of biomedical research: An international perspective.* New York: Oxford University Press.

Brody, B. (2001). Defending animal research: An international perspective. In E. F. Paul & J. Paul (Eds.), *Why animal experimentation matters: The use of animals in medical research.* New Brunswick: Transaction.

Carroll, M. E., & Overmier, J. B. (2001). *Animal research and human health.* Washington, DC: American Psychological Association.

Cohen, C. (1986). The case for the use of animals in biomedical research. *New England Journal of Medicine, 315,* 865-870.

Carruthers, P. (1992). *The animal issue: Moral theory in practice.* Cambridge, UK: Cambridge University Press.

DeGrazia, D. (1991). The moral status of animals and their use in research: A philosophical review. *Kennedy Institute of Ethics Journal, 1*(1), 48-70.

Dennis, W. (1935). The effect of restricted practice upon the reaching, sitting, and standing of two infants. *Journal of Genetic Psychology, 47,* 17-32.

Director addresses health research. (1989, February 27). *Michigan State News,* p. 8.

Forman, P. (1971). Weimar culture, causality, and quantum theory, 1918-1927: Adaptation by German physicists and mathematicians to a hostile intellectual environment. In R. McCormmach (Ed.), *Historical studies in the physical sciences* (pp. 1-116). Philadelphia: University of Pennsylvania Press.

Frey, R. (2002). Ethics, animals, and scientific inquiry. In J. Gluck, T. DiPasquale, & F. B. Orlans (Eds.), *Applied ethics in animal research: Philosophy, regulation, and laboratory applications* (pp. 13-24). West Lafayette, IN: Purdue University Press.

Gluck, J. P., & DiPasquale, T. (2002). Introduction and overview. In J. P. Gluck, T. DiPasquale, & F. B. Orlans (Eds.), *Applied ethics in animal research: Philosophy, regulation, and laboratory applications* (pp. 1-11). West Lafayette, IN: Purdue University Press.

Gluck, J. P., & Kubacki, S. R. (1991). Animals in biomedical research: The undermining effect of the rhetoric of the besieged. *Ethics and Behavior, 1*(3), 157-173.

Griffin, D. (1981). *The question of animal awareness.* New York: Rockefeller University Press.

Griffin, D. (1984). *Animal thinking.* Cambridge, MA: Harvard University Press.

Griffin, D. (1992). *Animal minds.* Chicago: University of Chicago Press.

Hahn, B., Shaw, G., Cock, K., & Sharp, P. (2000). Aids as a zoonosis: Scientific and public health implications. *Science, 287*(5453), 607-14.

Harlow, H. F., Harlow, M. K., & Suomi, S. J. (1971). From thought to therapy: Lessons from a primate laboratory. *American Scientist, 59,* 538-549.

Harvard Medical School. (1968). A definition of irreversible coma. Report of the ad hoc Committee of the Harvard Medical School to examine the definition of brain death. *Journal of the American Medical Association, 205,* 337-340.

Hauser, M. (2000). *Wild minds.* New York: Henry Holt.

Health Research Extension Act, Pub. L. 99-158 (1985).

Kuhn, T. (1973). *The structure of scientific revolutions.* Chicago: University of Chicago Press.

Laboratory Animal Welfare Act, Pub. L. 89-544 (1966).

Midgley, M. (1984). *Animals and why they matter.* Athens: University of Georgia Press.

Milgram, S. (1963). Behavioral study of obedience. *Journal of Abnormal and Social Psychology, 67,* 371-378.

Morrison, A. (2001). A scientist's perspective on the ethics of using animals in behavioral research. In M. Carroll & J. B. Overmier (Eds.), *Animal research and human health.* Washington, DC: American Psychological Association.

Novak, M. (1991, July). Psychologists care deeply about animals. *APA Monitor,* p. 4.

Office of Science and Technology Policy. (1985). U.S. government principles for the utilization and care of vertebrate animals used in testing, research, and training. *Federal Register, 50*(97).

Orlans, F. B. (1993). *In the name of science: Issues in responsible animal experimentation.* New York: Oxford University Press.

Orlans, F. B. (2002). Ethical themes of the national regulations governing animal experiments: An international perspective. In J. Gluck, T. DiPasquale, & F. B. Orlans (Eds.), *Applied ethics in animal research: Philosophy, regulation, and laboratory applications.* West Lafayette, IN: Purdue University Press.

Plous, S. (1996). Attitudes toward the use of animals in psychological research and education: Results from a national survey of psychologists. *The American Psychologist, 51*(11), 1167-1180.

Regan, T. (1983). *The case for animal rights.* Berkeley: University of California Press.

Roe v. Wade, 410 U.S. 113 (1973).

Rollin, B. (1989). *The unheeded cry: Animal consciousness, animal pain and science.* New York: Oxford University Press.

Russell, W., & Burch, R. (1959). *The principles of humane experimental technique.* London: Meuthen.

Sapontzis, S. (1987). *Morals, reasons and animals.* Philadelphia: Temple University Press.

Seligman, M. E. P. (1975). *Helplessness: On depression, development, and death.* San Francisco: Freeman.

Shapiro, K. (1998). *Animal models of human psychology.* Seattle, WA: Hogrefe and Huber.

Singer, P. (1975). *Animal liberation: A new ethics for our treatment of animals.* New York: New York Review.

Singer, P. (1990). *Animal liberation: A new ethics for the treatment of animals* (2nd ed.). New York: New York Review.

Tuan, Y-F. (1984). *Dominance and affection: The making of pets.* New Haven: Yale University Press.

U.S. Department of Agriculture. (1999). *Animal Welfare Act regulations,* Title 9, Volume 1, Code of Federal Regulations.

U.S. Department of Agriculture. (2001). *Animal Welfare Act regulations* (Rev.), Title 9, Volume 1 § 1.1, Code of Federal Regulations. (Also see the World Wide Web at: http://www.nal.usda.gov/awic/legislat/ regsqa.htm)

Veatch, R. (2000). *The basics of bioethics.* Upper Saddle River, NJ: Prentice Hall.

White, R. (1990, November/December). Animal ethics? *Hastings Center Report,* p. 43.

CHAPTER 16

Ethical Considerations in Psychological Assessment

HENRY E. ADAMS AND KRISTEN A. LUSCHER
University of Georgia

Assessment, as it relates to the field of psychology, serves an important function when working with others. Human beings by nature are intricately complicated, and assessment is a valuable tool that enables one to understand the many unique facets and ubiquitous dimensions of another individual. Carelessness or lack of knowledge in assessment sets the stage for encountering myriad problems and, in turn, can lead to detrimental consequences that jeopardize both the welfare of the individual being assessed and the psychologist performing the assessment. With this in mind, one should begin to reflect on the ethical considerations required of a psychologist who engages in assessment. This chapter is therefore dedicated to discussing the connection between ethicality and assessment in psychology.

The objectives for this chapter are twofold. First, the chapter will discuss the main areas in which assessment is typically implemented and highlight important ethical concerns and/or dilemmas that often accompany these areas. Second, the chapter will also devote time to outlining proper procedures for conducting a solid assessment, which will help to reduce the likelihood of encountering ethical violations.

AREAS OF ASSESSMENT

Sattler (1986) identified "four pillars" of assessment from which one is likely to gain valuable information. Specifically, the "four pillars" of assessment include norm-referenced tests, interviews, observation, and informal assessment. Implicitly, these individual components complement one another and provide a firm foundation from which one can make decisions and recommendations based on the accompanying assessment.

Norm-Referenced Tests

Norm-referenced tests are one type of assessment measure frequently encountered by psychologists. Norm-referenced tests are measurement tools standardized on a clearly defined group, often referred to as a *norm group,* such that each individual score reflects a rank within that particular group (Sattler, 1986). In the best-case scenario, these norm-referenced tests should have measures of both reliability and validity, which serve as indexes to aid the psychologist in deciphering the acquired score(s) for a particular individual in relation to how other individuals typically score on the same assessment measure(s). *Reliability* is referred to as the consistency of a measure, whereas *validity* refers to the content and whether the measure assesses a particular domain of interest (Kazdin, 1992). According to the American Psychological Association ethical code (APA, 1992) set for psychologists, using norm-referenced tests that are not reliable or not valid creates an ethical dilemma when making projections of an individual's ability from test scores, because one can never guarantee if the examiner's interpretation accurately represents that individual's performance in relation to the performance of others.

Moreover, Section 1.06 (Basis for Scientific and Professional Judgments) of the APA ethics code (1992) states that psychologists must rely on scientifically and professionally derived knowledge when making judgments, albeit with regard to a particular individual or the test scores that represent such an individual. In addition, psychologists must specifically define the purpose of using a particular testing measure, have viable reasons for its administration, and interpret any testing information in conjunction with the guidelines provided for that specific test. As stated by Loveland (1985), regardless of the type of assessment instrument being used, the most important issues of professional competence concern clearly defining what is to be measured. He stresses the notion that the implementation of any psychological instrument requires a clearly specified reason for its use.

In addition, a psychologist should use only those tests that one is competent to administer and avoid using testing materials that do not fall within his or her range of training and expertise. Section 1.04 (Boundaries of Competence) and Section 1.05 (Maintaining Expertise) of the APA ethics code (1992) emphasize the need for a psychologist to operate in only those areas in which he or she is competent. Specifically, Section 1.04 states that psychologists should recognize the areas of their competence as well as the limits of it, whereas Section 1.05 mandates maintaining knowledge of current information within an individual's field of activity. These standards support the notion that competence is not a permanent construct and individuals must maintain some degree of awareness regarding their level of competency to avoid ethical dilemmas. Competence can be maintained by reading current literature, attending professional workshops, attending conventions, and involving oneself in other related scholarly activities.

When using norm-referenced tests, one should never focus exclusively on an obtained score but, instead, should use this information in the appropriate context to address the initial reason for administering the test. Norm-referenced tests are useful in that administration occurs within a relatively short period of time and substantial information can be obtained from such tests (Sattler, 1986). Moreover, norm-referenced tests provide an objective measure with regard to a particular aspect of the individual being assessed. The information gained from this form of assessment, when used correctly, can be plentiful and create a foundation from which to base an assessment.

Interviews

Interviews are another means of gathering information about an individual, particularly as it relates to the subjective account of his or her presenting problem. Interviews also allow psychologists to assess and interpret information on the basis of interactions with the individual in a more or less open-ended format. Interviews can be either standardized (i.e., Structured Clinical Interview for the *DSM-IV* [SCID]) or unstandardized (i.e., initial intakes). Regardless of the format, the information garnished often supplements other forms of assessment techniques, such as norm-referenced tests. Psychologists are cautioned to interpret this information only within the context from which it was obtained, and overgeneralization should be avoided unless it is otherwise warranted. Because this information is considered confidential, the APA ethical code (1992) asserts that psychologists must maintain the privacy of the individual and present any interview material in a nonidentifiable manner unless otherwise required by law. This is reiterated in Section 5.03 (Minimizing Intrusions of Privacy) of the ethical standards, which states that no information should be released by a psychologist to anyone other than the individual being assessed and/or his or her guardian without consent from either relevant party except under court order. Care should be taken to avoid, when possible, interviewing a person without his or her consent.

Observation

Observation can be the most subjective technique employed to gather information, because it is generally filtered through the interpretation of the psychologist. Despite the subjectivity of this approach, observation is a means of gathering a substantial amount of information about an individual that would not otherwise be captured in formal testing procedures. Like interviewing, observation can be and is often used to interpret norm-referenced tests and increase the accuracy of test interpretation by confirming or disconfirming obtained results. Take, for instance, a case in which an individual is being administered an intelligence test during which he or she displays a high degree of anxiety. Observing the client's anxiety level can aid the psychologist in interpreting the standardized scores and may explain findings that would not otherwise be identified through the specified administration and interpretation procedures of the test, such as poor performance due to the interference of anxiety rather then cognitive deficits. Psychologists should be aware of the subjectivity related to this assessment technique and take the necessary means to avoid misinterpreting or overstating the observations made at any point during the assessment. However, some behavioral assessments have well-defined techniques for observation that are clearly documented. Because behavioral assessments tend to measure a narrow aspect of a specific behavior (i.e., tic frequency), the usefulness of this approach is limited.

Informal Assessment

In some cases, norm-referenced tests are supplemented with informal assessment procedures that may or may not be standardized or normed, such as *criterion-referenced tests* (Sattler, 1986). The main drawback associated with the use of such assessment techniques is the possibility of low reliability and validity. This is not to say that informal assessment tests are consistently characterized by poor reliability and validity; some of these assessment instruments have adequate reliability and validity indexes. Due to the existing possibility, however, it is important when using this type of measure to maintain an awareness of the psychometric properties of the assessment measure being used. As Stated in Section 1.06 (Basis for Scientific and Professional Judgments) of the APA ethical code (1992), tests should be scientifically based such that appropriate indexes of reliability and validity are stated. Thus, forms of assessment with these characteristics should be used with extreme caution, and psychologists are recommended to confirm findings of such tests with other forms of information, such as norm-referenced tests or observation. By matching the results of assessment measures with low reliability and validity to the results of tests with high reliability and validity, one can ensure that they are indeed measuring similar constructs of interest. Psychologists are also warned against using these types of assessment measures as independent sources from which to base assessments.

TECHNIQUES FOR PSYCHOLOGICAL ASSESSMENT

After considering some ethical standards related to assessment, it is essential to have a solid understanding of accurate assessment methodology. Adhering to a proper assessment protocol can avoid many ethical dilemmas. Based on years of personal involvement with assessment measures, several recommended guidelines will be outlined during this section of the chapter that are beneficial in helping one conduct a proper assessment.

First, all assessments should begin with an interview. It is likely that the interview will occur during the first meeting between a psychologist and client. During the interview, the goal of the psychologist is to gather relevant information pertaining to the individual's presenting problem, historical events that may have precipitated or contributed to the presenting problem, and observational data that may not be obtainable during formal testing procedures (i.e., appearance, speech, orientation, etc.). Because the psychologist and the client are entering the beginning stage of a working relationship, it is also paramount that the psychologist

establish rapport with his or her client and make reasonable efforts within the context of the interview to facilitate this process. Moreover, the interview is of fundamental importance because it determines the course of the subsequent assessment and guides the psychologist in selecting relevant devices to evaluate the client's presenting problem. It is also important that the interviewer inform the person about the nature of the assessment and obtain informed consent for the individual in written form (Koocher, 1994). A standard form that meets ethical guidelines should be maintained for this purpose.

When selecting relevant assessment devices, it is advised that one adhere to several guidelines. First, it is crucial to select assessment instruments that are based on the conceptualization of the client's presenting problem. The goal when choosing assessment devices is to use only those devices that will aid in identifying and describing the client's presenting problem previously obtained during the interview. It is inappropriate to haphazardly select a variety of devices that are not germane to the psychologist's conceptualization of the case. Some psychologists, for example, employ the "shotgun" approach in which they administer a plethora of assessment instruments under the assumption that more is better. The basis for using such a practice is the hope that some of the selected devices will by chance glean information relevant to the presenting problem, which may or may not have been originally conceptualized. This technique is counterproductive when considering the expense to both the psychologist and client. Binder and Thompson (1994) advise psychologists to refrain from the misuse of assessment techniques by using them for their specified purpose only, which will decrease the haphazard use of assessment devices. Therefore, sufficient rationale for the use of any assessment device, largely influenced by the hypotheses regarding the presenting problem obtained during the interview, must exist prior to its selection.

Furthermore, when selecting assessment devices, one must understand that no single device can measure all aspects of an individual's functioning. It is, therefore, more appropriate to use a "package" of measures that provide a complete and comprehensive picture of the individual guided by the psychologist's conceptualization of the client's presenting problem. Kazdin (1992) states that the presenting problem or "construct of interest" is multifaceted and therefore comprises many components. Because this is the typical situation most psychologists will encounter, he continues to reinforce the notion that no single measure will capture the different aspects related to the "construct of interest." Thus, implementing a package of measures designed to assess the different facets of the presenting problem will increase the effectiveness of the assessment procedure as it relates to identifying and evaluating the presenting problem.

When selecting appropriate measures, the psychologist must also be fully cognizant of the existing research or literature relevant to the chosen device (Binder & Thompson, 1994). This includes being aware of the measure's intended use, indexes of both reliability and validity, and normative data that specify the degree of generalizability that can be ascertained from the results. To select the most efficacious assessment measure, one must consider which tool will produce the most substantiated results, supported by its reliability and validity indexes. Situations may arise in which an individual chooses to administer a device that does not meet all of the earmarks outlined in the APA ethical code. According to Binder and Thompson (1994), examples of such devices include, but are not limited to, using experimental instruments without validity or standardization,

using assessment devices on populations in which use is not intended, and interpreting of assessment devices that are not supported by research. This is not to say that psychologists should always refrain from using "experimental" assessment devices, but awareness of the possibility of error related to such devices should be high.

If one chooses to use an experimental device, he or she should be prepared to demonstrate that there is at least minimal evidence of reliability and validity related in some meaningful way to the problem being assessed. At the very minimum, the examiner should include some research evidence supporting reliability and criterion-related validity that is based on normative data, as justification for employing such an experimental device is required. One way to justify its use is to administer other scales supported and fully documented by research that measure the phenomenon of interest. The psychologist can then compare the experimental devices with fully standardized devices to assess the convergent validity that exists between the two measures. *Convergent validity* refers to the extent to which two measures assess similar or related constructs (Kazdin, 1992). If the measures correlate highly with one another, one can assume that the two measures overlap. Furthermore, if there is a high convergent validity index, then one can assume that the experimental device is measuring the same construct intended to be assessed by the standardized measure. This helps to ensure that the experimental device is truly measuring the same phenomenon, particularly when compared with similar tests that have shown to accurately assess the specified target. Examiners should also carefully document the limitations and reservations about the accuracy of any assessment device that has not received full standardization when reporting findings (Binder & Thompson, 1994).

Finally, the psychologist must also evaluate his or her own level of competence with regard to assessing the client's presenting problem (Binder & Thompson, 1994; Kane, 1992; Loveland, 1985). Kane (1992) defined competence as "the ability to use professional knowledge and skills to solve the problems that arise in [assessment]" (p. 165). He further asserts that competence is comprised of two major components. One component includes the domain impossible interactions that the psychologist is expected to manage, and the other is the knowledge, skills, and judgment that he or she employs during these interactions (Kane, 1992). Domain is specified as any "professional encounter" involving a psychologist, a client, and a reason for professional intervention (Kane, 1992). The APA ethical code (1992) clearly states that it is unethical to administer any assessment devices in which an individual has not been properly trained. An example reflecting an ethical violation of competence would occur if a psychologist specializing in the assessment of adult schizophrenia chose to conduct an assessment of a child aimed at evaluating sexual victimization. This is not to say that this person is excluded from ever evaluating children presumably exposed to sexual abuse but, rather, that he or she is required to obtain appropriate training that specifically addresses the needs of the populations in which he or she is unfamiliar. If the occasion arises and one finds that he or she does not possess the competence to evaluate the client's presenting problem or administer relevant assessment measures, it is best for that professional to refer the client to another psychologist who is adequately and competently trained to conduct the necessary assessment.

Another issue relevant to the selection and administration of assessment measures occurs during situations that involve the legal system. It is not uncommon for psychologists

to find themselves involved in assessments deemed necessary by the legal system, such as custody evaluations, lawsuits regarding bodily injury, psychological evaluations for need-based programs, and even criminal cases. When this occurs, the psychologist should carefully document all assessment procedures implemented, and evidence supporting the use of such procedures is recommended in the event that the psychologist is asked to substantiate the findings in a court of law. Furthermore, the psychologist should also document information that supports his or her competency for administering such procedures and evaluating results gathered from the assessment process. This procedure ensures both the integrity of the administration techniques and the reputation of the psychologist making the requested evaluation.

The courts will usually have specified legal criteria in place before a psychologist is allowed to testify, which is typically indicated in the Daubert test. The Daubert test outlines standards that ensure that the administered test meets the requirements for use in a scientific community as well as its customary or common use. Specifically, the Daubert test ensures that any information given as expert testimony in a court case meet the following requirements: (a) the expert's theory or assessment methods have been tested, (b) the expert's testimony has been subjected to peer review or evaluation, (c) the assessment method being used has established a potential rate of error, and (d) the assessment technique is accepted by the scientific community for each of the given tests prior to testifying in the actual court proceedings (Ceci & Bruck, 1996).

CONDITIONS OF THE ASSESSMENT

Once the psychologist has determined the assessment devices that are to be used, he or she is ready to begin the actual administration of these devices. The next section will focus on outlining criteria that should be present during the actual assessment procedure.

Whenever a psychologist administers an assessment device to a client, he or she is required to clearly explain the purpose and procedures of the particular device. The client has the right to be fully informed about the assessment procedures, use of the results prior to engaging in the process, and information regarding confidentiality of the assessment (Koocher, 1994). All clients must give legally informed consent before assessment proceeding can begin. In cases involving a client who is a minor or who is incapable of giving consent (e.g., profoundly impaired, severely disturbed), a legal guardian must provide permission for the individual to engage in the specified assessment. During situations in which an assessment has been ordered by the court system, the psychologist must make clear to the client that his or her responses will not remain confidential and that it is the psychologist's obligation to supply the court system with any requested material.

Finally, the client should be given the opportunity to ask questions pertaining to any area of the assessment that he or she finds unclear (i.e., purpose, task instructions, etc.). Although the client may appear to understand the specified instructions, the psychologist should not take this assumption for granted, because many clients may not attend to all presented information or may not strictly adhere to the instructions for the test. Assessing for such an event will improve the chances of obtaining accurate information about the client.

During the administration process, the psychologist should be attuned to specific situations that occur within the testing environment. The psychologist must supervise the administration of all assessment devices to ensure that the client is following the directions of the tests and is demonstrating the required efforts necessary to meet the criteria of the administered devices. The client should never be allowed to take any assessment devices outside the testing environment (i.e., taking the test home). Taking assessment devices outside a secured area jeopardizes the integrity of the test, and the psychologist cannot conclude with absolute certainty that the assessment devices were completed accurately, or for that matter, even completed by the client at all.

Furthermore, the psychologist must also query the client about drug and/or alcohol use that may have occurred prior to the testing session. Obviously, a client who is under the influence of an intoxicating substance will not perform to his or her full potential. In addition, the psychologist should ensure that the client is well rested and mentally prepared to engage in the required tasks. Providing breaks throughout the testing session will reduce fatigue and increase accuracy of testing information supplied by the client. In short, it is the responsibility of the psychologist to evaluate outside influences that may alter the results obtained during the assessment process. If this criterion is not met, the results garnished may be inaccurate and may not generalize to the presenting problem.

WRITING THE REPORT

Report writing is the final aspect of the assessment process. It provides the primary means for presenting the results of the assessment, stating conclusions drawn from the results, and specifying recommendations for the future course of action. The purpose of the report is to share information found during the assessment with others who have a vested interest in the assessment outcome (including the client). The audience is the first factor to consider when writing a report. When assessing the audience, it is important to evaluate its level of understanding about assessment procedures and results. The vocabulary used within the report should match the level of the audience, and technical jargon that is not universally recognized should be avoided when possible. However, altering the vocabulary of the report to match the audience should not alter the report's thoroughness or professionalism.

Moreover, the report should not include dogmatic statements, because the results gathered from the assessment are under no circumstances absolute. Rather, the results reflect an individual's functioning within a given situation and during a circumscribed period of time. An assessment will also not provide absolute answers or truths, due to the fact that both tests and examiners are flawed. It would, therefore, be incorrect for a psychologist to include within his or her report a statement such as "The individual being assessed is schizophrenic," because results will not conclusively indicate the nature of this finding. Rather than dealing with absolute truth, the psychologist must contend with statistical probability when documenting and reporting assessment findings. Statistical probability will indicate the likelihood of the results given the natural occurrence of these results in the general population. Probability statements regarding the obtained results indicate the degree of certainty associated with the assessment findings and provide an index that specifies the degree to which the findings cannot conclusively "rule out" other arbitrary possibilities. In short, there may be error, and therefore it would be more appropriate to include a statement such as "From the results of the present assessment, the individual appears to demonstrate characteristics similar to those diagnosed with schizophrenia" within the report, as opposed to the first statement.

The written report should also include within its context a description of the circumstances surrounding the assessment. The description should include information pertaining to the relevant characteristics of the assessment procedure(s), typical behavior of the client during the assessment, and the relationship between the psychologist and the client (e.g., level of rapport). Based on these factors, the psychologist should also include an accuracy index of the obtained results designed to delineate the reliability of his or her findings and conclusions. Any recommendations pertaining to the relevant assessment should be clearly stated within the report and should be based on objective, rather than subjective, evidence assembled from the subsequent assessment devices. The findings and conclusions specified within the report should be documented in such a way that does not make them subject to a variety of interpretations.

When evaluating the client, the psychologist should not state within the report any information that cannot be documented, such as absolute statements and projections without proper foundation. Thus, the psychologist should not make statements that cannot be substantiated by the obtained data. This would include the overinterpretation of a finding without reasonable evidence to make such a finding. Overinterpretation can be avoided by using the scoring and interpretation criteria that accompany the assessment device. In turn, the psychologist should be cognizant of differences between objective versus subjective data when citing specific findings within his or her report.

Finally, the report should not include statements about anyone who has not been personally assessed by the psychologist. For instance, during the assessment of a child, the child reports being sexually abused by her father. The psychologist cannot include in his or her report a statement accusing the father of child abuse but, rather, can include only a statement indicating that the child reported such a scenario. If the report does not include descriptions of the latter type, the psychologist is considered to be engaging in slander, which would result in a variety of negative consequences (e.g., misinterpretation, facing a lawsuit).

SUMMARY AND CONCLUSIONS

Assessment is an important area within the field of psychology. Consistent with any approach used in psychology, many ethical considerations accompany the use of assessment as a psychological practice. This chapter has outlined several common issues that are specific to assessment and can arise as the result of improper or negligent behavior on the part of the individual conducting the assessment. It is crucial for an individual who is involved with assessment procedures to

have a clear understanding of the ethical guidelines specified by the APA ethical code that pertain to this particular area. An individual can avoid many ethical dilemmas by maintaining knowledge of the ethical code as it pertains to assessment and following the guidelines outlined therein.

Furthermore, this chapter also discussed recommendations for conducting an assessment procedure that will reduce the likelihood of encountering ethical concerns and/or violations when engaging in assessment. It is suggested that individuals continue to monitor all aspects of their assessment procedures from start to finish, while paying special attention and noting any issues that arise that may later cause ethical concerns. When possible, the psychologist should always make attempts to remedy these types of difficulties. Finally, it is important that the psychologist always adopt an assessment approach that meets the standards set by the APA ethical code.

REFERENCES

American Psychological Association. (1992). Ethical principles of psychologists and code of conduct. *American Psychologist, 47,* 1597-1611.

Binder, L. M., & Thompson, L. L. (1994). The ethics code and neuropsychological assessment practices. *Archives of Clinical Neuropsychology, 10*(1), 27-46.

Ceci, S. J., & Bruck, M. (1996). *Jeopardy in the courtroom* (1st ed.). Washington, DC: American Psychological Association.

Kane, M. T. (1992). The assessment of professional competence. *Evaluation and the Health Professional, 15*(2), 163-182.

Kazdin, A. E. (1992). *Research design in clinical psychology* (2nd ed.). Needham Heights, MA: Allyn & Bacon.

Koocher, G. P. (1994). The commerce of professional psychology and the new ethics code. *Professional Psychology, 25*(4), 355-361.

Loveland, E. H. (1985). Measurement of competence: Some definitional issues. *Professional Practice of Psychology, 6*(1), 129-143.

Sattler, J. M. (1986). *Assessment of children* (3rd ed.). San Diego, CA: Jerome M. Sattler.

Part IV

SPECIAL POPULATIONS

CHAPTER 17

Confidentiality in Psychotherapy and Related Contexts

Nancy E. Tribbensee and Charles D. Claiborn
Arizona State University

Whatever, in connection with my professional practice, or not in connection with it, I see or hear, in the life of men, which ought not to be spoken of abroad, I will not divulge, as reckoning that all such should be kept secret.

— Hippocratic Oath (5th cent., B.C.E.)

The public policy favoring protection of the confidential character of patient-psychotherapist communications must yield to the extent to which disclosure is essential to avert danger to others. The protective privilege ends where the public peril begins.

— *Tarasoff v. Regents of the University of California* (1974, p. 561)

Individuals enter therapeutic relationships and participate in psychological research with expectations and assumptions about the degree to which otherwise private information that they disclose will be maintained as confidential. An important feature of the relationship between therapist and client is the client's willingness to risk disclosing personal information pertinent to the client's concerns. The hope is that the disclosure will promote a better understanding and resolution of these concerns. Disclosure in confidence is thus essential to the therapeutic enterprise. Similarly, the value of data collected in research is directly related to the degree to which participants feel safe in disclosing personal information, some of which may be sensitive. The individual's willingness to disclose is based on trust that the researcher will not reveal such information without the consent of the participant. Disclosure in confidence is thus also essential to the scientific enterprise.

This chapter concerns issues of confidentiality in psychotherapy and other applied professional contexts. It does not extend to research, scholarship, or teaching, though many confidentiality concepts and principles apply to these professional activities as well and derive from the same basic values. The chapter begins with a discussion of basic concepts and ethical principles relevant to confidentiality and the related issue of informed consent, particularly as it regards the protection of client communications and records. Next, the general limitations on confidentiality are reviewed. The discussion then turns to an examination of confidentiality in specific applied contexts and with specific kinds of clients. The focus here is on situations that might pose particular difficulty and thus might require added consideration on the part of the practitioner. Included are situations in which confidentiality might necessarily be broken and how this may be most appropriately handled. The goals of the chapter are to leave the reader with a well-founded, practical understanding of confidentiality issues in practice.

BASIC CONCEPTS AND PRINCIPLES

Privacy, confidentiality, and privilege are related but distinct concepts. Although in informal situations, these terms may be used interchangeably, in ethical and legal discussions, *privacy* generally refers to some condition or right of an individual, *confidentiality* arises in the context of a relationship in which information is shared, and *privilege* is an exception under legal rules of evidence.

These concepts may be interrelated in the context of therapy, in which a client may disclose private information to the therapist, with the expectation that the therapist will not voluntarily break this confidence and, as a consequence of privilege, will not be required to disclose this information in a legal proceeding.

Privacy

An individual privacy right is the right of individuals to be free from unreasonable intrusion by the government or by individuals into their personal space, information, thoughts, or feelings. Legal rights to privacy may have an express basis in a state constitution, statutes, or case law. Although no right to privacy is articulated in the U.S. Constitution, the U.S. Supreme Court has interpreted various constitutional provisions to provide certain rights to privacy. For example, in reviewing cases involving contraception (*Griswold v. Connecticut,* 1965) and abortion (*Roe v. Wade,* 1973), the Court found individual rights to privacy to be implicit in the Constitution. Most states have statutes that protect the privacy of medical record information. In addition, state laws allow individuals to sue for damages for invasion of privacy. The U.S. Supreme Court declined to find a federal right to privacy in medical records, however, when it was faced with the issue in *Whalen v. Roe* (1976).

Confidentiality

Clients generally expect to disclose private information in the context of a confidential therapeutic relationship. Their disclosure is made with the understanding that with a few exceptions, the therapist will not share the information with anyone else. In any therapeutic situation, confidentiality is not absolute, but rather a number of limitations are placed on it; these are circumstances in which confidentiality might possibly or certainly be broken. Therapists do not assume that clients fully understand the confidentiality of the therapeutic relationship, including the ways in which it is limited. Rather, therapists inform their clients, typically at the outset of therapy, of the nature of confidentiality and its specific limits so that clients can develop a reasonable expectation regarding confidentiality (Braaten, Otto, & Handelsman, 1993). This is a necessary part of informed consent to treatment.

Limitations on confidentiality, in law and social policy, derive from circumstances in which a particular social interest is determined to outweigh the value of maintaining absolute confidentiality—for example, when disclosure might be necessary to protect someone from harm. As a consequence, limited disclosures of client communications or breaches of confidentiality may be permitted and in some cases are required. These limitations and the particular justifications for them are discussed fully in a subsequent section of this chapter. Whenever the disclosure of confidential information is permitted or required, however, such disclosure is narrowly construed—that is, only relevant information is disclosed, and it is disclosed only to appropriate individuals or organizational entities.

Privilege

In contrast to privacy and confidentiality, the doctrine of privilege is applicable only in the context of a legal proceeding. To say that a communication made by the client to the therapist is "privileged" means that the therapist cannot be compelled to disclose the content of the communication in the course of a legal proceeding unless the client has waived the protection of the privilege. The general rule of evidence in litigation is that evidence relevant to an issue before the court is admissible.

Privilege statutes are an exception to this rule and are narrowly construed. The protection of a privilege means that to protect some higher value, information that may be relevant to an issue being litigated will not be disclosed in a civil or criminal proceeding.

Legal privilege includes three elements. The first is the type of communication that the privilege protects. The second is the action—for example, compelled disclosure—from which eligible communications are protected. The third is the identity of the person protected, also referred to as the person who "holds" the privilege—in this context, the client. Legal privilege can arise by common law, state statue, or federal statue. The U.S. Supreme Court has recognized a federal "psychotherapist privilege" in the case of *Jaffe v. Redmond* (1996, pp. 9-10).

To be protected by privilege, a communication must be made by a client, in the context of a therapeutic relationship, with a reasonable expectation of privacy. If any one of these features is not present, the privilege will not apply. Thus, for example, a therapist may be required to testify as to a communication made by a nonclient, such as a family member, even if the statement is about a client. In addition, statements made by a client to a therapist may fall beyond the protection of the privilege if made under circumstances in which the client did not have a reasonable expectation of privacy. Examples of statements that would not be privileged include statements made by a client in a public or social setting and statements made by a client after the therapeutic relationship has terminated or before such a relationship has been initiated. Another feature of privilege statutes is that they typically protect *communications* and may not protect other elements of the relationship, such as the dates and times of appointments.

Finally, essential to the understanding of privilege is the recognition that the privilege is held by the client and not by the therapist. The client, not the therapist, has the right to waive the protection of the privilege. A client may intentionally or inadvertently waive the privilege. For example, a client may waive the privilege by making a legal claim for emotional or psychological damages or by making his or her mental state an issue in the litigation (DeKraai, Sales, & Hall, 1998). A privilege may also be waived inadvertently by failing to assert it when protected information is first sought. Privileges are construed narrowly by courts, and some have suggested that they are of diminishing value in the light of the numerous exceptions and waivers (Slovenko, 1998).

Smith-Bell and Winslade (1994) have criticized the concept of privilege on two grounds. First, they argue that because most clients are not aware of or do not understand the meaning of privilege law and what it protects, these laws do not influence client behavior. Second, they argue that the laws appear more frequently to insulate therapists from scrutiny than to protect client welfare.

THE ETHICAL BASIS OF CONFIDENTIALITY

The therapist's ethical obligation to maintain the confidentiality of client information is incorporated into the ethical guidelines of psychologists and other mental health professionals, where it is firmly rooted in the client's right to privacy. In particular, the Ethical Principles of Psychologists and Code of Conduct of the American Psychological Association (APA, 1992) identifies "Respect for People's Rights and Dignity" (p. 1599) as a fundamental principle and, by way of explication, states that psychologists "respect the rights of individuals to privacy, confidentiality, self-determination and autonomy" (p. 1599). More specifically, these principles state that

maintaining confidentiality is a "primary obligation" (p. 1606) of psychologists in all professional capacities, including service delivery and scientific research. The principles emphasize that psychologists make clear, as early as possible in their professional relationships, "relevant limitations on confidentiality" (p. 1606) and "the foreseeable uses of the information generated through their services" (p. 1606). Confidentiality in these principles extends to client records, which should contain "only information germane to the purpose for which the communication is made" (p. 1606), and whose contents may be disclosed "only for scientific or professional purposes and only with persons clearly concerned with such matters" (p. 1606). With respect to disclosure of confidential information to others, these principles state that the prior consent of the client be obtained, except in instances where disclosure without consent is "mandated ... or permitted by law" (p. 1606). Such instances, of course, constitute limitations on confidentiality about which clients should be informed at the outset of the professional relationship.

CONFIDENTIALITY AND INFORMED CONSENT

When an individual is considering whether to participate in psychotherapy or participate in research, the therapist or researcher must provide sufficient information to allow the individual to make an informed decision. In therapy, the informed consent process is the proper occasion for an explicit explanation of the client's rights and the limits of confidentiality. The process creates "an opportunity for the client to reflect" (Everstine et al., 1980, p. 83) on the consequences of disclosing information to the therapist, and this is an important part of the risk-benefit assessment that anyone entering therapy must make.

Informed consent requires that the individual has the capacity to consent and is competent to consent. Young children or incapacitated adults typically do not have the legal capacity to consent, and a parent or guardian must consent on their behalf. Informed consent also requires that the information provided is complete and relevant to the decision being considered by the client; confidentiality information is, of course, only a part of this. The information must also be provided in language the client can understand (Kitchener, 2000). The therapist will thus want to gauge explanations of confidentiality and its limitations to the comprehension of the client and certainly provide opportunities for client questions. Not only is confidentiality information provided as part of informed consent at the outset of therapy, but therapists should also remind clients of confidentiality and its limits as issues arise in therapy in which these might be at issue.

LIMITS OF CONFIDENTIALITY

Confidentiality as an ethical issue is complicated by its limitations, circumstances in which otherwise confidential information *may* or *must* be disclosed and in which disclosure may, in some cases, be made without the consent of the client. Even so, in each circumstance, the permitted or required disclosure of confidential information is itself limited to information relevant to the circumstance at hand and to individuals or entities in an appropriate position to act on it. The circumstances that constitute limitations on confidentiality are considered in turn.

Duty to Report Abuse or Neglect of Minors and Vulnerable Adults

Every state and the District of Columbia have statutes that require all mental health providers to report known or suspected child abuse or neglect (Crenshaw & Lichtenberg, 1993), although the Oregon statute protects privileged communications from required reporting (Oregon Revised Statutes, 2000). These states may also have parallel statutes that require the reporting of the abuse or neglect of an elderly or vulnerable adult. Therapists should become familiar with the laws in the state in which they practice and should include information about the disclosures—potential breaches of confidentiality—required by state law in obtaining informed consent from the client. These reporting statutes define who must report and what must be reported (Kalichman, 1993). Abuse is typically defined in terms of nonaccidental physical injury and may also include sexual molestation, emotional abuse, and neglect (Watson & Levine, 1989). Reports are to be made to law enforcement agencies or agencies charged with providing child protective services. *Client consent is not required* for reporting, with the exception of the statutory protection provided in the Oregon statute just mentioned. Nevertheless, it may often be therapeutically appropriate for the therapist to discuss the reporting requirement with the client prior to making the report. Those who report in good faith under these statutes may receive immunity from prosecution, even if the report later proves to be unfounded. The immunity, however, may extend only to the elements that the state specifies must be included in the report; therefore, in making reports, therapists should take care to avoid exceeding the protection of the applicable statute and risking liability for violation of privacy (Kalichman, 1993).

Some researchers have questioned the effectiveness of reporting statutes because a significant number of therapists have indicated that they would ignore or have ignored these requirements in certain circumstances

(Watson & Levine, 1989). Among the reasons given for failing to report as required by law are (a) reluctance to breach confidentiality and fear of damaging the therapeutic relationship, (b) concern that reporting would not be in the best interest of the client and might even increase the risk to the client, (c) fear of liability for disclosing confidential information, and (d) lack of confidence in the agency charged with responding to reports (DeKraai et al., 1998; Watson & Levine, 1989). On the other hand, concerns about damage to the therapeutic relationship may be overstated. Whether the client is the alleged abuser, present or past victim, or a witness to abuse, reporting may set appropriate limits in the relationship, assist the client in facing reality and moving past denial, and provide a supportive environment for the client as he or she faces the consequences of reported misconduct (Watson & Levine, 1989).

Duty to Warn

Statutes and case law have established a duty to warn, under which confidential communications must be disclosed if the therapist reasonably believes that the client may present a danger to self or others. *Client consent is not required* in making such a disclosure. This limit to confidentiality arose originally from the well-known case of *Tarasoff v. Regents of the University of California* (1974). State statutes vary, but generally the harm must be perceived to be imminent, and the breach of confidentiality must be related to a reasonable attempt to avoid the threatened harm. This means, for example, that the person to whom the disclosure is made should be in a position to minimize the risk. Risks may be minimized either by controlling the client (as with a disclosure in the course of involuntary commitment) or by protecting an identified or

identifiable victim (as with disclosure to the potential victim or law enforcement).

The duty to warn has been criticized as ineffective and unworkable (DeKraai et al., 1998). Among the problems identified with the requirement to warn a potential victim is that it appears to be based on an unwarranted assumption that therapists can accurately predict dangerous behavior. In addition, therapists fear that if they make a report in error, they may face liability for breaching confidentiality. Some argue that these laws may discourage therapists from seeing potentially dangerous clients, thereby depriving this population of an important resource. It has also been argued that issuing a warning may be either unnecessary and cause the identified victim to take unnecessary precautions and create unnecessary fear or, even if well-founded, may place the therapist at risk.

Tarasoff and the cases that follow it raise the question of a therapist's duty to warn of a risk presented by a client's threatened violent conduct. Analogous questions have arisen with regard to circumstances in which a client's nonviolent conduct poses risk danger, as when a client with HIV/AIDS engages in high-risk sexual acts or shares needles with partners who are not aware of the client's health status. In analyzing whether a duty to warn should be extended to therapists who are aware of these risks, commentators have identified factors in favor of and against requiring therapists to notify those who may be at risk from a client's conduct (Lamb, Clark, Drumheller, Frizzell, & Surrey, 1989). Primary among the factors that weigh in favor of notification are the potentially catastrophic consequences of the victim becoming infected. Among the considerations that do not support the therapist's disclosing confidential information are the uncertainties in many cases as to the identities of potential victims, the potential harm to the client and associated stigma of disclosing HIV/AIDS health status, and the low risk of transmission unless certain high-risk sexual practices or needle sharing are occurring. In addition, many states have statutes that expressly prohibit the disclosure of confidential HIV/AIDS information, and no cases have examined the effect of these statutes on the duty to warn. Knapp and VandeCreek (1990) proposed statutory solutions that would permit—but not require—the warning of potential victims. For the time being, therapists will need to evaluate each case on its merits to balance the potential costs and benefits of disclosure.

Mandatory Referrals

Mandatory or court-ordered referrals for evaluation or psychotherapy create another exception to the general rule that clients can expect their therapists to hold client communications in confidence. In cases of evaluation, the court will receive a copy of the evaluation, and the therapist who evaluated the client may be asked to provide testimony regarding the client. In cases of mandated therapy, the therapist will minimally provide the court with evidence that therapy sessions took place and may in addition be asked to provide evidence of client progress. *Client consent is not required* for these communications, though the client is informed of them as a limitation on confidentiality.

Other Limits

Other circumstances that may limit confidentiality include those in which a *client is required to consent* to disclosure of confidential information as a condition of obtaining a valuable service, such as insurance or employment. Technically, the client has consented to such disclosure to receive a benefit, so these examples are not true exceptions to therapists' obligations regarding confidentiality. The

circumstances of the consent may, however, have left the client with few or no acceptable alternatives. Insurance companies require that clients consent to the insurer's access to their medical and psychological records as a condition of coverage. In addition, an individual may be required to consent to disclosure of confidential information for an employment background check, to receive security clearance, or to be eligible to participate in certain other opportunities, such as the Peace Corps. Of course, in such circumstances, the individual is informed of (a) the specific limits on confidentiality; (b) the therapist's (or evaluator's) obligation to disclose confidential information; (c) exactly what information is to be disclosed, to whom, and for what purpose; and (d) possible risks of such disclosure. This, again, is part of the informed consent process.

Similar circumstances that limit confidentiality, though again always with client consent, are those in which the client is informed *at the outset of therapy* that professionals other than the client's therapist will or may have access to client information. Such professionals could include the therapist's supervisor or administrative staff at an agency. If the therapist is a student, other students in the therapist's practicum or internship might be included as well. All these professionals and students are, of course, under the same ethical obligations of confidentiality as the therapist, as should be made clear to the client in the informed consent process. These circumstances, like those just discussed, do not constitute true exceptions to therapist confidentiality because, again, the client may decline to give consent. But because this is likely to mean that the client cannot be seen by that therapist or perhaps in that agency, it is nevertheless a practical limitation on confidentiality.

It is worth noting how these circumstances differ from those in which client consent is sought *during the course of therapy* for the therapist to consult with (and therefore to disclose confidential information to) professionals independent of the therapist. Such professionals might include the client's physician, psychiatrist, or another therapist with whom the client is working. These latter circumstances do not in any way constitute a limit on confidentiality, because the client may decline to give consent with no adverse consequence. Of course, it may be in the client's interest to give consent, typically termed a *release,* and the therapist makes this clear to the client in providing a rationale for the requested release; however, as the therapist also makes clear, the choice is the client's.

Confidentiality of Client Records

Client records include any information preserved by the therapist about a current or former client, including session notes, diagnostic information, assessments, communications about the client sent to or received from others, and forms completed and signed by the client. It is the therapist's responsibility to maintain the confidentiality of client records and to insure that office procedures for handling records, including the behavior of office staff, are consistent with the standards of confidentiality to which the therapist is bound (APA, 1993). The therapist's procedures for maintaining client records should be in accordance with the relevant state laws or, in the absence of these, with the standards of the therapist's professional association. These include provisions for maintaining the records in a secure and accessible way, even in the event of the therapist's death, and for destroying the records at the appropriate time as specified by law. Therapists may routinely inform clients of these procedures, but if they do not, therapists should be prepared to inform clients on request. Just as the therapist informs the client of the confidentiality of

material disclosed in therapy and limits on confidentiality, so also does the therapist include the confidentiality of client records in this assurance and the relevant limitations (APA, 1993).

Clients may not be aware of the complete contents of their records nor realize the possible consequences of releasing the records to others. Therapists should help current clients (it is difficult to do this with former clients) anticipate these consequences when they request to have their records sent to others or when they are considering whether to comply with another's request for the release of their records. Specifically, therapists might explore with their clients matters such as (a) the intended purpose of releasing their records to others, including anticipated benefits; (b) whether certain information in the records could prove embarrassing or harmful to the clients if it became known to others (and if so, whether it is desirable to release the *entire* records or only a relevant part of them); (c) the standards of confidentiality that those receiving the records are obliged to maintain; and (d) whether those receiving the records may misinterpret or misuse them. It is not the therapist's role to discourage the release of records; after all, release may serve client interests. The therapist's responsibility is, rather, to guard against the misuse of records (APA, 1993) and to place their release in the context of informed consent. As records become out-of-date, the possibility of their misuse increases because descriptions of the client that were once valid may no longer be. In complying with a client's request to release records that contain obsolete information, the client should be informed, if possible, that some information is obsolete. In addition, obsolete information should be so noted in the records themselves, with the annotation signed and dated by the therapist at the time of release.

Clients receiving psychotherapy generally have legal access to their own records, a fact that therapists must keep in mind as they compile the records. In some cases, state law may provide for therapists to withhold records from a client if the therapist judges that access would be harmful to the client. In these instances, the therapist documents the client's request as well as the therapist's own rationale for not complying. Even here, of course, the client could challenge the therapist's decision and possibly gain access to the records. In contrast, individuals who are being assessed at the behest of organizational clients, such as potential employers, may not have access to the results of their assessments. If so, this should be made clear to the individuals assessed prior to the assessment (Committee on Psychological Tests and Assessments, 1996).

Issues surrounding the release of client records to others and clients' access to their own records are considerably more complicated when the clients are minors or adults under the guardianship of others. These issues are among the topics considered in the next section.

CONFIDENTIALITY IN SPECIAL CIRCUMSTANCES

Group and Family Therapy

Group and family therapies both present complications with respect to confidentiality as a consequence of creating a somewhat more "public" treatment environment. Clients disclose not merely to the therapist, but to other clients as well, and clients do not have the professional obligation to confidentiality that the therapist does. In group therapy, the therapist not only has the usual obligation of maintaining the confidentiality of each client's information within the limitations discussed in the previous section; the therapist must also confront the possibility that clients could disclose information about

other clients to individuals outside the group. The fact that clients do not have an obligation to maintain the confidentiality of other clients constitutes a risk of group therapy, and the therapist should inform potential clients of this risk as part of informed consent prior to the beginning of therapy. At the same time, in screening potential clients for the group, the therapist should emphasize the importance of confidentiality to the group and gain each client's commitment to maintain the confidentiality of information shared in the group. In this way, the therapist begins the establishment of a norm of confidentiality, which is further shaped as the group develops by the therapist's own modeling and explicit reminders to the group.

In a review of group therapist practices with respect to confidentiality, Roback, Moore, Bloch, and Shelton (1996) found that therapists generally discussed confidentiality with potential group therapy clients but that they were less likely to inform potential clients of the risk that confidentiality could be broken. Arguing (accurately) that informed consent information must include *all* risks that could affect a client's decision to enter treatment, Roback et al. provided an example of an informed consent statement for group therapy that clearly describes the confidentiality risks, client responsibilities regarding confidentiality, and possible consequences of clients' violating confidentiality:

> If you reveal secrets in the group, those secrets might be told outside the group by other members of the group. If your secrets are told outside the group, then people you know might learn your secrets. You could be hurt emotionally and economically if your secrets are told outside the group.
>
> Other group members may tell their secrets to you. If you tell those secrets outside the group, then the member whose secrets you tell might have legal grounds to sue you for money for telling those secrets.

> If you violate the confidentiality rules of the group, then the group leader may expel you from the group. (p. 135)

Despite the fact that family members know and interact with one another outside therapy, family therapy presents similar, though not identical, difficulties with respect to confidentiality. (In this discussion, the term *family* is used broadly to refer to adults with custody of children and to couples, regardless of marital status or sexual orientation.) After all, what clients share with members of their immediate family in therapy, especially if it is disclosed only in therapy, might reasonably be expected to be held in confidence by those family members. On the other hand, family members may not be sensitive to confidentiality concerns of other family members, and this lack of sensitivity could be considered symptomatic within the family and, as such, the focus of therapeutic attention (Margolin, 1982). This, of course, is a difference between family and group therapy. Nevertheless, confidentiality issues should be included as risks to family therapy, just as they are to group therapy, in the informed consent process. Family therapists should emphasize the importance of confidentiality in therapy and discuss with the members of the family the norms of confidentiality that are to apply in their work.

A confidentiality dilemma that is unique to family therapy arises when one member of the family wishes to disclose information to the therapist in private—that is, outside the presence of the other members—with the expectation that the therapist will hold this information in confidence even from the other members (Margolin, 1982). Is the therapist to allow this sort of disclosure at all? Arguments in favor of allowing it are that (a) it gives the individual family member full access to the therapist and thus may maximize the therapist's ability to meet the individual

client's needs, and (b) it is consistent with a respect for the family member's individual right to privacy. On the other hand, maintaining one family member's confidence may be ethically problematic, given the therapist's obligations to the other family members as individuals and to the family as a whole. Specifically, it is likely to create an imbalance in the therapist's alliances with family members. It could also put the therapist in the position of withholding information from the family that directly bears on the family's therapeutic work—or even a position of colluding with the one family member in deceiving the other members. To avoid such countertherapeutic consequences, many therapists prefer a confidentiality arrangement in which information is disclosed only in family sessions, not in private individual communications. A principal exception to this is often made for adults to be able to discuss matters with the therapist that are inappropriate for children. Otherwise, therapists might refer family members who have a need for private disclosure to a separate individual therapist.

Minors as Clients

In considering how to handle confidentiality with clients who are minors, therapists must first consult the laws of the state in which they work. In a review of such legislation, DeKraai and Sales (1991) noted that freedom to disclose within a confidential relationship is generally paired with consent to treatment. In other words, clients who are considered sufficiently autonomous to consent to their own treatment (rather than to require consent of a parent or guardian) are also entitled to confidentiality of therapeutic communications. (Hereafter in this discussion, the term *parent* refers to any person who has legal custody of the child—that is, the child's parent or guardian.) Though state laws vary with regard to specific ages, preadolescent clients typically require parental consent to receive treatment; correspondingly, parents are also likely to have access to any information these clients disclose in therapy, as well as access to client records. Adolescent clients, in some states, may be allowed to consent to treatment on their own; in these circumstances, parents may not have access to client communications or records.

Even when parents have a legal right of access to the information disclosed by minor clients, such access might not be in the best interests of the client (Taylor & Adelman, 1989). Minor clients might be unwilling to disclose relevant information in therapy if they believe that their parents, for example, will have access to it. Recognizing this, some states that have generally given parents access to minor clients' records have also given therapists the option of denying access when they judge that it would be detrimental to the client (DeKraai & Sales, 1991). More commonly, therapists working with minor clients often negotiate an arrangement with the clients and their parents whereby the parents will not expect to be informed of what the client discloses in therapy except under specified circumstances, usually those involving harm to the client. In this discussion, therapists provide a rationale for the client's confidentiality, emphasizing how it serves the client's therapeutic interests and how these are the parents' interests as well (Gustafson & McNamara, 1987). The agreement resulting from such a negotiation, of course, has no legal status, so that at a later point in therapy, parents who have legal access to client records may still request them.

Taylor and Adelman (1989) have drawn attention to the difficulty of building trust in therapeutic relationships with minor clients, given these limitations on confidentiality. They recommended a number of ways to address this difficulty: First, the therapist should clearly explain confidentiality and its limits to the client in the context of a discussion in which the client can ask questions about them. Second, the therapist should link client disclosure to the client's goals in therapy and to the therapist's desire to be helpful to the client in reaching those goals. Third, when faced with the necessity of revealing client information to others, the therapist should discuss with the client how this might be done with minimum harm and possible benefit to the client. Taylor and Adelman provided examples of the sorts of things the therapist might say to the client in the course of such a discussion:

> What you have shared today is very important. I know you're not ready to talk about this with your parents, but it is the kind of thing that I told you at the beginning that I am required to tell them. . . .
> I know that if I do . . . [tell your parents] you will be upset with me and it will be hard for you to trust me anymore. I feel caught in this situation. I'd like us to be able to work something out to make this all come out as good [sic] as we can make it. . . .
> [In terms of how to proceed,] this may work best for you if you tell them rather than me [sic]. Or, if you don't feel ready to handle this, we both could sit down with your parents while I tell them. (p. 82)

Though the specific wording will vary with the situation, these examples illustrate the kind of respect for and sensitivity to the client that the therapist should display in such circumstances.

Small Communities

Small communities refer, of course, to small towns and rural areas, but also to distinct communities within more populous areas—for example, a college campus, the gay and lesbian community, or the Mexican American community in a larger city. Small communities present therapists with numerous ethical challenges with respect to multiple relationships, and these create some confidentiality difficulties as well. Probably the most serious threat to confidentiality occurs when therapists become aware that two clients with whom they are working have some relationship with one another and that information disclosed by one client may have a bearing the therapist's work with the other (Spiegel, 1990). Sharkin (1995), in discussing therapy on college campuses, called these "entangled therapeutic relationships" (p. 184). These entanglements can often impair the therapist's work and can also give the therapist the feeling of deceiving both clients—a feeling that could be enhanced should the clients become aware of the situation and wonder why the therapist did not inform them of it. The therapist's efforts to resolve an entanglement *could* include breaking confidentiality to the extent of informing the clients of the situation. This course of action would presumably be a last resort but would be justified if client welfare required it and if the information disclosed about each client to the other were limited to the minimum information necessary. In addition, therapists practicing in small communities should certainly include this circumstance among the potential risks of therapy in the informed consent process.

Cyber-Therapy and E-Mail

Information technology can have many advantages in enhancing client communications, but if e-mail or Internet transactions are used to exchange personal or confidential information, the therapist must inform the client of security limits inherent in the technology. For example, when communicating electronically, it may not be possible to establish with certainty that the individual with whom the therapist is communicating is the client and not an electronic impersonator; messages can be inadvertently sent to someone outside of the therapeutic relationship. In addition, to the extent that communications are not made over a secure network, they may be intercepted. Either scenario could violate the client's privacy and to thwart later attempts to characterize the communication as privileged. Anonymous electronic communications or sessions may also raise ethical concerns about the duties to warn or to report child abuse. Without identifying information, the therapist may not have sufficient information to identify the individual (Hughes, 2000).

Assessment

Psychological assessment refers here to the set of activities that result in a description or evaluation of an individual at a particular time. It often involves the use of psychological instruments whose validity depends on their remaining secure from release to those not qualified to use them, namely, members of other professions and the general public.

In psychotherapy, the description or evaluation of a client, sometimes formalized in a psychological report, becomes part of the client's records and is therefore subject to the standards and procedures of confidentiality that apply to client records generally. Clients are informed of these standards and procedures when they consent to be assessed. As part of informed consent to assessment (which may be combined with consent to treatment), clients are informed about the instruments to be administered, their purpose, and how the results will be used (Committee on Psychological Tests and Assessments, 1996). Clients have access to the results of the assessments, just as they have access to the rest of their records except when the therapist judges that access would be harmful to the client. The release of client records to others, with the client's consent, would of course include any assessment results. To the extent that the assessment results are out of date, the therapist releasing the records should guard against their misuse by noting that the assessment was done at an earlier time in the client's life and that the results do not represent a valid current description or evaluation of the client. Any such annotation to the client's records should be signed and dated by the therapist at the time it is made.

When the assessment is performed in a context other than therapy, such as for an organizational client, the individuals assessed should nevertheless be informed about the assessment process and the use to which the results will be put, including who will have access to them (Committee on Psychological Tests and Assessments, 1996). As has already been noted, such individuals may not have access to their own assessment results; if this is the case, they should be so informed during the informed consent process.

Finally, the need to maintain the security of psychological instruments poses a different kind of confidentiality issue: the confidentiality of the instruments themselves. As stated by APA's Committee on Psychological Tests and Assessments (1996):

> Disclosure of secure testing materials (e.g., test items, test scoring, or test protocols) to unqualified persons may decrease the test's validity. Availability of test items to an unqualified person can not only render the test invalid for any future use with that individual, but also jeopardizes the security and integrity of the test for other persons who may be exposed to test items and responses. Such release imposes very concrete harm to the general public—loss of effective assessment tools. Because there are a limited number of standardized psychological tests considered appropriate for a given purpose . . . they cannot easily be replaced or substituted if an individual obtains prior knowledge of item content or the security of the test is otherwise compromised. (p. 646)

Therapists releasing client records may therefore include the client's scores on psychological instruments and the interpretation of the scores, but not such secure materials as the test booklet or scoring keys. The latter may be of interest to the client or others, but maintaining their security is essential to their effective (and ethical) use.

REFERENCES

American Psychological Association. (1992). Ethical principles of psychologists and code of conduct. *American Psychologist, 47,* 1597-1611.

American Psychological Association. (1993). Record keeping guidelines. *American Psychologist, 48,* 984-986.

Braaten, E. B., Otto, S., & Handelsman, M. M. (1993). What do people want to know about psychotherapy? *Psychotherapy, 30,* 565-570.

Committee on Psychological Tests and Assessments. (1996). Statement on the disclosure of test data. *American Psychologist, 51,* 644-648.

Crenshaw, W. B., & Lichtenberg, J. W. (1993). Child abuse and the limits of confidentiality: Forewarning practices. *Behavioral Sciences and the Law, 11,* 181-192.

DeKraai, M. B., & Sales, B. D. (1991). Liability in child therapy and research. *Journal of Consulting and Clinical Psychology, 59,* 853-860.

DeKraai, M. B., Sales, B. D., & Hall, S. R. (1998). Informed consent, confidentiality, and duty to report laws in the conduct of child therapy. In R. J. Morris & T. R. Kratochwill (Eds.), *The practice of child therapy* (3rd ed., pp. 540-559). Needham Heights, MA: Allyn & Bacon.

Everstine L., Everstine, D. S., Heymann, G. M., True, R. H., Frey, D., Johnson, H. G., & Seiden, R. H. (1980). Privacy and confidentiality in psychotherapy. *American Psychologist, 35,* 828-840.

Griswold v. Connecticut, 381 U.S. 479 (1965).

Gustafson, K. E., & McNamara, J. R. (1987). Confidentiality with minor clients: Issues and guidelines for therapists. *Professional Psychology: Research and Practice, 18,* 503-508.

Hughes, R. S. (2000). Cybercounseling and regulations: Quagmire or quest? In J. W. Bloom & G. R. Walz (Eds.), *Cybercounseling and cyberlearning.* Alexandria, VA: American Counseling Association and CAPS.

Jaffe v. Redmond, 518 U.S. 1 (1996).

Kalichman, S. C. (1993). *Mandated reporting of suspected child abuse: Ethics, law, and policy.* Washington, DC: American Psychological Association.

Kitchener, K. S. (2000). *Foundations of ethical practice, research, and teaching in psychology.* Mahwah, NJ: Lawrence Erlbaum.

Knapp, S., & VandeCreek, L. (1990). Application of the duty to protect to HIV-positive patients. *Professional Psychology: Research and Practice, 21,* 161-166.

Lamb, D. H., Clark, C., Drumheller, P., Frizzell, K., & Surrey, L. (1989). Applying Tarasoff to AIDS-related therapy issues. *Professional Psychology: Research and Practice, 20,* 37-43.

Margolin, G. (1982). Ethical and legal considerations in marital and family therapy. *American Psychologist, 37,* 788-801.

Oregon Revised Statutes. §419B.010[1] (2001).

Roback, H. B., Moore, R. F., Bloch, F. S., & Shelton, M. (1996). Confidentiality in group psychotherapy: Empirical findings and the law. *International Journal of Group Psychotherapy, 46,* 117-135.

Roe v. Wade, 410 U.S. 113 (1973).

Sharkin, B. S. (1995). Strains on confidentiality in college-student psychotherapy: Entangled therapeutic relationships, incidental encounters, and third-party inquiries. *Professional Psychology: Research and Practice, 26,* 184-189.

Slovenko, R. (1998). *Psychotherapy and confidentiality: Testimonial privileged communication, breach of confidentiality, and reporting duties.* Springfield, IL: Charles C Thomas.

Smith-Bell, M., & Winslade, W. J. (1994). Privacy, confidentiality, and privilege in psychotherapeutic relationships. *American Journal of Orthopsychiatry, 64,* 180-193.

Spiegel, P. B. (1990). Confidentiality endangered under some circumstances without special management. *Psychotherapy, 27,* 636-643.

Tarasoff v. Regents of the University of California, 529 P.2d 553 (1974); vacated 551 P.2d 334 (Cal. 1976).

Taylor, L., & Adelman, H. S. (1989). Reframing the confidentiality dilemma to work in children's best interests. *Professional Psychology: Research and Practice, 20,* 79-83.

Watson, H., & Levine, M. (1989). Psychotherapy and mandated reporting of child abuse. *American Journal of Orthopsychiatry, 59,* 246-256.

Whalen v. Roe, 429 U.S. 589 (1976).

CHAPTER 18

Ethical Principles of the Psychology Profession and Ethnic Minority Issues

GORDON C. NAGAYAMA HALL
University of Oregon

GAYLE Y. IWAMASA
University of Indianapolis

JESSICA N. SMITH
University of Oregon

The ethical issues involved in work with ethnic minority persons should be a primary concern for all psychologists. Over the past three decades, various scholars have developed proposals for culturally competent research, training, and clinical practice. However, these proposals have failed to become widely implemented, and the primary proponents and practitioners of cultural competence have been ethnic minority psychologists themselves. In this chapter, we suggest that the basis for ethical standards in work with ethnic minority persons was established nearly 30 years ago. We also discuss several major ethical issues that have been identified involving ethnic minority populations. Finally, we make recommendations toward a goal of cultural competence as a requirement for all psychologists and address potential resistance to such a goal.

Why should ethical issues regarding ethnic minority persons be of concern to psychologists? Doesn't the consideration of group differences compromise objectivity? Isn't this

AUTHOR'S NOTE: Preparation of this chapter was supported by National Institute of Mental Health grants R01 MH58726 and R25 MH62575.

tantamount to stereotyping? Wouldn't a "color-blind" approach be the most objective? Such reasoning may reflect the residual effects of Aristotelian science, in which scientific methods were separate from ethics (Stroud, 1994). The assumption is that objectivity can be achieved independently of social or cultural context. In other words, ethnicity and cultural issues are irrelevant in the development, implementation, and interpretation of a research study. Nevertheless, even those who seek objective reality operate within a cultural context. Proponents of "color-blindness" (i.e., everyone is the same) are ignorant of the possibility that everyone is, in fact, not the same, and that ethnic and cultural values can significantly influence the research, training, and clinical process (Iwamasa, 1997). These individuals may be construed as tending to perceive a single color—their own— and tend to evaluate others relative to themselves. Scientists are not immune from self-serving biases that influence person perception, particularly those who are unaware of or deny that such biases exist (Gilbert, 1998). Attempting to ignore sociocultural context will not cause its effects to disappear (Iwamasa, 1997; Thompson, 1998). Despite the reluctance of many psychologists to examine their own ethics (Pope & Vasquez, 1991), the examination of ethics with respect to ethnic minorities is critical to the survival of psychology in an increasingly multicultural society (Hall, 1997).

FOUNDATIONS OF ETHICAL ISSUES INVOLVING ETHNIC MINORITY GROUPS

The seeds for ethical standards regarding cultural competence in psychology were sown nearly 30 years ago. The very existence of human subjects review boards at research institutions is the result of the Tuskegee study, one of the worst abuses of ethnic minority persons for research purposes in U.S. history. This study of the effects of untreated syphilis on 600 African American men in Alabama, who were poor and uneducated, conducted by the U.S. Public Health Service, began in 1932 and continued for more than 40 years (Harris, 1996). These men were enticed to participate in the study with financial incentives and the encouragement of planters, who also were given incentives for allowing their sharecropper tenants to participate in the study (Harter, Stephens, & Japp, 2000). In addition, the all–African American Tuskegee Institute, a teaching hospital, cosponsored the project (Harter et al., 2000). The sponsorship of this project by this prestigious African American institution and the involvement of African American assistants in the project persuaded many of the participants of the legitimacy of the project.

The Tuskegee study came under investigation in 1972 by a panel appointed by the Department of Health, Education, and Welfare (Harris, 1996). It was determined that the participants did not voluntarily submit to the project, but were told that they would receive medical treatment from expert government doctors for "bad blood" (Harris, 1996). In 1974, the National Research Service Award Act was established, which required that human participants in research provide informed consent to protect their welfare (Harris, 1996). Institutional human subjects boards to review research projects to be federally funded were also required as part of this act. Ironically, the federal government did not acknowledge wrongdoing in the Tuskegee study until President Clinton apologized in a speech in May 1997.

A major issue in the Tuskegee study was the lack of community input in its planning and implementation, a major component of conducting culturally sensitive research with ethnic minority communities (Council of the National Psychological Associations for the Advancement of Ethnic Minority Interests [CNPAAEMI], 2000). One aspect of institutional review boards (IRBs) that is intended to be a voice for the community is the inclusion of community persons as voting members. However, any particular community member may not necessarily represent the community. Furthermore, as Scott-Jones (1994) pointed out, IRBs tend to review research with ethnic minority individuals differently from research on nonminority populations. A case in point is the African American Tuskegee Institute's cosponsorship of the Tuskegee study. It does not appear that the Tuskegee Institute had the African American community's best interests in mind. Ceci, Peters, and Plotkin's (1985) study of differential IRB decisions related to the sociopolitical content of the research demonstrates how the personal characteristics of IRB members themselves (including their own personal experience with the population of study) will influence their judgment of research with ethnic minorities. Rosnow, Rotheram-Borus, Ceci, Blanck, and Koocher (1993) emphasized that IRB members should understand the community standards and values of the group being studied. Nevertheless, the inclusion of community members on IRBs allows the potential for ethnic minority community concerns to be represented, assuming that credible and qualified individuals are selected. These individuals should be sanctioned by the community as representatives of the community and not necessarily selected by those unfamiliar with the community.

At the same time as the investigations into the Tuskegee study, two other important reports were written involving the American Psychological Association (APA) on ethical issues with respect to ethnic minority populations. The APA sponsored the Vail Conference in 1974 (Korman, 1974). A recommendation of the conference was that clinical psychologists should become knowledgeable about culture. It was contended that psychologists who work with persons of culturally diverse backgrounds but are not trained or competent to do so are engaging in unethical behavior. Unlike the National Research Service Award Act of 1974, the Vail Conference recommendation pertained to clinical practice and implied that cultural competence is a necessary component of training. In a prescient statement that has been recently echoed (Hall, Lopez, & Bansal, 2001), it was also recommended that training should help students to maintain a balance between their cultural group identity and acculturation to an identity as a psychologist (Korman, 1974). However, these recommendations essentially left cultural competence up to individuals and did not specify how individual psychologists could become culturally competent. Recently, researchers such as Yutrzenka (1995) are still calling for the need to incorporate training in ethnic and cultural diversity, indicating that the recommendations from the Vail Conference had yet to be implemented some 20 years later.

Also in 1974, a report on cross-cultural ethics to the APA Committee on International Relations in Psychology was published (Tapp, Kelman, Triandis, Wrightsman, & Coelho, 1974). The report recommended that the cultural acceptability of methods should be evaluated and that cultures in which research is conducted be respected. Collaboration with local researchers *from that culture* was also recommended. Researchers were also encouraged to ensure that participants benefited from the research. The advantage of this approach over the individual approach to cultural competence of the Vail Conference was that researchers were encouraged to collaborate with cultural communities. However, it appears that such collaboration was intended to occur after research ideas had been formulated outside the cultural community, rather than having a priori input from the cultural community into the design and development of the research ideas. Moreover, the report did not specify recommendations for training or practice. Again, as indicated by the *Guidelines on Research in Ethnic Minority Communities* (CNPAAEMI, 2000), such research collaboration with ethnic minority communities has not typically occurred in psychological research.

Eight years later, Derald Wing Sue and his colleagues (1982), who were members of the Education and Training Committee of the Counseling Psychology Division (17) of APA, recommended that the APA adopt specific cross-cultural counseling and therapy competencies. It was further recommended that these competencies be implemented into criteria for APA accreditation of *counseling, clinical, and school psychology* graduate training programs. *Cross-cultural counseling and therapy* was defined as any counseling relationship in which participants differ on cultural background, values, and lifestyle. The dimensions of competency included beliefs and attitudes, knowledge, and skills. The first dimension involves therapists' *beliefs* and attitudes concerning ethnic minorities, the need to examine biases and stereotypes, the development of a positive attitude toward multiculturalism, and the way therapists' values may interfere with cross-cultural counseling. *Knowledge* involves an understanding of one's own worldview, knowledge of the cultural groups with which one works, and understanding of sociopolitical influences. *Skills* are the specific intervention methods necessary in working with ethnic minority groups. These multicultural competencies were further developed and in 1991 were approved by the Association for Multicultural Counseling and Development (Sue, Arredondo, & McDavis,

1992). In August 2002, the APA Council of Representatives approved as APA policy the Guidelines on Multicultural Education, Training, Research, Practice, and Organization Change for Psychologists that were based, in part, on the Sue et al. (1992) multicultural competencies (http://www.apaorg/pi/multicul-turalguidelines.pdf). These guidelines are not mandatory, however, and do not include an enforcement mechanism as ethical standards do.

APA ETHICAL PRINCIPLES AND ETHNIC MINORITY ISSUES

The APA ethical principles have the broadest application among psychologists of any ethical codes. The APA is the largest professional organization of psychologists and is one of the largest professional organizations in any profession. Members of APA presumably adhere to APA's ethical principles as a condition of membership.

APA first developed a set of 10 ethical principles to guide research with human participants in 1973, soon after the Tuskegee study hearings. None of these principles addressed ethnic minority issues. It was not until 1981 that the APA ethical principles of psychologists mentioned issues relevant to ethnic minority groups. Under the moral and legal standards principle, it was indicated that psychologists do not engage in and/or condone illegal or inhumane practices, including those based on considerations of race and national origin in hiring, promotion, or training. This principle encouraged psychologists to "do no harm" by abiding by existing laws against discrimination. However, "doing no harm" is not equivalent to cultural competence or proactive efforts with respect to ethnic minority issues (Casas, Ponterotto, & Gutierrez, 1986). Encouraging psychologists not to discriminate may encourage "color-blindness" and may interfere with cultural sensitivity (Pedersen, 1997). Moreover, the principle was specific to hiring, promotion, and training, and there was no general admonition to the science and profession on discrimination. Many who reviewed the ethical principles criticized them for reflecting the values of men, particularly of European decent, and failing to consider the worldviews and values of nonwhite individuals, those not included in the middle class, and women (Gilligan, 1982; Harding, 1987; LaFromboise & Foster, 1989; Noddings, 1984, 1986).

Casas and Thompson (1991) provided an insightful review of the problems inherent in the ethical principles and standards and also provided suggestions for improvement in concrete and measurable ways. Specifically, they called for a change in the philosophical premises of the principles and standards that demonstrate explicit rather than implicit diversity concerns. For example, psychologists should attempt to develop ethical standards and resolve ethical dilemmas in consultation with the community (Hillerbrand, 1987; Ivey, 1987) and incorporate both caring and justice, particularly as they relate to ethnic minority ethical issues (LaFromboise & Foster, 1989). Potential changes in the standards and principles that can be tangibly measured included the areas of altruism, responsibility, justice, and caring (Casas & Thompson, 1991).

In 1985, the APA published *Standards for Educational and Psychological Testing.* Standards relevant to ethnic minority issues included 3.10, which stated that if item/test performance differs for particular kinds of tests for members of age, ethnicity, and gender groups in the population of test takers, research should be designed to detect and eliminate aspects of test design, content, or format that might bias test scores for particular groups. Standard 6.10 stated that individuals should not be evaluated if they

had special characteristics, including cultural background, that are outside the psychologist's range of academic training or supervised experience. In such cases, psychologists should seek consultation, necessary modifications of test procedures, or score interpretations from someone with relevant experience. In addition, standards were offered involving linguistic minorities. Psychologists should minimize threats to reliability from language differences (Standard 13.1), describe any linguistic modifications recommended by test developers (Standard 13.2), and establish reliability and validity again with minority groups if translating the test (Standard 13.4). Although these standards were more proactive than the 1981 APA ethical principles in attempting to eliminate bias, the 1985 standards were short on specifics and were targeted to educational and psychological testing rather than to the whole profession.

The APA ethical principles were revised in 1992. Although the 1992 APA ethical principles fell short of defining and requiring cultural competence, unlike the 1981 principles, some suggestions for being proactive were included. Similar to the 1981 APA ethical principles, the 1992 APA code encouraged psychologists not to discriminate or harass ethnic minority persons. Principle B on "Integrity" indicated that psychologists need to be aware of their own belief systems and to be respectful of others. Principle C, on "Professional and Scientific Responsibility," stated that psychologists need to adapt their methods to needs of different populations. For example, psychologists must try to identify situations in which particular interventions, assessment techniques, or norms may not be applicable or might require adjustment in administration/interpretation because of factors such as race and ethnicity. Principle D, on "Respect for People's Rights and Dignity," stated that psychologists need to be aware of cultural, individual, and role differences, including those due to race, ethnicity, national origin, and religion. Standard 1.08, on "Human Differences," indicated that where differences of race, ethnicity, national origin, religion, socioeconomic status, and so on significantly affects psychologists' work concerning particular individuals or groups, psychologists need to get training, experience, consultation, or supervision necessary to ensure the competence of their services or make an appropriate referral.

The APA Office of Ethnic Minority Affairs (APA, 1993) *Guidelines for Providers of Psychological Services to Ethnic, Linguistic, and Culturally Diverse Populations* recommended that psychologists recognize ethnicity and culture as significant parameters in understanding psychology processes and that cultural differences regarding language, family, community, religious, spiritual, and sociopolitical issues be understood and respected. However, the guidelines represent general principles that were intended to be aspirational in nature and were designed to provide suggestions to psychologists in working with ethnic, linguistic, and culturally diverse populations. Hence, these guidelines were ancillary to the APA ethical principles. Therefore, a failure to recognize ethnicity and culture in understanding psychological processes or a failure to understand and respect cultural differences would not necessarily comprise an ethical violation.

The most recent commentary from APA on ethical issues relevant to ethnic minorities is a report of a task force to develop guidelines for competent use of psychological tests (Turner, Demers, Fox, & Reed, 2001). This report advised that consideration of racial, gender, age, and linguistic variables is important for proper selection of tests and that in some cases (e.g., employment testing), use of these variables may be illegal. Issues involved

in test use with diverse groups include construct equivalence, orientations and values that may alter definition of constructs and interpretation of results, test bias, and how testing environment might affect performance of different groups. The need for psychology training programs to address cultural diversity was also addressed. However, similar to the 1985 standards for testing and the 1993 guidelines for providers, the 2001 report did not address the psychology profession as a whole.

At press time for this book, the APA was currently examining its ethics review process as well as the principles and standards themselves. Some have suggested that ethical issues related to psychologists should be dealt with by local "consumers" such as IRBs and state licensing boards, whereas others are concerned about the lack of professional guidelines for the conduct of psychologists. In addition, there are indications that the APA is moving toward discontinuing the practice of establishing guidelines for the psychology profession. Apparently, many psychologists have voiced concerns about the utility of guidelines that are aspirational in nature and thus nonenforceable. Whatever is decided by the APA, it is clear that major consequences related to accountability, credibility, and standards of the profession will be under close scrutiny.

ETHICAL ISSUES INVOLVING ETHNIC MINORITY POPULATIONS: RESEARCH, PRACTICE, AND TRAINING

In the ensuing years since the seminal events of the 1970s, multiple ethical issues that involve ethnic minority populations have been raised. These ethical issues have a bearing on research, training, and the practice of psychology. We might add that these issues are not new: They have repeatedly been raised without much tangible response from the profession. Our purpose is to summarize what we see as some of the primary ethical issues involving ethnic minorities.

Generalizability of Scientific Knowledge Base

Most theory and research in psychology has not included non–European American worldviews or participants (Sue, 1999). There has been a dearth of published literature on ethnic minority populations, particularly in the most prestigious psychology journals (Case & Smith, 2000; Graham, 1992; Hall & Maramba, 2001; Iwamasa & Smith, 1996; Iwamasa, Sorocco, & Koonce, 2002). This overemphasis on European American worldviews and participants creates a knowledge base that is not generalizable. The population of the United States is but 4% of the world population. Moreover, a European American psychology is not even representative of the United States. Indeed, according to the 2000 Census (U.S. Bureau of the Census, 2000), ethnic minority individuals comprise more than 40% of the United States population when individuals of Latino/Hispanic, Middle Eastern, and North African descent are added to the 25% ethnic minority (single race reported) and 2.4% multiracial individuals (U.S. Bureau of the Census, 2001).

The monocultural nature of psychology warrants cultural diversification, and the continued exclusion of ethnic minorities from theory and research could be considered unethical. Since 1994, the National Institutes of Health (NIH) have required the inclusion of ethnic minority participants in funded research projects (Hohmann & Parron, 1996). However, simple inclusion of ethnic minorities in research projects is far from a guarantee of culturally competent research. The NIH did not require the development of culturally relevant theories and research designs, culturally relevant constructs and measures, or even the separate analysis of ethnic minority subsamples (Hall, 2001). Therefore, it is not clear that simply including ethnic minorities in studies will lead to results that are different from those had ethnic minorities not been included. From both ethical and scientific perspectives, much more conceptually based, methodologically sound empirical research with ethnic minority populations is necessary. Recently, given the emphasis on racial disparities in health and mental health, the NIH is beginning to examine the impact of ethnicity on health. For example, in April 2002, the NIH held a conference and workshop entitled "Racial/Ethnic Bias and Health: Scientific Evidence and Methods." A goal of the conference and workshop was to explore the effects of racial/ethnic bias in scientific methods and potentially develop policy initiatives that would be implemented across the various NIH institutes. Time will tell if the outcome of the conference lived up to expectations.

When research that includes ethnic minority samples is conducted, these samples are often unrepresentative of ethnic minority communities. Research on ethnic minorities tends to be problem oriented, with a focus on persons in the lowest positions in the community (Fontes, 1998; Gil & Bob, 1999). The term *ethnic minority* has often become a euphemism for socioeconomic disadvantage or psychopathology (Hall, 2001). Thus, not only should research samples be representative of ethnocultural diversity but such samples should also represent the diversity within ethnoculturally diverse groups.

In the realm of practice, the limited empirical data on the effectiveness of clinical interventions with ethnic minority populations place clinicians in an ethical quandary. The assumption that interventions that have been empirically supported with European Americans are equally valid for ethnic minority populations may be unjustified. Indeed, Sue (1995) pointed out that there exists little scientific evidence for positive treatment outcome for ethnic minority populations. It has been recommended that approaches that have been empirically supported with European Americans be modified to be culturally relevant for use with ethnic minority populations (Hall, 2001). The relative utility and validity of existing approaches versus culturally specific approaches should be examined. Sue (1995) has called for practical research that focuses on identification of culturally derived interventions that are most effective for people of color, rather than examining effectiveness of mental health treatment in general.

It should be no surprise that a largely monocultural psychology has trained students in a primarily monocultural manner (Bernal & Castro, 1994; Hall, 1997). Similar to research and practice, training should be diversified (Lopez, 1997; Ponterotto, 1997; Yutrzenka, 1995). Ethnic minority students may undergo a process of acculturation to academic psychology that actually renders them less culturally competent than they were before their psychology training (Hall et al., 2001). Monocultural training does not instill cultural competence in European American students, either. The importance for ethnic minority students of developing and retaining competence in academic psychology as well as cultural competence was recognized at least as early as the Vail Conference in 1974 (Korman, 1974). Unfortunately, such calls for diversity training seem to have had limited impact on training programs.

Ethnic Comparisons

Psychologists tend to approach ethnic minority groups from a European American ethnocentric perspective. In most research on ethnic minority populations, ethnic minority groups are compared with European Americans (Graham, 1992). When ethnic minorities differ from European Americans, these differences are typically interpreted as deviance on the part of the minority groups. Moreover, comparative approaches tend to treat ethnic groups as homogeneous, ignoring important within-group variability (Iwamasa, 1997). Because of the many sociodemographic differences between ethnic minority and majority groups, Phinney (1996) has gone as far as arguing for a moratorium on ethnic comparative research.

Despite the potential problems of comparative approaches, these approaches can provide a context for understanding ethnic minority groups (Sue, 1991). Evidence of between-group differences can be a starting point from which to modify theories, methods, and interventions. For example, evidence that members of an ethnic group have interdependent tendencies could result in revisions of theories, methods, and interventions to consider the family, group, and community context of behavior in this group. Nevertheless, group characteristics should not be misunderstood to characterize all individuals in a group (Sue, 1991).

Knowledge about group differences can provide a useful context for hypothesis testing. Knowing that a person belongs to a group may help a psychologist target a domain (e.g., interdependence) for such hypothesis testing. Individual A belongs to Group B. Does this individual share characteristics with others in Group B? Failure to use knowledge about group differences may result in a failure to test relevant hypotheses or in testing the wrong hypotheses. For example, the assumption that an infant's inability to leave her mother and play independently in a new situation reflects insecure attachment may not be accurate in cultural groups in which interdependence is encouraged. Orientation to one's mother is common in interdependent cultures, whereas orientation to the environment is common in independent cultures (Rothbaum, Weisz, Pott, Miyake, & Morelli, 2000). Such cultural knowledge might result in culturally specific definitions of secure and insecure attachments.

Balancing the need to understand and accurately interpret between group differences and the need to better understand the complex and unique within-group differences of ethnic minority populations should be considered in the development of the research question. Researchers must ask themselves how answering the research question will benefit the population being studied and also how the methodology will culturally appropriately answer the research question (Iwamasa & Sorocco, 2002). Practitioners should also be able to understand that the way they interpret thoughts, behaviors, and feelings of their clients are influenced by their own ethnic and cultural values. Again, practitioners should be able to articulate how their interpretations are culturally relevant to their clients and also how implementation of interventions will be of benefit given clients' cultural contexts.

Cultural Equivalence of Measures

In instances in which psychologists desire to determine the generalizability of scientific knowledge, the most convenient method is to use an existing measure of a construct and apply it to a new sample, such as an ethnic minority group. This may involve translation of the measure into another language. Because these measures are usually standardized, such translations are usually literal, without consideration of cultural issues or context (Rogler, 1999). For example, the NEO Personality Inventory has been translated into

several languages, and its five-factor structure has been replicated in these languages (McCrae & Costa, 1997). However, replicating an existing factor structure in a translation is not a very demanding test, nor is it culturally sensitive to the meaning of the factors in particular cultural contexts (Hall, Bansal, & Lopez, 1999; Rogler, 1999; Saucier & Goldberg, in press). Moreover, there may be factors that are important or unique to cultural contexts not assessed by a measure originally developed in another culture. Similarly with the MMPI/MMPI-2, there is no evidence of test bias against ethnic minority groups, but absence of bias is not equivalent to a culturally sensitive test (Hall et al., 1999).

Sue, Kurasaki, and Srinivasan (1999) have suggested four issues to consider when adapting and selecting measures: (a) language equivalence, (b) cultural and socioeconomic equivalence, (c) conceptual equivalence, and (d) metric equivalence. Language equivalence exists when measures of constructs can be translated well across cultures. The effectiveness of translated measures depends on the degree of difference between the cultures (Rogler, 1999). To achieve such language equivalence, translation into the second language and back to the original language are necessary. Cultural and socioeconomic contextual factors also need to be considered to make the test understandable for particular groups (Sue et al., 1999). Conceptual equivalence involves the relevance of a construct in a particular cultural group and whether the construct is understood in a similar manner. Metric equivalence involves the comparability of test scores across cultural groups. For example, is a test score of 100 on a measure in one population equivalent to a score of 100 in another population, or on a translated form of the measure? Sue et al. (1999) recommended that multiple measures and methods be used to determine the convergent validity of measures. It was also recommended that consultants familiar with the target populations help develop measures.

Power Disparities Between Psychologists and Others

There exist inherent power disparities between psychologists and their research participants, students, and clients (Ivey, 1987; Kaiser, 1997). Psychologists typically have decision-making power that can affect these persons' futures, often in a dramatic fashion such as involuntary hospitalization. Such power disparities may be magnified when the psychologists are from the majority group and those with whom they work are from minority groups. Even when the psychologist is an ethnic minority person, this does not necessarily reduce the power disparity. An ethnic minority psychologist may be viewed as a pawn of the majority (Harris, 1996). Given that many ethnic minority psychologists are socialized and acculturated into traditional academic worldviews, this view is not unwarranted (Hall et al., 2001). In addition, although ethnic minority psychologists may be viewed as pawns of the majority culture by other ethnic minorities, ethnic minorities often are viewed as less powerful, credible, and able by their own colleagues (Committee on Women in Psychology and Commission on Ethnic Minority Recruitment, Retention, and Training in Psychology, 1998; Iwamasa, 1996).

For many ethnic minority persons, merely becoming a client or participating in research may be threatening (Fontes, 1998). For example, undocumented workers and other stigmatized groups may fear that their identities will be recorded and that they will face the negative consequences of detection (e.g., deportation). Others may fear retribution from family members if their participation in a study or in treatment is made public.

Principle E of the 1992 APA ethical principles on "Concern for Others' Welfare" indicates that psychologists are sensitive to real and ascribed differences in power between themselves and others. Sensitivity to the power disparity is a first step in preventing psychologists from exploiting research participants, students, and clients. Principle E also indicates that psychologists seek to contribute to the welfare of those with whom they interact professionally, although the principle is not specific about how this is to be accomplished other than avoiding or minimizing harm. Promoting the welfare of others could be an antidote to the power disparity between psychologists and those with whom they work.

Responsibilities for the Welfare of Ethnic Minority Persons

Principle F of the 1992 APA ethical principles indicates that psychologists are aware of their professional and scientific responsibilities to the community. Many psychologists contribute to the welfare of the community in terms of scientific knowledge, training, or interventions. Such contributions, however, are not necessarily beneficial to ethnic minority communities. Tangible contributions by psychologists to ethnic minority communities may require an activist stance that challenges social structures that oppress ethnic minority groups (Casas & Thompson, 1991; LaFromboise, Foster, & James, 1996). For example, culturally sensitive research, training, and interventions challenge existing paradigms and may have unique benefits for ethnic minority communities.

In the Tuskegee study, previously discussed, interventions for syphilis were denied. Denying an intervention to a group is common in research that involves a control group. It is typically argued that the efficacy of an intervention cannot be adequately evaluated without a control group. However, including a control group does not necessarily mean that a group is denied a potentially effective intervention. There are several potential alternatives to denying an intervention to a control group. These include providing the intervention after the study is complete, comparing two or more potentially beneficial treatments, comparing treatment group outcome with some established standard, and conducting intra-individual comparisons (Scott-Jones, 1994).

IS PSYCHOLOGY THE APPROPRIATE DISCIPLINE IN WHICH TO ADDRESS ETHNIC MINORITY ISSUES?

Most psychologists have not obtained the training, experience, consultation, or supervision to ensure the competence of their services to ethnic minority groups that is required by APA (1992) Principle 1.08 on "Human Differences." Research and training activities could also qualify as services, although the term *services* in the ethical principles implies clinical practice issues. Exposure to ethnic minority issues in most psychology graduate training programs is at best minimal (Bernal & Castro, 1994). Minimal exposure is not adequate to insure competence (Hall, 1997). Thus, it could be contended that most psychologists who work with ethnic minority persons are not competent and are therefore engaging in unethical behavior.

Does the prospect of engaging in unethical behavior motivate change among most psychologists? Given the limited response in psychology to ethical mandates for diversity over the past 30 years, the answer in most cases is probably "No." In most instances, psychologists can be culturally insensitive with relative impunity (Gil & Bob,

1999; Hall, 1997). For example, cultural incompetence is rarely a basis for professional sanctions, such as loss of one's psychology license. Even those psychologists who genuinely desire to obtain appropriate training, experience, consultation, or supervision to ensure cultural competence may find barriers. In training programs, ethnic minority and other diversity issues are often "assigned" to the only or few ethnic minority faculty, who are often expected to serve as experts on every facet of diversity and consistently speak on behalf of diversity issues in every context: classroom, departmental and university meetings, student theses and dissertations, and so on. These individuals are often expected to provide this additional service requirement, which is not expected of nonminority faculty, who often do not feel responsible for being knowledgeable about issues of diversity. Expertise on ethnic minority issues is in short supply (Bernal & Castro, 1994).

Are certain subdisciplines in psychology doing a better job with ethnic minority issues than others? Relative emphasis on ethnic minority issues is reflected in publications on these issues in the journals of subdisciplines. Ponterotto (1988) examined articles published in the *Journal of Counseling Psychology* from 1976 to 1986 and found that 5.7% of the articles contained ethnic minority participants. Iwamasa and Smith (1996) examined the behavioral psychology literature and found that 1.3% of the articles published in three leading behavioral journals focused on ethnic minorities. In a content analysis of the articles published in psychology journals from 1993 to 1999, the journals that published the greatest percentage of articles on ethnic minorities, other than those that specifically focused on ethnic minority issues (e.g., *Journal of Black Psychology),* were the *American Journal of Community Psychology (AJCP),* at 34%, and the *Journal of Community Psychology*

(JCP), at 29% (Hall & Maramba, 2001). This is an improvement over previous reviews of these journals, which found that between 1973 and 1985, *AJCP's* percentage of including ethnic minority participants was 17%, and *JCP's* was 16% (Loo, Fong, & Iwamasa, 1988). However, it is not necessarily the case that research on ethnic minorities in community psychology is being conducted from an ethnic minority perspective or that it is culturally competent. Indeed, the most productive researchers on ethnic minority issues do not have work published in community psychology journals (Hall & Maramba, 2001).

In psychology, there is a discipline-wide paucity of publications on ethnic minorities. Of the 24 flagship journals published by the APA or the American Psychological Society (APS) from 1993 to 1999, only 6% of all published articles involved ethnic minority populations or issues (Hall & Maramba, 2001). The only journal to devote more than 10% of its publications to ethnic minorities was the *Journal of Counseling Psychology*, at 14%. Many of the leading ethnic minority scholars have their work published in counseling psychology journals (Hall & Maramba, 2001). A relevant question is what the expected percentage of publications would be for an area that was considered important within a field. In an analysis of 16 top-tier psychology journals, it was concluded that an area represented by 18% of the publications (cognitive psychology) was prominent, whereas areas with less than 4% of the publications (behavioral, psychoanalytic, neuroscience) were in decline (Robbins, Gosling, & Craik, 1999). Ethnic minority issues at 6% in APA and APS journals are quite close to the areas in decline. Thus, with the exceptions of community psychology and possibly also counseling psychology, psychology has neglected ethnic minority populations and issues. Such neglect is an indication that most psychologists are not interested in ethnic minority issues, do not have ethnic minority competence, and have not been trained to be culturally competent.

Principle 1.08 (APA, 1992) indicates that when psychologists do not possess adequate expertise, they make appropriate referrals. Although referrals appear most germane to clinical practice, perhaps the concept of referral is relevant to psychology in a more general sense. Can ethnic minority issues be better addressed outside psychology? Should psychology refer ethnic minority issues to another field that is more culturally sensitive?

Other social science disciplines that address ethnic minority issues include cultural anthropology and sociology. Relatively speaking, cultural anthropology and sociology are descriptive, whereas psychology is explanatory. An advantage of the descriptive approach is that foreign theoretical and research frameworks are less likely to be imposed on the population of study than in an explanatory approach. The descriptive approach may for the most part preclude experimental manipulations or interventions common in psychological science. Moreover, cultural anthropology and sociology address issues at the group and community levels, whereas psychology has primarily examined individuals.

Ethnic minority issues are also approached in social policy and social welfare disciplines at a community policy level. Similar to cultural anthropology and sociology, phenomena are considered at the group and community levels. However, unlike cultural anthropology and sociology, interventions are an important component of social policy and social welfare. Interventions in social policy and social welfare tend to be at the community or societal level. Ethnic minority persons often have strong ties to their ethnic community, and many problems that ethnic minority persons face (e.g., discrimination) occur at the community or societal level. Individual interventions tend not to be emphasized unless they have implications beyond the individual (e.g., court cases on behalf of an individual that affect a group).

Referring ethnic minority issues to another discipline would leave psychology on the sidelines, in obsolescence (Hall, 1997). A European American psychology fails to explain the behavior of a significant percentage of the United States population and may be even more irrelevant in the global context from which many American ethnic minority persons have emigrated. Thus, psychology needs ethnic minority issues (Iwamasa, 1997). But do ethnic minority issues need psychology? It would be extremely ethnocentric and naive to assume that ethnic minority issues cannot survive outside psychology's sphere of influence. Despite the very limited attention that psychology has devoted to ethnic minority issues, they continue to be critical in society.

What psychology potentially brings to ethnic minority issues is the ability to address issues at a range of levels, from the molecular to the societal levels. Much psychology research has direct or indirect benefits to human welfare, including empirically based interventions that can be tailored to a variety of contexts. Psychology's scientific rigor also distinguishes it from many other social and behavioral sciences. Nevertheless, wholesale changes are needed in psychology if it is to be relevant to ethnic minority issues. In the absence of such changes, psychology risks being supplanted by other disciplines that are more responsive to ethnic minority issues.

RECOMMENDATIONS FOR ACTION

Christine Iijima Hall (1997) criticized APA for its support of diversity, which has not necessarily led to curricular and policy changes in psychology. As discussed previously,

ethical guidelines regarding cultural competence have long existed but appear not to have had an effect on most psychologists. Clear ethical standards do not necessarily insure improved services (Prilleltensky, 1997). There are few professional consequences for psychologists who work outside their areas of competence (Pedersen, 1995). Compliance with ethical standards is largely voluntary, which means that many psychologists will do nothing or the minimum required with respect to ethnic minority issues.

Rather than simply relying on the goodwill of psychologists by developing general ethical standards and guidelines, there is a need for psychology as a profession to take actions to increase its responsiveness to ethnic minority issues. Specific recommendations include the following:

1. Recruitment of minority students and faculty and the development of a culturally inclusive training curriculum that includes discussion of the political, economic, and social issues of race, gender, class, and sexual identity (Hall, 1997).

2. Multicultural research teams, IRBs, grant panels, and journal boards (Atkinson, 1993; Fontes, 1998; Gil & Bob, 1999; Hall, 2001; Scott-Jones, 1994).

3. Nonrepresentative samples and culturally insensitive research should not be supported by IRBs, government funding, or journal reviewers and editors.

4. Multicultural expertise on training program accreditation committees and enforcement of penalties (e.g., probation, nonaccreditation) against programs that pay only lip service to diversity.

5. Multicultural licensing boards that require the demonstration of multicultural competence for licensure and also require multicultural continuing education.

There undoubtedly has been and will continue to be resistance against such actions to diversify psychology. Persons in power benefit from the existing system of social, economic, and cultural dominance (D'Andrea et al., 2001). Becoming more inclusive of ethnic minority persons and issues will involve a reduction in the power of dominant groups. Some well-meaning psychologists who are philosophically liberal and supportive of ethnic minority issues may find it difficult to learn to collaborate with ethnic minority psychologists and community members. This collaboration is likely to mean deference on the part of nonminority psychologists toward ethnic minority persons. Many nonminority psychologists may be much more comfortable in an expert role than in a learner role. Rather than attempting to impose standards on ethnic minority populations, as has often been the case in cross-cultural psychology, nonminority psychologists will need to respect the standards developed within ethnic minority communities.

Persons from ethnic minority groups that are directly affected by the actions and inactions of the governing bodies of psychology should have a voice and may be in a better position than persons who are not ethnic minorities to determine what is ethically appropriate. Out-groups inherently have less power than in-groups to influence policy (Meara, Schmidt, & Day, 1996). It is important for ethical issues involving ethnic minorities to be codified by the governing bodies of the profession. Otherwise, attention to these issues is unlikely to be sustained. Without such codification, emphasis on ethnic minority issues is likely to vary depending on whom the leaders happen to be at the time.

Ethnic minority issues are not simply a "flavor of the month" that will soon lose their importance. It is a monocultural psychology, not ethnic minority issues, that risks becoming unimportant and irrelevant (Hall, 1997; Hall et al., 2001). Ethnic minority issues touch virtually every area of psychological research, training, and practice. Moreover, ethnic minority populations in the United States are rapidly and steadily growing, which suggests that these issues will only increase in importance rather than the reverse (Iwamasa, 1997).

REFERENCES

American Psychological Association. (1973). Ethical principles in the conduct of research with human participants. *American Psychologist, 28,* 79-80.

American Psychological Association. (1981). Ethical principles of psychologists. *American Psychologist, 36,* 633-638.

American Psychological Association. (1985). *Standards for educational and psychological testing.* Washington DC: American Psychological Association.

American Psychological Association. (1992). Ethical principles of psychologists and code of conduct. *American Psychologist, 47,* 1597-1611.

American Psychological Association. (1993). Guidelines for providers of psychological services to ethnic, linguistic, and culturally diverse populations. *American Psychologist, 48,* 45-48.

Atkinson, D. R. (1993). Who speaks for cross-cultural counseling research? *Counseling Psychologist, 21,* 218-224.

Bernal, M. E., & Castro, F. G. (1994). Are clinical psychologists prepared for service and research with ethnic minorities? Report of a decade of progress. *American Psychologist, 49,* 797-805.

Casas, J. M., Ponterotto, J. G., & Gutierrez, J. M. (1986). An ethical indictment of counseling research and training: The cross-cultural perspective. *Journal of Counseling and Development, 64,* 347-349.

Casas, J. M., & Thompson, C. E. (1991). Ethical principles and standards: A racial-ethnic minority research perspective. *Counseling and Values, 35,* 186-195.

Case, L., & Smith, T. B. (2000). Ethnic representation in a sample of the literature in applied psychology. *Journal of Consulting and Clinical Psychology, 68,* 1107-1110.

Ceci, S. J., Peters, D., & Plotkin, J. (1985). Human subjects review, personal values, and the regulation of social science research. *American Psychologist, 40,* 994-1002.

Council of National Psychological Associations for the Advancement of Ethnic Minority Interests. (2000). *Guidelines for research in ethnic minority communities.* Washington, DC: American Psychological Association.

Committee on Women in Psychology and the APA Commission on Ethnic Minority Recruitment, Retention, and Training in Psychology. (1998). *Surviving and thriving in academia: A guide for women and ethnic minorities.* Washington, DC: American Psychological Association.

D'Andrea, M., Daniels, J., Arredondo, P., Ivey, M. B., Ivey, A. E., Locke, D. C., O'Bryant, B., Parham, T. A., & Sue, D. W. (2001). Fostering organizational changes to realize the revolutionary potential of the multicultural movement. In J. G. Ponterotto, J. M. Casas, C. A. Suzuki, & C. M. Alexander (Eds.), *Handbook of multicultural counseling* (pp. 222-253). Thousand Oaks, CA: Sage.

Fontes, L. A. (1998). Ethics in family violence research: Cross-cultural issues. *Family Relations, 47,* 53-61.

Gil, E. F., & Bob, S. (1999). Culturally competent research: An ethical perspective. *Clinical Psychology Review, 19,* 45-55.

Gilbert, D. T. (1998). Ordinary personology. In D. T. Gilbert, S. T. Fiske, & G. Lindzey (Eds.), *The handbook of social psychology* (4th ed., Vol. 2., pp. 89-150). New York: McGraw-Hill.

Gilligan, C. (1982). *In a different voice.* Cambridge, MA: Harvard University Press.

Graham, S. (1992). "Most of the subjects were White and middle class": Trends in published research on African Americans in selected APA journals, 1970-1989. *American Psychologist, 47,* 629-639.

Hall, C. C. I. (1997). Cultural malpractice: The growing obsolescence of psychology with the changing U.S. population. *American Psychologist, 52,* 642-651.

Hall, G. C. N. (2001). Psychotherapy research with ethnic minorities: Empirical, ethical, and conceptual issues. *Journal of Consulting and Clinical Psychology, 69,* 502-510.

Hall, G. C. N., Bansal, A., & Lopez, I. R. (1999). Ethnicity and psychopathology: A meta-analytic review of 31 years of comparative MMPI/MMPI-2 research. *Psychological Assessment, 11,* 186-197.

Hall, G. C. N., Lopez, I. R., & Bansal, A. (2001). Academic acculturation: Race, gender, and class issues. In D. Pope-Davis & H. Coleman (Eds.), *The intersection of race, gender, and class: Implications for counselor training* (pp. 171-188). Thousand Oaks, CA: Sage.

Hall, G. C. N., & Maramba, G. G. (2001). In search of cultural diversity: Recent literature in cross-cultural and ethnic minority psychology. *Cultural Diversity and Ethnic Minority Psychology, 7,* 12-26.

Harding, S. (1987). The curious coincidence of feminine and African moralities: Challenges for feminist theory. In E. F. Kittay & D. T. Meyers (Eds.), *Women and moral theory* (pp. 296-315). Totowa, NJ: Rowman and Littlefield.

Harris, J. L. (1996). Issues in recruiting African American participants for research. In A. G. Kamhi & E. Pollock (Eds.), *Communication development and disorders in African American children: Research, assessment, and intervention* (pp. 19-34). Baltimore, MD: Brooks.

Harter, L. M., Stephens, R. J., & Japp, P. M. (2000). President Clinton's apology for the Tuskegee Syphilis Experiment: A narrative of remembrance, redefinition, and reconciliation. *The Howard Journal of Communications, 11,* 19-34.

Hillerbrand, E. (1987). Philosophical tensions influencing psychology and social action. *American Psychologist, 42,* 111-118.

Hohmann, A. A., & Parron, D. L. (1996). How the new NIH guidelines on inclusion of women and minorities apply: Efficacy trials, effectiveness trials, and validity. *Journal of Consulting and Clinical Psychology, 64,* 851-855.

Ivey, A. E. (1987). The multicultural practice of therapy: Ethics, empathy, and dialectics. *Journal of Social and Clinical Psychology, 5,* 195-204.

Iwamasa, G. Y. (1996). On being an ethnic minority cognitive behavioral therapist. *Cognitive and Behavioral Practice, 3,* 235-254.

Iwamasa, G. Y. (1997). Behavior therapy and a culturally diverse society: Forging an alliance. *Behavior Therapy, 28,* 347-358.

Iwamasa, G. Y., & Smith, S. K. (1996). Ethnic diversity in behavioral psychology: A review of the literature. *Behavior Modification, 20,* 45-59.

Iwamasa, G. Y., & Sorocco, K. H. (2002.) Aging and Asian Americans: Developing culturally appropriate research methodology. In G. C. H. Hall & S. Okazaki (Eds.), *Asian American psychology: The science of lives in context.* Washington, DC: American Psychological Association.

Iwamasa, G. Y., Sorocco, K. H., & Koonce, D. (2002). Ethnicity in clinical psychology: A review of the literature. *Clinical Psychology Review, 22,* 931-944.

Kaiser, T. L. (1997). *Supervisory relationships: Exploring the human element.* Pacific Grove, CA: Brooks/Cole.

Korman, M. (1974). National conference on levels and patterns of professional training in psychology: The major themes. *American Psychologist, 29,* 441-449.

LaFromboise, T. D., & Foster, S. L. (1989). Ethics in multicultural counseling. Ethics in multicultural counseling. In P. B. Pedersen, J. G. Draguns, W. J. Lonner, & J. E. Trimble (Eds.), *Counseling across cultures* (pp. 115-136). Honolulu: University of Hawaii Press.

LaFromboise, T. D., Foster, S., & James, A. (1996). Ethics in multicultural counseling. In P. B. Pedersen, J. G. Draguns, W. J. Lonner, & J. E. Trimble (Eds.), *Counseling across cultures* (4th ed., pp. 47-72). Thousand Oaks, CA: Sage.

Loo, C., Fong, K. T., & Iwamasa, G. (1988). Ethnicity and cultural diversity: An analysis of work published in Community Psychology journals, 1965-1985. *Journal of Community Psychology, 16,* 332-349.

Lopez, S. R. (1997). Cultural competence in psychotherapy: A guide for clinicians and their supervisors. In C. E. Watkins (Ed.), *Handbook of psychotherapy supervision* (pp. 570-588). New York: Wiley.

McCrae, R. R., & Costa, P. T. Jr. (1997). Personality trait structure as a human universal. *American Psychologist, 52,* 509-516.

Meara, N. M., Schmidt, L. D., & Day, J. D. (1996). Principles and virtues: A foundation for ethical decisions, policies, and character. *Counseling Psychologist, 24,* 4-77.

National Research Service Award Act, Pub. L. No. 93-348 (1974).

Noddings, N. (1984). *Caring: A feminine approach to ethics and moral education.* Berkeley: University of California Press.

Noddings, N. (1986). Fidelity in teaching, teacher education, and research for teaching. *Harvard Educational Review, 56,* 496-510.

Pedersen, P. B. (1995). Culture-centered ethical guidelines for counselors. In J. G. Ponterotto & J. M. Casas (Eds.), *Handbook of multicultural counseling* (pp. 34-49). Thousand Oaks, CA: Sage.

Pedersen, P. B. (1997). The cultural context of the American Counseling Association code of ethics. *Journal of Counseling and Development, 76,* 23-28.

Phinney, J. S. (1996). When we talk about American ethnic groups, what do we mean? *American Psychologist, 51,* 918-927.

Ponterotto, J. G. (1988). Racial/ethnic minority research in the *Journal of Counseling Psychology:* A content analysis and methodological critique. *Journal of Counseling Psychology, 35,* 410-418.

Ponterotto, J. G. (1997). Multicultural counseling training: A competency model and national survey. In D. B. Pope-Davis & H. L. K. Coleman (Eds.), *Multicultural counseling competencies: Assessment, education and training, and supervision* (pp. 111-130). Thousand Oaks, CA: Sage.

Pope, K. S., & Vasquez, M. J. T. (1991). *Ethics in psychotherapy and counseling.* San Francisco: Jossey-Bass.

Prilleltensky, I. (1997). Values, assumptions, and practices: Assessing the moral implications of psychological discourse and action. *American Psychologist, 52,* 517-535.

Robbins, R. W., Gosling, S. D., & Craik, K. H. (1999). An empirical analysis of trends in psychology. *American Psychologist, 53,* 1101-1110.

Rogler, L. H. (1999). Methodological sources of cultural insensitivity in mental health research. *American Psychologist, 54,* 424-433.

Rosnow, R. L., Rotheram-Borus, M. J., Ceci, S. J., Blanck, P. D., & Koocher, G. P. (1993). Institutional review board as mirror of scientific and ethical standards. *American Psychologist, 48,* 821-826.

Rothbaum, F., Weisz, J., Pott, M., Miyake, K., & Morelli, G. (2000). Attachment and culture: Security in the United States and Japan. *American Psychologist, 55,* 1093-1104.

Saucier, G., & Goldberg, L. R. (in press). The structure of personality attributes. In M. Barrick & A. M. Ryan (Eds.), *Personality and work.* New York: Jossey-Bass-Pfeiffer.

Scott-Jones, D. (1994). Ethical issues in reporting and referring in research with low-income minority children. *Ethics and Behavior, 4,* 97-108.

Stroud, W. L. (1994). Dewey's integrated logic of science, ethics, and practice. *American Psychologist, 49,* 968-970.

Sue, D. W., Arredondo, P., & McDavis, J. (1992). Multicultural counseling competencies and standards: A call to the profession. *Journal of Counseling and Development, 70,* 477-486.

Sue, D. W., Bernier, J. E., Durran, A., Feinberg, L., Pedersen, P., Smith, E. J., & Vasquez-Nuttall, E. (1982). Position paper: Cross-cultural counseling competencies. *Counseling Psychologist, 10,* 45-52.

Sue, D. W., & Sue, D. (1999). *Counseling the culturally different* (3rd ed.). New York: Wiley.

Sue, S. (1991). Ethnicity and culture in psychological research and practice. In J. Goodchilds (Ed.), *Psychological perspectives on human diversity in America* (pp. 51-85). Washington, DC: American Psychological Association.

Sue, S. (1995). The implications of diversity for scientific standards of practice. In S. C. Hayes, V. M. Follette, R. M. Dawes, & K. E. Grady (Eds.), *Scientific standards of psychological practice: Issues and recommendations.* Reno, NV: Context.

Sue, S. (1999). Science, ethnicity, and bias: Where have we gone wrong? *American Psychologist, 54,* 1070-1077.

Sue, S., Kurasaki, K. S., & Srinivasan, S. (1999). Ethnicity, gender, and cross-cultural issues in clinical research. In P. C. Kendall, J. N. Butcher, & G. N. Holmbeck (Eds.), *Handbook of research methods in clinical psychology* (2nd ed., pp. 54-71). New York: Wiley.

Tapp, J. L., Kelman, H. C., Triandis, H. C., Wrightsman, L. S., & Coelho, G. V. (1974). Continuing concerns in cross-cultural ethics: A report. *International Journal of Psychology, 9,* 231-249.

Thompson, A. (1998). Not the color purple: Black feminist lessons for educational caring. *Harvard Educational Review, 68,* 522-554.

Turner, S. M., Demers, S. T., Fox, H. R., & Reed, G. M. (2001). APA's guidelines for test user qualifications: An executive summary. *American Psychologist, 56,* 1099-1113.

U.S. Bureau of the Census. (2000). *The white population: Census 2000 brief.* Retrieved September 18, 2002, on the World Wide Web at: http://www. census.gov/prod/2001 pubs/c2kbr01-4.pdf.

U.S. Bureau of the Census. (2001). *Overview of race and Hispanic origin, 2000: Census 2000 brief.* Retrieved September 18, 2002, on the World Wide Web at http://www.census.gov/prod/2001pubs/c2kbr01-1.pdf.

Yutrzenka, B. A. (1995). Making a case for training in ethnic and cultural diversity in increasing treatment efficacy. *Journal of Consulting and Clinical Psychology, 63,* 197-206.

CHAPTER 19

Sexual Orientation and Professional Ethics

DAVID W. PURCELL, STEPHANIE SWANN, AND SARAH E. HERBERT

Treating gay, lesbian, and bisexual clients can be fraught with ethical dilemmas and conflict. However, clinicians can take steps to learn about these populations to assure that therapy is conducted in an ethical manner. Learning about the competent, ethical treatment of these clients is important for therapists of all theoretical and sexual orientations for at least four reasons. First, in a 1991 survey of almost 1,500 psychologists, 99% of the respondents reported that they had treated a lesbian or gay man (Garnets, Hancock, Cochran, Goodchilds, & Peplau, 1991). Thus, mental health clinicians are very likely to see such clients in practice. Second, gay men and lesbians are more likely to use psychotherapeutic services than are heterosexual men and women (Hancock, 1995). Third, well-trained therapists can offer ethical, competent, and sensitive care to this population and avoid some of the unethical practices found by Garnets and her colleagues, who were surprised to find that "despite APA's

formal repeatedly stated nondiscriminatory policy, understanding, acceptance, and adherence to those goals are seriously lacking" (Garnets et al., 1991, p. 971). In their article, Garnets and her colleagues highlighted 25 themes illustrating biased, inappropriate practice (such as attributing clients' problems to their sexual orientation without evidence) and 20 themes showing exemplary practice. Finally, attention to this topic is important because therapists often have more accurate information about sexual behavior, orientation, and identity than clients do, especially young people or those first struggling to accept their sexuality.

To define the scope of this chapter more clearly, we first address basic definitions regarding sexuality and gender, two concepts that are often confused. Then, we highlight the history of mental health treatment for homosexuality to provide a context for ethical work with these clients today. Next, we focus on three factors about which therapists must have basic information: (a) *therapist factors,* the strengths and weaknesses the therapist brings to a therapeutic relationship with clients, including an understanding of the effects of homophobia and heterosexism on them as therapists; (b) *cultural factors,* the richness and texture of gay, lesbian, and bisexual lives and culture; and (c) *client factors,* the extent of the client's involvement in and understanding of gay culture. Finally, we will address ethical therapy with adolescents under age 18 who present with concerns about their sexuality.

BACKGROUND INFORMATION ON SEXUALITY- AND GENDER-RELATED ISSUES

Various behaviors and "lifestyles" often are confused with or linked to homosexuality, making it important to understand the distinctions between sexual behavior, orientation, identity, and gender identity and role. Although expressions of sexuality and gender may be linked for clients, therapists must learn to assess and conceptualize sexuality and gender separately.

Definitions of Sexual Behavior, Sexual Orientation, and Sexual Identity

Sexual behavior is simply a term used to describe a person's behavior only, regardless of their sexual orientation or identity. In contrast, *sexual orientation* describes a person's pattern of sexual attraction, which may or may not match their actual sexual behavior. Most individuals experience erotic feelings and desires (i.e., orientation) early in life, and these are relatively stable and resistant to change (D'Augelli, 1991), whereas sexual behavior may vary depending on circumstances (e.g., prison, sexual experimentation). *Sexual identity* is defined as how people understand and make sense of their own sexual attractions (orientation) and behavior. Sexual orientation may be more stable over time than either sexual identity or behavior, although more research is needed to understand the development of all forms of sexuality (Bailey, 1995).

A few examples help to illustrate these concepts. A man's sexual orientation may be *homosexual* or *bisexual* (he is attracted to men or men and women), but he may choose to get married to a woman and not integrate his same-sex desires into his sexual identity. Thus, he would not call himself gay or bisexual, might not engage in sex with men, nor participate in any cultural expressions of being gay or bisexual, such as attending a pride march. Even if such a man did choose to sometimes have sex with men, his sexual identity may be heterosexual. Similarly, a woman who is primarily attracted to men or to men and women may adopt a lesbian identity due to her political or social beliefs. She might find it more empowering or personally fulfilling to hold such an identity and enter sexual relationships only with women, despite her sexual feelings.

Definitions of Gender Identity and Gender Role

Gender identity is defined as a person's internal, psychological sense of being male or female, regardless of anatomic reality, although in most cases a person's gender identity is consistent with his or her biological sex (Paul, 1993). A person's *gender role* is defined as personality traits, behavior, and appearance that are viewed as masculine or feminine by a particular culture. The *DSM-IV* (*Diagnostic and Statistical Manual of Mental Disorders,* 4th ed.), includes a diagnosis for "gender identity disorder" (GID) that requires (a) strong and persistent cross-gender identification and (b) persistent discomfort with assigned sex or a sense of inappropriateness in the gender role of that sex (American Psychiatric Association, 1994). There currently is controversy over the use of GID as a psychiatric diagnosis and how to differentiate it from gender-nonconforming behavior. Although developmental research with girls is sparse, research with boys diagnosed with GID indicates that by adolescence, most no longer meet diagnostic criteria and about 75% report a gay or bisexual orientation in adulthood (American Psychiatric Association, 1994; Green, 1987). Adults who continue to feel that their gender identity does not match their biological sex may live as the other sex, take sex hormones, and eventually have surgery to reflect their gender identity. *Transgender* or *transsexual* (after surgery) is the term applied to these people.

Although it is often confused with sexuality, gender identity is not directly related to sexual orientation. *DSM-IV* (American Psychiatric Association, 1994) indicates that gender identity and sexual orientation should be assessed independently. Unfortunately, addressing the full range of ethical issues for therapy with transgender individuals is beyond the scope of this chapter, and these issues are addressed elsewhere (Seil, 1996). It is important to note, however, the potential overlap of these issues, because clients or their families may present with confusion about the relationship between sexuality and gender. For example, some gay men, particularly when they are first coming out, may identify strongly with women and a female gender role, partially because they think that being gay means being effeminate. The client may come to therapy fearful that he is a girl because of his same-sex attractions, or an adolescent may be brought to therapy by his parents because of his cross-gender behavior or interests. The therapist's job would be to sensitively disentangle these issues with the client. Therapists should seek consultation or refer the client in accordance with standard ethical practice if they do not have experience with these complex issues.

BACKGROUND INFORMATION ON HOMOSEXUALITY

Historically, homosexual behavior was seen as a potential criminal or evil behavior in everyone that was controlled through laws or religious proscriptions (Goggin, 1993). During the 20th century, however, as the meaning of homosexual shifted from being used to describe sexual behavior to describing a type of person (Garnets & Kimmel, 1991), homosexuality came to be conceptualized as a pathological medical and/or psychiatric illness to be managed by doctors. In *DSM-I* (American Psychiatric Association, 1952), homosexuality was listed under sociopathic personality disturbances as a pathological sexual deviation, and the treatment focused on change to heterosexuality. Theorists posited that heterosexuality was the natural result of unimpeded development and that homosexuality was caused by severe early disturbances and an "inversion" of gender identity (Isay, 1989; Lewes, 1988). These early psychoanalytic theories reflect the cultural confusion about the differences between sexual orientation and gender identity.

A major methodological flaw in the development of early psychoanalytic models was biased sampling using clinical samples to draw broad conclusions of universal pathology (for a review, see Gonsiorek, 1991). Numerous studies, starting with Hooker's (1957) seminal research, have shown that lesbians and gay men are psychologically indistinguishable from heterosexuals and that homosexuality itself is not a sign of psychological maladjustment. The only significant differences found in some studies were higher rates of past suicide attempts and drug and alcohol abuse in late adolescence and early adulthood, differences that may be linked to the high levels of external stress often experienced when someone first becomes aware of their gay, lesbian, or bisexual orientations (Gonsiorek, 1995).

As a result of scientific and political pressure, in 1973, the American Psychiatric Association Board of Trustees removed homosexuality as a diagnosis from the *DSM* (Gonsiorek, 1991), and this controversial decision was upheld by a vote of members, with 58% voting for removal (Bayer, 1987). Other professional organizations soon followed this lead. In 1975, the American Psychological Association (APA) resolved that "Homosexuality per se implies no impairment in judgment, reliability, or general social and vocational abilities" and urged psychologists to "take the lead in removing the stigma of mental illness that has long been associated with homosexual orientations" (Conger, 1975, p. 633).

Despite the removal of homosexuality from the *DSM,* some therapists still assert that adult psychological adjustment in lesbians and gay men is pathological (Socarides & Volkan, 1991) and suggest methods to "cure" these defects with reparative therapy (Nicolosi, 1991) or prevent them from occurring in the first place (Van den Aardweg, 1986). Some therapists also do not support a client's homosexual orientation because of the therapist's religious or moral beliefs. There has been extensive debate about the ethics of "conversion" or "reparative" therapy, often practiced by those with strong religious beliefs, and there have been attempts to have these therapies declared unethical. However, no professional group has declared conversion therapies unethical or illegal. In August 1997, the APA passed a resolution on this issue reaffirming that homosexuality is not a mental illness and that therapists providing therapy to clients who are gay or lesbian or are questioning their sexuality should

(a) provide accurate information about sexual orientation, (b) provide informed consent as to the treatment offered, (c) offer information about alternative treatments, and (d) practice in a nondiscriminatory and value-neutral manner regarding sexual orientation. Practicing in a *value-neutral* manner means that the therapist is not invested in the outcome of the client's exploration of his or her sexuality; the therapist would support a heterosexual or homosexual orientation (or other variations, such as bisexual).

WORKING WITH LESBIAN, GAY, AND BISEXUAL CLIENTS

Since homosexuality was removed from the *DSM,* a number of books and articles on psychotherapy with lesbians and gay men have been published (Cabaj & Stein, 1996; Coleman, 1987; Cornett, 1993; Hancock, 1995; Stein & Cohen, 1986). The initial focus was on atheoretical "gay-affirmative" models of therapy. More recently, theoretically based, affirmative models have been advanced by psychodynamic (e.g., Cornett, 1993; Isay, 1989) and cognitive behavioral therapists (e.g., Bernstein & Miller, 1995; Purcell, Campos, & Perilla, 1996). This work has allowed clinicians to learn about lesbians and gay men as people and as therapy clients.

Next, we will examine three general classes of factors that may affect therapy with lesbians, gay men, and bisexual clients: therapist, cultural, and client factors. Understanding each is crucial to providing ethical, sensitive, and competent therapy to these clients.

Therapist Factors
Affecting Therapy With Lesbians, Gay Men, and Bisexuals

To be able to understand the second and third factors (the cultural context of clients and clients' individual issues), it is necessary for therapists to examine their own histories and how these histories have affected and continue to affect their thoughts and feelings about lesbians, gay men, and bisexuals. This type of self-examination may help the therapist to create an empathic environment and to understand some of the special mental health issues for these men and women. It has been argued that nearly everyone in Western culture has grown up surrounded by *homophobia* (fear and hatred of nonheterosexual persons) and *heterosexism* (the devaluation of any nonheterosexual form of behavior, identity, or relationship) (Stein, 1996b) and that these two forms of bias significantly affect therapists' work with this population (Brown, 1996). Poor ethical decision making becomes more likely when the therapist is biased (in this case due to culturally acquired homophobia and/or heterosexism) and when the course of action is not clearly addressed by ethical codes or laws (which is the case for most complex ethical dilemmas with lesbian, gay, and bisexual clients) (Brown, 1996).

Homophobia and Heterosexism

Although these two constructs are widely used, there is some controversy about the actual measurement of homophobia (O'Donohue & Caselles, 1993) and about the fact that the behavior, fear, or hatred of gay men and lesbians may not actually be a phobia (Rowan, 1994). Although the resolution of these issues is beyond the scope of this chapter, recently, researchers have tried to more precisely define homophobia and measure it in a psychometrically adequate manner (Herek, 1996; Shidlo, 1994; Shidlo & Hollander, 1998). For the purposes of this chapter, we will assume that homophobia and heterosexism are useful heuristics that can assist in our understanding of ethical

clinical practice with lesbian, gay male, and bisexual clients.

Therapeutic encounters are affected by the values and biases of the therapist (Lopez, 1989), and therapists should be sensitive to the possibility of biases based on sexuality. Individual prejudice and discrimination are theorized to arise from a combination of homophobia and heterosexism (Stein, 1996b). A recent APA survey reported that 58% of the almost 1,500 psychologists knew of incidents involving biased or inappropriate therapeutic services to lesbians or gay men, which in many cases were hypothesized to be related to homophobia and heterosexism (Garnets et al., 1991). On the basis of the responses to the survey, three broad areas were highlighted to illustrate biased, inadequate, or inappropriate practice. First, bias was found in assessment and intervention (e.g., automatically pathologizing the client on the basis of sexual orientation, attributing presenting problems to sexual orientation without evidence, not knowing that psychological symptoms or distress can be influenced by internalized homophobia, and discouraging a client from adopting a lesbian or gay identity). Second, bias was found regarding issues of identity, family, and intimate relationships (e.g., viewing a client's sexual orientation in terms of sexual behavior, minimizing fears of coming out or of societal intolerance, interpreting same-sex feelings as a phase, minimizing the importance of intimate relationships or saying that they cannot work between members of the same sex, and presuming that problems with a child are due to the sexual orientation of the parent or parents). Third, therapist expertise and training were found to be biased or inadequate (e.g., lacking of knowledge about gay and lesbian issues, relying too much on the client for education about issues, and teaching inaccurate or biased information to students or supervisees). Self-examination, training, and supervision can help to minimize these biases in therapists of all sexual orientations and help therapists of all sexual orientations to address their own homophobia and heterosexism.

Empirical research has demonstrated bias toward lesbian, gay, and bisexual clients by mental health clinicians. A recent study that asked psychoanalysts to rate identical clinical vignettes, which varied by level of pathology (high versus low) and sexual orientation (heterosexual versus homosexual), found a significant interaction between level of pathology and sexual orientation (Lilling & Friedman, 1995). Low-pathology clients were not rated differently, regardless of sexual orientation, whereas high-pathology gay or lesbian clients were rated more negatively. There was a trend to diagnose the gay or lesbian client with borderline personality disorder (versus obsessive-compulsive personality disorder for the heterosexual client), a result that is probably explained by the link between homosexuality and borderline pathology in many psychoanalytic theories. An earlier study using a similar methodology also found that lesbian and gay clients were rated as more pathological (Garfinkle & Morin, 1978). These studies make clear how homophobia and heterosexism can affect one's clinical and ethical judgment.

Treating Homophobia and Heterosexism

In behavioral terms, antigay therapeutic bias may be due to conditioned emotional responses that are maintained through avoidance (Spencer & Hemmer, 1993). Thus, in our society, people learn to have a negative emotional response to homosexuality from playground experiences as well as negative exposure in church, media, and school. As adults, therapists may continue to fear lesbians and gay men because exposure to

evidence that is contradictory to childhood learning is avoided or unavailable. This avoidance is negatively reinforced by escape from the feared stimuli. Thus, motivated avoidance of accurate information about lesbians and gay men may be one reason for some clinicians' lack of information. The most effective behavioral treatment for conditioned negative responses is cognitive restructuring to increase self-efficacy and exposure to feared stimuli with response prevention (Spencer & Hemmer, 1993). Therefore, therapists may be able to alter their faulty perceptions, homophobia, and heterosexism, and decrease avoidance by (a) critically evaluating belief systems and attitudes about lesbians, gay men, and bisexuals; (b) reading current affirmative literature on lesbian and gay issues and developing sensitive language to decrease anxiety and increase self-efficacy; (c) having direct experience with and exposure to such clients and communities; and (d) developing research, training guidelines, and policies to support lesbian, gay, and bisexual clients.

This model of "treatment" to help therapists become more competent clinicians and to decrease their homophobia and heterosexism also has applicability to gay, lesbian, and bisexual clients themselves. This type of conditioned, negative emotional response occurs in clients, too (as internalized homophobia), suggesting that clients whose primary issue is internalized negative feelings and thoughts about their sexual orientation might be successfully treated with cognitive restructuring and exposure with response prevention.

The Therapist's Sexual Orientation

It is not necessary for the therapist to be of the same gender and/or sexual orientation as the client for positive therapeutic outcome (Hancock, 1995; Stein, 1996b), although an openly lesbian or gay clinician can serve as an important role model (especially in the early stages of coming out). Generally, any therapist who has knowledge about the lives of lesbians and gay men, can maintain empathy, can monitor his or her reactions to the client, and has examined and is aware of homophobia and heterosexism can help a lesbian or gay client. Acceptance by itself is not enough; the therapist must try to understand and empathize with the client's experience of his or her sexual behavior, orientation, and identity (Stein, 1996b). However, a gay-affirmative stance is not a substitute for a thorough evaluation of the client and his or her presenting problem, and therapists must be aware of the potential to overcompensate for past homophobia by avoiding appropriate evaluation, diagnosis, and treatment (Stein, 1996b).

In summary, "therapist factors" in the therapeutic interaction can be managed when therapists who work with lesbian, gay, and bisexual clients (virtually all therapists) become aware of their own attitudes and prejudices and address the effects of heterosexism and homophobia on them so as to be able to provide ethical treatment to this population.

Cultural Factors Affecting Therapy With Lesbians, Gay Men, and Bisexuals

Most racial and ethnic groups are vertically integrated, cross-generational groups who transmit their culture from one generation to the next starting in childhood. Among lesbians, gay men, and bisexuals, however, sociocultural norms and information are not passed as easily between generations. For example, youth usually are not exposed to positive gay and lesbian images at home or at school (D'Augelli, 1996). Instead, the culture is horizontally organized, with most learning coming from peers rather than from parents,

teachers, or the media (Gonsiorek, 1995). Thus, gay men and lesbians must learn about their culture and find others like themselves after becoming aware of and wanting to act on their attractions, which usually occurs in adolescence or early adulthood. Because of the lack of role models, lesbians, gay men, and bisexuals may turn to mental health professionals for information and support.

In addition, discrimination and prejudice are important cultural factors that are still widespread in many societal institutions and prevalent among many individuals. Whereas many groups suffer from prejudice, lesbians, gay men, and bisexuals are particularly disadvantaged because discrimination and intolerance is often openly supported by governmental, religious, and social institutions. To provide competent therapy, clinicians must be able to acknowledge the prejudice and discrimination that clients may report and to try to understand the cultural context in which lesbians and gay men struggle to build healthy identities (Garnets et al., 1991).

Examples of institutional hostility toward lesbians and gay men are abundant (see Purcell & Hicks, 1996). Sexual relations between members of the same sex are illegal in almost 20 states ("sodomy" laws were upheld by the Supreme Court in 1986). Discrimination based on sexual orientation in employment, housing, and education is legal in most states and under federal law, and antidiscrimination laws protecting gay and lesbian citizens have been overturned in recent years by popular votes. In the most recent example, in February 1998, in a fiercely battled contest, the state of Maine voted to repeal its civil rights protections, sending a clear message to lesbian and gay citizens of the state that they were considered second-class citizens. Gay men and lesbians have no legal right to marry or to file a joint tax return, and rights of inheritance, hospital visitation, and sometimes health benefits can be obtained only with advance planning. Sexual orientation is often used during custody battles, in which societal myths are often treated as judicial fact (Falk, 1989), and openly gay men and lesbians are barred from military service and are involuntarily discharged if their sexuality is discovered.

The negative institutional attitudes and biases toward lesbians and gay men implicitly and explicitly support the persistence of individual hatred, fear, and violence toward lesbians and gay men (Herek, 1991b). This homophobia and heterosexism has led to thousands of incidents of defamation, harassment, intimidation, assault, vandalism, murder, and other abuses that have been reported since the late 1960s, and the problem appears to occur in both large and small cities across the nation (Berrill, 1992; Herek & Berrill, 1992). Although American culture has become more tolerant of homosexuality, it is important that therapists do not devalue clients' experience of discrimination and prejudice. Instead, the social context of institutional and individual discrimination and stigmatization must be acknowledged or recognized by clinicians, either implicitly or explicitly, to provide ethical therapy to this population.

Client Factors Affecting Therapy With Lesbians and Gay Men

Lesbians and gay men enter therapy with many of the same concerns as heterosexuals; at times, sexual orientation will be the primary focus, and at other times, it will be in the background (Stein, 1996b). In fact, it would be poor clinical practice, and perhaps unethical, for the therapist to focus on the client's sexual orientation when this is not an issue that the client chooses or needs to discuss (see Garnets et al., 1991). Frequent issues include antigay prejudice and homophobia, coming out and identity, love and family relationships, gay and lesbian parenting, and health (Hancock, 1995).

Beginning the Relationship: Terminology

When talking about sexuality with clients, it is important to understand the language used and what these terms mean for the client. In addition, certain standard terms have developed that can aid in developing a therapeutic relationship. The APA Committee on Lesbian and Gay Concerns suggested that *gay man* and *lesbian* are preferable terms because *homosexual* is unclear as to whom it refers and has long been associated with negative stereotypes and pathology (APA, 1991). Even the preferred terms can be confusing, however, as they suggest more than simply same-sex attraction; they also may indicate identification with a cultural community and the adoption of a distinct cultural identity (Boxer, Cook, & Herdt, 1991). The APA also suggests using *sexual orientation* rather than *sexual preference* or *homosexual lifestyle*. Orientation suggests that sexuality is basic to a person, whereas the latter two terms suggest a choice, something that has not been supported in research or by self-reports (APA, 1991). A therapist who is unsure of terminology (or who broaches the topic first) should use the neutral terms suggested by the APA Committee on Lesbian and Gay Concerns. The therapist also can ask the client what terms he or she prefers if the client uses terms that are unfamiliar to the therapist. It has been suggested that familiarity with terminology can decrease apprehension and help the therapist with self-efficacy regarding their treatment of lesbian and gay clients (Spencer & Hemmer, 1993).

Internalized Homophobia

The widespread societal and individual prejudice and discrimination against lesbians and gay men (homophobia and heterosexism) discussed earlier are hypothesized to lead to internalized homophobia in most people (Herek, 1996). Higher levels of internalized homophobia among gay men and lesbians have been found to be associated with more depressive symptoms, lower self-esteem, greater loneliness, and less social support from other gay men and lesbians (Shidlo, 1994). Shidlo suggested that internalized homophobia is an important construct for therapists to understand because (a) all lesbians and gay men as well as their therapists internalize some homophobia, (b) internalized homophobia often leads to psychological symptoms, (c) reduction in internalized homophobia is a useful therapy outcome measure, and (d) conversion or reparative therapies can reinforce and increase internalized homophobia and psychological symptoms.

Coming Out and Stages of Identity Development

Regardless of the age of a client, it is important to assess comfort with and openness about his or her sexuality and the extent to which orientation has been integrated into sexual identity. The process of identifying as lesbian or gay and then disclosing this identity to friends and family, known as *coming out,* involves a complex series of cognitive, affective, and behavior changes that result in the acceptance of a nontraditional identity (Stein, 1996b). Early in this process, the therapist may be much more comfortable with the client's emerging sexual orientation than the client is, so sensitivity to the client's comfort with and integration of his or her sexual orientation is essential. Coming out affects one's self-concept, interpersonal relationships, and relations with society, and this ongoing process may occur quickly or slowly, affecting different domains of one's life at different times. A variety of stage models have been developed to explain this

process (e.g., Cass, 1996; Troiden, 1989), although as with all stage models, people do not go through the same stages in the same order, if at all. However, these models provide a useful heuristic for conceptualizing the client's coming-out process. The clinician's task is to understand how coming out and adopting a lesbian or gay identity is experienced and expressed by the client (Stein, 1996b).

Troiden (1989) suggested four stages in his model. First, *sensitization,* when a child or adolescent feels "different" (often due to gender-nonconforming behavior, especially in boys) but does not see homosexuality as personally relevant. Second, *identity confusion* often occurs during adolescence, when the connection is made between these unexplainable thoughts and feelings and sexual orientation. A variety of behaviors might be observed at this stage, such as trying to block out same-sex feelings, trying to avoid thoughts, behaviors, and interests that are associated with homosexuality, attempting to repair or eradicate same-sex feelings (often with professional help), and redefining sexual behaviors (as "bisexual" or "It's only a phase"). High levels of internalized homophobia and sometimes the overt expression of antihomosexual thoughts and feelings are common (Goggin, 1993). Particularly in this stage, it is important that the clinician not push the client too quickly to become comfortable with his or her sexuality (e.g., the clinician may be more comfortable with a gay or lesbian identity than the client is).

In the third stage, *identity assumption,* a gay or lesbian identity first becomes tolerated, and later accepted and shared with a few significant others. This stage often begins with or shortly after first social contact with other lesbians and gay men. Good experiences at this stage can diminish isolation, whereas negative experiences can result in an attempt to reject same-sex behavior and identity (Troiden, 1989). This is often the time when bibliotherapy is helpful with clients (if they have not discovered lesbian and gay books on their own) and when a supportive therapy relationship can be immensely helpful (see "Suggested Readings" at the end of this chapter). Having a gay or lesbian therapist at this stage can be particularly helpful but is not necessary.

The last stage, *commitment,* involves embracing a lesbian or gay identity as a way of life because it is easier than trying to pass as a heterosexual. There are internal and external changes at this stage. Internally, increased feelings of happiness and satisfaction with a lesbian or gay self-identity are reported. Externally, entering a love relationship often marks the beginning of this stage, and coming out to friends and family indicates a new way of managing stigma.

Family Relationships

Lesbians, gay men, and bisexuals, like other clients, often come to therapy with concerns about their families of origin, their partners, or their children. Many gay and lesbian clients have good relationships with their parents and siblings, although conflict often occurs around the time that family members are told or discover their family member's homosexuality. Religion is another issue that often leads to family conflict, due to the explicit homophobia found in many religions (Haldeman, 1996). However, many lesbians, gay men, and bisexuals seek a spiritual connection, and they find it through more enlightened denominations, through a gay church, or through a reconciliation with their childhood religion (Haldeman, 1996). There are many books written on lesbians and gay men and religion or spirituality that can help clients with this struggle (see "Suggested Readings").

Regarding intimate relationships, the majority of lesbians and gay men are coupled.

Their couples' issues are similar to, as well as different from, those experienced by heterosexual couples (Cabaj & Purcell, 1998; Peplau & Cochran, 1990). Generally, there are more psychosocial stressors on lesbian and gay couples (e.g., disapproval from family, keeping the relationship secret at work, lack of socially sanctioned benefits), and the dynamics may be different due to gender-role socialization (Hancock, 1995). But, as with heterosexual couples, research has shown that lesbian and gay couples desire both attachment and autonomy, generally are satisfied with their relationships, use similar power strategies, go through similar stages (from infatuation to settling down), and have struggles over money and career intrusions into the relationship (Hancock, 1995). Supporting the development of healthy relationships is important because, as with heterosexual relationships, being in a relationship generally enhances psychological functioning and adjustment for lesbian and gay clients (Kurdek, 1994). Moreover, some clients may believe the myths that same-sex relationships are not sustainable or are inferior to heterosexual relationships (Herek, 1991a). Working with clients around these cognitive distortions can help them to be more open to the possibility of a sustained same-sex relationship.

Many lesbians and gay men are parents, either from a prior heterosexual marriage, from artificial insemination, or from adoption, and this appears to be an increasing trend (Patterson, 1995). Research on lesbian and gay parents began in a judicial context, because of the assumption that lesbian and gay parents were automatically unfit (Herek, 1991a; Patterson, 1995). Research has shown that this is an unfounded myth and that lesbian and gay men are fit parents (Golombok & Tasker, 1994; Patterson, 1995). Furthermore, no evidence has been found that a child's gender identity and adult sexual orientation are related to either the gender or sexual orientation of the child's primary caretakers (Bailey, Bobrow, Wolfe, & Mikach, 1995; Patterson, 1995).

Ethnicity

The lesbian and gay community is a heterogeneous collection of subcultures, and clients can benefit from learning about this diversity. The community is as diverse as the population in general and is made up of individuals who may differ based on race, ethnicity, class, education, age, physical condition, religion, and urban versus rural setting (Stein, 1996b). Lesbians and gay men may experience discrimination based on some of these factors, both within the lesbian and gay community and in society at large.

Only recently has work been done on the potentially painful and difficult struggle to integrate multiple identities, with a particular focus on lesbians and gay men of different races or ethnic cultures, such as African American (Jones & Hill, 1996; Peterson, 1992), Asian (Chan, 1995; Nakajima, Chan, & Lee, 1996), Hispanic (Gonzalez & Espin, 1996), and Native American (Tafoya, 1996). Adoption of a lesbian or gay identity may be particularly difficult for members of minority cultures because it may be personally and culturally perceived as a rejection of their ethnic culture and the acceptance of a Western or white perspective. In addition, the double discrimination and potential isolation from both the lesbian and gay community and the racial or ethnic community can be stressful (Stein, 1996b). Moreover, the balancing of racial or ethnic identity with sexual identity can be difficult because the notion of sexual identity is not relevant in some cultures (Chan, 1995) or because the notion of sexual orientation is rejected despite the covert tolerance of same-sex sexual behavior. For example, among Latin cultures, men who engage in sex with other men are not stigmatized as being homosexual unless they are the passive sexual partner (Carrier, 1989). The intersection of sexual and ethnic identities is complex, these issues should be considered in treatment planning, and consultation should be sought.

The Client's Desire to Change Sexual Orientation or Behavior

A difficult therapeutic issue occurs when a client comes to therapy or is brought by parents wanting the client to "become heterosexual." Implicit in many theories of homosexuality is the assumption that it is less permanent than heterosexuality and thus may be reversible (Goggin, 1993). Change therapies usually are based on either a religious model ("Homosexuality is a sin") or a psychiatric model. Religious-based treatments often involve having the patient engage in gender-typical behavior (e.g., men throw a football; women learn to apply makeup), another example of the confusion of gender identity and sexual orientation. Behavioral treatments focus on decreasing responsivity to homosexual stimuli while increasing responsivity to heterosexual stimuli.

Change therapies have been criticized because they are thought to reinforce prejudice, internalized homophobia, and lowered self-esteem in vulnerable clients (Haldeman, 1994; Stein, 1996a). Current research indicates that people do not choose to be heterosexual or gay. Although people can choose not to express their sexual feelings for moral, ethical, or personal reasons, the feelings are not chosen. As indicated in the APA's 1997 resolution, clinicians should not direct a client toward a specific sexual orientation, but should retain an open, inquiring, supportive stance to help the client explore the meaning of various sexual feelings (see also Sobocinski, 1990).

The clinician who has a client seeking change must perform a complete, culturally sensitive assessment of the reasons for such desires and the motivations for treatment, independent of the client's expressed desires for change (Spencer & Hemmer, 1993). That is, the therapist must be aware of, and sensitive to, the fact that the client's desire to change orientation might represent a reflection of societal biases against gays and lesbians. In such cases, clients would be responding to social or familial pressures to conform, and therapy could proceed to very different interventions (e.g., family therapy, assessment of attributions and self-efficacy). Such client-generated decisions might be based on the client's irrational assumptions about being lesbian or gay and might be an attempt to seek a socially conditioned remedy for emotional upheaval caused by his or her dysfunctional belief systems. For example, clients might desire to lead a family-oriented lifestyle in which they live with a significant other and raise children. They might see commitments and families as atypical of being gay or lesbian and may have some very restrictive views on what "being gay" involves (e.g., it is impossible to be in a committed relationship with someone of the same sex). They may not be aware that children raised by lesbian or gay male parents are as well-adjusted as children from more "traditional" families (Patterson, 1995). Furthermore, because society does not sanction same-sex marriage, the client's "pathology" view of being lesbian or gay and their desire to change may be reinforced (Cabaj & Purcell, 1998). If the client continues to insist on therapy to change, it is important for the therapist to let the client know that research on "conversion" therapies has found that they generally do not work (Haldeman, 1994; Stein, 1996a). Although behavior change might be possible for some clients (at least in the short term), change in sexual orientation is unlikely. The following case illustrates this conflict:

> The parents of a 19-year-old young woman named Joan called because they believed that their daughter was having a relationship with a woman at college. When the parents confronted Joan with a letter they had found in her room, Joan admitted to a relationship with a young woman on her softball team at college but denied that there had been any sexual involvement. Her father was so upset by this revelation that he insisted that Joan drop out of college. She returned home to work in the family business and attended church regularly. According to her father, she agreed with her parents that homosexuality was morally wrong and said she would agree to psychotherapy in order to help with the situation. The father and mother reported that they both felt terribly hurt by their daughter's homosexual attraction, that it was tearing their family apart, and that they could not understand how this could have happened in their family. The father asked the therapist if it were possible for his daughter to change and whether the therapist agreed that homosexuality was morally wrong.
>
> The therapist wanted to be truthful with the parents and felt that educating them about sexual orientation could ultimately be helpful for Joan. It was important that the parents understand the negative impact on their daughter's self-esteem of trying to change her sexual orientation and the consequences this could have—not only for her but also for their relationship with her in the future. Despite the therapist's

conviction that it would be helpful for this woman to have therapy, she knew it was unlikely that these parents would refer their daughter to her for therapy unless there were agreement with their view that homosexuality was morally wrong. The clinician did not feel she could portray herself as a person who shared their views, nor could she participate in treatment that could be damaging to this young woman's self-esteem. She had not had the opportunity to evaluate the young woman but felt that given her age and the circumstances that had been reported by the parents, respect for this young woman's autonomy dictated a need to provide a therapeutic environment in which she could come to terms with her sexual orientation, whether that was homosexual, heterosexual, or bisexual. The young woman appeared to be very confused about her sexual orientation and eager to avoid conflict with her parents. It was not clear whether her beliefs about homosexuality were actually those of her parents, an internalization of the antihomosexual bias of our culture, or genuinely her own. When the therapist discussed this with the parents, they were unwilling to have their daughter come for evaluation or treatment with her, and they asked for a referral to someone else who shared their beliefs about homosexuality.

In this case, the therapist shared the information that she had about sexuality with the parents, and they made the choice not to see her. Although this therapist did not believe in the efficacy of therapy to change sexuality, she had to allow the parent to try to follow this route.

The issues that arise when a client or the parents of a client want a heterosexual outcome are complex. In many cases, after providing the client or parents with accurate information, consent to engage in gay-affirmative therapy is obtained. These types of issues are even more complex in cases in which therapy is with an adolescent, which we turn to next.

ETHICAL ISSUES WITH ADOLESCENTS WHO HAVE CONCERNS ABOUT THEIR SEXUALITY

The general principles of professional ethics for psychotherapy with gay and lesbian clients apply to adolescent clients as well. However, treatment of adolescents also presents the clinician with specific legal and ethical dilemmas.

Background on Sexual Minority Youth

The idea of an adolescent who claims a lesbian, gay, or bisexual identity is a relatively new concept (Goggin, 1993), and these youth may feel intense pressure to deny such an identity. Research and clinical experience indicates that sexual behavior, orientation, and identity often are not integrated during adolescence as they typically are for adults. Based on a review of the developmental literature, Savin-Williams (1990) concluded that (a) not all lesbian and gay adolescents are sexually active, (b) many lesbian and gay adolescents are sexually active with members of the other sex, (c) many heterosexual adolescents are sexually active with members of the same sex, and (d) the relation between sexual identity and sexual behavior is highly variable (see also Herdt & Boxer, 1993; Savin-Williams, 1995;

Savin-Williams & Rodriguez, 1993). Whereas sexual behavior can be a poor indicator of sexual orientation during adolescence, at the same time, not all same- sex sexual behavior during this time is necessarily part of a "phase."

Due to the increasing visibility of gay and lesbian culture, youth with same-sex attractions increasingly are becoming aware of and acknowledging these feelings during adolescence. These youth face tremendous developmental challenges in often hostile school and home environments if they choose to act on this awareness or to self-identify as gay or lesbian (D'Augelli, 1996). Youth who identify as lesbian or gay at an earlier age, as well as gender-nonconforming youth (especially boys), are at increased risk for victimization (Pilkington & D'Augelli, 1995). Coming out during adolescence may be difficult for some youth because they face this difficult developmental challenge at a time when their psychological resources are less mature and their social and family support may be diminished or withdrawn. Although positive images of lesbian and gay individuals are more likely to be encountered today than even 10 years ago, most questioning youth are not exposed to positive images at home or at school, and getting accurate information to them can be difficult, even in urban areas (D'Augelli, 1996). In recent studies, sexual minority youth identified the following issues as primary concerns: telling family about their sexual orientations, relationship problems, fears about AIDS, homophobia, lack of positive role models, coming out, and depression (D'Augelli & Hershberger, 1993; Slater, 1988).

Working with parents and their underage children who identify as lesbian or gay or who are struggling with sexual identity issues requires special sensitivity to ethical issues (Sobocinski, 1990). For example, revealing an adolescent's sexual orientation concerns to parents could lead to verbal or physical abuse or even ejection from the family home. When parents first find out about their child's sexual orientation, they start on their own process of acceptance and "coming out" as parents of a lesbian, gay, or bisexual child, something that therapists can help them to work through. This process is even more delicate and ethically challenging if the clinician is trying to work with the parents and the youth, which is often the case.

One component of ethical work with these youth and their families, beyond awareness of laws and ethical codes and principles, is knowledge of community resources. For example, there are a growing number of support services in many cities specifically targeted for youth, which have been found to be very valuable by allowing the youth to interact with other gay and lesbian adolescents, develop social skills, exchange information, and obtain crucial social support (Sobocinski, 1990). There also are groups specifically for parents, even in small cities, organized by Parents, Families and Friends of Lesbians and Gays (PFLAG). Awareness of these resources can provide families and adolescents with invaluable connections and support.

Balancing Laws, Ethical Codes, and Ethical Principles

A number of legal and ethical issues are salient for gay, lesbian, and bisexual youth. Clinicians may be confronted with what the limits of confidentiality should be with respect to sexuality-related issues. If an adolescent has concerns about his or her sexual orientation, discloses this in therapy, and wants assurance from the clinician that parents will not be told, clinicians may feel they are in a legal and/or ethical bind. Issues of autonomy arise when the parents' or clinicians' beliefs regarding definitions of healthy sexuality conflict with the identity and goals of the adolescent. Questions may arise about whether parents or mental health clinicians should dictate what the adolescent's sexual orientation should be and set the goals of treatment to achieve this. The clinician faced with these complex questions may seek clarification from the law, from professional codes of ethics, or from general ethical principles. If the dilemmas that clinicians face are addressed in laws or professional codes of ethics, then these laws and codes generally should be followed, although as discussed below, this is usually not the case.

Legally, under most circumstances, parents must give consent for their minor children, even if adolescent, to receive health care, including psychotherapy. Children have been traditionally seen as the property of their parents or guardians who are responsible for protecting them, providing for their care, and making decisions for them even in situations in which the adolescent is competent (Enzer, 1985; Fraad, 1993). Thus, many of the customary protections afforded to adults by the U.S. Constitution have not traditionally applied to adolescents. Legal decisions in the past 20 years, however, have given increasing recognition to the independence of adolescents to consent to their own medical treatment. Statutory laws in many states have defined specific conditions, including venereal disease, pregnancy, and substance abuse, that define adolescents as "emancipated minors" and thus allow them to consent to their own medical treatment (Holder, 1996). In other states, however, laws have been passed restricting adolescents' access to counseling (Sobocinski, 1990). Common law uses a "mature minor" exception to the requirement for parental consent for treatment, such that young people may be judged to be mature enough to make medical decisions for themselves if they are old enough, understand the nature of a proposed treatment and its risks, can give the same degree of informed consent as an adult patient, and if the treatment does not involve very serious risks (Holder, 1996). This type of exception fits with research showing that children's cognitive ability to make rational decisions is well developed prior to adulthood (Moshman, 1993). However, legal decisions and statutes vary from state to state and are contradictory, so a familiarity with state law is important for any clinician treating children and adolescents.

Codes of ethics for various mental health professions often do not directly address difficult ethical issues that arise in treating lesbian, gay, and bisexual youth. The code of ethics for the APA is particularly nonspecific (APA, 1992). Most codes seem to recognize a need to balance the rights and needs of the parents with the rights and needs of the child, a balance that shifts as the child ages. Because neither laws nor professional codes of ethics directly address many difficult ethical dilemmas, the clinician is left to examine general ethical principles from which the professional codes were developed (Brown, 1996; Sobocinski, 1990). These principles include autonomy (recognizing individuals as self-determining if they are "competent"), fidelity (keeping one's trust or confidences), justice (being fair), beneficence (doing good), and nonmaleficence (doing no harm). Although ethical principles generally are considered universally applicable, most ethical dilemmas arise when competing principles are relevant and the clinician must balance these competing ethical principles.

In the following case, issues of confidentiality, beneficence, and autonomy, including criteria for competent decision making, are explored in greater depth.

Casey is a 16-year-old female who was referred for therapy after being caught skipping school. She is an only child whose parents both have busy work lives. Casey self-identified as a lesbian and reported that she had had several girlfriends in the past year. She had recently disclosed her sexual orientation to her parents and two female friends at school. She was upset at her friends for "outing" her at school and no longer associated with the two girls whom she considered her only friends. Casey reported that she did not enjoy school and that she was repeatedly harassed, often being teased for being a "boy" or a "dyke." She refused to return to school and appeared adamant that she would not finish high school.

During an individual session with her therapist, she disclosed the fact that she was going to bars and getting intoxicated with older lesbians from a local college. She bragged about her fake identification and her ability to associate with these women who were much older. She described several nights of excessive drinking, driving intoxicated, and an inability to remember aspects of the evening. However, she stated that for the first time, she had found friends that liked her and because of this she felt happy. After several discussions regarding the choices Casey was making, she became angry with her therapist and refused to change her behavior. Casey minimized the danger in which she was placing herself. Although there was a local gay and lesbian adolescent support group, Casey thought that it would be boring and too serious and did not consider this to be a viable way to meet other youth. Casey believed that the therapist did not understand her situation and interpreted the therapist's concerns as a desire to control her life, much like the ways in which she believed her parents tried to control her.

Casey did not want her parents to know about the types of behaviors in which she had been engaging or that she had encountered any danger in doing so, fearing that they would ground her and refuse to allow her to "hang out" with her new friends. She insisted that she had the freedom to choose her own way of living. She threatened that if her parents attempted to stop her from being with her friends she would have no alternative but to leave home. Due to Casey's inability to effectively conceptualize the dangers involved in her situation or effectively generate alternatives that would provide her with greater safety, it became necessary to inform her parents, thereby eliciting their support.

How do clinicians know whether a particular adolescent is able to determine his or her own treatment plan, including who is a part of the therapeutic process and what information is shared with other family members? Research on adolescent decision-making processes suggests that the abilities of adolescents in their mid- to late-teenage years are much closer to those of adults, even though they lack some of the life experiences (Mann, Harmoni, & Power, 1989). The ability to make a reasonable decision is one of the hallmarks of a mature adolescent. Tancredi (1982) defined competence as the "capacity to make rational or intelligent judgments." Embedded in competence is the ability to survey a wide range of alternative solutions, evaluate the positives and negatives of each possible consequence stemming from the options identified, incorporate new information from reliable sources even when it is offensive, and effectively implement the determined choice of action. It is assumed that the more adequately each of these steps is implemented, the more competent the decision maker (Mann et al., 1989). Patterns of impulsivity, rigidity, defensive avoidance, and complacent adherence or complacent change have been described as incompetent decision making (Janis & Mann, 1977).

At first glance, due to her age and above-average level of intelligence, Casey is an adolescent who might be viewed as a competent decision maker. However, her poor judgment, lack of insight, and impulsivity made it necessary for the therapist to place the ethical principle of beneficence above the principle of respect for her autonomy and self-determination. This was accomplished by requiring Casey's parents to be more involved with the treatment process, thereby usurping her right to formulate her own treatment plan. It also became necessary to violate her confidentiality to the extent that was needed to provide her with the safety she was unable to provide for herself.

The ethical conflicts involved in the decision to override Casey's autonomous decision making and violate her confidentiality were further complicated by the therapist's hesitance to disrupt the therapeutic alliance with her client. Involving her parents and violating her confidentiality diminished the trust and threatened the continuation of her therapy. After 4 months of weekly psychotherapy, Casey appeared to have begun trusting her therapist with her thoughts and, at times, her feelings of vulnerability. Realizing Casey's difficulty with basic trust made what might appear to be the only decision (to inform her parents of the dangerous behavior) less definitive. However, the life-threatening consequences of respecting her autonomous decision making in this case forced the clinician to take a more paternalistic stance despite the risk of negatively affecting the therapeutic relationship.

Another ethical dilemma arose during the therapeutic process. Having the knowledge that Casey was being harassed at school and offered no protection by the administration, including the school counselor, the therapist was compelled to examine her role as advocate. Adolescents are a group of individuals that experience powerlessness and oppression in many ways in society. Conoley and Larson (1993) state that "Children have suffered from not having powerful voices to support them" (p. 209). Gay and lesbian adolescents have suffered both physically and emotionally due to hostile environments, including school systems, with no or few advocates to protect them. As an informed and educated practitioner, the therapist understood the deleterious consequences that would occur from the continuous harassment Casey faced at school. Silence and hostility are often daily realities for gay and lesbian adolescents in high school. Gay teens experience verbal harassment and physical violence from peers and adults. In 1989, the U.S. Department of Health and Human Services reported that these types of abuse have resulted in 28% of gay and lesbian youth quitting school (Gibson, 1989). Lack of acceptance and overt hostility can lead to feelings of isolation, extreme low self-esteem, and subsequent efforts at self-destructive behaviors. Sexual minority youth, particularly boys, have been found to be at increased risk for suicidal ideation and attempts (Remafedi, French, Story, Resnick, & Blum, 1998). Casey's therapist decided to discuss her concern with Casey and her family because of her understanding of the consequences of harassment. Casey and her parents agreed to a meeting with the school counselor and school administrators in the hope that educating the school staff would secure more protection for Casey and make it possible for her to remain in school.

In the next case, issues of confidentiality, autonomy, and competence arose.

Duncan, a 17-year-old African American male, was brought to a child psychiatrist for evaluation and treatment because he had made two suicide attempts and admitted to being quite depressed. Sensitive questioning by the therapist revealed that he was depressed because he thought he might be gay. "I never felt attracted to girls before," he reported. Religious conflict about his sexual orientation was a significant factor in his depression and suicide attempts. He was raised as a Jehovah's Witness and was well aware that homosexuality was not at all acceptable in his religion. He said, "I'd be considered another 'Sodom and Gomorrah' if my friends at the Kingdom Hall found out; I'd be excommunicated." He acknowledged attraction to male peers and longed to meet gay peers. Duncan reported feeling enormously relieved by the opportunity to talk with an accepting clinician about his sexual orientation concerns, indicating that he was less depressed and no longer suicidal. However, he was very concerned about the impact of this knowledge on his family and did not want his parents told.

This posed an ethical dilemma for the treating clinician. Should she respect this patient's request for confidentiality and not disclose information regarding his sexual orientation concerns to his parents? Professional codes of ethics generally suggest respecting a minor's confidentiality unless a situation of danger to self or others exists. It did not appear that Duncan's concerns regarding his sexual orientation were putting himself or others in danger. He was not reporting suicidality, nor was he engaged in any behaviors at that time, sexual or otherwise, that could have put him at risk. What he appeared to need was a place where he could be free to discuss his emerging sexuality. Not respecting his desire for confidentiality would likely have disrupted this process.

Duncan felt alone and isolated in his peer group both at his school and at church, despite being a popular leader. He expressed a strong desire to meet other youth with concerns similar to his own. This presented another dilemma for the clinician. Awareness of the dearth of peer support in his current environment coupled with an understanding of the crucial role that a peer group plays in an adolescent's identity formation and consolidation led the clinician to consider referral to a community support group and other services for gay, lesbian, and bisexual youth. The question faced by the therapist was whether to inform Duncan and his parents of these resources. It was clear that Duncan did not know these resources existed. If the parents were informed, however, they probably would not have allowed him to attend the groups and might have stopped therapy. A decision was made to inform Duncan of the possible community resources and let him decide about informing his parents. The treating clinician felt that this young man was mature enough that his autonomy could be respected and he could be allowed to make the decision about whether to explore these community resources and inform his parents about them. The ethical principle of non-maleficence, however, led the treating clinician to discuss with Duncan the possible consequences of using the community resources for sexual minority youth. As a senior in high school, he was dependent on his family and religious community for social and emotional support, and his plans to attend college would require continued family financial support. If he were to be more overt about socializing with gay and lesbian peers, this might lead to feeling further alienated from or rejected by peers and family.

Complex ethical dilemmas for which there are no correct or easy answers arise in the treatment of gay, lesbian, and bisexual adolescents. Issues related to sexual orientation, behavior, and identity interface with issues involved in treating individuals who are minors according to the law and often still dependent on family for emotional and financial support. The clinician needs to keep as primary concerns the welfare and optimal development of the adolescent. It is important to remember that the adolescent exists within the context of family, school, and community, and the attitudes of these groups may have a significant impact on adolescent self-esteem and level of functioning. When it is possible, given an appropriate developmental level, the clinician should make an attempt to respect the individual adolescent's autonomous decision making. What we can know is that these adolescents are individuals whose struggles with their sexuality need to be listened to and responded to with respect and sensitivity.

CONCLUSION

The decision rests with each individual therapist as to whether they can or wish to work with lesbian, gay, and bisexual clients. Therapists who feel confident in their knowledge of gay and lesbian issues, who are comfortable working with diverse lifestyles and behaviors, who are sensitive to issues affecting these clients, and who are aware of their own homophobia and heterosexism will make competent, ethical decisions about treatment. If any of these conditions are absent (e.g., if the therapist is not comfortable working with gay men, lesbians, or bisexuals), the ethical duty is to recognize the boundaries of one's competence. Furthermore, as in the case of a therapist who is uncomfortable working with ethnic minority clients, discomfort working with gay and lesbian clients might spring from unfamiliarity with the population and culture. Therefore, it would be professionally and ethically responsible for such therapists to seek consultation and specific training in the cultural issues affecting lesbians and gay men so as to provide them sensitive mental health treatment. Those clinicians willing to take on the challenge of working with lesbians, gay men, and bisexuals will find themselves and their clients enriched by their work.

SUGGESTED READINGS FOR LESBIAN AND GAY CLIENTS

The list below is not exhaustive, because the number of books published for lesbians and gay men on a huge variety of fiction and nonfiction topics has exploded since the 1990s. In addition, lesbian and gay bookstores are found in most large cities, and mainstream bookstores increasingly are developing separate lesbian and gay sections.

Bernstein, R. A. (1995). *Straight parents, gay children.* New York: Thunder's Mouth Press.

Blumenfeld, W. J. (1992). *Homophobia: How we all pay the price.* Boston: Beacon.

Blumenfeld, W. J., & Raymond, D. (1993). *Looking at gay and lesbian life* (Rev. ed.). Boston: Beacon.

Borhek, M. V. (1993). *Coming out to parents: A two-way survival guide for lesbians and gay men and their parents* (Rev. ed.). Cleveland, OH: Pilgrim.

Bouldrey, B. (Ed.). (1995). *Wrestling with the angel: Faith and religion in the lives of gay men.* New York: Riverhead Books.

Cabaj, R. P., & Purcell, D. W. (Eds.). (1998). *On the road to same sex marriage: A supportive guide to psychological, political, and legal issues.* San Francisco: Jossey-Bass.

Caster, W. (1993). *The lesbian sex book.* Los Angeles: Alyson.

Clark, D. (1987). *Loving someone gay* (Rev. ed.). Berkeley, CA: Celestial Arts.

Clunis, D. M., & Green, G. D. (1988). *Lesbian couples.* Seattle: Seal Press.

Fairchild, B., & Hayward, N. (1989). *Now that you know: What every parent should know about homosexuality* (Rev. ed.). New York: Harcourt Brace Jovanovich.

Helminiak, D. A. (1994). *What the Bible really has to say about homosexuality.* San Francisco: Alamo Square.

Herdt, G., & Boxer, A. (1993). *Children of horizons: How gay and lesbian teens are leading a new way out of the closet.* Boston: Beacon.

LeVay, S., & Nonas, E. (1995). *City of friends: A portrait of the gay and lesbian community in America.* Cambridge: MIT Press.

Marcus, E. (1992). *The male couples guide.* New York: Harper Perennial.

Marcus, E. (1993). *Is it a choice? Answers to 300 of the most frequently asked questions about gays and lesbians.* New York: HarperCollins.

McNaught, B. (1988). *On being gay: Thoughts on family, faith, and love.* New York: St. Martin's.

Nelson, C. (1996). *Finding true love in a man-eat-man world.* New York: Dell.

Shyer, M. F., & Shyer, C. (1996). *Not like other boys, growing up gay: A mother and son look back.* New York: Houghton Mifflin.

Signorile, M. (1995). *Outing yourself: How to come out as lesbian or gay to your family, friends, and coworkers.* New York: Random House.

Silverstein, C., & Picano, F. (1992). *The new joy of gay sex.* New York: HarperCollins.

Sullivan, A. (1995). *Virtually normal: An argument about homosexuality.* New York: Knopf.

Thompson, M. (1995). *Gay soul: Finding the heart of gay spirit and nature.* New York: HarperCollins.

Vaid, U. (1995). *Virtual equality: The mainstreaming of gay and lesbian liberation.* New York: Doubleday.

REFERENCES

American Psychiatric Association. (1952). *Diagnostic and statistical manual of mental disorders* (1st ed.). Washington, DC: American Psychiatric Association.

American Psychiatric Association. (1994). *Diagnostic and statistical manual of mental disorders* (4th ed.). Washington, DC: American Psychiatric Association.

American Psychological Association. Committee on Lesbian and Gay Concerns. (1991). Avoiding heterosexual bias in language. *American Psychologist, 46,* 973-974.

American Psychological Association. Ethics Committee. (1992). Ethical principles of psychologists and code of conduct. *American Psychologist, 47,* 1597-1611.

Bailey, J. M. (1995). Biological perspectives on sexual orientation. In A. R. D'Augelli & C. J. Patterson (Eds.), *Lesbian, gay, and bisexual identities over the life span* (pp. 102-135). New York: Oxford University Press.

Bailey, J. M., Bobrow, D., Wolfe, M., & Mikach, S. (1995). Sexual orientation of adult sons of gay fathers. *Developmental Psychology, 31,* 124-129.

Bayer, R. (1987). *Homosexuality and American psychiatry: The politics of diagnosis.* Princeton, NJ: Princeton University Press.

Bernstein, G. S., & Miller, M. E. (1995). Behavior therapy with lesbian and gay individuals. In M. Hersen, R. M. Eisler, & P. M. Miller (Eds.), *Progress in behavior modification* (Vol. 30). Pacific Grove, CA: Brooks/Cole.

Berrill, K. T. (1992). Anti-gay violence and victimization in the United States: An overview. In G. M. Herek & K. T. Berrill (Eds.), *Hate crimes: Confronting violence against lesbians and gay men* (pp. 19-45). Newbury Park, CA: Sage.

Boxer, A. M., Cook, J. A., & Herdt, G. (1991). Double jeopardy: Identity transitions and parent-child relations among gay and lesbian youth. In K. Pillemer & K. McCartney (Eds.), *Parent-child relations throughout life* (pp. 59-92). Hillsdale, NJ: Lawrence Erlbaum.

Brown, L. S. (1996). Ethical concerns with sexual minority patients. In R. P. Cabaj & T. S. Stein (Eds.), *Textbook of homosexuality and mental health* (pp. 897-916). Washington, DC: American Psychiatric Press.

Cabaj, R. P., & Purcell, D. W. (1998). *On the road to same-sex marriage: A supportive guide to psychological, political, and legal issues.* San Francisco: Jossey-Bass.

Cabaj, R. P., & Stein, T. S. (Eds.). (1996). *Textbook of homosexuality and mental health.* Washington, DC: American Psychiatric Press.

Carrier, J. M. (1989). Gay liberation and coming out in Mexico. *Journal of Homosexuality, 17*(3/4), 225-252.

Cass, V. C. (1996). Sexual orientation identity formation: A Western phenomenon. In R. P. Cabaj & T. S. Stein (Eds.), *Textbook of homosexuality and mental health* (pp. 227-251). Washington, DC: American Psychiatric Press.

Chan, C. S. (1995). Issues of sexual identity in an ethnic minority: The case of Chinese American lesbians, gay men, and bisexual people. In A. R. D'Augelli & C. J. Patterson (Eds.), *Lesbian, gay, and bisexual identities over the life span* (pp. 87-101). New York: Oxford University Press.

Coleman, E. (Ed.). (1987). *Psychotherapy with homosexual men and women: Integrated identity approaches for clinical practice.* New York: Haworth.

Conger, J. (1975). Proceedings of the American Psychological Association, for the year 1974: Minutes of the annual meeting of Council of Representatives. *American Psychologist, 36,* 633-638.

Conoley, J. C., & Larson, P. (1995). Conflicts in care: Early years of the life span. In E. J. Rave & C. C. Larsen (Eds.), *Ethical decision making in therapy: Feminist perspectives* (pp. 202-222). New York: Guilford.

Cornett, C. (Ed.). (1993). *Affirmative dynamic psychotherapy with gay men.* Northvale, NJ: Jason Aronson.

D'Augelli, A. R. (1991). Gay men in college: Identity processes and adaptations. *Journal of College Student Development, 32,* 140-146.

D'Augelli, A. R. (1996). Lesbian, gay, and bisexual development during adolescence and young adulthood. In R. P. Cabaj & T. S. Stein (Eds.), *Textbook of homosexuality and mental health* (pp. 267-288). Washington, DC: American Psychiatric Press.

D'Augelli, A. R., & Hershberger, S. L. (1993). Lesbian, gay, and bisexual youth in community settings: Personal challenges and mental health problems. *American Journal of Community Psychology, 21,* 421-448.

Enzer, N. B. (1985). Ethics in child psychiatry—an overview. In D. H. Schetky & E. P. Benedek (Eds.), *Emerging issues in child psychiatry and the law* (pp. 3-21). New York: Brunner/Mazel.

Falk, P. J. (1989). Lesbian mothers: Psychosocial assumptions in family law. *American Psychologist, 44,* 941-947.

Fraad, H. (1993). Children as an exploited class. *Journal of Psychohistory, 21,* 37-51.

Garfinkle, E. M., & Morin, S. F. (1978). Psychologists' attitudes toward homosexual psychotherapy clients. *Journal of Social Issues, 34,* 101-112.

Garnets, L. D., Hancock, K., Cochran, S., Goodchilds, J., & Peplau, A. (1991). Issues in psychotherapy with lesbians and gay men: A survey of psychologists. *American Psychologist, 46,* 964-972.

Garnets, L. D., & Kimmel, D. (1991). Lesbian and gay male dimensions in the psychological study of human diversity. In J. D. Goodchilds (Ed.), *Psychological perspectives on human diversity in America* (pp. 143-189). Washington, DC: American Psychological Association.

Gibson, P. (1989). Gay male and lesbian youth suicide. *ADAMHA report of the secretary's task force on youth suicide* (Vol. 3, pp. 110-142; DHHS Publication No. ADM 89-1623). Washington DC: Government Printing Office.

Goggin, M. (1993). Gay and lesbian adolescence. In S. Moore & D. Rosenthal (Eds.), *Sexuality in adolescence* (pp. 102-123). New York: Routledge.

Golombok, S., & Tasker, F. (1994). Children in lesbian and gay families: Theories and evidence. *The Annual Review of Sex Research, 5,* 73-100.

Gonsiorek, J. C. (1991). The empirical basis for the demise of the illness model of homosexuality. In J. C. Gonsiorek & J. D. Weinrich (Eds.), *Homosexuality: Research implications for public policy* (pp. 115-136). Newbury Park, CA: Sage.

Gonsiorek, J. C. (1995). Gay male identities: Concepts and issues. In A. R. D'Augelli & C. J. Patterson (Eds.), *Lesbian, gay, and bisexual identities over the life span* (pp. 24-47). New York: Oxford University Press.

Gonzalez, F. J., & Espin, O. M. (1996). Latino men, Latina women, and homosexuality. In R. P. Cabaj & T. S. Stein (Eds.), *Textbook of homosexuality and mental health* (pp. 583-601). Washington, DC: American Psychiatric Press.

Green, R. (1987). *The sissy boy syndrome and the development of homosexuality.* New Haven, CT: Yale University Press.

Haldeman, D. C. (1994). The practice and ethics of sexual orientation conversion therapy. *Journal of Consulting and Clinical Psychology, 62,* 221-227.

Haldeman, D. C. (1996). Spirituality and religion in the lives of lesbians and gay men. In R. P. Cabaj & T. S. Stein (Eds.), *Textbook of homosexuality and mental health* (pp. 881-896). Washington, DC: American Psychiatric Press.

Hancock, K. A. (1995). Psychotherapy with lesbians and gay men. In A. R. D'Augelli & C. J. Patterson (Eds.), *Lesbian, gay, and bisexual identities over the life span* (pp. 398-432). New York: Oxford University Press.

Herdt, G., & Boxer, A. M. (1993). *Children of horizons: How gay and lesbian teens are leading a new way out of the closet.* Boston: Beacon.

Herek, G. M. (1991a). Myths about sexual orientation: a lawyer's guide to psychosocial research. *Law & Sexuality, 1,* 133-172.

Herek, G. M. (1991b). Stigma, prejudice, and violence against lesbians and gay men. In J. C. Gonsiorek & J. D. Weinrich (Eds.), *Homosexuality: Research implications for public policy* (pp. 60-80). Newbury Park, CA: Sage.

Herek, G. M. (1996). Heterosexism and homophobia. In R. P. Cabaj & T. S. Stein (Eds.), *Textbook of homosexuality and mental health* (pp. 101-113). Washington, DC: American Psychiatric Press.

Herek, G. M., & Berrill, K. T. (Eds.). (1992). *Hate crimes: Confronting violence against lesbians and gay men.* Newbury Park, CA: Sage.

Holder, A. R. (1996). Legal issues in professional liability. In M. Lewis (Ed.), *Child and adolescent psychiatry: A comprehensive textbook* (2nd ed., pp. 1145-1150). Baltimore, MD: Williams & Wilkins.

Hooker, E. A. (1957). The adjustment of the male overt homosexual. *Journal of Projective Techniques, 21,* 17-31.

Isay, R. A. (1989). *Being homosexual: Gay men and their development.* New York: Farrar, Straus, Giroux.

Janis, I. L., & Mann, L. (1977). *Decision making: A psychological analysis of conflict, choice, and commitment.* New York: Free Press.

Jones, B. E., & Hill, M. J. (1996). African American lesbians, gay men, and bisexuals. In R. P. Cabaj & T. S. Stein (Eds.), *Textbook of homosexuality and mental health* (pp. 549-561). Washington, DC: American Psychiatric Press.

Kurdek, L. A. (1994). The nature and correlates of relationship quality in gay, lesbian, and heterosexual cohabitating couples. In B. Greene & G. M. Herek (Eds.), *Lesbian and gay psychology: Theory, research and clinical applications* (pp. 133-155). Thousand Oaks, CA: Sage.

Lewes, K. (1988). *The psychoanalytic theory of male homosexuality.* New York: Simon & Schuster.

Lilling, A. H., & Friedman, R. C. (1995). Bias toward gay patients by psychoanalytic clinicians: An empirical investigation. *Archives of Sexual Behavior, 24,* 563-570.

Lopez, S. R. (1989). Patient variable biases in clinical judgment: Conceptual overview and methodological considerations. *Psychological Bulletin, 106,* 184-203.

Mann, L., Harmoni, R., & Power C. (1989). Adolescent decision-making: The development of competence. *Journal of Adolescence, 12,* 265-278.

Moshman, D. (1993). Adolescent reasoning and adolescent rights. *Human Development, 36,* 27-40.

Nakajima, G. A., Chan, Y. II., & Lee, K. (1996). Mental health issues for gay and lesbian Asian Americans. In R. P. Cabaj & T. S. Stein (Eds.), *Textbook of homosexuality and mental health* (pp. 563-581). Washington, DC: American Psychiatric Press.

Nicolosi, J. (1991). *Reparative therapy of male homosexuality: A new clinical approach.* North Vale, NJ: Jason Aronson.

O'Donohue, W., & Caselles, C. E. (1993). Homophobia: Conceptual, definitional, and value issues. *Journal of Psychopathology and Behavioral Assessment, 15,* 177-195.

Patterson, C. J. (1995). Lesbian mothers, gay fathers, and their children. In A. R. D'Augelli & C. J. Patterson (Eds.), *Lesbian, gay, and bisexual identities over the life span* (pp. 262-290). New York: Oxford University Press.

Paul, J. P. (1993). Childhood cross-gender behavior and adult homosexuality: The resurgence of biological models of sexuality, *Journal of Homosexuality, 24,* 41-54.

Peplau, L. A., & Cochran, S. D. (1998). A relational perspective on homosexuality. In D. P. McWhirter, D. P. Sanders, & S. M. Reinisch (Eds.), *Homosexuality/heterosexuality* (pp. 321-349). New York: Oxford University Press.

Peterson, J. L. (1992). Black men and their same-sex desires and behaviors. In G. Herdt (Ed.), *Gay culture in America: Essays from the field* (pp. 147-164). Boston: Beacon.

Pilkington, N. W., & D'Augelli, A. R. (1995). Victimization of lesbian, gay, and bisexual youth in community settings. *Journal of Community Psychology, 23,* 34-56.

Purcell, D. W., Campos, P. E., & Perilla, J. L. (1996). Therapy with lesbians and gay men: A cognitive behavioral perspective. *Cognitive and Behavioral Practice, 3,* 391-415.

Purcell, D. W., & Hicks, D. W. (1996). Institutional discrimination against lesbians, gay men, and bisexual: The courts, legislatures, and the military. In R. P. Cabaj & T. S. Stein (Eds.), *Textbook of homosexuality and mental health* (pp. 763-782). Washington, DC: American Psychiatric Press.

Remafedi, G., French, S., Story, M., Resnick, M. D., & Blum, R. (1998). The relationship between suicide risk and sexual orientation: Results of a population-based study. *American Journal of Public Health, 88,* 57-60.

Rowan, A. (1994). Homophobia: A new diagnosis for *DSM-V? The Behavior Therapist, 7,* 183-184.

Savin-Williams, R. C. (1990). *Gay and lesbian youth: Expressions of identity.* New York: Hemisphere.

Savin-Williams, R. C. (1995). Lesbian, gay male, and bisexual adolescents. In A. R. D'Augelli & C. J. Patterson (Eds.), *Lesbian, gay, and bisexual identities over the life span* (pp. 165-189). New York: Oxford University Press.

Savin-Williams, R. C., & Rodriguez, R. G. (1993). A developmental, clinical perspective on lesbian, gay male, and bisexual youths. In T. P. Gullotta, G. R. Adams, & R. Montemayor (Eds.), *Adolescent sexuality* (pp. 77-101). Newbury Park, CA: Sage.

Seil, D. (1996). Transsexuals: The boundaries of sexual identity and gender. In R. P. Cabaj & T. S. Stein (Eds.), *Textbook of homosexuality and mental health* (pp. 743-762). Washington, DC: American Psychiatric Press.

Shidlo, A. (1994). Internalized homophobia: Conceptual and empirical issues in measurement. In B. Greene & G. M. Herek (Eds.), *Lesbian and gay psychology: Theory, research and clinical applications* (pp. 176-205). Thousand Oaks, CA: Sage.

Shidlo, A., & Hollander, G. W. (1998, August). *Assessing internalized homophobia: New empirical findings.* Symposium presented at the 106th annual convention of the American Psychological Association, San Francisco, CA.

Slater, B. R. (1988). Essential issues in working with lesbian and gay male youths. *Professional Psychology: Research and Practice, 19,* 226-235.

Sobocinski, M. R. (1990). Ethical principles in the counseling of gay and lesbian adolescents: Issues of autonomy, competence, and confidentiality. *Professional Psychology: Research and Practice, 21,* 240-247.

Socarides, C. W., & Volkan, V. D. (Eds.). (1991). *The homosexualities and the therapeutic process.* Madison, CT: International Universities Press.

Spencer, S. B., & Hemmer, R. C. (1993). Therapeutic bias with gay and lesbian clients: A functional analysis. *The Behavior Therapist, 16,* 93-97.

Stein, T. S. (1996a). A critique of approaches to changing sexual orientation. In R. P. Cabaj & T. S. Stein (Eds.), *Textbook of homosexuality and mental health* (pp. 525-537). Washington, DC: American Psychiatric Press.

Stein, T. S. (1996b). Homosexuality and homophobia in men. *Psychiatric Annals, 26,* 37-40.

Stein, T. S., & Cohen, C. J. (Eds.). (1986). *Contemporary perspectives on psychotherapy with lesbians and gay men.* New York: Plenum.

Tafoya, T. N. (1996). Native two-spirit people. In R. P. Cabaj & T. S. Stein (Eds.), *Textbook of homosexuality and mental health* (pp. 603-617). Washington, DC: American Psychiatric Press.

Tancredi, L. (1982). Competency for informed consent. *International Journal of Law and Psychiatry, 5,* 51-63.

Troiden, R. R. (1989). The formation of homosexual identities. *Journal of Homosexuality, 17*(1-2), 43-73.

Van den Aardweg, G. J. M. (1986). *On the origin and treatment of homosexuality: A psychoanalytic reinterpretation.* New York: Praeger.

CHAPTER 20

Ethical Issues for Psychologists Working With Persons With Developmental Disabilities

W. Larry Williams and Kevin D. Williams
University of Nevada, Reno

T he ethical concepts and issues in the provision of educational and therapeutic services for persons with developmental disabilities (DD) comprise all those delineated for any other population and are outlined in the American Psychological Association (APA) Ethical Principles of Psychologists and Code of Conduct (1992). Indeed, the vulnerability of many persons with DD due to cognitive impairment and, in many cases, diagnoses of mental retardation (MR), mandates that educators, therapists, and a wide range of service practitioners must constantly act in ways that establish and maintain the most effective training methods and therapeutic treatments. It also requires informed and voluntary selection by consumers while simultaneously protecting those with limited intellectual abilities from inappropriate decisions with potentially deleterious effects (Millard & Rubin, 1992). Historically, there have been considerable problems in the field from the positioning of care providers' philosophical and service priorities unequally on either side of an apparent dichotomy of duty (see Weiner & Wettstein, 1993). Perhaps no other area of human services has been affected more by ethical and legal controversy as has Western society's acceptance and treatment of persons with DD as it has evolved from rejection and persecution in ancient societies: through subsistent accommodation and abuse after the Renaissance; to scientific interest, attempts at genetic elimination, and physical isolation at the turn of the past century; to deinstitutionalization, community integration, consumer-controlled service provision, and "person-first" professional attitudes developed over the last half of the 20th century (Scheerenberger, 1987; Williams, 1999). This evolution provides a unique opportunity for analysis of fundamental ethical principles and difficulties professionals have faced in their appropriate implementation.

FUNDAMENTAL PRINCIPLES OF PSYCHOLOGICAL SERVICE PROVISION

Autonomy, Beneficence, Nonmalevolence, and Justice

Fundamental to all ethical considerations in service provision are concepts derived from the very origins of philosophical inquiry. Early philosophy was concerned with establishing overreaching truths concerning the meaning and quality of life. Original analyses identified specific positions and choices reflective of then-understood human possibilities. The concepts of autonomy, beneficence, nonmalevolence, and justice form the core on which modern ethical principles and practices are based.

Autonomy has evolved as a concept in modern society that holds that every person should have the opportunity to determine their actions and be free to choose and make choices. Self-determination is basic to many Western political positions and holds a central position in democratic societies. Accompanying this basic respect for an individual's right to independent choice come the issues of a person's informed choice and whether the person is competent to choose. Does a person have all the information necessary to make a truly informed decision? Is the person cognitively or intellectually capable of comprehending the current and future facts and issues involved in the decision? Persons with DD who also have MR present a unique continuum of such abilities; we are obliged to determine the extent to which a person has all the information required to make a choice, the extent to which alternative resources and services are available for choosing among, and whether the individual is intellectually competent to actually comprehend and make such choices (Hayes, Adams, & Rydeen, 1994). Some persons

may be in need of extensive protection, even to the extent of excluding them from participation in certain activities and choice opportunities. Most recently (Bannerman, Sheldon, Sherman, & Harchik, 1990), these issues have been complicated with recognition that in our current indulgent Western way of living, most people often make choices that are not the best for their long-term benefit (e.g., many of us eat too much or consume harmful substances for immediate pleasure, which may result in long-term delayed health problems). Also relevant to this issue is the difference between choices made *by one's self* (i.e., the client) and choices made *for one's self by others* (e.g., direct care staff, interdisciplinary professionals, home staff, parents/legal guardians, etc.). When one is responsible for deciding on courses of action for individuals in public processes, one may come under considerable social/political pressure for "correctness" as perceived by others, and those decisions may differ considerably from those we all often make for ourselves that are less subject to such open public scrutiny (e.g., Howie, Gatens-Robinson, & Rubin, 1992). Such are the conditions for much controversy in legal actions and standards of practice that have become increasingly based on political merit and protection of professionals from litigation, as opposed to clear long-term benefits for consumers.

Beneficence refers to the ethical responsibility of educators, service providers, and therapists not only to respect the decisions of persons with DD and protect them from harm but also to secure their well-being. Two complementary rules have come to be associated with the professional provision of beneficence: (a) Do no harm, and (b) maximize possible benefits and minimize possible harms. The reader will recognize the former rule as the Hippocratic maxim of "Do no harm," the fundamental principle of medical ethical practice. In addition to the clear requirement to not worsen a person's situation through treatment or other services, we are also obliged to act in ways that maximize benefits for persons with DD in our services (see Cuvo & Thaw, 1986). To further complicate the issues, beneficence can be evaluated on both an individual and a societal level. This becomes especially relevant in standards for conducting research in which some risk may be involved for individuals participating in research in answering questions or performing tasks that significantly benefit others (e.g., publications, conference presentations, grant submissions, etc.). It also plays into protecting individuals from research or treatment actions for which possible benefits are small or nonexistent.

Nonmalevolence: As iterated, diligence in "doing no harm" is critical in DD due to relative degrees of incompetence indigenous in working with individuals with any level of MR. Indeed, this principle is most relevant to past and current dilemmas in clinical or educational service delivery in which long-term gains in independence of functioning may be sacrificed under current well-intentioned courses of action that do not address, or that even make worse, basic behavioral development. Such issues are present typically in state and provincial laws that seek to protect individuals from others' employment of perceived inhumane or unnecessarily punitive consequences for seriously harmful behaviors to one self or to others (e.g., Illinois Mental Health and Developmental Disability Code, Chapter 11, 1992, placing restrictions on behavioral programming). Although such legislation places a healthy burden on professionals to bring about behavior change using positive approaches, it can also effectively leave some individuals with long-standing behavioral abnormalities without treatment and destined to live out their lives in seclusion and with physical or chemical restraints. Ironically, at the other extreme, one can

often observe the negative effects of a lack of effective instruction and training for many individuals who show a variety of challenges in learning. Again, well-intentioned decisions to allow people to "choose" not to participate in educational or training activities (i.e., as the patient's right to refuse treatment) naturally result in developmentally disabled persons with little or no functional repertoires remaining dependent on human service providers and isolated from mainstream society—the exact opposite of the agreed-on overall goals for such individuals. Thus, the client's right to refuse treatment seems partly at odds with the right to effective treatment, just as the latter is partly at odds with the right to the least-intrusive treatment in the least-restrictive environment and raises the issue of justice in human service provision.

Further emphasis on the principle of nonmalevolence is also represented in professional domains as standards of practice. Schroeder, Oldenquist, and Rojahn (1990), for instance, presented a conceptual framework useful for human service providers to assess and evaluate the relative humaneness and effectiveness of prospective behavioral treatments. The reader must naturally ask, "Relative to what?" and the authors emphatically respond, "Relative to the individual's history, severity of the behavior problem, and the patient's and familial concerns, as well as those of other involved parties, state/provincial/federal statutes, and professional standards of practice." Only in addressing these issues comprehensively can human service providers evaluate the relative humaneness and effectiveness of any procedure. Similarly, human service providers must be aware of the law on aversive behavioral procedures (e.g., Herr, 1990) and legal restrictions pertaining to pharmacological protocol. For a comprehensive discussion of the latter, please see Kalachnik (1998).

Justice is concerned with the fair distribution of both benefits from and responsibilities or burdens for resources, research, or services across people. Injustice occurs when an entitled benefit is denied or when some burden is wrongly applied. To determine the fairness of distributions, it is necessary to explain the concept of *equality*. Further concepts are then necessary to provide dimensions of equality along which benefits and burdens should be assessed, shared, and evaluated. These concepts reflect the fundamental positions of long-established political viewpoints encompassed in libertarian and egalitarian positioning. Benefits and burdens can be distributed (a) to each person an equal share, (b) to each person according to individual needs, (c) to each person according to individual effort, (d) to each person according to societal contribution, and (e) to each person according to merit. Although these concepts affect standards of practice, they are the basis of federal standards for protection of human subjects in research and are particularly relevant in decisions concerning research with persons with DD, as well as other minority or disadvantaged groups. (For an explanation and analysis of theses and further concepts within the concept of justice applied to persons with acquired brain injury, see DeJong & Batavia, 1989.)

Moral Development

Moral development is critical to professional development in any profession, though human services is certainly a field in which moral development is likely to produce substantial changes in service delivery and professional decorum (e.g., Newman, Reinecke, & Kurtz, 1996). Hayes and Hayes (1994) defined moral behavior as "activity governed by and consistent with verbal rules about what is socially and personally good" (p. 46). Furthermore, the authors argued that two major processes are instrumental in moral development: relational framing and rule-governance. Relational frames are simply equivalence relations in which a substantial amount of empirical research has been conducted (e.g., Sidman, 1994). On the other hand, there are several types of rule-governance. *Pliance,* for instance, refers to "behavior due to a history of socially-mediated consequences for a correspondence between antecedent verbal stimuli and relevant behavior" (Hayes & Hayes, 1994, p. 51). Service providers are *pliant* in the sense that their behavior has a history of social consequences by other colleagues, employers, and advocates in correspondence between legal and ethical guidelines and professional practice. In layman terms, "I have to do what other legal and ethical representatives in developmental disabilities expect me to do."

Tracking is a second type of rule-governance relevant to our discussion of moral development and legal/ethical issues and refers to "behavior due to a history of correspondence between antecedent verbal stimuli and the contingencies contracted by formal and situational properties of the relevant behavior" (Hayes & Hayes, 1994, p. 51). Service providers *track* their behavior because they are told to do so by other colleagues, employers, and advocates (e.g., for clients', service providers', or others' protection) and because state statutes under the Department of Human Resources mandate it (i.e., formal/situational properties of service provision). In layman terms, "I have to do what others tell me to do and maintain what is expected of my professional practice with state statues."

Augmenting is the third type of rule-governance relevant to legal and ethical issues in DD and refers to "behavior due to antecedent verbal stimuli that temporarily alter the degree to which previously established consequences function as reinforcers or punishers" (Hayes & Hayes, 1994, p. 51). Service providers are expected, when applicable, to practice in ways under the dominant control of new antecedent stimuli, regardless of well-established practices that have proven useful and efficient for them in the past. In collective lay terms, "We do what others tell us to do, maintain what is expected of our professional practice in accordance with state statutes, and modify our professional decorum when either the former or latter tells us to do so." Hayes and Hayes (1994) further discuss augmenting in two forms: motivative and formative augmenting. The former colloquially refers to changes in professional practice due to *direct experience* (e.g., in service provision), whereas the latter refers to identical changes due to *indirect experience* (e.g., being informed of relevant consequences for noncompliance to professional practice standards).

There is also a second-level account necessary in rule-governance referred to as "support for systems of rule-governance" (Hayes & Hayes, 1994, p. 56) and is particularly relevant to our discussion of legal and ethical issues in DD. First and foremost, service providers maintain *social concern for pliance* by establishing practices highly correspondent to legal and professional ethic codes. Some specific activities conducted out of *social concern for pliance* may consist of licensure suspension or removal, loss of credentials, or professional censorship. In lay terms, "We have to maintain high correspondence in professional practice with what others say and do, what is expected of us by legal statutes in service provision, and be prepared to modify such practices when told or expected to do so." The implicit should also be said, in that we have to *avoid* differences between our professional practice and what is said and done by others, discrepancies between service provision and legal statutes, and immutability when change is clearly dictated. Inasmuch as a substantial amount of evidence is accumulated against service providers *implicitly* as acts of omission or commission, it is critical to assume both in all contexts.

Second, there is also considerable *social concern for tracking,* represented in the trend toward actuarial decision making and service accountability in recent years. Tracking activities typically conducted in service provision consist of employee performance evaluation; accurate reporting of service types, dates, deliveries, and so on; advocacy investigations, accreditation, and legal hearings and proceedings; interdisciplinary review; and all those not otherwise mentioned. Tracking activities usually result in final products in the form of meeting minutes, performance reviews, service evaluation and modification, and so on and serve as the basis on which commendable and disciplinary action are taken. The former is relatively improbable to the latter, though in either case, tracking activities, particularly those resulting in final products, become the fundamental basis on which the service provider's argument of adequate delivery of treatment is predicated. Thus, meticulous and thorough tracking activities are invaluable skills in attaining and maintaining professional credentials, membership, and practice, as well as civil privileges. In lay terms, "Service providers must track all their professional activities to ensure and justify pliance to legal and professional standards of practice."

Finally, *social concern for augmenting* becomes relevant to our discussion of legal and ethical issues in DD. Service providers are charged with affording "just" services to clients in accordance with legal and professional standards of practice. The "person-first" movement, for instance, originated from this concern seeking just treatment for individuals with DD. Typical activities of social concern for augmenting consist of continuing education, licensure and credential requirements, professional practice standards and disciplinary action, legal statutes and advocacy reviews, professional conferences of service providers, and the like. The social concern for augmenting is also the driving force in a trend toward actuarial decision making and full accountability, though it has considerably different outcomes for clients and professionals. For clients, service type and delivery must be *justified* or otherwise augmented on the basis of the client's needs, preferences, and activities, with special consideration to family members and affected parties. The assumption in justifying service delivery is that we increase the likelihood of not engaging in unjustified or reprehensible professional decorum. Moreover, the likelihood of positive outcomes for clients is similarly increased because a justified service delivery would presumably be pliant, tracked, and valid. The consequences are not so sweet for service providers. If all services must be justified, the opportunity for authentic experimental creativity is precluded. Furthermore, the social concern for augmenting becomes problematic because "unjustified" service delivery becomes reprehensible from either a legal or ethical perspective and therefore subject to disciplinary action by legal advocates or members of professional organizations. The severity of disciplinary action is, of course, directly related to tracking and any existing products to support or refute the sustaining conditions for punishment or censorship. Thus, social concern for augmenting needs to play an integral part in service delivery yet afford equal and adequate protection of professional, civil, and personal rights of service providers and clients by mutual tracking.

Summary of moral development: The authors argue that moral development is an instrumental process to improving the quality of human services and their delivery and

the professional decorum of its handmaidens. Behavioral service providers must always be pliant and they must track all professional activities and relevant products delineated in standards of practice or code of ethics. Most important, behavioral service providers must augment their professional activities when statutes, data, relevant parties, clients, or experience tells them to do so, without transgressing the confines exerted legally, ethically, or socially by the aforementioned. Pliance, tracking, and augmenting are critical for professional development at the level of service delivery, though more is needed for professional development in practice. Thus, social concern for pliance, tracking, and augmenting are tantamount requirements to adequate service delivery and accountability and play crucial roles in moral and, ultimately, professional development.

Working Assumptions

There are several assumptions made in analyzing legal and ethical issues in DD. First, individuals with DD have the right to *effective treatment* and full *community membership*. This includes, though is not limited to, deinstitutionalization, reform, remedial academics, vocational rehabilitation, social habilitation, and any other factors crucial to adaptive client functioning in their natural environment. The Americans With Disabilities Act (ADA, 1993) required that handicap children be provided with the least-restrictive school environment, and its expansion and refinement in the Individuals With Disabilities Education Act (IDEA, 1997) are legislative examples representative of this assumption at the molar level. Second, a corollary assumption is extended from the latter example such that mental health patients and individuals with DD are entitled to treatment in the least-restrictive *effective* environment (Effective is presumably a relative term justified or not by tracking activities and/or products in regard to pliance, tracking, and augmenting in professional practice.) The third assumption made is that clients have the right to treatment decisions directly predicated *on good data.* The assumption necessarily consists of elements of pliance (treatment is formulated from data), tracking (good data is presumably well-defined and tracked), and augmenting (treatment decisions are changed only when good data dictates). A fourth assumption states to certify *procedures,* not service providers, because the former can be objectively and reliably monitored and evaluated, whereas the latter cannot (Risley, 1975). In other words, procedures can be justified, though service providers cannot. Professional standards of practice and legislative action are two molar instances with demonstrable trends toward procedure certification and are representative of the preceding assumption.

There are additional assumptions made by the authors to elaborate and clarify legal and ethical issues in DD. Fifth, professional standards of practice and legislative action are primarily based in exercises related to moral development in professional and legal contexts, respectively. As such, a comprehensive understanding of moral development is needed (see Hayes & Hayes, 1994), sustaining legal and professional practices and integration of tracking activities such that professional and legislative action is justified a priori, ad hoc, or post hoc. Sixth, the authors assume that autonomy, benevolence, nonmalevolence, and justice are crucial facets to valid and effective service delivery and are instrumental in ensuring pliance, tracking, and augmenting in professional practice. These facets are given consideration in all regards prior to, during, and after treatment has been formulated, implemented, evaluated, discarded/modified, and terminated.

Seventh, the authors assume that tracking is the basis on which all service delivery is predicated, evaluated, extended, revised, and discarded. Service providers evaluate tracking products to assess, evaluate, modify, and discard existent and nonexistent treatment protocols, whereas clients, families/ guardians, and advocates evaluate tracking products to assess, evaluate, modify, and discard current and subsequent treatment providers. Finally and most important, the authors make these collective assumptions from the fallible vantage point of man and cannot account for the accuracy or entirety of the assumptions previously delineated, because they are necessarily tenuous.

APA CODE OF ETHICS AND DEVELOPMENTAL DISABILITIES

The general ethical considerations of a psychologist's activities with persons with DD are the same as those for working with any population. This includes general areas of competence, integrity, professional and scientific responsibility, respect for people's rights and dignity, and concern for others' welfare and social responsibility (APA, 1992). However, the nature of DD makes salient that several general considerations require closer scrutiny by professionals.

Competence and Behavioral Standards of Practice

DD and their frequent association with MR require an understanding of these conditions, adequate assessment, and potential interventions and treatments that are not widely available in most university undergraduate and graduate psychology curricula. Indeed, a long-standing problem of the DD field and its original "medical model" approach were probably due to the fact that the principle professionals "stepping up to the plate" in treatment of this population were physicians. Although many disciplines besides psychology are currently involved in the field, it is unusual to find many university level courses in psychology covering MR or DD. Typically, such topics are the subject of special education courses. In a current related issue, the same problem exists for the clearly effective approach of behavior analysis, most evident these days in the widespread increased demands for behavioral service provision for children with autism and related disorders (for example, the inclusion of functional analysis in the revised IDEA legislation). Clearly, the issue of a psychologist's competence to adequately assess and treat persons with DD or MR has become more salient. As a knowledge area within psychology, behavior analysis has made significant advances in the assessment and treatment of a variety of behavioral disorders over the last 20 years (e.g., Iwata, Dorsey, Slifer, Bauman, & Richman 1994). Several states have passed legislation recognizing a national standard certification process (Shook, 1993) for behavior analysts, and all indications are that this practice will expand. Although the APA has declared a separate specialty of behavioral psychology, its eventual relationship to behavior analysis and the current certification process for behavior analytic service provision is unclear.

Behavior analysis has become arguably the predominant psychological assessment and treatment approach in DD and MR. Although many psychologists openly conduct or supervise behavior analysis assessments and interventions, it is generally known that many have taken little more than one undergraduate course in behavior analysis, let alone comprehensive graduate levels of training. Only one university in Canada (Manitoba) and a handful of universities in the United States provide doctoral level

training specifically focused in behavior analysis. Perhaps twice that number provide master's level training, and twice that number provide a variety of undergraduate courses in behavior analysis. It appears that a major issue is arising in the DD and MR field concerning the competence and qualifications required by psychologists using behavior analytic approaches.

Finally, with the changing criteria during the 1980s of the third edition of the current *Diagnostic and Statistical Manual,* 4th edition *(DSM-IV),* of the American Psychiatric Association (1994), it became possible for persons with MR to also be diagnosed with a psychopathology. These so-called dual-diagnosis cases have also contributed to the field's new demand for more specialized training. Many practitioners in the DD/MR field have little or no training in assessment or treatment of persons with such a wide variety of pathologies, and those with traditional assessment training are typically lacking in appropriate instruments and knowledge about DD and MR. Assessments and treatments in this expanding specialty have been most successful with interdisciplinary teams from the areas of psychiatry, behavior analysis, pharmacology, and clinical psychology. These approaches manifest elements of pharmacological protocol, rigorous data-driven behavioral assessment and interventions, and some traditional therapies that ultimately have proven effective. As no formal graduate level training is available at this point, cautious and conservative interdisciplinary, team-based experience is called for in specializing in assessment and treatment of the dually diagnosed.

Integrity and Professional and Scientific Responsibility

Because practice in DD often involves third-party referrals, there is less direct countercontrol over professionals from consumers. As a whole, the field of DD has become increasingly affected by the availability of resources and highly variable effects of clinical and political decision making (e.g., Cuvo & Thaw, 1986). These variables taken together with regional differences in population and corresponding sophistication of services can lead a psychologist to be pressured into at least "agreement through abstention" concerning the lack of appropriate services for consumers. Although it is clearly the duty of a psychologist to point out and work toward change in systems that are at fault, a reality in many situations is that if one argues for too much change, too soon, one will be functionally excluded from having an effective role in services. Often, meaningful change will require years to bring about, especially in areas with poor or no services, and the psychologist must diligently maintain his or her position while still participating in the overall service effort and attempting to show relevant leadership toward appropriate services. In areas with few resources, a psychologists may find themselves in different levels of conflict of interest when only a few people provide myriad services, against an alternative of no services. *Integrity* is explicitly addressed under the provisions for "responsible conduct of a behavior analyst," whereas the issues of *professional and scientific responsibility* are likewise addressed throughout the remainder of standards of practice collectively known as the "Behavior Analyst Code of Ethical Conduct."

Respect for People's Rights and Dignity and Concern for Others' Welfare

As in all areas of psychological service, psychologists working in DD strive for the protection of consumer confidentiality and their self-determination and autonomy. Indeed, issues of confidentiality, dignity, and

autonomy have become central to the current widely accepted "person-centered" approaches to service delivery. The last 20 years have seen a true change in the service paradigm from one of early attempts at deinstitutionalization and community living to total community immersion and consumer-driven supports. Well-developed services provide all levels of support for persons with even pervasive (Luckasson et al., 1992) needs in community settings and through as many regular service channels as possible that provide other services to the population in general. Service design has become driven by allowing consumers to choose where they want to live and where they want to work and providing the supports necessary to realize these wants. Ironically, much controversy exists in the field between proponents of complete choice and those who argue that to be able to choose, one must be able to first discriminate between the chosen items. This argument is less relevant for persons with at least minimal language skills or other forms of functional communication. However, for many persons with DD functioning in the lower intellectual ranges, it is clear that they will consistently choose activities and actions that are not conducive to their development or are even outright dangerous to their physical well-being. An extreme example for these authors was a recent criticism of our day program activities for a person with long-standing PICA behavior in that we did not allow him to choose to engage in such behaviors. It is becoming increasingly difficult under such social-political positions by service agencies for psychologists to maintain and encourage activities for the developmentally disabled that will maximize beneficence, minimize malevolence, and all the while maintain the highest level feasible of autonomy for that person. The current controversy in the DD field appears to be mostly due to ignorance of such concepts or practical differences in the priorities with which they should be considered. For further discussion of generic socio-political and theoretical issues as well as professional practices in a trend of emerging responsive human services, please see Cuvo & Thaw (1986); Holburn (1997); and Weiner and Wettstein (1993).

Relevant to these issues is recent research concerning a possible hierarchy of visual and auditory discrimination skills that can be reliably measured in persons with DD (Martin & Yu, 2000). Basic auditory discrimination ability appears to follow visual "simple" and then "conditional" discriminations, comprising a crucial "keystone" activity that separates persons with eventual communication ability from those who remain perpetually nonverbal. Furthermore, this ability has predictive testability on standard intelligence tests (Richards, Williams, & Follette, 2002). In any case, the basic literature on simple and conditional discriminations (commonly employed in *stimulus equivalence* studies) with individuals with DD affords a rudimentary understanding of core requisite skills in developing subsequent appropriate verbal and social skills collectively known as *cognition.*

Social Responsibility

Given our discussion of extreme variability in services and their sophistication (notwithstanding clear federal legislation mandating service for persons with DD), psychologists have an increasing responsibility to make themselves available and to influence service decision making. This is especially true for human rights committees and behavior intervention committees that consistently need membership and guidance in trying to unravel and understand routine conflicting issues of general treatment policy, politically correct service movements, and the psychological reality and needs of individuals. One small but clear example

concerns the often demonstrable function of escape-maintained aggression or self-injurious behavior (Hagopian, Fisher, Sullivan, Acquisto, & LeBlanc, 1998) and the necessity to teach alternatives while eliminating the maladaptive relationship of escape (e.g., by extinction). This requires restricting the person's right to aggress, and because this procedure is often not carried out consistently, no appreciable change in the behavior occurs. Thus, it seems that psychologists require procedural fidelity checks on legal and ethical adherence to legal and professional standards of practice, as well as the stipulations of behavioral protocols in professional practice (Vollmer & Northup, 1996).

A lack of effective action by psychologists is also evident at the molar level in the passing of legislation in many states that, although well-meaning, restricts the clinical treatment options of professionals. Our own experience recently found us testifying to the state legislature against the death penalty for persons diagnosed with MR. Ironically, this same legislature has passed legislation forbidding the use of clinically applied, minor decelerative consequences for severe behavior disorder treatments. We cannot use clinically demonstrated effective methods to stop aggression or self-injury, but if the behavior escalates to the point where someone is killed, we can execute the perpetrator.

BEHAVIORAL STANDARDS OF PRACTICE

Because of its widespread presence in DD, behavior analysis standards of practice have also become necessary for any psychologist to know and follow. Although many state and provincial associations for behavior analysis have produced their own standards of conduct, all are affiliated with the Association for Behavior Analysis (ABA) and conform to that association's standards.[1] ABA has undertaken to provide a national exam in behavior analysis (Shook, 1993), subscribed to currently in several states. In Florida, Tennessee, and California, these standards of practice are adopted and sustained by legislative action, mandating behavioral service providers to adhere to its statutes. There are currently 10 general standards of practice in behavior analysis (with several substandards), though the number is likely to be expanded as the profession develops and evolves. For instance, there are currently no standards of practice mandating moral development in behavior analysis, though the authors are currently in the process of petitioning the ABA for emendations. The existing Florida general standards of conduct in behavior analysis (Florida Association for Behavior Analysis, 1995) are grouped under specific areas and are listed as follows:

1. Responsible conduct of a behavior analyst

2. The behavior analyst's responsibility to clients

3. The behavior analyst's preintervention behavior

4. The behavior analyst and the individual behavior change program

5. The behavior analyst as a teacher and/or supervisor

6. The behavior analyst and the workplace

7. Research guidelines

8. The behavior analyst's ethical responsibility to the field of behavior analysis

9. The behavior analyst's ethical responsibility to colleagues

10. The behavior analyst's ethical responsibility to society

It is noteworthy to know that these standards are predicated on and evolve beyond those delineated in the APA code of ethics (APA, 1992). These standards of practice are not mutually exclusive and collectively comprise what is deemed as competence in behavior analysis.

RELEVANT LEGISLATION AND STANDARDS OF PRACTICE IN DEVELOPMENTAL DISABILITIES

Psychologists working in DD need to become familiar with the developments over the past 30 years in crucial new legislation concerning services and rights of all persons with disabilities. Early legislation in DD fell under the auspices of the Rehabilitation Act of 1973, though in recent years legislation has primarily been under the ADA of 1990. The ADA is divided in three parts, addressing three different aspects of public domain: Title I addresses "Employment," Title II pertains to "State and Local Government Activities," and Title III involves "Public Accommodations." Several subsequent acts of legislation have been executed under the auspices of the ADA (e.g., Civil Rights of Institutionalized Patients, Fair Housing Act, Individuals With Disabilities Education Act, Voter Accessibility, Air Carrier Access, etc.), all of which provide blanket protection for individuals with DD and/or MR. The ADA is the major source of legislation at the federal level, and its statutes supersede those of state and local governments.[2]

Several states also have standards of practice for general psychology and in some cases for individuals with DD or MR. For instance, Illinois has such statutes and places restrictions on behavioral programming. All states are required by the federal government to maintain a Web page on-line, and direct access to the state Department Of Human Resources will provide a listing of divisions (e.g., Division of Mental Health and

Developmental Services in Nevada) where standards of practice can be easily and conveniently obtained.

There are also new lawsuits relevant to our discussion of legal and ethical issues in service provision to individuals with DD and MR. Mental disability case law of this sort falls under the auspices of the ADA and is further sustained by any or all of the three titles. For instance, *Lancaster v. City of Mobile, Alabama* (1992), a recent employment lawsuit against local government for hiring practices, falls under the auspices of Title I of the ADA. (A man with a second-grade reading level was denied the accommodation of taking a written examination orally and was, as a consequence, denied the fair opportunity for employment.) Cases of this sort become increasingly relevant as precedents when practice and positive outcomes in habilitative and rehabilitative contexts occur more frequently in work with individuals with DD. A second recent lawsuit was filed under the auspices of Title II of the ADA pertaining to "State and Local Government Activities" in the *United States vs. Commonwealth of Virginia* (1994). Virginia is charged with following:

> Violating Title II by failing to establish a process in which an individualized, professional determination is made as to what type of setting, among the range of institutional and community-based options available, is most appropriate for the needs of each resident.[3]

No current lawsuits have been filed for individuals with any kind of mental disability under the auspices of Title III of the ADA ("Public Accommodations"), though as the time goes by, so shall the number of lawsuits filed under the titles of the ADA be likely to change. Thus, familiarity with all facets of the ADA, that is, their individual titles and case law, affords human service providers

insight as what *not* to do in working with individuals with DD and whether professional standards of practice are consistent with the stipulations of the ADA. Most important, familiarity with the ADA also affords insight as to the unlimited possibilities of judicial censorship in provision and advocacy of services for individuals with DD and/or MR by private, state, and federal agencies. Consider the following controversial positions in terms of the ADA and whether such practices may be likely or unlikely to attract federal censorship.

Position on the Use of Intrusive Procedures

During the 1980s and 1990s, controversy increased concerning the use of intrusive consequences in the treatment of behavior disorders. Although certain decelerative consequences (e.g., social disapproval, overcorrection, fines, time-out, etc.) had been identified as effective when used with positive consequences for alternative behaviors, many held the position that no such consequences should ever be used with persons with DD, regardless of mitigating circumstances. Others with a history of treating extremely severe aggression and self-injury with deceleratives have argued that to not use these methods relegated consumers with such behaviors to life in mechanical and or chemical restraint. As in many medical treatments, a small amount of unpleasantness is often required to relieve long-term illness (such as Novocain administration and drilling decayed teeth to maintain one's teeth). In terms of standards of practice, intrusive procedures fall primarily under the auspices of "the behavior analyst's responsibility to clients" (2.0), "the behavior analyst's pre-intervention behavior" (3.0), "the behavior analyst and the individual change program" (4.0) and intermittently throughout the remainder of the code. Several other large organizations produced statements regarding the limits and descriptions they supported for treating severe behavior disorders and are represented in the behavior analyst code of ethics.[4]

Positions on the Use of Controversial Procedures

Over the last 25 years, the predominant organizations in the DD field have been forced to provide position papers on the use of treatment and educational methods that arise with little or no scientific or clinical support from the professional literature. Both the APA and the American Association on Mental Retardation have published position statements on the use of intrusive procedures and on specific treatment approaches that have yet to be demonstrated to be effective. Psychologists must make themselves aware of such treatments and the empirical evidence for their efficacy. A major problem with new, "strong effects" claiming methods is that consumers and their families will do or pay almost anything hoping for a "cure" for themselves or their family members. They and supporting professionals are unethically subjected to a form of emotional blackmail in undertaking the approach, usually to the detriment of existing methods.

Two such approaches, "gentle teaching" (McGee Menolascino, Hobbs, & Menousek, 1987) and "facilitated communication" (Biklen, 1990), have received extensive attention and have essentially been shown to have little or no scientific or clinical merit (Jacobson, Mulick, & Swartz, 1995; Jones & McCaughey, 1992). Assuming the code in the absence of data with persons with DD, controversial procedures are specifically addressed in "responsible conduct of a behavior analyst" (1.0), "the behavior analyst's responsibility to clients" (2.0), "the behavior

analyst's pre-intervention behavior" (3.0), "the behavior analyst and the individual behavior change program" (4.0), and secondarily throughout the remaining standards of practice (e.g., "Research Guidelines").

CONDUCTING RESEARCH WITH PERSONS WITH DEVELOPMENTAL DISABILITIES

Psychologists follow the APA (1992) ethical code of conduct when conducting research in any sense. When human participants are involved, psychologists typically also follow the specific federal policy for conducting research with humans, as described in "Protection of Human Participants."[5] This legislation enforces protection for human subjects involved in research that is conducted with federal funding and therefore also is typically followed by any institutions or organizations, such as universities, hospitals, research centers, and so forth, involved in research of any nature that includes human subjects. The Department of Health and Human Services, National Institutes of Health, Office for Protection From Research Risks enforces the regulations through the national system of institutional review boards (IRBs) that are established at each organization overseen by the regulations. Fashioned initially from the *Belmont Report* (National Commission for the Protection of Human Subjects of Biomedical and Behavioral Research, 1979), federal protection is based on the principles previously discussed in this chapter of respect for persons, beneficence, and justice. These principles generate the basic application principles of a competent, informed, and voluntary consent from an individual to participate in research that has been deemed to provide more benefit than any planned or possible risk.

Whereas the general features of any IRB approval are involved in research with persons with DD and MR, certain additional restrictions in procedures are often involved. For example, whereas certain categories of program evaluation or educational research may be exempt from securing formal informed consent from individuals and may be eligible for an expedited review not requiring the full "live" discussion by the complete IRB, studies involving DD and MR always require full IRB approval. This is due to this population's status as a group at risk or as particularly vulnerable to coercion. In addition, it is often necessary for researchers to provide a rationale as to why the participants in their proposed study are individuals with DD and MR, as opposed to individuals with other characteristics.

The issues of competence involved in DD and MR often involve the necessity of obtaining informed voluntary consent from family or guardians. In many clinical service and educational settings, this may promote a closer review of possible coercion of such third parties, due to conflict of interest relationships when providers approach guardians for such research project consents. In the DD and MR field, special consideration must be given to the recruitment of participants in ways that allow rejection of participation after preliminary or complete information about the research without having to directly interact with the researchers.

An interesting further phenomenon in research with DD and MR, particularly from a behavior analysis approach, is the confusion many people have surrounding the "research" nature of clinical and educational services via a "scientist-practitioner model" (Barlow, Hayes, & Nelson, 1986) when teaching or training interventions are demonstrated to be effective through single-subject designs as part of regular clinical or educational practice. The essential feature of such demonstrations that makes them necessary for IRB review is that the researchers want to publish the data—not that the data represent predetermined, esoteric manipulations of independent variables to test theoretical or applied hypotheses. Of course this, too, would make such undertakings "research," requiring IRB review and its corresponding voluntary, informed consent procedures. Furthermore, IRB approval does not then guarantee the right to conduct the research. An individual educational-planning team or an individual service plan team typically must agree to the research participation in their roles as planners of the best course of events for the individual involved. If such teams have biased views concerning what research is and who should participate, researchers can also approach human rights committees (which operate in most states) to decide on differences of opinion on a given individual's participation in a research endeavor.

NOTES

1. See Association of Behavior Analysis (2002) at: http://www.wmich.edu/~aba/.
2. For a copy of the Americans with Disabilities Act and all relevant legislative acts and case law, please visit www.ada.gov.
3. Retrieved on June 16, 2002, from: www.ada.gov.mental disability.caselaw.
4. Copies of their individual positions may be obtained through the ABA Web site at: http://www. wmich.edu/~aba/.
5. Code of Federal Regulations, Title 45, Part 46.

REFERENCES

American Psychiatric Association. (1994). *Diagnostic and statistical manual of mental disorders* (4th ed.). Washington, DC: American Psychiatric Association.

American Psychological Association. (1992). Ethical principles of psychologists and code of conduct. *American Psychologist, 47*(12), 1597-1611.

Americans With Disabilities Act, Pub. L. 94-142 (1993).

Bannerman, D. J., Sheldon, J. B., Sherman, J. A., & Harchik, A. E. (1990). Balancing the right to habilitation with the right to personal liberties: The rights of people with developmental disabilities to eat too many doughnuts and take a nap. *Journal of Applied Behavior Analysis, 23,* 79-89.

Barlow, D. H., Hayes, S. C., & Nelson, R. O. (1986). *The scientist practitioner: Research and accountability in clinical and educational settings* (3rd ed.). New York: Pergamon.

Biklen, D. (1990). Communication unbound: Autism and praise. *Harvard Educational Review, 60,* 291-314.

Cuvo, A. J., & Thaw, J. (1986). *Mental disability law-The politics of human rights.* In J. Thaw & A. Cuvo (Eds.), *Developing responsive human services* (pp. 191-228). Hillsdale, NJ: Lawrence Erlbaum.

DeJong, G., & Batavia, A. I. (1989). Societal duty and resource allocation for persons with severe traumatic brain injury. *Journal of Head Trauma Rehabilitation, 4*(1), 1-12.

Florida Association for Behavior Analysis. (1995). *Behavior analyst code of conduct.* Retrieved from the World Wide Web on June 18, 2002, at: http://fabaworld.org/code.html.

Hagopian, L. P., Fisher, W. W., Sullivan, M. T., Acquisto, J., & LeBlanc, L. A. (1998). Effectiveness of functional communication training with and without extinction and punishment: A summary of 21 inpatient cases. *Journal of Applied Behavior Analysis, 31,* 211-235.

Hayes, L. J., Adams, M. A., & Rydeen, K. L. (1994). Ethics choice and value. In L. J. Hayes, G. J. Hayes, S. C., Moore, & P. M. Ghezzi (Eds.), *Ethical issues in developmental disabilities.* Reno, NV: Context.

Hayes, S. C., & Hayes, G. J. (1994). Stages of moral development as stages of rule-governance. In L. Hayes, G. Hayes, S. Moore, & P. Ghezzi (Eds.), *Ethical issues in developmental disabilities.* Reno, NV. Context.

Herr, S. S. (1990). The law on aversive and nonaversive behavioral intervention. In S. L. Harris & J. S. Handleman (Eds.), *Aversive and nonaversive interventions: Controlling life-threatening behavior by the developmentally disabled* (pp. 80-118). New York: Springer.

Holburn, S. (1997). A renaissance in residential behavior analysis? A historical perspective and a better way to help people with challenging behavior. *The Behavior-Analyst, 20*(2), 61-85.

Howie, J., Gatens-Robinson, E., & Rubin, S. E. (1992). Applying ethical principles in the rehabilitation context. Illinois Mental Health and Developmental Disabilities Code. *Journal of Rehabilitation Education, 6,* 41-55.

Iwata, B., Dorsey, M. F., Slifer, K. J., Bauman, K. E., & Richman, G. S. (1994). Toward a functional analysis of self-injury. *Journal of Applied Behavior Analysis, 27,* 197-209.

Jacobson, J. W., Mulick, J. A., & Swartz, A. A. (1995). A history of facilitated communication: Science, pseudoscience, and antiscience. *American Psychologist, 50*(9), 750-765.

Jones, R. P., & McCaughey, R. E. (1992). Gentle Teaching and applied behavior analysis: A critical review. *Journal of Applied Behavior Analysis, 25,* 853-868.

Kalachnik, J. E. (1998). Guidelines for the use of psychotropic medication. In S. Reiss & M. G. Amen (Eds.), *Psychotropic medication and developmental disabilities: The international consensus handbook* (pp. 45-72). Columbus: Ohio State University, Nisonger Center.

Luckasson, R., Coulter, D. L., Polloway, E. A., Reiss, S., Shalock, R. L., Snell, M. E., Spitalnik, D. M., & Stark, J. A. (1992). *Mental retardation: Definition, classification & system of supports* (9th ed.). Washington, DC: American Association on Mental Retardation.

Martin, G. L., & Yu, D. C. T. (2000). Overview of research on the assessment of Basic Learning Abilities test. *Journal of Developmental Disabilities, 7,* 10-36.

McGee, J. J., Menolascino, F. J., Hobbs, D. C., & Menousek, P. E. (1987). *Gentle teaching: A nonaversive approach for helping persons with mental retardation.* New York: Human Sciences.

Millard, R. P., & Rubin, S. E. (1992). Ethical considerations in case management decision making. In R. T. Roessler & S. E. Rubin (Eds.), *Case management and rehabilitation counseling* (2nd ed., pp. 155-168). Austin, TX: Pro Ed.

National Commission for the Protection of Human Subjects of Biomedical and Behavioral Research. (1979). *The Belmont Report: Ethical principles and guidelines for the protection of human subjects of research.* Washington, DC: U.S. Government Printing Office.

Newman, B., Reinecke, D. R., & Kurtz, A. L. (1996). Why be moral: Humanist and behavioral perspectives. *The Behavior Analyst, 19,* 273-280.

Richards, D. F., Williams, W. L., & Follette, W. C. (2002). Two new empirically-derived reasons to use the Assessment of Basic Learning Abilities. *American Journal on Mental Retardation, 107,* 5, 329-339.

Risley, T. R. (1975). Certify procedures, not people. In W. S. Wood (Ed.), *Issues in evaluating behavior modification: Proceedings of the first Drake conference on professional issues in behavior analysis, 1974* (pp. 159-181). Champaign, IL: Research Press.

Scheerenberger, R. C. (1987). *A history of mental retardation: A quarter century of promise.* Baltimore, MD: Brookes.

Schroeder, S. R., Oldenquist, A., & Rojahn, J. (1990). A conceptual framework for judging the humaneness and effectiveness of behavioral treatment. In A. C. Repp & N. N. Singh (Eds.), *Perspectives on the use of nonaversive and aversive interventions for persons with developmental disabilities* (pp. 103-118). Sycamore, IL: Sycamore.

Vollmer, T. R., & Northup, J. (1996). Some implications of functional analysis for school psychology. *School Psychology Quarterly, 11,* 76-92.

Weiner, B. A., & Wettstein, R. M. (1993). *Legal issues in mental health-care.* New York: Plenum.

Williams, W. L. (1999). *An introduction to mental retardation and developmental disabilities.* Chicago: High.

CHAPTER 21

Ethical Principles of Correctional Psychology

LINDA E. WEINBERGER
University of Southern California, Keck School of Medicine
USC, Institute of Psychiatry, Law, and Behavioral Science

SHOBA SREENIVASAN
University of Southern California, Keck School of Medicine
Greater Los Angeles
Veterans Administration Medical Center

In recent years, there has been a burgeoning demand for psychologists to work for correctional agencies. This is a result of the dramatic increase in the number of persons with mental illness who have been arrested and/or convicted. Consequently, there is a great need to provide these individuals with treatment while they are in jail, prison, or living in the community as probationers or parolees. Psychologists working with individuals who are under the jurisdiction of correctional agencies face a significantly different set of rules than they are accustomed to when working for mental health facilities. These rules may present a host of both familiar and unfamiliar ethical and professional dilemmas for psychologists employed by correctional facilities.

This chapter reviews the history of corrections and its expectations of the role of mental health professionals. The struggle psychologists may have in maintaining ethical conduct while meeting the needs of correctional agencies and offenders is discussed and explored through the use of vignettes. Finally, recommendations will be offered to assist correctional psychologists in resolving some of the stresses and problems they encounter while working in this unique setting.

HISTORICAL PERSPECTIVE

Most societies have adopted a philosophy that individuals who commit criminal acts should be punished. Modern Western judicial systems have justified their use of punishment on the basis of four principles: retribution, deterrence, incapacitation, and rehabilitation (Grilliot, 1983). *Retribution* describes the earliest form of redressing wrongs and is based on the concept of "eye for eye, and tooth for tooth" (Allen & Simonsen, 1978). *Deterrence* is based on the assumption that those who see others punished will be deterred from following their example for fear of being punished themselves. *Incapacitation* protects society by rendering offenders unable to repeat their offenses; imprisonment embodies this concept. *Rehabilitation* is aimed at "correcting" offenders so that they can live in society and not reoffend.

The theory of rehabilitation is a relatively new objective used to justify punishment and has undergone many reformulations as society's attitude toward criminal offenders has changed (Travin, 1994). Until the late 18th century, colonial America believed that rehabilitation could be accomplished through severe punishment (e.g., stocks or gallows). The 19th century saw the development of the penitentiary stage in corrections. This stage reflected the belief that rehabilitation could be achieved if individuals were placed in well-designed prisons in which they engaged in solitude, hard labor, and contemplation of their criminal acts. However, there was strong opposition to this manner of rehabilitation; therefore, in the late 19th century, the reformatory model was established. This model endorsed the belief that offenders could be reformed if they could gain self-respect and determine their destinies. The reforms included the use of indeterminate sentences, education, vocational training, parole, a system to reward good behavior with early release, and aftercare supervision (Bartollas, 1985).

An additional reform advocated was that of individualized treatment, which eventually led to the emergence of the Progressive era, beginning in the early 20th century. This stage in corrections emphasized the individualized approach to the treatment of offenders and was based on the medical or treatment model. The Progressive era was marked by the hiring of psychologists and psychiatrists to treat prisoners and to use community-based programs as alternatives to incarceration. Initially, mental health professionals focused on the treatment of the individual inmate toward the goal of psychological behavioral changes wherein the inmate would become a law-abiding citizen (Adams, 1985). The community–based programs were an attempt to keep offenders in the community and help them "reintegrate" there (Bartollas, 1985).

The medical model or treatment approach as well as the "reintegration" effort lost favor beginning in the 1960s. Many factors contributed to this disillusionment, not the least of which was the failure to significantly lower recidivism rates (Roth, 1986). Consequently, mental health services in corrections today do not emphasize the treatment of offenders to become law-abiding citizens; rather, the services focus on treating mentally ill persons in the correctional system.

Beginning in the 1970s, large numbers of mentally ill persons entered American jails and prisons (Lamb & Weinberger, 1998); such a phenomenon had not been seen since the 19th century (Torrey, 1997). The reasons most commonly cited for this latest increase are deintstitutionalization and fewer long-term state hospital beds for persons with chronic and severe mental illness; more rigid criteria for civil commitment; a lack of adequate support systems in the community for mentally ill persons; the difficulty mentally ill persons released from correctional agencies have in gaining access to mental health community treatment; and the belief by law enforcement personnel that they can deal with deviant behavior more quickly and efficiently within the criminal justice system than in the mental health system (Lamb & Weinberger, 1998).

The number of persons with severe mental disorders in jails has ranged from 6% to 15% (Guy, Platt, Zwerling, & Bullock, 1985; Teplin, 1990; Teplin, Abram, & McClelland, 1996) and the number in prisons has ranged from 8% to 18% (Jemelka, Wiegand, Walker, & Trupin, 1992; Neighbors, 1987; Steadman, Fabisiak, Dvoskin, & Holohean, 1987). Although these illnesses generally include persons who suffer from schizophrenia, major depression, and bipolar disorder, many individuals in the correctional system suffer from other disorders that require periodic mental health services. In a recent nationwide report, 1 in every 8 state prisoners was involved in mental health treatment, with nearly 10% receiving psychotropic medications (Beck & Maruschak, 2001). One recent survey of correctional psychologists found that depression, anger, psychoses, anxiety, and adjustment issues were among the most frequently mentioned inmate problems (Boothby & Clements, 2000). There is also a high rate of substance abuse disorders found among offenders in the correctional system (Metzner, 1997a).

At about the same time the numbers of offenders with mental illness took a dramatic increase, a series of judicial decisions established that inmates had a right to receive adequate care to meet their medical needs. In 1976, the U.S. Supreme Court held that it was unconstitutional for prison officials to be deliberately indifferent to the serious medical needs of those in custody *(Estelle v. Gamble,*

1976). This decision was followed a year later by a U.S. Court of Appeals ruling that extended this requirement to serious mental health needs *(Bowring v. Godwin,* 1977). On the basis of the Eighth (prohibits "cruel and unusual punishment") and Fourteenth (guarantees due process) Amendments, other judicial cases have since clarified the rights inmates have to receive professional mental health services and the minimal requirements of the *services (Coleman v. Wilson,* 1995; *Farmer v. Brennan,* 1994; *Madrid v. Gomez,* 1995; *Ruiz v. Estelle,* 1980).

THE ROLE OF CORRECTIONAL PSYCHOLOGISTS

Due in part to both the large numbers of offenders with mental illness and the resulting litigation, there has been a significant increase in the recruitment of psychologists working in correctional agencies. The psychologists may be employees of the Department of Corrections and placed in such settings as prisons, parole clinics, or jails. Some states use employees of the Department of Mental Health or Mental Hygiene to provide psychological services to their correctional populations. In addition, some correctional agencies contract with psychologists in the private sector to provide treatment to their clients.

As stated earlier, the American criminal justice system became disillusioned with the rehabilitation efforts made to reduce recidivism; the emphasis in corrections has moved from a treatment model to a security model. In this respect, the use of psychological services for crime control following release into the community or for personal growth and enhancement for the offender is not emphasized (Travin, 1994; Van Voorhis, 1994). Rather, most mental health services today focus on reducing an offender's suffering caused by mental illness and decreasing an offender's unpredictable and violent actions that may jeopardize an institution's safety for staff, other offenders, volunteers, and visitors (Correia, 2001; Hafemeister, Hall, & Dvoskin, 2001; Metzner, 1997b; Weinstein et al., 2000). It has been found that when jails and prisons have inadequate mental health services, inmates with mental illness are frequently placed in segregation because their psychological condition prevents them from adjusting to living in a correctional setting and/or abiding by the rules of the institution (Weinstein et al., 2000).

The importance of treating symptoms or complaints that are disruptive to the overall functioning of the institution illustrates the correctional system's expectation that the role of mental health professionals is that of applying their expertise and skills to custody matters. Psychologists must understand that the primary emphasis in a correctional setting is on security, which takes precedence over all other concerns. Consequently, they are expected to respect custody-oriented activities that may at times override traditional mental health practices in which the interests of the client are primary (Ashford, Sales, & Reid, 2001; Weinberger & Sreenivasan, 1994). This is not to suggest that the therapeutic needs of the offender are not considered important by corrections; however, it is believed that effective treatment can be provided only in a safe environment (Weinstein et al., 2000).

In accordance with these objectives, psychologists provide a number of services to the offender. These include psychological intake screening, individual and group therapy, psychological assessment, crisis intervention, and training programs, such as anger management, stress management, and biofeedback (Correia, 2001; Hawk, 1997). Occasionally, psychologists may prepare aftercare release plans.

Correctional psychologists may also engage in other services. They may perform administrative tasks; identify sources of stress or dysfunctional activities within an institution and develop methods to remedy them; work in employee assistance programs, provide counseling to staff and their families during and after traumatic events; and train staff in areas such as recognizing symptoms of mental illness, confrontation-avoidance techniques, and stress management (Boothby & Clements, 2000; Hawk, 1997). Finally, psychologists may be involved in research activities.

The primacy of custodial/security issues is further corroborated when psychologists are expected to assume law enforcement tasks. In the federal system as well as in some local and state correctional agencies, psychologists receive the same basic training for dealing with institutional crises and disturbances as do other staff, including correctional officers (Correia, 2001). The psychologist may be expected to work in the role of a front line correctional officer; for example, search for contraband, use a firearm, drive a perimeter patrol vehicle with a variety of firearms to prevent escapes, and coordinate inmate movement within the institution.

Clearly, correctional administrations' underlying philosophy that all employees, including psychologists, are considered correctional officers first and foremost may at times undermine the traditional therapeutic goals and relationship between the psychologist-therapist and the client-inmate, thus causing ethical and professional dilemmas. Even without participating in these "law enforcement" type activities, some mental health professionals describe the emphasis on security and order as "unpleasant, unsettling, and antithetical to what they consider necessary for a therapeutic milieu" (Hafemeister et al., 2001, p. 429).

Other factors contribute to a psychologist's difficulty working with a correctional population and/or within a correctional setting. Apart from working with a population who have committed crimes, there are some mentally ill offenders who are dangerous, who are unpredictable, who require a disproportionate amount of attention, and who are treatment resistant (Cooke, Baldwin, & Howison, 1990; Hafemeister et al., 2001; Serin & Preston, 2001). In that these characteristics are difficult to handle and can contribute to tensions within the institution, administration often assigns psychologists the daunting responsibility of assisting in the management of these individuals. With respect to correctional personnel, it is not unusual to find that line staff and mental health professionals do not mutually respect one another as sources of valuable information in how to handle problematic situations (Correia, 2001; Hafemeister et al., 2001).

The correctional facility itself, with the physical requirements necessary for maintaining safety and security, can be anxiety arousing. In addition, there may be few other mental health professionals working in the correctional setting with whom a psychologist may consult. These stressors may all lead to feelings of distrust, isolation, overwhelming tasks, and eventual burnout.

Guidelines and Standards

With such a rapid expansion in the specialty area of correctional psychology—the varied responsibilities psychologists have and their potential for producing conflicts and stress, and the risk of liability for not providing "humane living environments" for the correctional population (including proper mental health services)—the need for ethical and practice standards is crucial in order to provide sound professional care and comply with legal and legislative mandates (American Association of Correctional Psychology [AACP], 2000).

The American Psychological Association's (APA) Ethical Principles of Psychologists and Code of Conduct (1992) should be the guiding authority for psychologists' professional conduct. It should be noted that in an effort to remain contemporary, the APA Council of Representatives adopted a new ethics code on August 21, 2002 that becomes effective June 1, 2003 (APA, 2002). In addition to the ethics code, laws and psychology board regulations must be considered in governing psychologists' practices. The Introduction of the ethics code states clearly how psychologists might resolve a conflict between its standards of conduct and those required by law. If the ethics code establishes a higher standard than that required by the law, psychologists must meet the higher ethical standard. If the ethics code standard conflicts with the law, then psychologists must make it known that they are committed to the ethics code and should take steps to resolve the conflict. The ethics code supports that psychologists consider other materials in their professional work, such as guidelines and standards adopted or endorsed by professional psychological organizations, the dictates of their conscience, and consultation with others.

Although many of the principles in the ethics code can be applied directly to work conducted by correctional psychologists, the standards of conduct are written broadly. In 1991, Division 41 of the APA published *Specialty Guidelines for Forensic Psychologists* in an effort to "provide more specific guidelines to forensic psychologists in monitoring their professional conduct" when functioning in correctional and forensic mental health facilities, as well as in other areas of forensic professional practice (Committee on Ethical Guidelines for Forensic Psychologists, 1991, p. 655). These guidelines, too, set the benchmark for ethical professional behavior for psychologists.

A variety of standards and guidelines developed specifically for correctional health care have been published by other national organizations. Some of the guidelines that are most relevant for psychologists who treat offenders are those established by the National Commission on Correctional Health Care (NCCHC) and the AACP *Standards for Psychology Services in Jails, Prisons, Correctional Facilities, and Agencies* (2000). The NCCHC published separate standards for jails (NCCHC, 1996), prisons (NCCHC, 1997), and juvenile facilities (NCCHC, 1995). In 1999, NCCHC published a volume addressing important issues in the delivery of mental health care (NCCHC, 1999). The primary purpose of the NCCHC is to assist correctional agencies in improving their health care delivery systems (Anno, 2001). Facilities that voluntarily comply with the NCCHC requirements may be accredited.

The standards developed by the AACP (2000) are more specific to psychologists and were recently modified in accordance with the standards of the NCCHC; the APA practice standards and ethical code of conduct (1987, 1992); the APA's *Specialty Guidelines for Forensic Psychologists* (Committee on Ethical Guidelines for Forensic Psychologists, 1991); and the American Psychiatric Association's *Psychiatric Services in Jails and Prisons* (1989). Thus, the AACP can be viewed as a set of standards used in corrections that augment the ethical and practice standards of the APA and the specialty guidelines of the American Psychiatric Association.

Despite the existence and recent revisions of these standards and guidelines, many professional and ethical dilemmas continue to plague psychologists working in corrections. Some of the reasons are that psychologists may not be familiar with or invoke the standards and guidelines, the standards and guidelines may not specifically address the predicament, and correctional personnel may not understand or support the standards and guidelines. In an effort to foster better familiarity with the standards and guidelines, to

demonstrate an analytic approach in applying the standards and guidelines when they appear vague or unspecific to the situation, and to emphasize the need for instructing others about the importance and relevance of the standards and guidelines, a number of vignettes will be presented and discussed. These vignettes are representative examples of dilemmas experienced by psychologists working in correctional agencies.

Scenarios

Scenario 1

Dr. C., a psychologist working at a women's jail, administers psychological tests to clarify the diagnosis of Ms. Y., a recent arrestee. Some of the tests assessing cognition and motivation identify malingering. Ms. Y. "fails" and is determined by Dr. C. to be a "malingerer." Ms. Y. is charged with a serious felony and is facing a potentially lengthy sentence. During the course of the assessment, Dr. C. asks Ms. Y. to detail the crime that led to her arrest. Later, when he enters his notes into Ms. Y.'s chart, he records a number of her statements related to the crime as well as his assessment of Ms. Y. having malingered her test results. Ms. Y.'s defense attorney raises a doubt as to her competency to stand trial due to cognitive impairment, because she was in special education classes. A court-appointed forensic expert is given access to the jail records. The forensic expert discovers that Ms. Y. recently underwent a neuropsychological exam in which she was determined to be malingering cognitive impairment as well as detailing her part in the crimes. Dr. C. did not obtain from Ms. Y. any informed consent as to the confidentiality limits of the records.

Discussion

Several ethical issues are raised by virtue of Dr. C.'s serious omission in not obtaining informed consent from Ms. Y. Of concern is the great risk that information solicited from pretrial defendants can be used against them. In this instance, Ms. Y. entered her mental condition into issue at trial (by her defense attorney raising a doubt as to her competency to stand trial). By doing so, her chart, which contains her test results and statements about the alleged crime, can be reviewed not only by defense counsel but also by the judge, prosecuting attorney, and any other parties deemed relevant to the criminal case.

The APA ethical standard (1992, 2002) related to "Privacy and Confidentiality" states that psychologists discuss with persons and organizations with whom they establish a professional relationship the limitations on confidentiality and the foreseeable uses of the information derived through their psychological activities. Dr. C. did not inform Ms. Y. of the limits of confidentiality. He should have outlined clearly to Ms. Y. the ramifications of the assessment measures, including how they could be interpreted psychologically and legally.

In the most recent edition of the APA ethics code (2002), the standard on "Assessment" states, "Psychologists obtain informed consent for assessments, evaluations, or diagnostic services" (Standard 9.03, "Informed Consent in Assessments"). The same standard acknowledges that there are exceptions to obtaining informed consent, but these are for instances when "testing is mandated by law or governmental regulations; . . . testing is conducted as a routine educational, institutional or organizational activity; . . . or to evaluate decisional capacity." Moreover, the ethics code states that the informed consent should be given to the individual using language that is reasonably understandable to the person.

The *Specialty Guidelines for Forensic Psychologists* (Committee on Ethical Guidelines for Forensic Psychologists, 1991) also addresses the issue of informed consent, under "Relationships,"

> Forensic psychologists have an obligation to ensure that prospective clients are informed of their legal rights with respect to the anticipated forensic service, of the purposes of any evaluation, of the nature of procedures to be employed, of the intended uses of any product of their services, and of the party who has employed the forensic psychologist. (p. 659)

If Ms. Y.'s mental condition were such that a doubt was raised as to her capacity to provide informed consent, her representative (such as her defense attorney) should have been contacted. The AACP *Standards for Correctional Psychology Services in Jails, Prisons, Correctional Facilities and Agencies* (2000) states in the section on "Inmate Treatment and Management,"

> If mental disturbance is identified in pre trial and/or presentenced detainees, the court and/or the inmate's attorney are notified according to a written policy or procedure approved by the facility's and/or organization's chief executive. Such notification will be documented and placed in the inmate's psychological services file. (p. 469)

Moreover, the *Specialty Guidelines for Forensic Psychologists* (Committee on Ethical Guidelines for Forensic Psychologists, 1991) note under the section on "Relationships" that in situations in which the client may not have the capacity to provide informed consent, "The forensic psychologist provides reasonable notice to the client's legal representative of the nature of the anticipated forensic service before proceeding" (p. 659).

Not only did Dr. C. create an ethical problem when he did not obtain informed consent, but he also asked Ms. Y. about the crime with which she was charged. Did he understand or could he foresee all the legal ramifications that might result from such questions and then be able to explain them to her? This is a key issue whenever one assesses/treats a pretrial inmate. The *Specialty Guidelines for Forensic Psychologists* (Committee on Ethical Guidelines for Forensic Psychologists, 1991), under "Methods and Procedures," states,

> Because forensic psychologists are not often in a position to know what evidence, documentation, or element of a written product may be or may lend to a "fruit of the statement," they exercise extreme caution in preparing reports or offering testimony prior to the defendant's assertion of a mental state claim or the defendant's introduction of testimony regarding a mental condition. Consistent with the reporting requirements of state or federal law, forensic psychologists avoid including statements from the defendant relating to the time period of the alleged offense. (p. 663)

Within the same section of the *Specialty Guidelines for Forensic Psychologists*, another guideline states clearly that forensic psychologists do not provide professional forensic services to a defendant prior to that individual's representation by counsel. However, there are exceptions (e.g., court ordered, defendant acting pro se, emergency). This is written in an effort to protect the legal rights of individuals facing court proceedings. This specific guideline and the one above, proscribing the inclusion of statements about the alleged offense by pretrial defendants, are intended for forensic psychologists.

Although Dr. C. was not acting officially as a forensic psychologist, but as a psychologist assessing a jail inmate for diagnostic purposes, his services had great forensic significance. Dr. C. should have been aware

of how his work product might affect Ms. Y.'s legal situation. Although the identification of malingering is not viewed favorably in the legal arena, it is a valid diagnostic assessment. On the other hand, asking Ms. Y. about details surrounding her alleged offense is not critical for determining an appropriate diagnosis. Indeed, one can see that there may be more potential for harm than benefit to defendants when queried about alleged criminal conduct for which they have yet to be tried.

Scenario 2

A parole agent refers a parolee, Mr. W., to a parole outpatient mental health clinic. The parole officer wants to know if Mr. W. is dangerous and in need of treatment. The only accompanying documents the parole clinic psychologist, Dr. L., receives for Mr. W. is the referral and a note stating that he received treatment in the community and in prison, where he also had two disciplinary infractions.

Discussion

Should the psychologist identify Mr. W. as dangerous or nondangerous as well as accept or reject him for treatment without any significant documentation (e.g., previous mental health treatment records, probation officer's report, arrest report, etc.)?

Let us assume in this case that the psychologist conducted a thorough clinical interview before giving an opinion to the parole officer's referral questions. Would this constitute a competent assessment? The APA ethical standard (1992, 2002) related to assessment states that psychologists base their professional recommendations and diagnostic statements on information and techniques that are sufficient to support their findings. According to the American

Psychiatric Association's latest guidelines on psychiatric services in jails and prisons, the principle on confidentiality states,

> Mental health professionals must be able to acquire patients' historical medical and mental health records from places where they have received previous services, within or outside of the correctional system, and ensure that records developed within the system move between facilities. (Weinstein et al., 2000, p. 13)

The AACP standard (2000) "Psychological Services File: Contents and Storage" addresses this issue specifically:

> The offender's psychological/mental health record is maintained in a psychological services file. This file contains, but is not limited to, historical mental health information, the completed admissions psychological screening form, test results (excluding raw data and/or protocols), findings, diagnoses, referral and consultation information, treatment plans and dictations (both psychological and psychiatric), dispositions, confidentiality, consent and release of information forms, terminations from treatment, and plans for community follow-up . . . If the offender has been released to community supervision, the psychological services file will be kept at a central location that facilitates access by correctional agency psychology staff. (p. 486)

It is not unusual to find a lack of close communication and collaboration between professionals in the mental health and criminal justice systems. Unfortunately, the majority of occasions in which the two professionals discuss parolees in any meaningful manner occur when parolees have failed to show for scheduled appointments, when they have done something to violate the terms of their parole, or when the parole officer is thinking about discharging them from parole.

The fact that Mr. W.'s mental health information did not accompany his referral does not preclude the parole clinic psychologist from obtaining it. Moreover, before answering the question related to Mr. W.'s possible dangerousness, it would be appropriate to have some documentation regarding his criminal record as well as past aggressive behavior. It would be advisable for the psychologist to read Mr. W.'s prison file, which most likely contains not only mental health information but also information about past criminal behavior and his behavior while incarcerated. Dr. L. should not be hampered by the limited information he was given initially by the parole officer. The psychologist should call the parole officer and request the specific information or, if necessary, the psychologist can get it from other sources. To assure ethical practice, Dr. L. should obtain sufficient material substantiating his opinion of whether Mr. W. needs treatment or is dangerous.

Scenario 3

A psychologist treating an inmate is asked by the parole board to evaluate whether the inmate is ready for parole.

Discussion

Although this is an instance of the parole board asking for the evaluation, would there be any ethical dilemma if the psychologist were asked by the court to perform an evaluation on a psychological-legal issue? Similarly, would there be any ethical dilemma if it were the inmate who asked the treating psychologist to perform an evaluation for a legal or administrative proceeding he or she was facing? When a psychologist is functioning as an individual's therapist and is then asked (regardless by whom) to function as the individual's evaluator, the psychologist is engaging in a multiple relationship.

The most recent edition of the APA ethics code (2002) includes a standard on "Human Relations," which defines and addresses *multiple relationships*. One definition is when a psychologist is in a professional role with a person and at the same time is in another role with the same person. The standard states that the psychologist should refrain from entering into a multiple relationship if it "could reasonably be expected to impair the psychologist's objectivity, competence, or effectiveness in performing his or her functions as a psychologist, or otherwise risks exploitation or harm to the person" (Standard 3.05, "Multiple Relationships"). The standard, however, acknowledges that there may be instances in which psychologists because of an institutional policy must serve in more than one role, such as in a judicial or administrative hearing. In such cases, they must clarify at the outset the role expectations and the extent of confidentiality. It could be argued that informing the client of the limits to confidentiality could well impede the effectiveness of the treatment; however, this dilemma is encountered whenever a psychologist gives proper informed consent.

Whereas the APA ethics code discusses multiple relationships in general, potential role conflicts in correctional settings are addressed more specifically by other specialty standards and guidelines. The American Public Health Association standards require that mental health professionals who participate in parole decisions should not provide direct therapeutic services to those inmates in order to decrease role conflicts for clinicians (Dubler, 1986). The NCCHC standards state that it is unethical for mental health staff who are in a treating relationship with an inmate to collect forensic information that may be used against the inmate, as in determining parole eligibility (Anno, 2001). Although correctional administrators may be tempted to use these individuals, the standards recommend that the services of an outside provider be obtained.

Clearly, there is the possibility that when a psychologist is engaged in such dual functions, the alliance established for treatment purposes could be viewed by the inmate as a guise for information gathering to be used when the psychologist will act as the parole board evaluator. These specialty guidelines recognize that the role of a clinician can become blurred if the clinician provides both treatment and a parole board evaluation for the same inmate (Metzner, 1997b). Thus, to decrease the risk of impairing a psychologist's objectivity as well as the potential for exploiting or harming the inmate, it is advisable that a psychologist not be involved in providing both treatment and any forensic evaluative services to the same individual. This would apply regardless of who asks the treating clinician to perform the evaluation. In addition, as stated in the guidelines, psychologists should inform the clients, the correctional agencies, and any other relevant parties of their positions.

It must be noted that by simply prohibiting treating psychologists from serving as evaluators, their position as neutral, caring professionals who do no harm is not necessarily assured. For example, there is no guarantee that during the course of treatment, a psychologist might not discover that the inmate has risk factors that identify him or her as having the potential to harm others. Just like psychologists practicing in the community, correctional psychologists are required by law to reveal information to protect the welfare of the public. If the situation is life threatening or security threatening, the correctional psychologist may have to breach confidentiality because of the "duty to warn." If there is no immediate risk of danger when prompt disclosure is indicated, the psychologist nevertheless may note this information in the inmate's record.

When the treating psychologist either discloses this material immediately or writes it in the chart, the possibility exists that the independent evaluator might become aware of the information and use it in opinions adverse to the inmate. Therefore, even when avoiding multiple roles, there is no certainty that information noted by treating clinicians will not be used forensically. As the AACP standard (2000) on "Limits of Confidentiality" states, the issue of most importance is that before treatment begins, the clinician gives the inmate informed consent and explains the limits of confidentiality and the possible uses of the information the offender provides in treatment.

Scenario 4

Dr. F. works in a prison unit with inmates who are seriously mentally ill and violent. During one of his therapy sessions, an inmate assaults him. Rather than return to work in the same unit, Dr. F. takes a position in which he conducts reception screenings. During an intake screening of a newly admitted inmate, he finds that this individual has some of the same features as his assailant. Dr. F.'s assessment is very strongly worded that the parolee is highly dangerous and should be committed to the most restrictive placement.

Discussion

What effect has Dr. F.'s previous assault had on his ability to make objective assessments? Are there lingering countertransference matters that have not been addressed adequately to assure Dr. F.'s fairness and impartiality when working with inmates? It could well be argued that in this scenario, we have a psychologist who because of his past may have unresolved issues regarding his assault.

In the most recent edition of the APA ethics code (2002), the "General Principle of Justice" was added. It states that "Psychologists exercise reasonable judgment and take precautions to ensure that their potential biases, . . . do not lead to or condone unjust practices" (Principle D: Justice). Dr. F.'s ability to dispassionately address dangerous risk factors appears to be affected by the experience of his personal assault. The latest version of the APA ethical standard on "Competence" elaborates on the issue of personal problems and conflicts. It states that "Psychologists refrain from initiating an activity when they know or should know that there is a substantial likelihood that their personal problems will prevent them from performing their work-related activities in a competent manner" (APA, 2002, Standard 2.06, "Personal Problems and Conflicts").

Another general principle added in the most recent edition of the APA ethics code (2002) is "Beneficence and Nonmaleficence." It states clearly that psychologists take care to do no harm for those with whom they work. It also asks that psychologists endeavor to be sensitive to the effect that their own physical and mental health may have on their ability to help the people with whom they work.

Countertransference issues are not uncommon when interacting with an offender population. As the APA ethical standard under "Avoiding Harm" states, "Psychologists take reasonable steps to avoid harming their patients or clients . . . and minimize harm where it is foreseeable and unavoidable" (APA, 1992, Standard 1.14; APA, 2002, Standard 3.04). With this in mind, although concern for one's safety is understandable within a prison setting, when such concern begins to bias the psychologist's judgment, several steps may be taken. The first would involve seeking consultation with fellow correctional mental health professionals to gain independent feedback as to whether one's concerns for safety were prejudicing the delivery of service. Second, if the concerns were found to be interfering with sound judgment, then the psychologist should refrain voluntarily from engaging in clinical activities affected by the countertransference. Third, the psychologist should seek counseling and/or treatment for these countertransference issues. Doing so not only encourages the psychologist to deal with and resolve these concerns but also could possibly allow the psychologist to resume former activities. Fourth, if such countertransference issues persist, the psychologist should not continue to be employed in a correctional setting. This recommendation is offered for the benefit of the affected psychologist, potential clients, and the correctional agency, which has certain expectations of a psychologist's ability to work with this population in an effective, fair, and unbiased manner.

Correctional psychologists encounter many difficult situations and clients. Therefore, it is imperative for the well-being of all concerned that staff meetings and other venues be available to psychologists on a regularly scheduled basis for the discussion of the stresses of working in such an environment and with this type of clientele.

Scenario 5

Dr. H. is a psychologist who works in a women's prison. She is told by administration that there may be some occasions in which she will be expected to assist the correctional staff in "lock-downs." She will be asked to pat down the inmate and search her possessions. Administration explains that this is necessary because of a shortage of correctional personnel. Administration understands that psychologists should not assume multiple roles; therefore, administration will not ask Dr. H. to perform these duties with inmates whom she is treating.

Discussion

Does the administration's belief that limiting psychologists' performance of correctional duties to nonclients is sufficient for avoiding multiple roles?

It could be argued that the administration's effort to avoid multiple roles is ineffective. There is no certainty that an inmate whom the psychologist "shakes down" today may not need her services tomorrow. The likelihood that if the institution is suffering from a shortage of less-skilled personnel such as custodial staff, then they most likely suffer as well from a shortage of skilled personnel such as mental health professionals. To deny an inmate the opportunity to obtain mental health services because the psychologist was previously involved in a pure custodial relationship with the individual is not in the best interests of the inmate.

More important, it must be recognized that when psychologists function in roles that are not related to mental health work, they lose the public's perception of them as professionals who provide only psychological services. Although this may be a requirement of employment at the institution, there is no psychological service when performing in this role. Thus, this custodial activity may be viewed as a conflict for the psychologist, particularly because it affects the way psychologists are viewed by both inmates and correctional personnel. That is, psychologists come to be viewed not as professionals whose only role is that of providing mental health services, but as persons who also can substitute as correctional officers.

The APA code of ethics states under "Resolving Ethical Issues" that if the demands of the organization where psychologists work are in conflict with this ethics code, "Psychologists clarify the nature of the conflict, make known their commitment to the Ethics Code, and . . . resolve the conflict in a way that permits adherence to the Ethics Code" (APA, 1992, Standard 8.03; APA, 2002, Standard 1.03).

The AACP standards (2000) under "Administration" acknowledge the distinctive nature of psychologists' work and how that should be maintained. Under "Professional Autonomy," the standard states, "Within the constraints of appropriate security regulations applicable to all institutional personnel, psychologists have professional autonomy regarding psychological services and psychology staff activities for which they are responsible" (p. 443). The standard also states,

> Psychological services should represent a separate and discrete entity—department—within the institution's . . . organizational structure . . . Within such a structure, psychological services staff can make their own unique contributions to the broader, non-medical mental health and human services provided at the facility or agency at the highest professional level. (AACP, 2000, Standard 5, pp. 443-444)

Some correctional psychologists (Correia, 2001) argue that assuming the duties of correctional officers (such as patrolling the perimeter of a facility, acting as a front line officer, etc.) has a number of benefits. It gives the psychologist a better perspective of the prison environment as well as the behavior of both employees and inmates. In addition, by performing these tasks, the psychologist is perceived by the inmates not only as a cooperating member of the correctional staff but also as someone whom they believe is concerned for their welfare occupying a position of authority. Moreover, engaging in these activities offers the further advantage of reducing the monotony of the usual functions

of a psychologist. It could also be argued that psychologists who decline such custodial duties do so out of inner fears that should be overcome. Although these statements may appear persuasive, they run counter to the ethical standards promulgated by psychologists' professional associations.

As discussed previously, correctional psychologists who are expected to provide psychological services as well as perform custodial tasks may be placed in multiple relationships. Clearly, if the psychologist is perceived by inmates as a cooperating member of the correctional staff who engages in security work, this could well impair their ability to be seen by the inmate as objective professionals who will not exploit or harm them. In an effort to avoid this occurrence, the AACP standard (2000) under "Ethical Guidelines" states, "To the greatest extent possible, psychological resources are used only for clearly defined psychological and mental health purposes" (p. 452). Under the standard "Roles, Services, Staffing, and Professional Development," AACP states, "The roles and services of correctional psychologists shall be directly related, or contribute to, mental health services, treatment, and programming for offenders" (p. 447). The AACP also states,

> It would not be appropriate for correctional psychologists to assume roles not consistent with and/or directly related to the provision of psychological mental health services to the offender and/or the correctional system such that (a) the scope of psychological services becomes blurred or blended with other services (e.g., security or social services) and (b) needed mental health treatment resources are decreased. (p. 448)

Correctional institutions that employ psychologists may have the expectation that the psychologists will perform correctional duties to promote the security of the institution.

Those duties that do not defray the professional identity of the psychologist and are concerned with the safety of the situation may not be inherently unethical. For example, psychologists may have to issue a "rules violation" when inmates come into the medical area when unauthorized to do so or when inmates miss scheduled appointments. Such duties enforce the rules of the prison and maintain security. On the other hand, other overtly correctional duties, such as strip searches, handcuffing inmates for custody purposes, and confronting inmates with a baton to secure cooperation, fall within an arena that significantly damages the professional role of psychologists. In addition, such assignments violate the APA Preamble to the ethics code to protect civil and human rights.

Working for correctional facilities in which security is the foremost concern is a situation that must be understood and accepted by psychologists; however, what also must be understood and accepted by correctional administrators is that psychologists can forward this agenda through their professional expertise as clinicians and not as persons replacing correctional officers. If a prison demands as a condition of employment that psychologists must function first as correctional officers, the likelihood is high that at some time they will be confronted with ethical conflicts. Consequently, those who agree to work in such situations must be prepared for this outcome and a means by which to reach an appropriate resolution.

IMPROVING THE QUALITY OF PSYCHOLOGICAL SERVICES IN CORRECTIONS

One of the most effective interventions for enhancing the delivery of services is education. Psychologists who want to work in correctional agencies should understand the nature of the work, the environment and its emphasis on security, the clients they will be evaluating and treating, and the staff with whom they will be working. Psychologists need to be aware of the similarities and differences between a correctional and community setting as well as the characteristics and needs of the population they will serve (Anno, 2001). One of the best means by which to experience and evaluate this is to complete a practicum or internship at these facilities (Boothby & Clements, 2000).

Another effective means by which to increase the psychologist's appreciation of the primary need for a correctional agency to maintain security is to expose psychologists to the basic training program given to correctional officers. Although they should not be expected to carry out these duties, learning about them can help psychologists understand the realities and stresses of life in jail and prison for both inmates and correctional officers. An additional educational experience for psychologists would be an orientation given by correctional officers regarding the "culture" of the jail or prison. This would include discussion about the social order in the facility, gangs, attitudes toward sex offenders, how staff can be manipulated by the offender, and so on (Weinstein et al., 2000).

Correctional officers can also benefit from training in mental health issues. As the persons in the best position to monitor an inmate's appearance or behavior over time, they are the first line of defense in preventing an inmate's decompensation. Thus, it is imperative that they receive training in how to recognize signs and symptoms of serious mental illness and suicidal behavior and how to access mental health services (Anno, 2001; Correia, 2001; Hafemeister et al., 2001; Metzner, 1997b). Clearly, those custody staff who work in special mental health housing units should have more detailed and intensive training.

When psychologists and correctional officers train each other in their respective areas of expertise, this fosters communication and cooperation between the two professional groups. They are encouraged to call on each other for advice and can develop mutually respectful and trusting relationships.

Another essential element for assuring quality mental health services is the opportunity for peer supervision and consultation. Correctional psychologists meeting together and discussing issues regarding their professional services, the stresses of working in corrections, and material constituting continuing education help psychologists engage in ethical and competent practice. However, there are many correctional agencies in which psychologists function as sole practitioners (Boothby & Clements, 2000). This type of isolation may not only lead to burnout but also precludes the psychologist from the benefit of having colleagues work in the same setting who can share experiences and offer support. For these situations, it is recommended that regional systems comprising correctional psychologists be established and have regularly scheduled meetings.

The life of a correctional psychologist can be quite challenging and stimulating. It can offer many rewards to one who understands the system and can manage the ethical dilemmas that derive from this specialty area.

REFERENCES

Adams, K. (1985). Addressing inmate mental health problems. *Federal Probation, 49,* 27-33.

Allen, H. E., & Simonsen, C. E. (1978). *Corrections in America: An introduction.* Encino, CA: Glencoe.

American Association of Correctional Psychology. (2000). Standards for psychology services in jails, prisons, correctional facilities, and agencies. *Criminal Justice and Behavior, 27,* 433-494.

American Psychiatric Association. (1989). *Psychiatric services in jails and prisons* (APA WM A512, No. 29). Washington, DC: Office of Psychiatric Services.

American Psychological Association. (1987). *General guidelines for providers of psychological services.* Washington, DC: Author.

American Psychological Association. (1992). Ethical principles of psychologists and code of conduct. *The American Psychologist, 47,* 1597-1611.

American Psychological Association. (2002). Ethical principles of psychologists and code of conduct 2002. Adopted by the APA's Council of Representatives, August 21, 2002. Washington, DC: Author.

Anno, B. J. (2001). National correctional health care standards. In J. B. Ashford, B. D. Sales, & W. H. Reid (Eds.), *Treating adult and juvenile offenders with special needs* (pp. 81-96). Washington, DC: American Psychological Association.

Ashford, J. B., Sales, B. D., & Reid, W. H. (2001). Political, legal, and professional challenges to treating offenders with special needs. In J. B. Ashford, B. D. Sales, & W. H. Reid (Eds.), *Treating adult and juvenile offenders with special needs* (pp. 31-49). Washington, DC: American Psychological Association.

Bartollas, C. (1985). *Correctional treatment: Theory and practice.* Englewood Cliffs, NJ: Prentice Hall.

Beck, A. J., & Maruschak, L. M. (2001). *Mental health treatment in state prisons, 2000.* Washington, DC: U.S. Department of Justice, Office of Justice Programs, Bureau of Justice Statistics.

Boothby, J. L., & Clements, C. B. (2000). A national survey of correctional psychologists. *Criminal Justice and Behavior, 27,* 716-732.

Bowring v. Godwin, 551 F.2d 44 (1977).

Coleman v. Wilson, 912 F.Supp. 1282 (1995).

Committee on Ethical Guidelines for Forensic Psychologists. (1991). Specialty guidelines for forensic psychologists. *Law and Human Behavior, 15,* 655-665.

Cooke, D. J., Baldwin, P. J., & Howison, J. (1990). *Psychology in prisons.* New York: Routledge, Chapman and Hall.

Correia, K. M. (2001). *A handbook for correctional psychologists.* Springfield, IL: Charles C Thomas.

Dubler, N. N. (Ed.). (1986). *Standards for health services in correctional facilities* (2nd ed.). Washington, DC: American Public Health Association.

Estelle v. Gamble, 429 U.S. 97 (1976).

Farmer v. Brennan, 511 U.S. 825 (1994).

Grilliot, H. J. (1983). *Introduction to law and the legal system* (3rd ed.). Boston: Houghton Mifflin.

Guy, E., Platt, J. J., Zwerling, I., & Bullock, S. (1985). Mental health status of prisoners in an urban jail. *Criminal Justice and Behavior, 12,* 29-53.

Hafemeister, T. L., Hall, S. R., & Dvoskin, J. A. (2001). Administrative concerns associated with the treatment of offenders with mental illness. In J. B. Ashford, B. D. Sales, & W. H. Reid (Eds.), *Treating adult and juvenile offenders with special needs* (pp. 419-444). Washington, DC: American Psychological Association.

Hawk, K. M. (1997). Personal reflections on a career in correctional psychology. *Professional Psychology: Research and Practice, 28,* 335-337.

Jemelka, R. P., Wiegand, G., Walker, E., & Trupin, E. W. (1992). Computerized offender assessment: Validation study. *Psychological Assessment, 4,* 138-144.

Lamb, H. R., & Weinberger, L. E. (1998). Persons with severe mental illness in jails and prisons: A review. *Psychiatric Services, 49,* 483-492.

Madrid v. Gomez, 889 F.Supp. 1146 (1995).

Metzner, J. L. (1997a). An introduction to correctional psychiatry: Part I. *Journal of the American Academy of Psychiatry and the Law, 25,* 375-381.

Metzner, J. L. (1997b). An introduction to correctional psychiatry: Part II. *Journal of the American Academy of Psychiatry and the Law, 25,* 571-579.

National Commission on Correctional Health Care. (1995). *Standards for health services in juvenile detention and confinement facilities.* Chicago: Author.

National Commission on Correctional Health Care. (1996). *Standards for health services in jails.* Chicago: Author.

National Commission on Correctional Health Care. (1997). *Standards for health services in prisons.* Chicago: Author.

National Commission on Correctional Health Care. (1999). *Correctional mental health care: Standards and guidelines for delivering services.* Chicago: Author.

Neighbors, H. W. (1987). The prevalence of mental disorder in Michigan prisons. *Diagnostic Interview Schedule (DIS) Newsletter, 7,* 8-11 (Department of Psychiatry, Washington University School of Medicine, St. Louis).

Roth, L. H. (1986). Correctional psychiatry. In W. J. Curran, A. L. McGarry & S. A. Shah (Eds.), *Forensic psychiatry and psychology: Perspectives and standards for interdisciplinary practice* (pp. 429-468). Philadelphia: F. A. Davis.

Ruiz v. Estelle, 503 F.Supp. 1265 (1980).

Serin, R. C., & Preston, D. L. (2001). Managing and treating violent offenders. In J. B. Ashford, B. D. Sales, & W. H. Reid (Eds.), *Treating adult and juvenile offenders with special needs* (pp. 249-271). Washington, DC: American Psychological Association.

Steadman, H. J., Fabisiak, S., Dvoskin, J. A., & Holohean, E. J. (1987). A survey of mental disability among state prison inmates. *Hospital and Community Psychiatry, 38,* 1086-1090.

Teplin, L. A. (1990). The prevalence of severe mental disorder among male urban jail detainees: Comparison with the epidemiologic catchment area program. *American Journal of Public Health, 80,* 663-669.

Teplin, L. A., Abram, K. M., & McClelland, G. M. (1996). Prevalence of psychiatric disorders among incarcerated women. *Archives of General Psychiatry, 53,* 505-512.

Torrey, E. F. (1997). *Out of the shadows: Confronting America's mental illness crisis.* New York: Wiley.

Travin, S. (1994). History of correctional psychiatry. In R. Rosner (Ed.), *Principles and practice of forensic psychiatry* (pp. 369-374). New York: Chapman & Hall.

Van Voorhis, P. (1994). *Psychological classification of the adult male prison inmate.* Albany: State University of New York Press.

Weinberger, L. E., & Sreenivasan, S. (1994). Ethical and professional conflicts in correctional psychology. *Professional Psychology: Research and Practice, 25,* 161-167.

Weinstein, H. C., Burns, K. A., Newkirk, C. F., Zil, J. S., Dvoskin, J. A., & Steadman, H. J. (2000). *Psychiatric services in jails and prisons* (2nd ed.). Washington, DC: American Psychiatric Association.

CHAPTER 22

The Central Role of Informed Consent in Ethical Treatment and Research with Children

DAVID F. RICHARDS
Area Cooperative Educational Services (ACES)

Many of the ethical principles that practitioners must consider when engaging adults in treatment and research also apply to children, such as obeying pertinent laws, delivering competent treatment and research, and safeguarding the welfare of clients and research participants (Koocher & Keith–Spiegel, 1990). However, there is one critical age-based ethical consideration that distinguishes children from adults: Children are not considered competent to consent to treatment and research. According to the U.S. Department of Health and Human Services (2001, 46.402a), "Children are persons who have not attained the legal age for consent to treatments or procedures involved in the research, under the applicable law of the jurisdiction in which the research will be conducted." (Hereafter, *consent* or *consenting* will refer to *consenting to treatment and research*.) The fact that federal code defines children in terms of their legal

right to consent emphasizes the importance of this age-based consideration. Although age of consent is established by statute on a state-by-state basis, persons below the age of 18 years are legally presumed incapable of consenting to participate in treatment and research throughout the United States (Glantz, 1996; Keith-Spiegel, 1983). This statutory distinction is based on a broadly held assumption (e.g., by parents, child professionals, politicians, legal professionals, etc.) that children do not have the ability to independently make major decisions about their lives (Hoagwood, Jensen, & Fisher, 1996; Koocher & Keith–Spiegel, 1990). The rational for legally limiting children's right to make decisions, or more specifically to consent, is to protect them from harm and to promote their welfare (Koocher & Keith-Spiegel, 1990; Thompson, 1992). Thus, the assumption is that children are not always able to make decisions in their best interests.

There are a number of ramifications associated with the practice of authorizing parents and other authorities to consent on behalf of children. These ramifications affect how practitioners conduct treatment and research with children. Before discussing these ramifications, the following background information is provided: (a) definition and description of informed consent, (b) importance of the role of informed consent in treatment and research, (c) rational for limiting children's right to consent, and (d) exceptions to restrictions on children's right to consent. A discussion of the ramifications of limiting children's consent will focus on particular issues related to the following: (a) children providing assent (or agreeing to participate), (b) complications associated with providing children with confidentiality, and (c) additional responsibility accrued to practitioners. Recommendations are provided to assist practitioners in avoiding potential problems that arise as a result of adults consenting on behalf of children.

INFORMED CONSENT

Definition and Description of Informed Consent

Informed consent means that individuals must understand their options, be capable of a competent decision, and independently agree to the option chosen. Legally adequate informed consent requires that decisions are informed, competent, and voluntary.

Informed means that individuals are provided with all information that might influence their willingness to participate. To determine whether treatment information provided to individuals is legally adequate, three standards typical of jurisdictions in the United States are usually followed: (a) The treatment must meet the standard of care, or an empirically validated or standard

treatment for the individual's concern; (b) the treatment must represent what a reasonable person would consider appropriate; and (c) the treatment must be consistent with the individual wishes or concerns of the individual receiving treatment. Information about research is considered legally adequate if it includes the following: (a) the purpose of the research, (b) the rational for asking individuals to participate (i.e., what characteristics they have that makes them desirable participants), (c) the procedures employed in the research, (d) the risks and benefits of the research, (e) the level of confidentiality that will be maintained, (f) the costs and compensations associated with participation, and (g) the right of individuals to refuse or withdrawal from treatment without consequences (National Committee for the Protection of Human Subjects of Biomedical and Behavioral Research, 1979).

Competence refers to the capacity to use the information provided to adequately weigh risks and benefits associated with participating in treatment and research. Currently, the legal standards for determining competency are vague, and in evaluating competency to consent, states tend to use *reasonable-person standards* (Melton, Ehrenreich, & Lyons, 2001). Reasonable person standards are most often defined by states in terms of either a reasonable process or reasonable outcome. A *reasonable process* is evaluated in terms of the degree to which the individuals comprehend the information about the treatment or research and the degree to which they weigh the information rationally. *Reasonable outcome of decision making* is not evaluated in terms of the process, but in terms of the competence of the actual decision made.

Voluntary means that the decision to participate is free of undue influence or coercion. Voluntary consent relates to information and competence in the sense that to be fully voluntary, the decision must be based on adequate information and a competent decision-making process (Melton et al., 2001). For example, undue influence or coercion can result if a practitioner withholds (or neglects to provide) information or provides information that is difficult to comprehend. A decision based on inadequate or poorly understood information cannot be considered voluntary.

Importance of Informed Consent

The most important ethical principal applying to treatment and research is the doctrine of informed consent. Failure of practitioners and researchers to obtain informed consent when conducting treatment and research can result in civil liability (DeKraai & Sales, 1991). In fact, health professionals and researchers can be held liable for battery and neglect if they provide treatment without adequately informing the person of risks, benefits, and alternatives to the treatment provided (Glantz, 1996).

Children and Informed Consent

With few exceptions (to be discussed below), children are presumed incompetent to make decisions about participation in treatment and research because of their limited autonomy, maturity, and experience (Pagliocca, Melton, Weisz, & Lyons, 1995). Thus, children are denied permission to consent and are required to rely on their parents or other legal authorities to consent on their behalf. Parents and other legal authorities are assigned the responsibility to act "in the best interest of the child" where consent is concerned. To understand the rational for limiting children's informed consent, their capacity to process information, make competent decisions, and independently volunteer will be discussed.

Information

Children's capacity to understand information varies widely across age and individual children. Some children can understand the same wording and complexity of information provided to adults, whereas others can not. Professionals often have to simplify the wording so a child can understand the information provided for informed consent. If practitioners or researchers have to simplify information before children can understand, the child has not received all the necessary information to competently weigh risks and benefits and make a reasoned decision. Thus, informed consent has not been accomplished.

Competency

The major area of concern regarding children's role in providing informed decisions involves competency in the decision-making process (which is different from competency to stand trial or competency of practitioners). There is no universally accepted definition of competency to make decisions in state laws. The definitions used by jurisdictions in the United States vary from considering a child competent (under certain situations) if they simply make a choice or express a preference to the more common requirement that the child must demonstrate an understanding of the proposed treatment or research, alternative treatments, and the relative risks and benefits of the proposed and alternative options (Roth, Meisel, & Lidz, 1977; Weithorn, 1982). To establish that a child has achieved an understanding of the treatment and alternatives, it may be necessary for them to demonstrate an awareness of potential consequences of treatments. To resolve the uncertainty of applying standards of competency to children, parents and other authorities usually assume that children are not competent to make decisions regarding treatment and research.

Children are unlikely to receive treatment even if they are allowed to consent, because they usually are not able to independently pay for treatment. In addition, children usually are not liable or legally obligated to pay for treatment. Instead, their parents, private institutions, or government entities must pay (Waldlington, 1983). For the purposes of liability for payment of services, minors are generally considered competent to enter into binding contracts only if these contracts are to purchase necessary treatment. This means that parents are generally liable for their children's necessary medical expenses but are not liable for payment of nonemergency treatment to which they have not authorized or consented or for which they have not been informed. Mental health services provided by psychologists and nonmedical professionals are usually not considered necessary by courts (Melton et al., 2001). Thus, parents are not likely to be required to pay for psychological services unless such services are considered absolutely necessary (Melton et al., 2001). For this reason alone, practitioners are ill advised to provide treatment without consent from parents or responsible entities. As for consent to research, institutional review boards (IRBs) require parental consent for research unless such consent poses a risk for the child. Such situations occur rarely.

Voluntariness

Voluntariness refers to the freedom to choose to or refuse to participate in treatment or research. Perceived risks and benefits must be intrinsic to the process of participating in the treatment or research for decisions to be considered voluntary (Melton et al., 2001). In other words, the choice is not based on influence or coercion applied externally to influence the decision, but is exclusively associated with weighing the risks and benefits of participating. Children are unlikely to be totally free of influence in making decisions because they are usually dependent on and influenced by adults. Because adults are continually influencing children, it is difficult to identify or be aware of the contingencies that distinguish between voluntary consent and consent resulting from pressure, undue influence, or coercion (Koocher, 1983; Melton, Lyons, & Spaulding, 1998). Voluntariness is often missing because children are usually "volunteered" for treatment.

Exceptions to Consent on Behalf of Children

Although the child's parents are generally the controlling authority in terms of consent, there are circumstances under which parental authority to consent on behalf of children can be bypassed. Under certain conditions, designees of states have the authority to order treatment over parental objection, for example, with a court order (Grisso, 1992). In addition, there are conditions under which children are presumably authorized to consent to treatment independent of their parent(s). These conditions include the following: (a) cases in which children have been emancipated from their parents or guardians, (b) cases in which children have been classified as *mature minors,* and (c) under minor consent statutes, which grant consent to children for specific types of treatment (for example, drug or alcohol treatment, abortion, and HIV treatment) (Grisso, 1992; Melton et al., 2001).

Children can be determined emancipated from their parents (i.e., most often through a court proceeding that designates them legally separated from their parents) and granted the authority to make their own decisions. Children who have been emancipated are designated by the courts to be sufficiently separated from their parents to justify treating the child as adults and are often presumed legally competent (Melton et al., 2001). In addition, there are other legally accepted exceptions to parental consent for children under 18 years of age that effectively emancipate them from parental authority (Goldberg, 1997). For example, parental authority may be bypassed when the child has graduated from high school, even if they are under age 18 years of age. Parental authority may also be bypassed if legal authorities believe that the parents may restrict their child's access to needed psychological or medical treatment. Other conditions under which parental consent may be bypassed include consent to receive treatment for (a) sexual abuse or rape, (b) substance abuse, (c) pregnancy, (d) sexually transmitted disease, and (e) a child who needs emergency treatment (Goldberg, 1997). These exceptions may vary from state to state.

Children designated as mature minors may be granted exemption from parental consent by the courts under the following vaguely defined conditions: (a) the child is of a relatively mature age, (b) the treatment is beneficial to the child independent of being beneficial to another person, (c) the child has the ability to understand the nature of the procedure, and (d) the treatment is not considered to be major (Davis, Scott, Wadlington, & Whitebread, 1997; Wadlington, 1983). The mature-minor rule used in many states holds that minors may consent to research if the minor is of sufficient intelligence to understand and appreciate the possible consequences of agreement (Melton et al., 2001; Weithorn, 1983). Few states have mature-minor laws, and at the federal level, such laws have been adopted most clearly to involve minors' access to abortion (Melton et al., 2001). Minor consent statutes

have been passed in cases in which the benefit from the treatment or the risk of not receiving the treatment outweighed the parental right to consent on behalf of their children. Some states have passed minor consent laws involving a minimum age at which children can consent to one or more of the following treatments: (a) pregnancy-related services, (b) general medical treatment, (c) treatment for sexually transmitted diseases, (d) mental health services, and (e) drug and alcohol abuse problems (Melton et al., 2001).

Practically speaking, practitioners are ill advised to provide treatment or research on the basis of the mature-minor principal. Few courts have clarified the issues to the point that psychologists can refer to them in deciding whether to provide treatment to minors. For example, determining the child's capacity to understand the nature of the treatment or research is difficult, and courts rarely provide guidelines that are helpful to psychologists in effectively establishing "maturity" (Melton et al., 2001). Although some states have enacted pertinent laws, the mature-minor principal is a judicially created doctrine in most and often applies to specific circumstances (e.g., access to abortions, treatment for sexually transmitted diseases, or drug and alcohol treatment). Even though there are conditions under which children can consent, clinicians are not free to treat consenting children, because clinicians can be liable if children are found to be incompetent at a later point in time or if their consent is not considered voluntary (Melton et al., 2001). Exceptions to the limitations typically placed on children's consent tend to raise more questions than answers. For example, the laws may authorize consent to treatment without specifying which specific professionals are to provide treatment. Also, laws often fail to specify the role of parents, if any, in the treatment process. If the child is deemed competent, can the parent still consent on his or her behalf, or must the child also consent to treatment? Can the clinician provide the parent with information regarding treatment? Given this uncertainty, even if children are authorized to independently consent to treatment, it is advised that the family be informed and consulted whenever possible, especially if the family's participation is anticipated (Grisso, 1992; Melton et al., 2001).

Ramifications of Consenting for Children

A number of complications arise when adults (e.g., parents, court officers, school officials, and mental health professionals) consent to, arrange for, and initiate children's participation in treatment and research (Drotar et al., 2000; Glantz, 1996; Keith-Spiegel, 1983; Koocher, 1983). For example, the need for parental consent on behalf of children adds a complication when a child is brought for treatment by a custodial divorced parent or a grandparent. Practitioners must identify all parties who have legal guardianship and obtain consent from all of them (Drotar et al., 2000). In addition, once consent has been obtained, treatment can be provided even over the child's objection (Melton et al., 2001). The course of treatment can vary depending upon whether treatment is provided over the child's objection. In addition, parental authority to consent on behalf of the child is often extended to granting parents or societal authorities the right to establish the goals and objectives of therapy independent of the child's wishes (Koocher, 1983). Practitioners should be mindful that such authority is not granted to responsible adults, parents in particular, because of their right to control their children's lives, but because of their responsibility to protect their children from unnecessary harm (Koocher, 1983; Melton et al., 2001). When it appears that decisions are not made in the best interest of the child, the

practitioner should challenge the decisions. In addition to these issues, two others deserve special consideration: (a) the need for children to assent to research and (b) the effect that consenting on behalf of children has on issues related to confidentiality.

Assent

According to Glantz (1996), children are particularly vulnerable as research participants for these reasons:

1. To the extent that children are not competent to provide consent, their participation in research is considered involuntary.

2. To the extent that parents or guardians are busy, overwhelmed, impaired, ill, limited, or possess conflicting motives, their consent may not solely represent concern for protecting or maintaining the welfare of the child.

3. Children who are institutionalized are more remote from "ideal" protective parents.

4. Children have historically been exploited as research participants.

In the 1970s, a debate raged between those who believed that no research should be conducted with children and those who believed that research should be conducted as long as there was no discernable risk to children (Areen, 1992). The current U.S. Department of Health and Human Services federal regulations represent an attempt to balance these two positions. The regulations require that an IRB approve proposed research and obtain both the consent of the parents and assent of the child (Areen, 2001; U.S. Department of Health and Human Services, 2001, 46.402, 46.403, 46.408). The risks of such research must be minimal as "not greater, considering probability and magnitude, than those ordinarily encountered in daily life or during the performance of routine physical or psychological examinations or tests" (Areen, 1992, pp. 8-9).

The regulations also allow the IRB to waive parental consent, although an appropriate substitute may be necessary. Regarding children who are wards of the state, federal regulations state that research on those children is permissible only if it involves their status as wards of the state (Koocher & Keith–Spiegel, 1990).

According to the U.S. Department of Health and Human Services (2001), "Permission means the agreement of parent(s) or guardian to the participation of their child or ward in research. . . . Assent means a child's affirmative agreement to participate in research." Furthermore, "Mere failure to object, should not, absent affirmative agreement, be considered as assent" (Part 46, 46.402). Taken together, these two definitions mean that children may not participate in research without parental consent and parents should not volunteer their children to participate in research without their children's approval (Tymchuk, 1992). Parents are granted the right to permit or deny their children's participation, whereas children are given the role to assent or dissent to participate (Grisso, 1992; Tymchuk, 1992).

The application of assent in the case of minors is a way to allow minors to indicate their willingness to participate in the research while recognizing that they may not fully understand the nature and purpose of the experiment (Keith-Spiegel, 1983; Porter, 1996). Child assent, however, does not relieve the researchers of the responsibility to ensure that the child understands the risks and benefits to the extent possible when giving assent (Goldberg, 1997). Clinicians should be sensitive to the competence and maturity of the child and present information about treatment, particularly risks and benefits, in an age-appropriate manner (Goldberg, 1997). To achieve this, children should be encouraged to ask questions.

Recent trends in the practices of IRBs include the requirement that researchers complete assent forms with children, written in age-appropriate language, as a way to ensure children's agreement (Oesterheld, Fogas, & Rutten, 1998). Because a specific age of assent is not provided by regulations, assessment of a child's capacity to assent should be made on a case-by-case basis. Often, individual IRBs decide on an age above which a signed assent form is required before research can begin with children. For example, the IRB at the University of Nevada, Reno, has decided that researchers shall obtain a signed assent form from all children 11 years of age or older who participate in research through that institution. It is recommended that researchers familiarize themselves with the rules governing assent within their own states or individual IRBs.

The legal and ethical restrictions on conducting research with children require researchers to produce informed consent forms that meet their local IRB requirements. The key elements that IRBs are likely to require in consent and assent forms include the following: (a) a clear statement that the study involves research, (b) an explanation of the purpose of the research, (c) the expected duration of the participants participation in the research, (d) clear identification of any procedures or interventions that are experimental, (e) foreseeable risks and potential benefits to the research participants and others, (f) alternative procedures or treatment, (g) confidentiality of research participation, (h) a clear statement that the research is voluntary and the participants can withdraw at any time, and (i) who to contact to answer questions or report problems encountered (Brock, 1994; Drotar et al., 2000; Koocher & Keith-Spiegel, 1994; Weithorn & Scherer, 1994). Often IRB committees have standardized wording that must be included in the forms. In addition, there is a general requirement for clear, understandable, comprehensive, and informative consent and assent forms (Drotar et al., 2000). At the same time, the form should be as concise and brief as possible. Often, it is difficult to write consent and assent forms that include all the required elements and wording and are at the same time brief, concise, informative, and understandable. However, there are some steps researchers can take to maximize the degree to which the informed consent and assent process is informative and understandable. For the purpose of making the forms as understandable as possible, it is suggested that researchers employ readability indexes included in most word processing software. They should design the consent form so that parental consent forms are at about the sixth-grade level and no higher than eighth-grade level. Assent forms should be no higher than third-grade level. In addition, supplemental handouts sufficient to enhance understanding of the research, particularly risks and benefits, should be provided. The purpose of the handout should be to provide the potential participants with a document that is brief, concise, and understandable. Investigators should role-play consent and assent meetings with research assistants to ensure that they are sensitive to literacy levels and cultural differences and that they identify and resolve issues that may interfere with informed consent (Drotar et al., 2000).

Confidentiality

When applied to treatment and research involving children, informed consent is assumed to include informing and consulting with parents, not the child (Melton et al., 2001). Thus, the practitioner is obligated to inform the parent about the treatment. This obligation raises issues related to the limitations on the level of confidentiality provided to the child.

Confidentiality in Therapy. Confidentiality is a well-established principle when applying therapeutic interventions (Koocher, 1983; Melton et al., 2001). Parents have the right to request information from the practitioner about treatment because their consent is required for treatment to occur (Goldberg, 1997; Melton et al., 2001). In addition, other authorities such as government institutions (i.e., such as child protective services or mental health entities), courts, or schools may also expect to receive information about treatment, especially if they are providing the funding. As a result, confidentiality is generally guaranteed to the parent or responsible adult rather than to the child (Drotar et al., 2000; Koocher, 1983; Melton et al., 2001). For example, parents may be guaranteed that people other than themselves, their child, and the therapist will not have access to information, but the child is not guaranteed that the parent will not be informed.

Confidentiality cannot be unequivocally promised to children, and as a result, it becomes the issue most dependent on the interpretation and judgment of the professional. The purpose of confidentiality is not only to protect the individual but also to facilitate trust between the individual and the professional (Goldberg, 1997; Koocher, 1983). Professionals working with children face the dilemma of either providing information to parents or other adult authorities (i.e., social workers, child case workers, mental health workers, or school officials) and risking the loss of the child's trust or withholding information from adult authorities (Koocher, 1983). In this situation, it is recommended that the professional be truthful with the child about the degree of confidentiality he or she can realistically expect. Modeling truthfulness, integrity, and personal respect are probably much more important in establishing a trusting relationship with a child than any promise of absolute confidentiality. Thus, the clinician should discuss with the child the extent and nature of information that will be provided to others (Koocher, 1983; Melton et al., 2001). It is recommended that professionals discuss this issue with parents and children together in the first session and encourage the parents to respect their children's need for confidentiality (Goldberg, 1997). Regardless of the level of confidentiality, practitioners should ensure that children are aware that their parents and possibly others will be informed of imminent risk of harm to themselves or someone else (Melton et al., 2001). Although a professional does not have a legal obligation to obtain consent from a child to disclose confidential information, it is ethically mandatory to attempt to obtain agreement from the child (Koocher, 1983). Such an agreement respects the child as a developing individual.

Confidentiality in Research. When conducting research involving children, a number of issues related to confidentiality arise. Maintaining confidentiality of data is particularly important for research with children because of their vulnerability. As with treatment, there are limitations to the degree to which confidentiality can be guaranteed to children when conducting research. These limitations result primarily from demands from parents and other authorities for information about the research. There are also circumstances under which the researcher may determine that it is necessary to disclose information.

Confidentiality of data is particularly important when working with children, given their vulnerability and the sensitivity of many psychological studies with children (Drotar et al., 2000). Any violation of confidentiality could result in legal action (DeKraii & Sales, 1991). As part of preserving confidentiality, researchers should separate demographic information from data and identify data with numbers or codes (Drotar

et al., 2000). In addition, investigators should provide specialized training to their research assistants regarding confidentiality (Attkisson, Rosenblatt, & Hoagwood, 1996; Drotar et al., 2000). It is advisable to conduct ongoing debriefing and supervision with research assistants regarding ethical issues (Attkisson et al., 1996). Also, researchers should have their research assistants complete confidentiality agreements (Drotar et al., 2000).

IRB committees are increasingly recognizing that parents do not have the absolute right to all information obtained during research at the expense of the participating children's privacy and confidentiality (Koocher & Keith-Spiegel, 1990). However, this tendency is limited by the reality of the pressures applied to researchers by parents, schools, and other agencies providing consent on behalf of the children involved. Parents often desire information about the progress and results of research involving their children. Schools and other agencies often have their own approval process for granting permission for investigators to conduct research and as a result, often demand access to information about the research. In addition to these demands, investigators themselves may recognize that providing parents and others with the information gained while conducting research may improve the child's life (Koocher & Keith-Spiegel, 1990). Given these limitations on children's confidentiality, researchers should ensure that children are aware of the information that will be provided to parents and other authorities. To determine the level of confidentiality that can be promised to children, investigators should agree in advance with parents, schools, and other agencies as to what information will be provided. They should then ensure that the child is aware of the extent to which they can be guaranteed confidentiality (Koocher & Keith-Spiegel, 1990). This information should be provided to children as part of the assent process.

In some cases, obtaining mutual agreement from parents and children regarding the level of confidentiality can result in conflicts between children and their parents. In these cases, it is recommended that investigators resolve these issues before beginning the research. If such issues cannot be resolved, then it is recommended that the child be excused from the study. The alternatives are to violate confidentiality with the child or to lie to the parents about disclosure. Both of these alternatives present ethical problems and model the wrong behavior for the child (Koocher & Keith-Spiegel, 1990).

The right of parents to be consulted and informed about the outcome of the research on their child can be limited or eliminated if such disclosure poses a risk to the child or would make the research impossible with such disclosure. For example, research involving adolescent drug use may not only pose a risk to children but may also be impossible if parents were consulted or informed. In such cases, informed consent must specifically include the parents' agreement to abrogate their right to be informed or consulted. In any case, decisions regarding consent and assent should be based on what is best for the child as opposed to what is beneficial for others.

Researchers may disclose some information without the consent of and even over the objections of the child. These conditions include situations in which children are in immanent danger from themselves or others. Investigators are not excluded from the requirements to disclose information necessary to avoid harm to research participants and are required to protect others from the participants (Koocher & Keith-Spiegel, 1990). In some states, researchers fall under statutes requiring mandatory reporting, such

as child abuse and neglect and HIV status (Attkisson et al., 1996; Koocher & Keith-Spiegel, 1990). Investigators should have specific knowledge of these requirements as they apply to the state or states in which they conduct research with children (Attkisson et al., 1996).

RESPONSIBILITY OF CHILD PRACTITIONERS

Child practitioners have a responsibility to ensure the protection and welfare of children because of the limited autonomy accorded children (i.e., as demonstrated by adults consenting to treatment and research on their behalf). One way to ensure that children's interests are considered is to include them in the decision-making process whenever possible. Although parents and other adult authorities generally believe that children do not have the capacity to make major decisions about their lives, research suggests that teenage minors can under some circumstances demonstrate an ability to make decisions commensurate with adults (Koocher & Keith–Spiegel, 1990). Even younger children (between 6 and 9 years of age) can demonstrate an ability to make reasonable choices regarding research participation. Given that children may be able to make reasonable choices, it is advisable that practitioners ensure that children are involved in the decision-making process with their parents whenever possible. Here again, it is important to bear in mind that the purpose for limiting children's permission to consent is to protect them from harm and to promote their welfare, not to control their lives.

In addition to including children in decision making, safeguards such as the following should be employed to ensure the protection of practitioners: (a) practitioners submitting themselves to peer review and (b) care in providing guidance to others. Whenever possible, child practitioners should seek out peers for consultation or submit to the review of other professionals on cases involving children (Koocher, 1983). The review should involve appropriateness not only of a specific treatment or research but also the course of that treatment or procedures of the research. Practitioners should provide guidance to parents and other authorities that emphasize importance of the interest of the child. In general, professionals providing treatment or conducting research with children bear a heavy social responsibility. They must at once act as advocates, researchers, information providers, and social-political change agents (Koocher, 1983).

SUMMARY

Many of the issues that involve ethical treatment and research with adults also apply to children. The one issue that distinguishes children from adults is the statutory limitation on their consent to participate in treatment and research. Informed consent requires that decisions about treatment and research be informed, competent, and voluntary. Informed means that practitioners have provided all information necessary and sufficient to weigh risks and benefits of participation. Competent means that the person making the decision understands the information and is able to employ it in making a reasoned choice. Voluntary means that decisions are made without undue influence or coercion.

Children are not allowed to consent to treatment and research except under specific circumstances. Legal standards usually authorize parents or other responsible adults to provide informed consent on behalf of the child. Even if children were allowed to consent, their consent would be irrelevant in many cases because they cannot pay for treatment themselves and cannot obligate their parents to pay unless the services are considered absolutely necessary. For the most part, parents and legal guardians have the legal authority to consent to treatment and research on behalf of the child. Children are reserved the right to assent or dissent to treatment and research, although such assent and dissent can be overridden by parents, guardians, courts, and other authority.

A number of complications arise from adults consenting for children. For example, custodial parents or guardians may not consent for the child without the knowledge or consent of a noncustodial parent. Child practitioners must ensure that responsible adults are involved in the consent process. Because the child is not providing consent, practitioners should ensure that decisions reflect the interests of the child, not the individual(s) providing consent. One way to ensure that the interests of children are addressed is to include them in the decision-making process and to obtain assent, or agreement, to participate. As with consent, assent requires that children be provided with all pertinent information in a way they can understand. Because parents and other adult authorities consent for children, they often require the practitioner to provide information about treatment and research. This demand for information by third parties limits the level of confidentiality that can be provided to children. The practitioner should determine the level of confidentiality that can be given the child before treatment and research begins and ensure that the child is informed about the limits to confidentiality as part of the assent process.

REFERENCES

Areen, J. (1992). Legal constraints on social research with children. In B. Stanley & J. E Sieber (Eds.), *Social research on children and adolescents*. Newbury Park, CA: Sage.

Attkisson, C. C., Rosenblatt, A., & Hoagwood, K. (1996). Research ethics and human subjects protection in child mental health services research and community studies. In K. Hoagwood, P. S. Jensen, & C. B. Fisher (Eds.), *Ethical issues in mental health research with children and adolescents*. Mahwah, NJ: Lawrence Erlbaum.

Brock, D. W. (1994). The law of human experiments with children. In A. Grodin & L. H. Glantz (Eds.), *Children as research subjects: Science and law*. New York: Oxford University Press.

Davis, S. M., Scott, E. S., Waldlington, W. L., & Whitebread, C. H. (1997). *Children in the legal system: Cases and materials* (2nd ed.). Westbury, NY: Foundation.

DeKraii, M. B., & Sales, B. D. (1991). Liability in child therapy and research. *Journal of Consulting and Clinical Psychology, 59*, 853-860.

Drotar, D., Overholser, J. C., Levi, R., Walters, N., Robinson, J. R., Palermo, T. M., & Reikert, K. A. (2000). Ethical issues in conducting research with pediatric and clinical child populations in applied settings. In D. Drotar (Ed.), *Handbook of research in pediatric and clinical child psychology: Practical strategies and methods*. New York: Kluwer Academic/Plenum.

Glantz, L. H. (1996). Conducting research with children: legal and ethical issues. *Journal of the American Academy of Child and Adolescent Psychiatry, 34*, 1283-1291.

Goldberg, R. (1997). Ethical dilemmas in working with children and adolescents. In D. T. Marsh & R. D. Magee (Eds.), *Ethical and legal issues in professional practice with families* (pp. 97-111). New York: John Wiley.

Grisso, T. (1992). Minor's assent to behavioral research without parental consent. In B. Stanley & J. E Sieber (Eds.), *Social research on children and adolescents*. Newbury Park, CA: Sage.

Hoagwood, K., Jensen, P. S., & Fisher, C. B. (1996). Toward a science of scientific ethics in research on child and adolescent mental disorders. In K. Hoagwood, P. S. Jensen, & C. B. Fisher (Eds.), *Ethical issues in mental health research with children and adolescents*. Mahwah, NJ: Lawrence Erlbaum.

Keith-Spiegel, P. (1983). Children and consent to participate in research. In G. B. Melton, G. P. Koocher, & M. J. Saks (Eds.), *Children's competence to consent* (pp. 179-211). New York: Plenum.

Koocher, G. P. (1983). Competence to consent. In G. B. Melton, G. P. Koocher, & M. J. Saks (Eds.), *Children's competence to consent* (pp. 21-37). New York: Plenum.

Koocher, G. P., & Keith-Spiegel, P. (1990). *Children, ethics, & the law: Professional issues and cases*. Lincoln: University of Nebraska Press.

Koocher, G. P., & Keith-Spiegel, P. (1994). Ethical issues in exposing children to risks in research. In A. Grodin & L. H. Glantz (Eds.), *Children as research subjects: Science and law*. New York: Oxford University Press.

Melton, G. B. (1983). Decision making by children: Psychological risks and benefits. In G. B. Melton, G. P. Koocher, & M. J. Saks (Eds.), *Children's competence to consent* (pp. 21-37). New York: Plenum.

Melton, G. B., Ehrenreich, N. S., & Lyons, P. M. (2001). Ethical and legal issues in mental health services for children. In E. C. Walker & M. C. Roberts (Eds.), *Handbook of clinical child psychology* (3rd ed., pp. 1074-1093). New York: John Wiley.

Melton, G. B., Lyons, P. M., & Spaulding, W. J. (1998). *No place to go: The civil commitment of minors.* Lincoln: University of Nebraska Press.

National Committee for the Protection of Human Subjects of Biomedical and Behavioral Research. (1979). *The Belmont Report: Ethical principals and guidelines for the protection of human subjects research.* Washington, DC: National Institutes of Health.

Oesterheld, J. R., Fogas, B., & Rutten, S. (1998). Ethical standards for research on children. *Journal of the American Academy of Child and Adolescent Psychiatry, 37,* 684-685.

Pagliocca, P. M., Melton, G. B., Weisz, V., & Lyons, P. M. Jr. (1995). Parenting and the law. In M. H. Bornstein (Ed.), *Handbook of parenting* (pp. 437-457). Hillsdale, NJ: Lawrence Erlbaum.

Porter, J. P. (1996). Regulatory considerations in research involving children and adolescents with mental disorders. In K. Hoagwood, P. S. Jensen, & C. B. Fisher (Eds.), *Ethical issues in mental health research with children and adolescents.* Mahwah, NJ: Lawrence Erlbaum.

Roth, L. H., Meisel, A., & Lidz, C. W. (1977) Tests of competency to consent to treatment. *American Journal of Psychiatry, 134,* 279-284.

Thompson, R. A. (1992). Developmental changes in research risk and benefit. In B. Stanley & J. E Sieber (Eds.), *Social research on children and adolescents.* Newberry Park, CA: Sage.

Tymchuk, A. J. (1992). Assent process. In B. Stanley & J. E. Sieber (Eds.), *Social research on children and adolescents.* Newbury Park, CA: Sage.

U.S. Department of Health and Human Services. (2001). *Federal code of regulations, Title 45 Subtitle A, Protection of human subjects; Subpart D, Additional protections for children involved as subjects of research* (46.401-46.408, pp. 123-125). Washington, DC: Office of the Federal Registrar National Archives and Records Administration, U.S. Government Printing Office.

Waldlington, W. J. (1983). Consent to medical care for minors. In G. B. Melton, G. P. Koocher, & M. J. Saks (Eds.), *Children's competence to consent* (pp. 21-37). New York: Plenum.

Weithorn, L. A. (1982). Developmental factors and competence to make informed treatment decisions. In G. B. Melton (Ed.), *Legal reforms affecting child and youth services* (pp. 85-100). New York: Hawthorn.

Weithorn, L. A. (1983). Involving children in decisions affecting their own welfare. In G. B. Melton, G. P. Koocher, & M. J. Saks (Eds.), *Children's competence to consent* (pp. 21-37). New York: Plenum.

Weithorn, L. A., & Scherer, D. G. (1994). Assessment of risk to children. In A. Grodin & L. H. Glantz (Eds.), *Children as research subjects: Science and law.* New York: Oxford University Press.

CHAPTER 23

Ethical Principles and Practice in Couple and Family Therapy

STEVEN R. THORP
Duke University Medical Center

ALAN E. FRUZZETTI
University of Nevada, Reno

T here has been a recent increase in ethical and legal concerns in psychological practice, but there does not appear to be a concomitant increase in training in ethics for therapists. Haas, Malouf, and Mayerson (1986) found that for a random sample of APA Division 29 (Psychotherapy) members, the modal number of hours in formal ethics training was zero. Moreover, despite the fact that many states now require ongoing continuing education in ethics for renewed licensure, few offerings really address the dilemmas that couple and family therapists face. The intent of this chapter is to highlight some of these special ethical challenges associated with couple and family therapy. We discuss ethical principles and applications, emphasizing avoiding harm and exploitation, issues in confidentiality in families, and the relevance of empirical evidence to ethical practice. The chapter concludes with recommendations for maximizing ethical conduct in couple and family therapy.

INDIVIDUAL VERSUS CONJOINT TREATMENTS

Although psychotherapy research and practice were dominated by a focus on the individual for most of the 20th century, recent decades have seen enormous growth in the practice of couple and family treatment (Fruzzetti & Jacobson, 1991). Couple therapy (also called *marriage counseling* or *marital therapy)* and family therapy have evolved to become popular and often effective forms of treatment for both individual and relationship problems.

Although couple and family therapies have been adopted more widely, the profession has been slow to adapt beyond an individual focus in many domains, including ethics. For example, despite a preponderance of data that show the importance of relationships with regard to psychopathology, the predominant diagnostic system does not include relational disorders (Fruzzetti, 1996; Kaslow, 1993). The *Diagnostic and Statistical Manual of Mental Disorders (DSM-IV),* developed by the American Psychiatric Association (1994), relegates such disorders to V-Codes. Although they may best represent the most appropriate diagnosis for a given case, V-Codes are not often reimbursed by insurance companies (Marsh, 1997). The few ethical guidelines associated with multi-person treatment have been derived from ethics codes designed for individual treatment. This is an important limitation, given that the ethical complexities of psychotherapy are often compounded when more than one client is involved (Margolin, 1986; Marsh, 1997).

ETHICAL PRINCIPLES AND ETHICAL GUIDELINES

Determining what constitutes ethical versus unethical practice could be accomplished in many ways. But perhaps the most important dimension to consider is that of principles versus prescribing/proscribing specific activities and behaviors. Presumably, even prescriptive/proscriptive systems are informed by some principles originally, and in reality, the principles on which ethical practices are determined are relatively few: (a) Do not harm clients/patients (which includes not engaging in poor practice or service delivery, maintaining confidentiality except when doing so causes more harm, etc.); (b) do not engage in exploitive practices toward clients (which includes not having sexual relationships with clients, abusing power for other gains, etc.); (c) get informed consent (provide information that the client can understand; ensure that the client's participation is voluntary, etc.); and (d) provide the best treatment possible (know and deliver the standard of care established by evidence, practice within competency, etc.).

Of course, these principles may at times be in conflict, or people may disagree about the instantiation of one or more of these principles. However, as we move away from principles to prescribing or proscribing certain activities or behaviors, the rules we create may themselves end up violating basic ethical principles. For example, service bartering (in lieu of direct fee payment) has at various times in the American Psychological Association guidelines (APA, 1992) been (a) not mentioned (implicitly; use principles to guide whether to barter); (b) specifically proscribed; and (c) specifically mentioned as allowable and dangerous, but not proscribed. Of course, the principle (doing no harm/not exploiting the client) was consistent over time; only the manner in which this principle was interpreted, and by whom, changed over time.

Most ethical codes have become more prescriptive/proscriptive and hence longer and more specific. These ethical guidelines provide summary statements about the views of the professional community and as such can be useful resources when global judgment and discretion are needed to resolve ethical problems (Butler & Gardner, 2001). The APA (1992) has established the ethical principles of psychologists (i.e., the ethics code) to govern the behavior of all APA members. The ethics code is by necessity quite broad, mixing principles with specifically prescribed and proscribed activities, and although useful in some ways, it is often too global for clinicians struggling with specific ethical quandaries. In determining principles and codes of conduct, there is often a conflict between the depth and breadth of the standards. In other words, to encompass the activities of 150,000 members serving various roles within the discipline, the APA has sacrificed specificity (and some principles) for generalizability and enforceability. The result is that the guidelines have been soundly criticized for lacking the precision and clarity needed by individual psychologists in complex situations, and that the frequent use of words such as *reasonable* and *feasible* serve only to dilute possible rules (and move away from principles) that may guide practitioners (Bersoff, 1994).

Moreover, there is a paucity of principles to direct decisions about multiperson (couple and family) therapies. Twenty years ago, Gayla Margolin (1982) decried the ambiguities involved in couple and family therapy that were not addressed in APA's ethical standards, and little has changed since her request for improvement. Lakin (1994) applauded the current (1992) APA ethics code as the first to contain a section specifically for couple and family therapies but lamented the lack of comprehensive or specific rules to pragmatically aid individual decisions. Indeed, the very brief section on "Couple and Family Relationships," Standard 4.03 of the principles, urges psychologists only to reduce or eliminate dual roles and to clarify from the beginning of treatment the relationship the psychologist will have with each person in the couple or family (including which members will be considered clients). Although Standard 4.03 holds promise, it is too broad and too brief to be of much service in many of the complicated issues that may arise in multiperson therapy (Magee, 1997). It is hoped that the upcoming revision of the APA

ethical code will offer more precise and more comprehensive standards for the practice of couple and family therapies.

The American Association for Marriage and Family Therapy (AAMFT) has also developed a code of ethical principles for marriage and family therapists (AAMFT, 1998). The AAMFT code provides similar content to the APA code, but is briefer, includes simpler language, and (by definition) is geared more toward providers of couple and family therapies. Conversely, the APA code devotes more space to research, teaching, assessment, and supervision, reflecting the mutlifaceted roles of psychologists.

Although ethics codes may be useful for documenting the state of the discipline's general views on ethical matters, it is not clear that the codes significantly guide behavior. Haas et al. (1986) found that APA Division 29 (Psychotherapy) members spent more time learning ethics via discussions with colleagues than from independent reading, internship supervision, graduate coursework, or continuing education courses combined. This may be due to the fact that situations that produce ethical dilemmas are difficult specifically because they do not fit neatly into prescribed or proscribed ethical practice guidelines provided by both the APA and AAMFT codes.

"Applying Empiricism to Ethics," Standard 1.06 in the 1992 APA code, mandates that psychologists rely on scientifically and professionally derived knowledge when making professional judgments, which implicitly includes ethical decisions. Although on the surface, this statement makes good sense, how to interpret the meaning of Standard 1.06 is not entirely clear. Ideally, professionally derived knowledge would be driven by science. However, data to guide decision making regarding ethical issues are largely absent. Butler and Gardner (2001) describe this problem in the area of dual relationships:

Our own review leaves us concerned that what currently exists are only incidental theoretical assertions or speculations and a few editorial ones rather than coherent and validated (e.g., effectiveness research) models for DRs (dual relationships). Advances in knowledge and practice often begin with creative, innovative speculation and discourse, and the willingness to see things through a new lens. Professional practice, however, should conscientiously follow only the *validation* of new methods and practice models. (p. 211)

Clearly, studies should be conducted to establish which practices do and do not cause harm and when and how often they cause harm, as well as to establish the benefits. The instantiation of our ethical principles would benefit from empirical practice.

The contents of the APA and AAMFT ethics guidelines are categorized into domains such as integrity, responsibility, confidentiality, competence, finances and fees, and advertising. Much of the content in these categories involves issues that may occur when professionals are acting as teachers, supervisors, researchers, businesspeople, forensic experts, and so on, and although sometimes relevant to couple or family therapists, these roles are beyond the scope of this chapter. Of course, many issues that are relevant to couple and family therapists (providing informed consent, ethical billing practices, etc.) transcend individual and multiperson therapies and rarely present unique challenges to couple and family therapists. Our concern is primarily with issues that are relevant specifically to the process of psychotherapy with couples or families. These issues will be discussed below, organized by relevant governing principles: (a) Do no harm, (b) do not exploit clients, and (c) provide the highest standard of care.

ETHICAL PRINCIPLES AND APPLICATIONS WITH COUPLES AND FAMILIES

Do No Harm

If you ask someone (a psychologist or lay person) to distill the essence of ethics for psychologists, you are likely to get responses that include the notion of nonmaleficence or the phrase "First, do no harm," which is summarized in the APA code (1992), Standard 1.14. However, it is not entirely clear what it means to minimize or avoid harm in psychotherapy. It is obvious that as therapists, we hope to improve our clients' lives (and conversely, to reduce the chances that their quality of life will be diminished in any way). However, much of the work in therapy involves exposing clients to short-term pain. This occurs when we discuss clients' difficult relationships, when we discuss traumatic events, and when we literally expose them to feared stimuli.

It is apparent that the simple proscription to "Do no harm" can be extremely complicated when considering the dyad of one therapist and one client, but the complexity is substantially compounded in multiperson therapy because additional people are involved. In couple therapy, for example, teaching assertiveness skills to one partner may lead the other partner to feel frustration, betrayal, anger, or fear. It could even lead to separation or divorce that is desirable to one person and deplored by the other. Is helping one person achieve her or his goals in such a situation a violation of the "Do no harm" principle? No, especially if appropriate informed consent orients all clients to the risks associated with family treatments. In family therapy, if caretakers are encouraged to address (rather than avoid) problems, the children involved may be upset by the ensuing (unfamiliar) arguments. Helping a battered woman to get to a shelter may compromise couple therapy and result in legal charges being filed against the battering partner. In these instances, what helps one member may harm another, at least in the short term, but whatever harm occurs is incidental to the treatment, not a result of malpractice.

There may also be conflicts between what is best for clients and what is best for mental health agencies or for the surrounding community. It is imperative to consider what Marsh (1997) calls the "ecological system" when working with couples or families, so that issues such as mental illness, disability, gender, and ethnicity or culture can be addressed appropriately. Blatant misunderstanding (or lack of knowledge) about the cultural meaning of certain behaviors may lead the therapist to less effective or even harmful treatment (as could cultural stereotyping). Although a society may dictate (through the judicial system or protective services, for example) that it is best if a child is removed from a home, that change may in fact harm family members socially, emotionally, and financially. In this sense, ethics are relative, and what is ethical or what reduces harm differs depending on the level of analysis (Kitchner, 1980). It is important to determine whether decisions will be made on the basis of what results in less harm to individuals, couples, families, the surrounding community, or the profession of psychology (Anderson & Barret, 2001).

It is critical that we be aware of the relevance of context to ethical practice and that we be explicit about our goals at each of these levels of analysis. Ethics codes would benefit from a general rule to guide decisions about conflicts among various levels. It has been argued that the good of the many outweighs the good of the few, but this perspective may not universally apply to all instances. Bersoff and Koeppl (1993) suggest that codes of ethics should provide guidance toward resolution of moral dilemmas that are likely to occur in the profession, with a primary emphasis on protecting the public. The APA ethics code (1992) does state that its primary goal is the "welfare and protection of the individuals and groups with whom psychologists work" (p. 1599). However, several psychologists have criticized the code as a document that is designed to minimize liability, in that it protects the profession more than the community the profession serves (Bersoff, 1994).

It is imperative that ethical decisions are made on the basis of minimizing malfeasance for each individual affected (directly or indirectly) by treatment, but it is equally important that decisions are informed by beneficence. That is, while minimizing harm is a necessary precondition to therapists' actions, it must also be apparent that a significant benefit is likely from the option chosen (Butler & Gardner, 2001). For example, a decision about violating confidentiality must take into account the reduction in harm and the potential advantage that results from doing so.

Pope and Vetter (1992) surveyed a random national sample of APA members in an effort to empirically determine the ethical dilemmas that have challenged or troubled psychologists. The dilemmas that were most frequently described involved issues of *confidentiality,* and the researchers emphasized the fact that the APA code (at that time, the 1991 draft form) did not adequately address confidentiality when multiple clients (groups, couples, or families) were involved (Pope & Vetter, 1992). Of course, the therapist should voice the standard exceptions to confidentiality at the outset of any treatment to minimize misunderstandings later. In couple or family therapy, it should also be made clear that information shared by all members during therapy may be used as evidence in legal proceedings for divorce or child custody (Margolin, 1998).

Many issues that do not compromise confidentiality in individual therapy may present dilemmas in multiperson therapy. Therapists conducting individual therapy can typically discuss all aspects of their clients' behaviors with little concern of sacrificing confidentiality, with the standard exceptions of the clients' threat to themselves or others, first-hand knowledge of child, elder, or dependent abuse, and legal demands for breaking confidentiality. However, individuals in couple and family therapy may be hesitant to share with partners or family members because they wish to avoid the rejection, anger, or disgust from others and their own humiliation and thus may not disclose in conjoint sessions information about which one or more family members may be unaware. For example, information about past crimes they have committed, details about prior divorces, their own histories as survivors of physical or sexual abuse, current use of substances, past experiences in therapy, their tumultuous relationship histories, or current sexual activities or desires may not be disclosed at all or may be disclosed only to the therapist and with the stipulation that he or she not disclose the information to family members. The therapist may be in a bind because this information may directly affect all clients in the therapy. For example, if an alcoholic family member privately tells a therapist that she has begun drinking again after 4 years of sobriety, the therapist may want to protect that confidence but may also realize that the drinking will affect other family members negatively and that family members might be helpful in reestablishing sobriety.

Discussions of extra-relational affairs pose a classic ethical dilemma, and how the dilemma is resolved may significantly alter the status of relationships between or among all of the clients involved in therapy. If a therapist complies with a request to keep information about a client's current affair private, the public silence on the matter may implicitly condone the affair, and it may be difficult to act as a true advocate for other members involved in the therapy (Birchler & Schwartz, 1994). However, breaking the person's confidence may result in a loss of trust and possibly premature termination (and may be an ethical breach if explicitly excluded from further disclosure by the client). But there is of course no "right" answer, as is the case with many ethical dilemmas. In response to an "affair vignette," approximately two thirds of therapists said they would keep news of an affair secret from the other partner if it emerged during ongoing couple therapy and if a policy about secrets had not been previously discussed with the couple (Haas et al., 1986).

Another common dilemma that occurs in couple therapy is how to handle the private disclosure by one partner to the therapist that he or she has tested positive for the human immunodeficiency virus (HIV) or acquired immune deficiency syndrome (AIDS) (Anderson & Barret, 2001). Although it is understandable that individuals who are diagnosed with HIV or AIDS may be fearful about sharing their status with others, the potential danger to the partner places the therapist in a difficult position. It is of course important to consider the potential harm that could result from breaking confidentiality (e.g., ending of the couple's relationship and/or damaging the therapeutic alliance with the therapist, risking possible, albeit unlikely, legal action) and the potential harm of not alerting the partner (e.g., the partner becoming infected with the virus, also risking possible, albeit unlikely, legal action). Although policies regarding this issue vary from state to state, general strategies have emerged to guide therapists faced with such a dilemma to work it through without violating either the principle of confidentiality nor the "duty to warn" principle (Anderson & Barret, 2001).

There are several options to choose from regarding such policies about individual disclosure to the therapist in general. One strategy is for a therapist to treat each member of the couple or family as an individual client and thus retain strict confidentiality for each person. This type of policy has the advantage of allowing each member of the dyad or group to reveal information that had been kept secret from the other members, which may unburden each member and fully inform the therapist. Clients might reveal material that is uncomfortable to share with others yet is critically relevant to treatment. However, this private sharing of secrets may substantially alter the course of treatment, and the shift in focus may confuse the members of the couple or family that are not privy to all the information. Each client will realize that the therapist may have information from others that will embarrass, anger, or hurt them in some way, and this "culture of secrets" may serve only to exacerbate members' guardedness and avoidance. Moreover, in long-term treatment, the therapist may forget whether information was obtained privately from individual meetings or publicly during meetings with the couple or family. This may lead a therapist to be overly cautious about which topics he or she submits for discussion. Finally, this approach may lead to unplanned alliances between the therapist and one or more of the people involved, which may alienate those who are not part of those alliances.

An alternative strategy for handling confidentiality is essentially to do the opposite of what was described above. That is, the therapist could decide to keep no secrets from others and make this policy explicit by including it in the informed consent procedure. This may foster a "culture of openness" that can model effective ways to disclose information and to respond to such disclosures. The therapist who adheres to this open model will not have to struggle as much with unintended alliances or the mistrust that can occur when clients realize that the therapist is keeping secrets. It is also not necessary for the therapist to be as cautious about revealing information to the couple or family, because it will be understood that everything previously shared with him or her is fair game for discussion. Ford (2001) suggests that the therapist get permission from each client to reveal all conversations with the therapist at the beginning of the next session. This establishes the open model, allows for explicitly informed consent, and allows time for discussion in session when potentially volatile topics are presented. We suggest that this model, if employed, be included in writing during the informed consent procedures at the beginning of treatment.

Although "strict confidentiality" or "full openness" approaches may be attractive because of their relative simplicity, some therapists may desire more flexibility. A third option is to take a dialectical stance toward confidentiality, or what Birchler and Schwartz (1994) call "limited confidentiality." Therapists choosing this alternative encourage clients to be fully open with them, with the understanding that full disclosure will help the therapist better understand the context of interactions and thus may improve the likelihood of a successful treatment outcome. The information obtained will be shared in conjoint sessions only if it will promote the welfare of the couple or family, which is left to the therapist's discretion. The exception to this general rule is that if clients request that certain information be kept confidential, the therapist will uphold the confidentiality—as long as the information does not violate legal and ethical limits to the confidentiality or compromise the goals of successful treatment. Because treatment goals will differ from case to case and goals may evolve or shift during the course of treatment, it is important that confidentiality be addressed and updated in both private and conjoint meetings with clients and is included in informed consent procedures. Although limited confidentiality is complex, for many therapists, it is the option that provides the most benefits and the fewest disadvantages (Birchler & Schwartz, 1994).

Do Not Exploit Clients: Dual Roles or Multiple Relationships

Dual roles and multiple relationships are of great concern to psychologists, second only to issues of confidentiality in the Pope and Vetter (1992) survey. Although some types of contact between therapists and clients outside the therapeutic context are relatively common and are certainly controversial, neither the APA code (1992) nor the AAMFT code (1998) define the term *multiple relationships* (Mamalakis, 2001). For the purposes of this chapter, we will use Hill and Mamalakis's (2001) definition of the term: "any concurrent or sequential relationship between a therapist and client that is distinct from the therapeutic relationship" (p. 199). Although some authors (Brodsky, 1985; Kagle & Grebelhausen, 1994; Pope, 1991) have suggested that multiple relationships between therapists and clients are simply unethical and should thus be avoided, others have recognized that such relationships may be unavoidable or even therapeutic (Catalano, 1997; Gottlieb, 1993; Pope & Vetter, 1992).

The APA code (1992, Standard 1.17) suggests that although multiple relationships with clients may occur, psychologists must be sensitive to the harm or exploitation that

could be caused by these relationships. Indeed, multiple relationships pose many risks to clients and therapists and to the therapy itself. However, APA's platitude provides nothing to guide therapists in terms of what is or is not permissible concerning interactions outside of traditional therapy roles. Guidance about how to handle multiple relationships is especially relevant in small communities, such as rural towns, religious groups, and communities formed to support racial minorities, gays, or lesbians. Therapists and clients will generally have fewer "degrees of separation" in such settings and are therefore more likely to share business and/or social connections and attend similar social functions (Schank & Skovholt, 1997). Given that multiperson therapy involves more relationships between the therapist and clients, the confusion that may develop about multiple relationships can be amplified.

A full discussion about all of the dilemmas that may emerge regarding multiple relationships in couple or family therapy is beyond the scope of this chapter. However, several issues are worth discussing here. Specifically, sexual involvement between therapists and clients, individual therapy to augment couple or family therapy, and contact outside the office will be discussed. The recommendations provided at the end of the chapter will offer guidance for minimizing the long-term harm that could result from multiple relationships.

Sexual Involvement Between Therapists and Clients

A topic that is tied closely to ethics in psychotherapy is the idea that ethics include a mandate against sexual involvement between therapists and clients, and between therapists and their former clients. The prohibition of therapists having sexual relationships with clients (APA, 1992, Standard 4.05) is one of the few absolute rules in the ethics code (Bersoff, 1994). Although controversy regarding this rule exists, there is a consensus that sexual activities with current or former clients may be harmful to the client (Lazarus, 1992; Gabbard, 1994; Pope & Vetter, 1991; Williams, 1992). Gabbard (1994) notes that much of this potential harm is a result of the power imbalance inherent in therapeutic relationships and the fact that some professional responsibilities of the therapist toward clients could persist for a lifetime. Indeed, sexual contact with one therapist may generalize to therapy in general, so that a client may be guarded about disclosing unflattering information or may mistrust the motives of future mental health professionals.

In multiperson therapy, the opportunities for sexual contact are greater, given that there are more people involved and the harmful consequences of such contact could be magnified. For example, if sexual involvement with the therapist occurs in couple therapy, either during treatment or any time after the treatment has ended, the result could be devastating. The sexual contact would bring into question the therapist's motives during treatment and the provision of quality care. The partner who was sexually involved with the therapist may later doubt his or her own motives, may feel confused, and may believe that the therapist was manipulative or seductive from the beginning of treatment. The other partner would likely feel betrayed, angry, and hurt if he or she learned of the therapist's behavior. If a therapist becomes involved with any treated family member, it could jeopardize the current treatment and the family's future interactions with professionals. Feelings of resentment, jealously, and loss may emerge even if the family member who is sexually involved with the therapist is not one of the identified patients. For example, if a child therapist begins a sexual relationship

with the sister of a child's mother, all three family members may be unclear about how to differentiate between the therapist's professional role and his role as the sister's partner.

On the other hand, proscribing romantic/sexual contact for several years could be unnecessary in some circumstances. For example, a family therapist might meet an extended family (grandparents, parents, and adult children) during a family consultation in a hospital concerning how to help the family adjust to a grandparent's medical problems and disability (e.g., stroke). Some time later, the therapist might meet one of the adult children in an entirely different context, and neither may initially remember their previous meeting. Could the development of a sexual relationship in this case be exploitive? Yes. Would it necessarily be such? Perhaps not. Because of the larger number of involved participants at varying levels of intensity and commitment, in family therapy, such dilemmas may be more common.

Individual Therapy to Augment Couple or Family Therapy

It is not uncommon for couple or family therapists to be faced with a dual-role dilemma when individual therapy for one of the family members is considered. It may become clear to the therapist that one of the clients in the couple or family has serious problems (e.g., substance use, depression, an eating disorder) that may be addressed more thoroughly in individual therapy (concurrently or following termination of family treatment). Or conversely, it may become clear that an individual client could benefit from couple or family sessions. Often, clients will want the same therapist to act as the individual therapist and the couple or family therapist, because the therapist is familiar and because he or she has already undertaken the initial process of assessment. The therapist may be tempted to augment the initial mode of treatment for the same reasons and perhaps also because of his or her own expertise in treating the identified problem(s) and the established relationships. This could be an opportunity for good practice, but may also present ethical problems. Confidentiality issues could become muddied because the therapist could forget where he or she learned certain information about the individual or family. In addition, the other partner or family may seek information about the individual sessions, either overtly or covertly. It may also be difficult to determine and maintain therapeutic priorities when administering concurrent therapies. When conducting couple and family treatments, it is important to consider the outcome for individual adults and children and for the couple or family as a unit (Christensen & Jacobson, 1998). It is not possible for the therapist to escape bias (for better or worse) when getting additional information about the family or couple from one person's perspective. Moreover, what is best for the individual may not be best for the couple or family, and vice versa. Although APA code does not prohibit one therapist from conducting individual therapy and multiperson therapy that involves that individual, these issues must be considered carefully. And again, explicitly orienting family members to these issues and obtaining informed consent go a long way toward delivering the best treatment without having to untangle ethical dilemmas.

Contact Outside the Office

One of the ethical challenges that can develop in multiple therapy relationships involves contact outside the therapist's office. This can range from incidental meetings in public places (such as accidentally meeting one or more family members at a grocery store or at a party of a mutual acquaintance) to planned excursions from the office (such as walking during planned sessions or eating meals together in restaurants). Telephone contact between sessions ranges widely among therapists, as well. For example, many therapists allow no after-hours phone contact and instead direct their clients to call crisis telephone lines if needed. Other therapists may encourage telephone contact and may give clients their home telephone numbers so that skills discussed in session can be generalized (see, for example, Linehan, 1993). Others may decide to have in-home visits to obtain a more contextual view of the couple or family.

Although incidental contact may be unavoidable, especially in small communities, the decision of whether to have or how to manage contact outside the office can be thorny issues. For example, if a therapist decides to meet a couple he is treating in a public setting, he or she must thoroughly consider concerns about confidentiality. For example, the therapist must be aware of proximity to other people (to prevent eavesdropping) and must decide how to react if the therapist or the members of the couple are greeted by acquaintances. Therapists should also be aware that meetings in less formal areas may invite more personal questions from clients, which could lead to a blurring of the lines between therapist as professional versus friend. Of course, the principles are still relevant: Is the out-of-office contact necessary to provide the best treatment? What harm could develop as a result of this activity? What can be done to avoid or mitigate potential harm?

Telephone calls, too, may be associated with a more familiar tone. It is possible that telephone conversations between the therapist and clients could devolve into "chatting" about external events rather than addressing the topics that are more appropriate to the therapy. When conducting conference calls with couples or families (perhaps as a kind of therapy session on the phone because of access difficulties), it is easier for quieter or more avoidant members to escape participation. The therapist would not have access to visual cues, and a client who would never leave a therapy office during a session might find it easier to hang up the phone. Therapists who accept after-hours telephone calls should be cautious about speaking with one member of a couple or family when others are not participating in the conversation or if there is a marked imbalance in the time spent talking to individual family members. These situations may lead to suspicion of the therapist having "favorites" or keeping secrets, even if that is not the case. As the saying goes, one should avoid both impropriety and the appearance of impropriety. It is also important to realize that contacts with clients outside the office increase the chance that the therapist will interact with friends and family who are associated with the clients but are not in treatment. For example, a family friend may inquire about the status of therapy for the family or may ask the therapist what to do about suspicious bruises seen on one of the children in the family. It is important to be clear with those individuals (ideally, early in the conversation) that client information will not be revealed and to explain to them issues that must be reported (e.g., information about child or elder abuse, or about clients' imminent danger to selves or others).

Provide the Highest Standard of Care: Competency and Empiricism

The APA ethics code (1992, p. 1599) states, "Psychologists work to develop a valid and reliable body of scientific knowledge based on research," that they "maintain knowledge of relevant scientific and professional information related to the services they render, and they recognize the need for ongoing education." In other words, psychologists are ethically bound to produce and use empirical data. Science should inform the practice of psychology in all domains, including teaching, supervision, and psychotherapy. Fortunately, couple and family therapy boasts a large and growing research literature to inform treatment decisions.

The empirical support for couple therapy has grown substantially in the past 30 years (Baucom & Hoffman, 1986; Baucom, Shoham, Mueser, Daiuto, & Stickle, 1998; Chambless et al., 1996; Christensen & Heavey, 1999; Fruzzetti & Jacobson, 1991). Traditional behavioral couple therapy[1] (Jacobson & Margolin, 1979) has received extensive empirical support; and both emotionally focused couples therapy (Greenberg & Johnson, 1988; Johnson & Greenberg, 1985) and insight-oriented therapy (Snyder & Wills, 1989; Snyder, Wills, & Grady-Fletcher, 1991) have shown promising results as couple therapies. Although family therapies in general have not received as consistent or rigorous empirical support, several types of family therapies do show improvement for treated families and individuals (Fruzzetti & Jacobson, 1991).

To demonstrate competence in the treatment of couples and families, therapists must be familiar with the research literature in these areas. This competence can be maintained by up-to-date monitoring of empirically supported assessments and interventions, through data-informed workshops, and through conferences in which research plays a central role. Unfortunately, it is clear that the proportion of couple and family therapists who deliver evidence-based services is not higher than that of individual therapists.

RECOMMENDATIONS
AND CONCLUSIONS

Butler & Gardner (2001) note that therapists are not always adept at spotting their own vulnerabilities to exploiting clients. When selecting the most appropriate choice among available alternatives in an ethical dilemma, it is important to consider several factors, all of which are related to the basic ethical principles noted earlier. Foremost among these considerations are potential client vulnerabilities, such as how the diagnosed problems will affect decision making, the client's history with relationships, and his or her ability to understand choices (especially when conducting therapy with children or cognitively compromised clients). It is also important to determine how a client will benefit (or be harmed) by a decision, relative to the therapist.

Therapists should be thoughtful about how decisions will affect the past, present, and future of therapy. In this way, therapists can make solid commitments about their future responses, and many decisions about how a therapist will act in a given situation (e.g., seeing a client at a party) will have been made before the situation even occurs. It is critical that therapists share their policies with clients during the first session and that discussion about potentially harmful events is encouraged throughout the therapy process.

In addition to consulting ethical guidelines, therapists will benefit from peer consultation and supervision to obtain external professional feedback about potential consequences of decisions. It is also useful to review case examples, such as those provided in the *AAMFT Casebook* (Brock, 1998). Although these may not mirror the specific problem a therapist is grappling with, there may be clear parallels that can aid in decision making and may help establish benchmarks for appropriate ethical practice. It is often helpful to dialogue with local and national ethics committees when interpretations of codes are unclear or when other means have not satisfactorily resolved the issue at hand. Similarly, legal resources and issues may also inform treatment decisions. Although concerns about malpractice and liability can interfere with common sense and good clinical judgment, it may be worthwhile to consider legal perspectives in some situations. Laws represent public values and precedents regarding professional practice and as such can provide guidance from the broader community (Butler & Gardner, 2001). Thus, it may be important or necessary to contact legal representatives before making ethical decisions.

But we must remember what Lazarus (1994) stated: "One of the worst professional or ethical violations is that of permitting current risk-management principles to take precedence over humane interventions" (p. 260). Understanding and embracing basic ethical principles may be as valuable or more valuable than trying to understand ethics from available guidelines for behavior that may be out of context, and it will lead to the provision of excellent, ethical couple and family services.

NOTE

1. Traditional behavioral couple therapy is often referred to as *behavioral marital therapy* (BMT), and indeed nearly all the subjects studied empirically have been legally married couples (Baucom et al., 1998).

REFERENCES

American Association for Marriage and Family Therapy. (1998). AAMFT code of ethics. *Family Therapy News, 29,* 10-11.

American Psychiatric Association. (1994). *Diagnostic and statistical manual of mental disorders* (4th ed.). Washington, DC: Author.

American Psychological Association. (1992). Ethical principles of psychologists and code of conduct. *American Psychologist, 47,* 1597-1611.

Anderson, J. R., & Barret, B. (Eds.). (2001). *Ethics in HIV-related psychotherapy: Clinical decision making in complex cases.* Washington, DC: American Psychological Association.

Baucom, D. H., & Hoffman, J. A. (1986). The effectiveness of marital therapy: Current status and application to the clinical setting. In N. S. Jacobson & A. S. Gurman (Eds.), *Clinical handbook of marital therapy* (pp. 597-620). New York: Guilford.

Baucom, D. H., Shoham, V., Mueser, K. T., Daiuto, A. D., & Stickle, T. R. (1998). Empirically supported couple and family interventions for marital distress and adult mental health problems. *Journal of Consulting and Clinical Psychology, 66,* 53-88.

Bersoff, D. N. (1994). Explicit ambiguity: The 1992 ethics code as an oxymoron. *Professional Psychology: Research and Practice, 25,* 382-387.

Bersoff, D. N., & Koeppl, P. M. (1993). The relation between ethical codes and moral principles. *Ethics and Behavior, 3,* 345-357.

Birchler, G. R., & Schwartz, L. (1994). Marital dyads. In M. Hersen & Samuel M. Turner (Eds.), *Diagnostic interviewing* (2nd ed., pp. 277-303). New York: Plenum.

Brock, G. W. (1998). *American association for marriage and family therapy casebook.* Washington, DC: American Association for Marriage and Family Therapy.

Brodsky, A. M. (1985). Sex between therapists and patients: Ethical grey areas. *Psychotherapy in Private Practice, 14,* 57-62.

Butler, M. H., & Gardner, B. C. (2001). Ethics and the ideal helping relationship: Response to Hill and Mamalakis. *Family Relations, 50,* 209-214.

Catalano, S. (1997). The challenges of clinical practice in small or rural communities. Case studies in managing dual relationships in and outside of therapy. *Journal of Contemporary Psychotherapy, 27,* 23-35.

Chambless, D. L., Sanderson, W. C., Shoham, V., Johnson, S. B., Pope, K. S., Crits-Christoph, P., Baker, M., Johnson, B., Woody, S. R., Sue, S., Beutler, L., Williams, D. A., & McCurry, S. (1996). An update on empirically valid therapies. *Clinical Psychologist, 49,* 5-18.

Christensen, A., & Heavey, C. L. (1999). Intervention in couples. *Annual Review of Psychology, 50,* 165-190.

Christensen, A., & Jacobson, N. S. (1998). Acceptance and change in couples therapy. In K. S. Dobson & K. D. Craig (Eds.), *Empirically supported therapies: Best practice in professional psychology* (pp. 133-156). Thousand Oaks, CA: Sage.

Ford, G. G. (2001). *Ethical reasoning in the mental health professions.* Boca Raton, FL: CRC.

Fruzzetti, A. E. (1996). Causes and consequences: Individual distress in the context of couple interactions. *Journal of Consulting and Clinical Psychology, 64,* 1192-1201.

Fruzzetti, A. E., & Jacobson, N. S. (1991). Marital and family therapy. In M. Hersen, A. Kazdin, & A. Bellack (Eds.), *The clinical psychology handbook* (2nd ed., pp. 643-666). New York: Pergamon.

Gabbard, G. O. (1994). Reconsidering the American Psychological Association's policy on sex with former patients: Is it justifiable? *Professional Psychology: Research and Practice, 25,* 329-335.

Greenberg, L. S., & Johnson, S. M. (1988). *Emotionally focused couples therapy.* New York: Guilford.

Haas, L. J., Malouf, J. L., & Mayerson, N. H. (1986). Ethical dilemmas in psychological practice: Results of a national survey. *Professional Psychology: Research and Practice, 17,* 316-321.

Hill, M. R., & Mamalakis, P. M. (2001). Family therapists and religious communities: Negotiating dual relationships. *Family Relations, 50,* 199-208.

Jacobson, N. S., & Margolin, G. (1979). *Marital therapy: Strategies based on social learning and behavior exchange principles.* New York: Brunner/Mazel.

Johnson, S. M., & Greenberg, L. S. (1985). Differential effects of experiential and problem-solving interventions in resolving marital conflict. *Journal of Consulting and Clinical Psychology, 53,* 175-184.

Kagle, J. D., & Grebelhausen, P. N. (1994). Dual relationships and professional boundaries. *Social Work, 39,* 213-220.

Kaslow, F. (1993). Relational diagnoses: Past, present and future. *American Journal of Family Therapy, 21,* 195-204.

Kitchner, R. (1980). Ethical relativism and behavior therapy. *Journal of Consulting and Clinical Psychology, 48,* 1-7.

Lakin, M. (1994). Morality in group and family therapies: Multiperson therapies and the 1992 ethics code. *Professional Psychology: Research and Practice, 25,* 344-348.

Lazarus, A. A. (1994). How certain boundaries and ethics diminish therapeutic effectiveness. *Ethics & Behavior, 4,* 255-261.

Lazarus, J. A. (1992). Sex with former patients is almost always unethical. *American Journal of Psychiatry, 149,* 855-857.

Linehan, M. M. (1993). *Cognitive behavioral treatment of borderline personality disorder.* New York: Guilford.

Magee, R. D. (1997). Ethical issues in couple therapy. In D. T. Marsh & R. D. Magee (Eds.), *Ethical and legal issues in professional practice with families* (pp. 112-126). New York: John Wiley.

Mamalakis, P. M. (2001). Evaluating potential dual relationships: A response to Butler and Gardner. *Family Relations, 50,* 214.

Margolin, G. (1982). Ethical and legal considerations in marital and family therapy. *American Psychologist, 37,* 788-801.

Margolin, G. (1986). Ethical issues in marital therapy. In N. S. Jacobson & A. S. Gurman (Eds.), *Clinical handbook of marital therapy* (pp. 621-638). New York: Guilford.

Margolin, G. (1998). Ethical issues in marital therapy. In R. M. Anderson Jr., T. L. Needels, & H. V. Hall (Eds.), *Avoiding ethical misconduct in psychology specialty areas* (pp. 78-94). Springfield, IL: Charles C Thomas.

Marsh, D. T. (1997). Ethical issues in professional practice with families. In D. T. Marsh & R. D. Magee (Eds.), *Ethical and legal issues in professional practice with families* (pp. 3-26). New York: John Wiley.

Pope, K. S. (1991). Dual relationships in psychotherapy. *Ethics and Behavior, 1,* 21-34.

Pope, K. S., & Vetter, V. A. (1991). Prior therapist-patient sexual involvement among patients seen by psychologists. *Psychotherapy, 28,* 429-438.

Pope, K. S., & Vetter, V. A. (1992). Ethical dilemmas encountered by members of the American Psychological Association: A national survey. *American Psychologist, 47,* 397-411.

Schank, J. A., & Skovholt, T. M. (1997). Dual-relationship dilemmas of rural and small-community psychologists. *Professional Psychology: Research and Practice, 29,* 44-49.

Snyder, D. K., & Wills, R. M. (1989). Behavioral vs. insight oriented marital therapy: A controlled comparative outcome study. *Journal of Consulting and Clinical Psychology, 57,* 39-46.

Snyder, D. K., Wills, R. M., & Grady-Fletcher, A. (1991). Long-term effectiveness of behavioral versus insight-oriented marital therapy: A 4-year follow-up study. *Journal of Consulting and Clinical Psychology, 59,* 138-141.

Williams, M. H. (1992). Exploitation and inference: Mapping the damage from therapist-patient sexual involvement. *American Psychologist, 47,* 412-421.

CHAPTER 24

Ethics And The School Psychologist

SUSAN JACOB
Central Michigan University

S chool psychology is the branch of psychology concerned with the application of psychological knowledge to the problems of schools and school children. There are approximately 22,000 school psychologists in the United States. Most are employed in the public schools, but some work in private schools, hospitals, mental health agencies, correctional facilities, or private practice (Fagan & Wise, 1994). The primary professional responsibility of the school psychologist is to promote the mental health and optimal learning of school children. Surveys of practitioners have found that they typically spend the greatest proportion of their time in psychoeducational assessment and consultation for pupils with learning and behavior problems (Reschly & Wilson, 1995). Practitioners also provide direct intervention services (academic or social skills training, behavioral intervention, counseling, parent training, crisis intervention), problem-solving consultation to teachers and parents, systems/organizational consultation, and research and evaluation services. Most practitioners in the schools

were trained at the specialist degree level; about 20% hold a doctoral degree (Reschly & Wilson, 1995).

SOURCES OF GUIDANCE

Ethical Codes

Two professional organizations represent school psychologists: the American Psychological Association (APA) and the National Association of School Psychologists (NASP). APA's Division 16 (Division of School Psychology) is largely composed of those who hold doctorates. NASP was formed in 1969 to better represent the school psychology practitioner, and it now has more than 17,000 members. Both organizations have developed ethical codes and professional standards for the delivery of services, and both require formal ethics coursework in their standards for accreditation of training programs.

Ethical codes are based on a consensus of association members about what constitutes appropriate professional conduct. NASP's "Principles for Professional Ethics," or PPE (most recently revised in 1997), were developed to provide guidelines specifically for school psychologists employed in the schools or working in private practice. NASP's code focuses on protecting the well-being of the student/client but also prescribes conduct to protect the rights and welfare of the parent, teachers, and other consumers of school psychological services. The code provides guidelines in the following areas: professional competence; professional relationships and responsibilities to students, parents, the school, the community, related professions, and other school psychologists; advocacy of the rights and welfare of the student/client; professional responsibilities in assessment and intervention; use of materials and technology; research, publication, and presentation; reporting data and sharing results; and professional responsibilities in private practice settings.

APA's Ethical Principles of Psychologists and Code of Conduct (APA, 1992), consists of general principles and specific ethical standards to protect the welfare of individuals and groups with whom psychologists work. APA's code of ethics differs from NASP's ethical principles in that the APA code was developed for psychologists with training in diverse specialty areas (e.g., clinical, industrial-organizational, school) who work in a number of different settings (private practice, industry, hospitals and clinics, public schools, university teaching and research).

Professional Standards

Both NASP (1997) and APA (1981) have developed professional standards for the delivery of school psychological services. Professional standards differ from ethical codes in both scope and intent. The standards represent a consensus of trainers and practitioners about roles and duties of school psychologists, desirable conditions for the effective delivery of services, and the nature of competent professional practice. NASP and APA seek to ensure that members abide by their respective ethical codes and will investigate and adjudicate code violations. In contrast, professional standards provide a model for excellence in the delivery of quality comprehensive school psychological services, and it is recognized that not all school psychologists or school psychological service units will be able to meet every standard outlined (NASP, 1997).

FOUR BROAD ETHICAL THEMES

School psychologists consider the student to be their primary responsibility (NASP, 1997, IV, A, #1). Concern for protecting the rights and welfare of students is "the top priority in determining services" (NASP, 1997, IV, A, #2). However, practitioners also strive to protect the rights of parents, teachers, and other recipients of services (NASP, 1997, IV, A, #1).

A number of writers have identified general principles that provide the foundation for ethical choices in psychology (e.g., Bersoff & Koeppl, 1993; Kitchener, 1986). Jacob-Timm and Hartshorne (1998) identified four broad themes or principles underlying ethical choices in school psychology. Their four principles were adapted from the Canadian Code of Ethics for Psychologists (Canadian Psychological Association, 1991). The first principle was *respect for the dignity of persons* (welfare of client). Consistent with this principle, school psychologists value client autonomy and safeguard the client's right to self-determination, respect client privacy and the confidentiality of disclosures, and are committed to fairness and nondiscrimination in interactions with the client and others. The second broad principle was *responsible caring*. According to this principle, school psychologists are obligated to work within the boundaries of their professional competence and accept responsibility for their actions. The third broad principle was *integrity in professional relationships*. School psychologists are candid and honest about the nature and scope of the services they have to offer and work in full cooperation with other professionals to meet the needs of children in the schools. The fourth broad principle was *responsibility to community and society*. School psychologists recognize that their profession exists within the context of society and work to ensure that the science of psychology is used to promote the welfare of all school children and to improve schools, neighborhoods, and communities.

LEGAL REGULATION OF SCHOOL PSYCHOLOGY

Many aspects of school psychological practice are regulated by federal and state law. This is one of the special challenges of school psychology. School psychologists are ethically obligated to know and respect federal and state law and school policies. Practitioners also must be knowledgeable about law to safeguard the rights of pupils and their parents in the school setting.

The U.S. Constitution does not refer to education as a duty of the federal government. Under the Tenth Amendment, the duty to educate children and the power to do so have been left to the states. As education is a duty of the states, the federal government avoided involvement in public school matters for many years. Beginning in the 1950s, however, the federal courts became involved in school-related issues because of school actions that violated the constitutional rights of pupils (e.g., *Brown v. Board of Education,* 1954). Court decisions since *Brown* have sent a clear message that public schools must

provide equal educational opportunity for all school children, regardless of race, color, national origin, native language, gender, and handicapping condition. Furthermore, a state may not deny a child's right to a public school education without some sort of fair, impartial due process procedures to safeguard the child from arbitrary infringement of that right. School psychologists have an important role to play in ensuring equal educational opportunity for all pupils, including those with mental health, behavior, and learning problems.

The U.S. Congress also avoided involvement in matters relating to public school education for many years. Since the mid-1960s, however, Congress has accepted the proposition that the federal government must ensure a basic floor of opportunity in public education. Congress has shaped educational policies and practices by offering monies to states contingent on compliance with federal mandates or by threatening to remove federal funding from schools that fail to comply with federal policies. Three important federal laws are the Individuals with Disabilities Education Act of 1990 (IDEA), Section 504 of The Rehabilitation Act of 1973, and the Family Educational Rights and Privacy Act of 1974 (FERPA). IDEA (Part B) allocates funds to states that provide free and appropriate education to all children with disabilities as defined by the law. To receive monies, each state must have developed a plan to assure that every child with disabilities receives special education and related services in conformance with an individualized education program. The individualized education program is developed by a team that includes the pupil's parents. In accordance with IDEA, pupils with disabilities must be educated in the least-restrictive (most normal) setting feasible. IDEA (Part C) also provides funds to states that offer early intervention programs for infants and toddlers with known or suspected disabilities in conformance with an individualized family service plan.

Section 504 of The Rehabilitation Act of 1973 is civil rights legislation that specifically prohibits discrimination against any otherwise qualified individual solely on the basis of a handicapping condition in any program or activity receiving federal financial assistance. School districts must comply with antidiscrimination legislation if they receive any federal funds for any purpose. Section 504 requires schools to make special accommodations for students with handicaps to ensure that they are afforded educational opportunity equal to their nonhandicapped peers. *Handicap* under Section 504 is more broadly defined than *disability* under IDEA; consequently, a number of pupils who are not eligible for special education under IDEA are protected by 504.

FERPA (1974) was enacted to protect confidentiality of school records and ensure parent access to the records of their own children. Under FERPA, no federal funds will be made available to schools unless they adhere to the pupil record-keeping requirements outlined in the law.

School practitioners must have a sound working knowledge of IDEA, Section 504, and FERPA. School practice is also highly regulated by state law. Practitioners must also be familiar with state law and school district policies pertinent to practice.

RELATIONSHIP BETWEEN ETHICS AND LAW

Professional ethics is a combination of broad ethical principles and rules that guide the conduct of a practitioner in his or her professional interactions with others. Professional associations such as APA and NASP develop ethical codes to protect the welfare of consumers of psychological services and to maintain the public trust in psychology. When practitioners violate professional ethical codes, they may face sanctions by their professional organizations. *Law* is a body of rules of conduct prescribed by the state that have binding legal force. Failure to comply with law can result in legal action against the practitioner (e.g., malpractice suits) or the school, and possible loss of certification or licensure to practice.

Both APA and NASP ethical codes require practitioners to know and respect law. Ethical behavior must conform with the law, not defy it (Ballantine, 1979). Professional ethical codes are generally viewed as requiring decisions that are "more correct or more stringent" than required by law (Ballantine, 1979, p. 636). APA and NASP require practitioners to adhere to ethical codes when ethical codes establish a higher standard than required by law. When ethical codes and law conflict, psychologists are obligated to work to resolve the conflict through legal channels (APA, 1992, 1.02; NASP, 1997, III, D, #2; E, #5).

In the delivery of school psychological services, practitioners may face decisions involving conflicts between ethics and law. In unusual circumstances, a practitioner may believe that conforming to law will violate fundamental ethical principles. As Ballantine has observed (1979), society may be forgiving of the practitioner who engages in an illegal act because of the dictates of his or her conscience. However, practitioners who choose to violate law should do so with full awareness of the possible sanctions. In a courtroom, law is supreme (Woody, 1998). Although there are no simple solutions to such dilemmas, use of a systematic decision-making model or procedure may assist the practitioner in making informed, well-reasoned choices (Keith-Spiegel & Koocher, 1985; Tymchuk, 1986). Decision-making models encourage careful consideration of the ethical and legal dimensions of a situation;

consultation with colleagues, review of available guidelines; and evaluation of the rights, responsibilities, and welfare of all affected parties before making a decision. Use of a systematic decision-making procedure also will allow the practitioner to describe how a decision was made. This may afford some protection when difficult decisions come under the scrutiny of others.

It is often difficult to interpret ethical principles as they relate to the delivery of psychological services in public school settings. The remaining portion of this chapter focuses on privacy and informed consent, confidentiality, and record keeping; ethical issues associated with psychoeducational assessment; identification, placement, and instruction for pupils with special needs; and behavioral interventions.

PRIVACY AND INFORMED CONSENT, CONFIDENTIALITY, AND RECORD KEEPING

Privacy and Informed Consent

Privacy has been defined as "the freedom of individuals to choose for themselves the time and the circumstances under which and the extent to which their beliefs, behaviors, and opinions are to be shared or withheld from others" (Siegel, 1979, p. 251). The school child's right to privacy is a legal and an ethical issue. Statutory and case law have recognized the need to balance the interest of the state (school) in fulfilling its duty to maintain order, ensure pupil safety, and educate children, with the personal freedoms and rights generally afforded citizens. Consequently, in the school setting, students do not have the full range of privacy rights afforded adult citizens, but they are not without privacy protections. Federal laws (FERPA, Protection of Pupil Rights Amendment of 1978, IDEA) protect pupil and family privacy by requiring informed parent

consent prior to the gathering of certain types of personal information, and by requiring informed parent consent prior to disclosure of information about a pupil to agencies or individuals outside the school setting.

Respect for client privacy is also an ethical mandate. Consistent with the general principle of respect for the dignity of persons and the valuing of autonomy, school psychologists are obligated to respect pupils' (or other clients') right to self-determine the circumstances under which they disclose private information. Furthermore, every effort is made to minimize intrusions on privacy (APA, 1992, Principle D, 5.03; NASP, 1997, III, B, #1). School psychologists do not seek or store personal information about pupils, parents, teachers, or others that is not needed in the provision of services.

Ethical codes, professional standards, and law are consistent in requiring parent consent (or the consent of an adult student) for school actions that may result in a significant intrusion on personal or family privacy beyond what might be expected in the course of ordinary classroom and school activities (Corrao & Melton, 1988). IDEA and the Protection of Pupil Rights Amendment of 1978 indicate "clear Congressional intent to require parent consent to school-based psychological services" (Corrao & Melton, 1988, p. 381). Consequently, with the exception of unusual situations, informed consent is obtained prior to the provision of psychological services (NASP, 1997, A, #4; C, #2). In the delivery of psychological services in the schools, as elsewhere, the three key elements of informed consent are that it must be knowing, competent, and voluntary. *Knowing* means the individual giving consent has a clear understanding of what it is they are consenting to. *Competent* means legally competent to give consent. In law, adults are presumed to be competent, whereas minors are presumed to be not capable of making legally binding decisions (Bersoff, 1983); consequently, consent typically is sought from the parent or guardian of a minor child prior to the provision of services. Parent consent may be bypassed in emergency situations (e.g., when the student is suicidal), and in some states, minors may self-refer for psychological assistance independent of parent notice or consent (see discussion below). The third element of informed consent is that it must be *voluntary;* that is, consent is obtained without coercion or undue enticement. Federal law outlines specific requirements for informed consent for psychological evaluation of students with suspected disabilities (IDEA) and for the release of information from school records (FERPA). To safeguard the right of pupils with disabilities to special education services, IDEA also outlines procedures for schools to follow when parents refuse to consent to assessment of a child with a suspected disability.

Although minors are not generally seen as legally competent to consent autonomously to (or refuse) psychological services in the schools, practitioners are ethically obligated to respect the dignity, autonomy, and self-determination of their pupil-clients. However, at times it is necessary to balance the child's rights to privacy and self-determination against concerns for the welfare of the child. In the delivery of school services, it is ethical to proceed without the child's explicit assent if the service is considered to be of direct benefit to the child. School psychologists do not seek the child's assent if refusal will not be honored (Corrao & Melton, 1988).

Practitioners have an ethical obligation to inform pupil-clients of the scope and nature of psychological services whether or not children are given a choice about participating in the services (NASP, 1997, III, B, #2). Also, consistent with the principle of respect for autonomy, practitioners permit and encourage pupil-client involvement in intervention

decisions (e.g., selection of goals) to the maximum extent appropriate to the child and the situation (Weithorn, 1983). A child's participation in intervention decisions may lead to enhanced motivation for treatment, an increased sense of personal responsibility for self-care, greater treatment compliance, and reduced rates of early treatment termination (Holmes & Urie, 1975; Kaser-Boyd, Adelman, & Taylor, 1985; Weithorn, 1983). However, psychologists must guard against overwhelming children with choices they do not wish to make for themselves.

Self-referrals for counseling pose a particularly challenging dilemma for school psychologists. Students who are minors may wish to see psychologists on the condition that their parents not be notified. A reasonable, ethically sound approach to this situation was suggested by C. Osip (as quoted in Canter, 1989). Osip recommends allowing one precounseling screening session without parental permission. This precounseling meeting can serve to ensure that the pupil is safe and not in danger. At this time, the school psychologist can discuss the need for parental consent for further counseling sessions, offer to contact the parent on behalf of the student, or offer to meet jointly with the student and parents to discuss consent and ensure ongoing parent support.

In some states, minors are given the right to access to certain types of treatment (usually limited to conditions of a medical nature) without parent notice or consent. School practitioners need to consult their state laws to determine whether minors are given the right to seek psychological treatment independent of parental notice or consent in their state (Corrao & Melton, 1988). If state laws are silent on this issue, practitioners may wish to work with school administrators to develop a district policy that allows minors to been seen for a precounseling session by the psychologist independent of parent notice or consent.

Confidentiality and Privileged Communication

School psychologists are ethically obligated as follows:

> [To] respect the confidentiality of information obtained during their professional work. Information is revealed only with the informed consent of the client, or the client's parent or legal guardian, except in those situations in which failure to release information would result in clear danger to the client or others. (NASP, 1997, III, A, #9)

The interpretation of the principle of confidentiality as it relates to the delivery of psychological services in the school setting is a complicated matter. However, one clear guideline emerges from the literature on confidentiality in the school setting. School psychologists define the parameters of confidentiality at the onset of offering services (NASP, 1997, A, #11; also APA, 1992, Standard 5.01; Davis & Sandoval, 1982). The parameters of the promise of confidentiality will vary depending on the nature of the services offered.

Direct Services to the Pupil-Client

The provision of direct services to the student means that the practitioner works with the student directly (e.g., individual counseling) and there is little or no collaboration with others. The initial interview with the student/client "should include a direct and candid discussion of the limits that may exist with respect to any confidences communicated in the relationship" (Keith-Spiegel & Koocher, 1985, pp. 57–58; also APA, 1992, Standard 5.01; NASP, 1997, III, A, #11). Much has been written about the importance of confidentiality for building and maintaining the trust essential to a helping relationship (Siegel, 1979; Watson & Levine, 1989). However, as Taylor and Adelman (1989)

have observed, the promise of confidentiality can limit the psychologist's ability to help when the client is a minor child. Consequently, school psychologists must weigh a number of factors in deciding the boundaries of a promise of confidentiality (e.g., age and maturity of the student-client, self-referral or referral by others, reason for referral). Whatever the parameters, the circumstances under which the psychologist might share confidences with others must be clear. Discussion of the limits of confidentiality does not tend to limit client self-disclosure if self-disclosure is verbally encouraged (Muehleman, Pickens, & Robinson, 1985).

In the provision of direct services to the student, there are three situations in which the school psychologist is obligated to share confidential student-client disclosures with others: (a) when the student requests it, (b) when there is a situation involving danger to the student or others (e.g., suspected child abuse or neglect, a student who is danger to self or others), and (c) when there is a legal obligation to testify in a court of law (Hummel, Talbutt, & Alexander, 1985).

Consistent with court rulings (e.g., *Tarasoff v. Regents of California*, 1976) and ethical codes (APA, 1992, Standard 5.05; NASP, 1997, III, A, #9), school psychologists are legally and ethically obligated to disclose confidential information if the disclosure is necessary to protect the client or others from harm. Because of their work setting and clientele, school psychologists must place a high priority on parent involvement and recognize the legal obligation of school personnel to protect the health and safety of all students under school supervision. Court cases (e.g., *Eisel v. Board of Education of Montgomery County*, 1991) have been interpreted to suggest that school personnel have little discretion regarding whether to contact parents once information suggests a potential student suicide; parents must be warned when there is any reason to believe a pupil has suicidal intentions. Also, when a student is determined to be a threat to another pupil, the intended victim and the parents of the intended victim must be notified *(Phillis P. v. Claremont Unified School District,* 1986). School professionals also are legally required to report suspected child abuse to a child protection agency.

Thus, school practitioners are obligated to share student confidences with others in situations involving potential student suicide or other self-injurious behavior, students who are a threat to others, and suspected child abuse. In addition, students may report any number of behaviors that although not immediately dangerous, have the potential to be so (e.g., substance abuse, eating disorders, risky sexual behaviors). Determining an appropriate course of action in such situations can be difficult. However, if it becomes apparent in working with a student-client that confidentiality must be broken, the decision to divulge confidential information should be discussed with the student-client if possible.

School practitioners also may be obligated to disclose confidential information in a legal proceeding. Privileged communication refers to the right of the client (the parent or guardian of a minor child) to prevent disclosure of confidential information in a legal proceeding. The client may voluntarily waive privilege, and then the psychologist must provide the relevant testimony. Practitioners need to consult their state laws to determine whether their state grants privileged communication to school psychologists. Even in states that do so, the court may not view all disclosures to the psychologist as privileged, and the judge may waive privilege during a court proceeding to ensure justice. The issue of whether communication between the school psychologist and client has privileged communication status can raise difficult legal

questions (see Glosoff, Herlihy, Herlihy, & Spence, 1997); practitioners should consult their school attorneys when questions arise.

Collaboration

School psychologists may provide direct services to the student-client. However, they typically work in collaboration with teachers, parents, and others to assist the student, a situation that complicates the translation of the principle of confidentiality into appropriate action. In collaboration, the individuals involved generally carry joint responsibility for assisting the pupil (Hansen, Himes, & Meier, 1990), and information to assist the student will most likely be shared by those involved in the collaborative effort. At the onset of offering services, the psychologist needs a clear prior agreement about confidentiality and the limits of confidentiality with those involved in the collaborative effort (NASP, 1997, III, A, #4, #11; B, #2). If information received in a confidential situation is subsequently disclosed to assist the teacher or parent in meeting the needs of a student, it is recommended that *only generalizations, not specific confidences* are shared (Davis & Sandoval, 1982; also NASP, 1997, III, A, #10). Furthermore, generalizations are shared with others involved in the collaborative effort only if those generalizations "are essential to the understanding and resolution" of the student's difficulties (Davis & Sandoval, 1982, p. 548).

Teacher Consultation

In providing consultation services, the school psychologists work with teachers or other school professionals to aid them in professional functioning (e.g., classroom management, working with a difficult student). The parameters of confidentiality must be discussed at the onset of the delivery of services, and at a minimum, teachers should clearly understand what and how information will be used, by whom, and for what purposes (Newman, 1993). The psychologist also should have a prior agreement about those parameters with others in the school setting (APA, 1992, Standard 5.06; NASP, 1997, III, A, #11).

In general, in consultation with the teacher or other school staff, the guarantees of client confidentiality apply to the consultant–consultee relationship (Fanibanda, 1976). All that is said between the psychologist and consultee is kept confidential by the psychologist, unless the consultee requests that information be disclosed to others (Davis & Sandoval, 1982). Violation of confidentiality in consultation with teachers or other staff is likely to result in a loss of trust in the school psychologist and impair his or her ability to work with the consultee and others.

In providing consultative services to teachers, ethical responsibility requires that limits to the promise of confidentiality be identified (Conoley & Conoley, 1982; Hughes, 1986; Newman, 1993). Thus, for example, the practitioner may want to ensure a prior agreement that the consultant may breach confidentiality in those unusual instances in which the consultee "chronically and stubbornly" persists in unethical activities (Conoley & Conoley, 1982, p. 216). However, "Before breaching confidentiality, the consultant must have expended all resources at influencing the consultee to take collaborative action" (Hughes, 1986, p. 491). Such a breach of confidentiality should be given careful consideration and would be appropriate only when the consultee's actions are harmful or potentially harmful to the student-client. "The consultee's approach toward the client actually must be detrimental to the child rather than a less than optimal approach" (Hughes, 1986, p. 491). The consultant is obligated to discuss the need to disclose confidential information with the consultee prior to disclosure.

Record Keeping in the Schools

In accordance with FERPA, no federal funds will be made available to schools unless they adhere to the pupil record-keeping procedures outlined in the law. FERPA record-keeping guidelines were developed to ensure confidentiality of pupil records and parent access to school records concerning their children. FERPA grants parents access to all official school records of their children, the right to challenge the accuracy of records, and the right to a hearing when disagreements arise regarding the accuracy of records. Pupil records are to be available only to those in the school setting with legitimate educational interests, and parent consent must be obtained before records are released to agencies or individuals outside the school.

Working within the boundaries of FERPA poses special ethical-legal challenges for school practitioners. *Education records* are defined as any records maintained by the school (or its agent) that are directly related to the student. Under FERPA, parents have the right to review school psychological records. Parental separation, divorce, and custody do not affect this right unless there is a legally binding document specifically revoking access. Consequently, in situations involving separation and divorce, the practitioner must take care to inform the custodial parent that the noncustodial parent also has access to school psychological records regarding the child. Practitioners must take care not to store information that is intrusive of parental privacy. In decisions regarding storage of sensitive family information, practitioners also need to remember that under FERPA, students have access to their own records once they reach the age of majority.

The psychologist's private notes are excluded from the definition of education records as long as the information contained within the notes is not shared with anyone except a substitute. However, psychological test answer sheets and protocols that contain personally identifiable information are considered to be part of a pupil's education records. Policy letters (FERPA Office, 1986; Hehir, 1993; Irvin, 1979); legal opinion (Bersoff & Hofer, 1990); and at least one court ruling (*John K. and Mary K. v. Board of Education for School District #5, Cook County,* 1987) suggest that test protocols cannot be considered to be private notes.

The parent access requirements of FERPA consequently conflict with the school psychologist's obligation to maintain test security. Practitioners may be able to avoid parent requests to inspect test protocols by (a) establishing a good collaborative relationship early in the assessment process by explaining the conflict between their professional obligation to maintain test security and the parents' right to review records and (b) by communicating assessment findings in a manner that satisfies the parents' need for information about their child (Jacob-Timm & Hartshorne, 1998). If, nevertheless, parents do request to see their child's test protocols, FERPA requirements are met if the school allows the parent to examine and discuss the protocols under school supervision (Irvin, 1979). APA's Division 16 Ethics Committee recommended that this inspection include a discussion of sample test items and responses to them. This should be done under the supervision of the school psychologist or other appropriately trained persons, and the parent should not be allowed to copy down questions and answers (Martin, 1985). Psychologists have no obligation under FERPA to disclose "nonidentifying information" to parents. Thus, it is appropriate to deny parent requests to inspect test materials (e.g., manuals and stimulus materials) that are

not part of the child's individual performance record (Hehir, 1993).

PSYCHOEDUCATIONAL ASSESSMENT

Prior to the passage of the Education of All Handicapped Children Act of 1975 (now IDEA), many children were institutionalized on the basis of a single IQ score. Racial and ethnic minority children were often misclassified as mentally retarded, placed in inferior education programs, and segregated from the mainstream. In an effort to protect school children from misclassification, special education law encourages schools to attempt to remediate learning and behavior problems in the regular classroom setting before referring a child for psychological assessment. Ethically, a child should not be exposed to the risk of misdiagnosis unless deficiencies in instruction have first been ruled out (Messick, 1984). IDEA also outlines standards with regard to the content and process of assessment of pupils with suspected disabilities to protect them from misclassification.

Five broad ethical-legal concerns emerge from an analysis of ethical codes, professional standards, and federal laws that address psychological assessment: Psychologists must strive to ensure that psychoeducational evaluations are *multifaceted, comprehensive, fair, valid,* and *useful* (Jacob-Timm & Hartshorne, 1998).

Multifaceted. Psychoeducational assessment of a child with learning or behavior difficulties must be based on a variety of different types of information from different sources. No decisions should be made on the basis of a single test score (IDEA, 1990, 34 C.F.R. § 300.532).

Comprehensive. Children with learning or behavior difficulties must be assessed "in all areas related to the suspected disability, including, if appropriate, health, vision, hearing, social and emotional status, general intelligence, academic performance, communicative status, and motor abilities" (IDEA, 1990, 34 C.F.R. § 300.532).

Fair. In the selection of assessment tools, psychologists strive to choose the most appropriate instruments and procedures in light of the child's age, gender, native language, disabilities, and socioeconomic and ethnic background (NASP, 1997, IV, B, #1). Regulations implementing IDEA require that tests and other evaluation materials used in the evaluation of children with suspected disabilities "are provided and administered in the child's native language or other mode of communication, unless it is clearly not feasible to do so" (IDEA, 1990, 34 C.F.R. § 300.352).

IDEA also mandates careful selection of assessment procedures for children with sensory, motor, or speech impairments. Regulations implementing the law require the following,

> Tests are selected and administered so as best to ensure that if a test is administered to a child with impaired sensory, manual, or speaking skills, the test results accurately reflect that child's aptitude or achievement level, or whatever other factors the test purports to measure, rather than reflecting the child's impaired sensory, manual, or speaking skills (unless those skills are the factors that the test purports to measure). (IDEA, 1990, 34 C.F.R. § 300.352)

In other words, evaluation procedures must be selected so that a child with disabilities is not penalized on measures of cognitive ability, achievement, and adaptive behavior because of failures due to his or her disability.

Ethical codes, professional standards, and special education law also mandate *nonbiased* assessment of children from minority cultural, ethnic, and racial backgrounds. "Testing and evaluation materials and procedures used for the purposes of evaluation and placement of children with disabilities must be selected and administered so as not to be discriminatory on a racial or cultural basis" (IDEA, 1990, 34 C.F.R. § 300.530; see also NASP, 1997, IV, B, #1). *Test bias* refers to the psychometric adequacy of the instrument itself. Practitioners are obligated to evaluate research evidence indicating whether a test or procedure is equally valid when used with children from differing ethnic or racial backgrounds and choose the fairest and most appropriate instruments available (Coles, 1981; Reynolds & Kaiser, 1990). *Bias in clinical application* refers to fairness in administration, interpretation, and decision making (Messick, 1980; Reynolds & Kaiser, 1990). To minimize bias in interpretation, school psychologists must be keenly sensitive to culture and ethnicity as factors that affect behavior (APA, 1993). *Fairness of consequences* concerns the way in which test results are used. If testing and assessment practices result in children from a particular ethnic group being placed in inferior programs, then the outcomes or consequences of testing are biased and unfair (Reschly, 1997).

Valid. *Standards for Educational and Psychological Testing* (American Educational Research Association, American Psychological Association, & National Council on Measurement in Education, 1985) provides guidelines for psychologists and educators to use in evaluating whether their tests and assessment procedures meet acceptable technical standards. Evaluation of the technical adequacy of assessment instruments and procedures involves consideration of the evidence for test reliability, validity, and the adequacy of the standardization norms. School psychologists are obligated to select tests and other evaluation procedures that meet high professional standards and are valid for the purpose for which they are used (NASP, 1997, IV, B, #2; see also IDEA, 1990). They are also obligated to ensure that instruments are administered and interpreted by qualified examiners in a manner consistent with sound professional practice.

Useful. Evaluation instruments must be selected to provide a profile of the child's strengths and difficulties to aid in instructional planning. "Tests and other evaluation materials include those tailored to assess specific areas of educational need and not merely those that are designed to provide a single general intelligence quotient" (IDEA, 1990, 34 C.F.R. § 300.532). The assessment is planned to ensure that the information gathered will result in maximum feasible assistance to the child (NASP, 1997, IV, B, #2).

School psychological assessment often results in the assignment of a formal diagnostic label. Legally and ethically, practitioners are obligated to ensure that when labels are assigned, they are based on valid assessment procedures and sound professional judgment. When labels are used, "The least stigmatizing labels, consistent with accurate reporting, should always be assigned" (American Educational Research Association, American Psychological Association, & National Council on Measurement in Education, 1985, p. 86).

The school psychologist shares his or her findings through the written report and in conferences with the parent, student, and teacher. In accordance with IDEA and FERPA, parents have access to psychological reports. Consequently, the writer must take into account the fact that reports will be read by professionals and nonprofessionals (Harvey, 1997). Reports should emphasize recommendations and interpretations rather than a simple passing along of test scores (NASP, 1997,IV, E, #3). Practitioners "strive

to propose a set of options which takes into account the values and capabilities of each parent" (NASP, 1997, III, C, #1). Discussion includes recommendations for assisting the student and alternatives associated with each set of plans.

IDENTIFICATION, PLACEMENT, AND INSTRUCTION FOR PUPILS WITH SPECIAL NEEDS

As mentioned, the most important special education law, the Education of All Handicapped Children Act, was passed in 1975, renamed the Individuals with Disabilities Education Act in 1990, and most recently amended in 1997. IDEA, Part B, allocates funds to states that provide a free and appropriate education to all children with disabilities as defined by the law. IDEA, Part C, provides funds to states that offer early intervention programs for infants and toddlers with known or suspected disabilities in conformance with an individualized family service plan.

To qualify for special education and related services under IDEA, Part B, a child must have a disability as outlined in one of the 13 disability categories, and he or she must need special education because of that disability. In accordance with IDEA, a pupil with a disability has the right to a free, individualized, and appropriate education in the least-restrictive (most normal) setting appropriate for the child. Individualized education is achieved through the development of an individualized education program (IEP) for the pupil by a team that includes the parents. The IEP outlines the pupil's annual educational goals and short-term objectives; how the child's progress will be assessed; and the special education, related services, and supplementary aids and services that will be provided. The school is accountable for providing the special instruction and related services outlined in the IEP. Pupils with disabilities also are entitled to an appropriate education. *Appropriate* means the IEP is reasonably designed to confer benefit.

In addition, pupils with disabilities have the right to an education in the least-restrictive environment appropriate for the child. Removal from the regular classroom occurs only when the nature or severity of the disability is such that education in the regular classroom with the use of supplementary aids and services cannot be achieved satisfactorily. IDEA also outlines a number of safeguards to ensure the rights of pupils with disabilities and their parents. For example, parents have a right to mediation or an impartial due process hearing on any matter regarding the identification, evaluation, educational placement, or education program of their child.

School practitioners must also be familiar with Section 504 of the Rehabilitation Act of 1973. Section 504 is antidiscrimination legislation that prohibits schools from discriminating against individuals on the basis of handicapping condition. It does not provide funds to schools, but federal funds can be denied to districts that fail to comply with its requirements. Section 504 requires schools to make accommodations for students with handicaps to ensure that they are afforded educational opportunity equal to their non-handicapped peers. The broad definition of *handicapped* in Section 504 includes a number of students who may not qualify as disabled under IDEA (e.g., pupils with attention deficit disorders or health impairments such as epilepsy).

In advocating for pupil rights under IDEA and Section 504, school psychologists encounter the ethical conflicts inherent in the dual roles of pupil advocate and school employee. Because of the many pressures affecting schools (especially financial), the interests and needs of the pupil-client may conflict with the interests of school administrators (Greenspan & Negron, 1994). Surveys have found that school psychologists may be pressured to put administrative interests ahead of the interests of pupils or the ethical mandates of the profession (Jacob-Timm, 1998; Jann, Hyman, & Reinhardt, 1992; Pope & Vetter, 1992). Practitioners have reported pressure from supervisors to limit school obligations to students with special needs, including directives to avoid finding students eligible for special education, to avoid recommending certain placements or services, and to withhold information from parents regarding their legal rights. School psychologists also report pressures to "make students eligible" who do not meet IDEA requirements.

In the face of administrative pressure to act unethically, most school practitioners resist (Jann et al., 1992). However, psychologists who resist pressure from school administrators have reported threats to their job security, loss of prestige, negative criticism, or ostracism (Greenspan & Negron, 1994; Jacob-Timm, 1998; Jann et al., 1992). Research is needed to explore ways to lessen organizational pressures on school psychologists (Helton, 1992).

BEHAVIORAL INTERVENTIONS

In recent years, the use of *applied behavior analysis* techniques has gained popularity in the public schools. IDEA requires schools to develop behavioral intervention plans for pupils with disabilities who have been removed from their placements for disciplinary reasons for more than 10 days. School psychologists are often some of the few school professionals with formal training in behavioral methods, ethical principles of psychology, and treatment decision making. Consequently, psychologists who have expertise in applied behavior analysis techniques have an important role to play in developing behavioral interventions in the schools.

An ethical concern that arises during the problem clarification stage is whether the goals of intervention are in the best interests of the child. Classroom behavior-modification programs introduced in the late 1960s often focused on teaching children to "be still, be quiet, and be docile" (Winett & Winkler, 1972), what Conoley and Conoley (1982) later referred to as "dead man behaviors." Such goals may assist the teacher in maintaining a quiet, orderly classroom, but they are not likely to improve learning or foster the healthy personal-social development of children (Winett & Winkler, 1972). The psychologist and teacher are ethically obligated to select target behaviors that "enhance the long-term well-being of the child" (Harris & Kapache, 1978, p. 27) and are consistent with the long-range goal of self-management. Goals must be selected to ensure that the pupil will develop appropriate adaptive behaviors and not just suppress inappropriate ones (Van Houten et al., 1988).

During the intervention stage, school psychologists are ethically obligated to select (or assist in the selection of) change procedures that have demonstrated effectiveness. Practitioners also are obligated to select the least-drastic procedures and those that minimize the risk of adverse side effects that are likely to be effective. There is some consensus in the literature about the procedures that are the most acceptable and those that are least acceptable in schools. First-choice strategies are based on differential reinforcement (e.g., reinforcing appropriate behaviors incompatible with problem behaviors). Second-choice strategies are based on extinction (withdrawing of reinforcement for undesired behavior). Third-choice strategies include removal of desirable stimuli (e.g., time-out procedures). The

least-acceptable, or fourth-choice, strategies involve presentation of aversive stimuli (Alberto & Troutman, 1982, p. 206).

The courts have scrutinized the use of behavioral interventions with children. Such methods must not deprive pupils of their basic rights to food; water; shelter, including adequate heat and ventilation; sleep; and exercise periods. *Time-out* is a popular intervention strategy, and the courts have found its use in the schools to be permissible. However, practitioners are ethically obligated to ensure that time-out is used in a manner that safeguards the rights and welfare of pupils. More specifically, school personnel must monitor a secluded student to ensure his or her well-being, the time-out room itself must not present a fire or safety hazard, the door must remain unlocked, and students must be permitted to leave time-out for appropriate reasons. Students should be given prior notice about the types of behaviors that will result in being placed in time-out, and school personnel must ensure that time-out, when used as punishment, is "not unduly harsh or grossly disproportionate" to the offense (*Dickens by Dickens v. Johnson County Board of Education,* 1987, p. 158). The length of the time-out should be appropriate for the child's age, and placement in time-out should not result in "a total exclusion from the educational process for more than a trivial period" (*Goss v. Lopez,* 1975, p. 575). Creating a time-out by segregating or secluding the child within the classroom or requiring the child to do schoolwork while in the time-out room is recommended *(Dickens by Dickens v. Johnson County Board of Education,* 1987).

A highly controversial issue in the schools is the use of aversive conditioning, whereby a discomforting stimulus is presented contingent on the child's undesirable behavior. Some psychologists and educators believe that aversive conditioning must never be used; others believe the use of aversive conditioning may be justified in the treatment of extremely self-injurious or dangerous aggressive behaviors. Interested readers are referred to Jacob-Timm (1996); National Institutes of Health (1991); and Repp and Singh (1990).

Consistent with the principle of responsible caring, school psychologists "modify or terminate the treatment plan when the data indicate the plan is not achieving the desired goals" (NASP, 1997, IV, B, #6).

ETHICS, LAW, AND SCHOOL PSYCHOLOGY: CURRENT STATUS

Professional ethical codes are imperfect guides to behavior. They are at times vague and difficult to interpret; competing principles may apply in a given situation; and codes often fail to address new and emerging issues (Hughes, 1986). However, taken together, the APA Ethical Principles of Psychologists and Code of Conduct (1992) and the NASP Principles for Professional Ethics (1997) generally provide imperfect but satisfactory guidance for ethical decision making in school psychology. The APA code of ethics provides a sound articulation of general principles that underlie ethical choices in psychology. The NASP code provides more specific guidance for many of the concerns likely to arise in the provision of services to school children.

As noted previously, many aspects of school psychological practice are regulated by law. IDEA, Section 504, and FERPA are good and important federal laws. Public Law No. 94-142 (now IDEA) opened the school doors for children with disabilities who were previously denied a public school education. Since that time, there have been numerous amendments to IDEA as well as changes in the regulations implementing the law, state interpretations, and district policies. Despite the many changes, aspects of IDEA and state interpretations of the law have been and continue to be ethically problematic. For example, there are many pupils who need extra help to succeed in school but who do not qualify as disabled under IDEA. Unfortunately, many districts do not provide adequate assistance to pupils who do not qualify for special education funding. In those districts, school psychologists often face the dilemma of whether a child should be inappropriately labeled as disabled under IDEA to secure the extra help and services the pupil needs. School psychologists have taken an active role in shaping changes in law and school policies to ensure a quality education for all children, and they must continue to do so.

Ethical codes are a mechanism of self-regulation of a profession, whereas law is a mechanism of external regulation. In school psychology, professional ethical codes and legislation can function together to safeguard the interests and well-being of school children. For this to occur, school practitioners must provide services consistent with their ethical codes and highest professional standards and take an active role in advocating for legislation and school policies and practices that are in the best interests of schools and school children.

REFERENCES

Alberto, P. A., & Troutman, A. C. (1982). *Applied behavior analysis for teachers.* Columbus, OH: Merrill.

American Educational Research Association, American Psychological Association, & National Council on Measurement in Education. (1985). *Standards for educational and psychological testing.* Washington, DC: American Psychological Association.

American Psychological Association. (1981). Specialty guidelines for the delivery of services by school psychologists. *American Psychologist, 36,* 670–681.

American Psychological Association. (1992). Ethical principles of psychologists and code of conduct. *American Psychologist, 47,* 1597-1611.

American Psychological Association. (1993). Guidelines for providers of psychological services to ethnic, linguistic, and culturally diverse populations. *American Psychologist, 48,* 45-48.

Ballantine, H. T. (1979). The crisis in ethics, anno domini 1979. *New England Journal of Medicine, 301,* 634-638.

Bersoff, D. N. (1983). Children as participants in psychoeducational assessment. In G. B. Melton, G. P. Koocher, & M. J. Saks (Eds.), *Children's competence to consent* (pp. 149–177). New York: Plenum.

Bersoff, D. N., & Hofer, P. T. (1990). The legal regulation of school psychology. In C. R. Reynolds & T. B. Gutkin (Eds.), *The handbook of school psychology* (2nd ed., pp. 937-961). New York: Wiley.

Bersoff, D. N., & Koeppl, P. M. (1993). The relation between ethical codes and moral principles. *Ethics and Behavior, 3,* 345-357.

Brown v. Board of Education, 347 U.S. 483 (1954).

Canadian Psychological Association. (1991). *Canadian code of ethics for psychologists* (Rev. ed.). (Available from Canadian Psychological Association, 151 Rue Slater St., Suite 205, Ottawa K1P 5H3)

Canter, A. (1989, November). Is parent permission always necessary? *Communique,* p. 9.

Coles, N. S. (1981). Bias in testing. *American Psychologist, 36,* 1067–1077.

Conoley, J. C., & Conoley, C. W. (1982). *School consultation: A guide to practice and training.* New York: Pergamon.

Corrao, J., & Melton, G. B. (1988). Legal issues in school-based behavior therapy. In J. C. Witt, S. N. Elliot, & F. M. Gresham (Eds.), *Handbook of behavior therapy in education* (pp. 377–399). New York: Plenum.

Davis, J. M., & Sandoval, J. (1982). Applied ethics for school-based consultants. *Professional Psychology, 13,* 543–551.

Dickens by Dickens v. Johnson County Board of Education, 661 F.Supp. 155 E.D.Tenn. (1987).

Education for All Handicapped Children Act of 1975, Pub. L. No. 94-142; renamed the Individuals with Disabilities Education Act, 20 U.S.C. Chapter 33 (1990).

Eisel v. Board of Education of Montgomery County, 597 A.2d 447 (1991).

Fagan, T. K., & Wise, P. S. (1994). *School psychology: Past, present, and future.* New York: Longman.

Family Educational Rights and Privacy Act of 1974 (also "FERPA" or "The Buckley Amendment"), Pub. L. No. 93-380 20 U.S.C. § 1232g (1974). Regulations implementing FERPA appear at 34 C.F.R. § Part 99 (1996).

Fanibanda, D. K. (1976). Ethical issues of mental health consultation. *Professional Psychology, 7,* 547–552.

FERPA Office. (1986, December 2). Response to letter of inquiry from R. E. Thomas. Reprinted in 1987, *Education for the Handicapped Law Report, 211,* 420-424.

Glosoff, H. L., Herlihy, S. B., Herlihy, B., & Spence, E. B. (1997). Privileged communication in the psychologist-client relationship. *Professional Psychology: Research and Practice, 28,* 573-581.

Goss v. Lopez, 419 U.S. 565, 95 S.Ct. 729 (1975).

Greenspan, S., & Negron, E. (1994). Ethical obligations of special services personnel. *Special Services in the Schools, 8,* 185-209.

Hansen, J. C., Himes, B. S., & Meier, S. (1990). *Consultation: Concepts and practices.* Englewood Cliffs, NJ: Prentice Hall.

Harris, A., & Kapache, R. (1978). Behavior modification in schools: Ethical issues and suggested guidelines. *Journal of School Psychology, 16,* 25–33.

Harvey, V. S. (1997). Improving readability of psychological reports. *Professional Psychology: Research and Practice, 28,* 271-274.

Hehir, T. (1993, October 25). Response to letter of inquiry from McDonald. *Individuals with Disabilities Education Law Report, 20,* 1159-1160.

Helton, G. (1992, March). *School psychologist's response to administrative pressure to act unethically.* Paper presented at the National Association of School Psychologists Convention, Nashville, TN.

Holmes, D. S., & Urie, R. C. (1975). Effects of preparing children for psychotherapy. *Journal of Consulting and Clinical Psychology, 43,* 311–318.

Hughes, J. N. (1986). Ethical issues in school consultation. *School Psychology Review, 15,* 489–499.

Hummel, D. L., Talbutt, L. C., & Alexander, M. D. (1985). *Law and ethics in counseling.* New York: Van Nostrand Rienhold.

Individuals with Disabilities Education Act of 1990, Pub. L. No. 101-476 20 U.S.C. chap. 33 (1990). Amended by Pub. L. No. 105-17 (1997, June). Regulations appear at 34 C.F.R. Part 300. Proposed regulations appeared in the *Federal Register* on October 22, 1997, 62 (204), 55025-55075. Final regulations expected by June 1998.

Irvin, T. B. (1979, January 9). Response to a letter of inquiry from W. A. Hafner. Reprinted in 1980, *Education for the Handicapped Law Report, Suppl. 23,* 181-182.

Jacob-Timm, S. (1996). Ethical and legal issues associated with the use of aversives in the public schools: The SIBIS controversy. *School Psychology Review, 2,* 184-198.

Jacob-Timm, S. (1998, April). *Ethically challenging situations encountered by school psychologists.* Paper presented at the National Association of School Psychologists Convention, Orlando, FL.

Jacob-Timm, S., & Hartshorne, T. S. (1998). *Ethics and law for school psychologists* (3rd ed.). New York: Wiley.

Jann, R. J., Hyman, I. A., & Reinhardt, J. A. (1992, March). *The consequences of supervisory pressure to act unethically: A national survey.* Paper presented at the National Association of School Psychologists Convention, Nashville, TN.

John K. and Mary K. v. Board of Education for School District #65, Cook County, 504 N.E.2d 797 Ill.App. 1 Dist. (1987).

Kaser-Boyd, N., Adelman, H. S., & Taylor, L. (1985). Minors' ability to identify risks and benefits of therapy. *Professional Psychology: Research and Practice, 16,* 411-417.

Keith-Spiegel, P., & Koocher, G. P. (1985). *Ethics in psychology.* Hillsdale, NJ: Erlbaum.

Kitchener, K. S. (1986). Teaching applied ethics in counselor education: An integration of psychological processes and philosophical analysis. *Journal of Counseling and Development, 64,* 306–310.

Martin, R. P. (1985, April). Ethics column—Parents' rights to copies of test protocols: A draft position statement of the Division 16 Ethics Committee. *The School Psychologist,* p. 9.

Messick, S. (1980). Test validity and the ethics of assessment. *American Psychologist, 35,* 1012–1027.

Messick, S. (1984). Assessment in context: Appraising student performance in relation to instructional quality. *Educational Researcher, 13,* 3-8.

Muehleman, T., Pickens, B. K., & Robinson, F. (1985). Informing clients about the limits to confidentiality, risks, and their rights: Is self-disclosure inhibited? *Professional Psychology: Research and Practice, 16,* 385–397.

National Association of School Psychologists. (1997). *Professional conduct manual.* Bethesda, MD: Author.

National Institutes of Health. (1991). National Institutes of Health consensus development conference statement. In *NIH consensus development conference on the treatment of destructive behaviors in persons with developmental disabilities* (NIH Publication No. 91-2410, pp. 1-29). Washington, DC: U.S. Government Printing Office.

Newman, J. L. (1993). Ethical issues in consultation. *Journal of Counseling and Development, 72,* 148-156.

Phillis P. v. Claremont Unified School District, 183 Cal.App.3d 1193 (1986).

Pope, K. S., & Vetter, V. A. (1992). Ethical dilemmas encountered by members of the American Psychological Association. *American Psychologist, 47,* 397-411.

Protection of Pupil Rights Amendment of 1978. Amended by Pub. L. No. 103-227 (1994). Regulations at 34 C.F.R. Part A § 98 (1996). New regulations due late 1997.

Rehabilitation Act of 1973, Pub. L. No. 93-112 29 U.S.C. § 794. Regulations implementing Section 504 appear at 34 C.F.R. Part 104 (1996).

Repp, A. C., & Singh, N. N. (Eds.). (1990). *Perspectives on the use of nonaversive and aversive interventions with persons with developmental disabilities.* Pacific Grove, CA: Brooks/Cole.

Reschly, D. J. (1997). Diagnostic and treatment utility of intelligence tests. In D. P. Flanagan, J. L. Genshaft, & P. L. Harrison (Eds.), *Contemporary intellectual assessment* (pp. 437-456). New York: Guilford.

Reschly, D., & Wilson, M. S. (1995). School psychology practitioners and faculty: 1986 to 1991-92 trends in demographics, roles, satisfaction, and system reform. *School Psychology Review, 24,* 2-80.

Reynolds, C. R., & Kaiser, S. M. (1990). Test bias in psychological assessment. In C. R. Reynolds & T. B. Gutkin (Eds.), *The handbook of school psychology* (2nd ed., pp. 487-525). New York: Wiley.

Siegel, M. (1979). Privacy, ethics, and confidentiality. *Professional Psychology, 10,* 249–258.

Tarasoff v. Regents of California, 118 Cal. Rptr. 129, 529 P.2d 553 (Cal. 1974, Tarasoff I); Tarasoff v. Regents of California, 131 Cal.Rptr.14, 551 P.2d 334 (Cal. 1976, Tarasoff II).

Taylor, L., & Adelman, H. S. (1989). Reframing the confidentiality dilemma to work in children's best interests. *Professional Psychology: Research and Practice, 20,* 79–83.

Tymchuk, A. J. (1986). Guidelines for ethical decision making. *Canadian Psychology, 27,* 36-43.

Van Houten, R. Axelrod, S., Bailey, J. S., Favell, J. E., Foxx, R. N., Iwata, B. A., & Lovaas, O. I. (1988). The right to effective behavioral treatment. *The Behavior Analyst, 11,* 111-114.

Watson, H., & Levine, M. (1989). Psychotherapy and mandated reporting of child abuse. *American Journal of Orthopsychiatry, 59,* 246-256.

Weithorn, L. A. (1983). Involving children in decisions affecting their own welfare: Guidelines for professionals. In G. B. Melton, G. P. Koocher, & M. J. Saks (Eds.), *Children's competence to consent* (pp. 235–260). New York: Plenum.

Winett, R. A., & Winkler, R. C. (1972). Current behavior modification in the classroom: Be still, be quiet, be docile. *Journal of Applied Behavior Analysis, 5,* 499-504.

Woody, R. H. (1998, April). *Legal and ethical issues for trainers.* Paper presented at the Trainers of School Psychology Conference, Orlando, FL.

CHAPTER 25

Issues in the Ethical Treatment of Older Adults

JANE E. FISHER AND CRAIG A. YURY
University of Nevada, Reno

This chapter focuses on ethical issues regarding psychological services and research with older adults. As a matter of convention, the term *older adults* includes individuals aged 65 and over. This demarcation is not intended to imply group homogeneity, but rather serves only as a heuristic for the likely relevance of certain age-associated issues. Psychologists working with older adults frequently must navigate ethical challenges involving issues such as the ability of a client to provide informed consent when the client's mental competence is questionable due to a cognitive disorder, confidentiality conflicts in the psychologist's role on multidisciplinary teams, and the need to mediate intergenerational conflicts when an older adult is dependent on adult children or grandchildren due to a physical or cognitive limitation.

In organizing the chapter, we first discuss levels of ethics and how they can be applied to clarify the types of ethical challenges psychologists confront in working with older adults.

We then present an overview of considerations in ethical professional conduct in working with older adults, with particular attention focused on issues regarding the assessment of competencies, obtaining informed consent, and the conduct of research. Finally, the chapter concludes with a discussion of implications and recommendations for professional training in mental health services and research with older adults.

LEVELS OF ETHICS

Several questions emerge regarding the relationship between ethical judgments and standards and applications to older adults. For example, do ethical priorities differ between elderly individuals and those responsible for their care and related decisions? Research has not addressed age- or cohort-associated ethical concerns and ideals of the elderly and how these may change over the life span or differ in a manner more consistent with cohort effects than with aging effects. Different types of ethical questions emerge when considering age- and cohort-associated differences, such as those that focus on values reflected in a client's behavior and those that focus on what should be valued, or even would be valued, under specified circumstances. Ethical terms can have various meanings and functions in different contexts, such as in the context of the lives of older adults and professional decisions involving elderly individuals (O'Donohue, Fisher, & Krasner, 1986). Nielson (1967) considered three levels of ethics: *descriptive ethics, normative ethics,* and *metaethics.* First, based on empirical evidence provided by observation of behavior, descriptive ethics refer to what *is* valued. Descriptive ethics refer to standards people employ for judging acts as ethically good or bad. The next level of discourse, normative ethics, refers to what individuals *should do* or *ought to* value. This level concentrates on identifying morally acceptable means and ends of human actions and interactions. Three principles are generally considered the basis of normative ethics: *autonomy, beneficence,* and *justice* (e.g., Moody, 1992a). Normative ethics cannot be adequately addressed by scientific method, for definitions of what individuals should do or ought to value are too vague to test empirically. Although questions of normative ethics cannot be answered by science, they are inherently intertwined with scientific endeavors. For instance, an investigator ought to regard the safety of participants as paramount, as opposed to disregarding the safety of participants in hopes of producing desirable findings. The connections between science and ethics have implications for training of professionals in a scientist-practitioner model, in that science and accumulation of empirical evidence do not adequately inform professionals of normative ethics. Thus, a gap frequently exists in the training

of professionals in the realm of ethics. Whereas descriptive ethics may be empirically studied and have some reciprocal influence with normative ethics, mental health professionals cannot rely solely on what *is* valued to inform what *ought to* be valued and subsequent actions (O'Donohue, Fisher, & Krasner, 1987). Religion is traditionally tied to normative ethics for many, including the elderly, who may have been exposed to ethical training in primarily religious contexts. This interconnection must be taken into account when engaging elderly individuals of religious backgrounds in ethical decision-making processes. The level of ethics furthest removed from the descriptive level, what people actually do, is that of metaethics. Metaethics focus on the meaning of ethical terms and the logic of ethical discourse (Sumner, 1966). For example, it may be considered ethical to deprive animals of food to a more severe extent than depriving children of food.

Scientist practitioners operate under the factual dictates of science as well as the "ought statements" of value-based ethics (e.g., Bahm, 1974; Krasner & Houts, 1984). It is necessary for psychologists to identify the values they apply to their research and practice in the field (Krasner & Houts, 1984). In summary, ethical standards cannot be directly deduced from factual premises, but must be derived via the application of analytic statements to factual claims (O'Donohue et al., 1987).

ETHICAL PRINCIPLES AND PROFESSIONAL STANDARDS

It is generally understood that members of a profession such as psychology function as a community. The community of professionals control entry into the profession and mandate appropriate behavior of its members.

Values of the psychological community evolve into formal statements of what is considered ethical behavior on behalf of the population served by the profession (see Bersoff, 1999). Regardless of whether ethical codes of conduct are followed in letter or in spirit, they are considered to be contractual agreements with the population served by professionals in the field of psychology. Codes of conduct derived from general ethical principles are designed to protect both parties from harm from aspects of the professional practices addressed. However, these types of codes may lean in favor of protecting professionals in psychology, such that the intent to protect the rights of the individuals served by professionals is overlooked or subverted. It has been suggested that the expansion of specific rules has occurred in response to an increase in litigious cases and may serve only to obscure the ethical principles on which enforceable codes of behavior were founded (Sinclair, Simon, & Pettifor, 1996).

The general ethical principles from which enforceable behaviors of psychologists are derived are contained in the most recent version of the Ethical Principles of Psychologists and Code of Conduct, published by the American Psychological Association (APA, 1992). The six general principles are aspirational goals for professionals in the field of psychology. Specifically, they are principles of competence, integrity, professional and scientific responsibility, respect for people's rights and dignity, concerns for others' welfare, and social responsibility that members of the community of psychologists are bound to monitor in themselves and others. The APA code "has as its primary goal the welfare and protection of the individuals and groups with whom psychologists work" (APA, 1992, Preamble). Codes are simply statements about what one ought to do. However, principles explain why one ought to behave in a particular fashion under particular circumstances. Codes may be considered superfluous if one understands the spirit of the principles from which the codes are derived (Bahm, 1974). The most recent APA document is not only the code of ethics for professional psychologists but it is also representative of ethical principles underlying ethical codes of conduct in Western cultures (Sinclair, 1996).

Several ethical problems have been identified that may have particular relevance in practice with older adults (Peterson, 1996). Test misuse and practicing outside the limits of one's competence or area of expertise are critical issues in providing ethical standards of service to older adults, both via practice and research. The issue of providing competent services to older adults is broad in scope, because there are not enough professionals clearly competent in providing psychological services to older adults or conducting research with older adults as participants. Peterson (1996) also lists informed consent and confidentiality as prime principles under which unethical behavior frequently occurs. Specific issues regarding informed consent for treatment and/or research with older adults will be addressed in more detail in sections to follow.

CHARACTERISTICS AND SUBPOPULATIONS OF OLDER ADULTS

Professional ethics require knowledge of characteristics common to the population from which individual clients and research participants are selected or recruited. Specifically, competence to provide services to older adults is predicated on familiarity with characteristics and corresponding needs of this population. In an effort to familiarize psychologists with pertinent aspects of working with older adults, the APA published a set of guidelines titled *What Practitioners Should Know About Working With Older Adults* (Cooley et al., 1997). By virtue of living into advanced age, older adults are likely to face a number of significant adjustments, such as those associated with changes in functional capacities, financial resources, familial and social relations, societal attitudes, illness, and bereavement. Information summarized in the APA pamphlet includes clarification of common myths about older adults, aspects of normal aging, psychological problems experienced by some older adults, and acceptable treatment options (Cooley et al., 1997). Subpopulations of older adults that may be particularly at risk for ethical abuse are those with diminished mental or physical capacities and/or limited resources. Cognitively impaired elderly, minority elderly, and physically frail, dependent elderly are most susceptible to being taken advantage of, directly or inadvertently, and so are addressed in turn.

WHEN AUTONOMY IS THREATENED: OLDER ADULTS WITH DEMENTIA

Autonomy is often confounded with ethical decisions involving those with diminished functional capacities, such as the frail elderly. Rather than the conventional focus on the primacy of normative ethics based on the principles of autonomy, beneficence, and justice, Moody (1992a) advocates the primacy of *communicative ethics*. Specifically, communicative ethics focus on respect for individuals on the basis of concrete experiences rather than on abstract ethical principles. Communicative ethics are derived from the life experience of individuals and can be used at a practical level. Whereas the principles of normative ethics focus on the individual, communicative ethics refers to the social context of the individual. This position leads to the idea of negotiated consent, as opposed to the traditional informed consent (Moody, 1988). Variations on the concept of autonomy are discussed in a later section that focuses on professional ethics and older adults with dementia.

The perception that individuals with mental illness are different from individuals without mental illness in their capacity to consent may arise from protective instincts but raises the dual specter of stigmatization and discrimination that have haunted mental health for centuries (Candilis, 2001). Approximately 30% of adults over the age of 85 years experience some type of dementia (Cooley et al., 1997). By virtue of changes in the age demographics of the population, it is expected that an increasing number of individuals who are living longer will be living with dementia. Alzheimer's and vascular dementia are the most common forms of dementia and may coexist. Other common forms of comorbidity involve delirium, depression, and/or physical ailments. Specific implications of the shifting age demographics, barring an abrupt change in the research on prevention or cure of dementias, are discussed in the context of informed consent for procedures and also in terms of the paternalistic nature of care of individuals with dementia.

The aforementioned conflation of autonomy and dignity is particularly relevant here; it can be argued that one does not necessarily imply the other. Dignity of an individual is often honored by respecting that person's autonomy, as evidenced by compliance with decisions made by that individual regarding his or her use of services or participation in research. However, autonomy erodes as dementia progresses, and cognitive decline complicates acceptance of the basic value of autonomy. Problems with beneficence include caregiver burden influencing decision making in older adults' best interests.

Paternalistic interventions are common with older adults experiencing dementia (Moody, 1992a, 1992b). Although dementia, by definition, always involves cognitive impairment, the diagnosis does not necessarily imply mental incompetence. Contextual definitions, or the meaning of beneficence and nonmaleficence in certain situations, come into play here. A prime example is ethical defense of restraint of individuals with dementia. Defending a position that advocates uses of restraint in the best interest of the individual with dementia is increasingly difficult in light of research indicating that restraints are more likely to be beneficial to the care staff than to the individual. In addition, the appeal to the prevention of falls is not supported by research (Miles & Meyers, 1994).

Dignity via involvement to the extent of the individual's capabilities is perhaps a more appropriate value than autonomy for the individual with dementia. Behaving in the interest of justice, such that no one's rights to a reasonable quality of life are usurped, becomes increasingly complicated in dementia when caregiver and/or familial interests are taken into account (Moody, 1992a). This is when a communicative ethics among parties involved, including the elderly individual with dementia, is imperative in establishing just treatment of the individual (Moody, 1992b). The goal of communication and negotiation of consent is further challenged by the paternalistic nature of involving others in quality-of-life issues pertaining to the individual with dementia. An advanced directive may be seen as a solution to questions regarding consent for treatment but fails to consider issues of fluctuating competency, for example. If the person is no longer considered himself or herself such that former functional abilities cease to be exhibited, then ethical application of advanced directives is questionable. In addition, advanced directives tend to be more effective in halting treatments than in procuring treatments. This may limit beneficent therapeutic interactions with the individual, whereas an advanced directive is composed prior to the experience of dementia, after which the individual cannot reliably recant the directive.

Another issue worth noting is that the nature of dementia must be understood for one to behave in an ethically appropriate manner with older adults. Networking with other health care providers allows for mutual information exchange regarding the condition of the individual. Although an interdisciplinary approach to care of adults in general will be advocated in a subsequent portion of this chapter, such an approach involving various professionals at different levels of care is particularly adaptive to work with cognitively impaired older adults. For example, a psychologist may have observed behavioral excesses or deficits not available to a neurologist. In turn, a neurologist is likely to have access to test results relevant to the deterioration patterns of the individual's brain structure, and an internist may have information regarding a thyroid condition. Furthermore, a general practitioner may have access to reports of somatic symptoms that the psychologist may find as resulting from depression rather than a diagnosed physical condition.

ELDER ABUSE

Abuse of older adults occurs at high rates in institutional settings (U.S. Government Accounting Office, 2002) but occurs at the highest rates in private homes, typically between caregivers and older adult and/or between family members (U.S. Department of Health and Human Services, 1998). Situations that result in abuse of younger individuals hold true in this population as well, but there is increased likelihood of dependence and isolation, as well as a sense of finitude that contributes to the abuse of older adults. Older adults are susceptible to physical, sexual, verbal, and also financial abuse or exploitation. Dependency and isolation foster abuse and neglect of elderly individuals. Ethical and moral standards of those in caregiving roles, as well as their views on aging people in general, can contribute to instances and patterns of abuse. The abuse may be a continuation or exacerbation of behaviors that occurred earlier in the life span, may be a complex product of former abuse by the older adult, or may be the result of overburdened caregiver factors, just to identify a few common scenarios for abuse. Neglect is also an issue that may arise out of maleficence or ignorance in meeting the needs of older adults (Fisher, Henderson, & Buchanan, 2002). It is the ethical responsibility of the mental health professional as a mandated reporter to attend to signs of abuse and neglect. These include, but are not limited to, the following: bruises, burns, or other injuries; crying, fear, and distrust; inability to pay bills or purchase necessities; uncleanliness and poor hygiene (e.g., Fulmer & Gould, 1996; Pugh, 1996; Ramsey-Klawsnik, 1996).

CONSIDERATIONS FOR PROFESSIONAL CONDUCT WITH ELDER INDIVIDUALS

Assessing Competency in Older Adults

All individuals are presumed legally competent until a judicial hearing determines otherwise. Here, the issue of ambiguity in definition becomes apparent. The term *competency* is usually reserved for the legal arena, although it is often used in a less formal sense in the context of assessing one's abilities to understand and/or perform certain acts. There is no universally accepted legal definition of competence as a construct, nor is there a generally cited definition of a *competent person*. The legal definition of competency has evolved from an earlier emphasis on the single criterion of a disabling condition (e.g., diagnosis of a mental illness) to include the additional criteria of evidence that the condition causes mental impairment and that the impairment affects the person's ability to perform the activity in question (Sabatino, 1996).

Assessment of competence is defined here as *identification of functional abilities,* rather than global determination of competence versus incompetence of older adults to participate in decision-making processes (for an expanded discussion of this issue, see Smyer, Schaie, & Kapp, 1996). Distinctions between global competence versus incompetence have no place in the assessment of older adults by professionals engaging in ethical practice. The goal of a mental health professional is emphasized in the current context as accurate assessment of an older individual's functional abilities. The degree of congruency between functional abilities of an older adult and the demands of the environment in which he or she must engage in particular behaviors is of utmost importance.

Capacity is used to describe functional ability of an individual. Decisional capacity, or the mental capacity to make decisions, can fluctuate over time (Artnak, 1997). A major threat to autonomy of older adults is the stereotypical assumption that an individual's mental capacities are deficient due to age. This becomes a particularly dangerous assumption to make when the decision of an older adult regarding provision of treatment, for example, differs from that of others involved, such as family members and professionals.

Assessment of mental capacities in general is hindered by issues of definition. First, the term *mental* is not particularly useful in the description or measurement of functional abilities. Focus on *behavioral* capacities reflects appropriate terminology that lends itself more readily to assessment by mental health professionals. Second, the issue of assessing behavioral capacities is more accurately represented by multiple aspects or levels of ability, hence the use of the terms *capacities* or *competencies*. Five basic questions have been identified in the literature as being key in determining decisional competencies, such as abilities to consent to treatment and to care for one's self and/or property: (a) Can the individual make and express choices about his or her life? (b) Are the outcomes of these choices reasonable? (c) Are the choices based on rational reasons? (d) Is the individual capable of understanding the personal implications of choices? (e) Does the individual understand the implications of choices about his or her life? (Appelbaum & Gutheil, 1991; Kapp, 1992; Smyer et al., 1996). Essentially, these questions involve the distinction between what is explained versus what is understood.

A particularly important study in the area of competence, the MacArthur Treatment Competence Study, was conducted by Grisso and Appelbaum in 1995. In this study, three instruments for assessing abilities were used: (a) understanding treatment disclosures, (b) perceptions of disorders, and (c) thinking rationally about treatment. Standardized interviews and assessments were applied to differing mentally ill and medically ill populations in multiple sites. The findings indicated that patients with diagnosed mental illness more often manifested deficits in competence than did the medically ill and their non-ill control groups. Interestingly, the majority of mentally ill patients did not perform more poorly than other medically ill and non-ill patients. The lower group mean for mental ill patients was due to a minority in that group that significantly lowered the mean.

Assessment of competencies and potential to overcome deficits is a more productive aspect of assessment that should be conducted in addition to the assessment of deficits exhibited by an older adult. In addition, assessments should be conducted under the ethical principles of beneficence and the duty to do no harm. The principles and nonmaleficence may seem in opposition in the context of recommendations based on neurological assessments, for example (Binder & Thompson, 1994). In cases in which a client is likely to be significantly distressed by a diagnosis, such as probable Alzheimer's, steps are taken to minimize the distress and provide accurate diagnostic information. Here, the psychologist would ideally provide supplemental information about what can be expected and what treatments are available.

Decisional capacities identified by the itemized questions above are often assessed by physicians or mental health professionals on an informal basis in conjunction with the individual and if appropriate, the individual's family. In informal, nonlegal settings, assessment instruments are not frequently used to assess these capacities. However, in legal cases, it is particularly important to use a standardized assessment instrument to communicate with other professionals in the field as well as legal counsel and a judge. A few measures exist (e.g., the Multidimensional Functional Assessment Questionnaire developed by the Older Americans Resources and Service Program of Duke University; Fillenbaum, 1988) but are not widely used in practice or research. Given the paucity of assessment instruments in this area and the likelihood that most psychologists will be involved in this type of assessment at some time, at least in an informal setting, we will discuss trends in this area. We then review an idiographic approach to the assessment of functional abilities based on a consideration of learning histories, situational variables, and overall environmental influences.

Guardianship Issues

Assessment of the functional abilities to care for self or property encompasses the assessment of competence to consent to treatment in many cases. Guardianship issues are the main focus of the discussion of functional abilities here. Lawton (1988) describes a hierarchy of behavioral competence that is useful for understanding the context of older adult guardianship issues. In ascending order on the dimension of functional health, physical activities of daily living (ADLs) are followed by instrumental activities of daily living (IADLs), which are lower on the behavioral-competence hierarchy than financial management and paid employment. These behavioral competencies, as well as cognitive abilities, are of interest in a competence evaluation of older adults in terms of whether it may be appropriate to establish a legal guardian for the individual. Relevant prevalence rates include the percentage of adults over age 65 who have difficulty or receive help with physical ADLs, self-maintenance behaviors such as eating, toileting, dressing, walking, getting outside, bathing, and transferring; 22.7% have difficultly with one or more of these activities, and 9.6% receive help with one or more of these activities. Moving up the previously identified hierarchy for IADLs, specifically using a telephone, managing money, preparing meals, housework, and shopping, 26.9% of older adults over age 65 have difficulty with one or more of these activities, and 22.2% receive help with one or more (National Center for Health Statistics, 1987). Functional disabilities or the need for assistance in these areas are often what precipitate an evaluation of relevant competencies.

The most comprehensive instrument for assessment of functional abilities of older adults is the Multidimensional Functional Assessment Questionnaire (MFAQ), also known as OARS, in reference to the group that developed it, the Older Americans Resources and Services programs at Duke University. The purpose in developing this instrument was to provide a reliable and valid method of describing older adults that would be "useful to clinicians, program analysts, resource allocations, and research scientists in a variety of disciplines" (Fillenbaum, 1988).

Many of the measures of functional abilities that are available either have not been tested for validity or do not meet reasonable reliability standards to warrant validity testing. Existing assessment instruments are subject to significant biases, should not be used in isolation, and would benefit from the addition of behavior-observational techniques. Lack of theoretical underpinnings appears to be the greatest flaw in assessment of competencies in general. Without a theoretical base to build on, it makes sense that the assessment instruments in the area of functional abilities of older adults are piecemeal at best. Overall, assessors should strive toward an idiographic multimodal assessment involving behavior-observational components relevant to the competencies in question.

MENTAL HEALTH SERVICES AND PSYCHOTHERAPY

The discussion of informed consent for treatment should be influenced by recognition of the importance of the role played by the source of and reason for the referral for treatment. Who decides to pursue treatment resources for the older adult and related issues of voluntary versus involuntary care decisions are inherently intertwined. In addition, implications of health care rationing, specifically mental health services for older adults, will be discussed in light of issues such as undertreatment of conditions based on agism rather than empirical evidence.

Because *rationing* denotes a crisis situation, the term is perhaps not the most useful way of looking at what is better described as *allocation of resources* (Moody, 1992b). Whereas the burgeoning older adult population may be construed as a crisis, health care deficits are more of a long-term planning issue. Activities most commonly involving psychologists are the provision of psychotherapy and the conduction of research. It is imperative when working with older adults that an interdisciplinary approach to the individual case is the most ethically responsible means.

Negotiated consent is a reasonable alternative to standard informed consent procedures, particularly when the individual in question is cognitively impaired, such as in the case of progressive dementia, for example (Moody, 1992a, 1992b). The individual's values and life goals must be taken into account to the greatest extent possible in making treatment decisions. It is imperative that the individual be well informed and have opportunity to address questions and concerns prior to implementation of a treatment plan and/or procedures. Rapport building with the client is facilitated by the availability of professional, active listening skills and minimal inferences by the professional, which are likely to be invaluable aspects of ethical interactions with elderly clients.

Normative ethics have a central role in provision of psychological services for the elderly. This implicitly requires identification of what one ought to be valued in terms of quality of life. Who is most concerned with the elderly individual's quality of life? Is the elderly individual presenting for services, or has a concerned family member referred him or her for psychological services? Does the elderly individual value treatment goals identified in conjunction with a therapist, or does that individual feel that his or her needs would be better addressed by clergy or medical practitioners? Therapy inherently suggests a change from a less desirable state to a more desirable one. Not only are the ends of psychotherapy, a better quality of life in some respect, dependent on value judgments, but so, too, are the means chosen to reach such ends (O'Donohue et al., 1987). The values of the elderly individual, significant others, and the psychotherapist are brought to bear on the therapy process and desired outcome.

Psychological disorders in late life tend to be continuations of problems first experienced in young adulthood or middle age. The treatment of psychological disorders in older adults is as effective as in younger adults (Fisher, Zeiss, & Carstensen, 2001). Therefore, the withholding of treatment from older adults is not compliant with aspirational goals or mandated conduct.

Ethical judgments are made by the psychotherapist in evaluating the goals of the elderly client and what the therapist should do in light of those goals. The desired end state may differ dramatically for all parties involved. For example, if the elderly individual presents with suicide as the end goal, the therapist makes an ethical decision in choosing to act in accordance with the client's goals or to act in accordance with the psychotherapist's own values, including those outlined in ethical codes for professionals, such as that of the APA (1992). Other concerns raised by O'Donohue and colleagues (1987) include the implicit endorsement of certain end states and the means to achieve them by professionals who agree to assist clients with particular goals. Level of intervention also requires ethical decision making by psychotherapists. Specifically addressing the latter, can the psychotherapist ethically intervene only at the level of the individual without implying that the individual is responsible for the presenting undesirable state of affairs? Issues regarding who the identified client is become complicated because family members are often involved in the care of older adults at some level, and these family members may disagree on aspects of the care of the identified client (Wetle, 1991).

Coercion to participate in therapy is not ethically acceptable, and therapy should not be initiated prior to obtaining informed consent from the potential client. Informed consent obtained in a noncoercive fashion includes explanation of therapy in terms understood by the elderly individual, description of potential risks and benefits of therapy, frequent opportunities for summarization of information covered, and opportunities for the elderly individual to ask questions. In addition, information is provided that the individual may withdraw consent without a negative consequence imposed by the psychotherapist.

Ethical risks for older adults include not being adequately involved in treatment planning and not being considered appropriate for particular treatments on the basis of age (Wetle, 1991). For example, older adults are prescribed antidepressants far more often than they are offered psychotherapy for depression. Delivery of treatment and treatment setting are likely to diverge from the conventional psychotherapeutic practices in order to enhance and build on the relevant competencies of older adults. For example, treatment planning is more likely to include modules to be conducted by other members of an interdisciplinary team, such as psychotherapy for depression accompanied by pharmacotherapy for medical problems and social assistance care for financial issues. Each of these are contributors to the individual's experience of depression, or accompanied by efforts to locate affordable housing, as financial difficulties are also frequently related to the experience of depression.

Given the complex combination of physical and psychological influences on the symptom presentation of many older adults,

a multidisciplinary approach to assessment is consistent with ethical standards and mandated codes of conduct. Continuous or ongoing assessments are necessary because the individual's functional capacities may fluctuate over time, or even over the course of a day. Thus, finding out what is typically a good time of day for the individual can be helpful in attaining an accurate assessment of functional abilities. A lack of awareness of the purpose of assessment or right to refuse increases older adults' risk for receiving unethical practices (Moye, 2000). Elderly individuals, even those with dementing illnesses, must always be informed of the purpose of assessments. Only relevant assessments or standardized tests appropriate for older adults, as indicated by established norms for the age range of the individual to be assessed, are acceptable for use. Relevant assessments are considered those that have treatment utility, in that they inform treatment selection and intervention.

Several additional factors should be taken into account when working with older adults, many of which are not specific to this population. These include awareness of physical and social limitations, time-limited contact due to possibility of fatigue, optimizing environmental variables such as lighting and noise level, assessment of physical or drug-related changes that may effect mental abilities, and use of concrete therapeutic goals. It is the responsibility of the psychologist to use language that the elderly client can understand and to make frequent checks, either verbal or written, to assure comprehension on the part of the elderly client. This can be achieved by stating concrete goals for therapy, preferably in the form of language used by the client, asking the client for further input or suggestions, and encouraging questions about therapy. A written treatment plan to this effect can be beneficial to document the understanding of the older adults;

the plan can be itemized with spaces for initials of the client, date, and signature space. Updating the treatment plan and having addendums initialed by the older adult may also be an effective way of maintaining informed consent to treatment in an ethical fashion. This process, of course, should be carried out in conjunction with ongoing assessment of functional competencies, specifically competency to consent to treatment (O'Donohue et al., 1987).

Provided that the client is interested and understands the treatment plan and goals, as well as basic tenets of the type of therapy intervention to be employed, the treatment plan should focus on minimizing dependence and maximizing autonomy. Perhaps the most clear example of the threat to independence occurs in long-term care facilities (see Moye, 2000; Norris, in press). For example, many institutionalized older adults capable of performing ADLs have the tasks completed for them. For a variety of reasons, dependence tends to be reinforced within long-term care settings (Carstensen, Fisher, & Malloy, 1987). For example, caregivers may perform these ADLs to save time, and in the process reinforce dependency through social contact (Baltes & Reisenzein, 1986). Skills-training components of therapy are particularly important because they allow elderly clients to more competently control their environment.

Finally, in the area of psychological service delivery, it is important to note the consistent reports of the elderly as an underserved population. This underutilization may be due in part to lack of communication between professionals across care modalities (Greene, 1995). Issues of affordability and accessibility also affect the existing health care structure. In addition, reimbursement mechanisms affect the communication gaps between interdisciplinary service providers (Knight & Kaskie, 1995). Finally, the inadequate number of professionals who meet the criteria of training and competence in working with older adults further limits access to appropriate psychological services.

RESEARCH

A major focus of professional ethics in conducting research with older adults is the process of informed consent and the right to withdraw from participation in research. In accordance with the above recommendations for obtaining consent for treatment, guidelines for research with older adults include assessment of competencies as well as multiple assessment interviews over time (e.g., O'Donohue et al., 1987). Specific recommendations for conducting research with older adults are delineated by O'Donohue and colleagues (1987). These include: (a) an ongoing process of obtaining consent to participate due to fluctuating capacities, (b) provision of consent forms that are typed clearly in a large font with simple wording, (c) objective assessment of relevant functional capacities performed and recorded when the individual's competence regarding aspects of research-related tasks is in question, (d) objective assessment of the potential participant's understanding of the procedures described during the process of obtaining informed consent (this may be checked via simple questionnaires that ask the potential participant to answer questions about the information provided in the consent forms and by the experimenter), and (e) obtain copies of relevant documents regarding the research participant, such as legal guardianship or power of attorney papers.

Legal documents become necessary in instances of obtaining consent by proxy. Informed consent by proxy is the norm in long-term care facilities when individuals are not considered capable of providing consent (Franzi, Orgren, & Rozance, 1994). However, state laws themselves differ on the permissibility of enrolling individuals in research trials in the absence of competence to give informed consent (DeRenzo, 1997). It is often unclear whether even informal assessments of the functional capacities regarding ability to provide informed consent are conducted with elderly individuals in long-term care. Rather, it is conventionally assumed that physically frail and/or cognitively impaired adults are incapable of providing even minimal consent. The most prominent danger in this assumption is that if consent is attained by proxy, the older adult recruited to participate in research is typically not informed of the nature or purpose of the psychological research. This may be less of a problem for nonintrusive observational research that poses minimal risk to participants and has a potential for direct benefits. Guidelines for conducting research with cognitively impaired individuals indicate that in situations in which breach of confidentiality is not seriously detrimental, risks are minimal to none, and the research questions require inclusion of cognitively impaired elderly, consent by proxy of a legal guardian is acceptable in lieu of informed consent from the participant. Such research protocols should be reviewed and approved by ethics committee and or internal review board (IRB) prior to activation (Melnick, Dubler, Weisbard, & Butler, 1984).

The ethics code for psychologists (APA, 1992) indicates that psychologists are bound to consult with colleagues deemed knowledgeable about the populations participating in research (Cantor, Bennett, Jones, & Nagy, 1996). However, specific criteria of knowledge are vague or unmentioned, as are appropriate procedures for obtaining sufficient knowledge to be considered a consultant. These ambiguities are likely the primary sources of discrepancies in ethical conduct. Secondary-gain issues and negligence appear to be more adequately addressed and may be more likely to be monitored by fellow members of the professional community, whose reputation and credibility are influenced by poor ethical decisions made by its members. It is included in the general standard of nondiscrimination that age is not an acceptable factor in determining whether services, either practice or research, may be provided (Cantor et al., 1996).

It is considered unethical to withhold empirically validated treatments from older adults, to supply insufficiently tested treatments, or to fail to conduct relevant research in developing basic knowledge and treatment implementation and outcome data. Psychologists must also recognize when assessment techniques are not applicable to older adults. Appropriate adjustments may be made in accordance with the reliability and validity data available, or steps should be taken to conduct research to modify, establish appropriate norms, or create new instruments or techniques that are applicable to and address the needs of older adults. Research into appropriate treatments for older adults requires expansion to include establishment of older adult norms for existing assessments and/or development of new assessments appropriate for use with older adults. Frequently, existing assessments are not indicated for use with older adults or individuals with particular functional capacities or deficits. Although many forms of treatment are appropriate to older adults unless otherwise indicated, further development of treatment modalities remains important. The literature to date on application of empirically validated treatments to the problems of older adults is unacceptably small given the percentage of older adults currently in the population as well as the expected increasing percentage.

IMPLICATIONS FOR PROFESSIONAL TRAINING

Applying the current prevalence rates for mental disorders to the projected proportion of older adults in the year 2000, 7.5 million individuals over the age of 65 are estimated to experience mental health problems. Dementias occurring in adults over the age of 85 can be expected to double by the year 2010, implicating shifts in resource allocation. This indicates continuance in the movement to time-limited services consisting of empirically based treatments (Gatz & Finkel, 1995). Guidelines offered for training of professionals include knowledge of assessment, intervention, research, normal aging, abnormal aging (psychopathology), interdisciplinary roles and responsibilities, and ethics (Gatz & Finkel, 1995). Thus, some gerontology training should be advocated in all programs as being more important than creating a small number of specialists.

Additional training in professional ethics is advocated in the areas of research and applied practices with older adults (Knight, Santos, Teri, & Lawton, 1995). Seventeen explicit recommendations to the APA from the National Conference on Clinical Training in Psychology for improving psychological services for older adults (Knight et al., 1995) include issues of public policies and services and professional competencies in training and research. Although enumeration and explanation of each of these recommendations is beyond the scope of the current chapter, highlights are outlined here. The conference recommendations advocate for the APA to establish a clinical psychology work group to create and monitor policies regarding provision of mental health services for older adults and conduction of relevant research. They also call for lobbying of research initiatives to foster geropsychological research. Such research endeavors are recommended to be shared with professionals in other health care fields to facilitate the highly recommended inter-disciplinary nature of providing health care, including mental health care for older adults.

Training recommendations to the APA include expansion of training at the undergraduate, graduate, postdoctoral, and professional levels in life span development and mental health, as well as mental illness in older adults. Exposure to healthy older adults is important to balance the perception of older adults as stereotypically dysfunctional (Burgess, 1995). It is important to recognize and identify normal aspects of aging from abnormal aspects of the aging process. In general, this distinction sounds like the golden key to dealing effectively and ethically with older adults. However, it is a much more complex proposition than it appears on the surface. Specifically, there are numerous factors to take into account when determining whether experiences of older adults fall within the realm of normal aging, such as family history, genetic endowment, personal history, current physical complaints, current medications, and current environmental factors.

Minimum basic competencies listed as necessary for ethical work with older adults are normal life span development, abnormal development (including psychopathology), assessment, networking with medical and social services professionals, treatments/therapies, and psychopharmacology. Also called for was the inclusion of at least some experience in working with older adults through APA-accredited internships. This may seem overzealous, in that not all psychologists are interested in working with older adults any more than they are all interested in working with children. If APA is to implement a requirement for working with older adults at each accredited internship site, it could be argued that each accredited site must also include training opportunities with children. A reasonable and accurate counterargument is based on the ever-increasing elderly population that increases the likelihood of all professionals interacting with older adults in some capacity. Although the spirit of such recommendations is admirable, the application may be interpreted as excessive in nature, as well as very unlikely in reality. Those interested in preserving and expanding the integrity of geropsychology would do well to advocate for the basic ideals, increased research and practice opportunities, and funding made available via APA and other organizations concerned with providing ethical ideals and guidelines to mental health professionals. Attracting professionals dedicated to working with older adults needs to be facilitated by increased likelihood of reimbursement for professional time and services, because they may be more extensive and interdisciplinary than what is typically accommodated under current reimbursement structures.

In summary, the recommendations encompass three levels of professional competencies in working with older adults: (a) exposure to developmental and practical aspects of aging via coursework and direct contact with older adults, (b) experience in working with older adults, and (c) expertise developed through a combination of training, continuing education, and interdisciplinary focus. In general, these recommendations are a step in the right direction in enhancing professional competencies in working with older adults and thus contribute to the upholding of the general principles and ethical standards of the APA Ethical Principles of Psychologists and Code of Conduct.

CONCLUDING COMMENTS

Perhaps the core issue for most ethical dilemmas in dealing with older adults is the conflict between the basic values on which ethical principles are based. Specifically, beneficence, or acting in accordance with what is deemed the elderly individual's best interests, can conflict with the value of autonomy (Artnak, 1997). However, ethical challenges must not serve to hinder research and practice with an ever-increasing proportion of the population. First, it seems imperative to acquaint ourselves with normative aspects of older adulthood, at least for the current cohort of older adults. However, who decides what constitutes competency in working with older adults? Surely, the summary brochure published by the APA working committee on providing basic information for professionals who may work with older adults cannot intimate competency in the issues pertinent to such work. Is certification in geropsychology necessary? Certification, of course, does not guarantee ethical conduct. However, a minimum recognized standard of competence in working with older adults is desirable. Perhaps documented coursework and continuing education accompanied by direct service or research training with older adults is the most reasonable answer at this juncture. This is based on the precedence set by child psychologists of various levels of specialization.

Assessment of cultural values regarding old age and continued efforts to dispel stereotyping and discrimination of older adults are necessary yet insufficient means of addressing professional ethics and the elderly. Research, publication, direct service provision, and education in mental health issues focusing on older adults must move from the level of normative ethics, or what *ought* to be valued, to the level of descriptive ethics, or what *is* valued, as indicated by the behavior of relevant professionals working collaboratively.

REFERENCES

American Psychological Association. (1992). *Ethical principles of psychologists and code of conduct.* Washington; DC: American Psychological Association.

Appelbaum, P. S., & Gutheil, T. G. (1991). *Clinical handbook of psychiatry and the law.* Baltimore, MD: Williams & Wilkins.

Artnak, K. E. (1997). Informed consent in the elderly: Assessing decisional capacity. *Seminars in Perioperative Nursing, 6*(1), 59-64.

Bahm, A. J. (1974). Ethics as a behavioral science. Springfield, IL: Charles C Thomas.

Baltes, M. M., & Reisenzein, R. (1986). The social world in long-term care institutions: Psychosocial control toward dependency? In M. M. Baltes & P. B. Baltes (Eds.), *The psychology of control and aging.* Hillsdale, NJ: Lawrence Erlbaum.

Bersoff, D. N. (1999). Ethics codes and how they are enforced. In D. N. Bersoff (Ed.), *Ethical conflicts in psychology* (2nd ed.). Washington, DC: American Psychological Association.

Binder, L. M., & Thompson, L. L. (1995). The ethics code and neuropsychological assessment practices. *Archives of Clinical Neuropsychology, 10*(1), 27-46.

Burgess, L. (1995). Foreword: The mental health care needs of older adults. In B. G. Knight, L. Teri, P. Wohlford, & J. Santos (Eds.), *Mental health services for older adults: Implications for training and practice in geropsychology.* Washington, DC: American Psychological Association.

Candilis, P. J. (2001). Advancing the ethics of research. *Psychiatric Annals, 31*(2), 119-124.

Cantor, M. B., Bennett, B. E., Jones, S. E., & Nagy, T. F. (1996). *Ethics for psychologists: A commentary on the APA ethics code.* Washington, DC: American Psychological Association.

Carstensen, L. L., Fisher, J. E., & Malloy, P. M. (1995) Cognitive and affective characteristics of socially withdrawn nursing home residents. *Journal of Clinical Geropsychology, 1*(3), 207-218.

Cooley, S., Deitch, I. M., Harper, M. S., Hinrichsen, G., Lopez, M. A., & Molinari, V. A. (1997). *What practitioners should know about working with older adults.* Washington, DC: American Psychological Association.

DeRenzo, E. G. (1997). Decisionally impaired persons in research: Refining the proposed refinements. *Journal of Law, Medicine, and Ethics, 54,* 139-149.

Fillenbaum, G. G. (1988). *Multidimensional functional assessment of older adults: The Duke older Americans resources and services procedures.* Hillsdale, NJ: Lawrence Erlbaum.

Fisher, J., Henderson, D., & Buchanan, J. A. (2002). Primary prevention of elder abuse. In T. Gullotta & M. Bloom (Eds.), *The encyclopedia of primary prevention.* New York: Plenum.

Fisher, J. E., Zeiss, A., & Carstensen, L. L. (2001). Psychopathology in the aged. In P. B. Sutker & H. E. Adams (Eds.), *Comprehensive handbook of psychopathology* (3rd ed.). New York: Plenum.

Franzi, C., Orgren, R. A., & Rozance, C. (1994). Informed consent by proxy: A dilemma in long-term care research. *Clinical Gerontologist, 15*(2), 23-35.

Fulmer, T. T., & Gould, E. S. (1996). Assessing neglect. In L. A. Baumhover & S. C. Beall (Eds.), *Abuse, neglect, and exploitation of older persons: strategies for assessment and intervention.* Baltimore, MD: Health Professions Press.

Gatz, M., & Finkel, S. I. (1995). Education and training of mental health service providers. In M. Gatz (Ed.), *Emerging issues in mental health and aging.* Washington, DC: American Psychological Association.

Greene, R. R. (1995). Family involvement in mental health care for older adults: From caregiving to advocacy and empowerment. In M. Gatz (Ed.), *Emerging issues in mental health and aging.* Washington, DC: American Psychological Association.

Grisso, T., & Appelbaum, P. S. (1995). The MacArthur Treatment Competence Study III: Abilities of patients to consent to psychiatric and medical treatments. *Law and Human Behavior, 19*(2), 149-174.

Kapp, M. B. (1992). *Geriatrics and the law: Patient rights and professional responsibilities* (2nd ed.). New York: Springer.

Knight, B. G., & Kaskie, B. (1995). Models for mental health service delivery to older adults. In M. Gatz (Ed.), *Emerging issues in mental health and aging.* Washington, DC: American Psychological Association.

Knight, B. G., Santos, J., Teri, L., & Lawton, M. P. (1995). The development of training in clinical geropsychology. In B. G. Knight, L. Teri, P. Wohlford, & J. Santos (Eds.), *Mental health services for older adults: Implications for training and practice in geropsychology.* Washington, DC: American Psychological Association.

Krasner, L., & Houts, A. C. (1984). A study of the "value" systems of behavioral scientists. *American Psychologist, 39,* 840-850.

Lawton, M. P. (1988). Scales to measure competence in everyday activities. *Psychopharmacology Bulletin, 24*(4), 609-614.

Melnick, V. L., Dubler, N. N., Weisbard, A., & Butler, R. N. (1984). Clinical research in senile dementia of the Alzheimer type: Suggested guidelines addressing the ethical and legal issues. *Journal of the American Geriatrics Society, 32,* 531-536.

Miles, S. H., & Meyers, R. (1994). Untying the elderly, 1989 to 1993 update: *Clinical Ethics, 10*(3), 513-525.

Moody, H. R. (1988). From informed consent to negotiated consent. *Gerontologist 28*(Suppl.), 76-90.

Moody, H. R. (1992a). A critical view of ethical dilemmas in dementia. In R. H. Binstock, S. G. Post, & P. J. Whitehouse (Eds.), *Dementia and aging: Ethics, values, and politics.* Baltimore, MD: Johns Hopkins University Press.

Moody, H. R. (1992b). *Ethics in an aging society.* Baltimore, MD: John Hopkins University Press.

Moye, J. (2000). Ethical issues. In V. Molinari (Ed.), *Professional psychology in long-term care* (pp. 329-348). New York: Hatherleigh.

National Center for Health Statistics. (1987). *Functional limitations of individuals age 65 years and over.* Hyattsville, MD: U.S. Public Health Service.

Nielson, K. (1967). Problems of ethics. In P. Edwards (Ed.), *The encyclopedia of philosophy.* New York: Macmillan.

Norris, M. P. (in press). *Psychologists' multiple roles in long-term care: Untangling confidentiality quandaries.* Clinical Geropsychologist.

O'Donohue, W. T., Fisher, J. E., & Krasner, L. (1986). Behavior therapy and the elderly: A conceptual and ethical analysis. *International Journal of Aging and Human Development, 23*(1), 1-15.

O'Donohue, W. T., Fisher, J. E., & Krasner, L. (1987). Ethics and the elderly. In L. L. Carstensen & B. A. Edelstein (Eds.), *Handbook of clinical gerontology.* New York: Pergamon.

Peterson, C. (1996). Common problem areas and their causes resulting in disciplinary action. In L. J. Bass, S. T. DeMers, J. R. P. Ogloff, C. Peterson, J. L. Pettifor, R. P. Reaves, T. Retfalvi, N. P. Simon, C. Sinclair, & R. M. Tipton (Eds.), *Professional conduct and the discipline of psychology.* Washington, DC: American Psychological Association.

Pugh, S. (1996). Abuse directed towards older people. In L. Matthew (Ed.), *Professional care for the elderly mentally ill.* London: Chapman & Hall.

Ramsey-Klawsnik, H. (1996). Assessing physical and sexual abuse in health care settings. In L. A. Baumhover & S. C. Beall (Eds.), *Abuse, neglect, and exploitation of older persons: Strategies for assessment and intervention.* Baltimore, MD: Health Professions Press.

Sabatino, C. (1996). Competency: Refining our legal fictions. In M. Smyer, K. W. Schaie, & M. B. Kapp (Eds.), *Older adults' decision making and the law.* New York: Springer.

Sinclair, C., Simon, N. P., & Pettifor, J. L. (1996). The history of ethical codes and licensure. In L. J. Bass, S. T. DeMers, J. R. P. Ogloff, C. Peterson, J. L. Pettifor, R. P. Reaves, T. Retfalvi, N. P. Simon, C. Sinclair, & R. M. Tipton (Eds.), *Professional conduct and the discipline of psychology.* Washington, DC: American Psychological Association.

Smyer, M. A., Schaie, K. W., & Kapp, M. B. (1996). Older adults decision making and the law. *In Springer series on ethics, law and aging.* New York: Springer.

Sumner, L. W. (1966). Normative ethics and metaethics. *Ethics, 77,* 95-106.

U.S. Department of Health and Human Services. (1998). *Elder abuse and neglect* [On-line]. Available at: http://www.ojp.usdoj.gov/ovc/ ncvrw/2001/stat_over_7.htm.

U.S. Government Accounting Office. (2002). *Long term care: Elderly individuals could find significant variation in the availability of Medicaid home and community services* [On-line]. Available at: http://www.gao.gov/ new.items/d021131t.pdf.

Wetle, T. (1991). Successful aging: New hope for optimizing mental and physical well-being. *Journal of Geriatric Psychiatry, 24*(1), 3-12.

Author Index

Subject Index

About the Editors

William T. O'Donohue is a professor of psychology at the University of Nevada at Reno. He received a doctorate in clinical psychology from the State University of New York at Stony Brook and a master's degree in philosophy from Indiana University. He is editor and coeditor of a number of books, including the *Handbook of Behaviorism; Learning and Behavior Therapy; Management and Administration Skills for the Mental Health Professional* (with Jane Fisher); *The Philosophy of Psychology* (with Richard Kitchener); and *Theories of Behavior Therapy* and the *Handbook of Psychological Skills Training* (both with Leonard Krasner). He coauthored the recent Sage book *The Psychology of B.F. Skinner* (2001) with Kyle E. Ferguson.

Kyle E. Ferguson is pursuing his Ph.D. in psychology at the University of Nevada, Reno. He received a master's degree in behavior analysis from Southern Illinois University and a bachelor's degree from the University of Alberta. He coauthored a previous book, *Working Through Anger* (with Mark Dixon), and two manuals, *Working Through Anger: Therapist's Manual* (with John Guercio and Martin McMorrow) and *A Practitioner's Guide to Behavioral-Medical Interventions* (with John Guercio). He coauthored the recent Sage book *The Psychology of B.F. Skinner* (2001) with William T. O'Donohue.

About the Contributors

Henry E. Adams is Emeritus Research Professor of clinical psychology at the University of Georgia. He received his bachelor's degree in psychology at the University of California, Berkeley, and his M.A. and Ph.D. in clinical psychology from Louisiana State University. He was director of clinical psychology training (1965-1978) at the University of Georgia, Chair of the Division of Social and Behavioral Sciences (1978-1982), and a research professor (1983-1997) at the institution. His primary research interest has been in behavioral approaches to sexual deviations and other disorders.

Devjani Banerjee-Stevens is a doctoral student in counseling psychology at the University of Minnesota, where she also received her M.A. in counseling and student personnel psychology. Her research interests include bicultural identity development in college students and multicultural competence development in counseling trainees.

Jordan B. Bell received his bachelor's degree in 1994 at the Pennsylvania State University, where he specialized in Eastern philosophy and values. He is currently a senior graduate student in clinical psychology with interests in cross cultural psychology, substance abuse, and the ethics of animal research. He is also Research Associate for the Research Ethics Service Project at the University of New Mexico.

Jeffrey A. Buchanan is a doctoral student in clinical psychology at the University of Nevada, Reno, and an intern at the Minneapolis VA Medical Center. He received his M.A. in clinical psychology from Minnesota State University at Mankato. His research interests are in the areas of behavior analysis, managing challenging behaviors in persons with dementia, and psychological interventions for caregivers of patients with Alzheimer's disease.

Charles D. Claiborn is associated with Arizona State University.

Nicholas A. Cummings, Ph.D., Sc.D., is President of the Foundation for Behavioral Health and Chairman of the Nicholas & Dorothy Cummings Foundation, Inc. He is the founding CEO of American Biodyne (MedCo/Merck, then Merit, now Magellan Behavioral Care). Cummings is a former president of the American Psychological Association. He is founder of the four campuses of the California School of Professional Psychology, the National Council of Professional Schools of Psychology, the American Managed Behavioral Healthcare Association, and the National Academy of Practice. He was Chief Psychologist at Kaiser Permanente and is the former Executive Director of the Mental Research in Palo Alto, California. Cummings currently serves as Distinguished Professor at the University of Nevada, Reno.

Deborah Davis received her Ph.D. from Ohio State University in 1973. She taught at Southern Illinois University and Georgia State University before coming to the University of Nevada-Reno in 1978. Dr. Davis pursues research in the areas of romantic relationship behavior across the lifespan, adult attachment theory, and several areas in psychology and law, including perceptions of rape victims, witness memory, and empirical approaches to evidentiary rulings. She has served on the editorial boards of the *Journal of Personality and Social Psychology* and the *Journal of Experimental Social Psychology*. Dr. Davis is also the founder and President of *Sierra Trial and Opinion Consultants*, a firm offering jury research and a variety of trial preparation services for attorneys.

Jane E. Fisher, Ph.D., is Associate Professor of psychology at the University of Nevada, Reno. She completed her B.S. degree at the University of Illinois, Champaign-Urbana and a Ph.D. in clinical psychology at Indiana University, Bloomington. She is the founder of the Nevada Caregiver Support Centre, a statewide facility that offers assistance to caregivers of patients with dementia. Her research interests include clinical gerontology, lifespan development, and environmental design for dementia and healthy aging.

Victoria Follette is a clinical scientist with a special emphasis in theory-based empirical research on the longterm impacts of trauma. Extending these findings to therapeutic practices that can be implemented in the community is central to her work. Dr. Follette is particularly interested in the links between interpersonal victimization, substance abuse, and high risk sexual behaviors. She has conducted research in the areas of child sexual abuse, adult rape, and domestic violence. Her current and future research will emphasize substance abuse both as a result of victimization and as a risk factor for future abuse. Currently she supervises six doctoral level students who conduct both basic and applied research related to trauma. In addition, she supervises a clinical team that provides individual, couples, and group therapy for issues related to trauma.

William C. Follette received his Ph.D. in clinical psychology from the University of Washington in 1984. He is currently an associate professor in the Department of Psychology at the University of Nevada, Reno. Dr. Follette is involved in psychotherapy research and treatment development, research design, philosophy of science, and conceptual challenges associated with empirically supported treatments.

Alan E. Fruzzetti, Ph.D., is Associate Professor of psychology and Director of the Dialectical Behavior Therapy (DBT) and Research Program at the University of Nevada at Reno. He received his B.A. from Brown University and M.S. and Ph.D. from the University of Washington in Seattle. His research focuses on the interplay between psychopathology and couple and family interactions, and the development of effective treatments for these problems. Dr. Fruzzetti is Research Advisor and Member of the Board of Directors of the National Educational Alliance for Borderline Personality Disorder, maintains a clinical practice with individuals and families, and has provided extensive training in the United States, Europe, and Australia in DBT with individuals, couples, and families.

John P. Gluck received his Ph.D. from the University of Wisconsin – Madison in 1971. For many years he researched the effects of early experience on learning in nonhuman primates. He is currently Professor of psychology, Director of the Research Ethics Service Project, and Senior Bioethicist at the Health Science Center Institute for Ethics at the University of New Mexico. He is also Faculty Affiliate at the Kennedy Institute of Ethics, Georgetown University.

Lori Goodkey is a Ph.D. candidate in counseling psychology at the University of Alberta in the department of educational psychology. Her research interests include ethics in psychology, forensics, and qualitative inquiry. For her dissertation, she is examining the counseling experience of incarcerated women.

Gordon C. Nagayama Hall is Professor of psychology at the University of Oregon. He was previously a professor of psychology at Kent State University and the Pennsylvania State University. His research interests are in the cultural context of psychopathology, particularly sexual aggression. Dr. Hall has grants from the National Institute of Mental Health to study culture-specific models of men's sexual aggression and monocultural versus multicultural academic acculturation. He coauthored *Multicultural Psychology* with Christy Barongan and coedited *Asian American Psychology: The Science of Lives in Context* with Sumie Okazaki. Dr. Hall was president of the American Psychological Association Society for the Psychological Study of Ethnic Minority Issues and received the Distinguished Contribution Award from the Asian American Psychological Association.

John Hansen is a psychology student at the University of Nevada, Reno. He is the project coordinator of a research grant using mathematical modeling techniques to capture change within therapy. His current research interests include psychotherapeutic process, relational learning, and decision-making.

Gregory J. Hayes is associated with the University of Nevada.

Karl H. Hennig is Assistant Professor of psychology at St. Francis Xavier University. He received his Ph.D. from the University of British Columbia and did postdoctoral work at the University of Western Ontario. His current research examines the role of family and peer processes in the development of healthy, nonviolent relationships among youth at risk for delinquency and dating violence and the efficacy of family and peer group interventions.

Sarah E. Herbert, M.D., M.S.W., is Assistant Professor in the department of psychiatry and behavioral sciences at Emory University School of Medicine in Atlanta, Georgia. She is Director of the Psychiatry Obstetrics Consultation/Liaison Service at Grady Memorial Hospital. She currently is President of the Lesbian and Gay Child and Adolescent Psychiatrist Association. She is one of the founding board members of YouthPride, a nonprofit organization that provides services for lesbian, gay, bisexual, transgender, and questioning youth in Georgia.

Gayle Y. Iwamasa is Associate Professor at DePaul University. She received her Ph.D. from Purdue University and has been on the faculties of Ball State University, Oklahoma State University, and the University of Indianapolis. Her reserch and clinical interests are in multicultural mental health across the life span. Her research has been supported by the National Institute of Mental Health. Dr. Iwamasa won the Emerging Professional Award from the American Psychological Association Society for the Psychological Study of the Ethnic Minority Issues and the Early Career Achievement Award from the Asian American Psychological Association (AAPA). She also was president of AAPA. She is the coeditor of *Culturally Diverse Mental Health: The Challenges of Research and Practice* and is an associate editor for *Cultural Diversity and Ethnic Minority Psychology.*

Susan Jacob, Ph.D., is Professor of Psychology at Central Michigan University. Her areas of professional interest include ethical and legal issues for school psychologists and intellectual assessment. She is author (with T. S. Hartshorne) of *Ethics and Law for School Psychologists*, now in its fourth edition, and is author or co-author of more than 30 book chapters and journal articles. She was Director of CMU's School Psychology Programs 1991-1998 and was coordinator of the University's Institutional Review Board for Review of Research Involving Human Subjects 1997-2000. She has served on professional ethics committees at the national and state levels. Dr. Jacob earned her Ph.D. in educational psychology from Michigan State University in 1981.

Markus Kemmelmeier received his Ph.D. in psychology from the University of Michigan in 2001. He is currently an assistant professor in the Interdisciplinary Ph.D. Program in Social Psychology at the University of Nevada. His research focuses on culture, attitudes and social-cognitive processes in interpersonal interaction.

Michael Lavin is in private practice in Washington, DC. He holds a Ph.D. in philosophy and humanities from Stanford (1983) and a Ph.D. in clinical psychology from the University of Arizona (1999). He is formerly an assistant and then Associate Professor of philosophy at the University of Tennessee at Knoxville (1983-1994). He has held postdoctoral positions at the University of Wisconsin (1982-83) and at University of Minnesota Medical School's Program in Human Sexuality (1999-2000). He has worked as a clinical administrator at St. Elizabeth Hospital's John Howard Pavilion. In his private practice, he treats persons facing a variety of psychological issues, including compulsive sexual behavior and illegal sexual behavior. He is a candidate at the Baltimore-Washington Institute for Psychoanalysis. He can be reached at ML1952@stanfordalumni.org.

Andrew Lloyd earned his M.A. in philosophy from the University of Nevada, Reno (UNR) in 1998. Since then he has been working toward his Ph.D. in psychology and is currently an advanced student in the clinical psychology program at UNR. Andrew has published in the areas of self control, delusional disorders, and philosophy. He enjoys working, writing, teaching, and researching on topics that share both philosophical and psychological features.

Kristen A. Luscher, Ph.D., is a recent graduate from the University of Georgia Clinical Psychology Program. Her current research interests include risk factors associated with sexual victimization and sexual violence, as well as psychological consequences associated with sexual victimization.

Brian P. Marx is a licensed clinical psychologist and Assistant Professor of psychology at Temple University. He received his Ph.D. in 1996 from the University of Mississippi. His research focuses on risk factors for and responses to sexual victimization and emotion and psychopathology. His research has been published in the *Journal of Consulting and Clinical Psychology, Behavior Therapy, Journal of Traumatic Stress*, and *Experimental and Clinical Psychopharmacology*.

Robert Miranda, Jr., Ph.D., is a postdoctoral fellow at the Center for Alcohol and Addiction Studies at Brown University. Upon completion of an internship through the Clinical Psychology Training Consortium at Brown, he received a Ph.D. in clinical psychology from Oklahoma State University. In addition to training in clinical psychology, he formally respecialized in biological psychology at the University of Oklahoma Health Sciences Center, with an emphasis in psychophysiology and affective neuroscience. His primary research interests center on how abnormalities in brain regions important for the generation of emotional reactivity and regulation confer liability for antisocial behavior and drug abuse.

Melody Pearson-Bish received her bachelor's degree from York College in 1995 and a M.A. degree from Towson University in 1998. She is currently a senior level clinical graduate student at the University of New Mexico. Her research interests include evolutionary psychology, bioethics, ethical decision making in animal and human research, and ethics education.

Ype H. Poortinga, Ph.D., is part-time Professor of cross-cultural psychology at Tilburg University in the Netherlands and at the University of Leuven in Belgium. He has conducted research on similarities and differences in behavior across a variety of cultural populations and aspects of behavior. He has been president of the International Association for Cross-Cultural Psychology (IACCP), the Netherlands Institute of Psychologists (NIP), and the European Federation of Psychologists Associations (EFPA). Currently he is on the executive committees of the International Association of Applied Psychology (IAAP) and the International Union of Psychological Science (IUPsyS).

David W. Purcell, J.D., Ph.D., is an attorney and clinical psychologist. He currently works as a behavioral scientist at the Centers for Disease Control and Prevention, Division of HIV/AIDS Prevention in Atlanta, Georgia. He also maintains a private practice in Atlanta, where many of his clients are gay men and male couples. He is coeditor of *On the Road to Same-Sex Marriage* (1998). He is one of the founding board members YouthPride Inc., a nonprofit organization that provides services for lesbian, gay, bisexual, transgender, and questioning youth in Georgia.

David F. Richards, Ph.D., holds bachelor degrees in mechanical engineering (University of Florida) and psychology (Arizona State University), a master's dgree in clinical psychology (Millersville University), and a Ph.D. in behavior analysis (University of Nevada, Reno). He holds a staff position as a behavior analyst at Area Cooperative Educational Services (ACES), North Haven, CT. He provides behavioral services and training to approximately 160 teachers in support of three magnet schools with a total of approximately 1,500 children. His research interests include conducting functional based behavioral assessments within the school setting and developing and evaluating techniques for improving teacher classroom behavior management skills.

Natalie M. Rice is a doctoral candidate in clinical psychology at the University of Nevada, Reno, where she also received her M.A. in psychology. Her master's project examined the characteristics, potential moderating factors, and longterm correlates of child and adolescent sexual abuse in a Latina community sample. Her current research interests include trauma, cultural issues in psychology, and emotion regulation.

Janet E. Schank, Ph.D., is a licensed psychologist and counseling supervisor at a social services agency in St. Paul, Minnesota. She received her M.A. and Ph.D. in counseling and student personnel psychology/educational psychology from the University of Minnesota—Twin Cities. She is a former Chair of the Minnestoa Psychological Association Ethics Committee and has written, consulted, and presented on a number of issues related to ethics in psychology. Her primary interest is in ethical dilemmas of psychologists who practice in a range of small communities, including rural areas, communities of color, small colleges, and others.

Thomas Skovholt, Ph.D. is Professor of counseling and student personnel psychology at the University of Minnesota. He is an author or editor of six books, including *Ethics in Small Worlds: A New Definition of Small-Community Psychology* (with Janet E. Schank), now in press. He is a Fellow of APA, Diplomate of ABPP, Fulbright Lecturer in Turkey, and Member of the Academy of Distinguished Teachers at the University of Minnesota. He has been an active part-time practitioner for over 25 years.

Rachel P. Slater is a doctoral student in counseling psychology at the University of Minnesota. She received her M.A. in counseling psychology from Saint Mary's University of Minnesota. Current interests include exploring new clients' expectations of the counseling process and applying reflexive research methods to the practice of therapy.

Jessica N. Smith is a doctoral student of developmental psychology at the Univeristy of Oregon in Eugene. She received her B.A. degree in psychology from Gonzaga University and an M.S. from the University of Oregon. Her current reseach interests lie in the broad area of developmental psychopathology; more specifically, she is interested in the influence of the cultural context and familiar relationships on both normal and problematic social-emotional development.

Karel A. Soudijn obtained his Ph.D. at the University of Amsterdam and is Associate Professor of psychology at Tilburg University. He has published several books and numerous articles on methodology, psychotherapy, the writing of scientific papers, and professional ethics for psychologists. He is a member of the Ethics Committee of the Netherlands Institute of Psychologists (NIP).

Shoba Sreenivasan, Ph.D., is Clinical Professor of psychiatry and the behavioral sciences at the University of Southern California, Keck School of Medicine, Department of Psychiatry. She is also the Coordinator of Forensic Neuropsychology at the USC Institute of Psychiatry, Law, and Behavioral Science. In addition, Dr. Sreenivasan is the Director of Forensic Outreach Services at the Greater Los Angeles V.A. She received her doctorate in clinical psychology from the University of California, Los Angeles. She also serves as a forensic psychology expert for local county courts and is on the California State Department of Mental Health Sexually Violent Predator evaluation panel. Her research interests and publications have been in the area of assessment of violence, forensic ethical issues, and suicide among adults and minors.

Stephanie K. Swann, L.C.S.W., is a licensed clinical social worker who is currently working on a Ph.D. in clinical social work at Smith College in Northhampton, MA. She also maintains a private practice in Atlanta, Georgia, where she spends most of her time (except summers, when she is in Northhampton). She is founder YouthPride, Inc., a nonprofit organization that provides services for lesbian, gay, bisexual, transgender, and questioning youth in Georgia.

Steven R. Thorp, Ph.D., is a postdoctoral research fellow at Duke University Medical Center. He received his doctorate in clinical psychology from the University of Nevada, Reno, and completed his internship training at the University of California, San Diego. He investigates cognitive-behavioral treatments for adult clients, and he has applied these treatments in VA hospitals, community and university outpatient clinics, a state hospital inpatient unit, and a locked forensic unit. His primary research interests include how interactions with family members, romantic partners, or caregivers influence clients' anxiety, depression, or personality disorders. He studies the mechanisms of change involved in Integrative Couple Therapy (ICT), Dialectical Behavioral Therapy (DBT), and other treatments that address acceptance and change, especially as they apply to older adults. He is also actively involved in discussions of professional issues, including ethics, training practices, and dissemination of science-based practice in psychology.

Nancy E. Tribbensee is Deputy General Counsel at Arizona State University and a member of the Board of Directors for the Association for Interdisciplinary Initiatives in Higher Education Law and Policy. Her primary areas of practice include student affairs, academic affairs, risk management, research, computer use, intellectual property, and free speech issues. She received her law degree and an M.A. and a B.A. in philosophy from Arizona State University. She is currently a doctoral candidate in the counseling psychology program. Her research interests include professional ethics, confidentiality, and appropriate response to issues that arise in graduate clinical training.

Derek Truscott, Ph.D., is Associate Professor of counseling psychology at the University of Alberta in the department of educational psychology. He is also currently Chair of the Practice Review Committee of the College of Alberta Psychologists and has served in numerous regulatory capacities. He is in the process of writing (with Kenneth Cook) *Ethics for the Practice of Psychology in Canada*. His interests include ethics, standards of professional practice, life-threatening behavior, and psychotherapeutic processes.

Lawrence J. Walker is Professor of psychology and coordinator of the graduate program in psychology at the University of British Columbia, having received his Ph.D. from the University of Toronto in 1978. He is past-president of the Association for Moral Education and currently serves as associate editor for the *Merrill-Palmer Quarterly*. His research focuses on issues relating to the psychology of moral development, including processes in the development of moral reasoning and the formation of moral personality.

Linda E. Weinberger, Ph.D., is Professor of clinical psychiatry and the behavioral sciences at the University of Southern California, Keck School of Medicine, Department of Psychiatry. She is also the Chief Psychologist at the USC Institute of Psychiatry, Law, and Behavioral Science. She received her doctorate in clinical psychology from the University of Houston. For more than 20 years, she has trained clinical psychologists and psychiatrists in a postdoctoral fellowship program in forensic psychology/psychiatry. In addition, she is a consultant to a number of agencies, including the Federal Bureau of Prisons, California Department of Corrections, parole and probation departments, jails, district attorneys' and public defenders' offices, superior courts, coroners' departments, and the California Board of Psychology. Her publications reflect her interests in mental health laws, evaluation and treatment of mentally disordered offenders, and psychological autopsies.

Kevin D. Williams is associated with the University of Nevada, Reno.

W. Larry Williams, Ph.D. (University of Manitoba, 1977), has worked in the field of developmental disabilities for over 30 years. He helped design, implement, and chair the first master's degree program in special education in Latin America at the University of Sao Carlos in Sao Paulo Brazil. From 1984-1994, he directed several clinical behavior analysis programs in developmental disabilities as a senior manager at Surrey Place Center in Toronto, Canada, where he oversaw intervention services for over 1,000 cases and trained 50 behavior therapists. He is the founder and member emeritus of the Ontario Association for Behavior Analysis and is a registered psychologist in Ontario. As an Associate Professor of psychology at the University of Nevada, Reno since 1995, his teaching and research interests are in basic learning processes in persons with developmental disabilities and organizational behavior analysis applied to human service delivery. He is also the director of the UNR PATH program for adults with developmental disabilities. Williams is the author of a book on mental retardation, co-author of two books concerning autism and education, and is currently preparing a book on recent advances in mental retardation as well as a book on anger management. He is on the board of editors of two professional journals, has published over 35 book chapters and professional research articles, and has made over 200 professional and research presentations over the last 20 years.

Craig A. Yury is a doctoral student at the University of Nevada, Reno. He received his B.A. with honors in psychology from the University of Manitoba. His current research interests include geriatric care, dementia related illnesses, and behavioral pharmacology.